L'Académie de droit international de La Haye
honorée du prix Wateler de la Paix (1936, 1950), du prix Félix Houphouët-Boigny
pour la recherche de la paix (1992), de l'ordre du Rio Branco, Brésil (1999), et de
la médaille de l'Institut royal d'études européennes, Espagne (2000)

The Hague Academy of International Law
awarded the Wateler Peace Prize (1936, 1950), the Félix Houphouët-Boigny Peace
Prize (1992), the Order of Rio Branco, Brazil (1999), and the Medal of the Royal
Institute of European Studies, Spain (2000)

© Académie de droit international de La Haye, 2024
The Hague Academy of International Law, 2024

Tous droits réservés   All rights reserved

ISBN 978-90-04-70805-1

International Biodiversity Law

ACADEMIE DE DROIT INTERNATIONAL DE LA HAYE
THE HAGUE ACADEMY OF INTERNATIONAL LAW

International Biodiversity Law

Sandrine Maljean-Dubois

BRILL | NIJHOFF
2024
Leiden/Boston

TABLE OF CONTENTS

Introduction	29
1. The invention of biodiversity	29
• From a scientific concept to a social and political construct	29
• Biodiversity and its characteristics	31
2. The crisis of biological diversity and the issues at stake	34
• The manifestations of the crisis	34
• The biodiversity crisis and the entry into the Anthropocene	37
• The causes of the crisis	38
• The consequences of the crisis	40
3. What is international biodiversity law?	42
Chapter I. The legal and institutional framework	44
Section 1. The construction of the international law on biodiversity	44
1) The infancy (1885-1946)	45
2) The development phase (1946-1992)	49
3) The consolidation phase (since 1992)	55
a) The invention of biological diversity and the adoption of the Rio Convention on Biological Diversity	55
b) A convention designed to be modern and scientifically based	58
c) A threefold objective	59
d) A framework convention supplemented by subsequent protocols	62
• The Cartagena Protocol	62
• The Kuala Lumpur Protocol	63
• The Nagoya Protocol	63
e) Defining a strategic framework: From the Aichi Targets to the Sustainable Development Goals and the post-2020 framework	64
f) The Convention on Biological Diversity in the international governance of biodiversity	66
Section 2. The apprehension of biodiversity by international institutions	73
1) The role of intergovernmental organisations	73
a) A major role	73
b) A wide range of missions	74
c) The creation of the Intergovernmental Science-Policy Platform for Biodiversity and Ecosystem Services	77
• A difficult start	78
• Structure and composition of IPBES	80
• The missions of IPBES	82
• Operating principles of IPBES	84
2) The multifaceted institutionalisation of co-operation within the conventional framework	85
a) The institutions created pursuant to the Convention on Biological Diversity	87
• The political body	87
• The secretariat	90
• The subsidiary bodies	90
• Proliferation	92

	b) The profusion beyond the Convention on Biological Diversity. .	93
	• Conference of the Parties.	93
	• Smaller political bodies	96
	• Expert bodies.	98
	• Secretariats.	101
	c) Institutional fragmentation and defragmentation	103
	• A fragmented institutional landscape.	103
	• Strengthening co-operation between biodiversity conventions .	105
	• The challenge of the disconnect with international organisations outside the environmental field	109
3) Non-State actors		110
	a) Non-State actors as observers in treaty institutions .	110
	• A wide variety of actors	111
	• The observer status.	113
	b) Various forms of co-operation	116
	c) Public-private partnerships and the "Action Agenda"	119
Chapter II. The status of biodiversity in international law		122
Section 1. The legal regime of biodiversity in international law		122
1) Biodiversity within the States' territorial jurisdiction		122
	a) Territorial sovereignty over natural resources	123
	b) Excessive claims	127
	c) The prohibition of abuse of rights and the principle of damage prevention	128
	d) Shared natural resources	131
2) Biodiversity outside territorial jurisdiction.		134
	a) Marine biodiversity beyond national jurisdiction	134
	• An initial status of *res nullius*	134
	• Extending due diligence obligations to biodiversity on the high seas.	135
	b) Biodiversity in the Antarctic	138
Section 2. The values of biodiversity in international law		140
1) The instrumental value of biodiversity.		141
	a) Strictly utilitarian approaches	142
	b) Broader utilitarian approaches	143
2) The heritage value of biodiversity		145
3) The intrinsic value of biodiversity		148
4) From the value of biodiversity to ecosystem services: The return to an instrumental approach.		150
Chapter III. International law and biodiversity conservation.		157
Section 1. The focus of conservation		157
1) Global approaches		157
	a) Nature	157
	b) Wildlife	159
	c) Biological diversity.	160
2) Targeted approaches		166
	a) Specific species.	166
	b) Specific areas.	172
	• Protected areas .	172

• Buffer zones	177
• Ecological corridors	178
Section 2. The substance of protection measures	179
1) General prevention obligations	180
a) The obligation to take all appropriate measure to prevent damage	180
b) The precautionary approach	183
2) Protection against exploitation	184
a) Hunting and fishing	184
• The guiding principle of rational use	185
• Hunting regulations	188
– Prohibitions	188
– Identifying game species	188
– Defining hunting seasons	189
– Specifying the means of hunting	191
– Quotas	193
– Co-operation	194
• Fishing regulations	195
– Sea fishing	195
– Freshwater fishing	197
b) Trade and transport	198
• National trade regulations	198
• Regulating international trade	200
3) Protecting environments	206
a) The protection of specific areas	206
• On a universal scale	207
• On a regional scale	210
b) General protection against harmful activities	215
• The development of instruments complementary to the institution of protected areas	216
• Controlling activities and processes that damage biodiversity	218
• Regulating the introduction of alien species	223
• Taking into account biodiversity in planning and development policies	227
• The obligation to carry out an impact assessment	229
• Climate change and biodiversity	235
4) *Ex situ* conservation	237
Section 3. New perspectives	239
1) Offsetting	239
2) Rights-based approaches	242
a) Human rights	242
b) The rights of nature	250
Chapter IV. International law and biosafety	255
Section 1. The Cartagena Protocol on Biosafety to the Convention on Biological Diversity	260
1) Two conflicting logics	260
a) The Protocol's ties with the Rio Convention and international environmental law	260
• The first protocol to the Convention on Biological Diversity	260

- The Protocol and international environmental law 261
  - *b)* WTO law and biosafety 262
  - *c)* Lengthy and difficult negotiations 263
- 2) A progressive approach 265
  - *a)* A relatively broad scope of application. 265
  - *b)* The advance informed agreement procedure 267
  - *c)* The endorsement of the precautionary principle 271
  - *d)* The labelling obligation 273
- 3) The implementation of the Protocol 275
  - *a)* Taking into account the needs of developing countries 275
  - *b)* The Protocol versus WTO law 277
  - *c)* The institution of a non-compliance mechanism 282
  - *d)* Co-operation with other organisations 285

Section 2. The Nagoya-Kuala Lumpur Supplementary Protocol on Liability and Redress to the Cartagena Protocol on Biosafety. 286
- 1) Lengthy negotiations. 286
- 2) The content of the Protocol 287
  - *a)* The scope of the Protocol. 288
  - *b)* Administrative and civil liability 289
- 3) The impact of the Protocol 291

Chapter V. International law and access and benefit-sharing 293

Section 1. The need for a Protocol to the Convention on Biological Diversity on access and benefit-sharing 294
- 1) A novel approach? 294
  - *a)* Access to genetic resources. 295
  - *b)* Benefit-sharing 295
- 2) The ambiguities of the Convention 297
  - *a)* The Convention and patent law 297
  - *b)* The relationship between the CBD and the FAO on agricultural biodiversity 305
- 3) The need to expand the rules laid down in the Rio Convention and the launch of negotiations for a new Protocol to the Convention . . 307

Section 2. The contribution of the Nagoya Protocol on Access to Genetic Resources and the Fair and Equitable Sharing of Benefits Arising from their Utilization 309
- 1) The general economy of the Protocol 309
  - *a)* The principles governing access and benefit-sharing 309
  - *b)* Adapting to technological change 312
  - *c)* Implementation mechanisms under the Protocol 313
- 2) The challenging relationship of the Protocol with other international agreements 316
- 3) A limited impact 321

Chapter VI. Supporting States in the implementation of the international law on biodiversity. 324

Section 1. Technical and financial co-operation tools. 324
- 1) Technical co-operation. 324
- 2) Financial co-operation 329

Section 2. International implementation monitoring and sanctions for
non-compliance 335
   1) The institution of specific and non-judicial compliance procedures . 336
      a) The development of these procedures in the field of biodiversity. 337
- At the universal level 338
- At the regional level 339
      b) The content of these procedures 339
- The main characteristics of these procedures. 340
- Monitoring and compliance techniques 341
    – Systematic monitoring. 342
    – Reactive monitoring 347
- The response to identified violations 350
    – Incentives and measures to promote compliance 351
    – Sanctions. 352
   2) Judicial review. 356
      a) International judicial review 356
      b) Judicial review by national courts 363

Conclusion 367

Bibliography 369

BIOGRAPHICAL NOTE

Sandrine Maljean Dubois, Born 29 June 1969 in Manosque (Alpes de Haute-Provence, France).

Director of research at the CNRS, CERIC, member of the "DICE" International, Comparative and European Law laboratory in Aix-en-Provence, Aix-Marseille University.

Graduate of the Aix-en-Provence Institute of Political Studies (1989); Saint-John Perse Foundation Prize. Master's degree in international public law, Paul Cézanne University (1990). Doctorate in public law, Paul Cézanne University (1996). Accredited research supervisor, Paul Cézanne University (2000).

Visiting professor at the Catholic University of Louvain, Laval University in Canada, the University of Brasilia in Brazil, Senghor University in Alexandria, Egypt, the Pearl Delta River Academy in Shenzhen and The Hague Academy of International Law (external programme in Beijing in 2010 and Yaoundé in 2017); summer programme in The Hague in 2019.

Director of the French-speaking section of The Hague Academy of International Law's Research Centre on *Implementation of International Environmental Law* (2008) and in 2022 on *Climate Change and the Testing of International Law* (2022).

Involved in various international negotiation processes (COP 21, UNESCO Expert Group on a Declaration of Ethical Principles in relation to Climate Change, Global Pact for the Environment, Global Framework for Biodiversity post-2020) and international proceedings before the ITLOS or the ICJ.

Member of the World Commission on Environmental Law of the International Union for Conservation of Nature.

PRINCIPAL PUBLICATIONS

Monographs

Quel droit pour l'environnement? Hachette, Paris, *Les fondamentaux*, 2008.
La diplomatie climatique de Rio 1992 à Paris 2015, Pedone, Paris, 2015, 2nd ed., with M. Wemaëre.
Le droit international de la biodiversité, Recueil des cours, Brill/Martinus Nijhof, 2020, tome 407, pp. 123-538; Les livres de poche de l'Académie de droit international de La Haye, Brill/Martinus Nijhof, 2021.

Edited Books

Climate Change and the Testing of International Law. Le droit international au défi des changements climatiques, with J. Peel, Brill, London, 2023.
La définition des limites planétaires. Quelles implications pour le droit et la gouvernance internationale? Pedone, Paris, 2023.
Biodiversity Litigation, with G. Futhazar and J. Razzaque, Oxford University Press, Oxford, 2022.
The Effectiveness of Environmental Law, Intersentia, 2017, Cambridge, UK.
Circulations de normes et réseaux d'acteurs dans la gouvernance internationale de l'environnement, coll. Confluence des droits, DICE, Aix-en-Provence, 2017.
Les 70 ans des Nations Unies: quel rôle dans le monde actuel? Journée d'études en l'honneur du Professeur Y. Daudet, with K. Bannelier-Christakis, T. Christakis, M.-P. Lanfranchi and A.-T. Norodom, Pedone, 2014.
Environmental Protection and Sustainable Development from Rio to Rio+20. Protection de l'environnement et développement durable de Rio à Rio+20, with M. Fitzmaurice and S. Negri, 2014, Brill.
La mise en œuvre du droit international de l'environnement. Implementation of International Environmental Law, with L. Rajamani, The Hague Academy of International Law, 2011, Martinus Nijhoff.
L'implication des entreprises dans les politiques climatiques. Entre corégulation et autorégulation, with A. Roger, La Documentation française, Paris, 2011.
The Transformation of International Environmental Law, with Y. Kerbrat, Hart Pub. & Pedone, 2011.
Le droit international face aux enjeux environnementaux, with Y. Kerbrat, Pedone, Paris, 2010.
Le rôle du juge dans le développement du droit de l'environnement, with O. Lecucq, Bruylant, Bruxelles, 2008.
Changements climatiques. Les enjeux du contrôle international, La Documentation française, Monde européen et international, Paris, 2007.
Les Nations Unies et les grandes pandémies, Pedone, Paris, 2007, with R. Mehdi.
La société internationale et les enjeux bioéthiques, Pedone, Paris, 2006.
Natura 2000: de l'injonction européenne aux négociations locales, La Documentation française, coll. Monde européen et international, 2005, with J. Dubois.
Droit de l'OMC et protection de l'environnement, Bruylant, Bruxelles, 2003.
La régulation du commerce international des OGM. La Documentation française, coll. Monde européen et international, 2002, with J. Bourrinet.
L'outil économique en droit international de l'environnement, La Documentation française, coll. Monde européen et international, 2002.
L'effectivité du droit européen de l'environnement. Contrôle de la mise en œuvre et sanction du non-respect, La Documentation française, Monde européen et international, Paris, 2000.
Les Nations Unies et la protection de l'environnement: la promotion d'un développement durable, Pedone, Paris, 1999, with R. Mehdi.

Co-ordination of Special Journals Issues

L'urgence environnementale, with Y. Kerbrat, *Annuaire français de droit international*, 2022.
International Investment Law and Climate Change, The Journal of World Investment & Trade, with H. Ruiz Fabri and S. Schill, Double issue, 2022, pp. 737-745.
International Law and Climate Litigation. Brazilian Journal of International Law, 2022, Vol. 19, No. 1.
Changements climatiques : quelles responsabilités, quelles réparations ?, Journal international de bioéthique, with Mathilde Hautereau-Boutonnet, Vol. 30, 2/2019.
The Paris Agreement, Carbon Climate Law Review, 1/2016, with M. Wemaëre.

Articles

Articles in Journals

Combining Tools and Actors for a Better Enforcement: A Case of the 2015 Paris Agreement on Climate Change, *Environmental Policy and Law*, vol. 53, No. 5-6, pp. 415-424, 2023 (with M. Hautereau-Boutonnet).
Prendre au sérieux l'urgence environnementale : quelle contribution du droit international ?, in *L'urgence environnementale*, introduction to the special issue, *Annuaire français de droit international*, 2022 (with Y. Kerbrat).
Climate Change in International Law, The Paris Agreement: A Renewed Form of States' Commitment? *French Yearbook of Public Law*, Issue 1, 2023, pp. 35-50.
The Paris Agreement on Climate Change: A Subtle Combination of Tools and Actors for Better Enforcement?, with Mathilde Hautereau-Boutonnet, *Environmental Policy and Law*, 52 (2022), pp. 389-398.
Climate Litigation: The Impact of the Paris Agreement in National Courts, *Taiwan Law Review*, May 2022, pp. 211-222.
International Law as Fuel for Climate Litigation, *Brazilian Journal of International law*, 2022, Vol. 19, No. 1.
A quand un contentieux interétatique sur les changements climatiques ?, *Questions of International Law*, November 2021.
The Paris Agreement Compliance Mechanism: Beyond COP 26, *The Wake Forest Law Review*, 22 November 2021, with I. A. Ibrahim and J. Owley.
Was the Global Pact for the Environment a Good Idea?, *Yearbook of International Disaster Law*, Vol. 2, 2021, pp. 283-313.
Le Pacte Mondial pour l'environnement, un nouveau traité pour sauver la planète ?, *Annuaire français de droit international*, 2019.
Liability and Compensation for Marine Plastic Pollution: Conceptual Issues and Possible Ways Forward, with B. Mayer, *American Journal of International Law Unbound*, July 2020.
22nd Conference of the Parties (Marrakesh) of United Nations Framework Convention on Climate Change: A Meeting Prior to Deadlines *[in Chinese]*, The Taiwan Law Review, June 2019, pp. 38-70.
Climat. La responsabilité de l'État en droit international public, stratégies d'évitement et pistes prospectives, *Journal international de bioéthique*, Vol. 30, 2/2019, pp. 95-118.
La contribution en demie teinte de la CIJ au droit international de l'environnement dans les affaires Costa Rica-Nicaragua, *Journal du droit international*, November 2018, with Y. Kerbrat, pp. 1133-1154.
International Litigation and State Liability for Environmental Damages: Recent Evolutions and Perspectives, *Revue de droit de l'environnement Kankyoho-kenkyu*, 2018, No. 7, pp. 159-144.
La reconnaissance du préjudice écologique par la Cour internationale de Justice, *Droit de l'environnement*, March 2018, No. 265, with Y. Kerbrat, pp. 90-91.
"Complex is Beautiful". What Role for the 2015 Paris Agreement in Making the Effective Links within the Climate Regime Complex?, *Brazilian Journal of International Law*, with M. Wemaëre, Vol. 14, No. 3, 2017, pp. 21-30.

L'Accord de Paris sur les changements climatiques du 12 décembre 2015, *Annuaire français de droit international*, with L. Rajamani, 2015, Vol. 61, pp. 615-648.
A propos de "Environmental warfare and écocide. Facts, appraisal and proposal" de Richard Falk (1973-I): l'écocide et le droit international de la guerre du Vietnam à la mise en péril des frontières planétaires, *Revue belge de droit International*, Vol. XLVIII, 2015-1/2, pp. 359-367.
Accord de Paris sur le climat: quels effets un an plus tard?, *Recueil Dalloz*, 17 November 2016, No. 39, p. 2328 (with M. Hautereau-Boutonnet).
The Paris Agreement: A Starting Point Towards Achieving Climate Neutrality?, Guest editor (ed.) M. Wemaëre du numéro spécial sur l'Accord de Paris, *Carbon Climate Law Review*, 1/2016, pp. 1-4.
The Paris Agreement: A New Step in the Gradual Evolution of Differential Treatment in the Climate Regime?, *RECIEL*, 25(2) 2016, pp. 151-160.
L'Accord de Paris: fin de la crise du multilatéralisme climatique ou évolution en clair-obscur?, *Revue juridique de l'environnement*, 2016/1, pp. 19-36, with S. Lavallée.
L'Accord de Paris sur le climat: urgence à agir et temps longs de la diplomatie, Guest Editorial, *European Society of International Law Newsletter*, March 2016, p. 1.
Conférence internationale de Paris sur le climat en décembre 2015: comment construire un accord évolutif dans le temps?, *Journal du droit international*, No. 4, 2015, with Y. Kerbrat and M. Wemaëre, pp. 1115-1130.
Quelles perspectives en droit international de l'environnement?, *Revue de droit d'Assas*, No. 11, October 2015, pp. 132-315 (with Y. Kerbrat).
L'accord à conclure à Paris en décembre 2015; une opportunité pour "dé" fragmenter la gouvernance internationale du climat? *Revue juridique de l'environnement*, No. 4/2015, pp. 649-671 (with M. Wemaëre).
Os limites dos termos bem público mundial, patrimônio comum da humanidade e bens comuns para delimitar as obrigações de preservação dos recursos marinhos, Revista de direito internacional. *Brazilian Journal of International Law*, No. 2-2015, pp. 109-125, with C. Costa de Oliveira.
La forme juridique du futur accord de Paris sur le climat: enjeux et principales options, *Cahiers droits, sciences et technologies*, No. 5/2015, pp. 177-210, with T. Spencer and M. Wemaëre.
Quel droit international face au changement climatique?, *Recueil Dalloz*, November 2015, No. 39, pp. 6-8.
The Legal Form of the Paris Climate Agreement: A Comprehensive Assessment of Options, *Carbon and Climate Law Review*, with T. A. Spencer and M. Wemaëre, No. 1/2015, pp. 1-17.
Questionnements juridiques autour de la négociation d'un nouvel accord international sur le climat, with M. Wemaëre, *Responsabilité & Environnement – Annales des mines*, January 2015, No. 77, pp. 29-32.
La plateforme intergouvernementale scientifique et politique sur la biodiversité et les services écosystémiques, *Journal international de bioéthique et d'éthique des sciences*, 2014, Vol. 25, No. 1, pp. 55-73.
La Conférence des Nations Unies sur le développement durable Rio+20, with M. Wemaëre, *Annuaire français de relations internationales*, 2014, pp. 721-735.
L'enjeu de protection de l'environnement dans l'exploration et exploitation de la Zone: l'apport de l'avis de la Chambre du Tribunal international du droit de la mer du 1er février 2011, *Annuaire du droit de la mer 2011*, Vol. 16, December 2012, "Le régime juridique des grands fonds marins, enjeux théoriques et pratiques à la lumière de l'avis consultatif du 1er février 2011", pp. 367-380.
After Durban, What Legal Form for the Future International Climate Regime?, *Carbon Climate Law Review*, 2012, with M. Wemaëre, Issue 3/2012, pp. 187-196.
Actualités de la Convention sur la diversité biologique: Science et politique, Equité, Biosécurité, *Annuaire français de droit international*, 2011, pp. 399-437, with M.-A. Hermitte and E. Truilhé-Marengo.
Après Durban, quelle structuration juridique pour un nouvel accord international sur le climat?, *Revue juridique de l'environnement*, No. 2/2012, with M. Wemaëre, pp. 269-282.
The Drafting of the Future International Climate Regime (in Chinese), *Journal*

of Shanghai University (Social Sciences), Vol. 29, No. 2/2012, pp. 1-14 (with V. Richard).

La portée des normes du droit international de l'environnement à l'égard des entreprises, *Journal du droit international*, No. 1/2012, pp. 93-114.

La Cour internationale de Justice face aux enjeux de protection de l'environnement: réflexions critiques sur l'arrêt du 20 avril 2010. Réflexions critiques sur l'arrêt du 20 avril 2010, Usines de pâte à papier sur le fleuve Uruguay *(Argentine c. Uruguay)*, *RGDIP*, No. 1, 2011, Vol. CXV, pp. 39-75 (with Y. Kerbrat).

Non-Compliance Mechanisms: Interaction between the Kyoto Protocol System and the European Union, *European Journal of International Law*, 2010, Vol. 21, pp. 749-763 (with A.-S. Tabau).

An Outlook for the Non-Compliance Mechanism of the Kyoto Protocol on Climate Change, *Amsterdam Law Forum*, No. 2/2010, pp. 77-80.

L'Accord de Copenhague: quelles perspectives pour le régime international du climat?, in *Revue du droit de l'Union Européenne*, No. 1/2010, pp. 5-40 (with M. Wemaëre).

Les changements climatiques dans la politique de coopération au développement de l'Union européenne, Revue du Marché Commun et de l'Union européenne, No. 530/2009, pp. 451-463 (with M.-P. Lanfranchi).

Le "post-2012": quel avenir pour le régime juridique international de lutte contre le réchauffement climatique?, Les Cahiers droit, sciences et techniques, 2009, pp 108-123.

Le Comité de contrôle du Protocole de Kyoto rend ses premières décisions, Droit de l'environnement, No. 162, October 2008, pp. 11-15.

Le spectre de l'isolation clinique: quelle articulation entre les règles de l'OMC et les autres règles du droit international?, in Revue européenne de droit de l'environnement, No. 2/2008, pp. 159-176, and in Chinese, *Chung-Hsing University Law Review*, 2008/5, pp. 127-143.

As repostas da sociedade internacional aos problemas ambientais globais: o direito e a governanca internacional do meio ambiente, *Artigos*, Centro Brasileiro de Relaçoes Internacionais, Vol. 3, ano II, 2007.

La Convention sur la diversité biologique a quinze ans, Annuaire français de droit international 2006, pp. 351-390 (with M.-A. Hermitte *et al.*).

L'affaire de l'Usine Mox devant les tribunaux internationaux, *Journal du droit international*, Vol. 134, No. 2/2007, pp. 437-472, with J.-C. Martin.

L'ONU et la protection de l'environnement. Eléments pour un bilan, *L'Observateur des Nations Unies*, No. 2/2006, pp. 315-330.

La mise en route du protocole de Kyoto à la convention-cadre des Nations Unies sur les changements climatiques, *Annuaire français de droit international* 2005, pp. 433-463.

Le conflit entre les pêcheurs de l'étang de Berre et EDF. Quelques remarques à propos des arrêts CJCE des 15 juillet et 7 octobre 2004, *Droit de l'environnement*, No. 131, septembre 2005, with E. Truilhé, pp. 186-190.

L'article 10 de la Charte de l'environnement: la Charte de l'environnement et la diplomatie française, *Environnement du Juris-classeur* n° 4, April 2005, pp. 36-38.

Le projet de Charte française de l'environnement au regard du droit international et européen, *Revue européenne de droit de l'environnement*, 2003, No. 4, pp. 409-425.

Environnement, développement durable et droit international. De Rio à Johannesburg: et au-delà?, *Annuaire français de droit international*, 2002, pp. 592-623.

Accès à l'information environnementale et règles d'étiquetage des denrées alimentaires produites à partir d'organismes génétiquement modifiés. L'arrêt de la Cour de Justice des Communautés Européennes du 12 juin 2003 Eva Glawischnig et Bundesminister für soziale Sicherheit und Generationen, *Droit de l'environnement*, No. 111, September 2003, pp. 152-156, with E. Brosset.

Le droit communautaire de la conservation de la nature devant la CJCE (1999-2001). Récente jurisprudence européenne relative aux directives "oiseaux" et "habitats", with C.-H. Born, *Revue juridique de l'environnement*, 4/2001, pp. 597-649.

Le protocole de Carthagène sur la biosécurité et le commerce international des organismes génétiquement modifiés, *L'Observateur des Nations Unies*, No. 11, automne-hiver 2001, in Dossier spécial "Droit international de l'environnement – Développements conventionnels récents".

Bioéthique et droit international, *Annuaire français de droit international*, 2000, pp. 83-110.

Biodiversité, biotechnologies, biosécurité. Le droit international désarticulé, *Journal du droit international*, No. 4/2000, pp. 947-994.

Vers une gestion concertée de l'environnement. La directive "habitats" entre l'ambition et les possibles, with J. Dubois, *Revue juridique de l'environnement*, No. 4/1999, pp. 531-555.

La Convention européenne des droits de l'homme et le droit à l'information en matière d'environnement. A propos de l'arrêt rendu par la CEDH le 19 février 1998 en l'affaire *A. M. Guerra et 39 autres c. Italie*, *Revue générale de droit international public*, 1998/4, pp. 995-1022.

L'arrêt rendu par la Cour internationale de Justice le 25 septembre 1997 en l'affaire relative au projet Gabcikovo-Nagymaros (Hongrie/Slovaquie), *Annuaire français de droit international*, 1997, Vol. XLIII, pp. 286-332.

L'Accord du 16 juin 1995 relatif à la conservation des oiseaux d'eau migrateurs d'Afrique-Eurasie, with C. de Klemm, *Revue juridique de l'environnement*, No. 1/1998, pp. 5-30.

L'affaire relative à l'application de la convention pour la prévention et la répression du crime de génocide *(Bosnie-Herzégovine c. Yougoslavie)*, CIJ, arrêt du 11 juillet 1996, exceptions préliminaires, *Annuaire français de droit international*, 1996, Vol. XLII, pp. 357-386.

Note sous l'arrêt rendu par la Cour internationale de Justice le 11 juillet 1996 en l'affaire "Application de la convention pour la prévention et la répression du crime de génocide", *L'Observateur des Nations Unies*, No. 1/1997, pp. 107-117.

La clause du "mieux-disant social" dans l'attribution des marchés publics. Note sous Conseil d'Etat, 10 mai 1996, Fédération nationale des travaux publics, Fédération nationale du bâtiment, *Actualité Juridique – Droit Administratif*, 20 February 1997, pp. 197-202.

Book Chapters

La diplomatie climatique, *Revista Brasileira De Relaçoes Internacionais no Mundo Atual*, 2023; *Diplomacia de Sustentabilidade*, C. Ferreira Macedo D'Isep (ed.), Instituto Memoria, 2023, pp. 44-63.

La fabrique du consensus multilatéral dans le champ de l'environnement, in *Droit international multilatéral*, Actes du Colloque de la Société française pour le droit international, Perpignan, Pedone, 2023, pp. 133-146.

The Progressive "Climatization" of International Law, pp. 3-39; La "climatisation" progressive du droit international, pp. 41-81, in *Climate Change and the Testing of International Law. Le droit international au défi des changements climatiques*, S. Maljean-Dubois et J. Peel (eds.), Brill, London, 2023.

The Paris Agreement on Climate Change: A Subtle Combination of Tools and Actors for Better Enforcement?, with M. Hautereau-Boutonnet, in *Regulating Global Climate Change. From Global Concern to Planetary Concern*, 2023, IOS Press, B. H. Desai (ed.), pp. 151-160.

Droits de l'homme, droit de la nature, droits de l'animal : les approches par les droits peuvent-elles sauver la biodiversité?, in Mélanges en l'honneur de J.-C. Ricci, *Grandeur et servitudes du bien commun*, Dalloz, Paris, 2023, pp. 393-406.

Les Etats, la nature et le droit… La Convention sur la diversité biologique à l'heure de la sixième extinction de masse, in *Le droit à l'épreuve de la société des sciences et des techniques*, "Liber amicorum" en l'honneur de M.-A. Hermitte, Academia University Press, N. Baya-Laffite, M. Valeria Berros and R. Míguez Núñez (eds.), 2022, pp. 191-205.

La définition des "limites planétaires". Quelles implications pour le droit et la gouvernance internationale?, in *La définition des "limites planétaires". Quelles implications pour le droit et la gouvernance internationale?*, S. Maljean-Dubois (ed.), Pedone, 2022, pp. 7-20.

Biodiversity Litigation. Introduction, in Guillaume Futhazar, S. Maljean-Dubois, Jona Razzaque, *Biodiversity Litigation,* OUP, 2022, pp. 1-32 (with G. Futhazar and J. Razzaque).

The Increasing Emphasis on Biodiversity Law before International Courts and Tribunals, with Elisa Morgera, in *Biodiversity Litigation,* G. Futhazar, S. Maljean-Dubois and J. Razzaque (eds.), OUP, 2022, pp. 331-358.

Concluding Remarks, *Understanding Vulnerability in the Context of Climate Change,* Co-ed., M. Campins Eritja and R. Bentirou Mathlouthi, ed. Atelier, 2022, pp. 183-187.

L'éloge du flou? L'Accord de Paris devant les juges nationaux, Mélanges en l'honneur de Mireille Delmas-Marty, Mare et Martin, Paris, 2022, pp. 367-378.

Changement climatique. Revisiter et démêler la pelote des consensus, *Cahiers droit, sciences & technologies,* 12 | 2021, with A. Dahan.

Les obligations de due diligence des Etats pour préserver le milieu marin et à leurs conséquences en termes de responsabilité, in *A função do direito na gestão sustentável dos recursos minerais marinhos La fonction du droit dans la gestion durable des ressources minerales marines,* C. Costa De Oliveira, M.-P. Lanfranchi, A. Flávia Barros-Platiau and G. Rodrigo Bandeira Galindo (eds.), editora Proceso, Rio de Janeiro, 2021, pp. 129-150.

Voyage au cœur de la machine: la fabrique d'un droit climatique pour construire un monde à 1,5 degré, in *La fabrique d'un droit climatique au service de la trajectoire 1.5,* C. Cournil (ed.), Pedone, 2021, pp. 465-478.

Chapter 38. Regional Organizations: The European Union, *Oxford Handbook of International Environmental Law,* L. Rajamani and J. Peel (eds.), OUP, 2021, pp. 650-665.

The No-Harm Principle as the Foundation of International Climate Law, Debating Climate Law, B. Mayer and A. Zahar (eds.), Cambridge University Press, 2021, pp. 15-28.

L'Accord de Paris du 12 décembre 2015 sur le climat, illustration des évolutions de la garantie normative en droit international ?, with M. Hautereau-Boutonnet, in C. Thibierge (ed.), *La garantie normative. Exploration d'une notion-fonction,* 2021, pp. 223-240.

Entre les règles et l'esprit des règles, with M. Delmas-Marty and Linxin He, in *Sur les chemins d'un* jus commune *universalisable,* M. Delmas-Marty, K. Martin-Chenut and C. Perruso (eds.), 2021, Mare et Martin, Paris, pp. 397-412.

Outils juridiques d'articulation entre le commun et le particulier, with Marie Rota, Jean-Michel Servais, in *Sur les chemins d'un* jus commune *universalisable,* M. Delmas-Marty, K. Martin-Chenut and C. Perruso (eds.), Mare et Martin, Paris, 2021, pp. 363-380.

L'ouverture du procès environnemental dans l'ordre international, in M. Hautereau-Boutonnet and E. Truilhé (eds.), *Le procès environnemental. Du procès sur l'environnement au procès pour l'environnement,* Dalloz, Thèmes et commentaires, Paris, 2021, pp. 105-120.

Due Diligence, with C. Costa De Oliveira and H. Mpoto Bombaka, in *Dicionario sobre a função do direito na gestao sustentavel dos recursos minerais marinhos, Dictionnaire sur la fonction du droit dans la gestion durable des ressources minérales marines,* C. Costa de Oliveira, M.-P. Lanfranchi and N. Monebhurrun (eds.), Pontes, Sao Paulo, 2020, pp. 149-160 (in French and Portuguese).

Responsabilité de l'Etat patronnant – Responsabilidade do estado patrocinador, with Harvey Mpoto Bombaka, in *Dicionario sobre a função do direito na gestao sustentavel dos recursos minerais marinhos, Dictionnaire sur la fonction du droit dans la gestion durable des ressources minérales marines,* C. Costa de Oliveira, M.-P. Lanfranchi and N. Monebhurrun (eds.), Pontes, Sao Paulo, 2020, pp. 445-456 (in French and Portuguese).

Responsabilité (notion juridique), in *Dictionnaire des biens communs*, M. Cornu, F. Orsi and J. Rochfeld (ed.), PUF, 2021, with Mathilde Hautereau-Boutonnet, pp. 1142-1146.

Pétition Inuits (2005) et Petition Arctic Athabaskan (2013): un échec pour un succès?, in *Les grandes affaires climatiques*, C. Cournil (ed.), Confluence des droits, 2020, pp. 63-73.

Compliance and Implementation, in Morin, J.-F. and A. Orsini, *Essential Concepts of Global Environmental Governance*, Abingdon, Routledge, 2020, 2nd ed., pp. 49-52.

Paris Agreement, EU Climate Law and the Energy Union, in *Research Handbook on EU Environmental Law*, M. Eliantonio and M. Peeters (eds.), Edward Elgar, 2020 (with E. Brosset), pp. 412-427.

Le multilatéralisme est-il vraiment en crise? Quelques réflexions à partir de l'exemple des enjeux environnementaux, in Mélanges Doumbe-Bille, *Droit, humanité et environnement*, M. Prieur and A. Mekouar (eds.), Larcier, 2020, pp. 739-756.

Quelles perspectives pour la mise en œuvre de l'Accord de Paris?, in D. Dormoy and C. Kuyu (eds.), *Changement(s) climatique(s) et droit*, Les éditions du Net, 2020, pp. 139-162.

The Role of International Law in the Promotion of the Precautionary Principle, with Yann Kerbrat, in C. Costa de Oliveira, G. G. B. Lima Moraes and F. Ramos Ferreira (eds.), *A interpretação do princípio da precaução no direito brasileiro, no direito comparado e no direito internacional*, Pontes, Brasilia, 2019, pp. 275-284.

Climate Change Litigation, in *Max Planck Encyclopedia of International Procedural Law (EiPro)*, H. Ruiz Fabri (ed.), Max Planck Institute Luxembourg for International, European and Regulatory Procedural Law, 2019.

Research and Innovation, in *A Global Pact for the Environment – Legal Foundations*, Y. Aguila and J. Vinuales (eds.), Cambridge University Press, 2019, pp. 115-121 (with G. Futhazar).

La convention de Berne relative à la conservation de la vie sauvage et du milieu naturel de l'Europe; Directive oiseaux, in *Encyclopædia Universalis*, 2019, "La Science au présent", Anniversaires.

La responsabilité internationale de l'Etat pour les dommages climatiques, *Les procès climatiques: du national à l'international*, C. Cournil and L. Varison (eds.), Pedone, 2018, pp. 197-215.

Climat, *Dictionnaire juridique des transitions écologiques*, Institut Universitaire Varenne, 2018, pp. 197-204.

Au milieu du gué: le mécanisme de Varsovie relatif aux pertes et préjudices liés aux changements climatiques, in *Quel droit pour l'adaptation des territoires aux changements climatiques? L'expérience de l'île de La Réunion*, A.-S. Tabau (ed.), Confluence des droits, Aix-en-Provence, 2018, pp.123-134.

La quête de l'effectivité du droit international de l'environnement, in *A quoi sert le droit de l'environnement?*, D. Misonne (ed.), Bruylant, 2018, pp. 251-270.

L'Accord de Paris, un renouvellement des formes d'engagement de l'Etat?, in *Quel(s) droit(s) pour les changements climatiques?*, éditions Mare et Martin, M. Torre-Schaub, C. Cournil, S. Lavorel and M. Moliner-Dubost (eds.), 2018, pp. 55-74.

Après l'Accord de Paris, quels droits face au changement climatique? Introduction, with M. Hautereau-Boutonnet, *Revue juridique de l'environnement*, Numéro spécial 2017, M. Hautereau-Boutonnet and S. Maljean-Dubois (eds.), pp. 9-22.

La due diligence dans la pratique: la protection de l'environnement, in *Le standard de due diligence et la responsabilité internationale*, Pedone, Paris, 2018, pp. 145-162.

La gouvernance globale de la biodiversité marine dans les zones situées au-delà des limites de la juridiction nationale: vers une cohérence accrue?, with A. Flávia Barros-Platiau, in *La gouvernance globale de la biodiversité marine dans les zones situées au-delà des limites de la juridiction nationale: fragmentation et défragmentation dans le régime juridique de la biodiversité marine en haute mer*, D. Compagnon and E. Rodary (eds.), *Les politiques de biodiversité, du local ou global*, Presses de Sciences Po, Paris, 2017.

The Contribution That the Concept of Global Public Goods Can Make to the Conservation of Marine Resources, in *Protecting Forest and Marine Biodiversity: The Role of Law*, E. Couzens, A. Paterson, S. Riley and Y. Fristikawati, The IUCN Academy of Environmental Law Series, Edward Elgar, 2017 (with C. Costa de Oliveira), pp. 290-314.

The Effectiveness of Environmental Law: A Key Topic, Introduction to *The Effectiveness of Environmental Law*, S. Maljean-Dubois (ed.), *Intersentia*, Cambridge, UK, 2017, pp. 2-12.

Circulations de normes et réseaux d'acteurs. La gouvernance internationale de l'environnement entre fragmentation et défragmentation, Introduction, with D. Pesche, in Circulations de normes et réseaux d'acteurs dans la gouvernance internationale de l'environnement, *Confluence des droits*, UMR DICE, Aix-en-Provence, S. Maljean-Dubois (ed.), 2017, pp. 9-36.

Climate Change and Biodiversity, *Encyclopedia of Environmental Law - Biodiversity and Nature Protection Law*, Edward Elgar Publishing, J. Razzaque and E. Morgera (eds.), 2016 (with M. Wemaëre), pp. 295-308.

Le traitement du risque climatique. La réponse du droit international. L'atténuation du risque climatique en droit international, in *Regards juridiques franco-japonais sur le traitement du risque environnemental et sanitaire*, K. Yoshida and M. Hautereau-Boutonnet (eds.), Waseda University Press, Tokyo, 2017, pp. 91-109.

International Litigation and State Liability for Environmental Damages: Recent Evolutions and Perspectives, in *Climate Change Liability and Beyond*, Jiunn-rong Yeh (ed.), National Taiwan University Press, Taipei, 2016, pp. 28-77.

The International Court of Justice's Judgement of 20 April 2010 in the Pulp Mills on the River Uruguay *(Argentina* v. *Uruguay)* case, with Vanessa Richard, in Latin America and the International Court of Justice, J.-M. Sorel and P. Wojcikiewicz Almeida (eds.), Routledge, 2016, pp. 309-320.

IPBES Mandate and Governance, in *The Intergovernmental Platform on Biodiversity and Ecosystem Service (IPBES): Challenges, Knowledge and Actors*, Routledge, 2016, M. Hrabanski and D. Pesche (eds.) (with D. Pesche and G. Futhazar), pp. 78-101.

La Convention de Rio sur la diversité biologique, in *La diversité dans la gouvernance internationale. Perspectives culturelles, écologiques et juridiques*, V. Négri (ed.), Bruylant, 2016, pp. 97-118.

Les métamorphoses de la responsabilité de l'Etat dans le champ de l'environnement, in *L'environnement et ses métamorphoses*, C. Bréchignac, M. Delmas-Marty and G. de Broglie (eds.), Hermann, 2015, pp. 167-177.

Conventions, *Dictionnaire de la pensée écologique*, PUF, Paris, 2015, D. Bourg and A. Papaux (eds.), pp. 215-220.

Principe de précaution (Droit), in *Dictionnaire de la pensée écologique*, PUF, Paris, 2015, D. Bourg and A. Papaux (eds.), pp. 801-804 (with M. Hautereau-Boutonnet).

Principle 9, *The Rio Declaration. A Commentary*, J. Vinuales (ed.), Oxford Commentaries on International Law, OUP, 2015, pp. 269-286.

La gouvernance globale de l'environnement : enjeux et perspectives après la Conférence des Nations Unies sur le développement durable "Rio+20", in Environmental Protection and Sustainable Development from Rio to Rio+20. *Protection de l'environnement et développement durable de Rio à Rio+20*, M. Fitzmaurice, S. Maljean-Dubois and S. Negri (eds.) (Queen Mary Studies in International Law with la Brill/Martinus Nijhoff Publishers), 2014, pp. 27-39.

Compliance and Implementation, in Morin, J.-F. and A. Orsini, *Essential Concepts of Global Environmental Governance*, Abingdon, Routledge, 2014, pp. 37-40.

Les juridictions internationales face au principe de précaution, entre grande prudence et petites audaces, with Y. Kerbrat, in *Unity and Diversity of International Law, Essays in Honour of Professor Pierre-Marie Dupuy*, D. Alland, V. Chetail, O. de Frouville and J. E. Vinuales (eds.), Martinus Nijhoff, 2014, pp. 929-948.

Complexes de régimes internationaux et protection des forêts, in *L'Observateur des Nations Unies, La protection des forêts tropicales*, 2014-1, Vol. 36, pp. 9-17.

Marché(s) et lutte contre les changements climatiques à l'échelle internationale, in

Marché et environnement, J. Sohnle and P.-P. Camproux-Duffrène (eds.), Bruylant, Bruxelles, 2014, pp. 241-245.
Le principe des responsabilités communes mais différenciées dans le régime international du climat, with Pilar Moraga, *Les cahiers de droit*, Vol. 55, No. 1-2, June 2014, pp. 83-113.
Présentation, *Les cahiers de droit*, Vol. 55, No. 1-2, June 2014, pp. 3-8, S. Lavallée and K. Bartenstein (eds.).
Environnement et développement durable. Que peuvent les Nations Unies?, Journée d'études en hommage à Yves Daudet, *Regards croisés sur les Nations Unies*, 18 octobre 2013, Aix-en-Provence, Pedone, Paris, 2014, pp. 111-124.
La prise en compte des exigences de protection de l'environnement dans l'élaboration et la mise en œuvre des contrats transnationaux d'investissement [in Japanese], *Waseda University Institute of Comparative Law*, No. 42, *L'environnement et le contrat : regards croisés franco-japonais*, K. Yoshida and M. Boutonnet (eds.), pp. 147-181.
La responsabilité internationale de l'Etat pour les dommages environnementaux : quelles évolutions? Quelles perspectives?, dans Mélanges en l'honneur de Gilles Martin, *Pour un droit économique de l'environnement*, Frison-Roche, Paris, 2013, pp. 309-330.
Les droits de l'homme dans les politiques extérieures européennes de développement et d'adaptation aux changements climatiques, *Changements climatiques et droits de l'Homme : les options politiques de l'Union européenne*, Larcier, 2013, C. Cournil and A.-S. Tabau (eds.), with V. Richard.
The Drafting of the Future International Climate Regime: From the Copenhagen Accord to the Cancún Accords, in *Global Change, Energy Issues & Regulation Policies*, J.-B. Saulnier and M. Varella (eds.), Springer, 2013, pp. 239-258 (with V. Richard).
La contribution de l'Union africaine à la protection de la nature en Afrique : de la Convention d'Alger à la Convention de Maputo, in *Liber Amicorum* Raymond Ranjeva, *L'Afrique et le droit international. Variations sur l'organisation internationale*, Pedone, Paris, 2013, pp. 205-218.
The Applicability of International Environmental Law to Private Enterprises, in *Harnessing Foreign Investment to Promote Environmental Protection*, P.-M. Dupuy and J. E. Vinuales (eds.), Cambridge University Press, Cambridge, 2013, pp. 69-96.
La aplicacion juridica en Francia, in *La bioseguridad en la encrucijada europea. La aplicacion juridica en Francia y Espana*, Tirant Monografias 784, Valencia, J. Francisco Escudero Espinosa (ed.), 2012, pp. 161-198 (with M.-P. Lanfranchi).
From the Kyoto Protocol Compliance System to MRV: What is at Stake for the European Union?, in *Promoting Compliance System in an Evolving Climate Regime*, J. Brunnée, M. Doelle and L. Rajamani (eds.), Cambridge University Press, Cambridge, 2012, pp. 317-338 (with A.-S. Tabau).
Justice et société internationale : l'équité en droit international de l'environnement, in *Equité et environnement. Quel(s) modèle(s) de justice environnementale?*, A. Michelot (ed.), Larcier, Bruxelles, 2012, pp. 355-376.
L'efficacité des normes juridiques : quelles spécificités? Illustrations à partir du droit international de l'environnement, in *L'efficacité de la norme juridique : nouveau vecteur de légitimité?*, M. Fatin-Rouge, L. Gay and A. Vidal-Naquet (eds.), Bruylant, Bruxelles, 2012, pp. 233-252 (with V. Richard).
Bilan de recherche des sections francophone et anglophone – rapport des directeurs d'études/The Present State of Research Carried Out by the English-speaking and the French-speaking Sections – Report of the Directors of Studies, in *La mise en œuvre du droit international de l'environnement / Implementation of International Environmental Law*, S. Maljean-Dubois and Lavanya Rajamani (eds.), The Hague Academy of International Law, Martinus Nijhoff, 2011, pp. 3-205 (with L. Rajamani).
Originalités et faiblesses de la procédure de contrôle du respect du Protocole de Kyoto sur les changements climatiques, in *Vingt ans après : Rio et l'avant-goût de*

l'avenir, P. Leprestre (ed.), Presses de l'Université de Laval, Québec, 2011, pp. 137-141.

The Making of International Law Challenging Environmental Protection, in *The Transformation of International Environmental Law*, Hart Pub. & Pedone, 2011, Y. Kerbrat and S. Maljean-Dubois (eds.), pp. 25-54.

The Drafting of the Future International Climate Regime: From the Copenhagen Accord to the Cancun Accords, in *Climate Change Law: International and National Approaches*, He Weidong and Peng Feng (eds.), Shanghai Academy of Social Sciences Press, Shanghai, pp. 1-24 (with V. Richard).

Negociaciones internacionales sobre cambio climatico: perspectivas Post-Copenhague [in Spanish], in *Derecho ambiental en tiempos de reformas*, Actas de las V Jornadas de Derecho Ambiental and V. Duran Medina *et al.* (ed.), Université du Chili, Faculté de droit, Centre de droit de l'environnement, Abeledo Perrot Legal Publishing, 2010, pp. 569-592.

Conclusions, in *Preuve scientifique, preuve juridique*, E. Truilhé-Marengo (ed.), Larcier, Bruxelles, 2011, *La preuve entre sciences et droit* (with R. Mehdi), pp. 331-350.

L'"observance" du Protocole de Kyoto sur les changements climatiques : les enjeux du contrôle international du respect des engagements, in *Changement climatique et pollution de l'air. Droits de propriété, économie et environnement*, M. Falque and H. Lamotte (eds.), Bruylant, Bruxelles, 2010, pp. 221-230.

Les organes de contrôle du respect des dispositions internationales, in *Acteurs et outils du droit de l'environnement : développements récents, développements (peut-être) à venir*, Benoît Jadot (ed.), Anthémis, Bruxelles, 2010, pp. 249-278.

La "fabrication" du droit international au défi de la protection de l'environnement. Rapport général sur le thème de la première demi-journée, in *Le droit international face aux enjeux environnementaux*, Société française pour le droit international, Colloque of Aix-en-Provence, Pedone, Paris, 2010, pp. 9-37.

L'équité dans les relations internationales : des revendications d'un Nouvel Ordre Economique International à l'Accord de Copenhague, In *Vers une société sobre et désirable*, D. Bourg and A. Papaux (eds.), PUF, Paris, 2010, pp. 243-283.

L'environnement saisi par le droit, in P.-H. Gouyon and H. Leriche (eds.), *Aux origines de l'environnement,* Fayard, Paris, 2010, pp. 421-431.

Les aléas climatiques de l'aide européenne, in *Regards sur la Terre, l'Annuel du développement durable*, Presses de Sciences Po, Paris, 2010, p. 35 (with M.-P. Lanfranchi).

Le rôle du(des) juge(s) dans la mise en œuvre du droit de l'environnement [in Chinese], in *L'établissement du cadre juridique d'une société respectueuse de l'environnement*, He Weidong (ed.), Académie des sciences sociales de Shangaï, 2009, pp. 269-295.

Climate Change in the European Union Development Cooperation Policy, Article in *Climate Law and Developing Countries*, Edward Elgar Publishing, B. Richardson and Y. Le Bouthillier (eds.), 2009, pp. 386-406, with M.-P. Lanfranchi.

Conclusions, in *Le droit international et européen du vivant. Quel rôle pour les acteurs privés ?*, E. Brosset (ed.), La Documentation française, Monde international et européen, 2009, pp. 175-192.

Juge(s) et développement du droit de l'environnement. Des juges passeurs de frontière pour un droit cosmopolite?, in *Le rôle du juge dans le développement du droit de l'environnement*, Bruylant, Bruxelles, 2008, O. Lecucq and S. Maljean-Dubois (eds.), pp. 17-40.

L'émergence du développement durable : sa traduction juridique sur la scène internationale, in *Appropriations du développement durable. Emergences, Diffusions, Traductions*, B. Villalba (ed.), Septentrion, 2009, pp. 67-105.

Corée – Taxes sur les boissons alcooliques, in *La jurisprudence de l'OMC, The Case-Law of the WTO*, 1999-1, Martinus Nijhoff Publishers, H. Ruiz Fabri and B. Stern (eds.), pp. 13-38.

Canada – Mesures visant l'importation de lait et l'exportation de produits laitiers, *in*

La jurisprudence de l'OMC, The Case-Law of the WTO, 1999-2, Martinus Nijhoff Publishers, H. Ruiz Fabri and B. Stern (eds.), pp. 34-54.

Chili – Taxes sur les boissons alcooliques, in *La jurisprudence de l'OMC, The Case-Law of the WTO, 1999-2*, Martinus Nijhoff Publishers, H. Ruiz Fabri and B. Stern (eds.), pp. 81-100.

Projet Gabcikovo-Nagymaros (Hongrie/Slovaquie), in *La jurisprudence de la Cour internationale de Justice*, P.-M. Eisemann and P. Pazartis (ed.), Pedone, Paris, 2008, pp. 487-503.

Droit du Conseil de l'Europe et droit communautaire: actions et interactions normatives pour la protection de l'environnement, in *Pour un droit commun de l'environnement*, Dalloz, Paris, 2007 (with S. Mabile), pp. 779-802.

L'enjeu du contrôle dans le droit international de l'environnement et le Protocole de Kyoto en particulier, in *L'observance: l'enjeu du contrôle de la mise en œuvre du Protocole de Kyoto*, S. Maljean-Dubois (ed.), La Documentation française, Paris, 2007, pp. 17-28.

Le rôle du juge dans le développement des principes d'intégration et de développement durable.

Introduction and contribution on "La contribution du juge international", *Le rôle du juge dans le développement du droit de l'environnement*, actes de la 3e journée d'études de l'UMR 6201, Pau, 12 octobre 2007, Bruylant, Bruxelles, 2008, O. Lecucq and S. Maljean-Dubois (eds.), pp. 201-207.

Ethique et droit international du développement, in *Ethique et développement*, Aix-en-Provence, 29-30 juin 2006, PUAM, 2007, with J.-C. Martin collab.

World Trade and International Standardization: The Codex Alimentarius. Article pour un ouvrage collectif sur *WTO Obligations and Opportunities: Challenges of Implementation*, K. Van der Borght et al. (eds.), Cameron May, 2006, with E. Etchelar, 2007, pp. 121-153.

Politique agricole et conservation de la biodiversité: un enjeu non traité par le droit international de l'environnement?, in *Politique agricole commune et conservation de la biodiversité*, I. Doussan and J. Dubois (eds.), La Documentation française, Paris, 2007, pp. 318-337.

Acteurs non étatiques, droit international de la bioéthique et droit international de l'environnement, in 8es Rencontres internationales de la Faculté des sciences juridiques, politiques et sociales de Tunis, 13-15 avril 2006, Slim Laghmani (ed.), *Acteurs non étatiques et droit international*, Pedone, 2007, pp. 273-284.

Les réseaux écologiques méditerranéens, in M. G. Melchioni (ed.), *Le Relazioni transmediterranee nel tempo presente,* Rubettino, Atti del Colloquio Internazionale, Roma, 15-16 novembre 2004, 2006, pp. 513-535.

Relations entre normes techniques et normes juridiques: illustrations à partir de l'exemple du commerce international des produits biotechnologiques, in *Les enjeux de la normalisation internationale. Entre environnement, santé et commerce international*, E. Brosset and E. Truilhé-Marengo (ed.), La Documentation française, 2006, pp. 199-231.

Rapport introductif: les timides développements d'un bio-droit mondial face aux rapides avancées des sciences de la vie, in *La société internationale et les enjeux bioéthiques*, Pedone, 2006, pp. 13-32.

La procédure de non-respect du Protocole de Montréal relatif à des substances qui appauvrissent la couche d'ozone, in *L'observance: l'enjeu du contrôle de la mise en œuvre du Protocole de Kyoto*, S. Maljean-Dubois (ed.), *La Documentation française*, Paris, 2007, with C. Nègre, pp. 332-358.

La biodiversité dans les négociations internationales: de la Convention de Rio sur la diversité biologique au Protocole de Carthagène sur la biosécurité, in *Les biodiversités. Objets, théories, pratiques*, P. Marty, F.-D. Vivien, J. Lepart and R. Larrère (eds.), CNRS éditions, 2005, pp. 211-226.

As relacoes entre o Direito Internacional Ambiental e o direito da OMC, tomando-se como exemplo a regulamentacao do comercio internacional dos organismos geneticamente modificados [in Portuguese], in *Governo dos Riscos*, C. Caubet *et al.* (ed.), *Rede Latino-Americana – Europeia sobre Governo dos Riscos*, Uniceub, Unitar, Alfa, Brasil, 2005, pp. 164-215.

La "gouvernance internationale des questions environnementales". Les ONG dans le fonctionnement institutionnel des conventions internationales de protection de l'environnement, in *Une société internationale en mutation : quels acteurs pour une nouvelle gouvernance?*, L. Boisson de Chazournes and R. Mehdi (eds.), Bruylant, Bruxelles, 2005, pp. 86-103.

As relaçoes entre of direito internacional ambiental e o direito da OMC, à luz do exemplo da regulamentaçao do comércio internacional dos organismos geneticamente modificados [in Portuguese] *[La régulation du commerce international des organismes génétiquement modifiés : entre le droit international de l'environnement et le droit de l'Organisation mondiale du commerce]*, in *Organismos geneticamente modificatos*, M. Dias Varella and A. Flavia Barros-Platiau (eds.), DelRey, Belo Horizonte, 2005, pp. 173-210 (capitulo 7).

Natura 2000: incertitudes scientifiques, incertitudes juridiques, in *Natura 2000. Gérer la biodiversité de l'Europe au local*, La Documentation française, Monde européen et international, 2005, pp. 45-64.

Le Protocole de Carthagène sur la biosécurité et le commerce international des organismes génétiquement modifiés, *Les ressources génétiques végétales et le droit dans les rapports Nord-Sud*, M.-A. Hermitte and P. Kahn (eds.), Bruylant, Bruxelles, 2004, pp. 249-271.

Japon – Taxes sur les boissons alcooliques/Japan – Taxes on Alcoholic Beverages, in *La jurisprudence de l'OMC/The Case-Law of the WTO 1996-1997*, B. Stern and H. Ruiz-Fabri (eds.), Martinus Nijhoff Publishers, 2004, pp. 27-61.

Les dimensions internationales de la politique communautaire de protection de l'environnement, in Mélanges en l'honneur de Jacques Bourrinet, *L'intégration européenne au XXIe siècle*, La Documentation française, Paris, 2004, pp. 279-309.

Regulating International GMOs Trade. An Outlook on the Future Relations between the CBD Cartagena Protocol on Biosafety and the WTO Trading Agenda, in *Essays on the Future of WTO. Finding a New Balance*, Kim Van der Borght, E. Remacle and J. Wiener (eds.), Cameron May, 2004, pp. 185-204.

Le rôle des ONG internationales et de la soft-law, in *Normativité et biomédecine*, with L. Boisson de Chazournes and B. Le Mintier-Feuillet (edS.) Economica, Etudes juridiques, Paris, 2003, pp. 213-224.

L'insertion du modèle européen dans le système commercial multilatéral, in *La sécurité alimentaire dans l'Union européenne*, J. Bourrinet and F. Snyder (eds.), with E. Truilhé, Bruylant, Bruxelles, 2003, pp. 147-175.

La régulation du commerce international des organismes génétiquement modifiés (OGM) : entre le droit international de l'environnement et le droit de l'Organisation mondiale du commerce (OMC), in *La régulation du commerce international des OGM*, la Documentation française, Monde européen et international, Jacques Bourrinet, S. Maljean-Dubois (ed.), 2002, pp. 27-58.

Le recours à l'outil économique en droit international et européen de l'environnement : des habits neufs pour les politiques environnementales?, in *L'outil économique en droit international de l'environnement*, S. Maljean-Dubois (ed.), La Documentation française, 2002, pp. 9-40.

Le système communautaire de management environnemental et d'audit (EMAS), in *L'outil économique en droit international de l'environnement*, S. Maljean-Dubois (ed.), La Documentation française, 2002, pp. 379-389.

La diversité biologique et la Convention internationale sur le commerce des espèces menacées d'extinction (CITES), in *La diversité biologique et le droit de l'environnement*, Conseil de l'Europe, Strasbourg, 2001, pp. 55-68.

Le rôle de l'équité dans le droit de la succession d'Etats, in *La succession d'États. La codification à l'épreuve des faits*, P.-M. Eisemann and M. Koskienniemi (eds.), The Hague Academy of International Law, Editions Martinus Nijhoff, Dordrecht, 2000, pp. 137-184.

Accès à l'information et reconnaissance d'un droit à l'information environnementale.

Le nouveau contexte juridique international, in *L'effectivité du droit européen de l'environnement. Contrôle de la mise en œuvre et sanction du non-respect*, S. Maljean-Dubois (ed.), La Documentation française, 2000, pp. 25-48.

Le contrôle du juge international. Un jeu d'ombres et de lumières, with M.-P.Lanfranchi, in *L'effectivité du droit européen de l'environnement. Contrôle de la mise en œuvre et sanction du non-respect*, S. Maljean-Dubois (ed.), La Documentation française, 2000, pp. 247-284.

Environnement et développement. Les Nations Unies à la recherche d'un nouveau paradigme, with Rostane Mehdi, in *Les Nations Unies et la protection de l'environnement: la promotion d'un développement durable*, ed. Pedone, Paris, 1999, S. Maljean-Dubois and R. Mehdi (eds.), pp. 9-33.

Les fonctions de contrôle dans des conventions à vocation mondiale. Les conventions sur la biodiversité, *Vers l'application renforcée du droit international de l'environnement*, ed. Frison Roche, 1999, pp. 3-17.

Le foisonnement des institutions conventionnelles, in *L'effectivité du droit international de l'environnement. Contrôle de la mise en œuvre des conventions internationales*, C. Imperiali (ed.), ed. Economica, Paris, Collection Coopération et Développement, 1998, pp. 25-56.

Un mécanisme original: la procédure de non compliance du Protocole relatif aux substances appauvrissant la couche d'ozone, in *L'effectivité du droit international de l'environnement. Contrôle de la mise en œuvre des conventions internationales*, C. Imperiali (ed.), ed. Économica, Paris, Collection Coopération et Développement, 1998, pp. 225-247.

INTRODUCTION

1. The invention of biodiversity

1. Biodiversity is a relatively recent scientific concept that also quickly became a social and political construct. It is important to understand its meaning and main characteristics.

- *From a scientific concept to a social and political construct*

2. The term biological diversity was coined in the 1980s to designate the diversity of life forms on Earth. Its invention is attributed to American biologist Thomas Lovejoy [1]. Following the publication of the seminal article by ecologist Edward Wilson in 1985, who described biological diversity as under severe threat and relatively unexplored [2], a new scientific discipline was born: conservation biology. This new discipline places at its heart what it sees as a "crisis" of biological diversity, because of the speed and scale of the phenomenon. Conservation biology studies the causes and consequences of the loss of biological diversity and proposes and tests new ways of curbing it [3]. It is described by its founders as *the science of scarcity and diversity* [4].

3. The contraction of the expression into the term "biodiversity" was suggested in 1985 by Walter Rosen, another American biologist. Shorter and more impactful, this term entered everyday language and quickly enjoyed considerable success, winning over environmental activists, decision-makers, the media and finally the general public [5]. The transition from biological diversity to biodiversity is thus one from a technical concept used in scientific circles to an interdisciplinary concept brought into the public debate to attract attention, socially built

---

1. T. Lovejoy, "Changes in Biological Diversity" 2 (1980), *The Global 2000 Report to the President.*
2. V. Devictor, *Nature en crise. Penser la biodiversité*, Seuil, 2017, 17.
3. *Ibid.*, 21.
4. M. E. Soulé, *Conservation Biology. The Science of Scarcity and Diversity*, Sinauer Associates, 1986; M. E. Soulé, "What is Conservation Biology? A New Synthetic Discipline Addresses the Dynamic and Problems of Perturbed Species, Communities and Ecosystems" 35 (1985), 11 *Biosciences,* 727-734.
5. P. Huneman, "Introduction. Diversités théoriques et empiriques de la notion de biodiversité. Enjeux philosophiques, éthiques et scientifiques", *La biodiversité en question*, ed. Matériologiques, 2014, 13.

around institutional, legal, political, economic and cultural issues [6]. Very quickly, the concept gained a negative connotation. From a scientific object, biodiversity rapidly became a *global environmental issue:* the manifestation of a "planetary ecological crisis" [7]. This discovery more or less coincided with the discovery of other global threats, such as climate change or the destruction of the ozone layer. These threats are global because of their global scale, but also because they highlight the interdependence of States in these matters. Sources of pollution produce consequences at sometimes very distant points of the planet. This is all the more true as biodiversity is not spread equally across the globe. The thirty-four biodiversity hot spots, which are threatened areas characterised by a great wealth of biodiversity and an exceptional concentration of endemic species [8], are not located in the economically richest countries but mostly in tropical areas. Awareness of the global nature of biodiversity led States to recognise, at the Rio Conference in 1992, "the integral and interdependent nature of the Earth, our home" [9].

4. This process of social and political construction has resulted in a certain exploitation of biodiversity, which has become a political argument. Sometimes, it is seen as a heritage over which indigenous peoples have rights and provides an argument to challenge the Western vision of the place of humans in nature. Other times, it finds itself at the heart of controversies that could cause one to reassess economic development and technical progress [10]. In reality, more than a complex category of life sciences, the emergence and dissemination of this term reflects the emergence of a field of thought and action, at the intersection of science and politics, aimed at the appropriation and management of nature [11].

5. Bearing in mind this terminological shift and its consequences, we will nevertheless use biological diversity and biodiversity inter-

---

6. M. Hufty, "La gouvernance internationale de la biodiversité" 32 (2011), 1 *Etudes internationales*, 9.

7. C. Aubertin, "L'ascension fulgurante d'un concept flou" 13 (2000), 4 *La Recherche*, 15-21.

8. N. Myers, "Threatened Biotas: 'Hot Spots' in Tropical Rainforests" 8 (1988), *Environmentalist*, 187-208.

9. Rio Declaration on Environment and Development, https://www.un.org/en/development/desa/population/migration/generalassembly/docs/globalcompact/A_CONF.151_26_Vol.I_Declaration.pdf, accessed on 26 October 2023.

10. C. Aubertin (n. 7), 15-21.

11. V. Boisvert and F.-D. Vivien, "Gestion et appropriation de la nature entre le nord et le sud. Trente ans de politiques internationales relatives à la biodiversité" 202 (2010), 2 *Revue Tiers Monde* 15-32.

changeably as they cover the same reality in scientific terms. What does this reality entail?

- *Biodiversity and its characteristics*

6. The concept of biodiversity is all-encompassing, complex and elusive.

7. *An all-encompassing concept.* Biodiversity involves far more than species of wild fauna or flora, or even their habitats. It refers to the diversity of life, i.e. all living things [12], from fauna and flora to bacteria and genes, but also ecosystems as well as a whole range of ordinary biodiversity made up of common, but not necessarily remarkable organisms. It encompasses the countless productions of Nature, including humans [13]. Thus, biodiversity can be assessed and measured from the macro to the micro, at different levels (the gene, the species, the ecosystem) and on different scales (the biocenosis, the landscape, the biosphere). It is a unifying concept, a whole defined by the addition of various elements.

8. Thinking in terms of biodiversity rather than "wildlife" or "nature" involves a change of perspective, both spatially and temporally. Spatially first, because with the invention of biodiversity, the disappearance of a species, even if it is endemic to a specific area or to an isolated area such as an island, has an impact that is no longer just local. It becomes a global issue. Such disappearance contributes to the biodiversity crisis as a global crisis. Although biodiversity is a multiscale concept that is therefore not conceived solely on a global level, it is also a global concept. Temporally as well, because the disappearance of a species has consequences beyond the here and now. The notion of biodiversity requires us to think on a geological scale.

9. The concept of biodiversity is narrower than the concept of *nature* that was used until then in the scientific or political vocabulary. Nature includes the physiochemical environment (water, soil, rocks, climate, etc.) and therefore goes beyond biodiversity, which refers to the living part of nature [14].

---

12. F. Jacob, *The Logic of Life. A History of Heredity*, Gallimard, 1970 (Princeton University Press, 1993).
13. Buffon, *Œuvres*, Gallimard, Bibliothèque de la Pléiade, 2007, 30.
14. G. Bœuf, "Préface", in V. Maris, *Philosophie de la biodiversité. Petite éthique pour une nature en péril*, Buchet Chastel, La Verte, 2nd ed., 2016, 9.

10. The concept of biodiversity is, however, broader than the *wild*, which covers free-living animals or plants that grow naturally without being cultivated. Biodiversity encompasses all living things, including domesticated animals or cultivated plants. However, the line between what is wild and what is artificial tends to become blurred, if it has only made sense one day. Humans themselves host an untamed biodiversity through bacteria. The increasing artificiality of nature – with, for example, the alteration of most landscapes or the creation of genetically modified organisms – is also reducing the "wild part of the world" [15]. This has led Philippe Roqueplo to speak of a "Technonature". For him, this "artificialisation" of Nature by technology has produced a Technonature that society must now manage and maintain, and this is a new situation [16].

11. *A complex concept.* Biodiversity covers all living things in all of their variety and variability; it is therefore a complex concept. It is not an exhaustive category [17], but rather a living and evolving object. The Earth's biodiversity is made up of thousands of entities that constitute as many complex systems and sub-systems because they are themselves made of a large number of entities in constant interaction, varying in size from a tree stump to a savannah or a small wetland. The concept therefore covers not only an addition of entities, but more importantly relationships and processes. These systems and sub-systems are unstable; they evolve both naturally and as a result of human activities. They move and change in space and over time. Conservation biology itself is anything but fixist; it takes into account ecological interactions and evolutionary dynamics [18]. According to this discipline, it is with all its complexity and evolvability that biological diversity must be protected for its intrinsic value, irrespective of any usefulness [19]. The approach is Darwinist if one considers the essential contribution of Darwin's work to be that the adaptability of living organisms depends on their diversity, and that what counts is not to save a species, but to save its evolutionary potential [20].

---

15. V. Maris, *La part sauvage du monde. Penser la nature dans l'anthropocène*, Seuil, 2018 (our translation).
16. P. Roqueplo, *Entre savoir et décision, l'expertise scientifique*, INRA ed. 1997.
17. V. Devictor (n. 2) 13.
18. *Ibid.*, 22.
19. *Ibid.*, 202.
20. I. Michallet, "La notion de diversité biologique en droit international", in V. Négri (ed.), *La diversité dans la gouvernance internationale. Perspectives culturelles, écologiques et juridiques*, Bruylant, 2016, 80.

12. Here arises the "how" question. What should be protected and where? How to choose? What to prioritise and on what basis? Optimisation logics seem to be – sometimes even claim to be – based on science, but there are always choices and values behind them [21]. In reality, biodiversity is somewhat of a paradox: its scientific study purports to understand its complexity while its management seeks to reduce it to a set of simple elements that can be translated into indicators, easy to measure and communicate. A dual tendency to both simplify and complexify biodiversity thus structures scientific ecology and nature conservation [22]. In order to properly understand biodiversity, one must therefore be wary of reductionism.

13. *An elusive concept.* Biodiversity is difficult to apprehend in and of itself, because the very concept remains rather theoretical and abstract. The degree of biodiversity is not necessarily apparent to anyone walking through a natural environment. It can only be understood as a tangible, visible and measurable reality through its components, basically by breaking it down. However, the separate components do not account for the whole, which is also characterised by the relationships between these components. Biodiversity is more of a "dynamic and living multilevel concept", which makes it difficult to apprehend [23]. Both approaches, classificatory and evolutionary, are in fact necessary to understand biodiversity [24].

14. Furthermore, the concept of biodiversity syncretises concepts that are vague themselves, such as those of species, gene or ecosystem, the definitions and boundaries of which are still debated by scientists [25].

15. For these very reasons, biodiversity is somewhat immeasurable. Even though many figures are available, ultimately, it is beyond quantitative evaluation. What measurement tool, what index should be used? How can we move from field surveys to reliable statistical tools? Although they are necessary, inventories do not provide a global understanding of the links between the elements inventoried. Moreover, we do not know the baseline state of biodiversity. It is therefore difficult to put a figure on its loss; estimated ranges are huge [26]. There could be

---

21. V. Devictor (n. 2) 208.
22. V. Maris *et al.*, "Les valeurs en question", in P. Roche *et al.*, *Valeurs de la biodiversité et services écosystémiques*, ed. Quæ, 2016, 30.
23. V. Devictor (n. 2) 110 (our translation).
24. *Ibid.*, 194-195.
25. H. Le Guyader, "La biodiversité : un concept flou ou une réalité scientifique?", 55 (2008) *Le Courrier de l'environnement*, pp. 11-12.
26. V. Vincent (n. 2) 113.

around ten million species in total, excluding viruses, bacteria, yeasts, etc. which cannot be measured. It is thought that 90 per cent of species have yet to be discovered [27]. The famous Red Lists of the International Union for Conservation of Nature (IUCN), a major NGO in the field of biodiversity whose work inspires "biodiversity diplomats", list only 859 species as extinct, i.e. less than 0.05 per cent of the two million species listed. But the species whose conservation status is well known – vertebrates and a few other small groups such as butterflies, reef-building corals or dragonflies – represent only a tiny part of global biodiversity; thus, less than 5 per cent of known species have been assessed for the purposes of the IUCN Red List [28]. The global extinction rate itself is difficult to establish (there is talk of 1 to 5 per cent per decade) and may not be meaningful at all. Estimates, like projections, are calculated on fragile and shifting bases. In this context, one should be wary of figures. On top of that, when looking at the crisis through the prism of extinctions, we do not take into account population collapses even though they are a harbinger of massive extinction in the future.

16. Inevitably, it is far from easy for the law to take into account this complex and elusive object.

2. The crisis of biological diversity and the issues at stake

17. For nearly four billion years, life grew on Earth in the simple form of single-celled organisms. It has since greatly diversified, although the evolutionary process has also regularly led to extinctions, including mass extinctions. But biological diversity is now being eroded. This crisis is one of the symptoms of the entry into the Anthropocene and of the transgression of planetary boundaries. It is important to identify its manifestations and to understand its causes and consequences.

- *The manifestations of the crisis*

18. Biodiversity is deteriorating across the globe. This is not a new phenomenon [29]. However, the biomass – the mass of living matter – whether terrestrial or marine, is decreasing in very significant pro-

---

27. *Ibid.*, 114.
28. B. Fontaine *et al.*, "Espèces en voie d'extinction, le compte n'y est pas", *The Conversation*, 14 January 2018. According to IUCN, more than 40,000 species are threatened with extinction (28 per cent of all assessed species).
29. See the seminal book by R. Carson, *Silent Spring*, Houghton Mifflin, 1962; Mariner Books, 2002.

portions. We are witnessing the demographic decline of a large number of species, with current and future consequences for the way ecosystems and ecosystem services work. Some manifestations are highly visible, such as the virtual disappearance of insects on car windscreens [30], the increasing scarcity of birds in the European countryside [31], the death of corals or the drastic reduction in fish stocks.

19. The collapse of the biomass could herald a "mass" extinction, defined by palaeontologists as a relatively short geological period of time when a large proportion of species becomes extinct. For ecologists, the rate and magnitude of the current extinction of species are comparable to those observed during past major extinctions, of which "widespread defaunation" is only one symptom [32]. Even the most popular wild species, the ones most traded or seen in the media (through films, toys, advertising, etc.) are under serious threat despite the fact that they enjoy the greatest attention and the oldest protection measures [33]. This would be the sixth such crisis, the last of which took place sixty-five million years ago and led to the extinction of the dinosaurs [34]. However, the present crisis is unique, for two reasons. First, this sixth crisis is linked to the rapid expansion of the human species on Earth. Second, this crisis is taking place at a much faster pace than the previous ones (1,000 times, 10,000 times faster?), leaving no time for species to adapt. This could jeopardise the re-diversification of species that followed all the previous crises, facilitated at the time by continental drift and climate changes.

20. To inform policy on these issues, an expert institution was created in 2012 at the international level: the Intergovernmental Science-Policy Platform on Biodiversity and Ecosystem Services, or IPBES, which is often referred to as the "IPCC [35] of biodiversity". It released its first regional assessment reports in March 2018. These reports gave an alarming picture of the state of biodiversity in Africa, the Americas,

---

30. C. A. Hallmann et al., "More Than 75 Percent Decline over 27 Years in Total Flying Insects in Protected Areas" (18 October 2017), *PLOS One*; F. Sánchez-Bayo and K. A. G. Wyckhuys, "Worldwide Decline of the Entomofauna: A Review of its Driver" 232 (2019), *Biological Conservation*, 8-27.
31. S. Rigal et al., "Farmland Practices Are Driving Bird Population Decline Across Europe" 120 (2023), 21 *PNAS*.
32. V. Devictor (n. 2) 29 (our translation).
33. S. Musacchio, "Ces animaux stars menacés d'extinction", 13 April 2018, *Le Journal du CNRS*, https://lejournal.cnrs.fr/articles/ces-animaux-stars-menaces-dextinction, accessed on 26 October 2023.
34. V. Devictor (n. 2) 27.
35. IPCC for Intergovernmental Panel on Climate Change.

Asia-Pacific, Europe and Central Asia. They concluded that biodiversity is under threat on every continent and in every country. Today, less than 25 per cent of the land is believed to have escaped the substantial effects of human activities. By 2050, it is estimated that this will drop to only 10 per cent of the land, some of which unusable – deserts, mountainous regions or polar territories. In Central Asia, almost 42 per cent of land animals and plants have already disappeared in the last ten years. In Asia-Pacific, experts estimate that 90 per cent of corals will be severely degraded by 2050, even under optimistic climate change scenarios. The African continent could see half its bird and mammal populations become extinct by the end of the century [36].

21. The following year, in May 2019, IPBES released its global assessment report on biodiversity and ecosystem services. Prepared by 150 leading experts from 50 countries, with backgrounds in natural and social sciences, it is based on the 2005 *Millennium Ecosystem Assessment* [37], but also on the analysis of 15,000 scientific references and governmental sources, as well as – in an innovative way – on indigenous and local knowledge. This report analyses the changes that have taken place over the last fifty years and presents a range of possible scenarios for the future. It states: "Nature across most of the globe has now been significantly altered by multiple human drivers, with the great majority of indicators of ecosystems and biodiversity showing rapid decline" [38]. It estimates that around one million plant and animal species are now threatened with extinction, particularly in the coming decades, which is unprecedented in human history. Since 1900, the average abundance of native species in most major terrestrial habitats has declined by an average of at least 20 per cent. More than 40 per cent of amphibian species, nearly 33 per cent of coral reefs and more than one-third of all marine mammals are threatened. The situation is less clear-cut for insects, but the available data supports a provisional estimate of 10 per cent of species threatened. At least

---

36. IPBES, *The IPBES Regional Assessment Report on Biodiversity and Ecosystem Services for Africa*, E. Archer et al. (eds.) (Secretariat of the Intergovernmental Science-Policy Platform on Biodiversity and Ecosystem Services 2018).

37. Millennium Ecosystem Assessment, *Ecosystems and Human Well-being: Biodiversity Synthesis* (World Resources Institute 2005), http://www.millenniumassessment.org/documents/document.354.aspx.pdf, accessed on 26 October 2023.

38. IPBES, *Summary for Policymakers of the Global Assessment Report on Biodiversity and Ecosystem Services of the Intergovernmental Science-Policy Platform on Biodiversity and Ecosystem Services*, S. Díaz et al. (eds.) (IPBES secretariat 2019), https://ipbes.net/news/Media-Release-Global-Assessment, accessed on 28 October 2023.

680 vertebrate species have become extinct since the sixteenth century and more than 9 per cent of all domesticated breeds of mammals used for food and agriculture had disappeared by 2016; 1,000 more breeds are thought to be threatened [39]. Agricultural biodiversity is experiencing unprecedented erosion, having decreased by 75 per cent during the twentieth century. Twelve plant species and fourteen animal species now provide most of the world's food, whereas in the past, 10,000 species were grown to feed the world's population [40].

- *The biodiversity crisis and the entry into the Anthropocene*

22. This crisis is not just a biodiversity crisis and it must be viewed in a larger context. It marks the transgression of certain planetary boundaries. Scientists tell us that humans have now taken the Earth "to the limit". According to the authors of an article published in the journal *Nature* in 2009 [41], the Earth has nine biophysical thresholds – with links between them all – that are real boundaries which cannot be crossed without risking catastrophic consequences. Biodiversity loss is one of them, along with climate change, stratospheric ozone depletion, ocean acidification, change in land use, global freshwater use, interference with the nitrogen and phosphorus cycles, atmospheric aerosol loading and chemical pollution. In their 2015 update [42], these authors underlined the fact that we have already reached the tipping point for at least four limits: with regard to the integrity of the biosphere and in particular the loss of biodiversity, but also biogeochemical cycles (nitrogen, phosphorus), deforestation and climate change. The authors concluded that, from this point of view, we have left a "safe operating space for humanity" and entered a "danger zone", testing the resilience of our biosphere beyond reason [43]. In January 2022, scientists concluded that a fifth limit, relating to chemical pollution, had been exceeded [44]. In May

---

39. *Ibid.*
40. I. Trépant, *Biodiversité. Quand les politiques européennes menacent le vivant. Connaître la nature pour mieux légiférer*, ed. Yves Michel, 2017, 27.
41. J. Rockström *et al.*, "A Safe Operating Space for Humanity" 461 (2009), *Nature*, pp. 472-475.
42. W. Steffen *et al.*, "Planetary Boundaries: Guiding human development on a changing planet" 347 (2015), *Science*.
43. J. Rockström *et al.* (n. 41) 473. J. Richardson, W. Steffen, W. Lucht, J. Bendtsen and S. E. Cornell *et al.*, "Earth Beyond Six of Nine Planetary Boundaries" 9 (2023), *Science Advances* 37.
44. L. Persson *et al.*, "Outside the Safe Operating Space of the Planetary Boundary for Novel Entities" 56 (2022), 3 *Environ. Sci. Technol.* 1510-1521.

2022, a sixth limit, relating to freshwater, was considered to have been crossed [45]. While the state of the ozone layer is improving, giving us hope that it will be restored by 2050 or 2060, the situation for the other variables is worsening.

23. This reflection on planetary boundaries is part of the wider reflection on the Anthropocene, which some argue is a new geological epoch, succeeding the Holocene after the Industrial Revolution. The Anthropocene is marked by the significant impact of humans on the Earth's ecosystem, a major impact that establishes humans as a defining geological force for the first time.

24. Still disputed, the notion of the Anthropocene has the advantage of inviting us to change our view on the planet, to see it as a complex system. According to "anthropocenologists", we should no longer speak of an environmental "crisis", because a crisis is transitory by nature, whereas the transgression of planetary boundaries in some respects marks a point of no return. Thus, even if we managed to drastically reduce our ecological footprint and invent a sustainable civilisation, it would take tens or even hundreds of thousands of years for the Earth to return to the climate and biogeological regime of the Holocene: "The traces of our urban, industrial, consumerist, chemical and nuclear age will remain for thousands or even millions of years in the geological archives of the planet." [46] This was confirmed by a study which indicated that biodiversity could take millions of years to recover [47].

- *The causes of the crisis*

25. The 2005 *Millennium Ecosystem Assessment*, a report commissioned by the UN Secretary-General, concluded that over the past fifty years humans have altered ecosystems more extensively than in any comparable period of time in human history, mainly to meet the rapidly growing needs for food, water, timber and energy resources such as oil [48]. This has been the source of many benefits but has also caused a substantial and largely irreversible loss of biodiversity.

---

45. L. Wang-Erlandsson, "A Planetary Boundary for Green Water" 3 (2022), *Nature Reviews Earth & Environment* 380-392.

46. C. Bonneuil and J.-P. Fressoz, *L'événement anthropocène, la terre, l'histoire et nous*, Seuil, 2013 (our translation).

47. J. Gabbatiss, "Earth Will Take Millions of Years to Recover from Climate Change Mass Extinction, Study Suggests. 'Speed Limit' on Rate of Evolution Means Diversity Would Be Slow to Return to Previous Levels", 9 April 2019, *The Independent*.

48. UN, *Millennium Ecosystem Assessment*, UN (2005), https://www.millenniumassessment.org/en/index.html, accessed on 25 October 2023.

26. According to the recent IPBES report mentioned above [49], the five direct drivers of change affecting nature that have the strongest impacts on a global scale are, in descending order:

(1) changes in land and sea use;
(2) direct exploitation of organisms;
(3) climate change;
(4) pollution and
(5) invasion of alien species.

The report stresses that climate change, another consequence of human activities, is already having a strong impact on biodiversity, from the level of ecosystems down to that of genetic diversity. The impact is all the greater that climate change is happening quickly, making it difficult for living organisms and ecosystems to adapt. Major ecological balances are being disrupted by the increase in the frequency and intensity of extreme weather events (heatwaves, droughts, floods, storms and hurricanes, etc.) and by the changes in water regimes and in the acidity of the marine environment. This is resulting in the reduction, migration or disappearance of species. But the biodiversity crisis in turn reinforces climate change. The collapse of phytoplankton, the increased acidity of oceans and massive deforestation destroy natural carbon sinks and lead to changes in water regimes. It is a vicious circle [50]. Given the lack of ambition of climate policies, the impact of climate change on biodiversity is expected to increase in the coming decades and, in some cases, to outweigh the impact of land and sea-use change and other stressors [51]. In its special report on 1.5°C, the IPCC highlighted the dramatic effects of an average temperature increase of more than 3.2°C compared to the pre-industrial era. This is the increase that current policies are leading us to. The IPCC has also established that every tenth of a degree matters. Thus, between a 1.5°C and a 2°C increase, two extremely different scenarios would emerge for biodiversity [52].

---

49. IPBES, *Summary for Policymakers of the Global Assessment Report on Biodiversity and Ecosystem Services of the Intergovernmental Science-Policy Platform on Biodiversity and Ecosystem Services* (n. 38).

50. The Shift Project, *Biodiversité et changement climatique: The Shift Project défend une vision coordonnée, Note d'analyse et proposition à destination des pouvoirs publics*, The Shift, March 2019, 1.

51. IPBES, *Summary for Policymakers of the Global Assessment Report on Biodiversity and Ecosystem Services of the Intergovernmental Science-Policy Platform on Biodiversity and Ecosystem Services* (n. 38).

52. R. Warren *et al.*, "The Projected Effect on Insects, Vertebrates, and Plants of Limiting Global Warming to 1.5°C Rather Than 2°C" 360 (2018), 6390 *Science* 791-795.

The IPCC and IPBES have produced a joint report on biodiversity and climate change, which underlines the interconnection between these two pressing issues of the Anthropocene that in practice are largely addressed in their own domains [53].

- *The consequences of the crisis*

27. Looking only at the effects on humans, this crisis has and will continue to have major consequences. According to some, with the crossing of the other planetary boundaries, it even gives us a glimpse, if not of planetary finitude, at least of human finitude [54]. As underlined by the One Health concept and the COVID-19 pandemic [55], our life, our development and our well-being largely depend on nature. Useful plants (wheat, spices, coffee, rubber trees, etc.) have always been strategic economic resources and have been considered as such from Ancient Rome through colonisation to the present day [56]. Intensive agriculture and the selection of high-yielding varieties are creating new risks for world food security, as shown by the 1969-1970 corn leaf blight epidemic in the United States. The solution was found by crossing these high-yielding varieties with a wild maize species from Mexico on the verge of extinction. This crisis highlighted the need to protect potentially useful wild species and even hardy varieties used by small farmers [57]. The development of biotechnologies from the 1980s onwards, with potentially unlimited applications in the agri-food, medical and even chemical sectors, further bolstered interest in biodiversity, at a time when it was perceived to be increasingly under threat.

28. But biodiversity is not just a reservoir of useful genetic resources. Much more than that, it provides on a daily basis and on a large scale what many authors refer to as "ecosystem services", i.e. services provided by ecosystems to humans for free, such as pollination, soil erosion mitigation, recycling of organic waste, natural water purification, production of oxygen for the air, natural carbon sequestration in wood,

---

53. H. O. Pörtner *et al.*, *IPBES-IPCC Co-sponsored Workshop Report on Biodiversity and Climate Change*, IPBES and IPCC, 2021, https://www.ipcc.ch/site/assets/uploads/2021/07/IPBES_IPCC_WR_12_2020.pdf, accessed on 25 October 2023.
54. D. Bourg, "L'impératif écologique" (2009), *Esprit* 7.
55. H. Keune *et al.*, "One Health and Biodiversity", *Transforming Biodiversity Governance*, I. J. Visseren-Hamakers (ed.), CUP, 2022, pp. 93-114.
56. M. Hufty, "La gouvernance internationale de la biodiversité" 32 (2001), 1 Etudes internationales 5.
57. *Ibid.*

oceans, soils and subsoil, etc. These services are estimated to be worth more than one and a half times the world's GDP, i.e. from 125,000 to 140,000 billion US dollars per year [58].

29. This notion of ecosystem services was a great success. It is now relied on by various actors and for different reasons. Indeed, the concept makes it possible to develop a rhetoric designed to boost fundraising for protected areas and to clarify what the monetary values of biodiversity could represent by providing a detailed description of the benefits that biodiversity offers to humans [59].

30. Commissioned by the UN, the *Millennium Ecosystem Assessment* has done much to popularise this concept. This study, published in 2005, emphasised the fact that, while changes have led to substantial gains in well-being and economic development, these benefits are being achieved at increasing costs in ecological and social terms. Without significant changes in current policies, institutions and practices, there will be a substantial reduction in the services that ecosystems could provide for future generations. Ecosystem degradation could increase in the first half of the twenty-first century. It is a barrier to achieving the Millennium Development Goals, which are primarily economic and social goals [60].

31. Following this study, the G8 Environment Ministers and five major developing countries commissioned, in March 2007, the study *The Economics of Ecosystems and Biodiversity* (TEEB) to define a conceptual and methodological framework for taking into account the value of biodiversity and ecosystem services in economic activities with a view to halting their degradation [61]. This study further highlighted the importance of the services provided by nature to humans for free – water, food, medicine, clothing, security, well-being, recreation, etc.

---

58. See in particular the major contribution by R. Costanza *et al.*, "The Value of the World's Ecosystem Services and Natural Capital" 387 (1997), *Nature*, 253-260; R. Mongruel, P. Méral, I. Doussan and H. Levrel, "L'institutionnalisation de l'approche par les services écosystémiques: dimensions scientifiques, politiques et juridiques", in P. Roche *et al.*, *Valeurs de la biodiversité et services écosystémiques*, ed. Quæ 2016, 191-216.
59. OECD, *Biodiversity: Finance and the Economic and Business Case for Action*, OECD Publishing, 2019, 1.
60. UN, *Millennium Ecosystem Assessment* (n. 48).
61. P. Ten Brink (ed.), *The Economics of Ecosystems and Biodiversity: Mainstreaming the Economics of Nature: A Synthesis of the Approach, Conclusions and Recommendations of TEEB* (2010), https://www.academia.edu/14081672/The_economics_of_ecosystems_and_biodiversity_mainstreaming_the_economics_of_nature_a_synthesis_of_the_approach_conclusions_and_recommendations_of_TEEB, accessed on 28 July 2023.

– and their economic invisibility. Many ecosystem services are now threatened by changes in our environment: decomposition, cycles of matter, water purification, climate regulation (absorption of CO_2 by the oceans and forests) and pollination. This study was followed by the publication of a report highlighting the cost of inaction on biodiversity protection, as the Stern Review had done for climate change [62]. The cost of inaction in the face of biodiversity loss is huge and will continue to increase. It is estimated that the world lost between 4 and 20 trillion US dollars per year in ecosystem services between 1997 and 2011 due to land-cover change, and between 6 and 11 trillion US dollars per year due to land degradation [63].

3. What is international biodiversity law?

32. In this book, international biodiversity law will be understood in a broad sense, encompassing all rules of international law that relate to biodiversity.

33. On the one hand, our approach is broad because in terms of treaties and conventions, it includes not only instruments on biodiversity itself, but also those regarding the components of biodiversity, even when they predate the invention of the concept of biodiversity. These instruments protected biodiversity, at least in part, even before the term was invented.

34. On the other hand, looking at biodiversity means going beyond the admittedly essential issues of protection and preservation to address issues raised by the use and exploitation of biodiversity: fishing, hunting, biosafety issues, to deal with the resulting risks, but also access to biodiversity and the sharing of the benefits arising from its use. In this respect, discussing international biodiversity law will take us well beyond international environmental law, in particular towards international trade, investment and human rights law.

35. For these reasons, it would be futile to try to produce an exhaustive presentation of a subject that is so abundant. Our ambition is rather to introduce the reader to international biodiversity law by presenting its history, founding principles and main directions as

---

62. L. C. Braat and P. Ten Brink (eds.), *The Cost of Policy Inaction (COPI): The Case of Not Meeting the 2010 Biodiversity Target* (Report to the European Commission under contract, ENV.G.1./ETU/2007/0044, Alterra report 1718, 2008).
63. OCDE, *Biodiversity: Finance and the Economic and Business Case for Action Executive Summary and Synthesis prepared by the OECD for the French G7 Presidency and the G7 Environment Ministers' Meeting*, 5-6 May 2019 (OECD 2019) 8.

well as the challenges linked to its implementation. In doing so, we would like to contribute to the conceptualisation of a subject that is still scattered. It should also be added that the international biodiversity law is, of course, international law, in this case applied to biodiversity. One can therefore see it as a laboratory for the study of current developments in contemporary international law. The institutionalisation of co-operation, the development of secondary law of uncertain normativity, fragmentation, the interactions between customary and treaty-based rules, the role of international courts and tribunals, innovative mechanisms to monitor and support State action, compensation for damage: these are all fundamental issues that go far beyond the international law on biodiversity, but it remains very instructive to approach them through the prism of biodiversity.

36. Insofar as international biodiversity law is complex and fragmented, we will begin by presenting its legal and institutional framework (Chap. 1) before focusing on the status of biodiversity in international law (Chap. 2). We will then discuss the more specific issues of conservation (Chap. 3), biosafety (Chap. 4) and access and benefit-sharing (Chap. 5). We will conclude by analysing the mechanisms available to support States in the implementation of the international law on biodiversity (Chap. 6).

CHAPTER I

THE LEGAL AND INSTITUTIONAL FRAMEWORK

37. In this chapter, we examine the construction of the international law on biodiversity (Sec. 1) and how international institutions apprehend biodiversity issues (Sec. 2).

Section 1. The construction of the international law on biodiversity

38. The construction of the international law on biodiversity has been gradual: treaty by treaty, step by step. As for all of international environmental law, this construction has been somewhat chaotic; it did not stem from a rationally designed overall plan. On the contrary, States have responded to the various issues and threats as and when they were identified, warned by scientists and under pressure from very active environmental groups.

39. International co-operation on this matter goes back a relatively long time – to the end of the nineteenth century. However, for many years international law apprehended biological diversity only through some of its components. International conventions first sought to protect animals, including emblematic species or useful and exploited species (fish, insectivorous birds, migratory birds, whales, turtles, fur seals, etc.). Later came the realisation that it was also necessary, in order to preserve these species, to protect their habitats as well as ecologically rich natural environments. This led to a new generation of instruments focusing on nature conservation, on certain types of particularly threatened habitats (wetlands) or on certain specific threats (international trade). In 1992, the Convention on Biological Diversity was added to an already imposing edifice of treaties and conventions – one of its last building blocks.

40. This section outlines the major stages in the construction of the international law on biodiversity. On the path from the protection of wild fauna and/or flora to the protection of biodiversity, three major phases can be identified: the infancy from the end of the nineteenth century to World War II; the development until 1992; and then the consolidation with the adoption of the Rio Convention on Biological Diversity.

1) The infancy (1885-1946)

41. Adopted shortly after the Convention on Measures to Be Taken Against Phylloxera Vastatrix of 17 September 1881, which sought to fight the spread of phylloxera (an insect that destroys vineyards), the Treaty concerning the Regulation of Salmon Fishery in the Rhine River Basin of 30 June 1885 was the first international convention protecting a species of wild fauna. Signed by Switzerland, the Netherlands, Germany and Luxembourg, it was aimed not at the protection, but rather at the sustainable management of fishing resources "shared" between various riparian States. To this end, the treaty essentially purported to regulate fishing (minimum size of salmon, methods, periods, etc.). It did not concern all riparian States.

42. Towards the end of the nineteenth century, the first parks and wildlife reserves were created in British colonial settlements: Yellowstone in the United States in 1872, the Royal National Park near Sydney in 1879 and the Hluhluwe-Umfolozi game reserves in Zululand in 1895 [64]. At the time, colonial powers were particularly concerned about the destruction of African fauna. The arrival of Europeans in Africa had led to the over-exploitation of wild fauna, which was not sustainable in the long-term [65]. And so the first multilateral convention on nature protection pertained to Africa, still colonised at the time. It was mainly to protect their commercial interests that European countries sought to harmonise the regime applicable to their African possessions. They probably also wished to reserve "areas of hedonic recreation for white populations in search of exoticism" [66]. As a result, they decided to adopt an international convention aimed at "preventing the uncontrolled massacre and ensuring the conservation of the diverse wild animal species that are useful to man" [67]. The Convention for the Preservation of Wild Animals, Birds and Fish in Africa (London, 19 May 1900) was signed by Germany, Belgium, Spain, France, Great

---

64. E. Rodary and C. Castellanet, "Les trois temps de la conservation", in E. Rodary, C. Castellanet and G. Rossi (dir.publ.), *Conservation de la nature et développement: l'intégration impossible?*, Paris, Karthala/GRET, Economie et développement, 2004, p. 13.
65. P. Fauchille, "Protection des animaux en Afrique. Convention de Londres du 19 mai 1900", Chronique des faits internationaux, *Revue générale de droit international public*, 1900, p. 521.
66. E. Rodary and C. Castellanet, "Les trois temps de la conservation" (n. 64), p. 10 (our translation).
67. M. Kamto, "Les conventions régionales sur la conservation de la nature et des ressources naturelles en Afrique et leur mise en œuvre", *Revue juridique de l'environnement*, 1991/4, p. 417 (our translation).

Britain, Italy and Portugal. The Convention protected "useful" or rare and endangered species of wild animals and organised the destruction of "harmful" species [68]. It also encouraged the signatories to create "wildlife reserves" [69]. This pioneering instrument never came into force as most of the signatories never ratified it. Nevertheless, this first initiative encouraged some signatories to adopt legislation to protect wildlife in their respective colonial territories. In France, "colonial experimentation" helped develop the prototypes of nature protection schemes [70].

43. Two years later, the Paris Convention for the Protection of Birds Useful to Agriculture (19 March 1902) was adopted, under the pressure of associations of naturalists – ornithologists in particular – who were very active especially in the UK [71]. This time, the convention covered the territory of the European States [72]. This instrument clearly reflected the utilitarian and short-term perspective of that time. It drew a distinction between birds considered "useful" to agriculture (essentially insectivores known as "insect-eaters"), which had to be protected, and "noxious" species (common ravens, magpies, cormorants, common jays, eagle-owls as well as grey and purple herons and night herons, etc.). It prohibited the killing of protected species, the destruction of their nests, eggs and broods, as well as any trade in these species. The destruction of vermin was however authorised [73]. In view of the advances in ecology, the content of this convention was soon deemed inadequate. Therefore, on 18 October 1950, the International Convention for the Protection of Birds was signed in Paris, replacing the 1902 Convention for its signatories. More "modern", this convention is no longer based on a binary distinction between useful species to be protected and harmful species to be destroyed. On the contrary, it establishes the principle that *all* birds in the wild should be protected [74].

---

68. Articles II (1), II (13) and II (15).
69. Article II (5), IUCN, *An Introduction to the African Convention on the Conservation of Nature and Natural Resources*, IUCN Environmental Policy and Law Paper No. 56 Rev., 2nd ed., 2006, p. 38.
70. S. Adel, "L'émergence de l'idée de parc national en France. De la protection des paysages à l'expérimentation coloniale", Raphaël Larrère éd., *Histoire des parcs nationaux. Comment prendre soin de la nature?*, Editions Quæ, Versailles, 2009, pp. 43-58 (our translation).
71. E. Rodary, C. Castellanet, "Les trois temps de la conservation" (n 64), pp. 5-44.
72. It came into force on 6 December 2006 and was ratified by Austria, Czechoslovakia, France, Germany, Hungary, Liechtenstein, Monaco, Poland, Portugal and Switzerland.
73. Article 9.
74. Preamble, Articles 1 and 2.

It then distinguishes between, on the one hand, the protection offered to all birds – at least during their breeding period – and to migratory species during their return journey to their nesting grounds, and on the other hand, the protection offered to species in danger of extinction or of scientific interest, which applies throughout the year. In Europe, the conventional edifice was supplemented by the Benelux Convention on the Hunting and Protection of Birds (Brussels, 10 June 1970). These two instruments do not so clearly reflect a utilitarian approach, but their aim is primarily to protect huntable birds.

44. On the American continent too, focus was first placed on birds, this time through a series of bilateral agreements at the initiative of the United States and concluded with some of the States located on the same migratory route. The Migratory Bird Treaty of 16 August 1916 between Canada and the United States was thus adopted, later supplemented by the Migratory Bird Treaty of 7 February 1936 between Mexico and the United States and its Protocol of 10 March 1972, the Convention Between the Government of the United States of America and the Government of Japan for the Protection of Migratory Birds and Birds in Danger of Extinction, and Their Environment, (Tokyo, 4 March 1972) and the Convention Between the United States and the USSR concerning the Conservation of Migratory Birds and Their Environment (Moscow, 19 November 1976).

45. Another species was the focus of an international treaty at the beginning of the twentieth century: the northern fur seal. Much sought after by fur traders at the time, it had been hunted almost to extinction. In 1893, an arbitration award settled a dispute between the United States and Great Britain (acting for its dominion of Canada) over fur seals in the Pribilof Islands [75]. In 1911, the North Pacific Fur Seal Convention was signed between the United States, Great Britain (acting for Canada), Japan and Russia. Pelagic seal hunting (on the high seas) was prohibited and the taking of sea lions was restricted. This first convention was replaced by a new one in 1957: the Interim Convention (with schedule) on conservation of North Pacific fur seals signed at Washington between the United States of America, Canada, Japan and the USSR. This instrument also prohibited pelagic sealing, but it allowed the United States and Canada to take female seals for

---

75. Award between the United States and the United Kingdom relating to the rights of jurisdiction of United States in the Bering's Sea and the preservation of fur seals, 15 August 1893, *Reports of International Arbitral Awards*, Vol. XXVIII, pp. 263-276. See below, Chapter 2.

research purposes. In addition, commercial harvesting on the Pribilof Islands was still permitted [76].

46. The 1930s saw the adoption of a new regional nature protection convention for Africa, the Convention relative to the Preservation of Fauna and Flora in their Natural State (London, 8 November 1933) [77]. Taking a more modern approach than the 1900 Convention, it encouraged the creation of the first African national parks and the protection of a number of wild species. It contributed to raising awareness in Africa of the need to protect nature and natural resources. Of course, it still reflected utilitarian concerns [78]. But it also explicitly recognised, for the first time, the notion of endangered species. It was also one of the first international instruments to adopt an integrated conservation approach, addressing both the protection of species and their habitats. It required States to protect the ecosystems most representative of their territories, especially those that are in some way specific to these territories, and to ensure the conservation of all species and especially those listed in the annex to the Convention [79]. It distinguished three types of protected areas: strict natural reserves, national parks and special reserves. Member States were under the obligation to maintain or enlarge the natural reserves existing when the Convention came into force and were to consider the need to create new ones. The Convention even provided for the creation of buffer zones around natural reserves. It also regulated the import and export of hunting trophies. Following the decolonisation movement, this treaty was replaced by the African Convention on the Conservation of Nature and Natural Resources of 15 September 1968, known as the Algiers Convention. As the first regional nature protection convention of the modern era, the Algiers Convention replaced the London Convention. It quickly came into force on 16 June 1969.

---

76. In 1984, the Convention was not renewed because the US Senate refused to ratify the protocol of extension. COSEWIC, *COSEWIC Assessment and Update Status Report on the Northern Fur Seal (Callorhinus ursinus) in Canada 2006*, Ottawa, 2010. Still considered vulnerable by the IUCN, the fur seal population has stabilised at 650,000 individuals and is now hunted only to a very limited extent by indigenous populations for food.

77. Société des Nations, *Recueil des Traités*, 1936, No. 3995, p. 241 ss.

78. See its Article 8.4 according to which the Parties provide that "[t]he competent authorities shall also give consideration to the question of protecting species of animals or plants which by general admission are useful to man or of special scientific interest".

79. M. Kamto, "Les conventions régionales sur la conservation de la nature et des ressources naturelles en Afrique et leur mise en œuvre" (n. 67), p. 418.

47. A few years after the 1933 London Convention, a convention on nature protection was adopted on the American continent: the Washington Convention of 12 October 1940 on Nature Protection and Wild Life Preservation in the Western Hemisphere. It contains similar, but on the whole less restrictive, provisions. Article 5 provides as follows:

> "The Contracting Governments agree to adopt, or to propose such adoption to their respective appropriate law-making bodies, suitable laws and regulations for the protection and preservation of flora and fauna within their national boundaries but not included in the national parks, national reserves, nature monuments, or strict wilderness reserves ... and recommend that their respective legislatures adopt laws which will assure the protection and preservation of the natural scenery, striking geological formations, and regions and natural objects of aesthetic interest or historic or scientific value."

In particular, Article 8 specifies that

> "[t]he protection of the species mentioned in the Annex ... is declared to be of special urgency and importance. Species included therein shall be protected as completely as possible, and their hunting, killing, capturing, or taking shall be allowed only with the permission of the appropriate government authorities in the country".

The Convention also includes an original possibility: a living animal species "of aesthetic, historic or scientific interest" can be declared by the signatories as a "nature monument", thus making it "an inviolate nature monument, except for duly authorized scientific investigations or government inspection" (Art. 1 (3)).

2) The development phase (1946-1992)

48. It was in 1946 that the first nature protection convention designed to be universal was adopted: the Convention for the Regulation of Whaling, signed on 2 December 1946 by fifteen States. It is open to accession by other States and currently has eighty-eight Parties[80]. Originally, it was not an environmental protection instrument protecting

---

80. As of 25 October 2023.

an emblematic species. In reality, it simply organised the sustainable hunting of a *resource* on an international scale. As stated in the preamble, "a system of international regulation" will "ensure proper and effective conservation and development of whale stocks", and "increases in the size of whale stocks will permit increases in the numbers of whales which may be captured without endangering these natural resources", the objective being to "make possible the orderly development of the whaling industry"[81]. Other universal agreements were later adopted with similar objectives (for instance, the Geneva Convention of 29 April 1958 on Fishing and Conservation of the Living Resources of the High Seas), as well as regional agreements, for example, the Agreement on the Exploitation and Conservation of the Maritime Resources of the South Pacific (18 August 1952), the Agreement concerning the Protection of the Salmon in the Baltic Sea of 20 December 1962, the Convention for the Conservation and Management of Vicuna between Bolivia, Chile, Ecuador and Peru (Lima, 20 December 1979), the Convention for the Conservation of Antarctic Seals (London, 1 June 1972) in the framework of the Antarctic Treaty System and the Agreement on the Conservation of Seals in the Wadden Sea (Bonn, 16 October 1990).

49. With regard to plants, mention should be made of the International Plant Protection Convention, adopted in Rome on 6 December 1951 under the auspices of the Food and Agriculture Organization (FAO), which aims to co-ordinate international action to prevent and control the introduction and spread of organisms that are harmful to plants and plant products. It primarily deals with cultivated plant species, but also seeks to protect "wild flora". As for the International Tropical Timber Agreement (Geneva, 18 November 1983), it provided a framework for co-operation between producer and consumer countries of tropical timber[82].

50. Regarding the Antarctic, the Agreed Measures for the Conservation of Antarctic Fauna and Flora were adopted in Brussels on 2 June 1964 and came into force on 1 November 1982. They designate the area south of 60° S latitude as a special conservation area and set out various measures to protect the fauna and flora, in particular plants, mammals and birds known as "indigenous" or "native"[83]. They were

---

81. Preamble.
82. This agreement was succeeded by the International Tropical Timber Agreement of 26 January 1994 and the International Tropical Timber Agreement of 27 January 2006.
83. See *Report of the Third Antarctic Treaty Consultative Meeting*, Doc.17/final, 13 June 1964.

later supplemented by the Convention for the Conservation of Antarctic Marine Living Resources (20 May 1980), then by the Protocol on Environmental Protection to the Antarctic Treaty (4 October 1991) and finally by the Agreement on Conservation of Polar Bears (Oslo, 15 November 1973). With these instruments, the Antarctic has become one of the most advanced international regimes and the first to have created a truly international protected area [84].

51. In 1968, at a conference organised by UNESCO on the Rational Use and Conservation of the Resources of the Biosphere, the idea was introduced to start an international and interdisciplinary research programme aimed essentially at providing scientific knowledge and qualified personnel for a sustained and sound management of terrestrial ecosystems. The Man and Biosphere (MAB) programme was thus launched in 1970 at the sixteenth session of the UNESCO General Conference, with the aim of creating a worldwide network of protected areas known as "biosphere reserves". The constitution of the network began in 1976. Its objective is to preserve representative ecosystems as well as genetic resources, but also to conduct scientific research, continuously monitor the state of the environment in these areas and lastly, educate the public about the environment. Designation is optional and left to the discretion of the States, whose proposals are then submitted to the MAB Council for approval. This is the first global and co-ordinated network of protected areas. The first protected areas were designated in 1976 and there are now a total number of 748 protected areas in 134 States [85].

52. Another convention designed to be universal is the Convention on Wetlands of International Importance Especially as Waterfowl Habitat (Ramsar, 2 February 1971). It came into force on 21 December 1975 and now has 172 Contracting Parties. It provides a framework for national action and international co-operation for the conservation and wise use of wetlands and their resources. Originally designed for the conservation of waterfowl habitat, its scope was later broadened as States recognised the importance of wetlands for biological diversity and for the well-being of humans more generally. Each Party undertakes to designate at least one site that meets the criteria for inclusion in the Ramsar List of wetlands of international importance and to ensure that the ecological character of each recognised site is maintained. A total

---

84. P.-M. Dupuy and J. Vinuales, *Introduction au droit international de l'environnement*, Bruylant, Bruxelles, 2015, p. 251.
85. UNESCO, https://en.unesco.org/biosphere/wnbr, accessed on 25 October 2023.

of 2,494 wetland sites, covering almost 257 million hectares, are now included in the Ramsar List ("Ramsar Sites"). As for the Montreux Record, it is a register of wetland sites on the List of Wetlands of International Importance where changes in ecological character have occurred, are occurring or are likely to occur as a result of technological developments, pollution or other human interference. It is maintained as part of the Ramsar List [86].

53. The following year, the UNESCO Convention concerning the Protection of the World Cultural and Natural Heritage was adopted in Paris on 16 November 1972 [87]. The purpose of this universal treaty is to protect the most remarkable sites and monuments, whether natural, cultural or both, provided that they have an "outstanding universal value" [88].

54. The Washington Convention on International Trade in Endangered Species of Wild Fauna and Flora (CITES), which regulates international trade in endangered species of wild fauna and flora, is relatively well known, including among the general public. Since the beginning of the twentieth century, the trade in live or dead wild species, or products or parts of wild species (bird feathers, elephant ivory, rhinoceros horns, cat skins, tortoise shells, etc.) had raised concern among naturalists, who pleaded for restrictions to be placed on international trade [89]. Yet this trade, whether in ornamental or medicinal plants, pets or animals for scientific research, trophies or decorative objects, grew rapidly. The bulk of the trade went from South to North, with developing countries being the main suppliers and developed countries, the main customers. In this respect, animals and plants were not spared by globalisation. With this in mind, in 1963, IUCN began drafting an international convention on the export, transport and import of rare or endangered species of wild fauna. Building on the impetus of the Stockholm Conference, CITES was finally adopted in Washington in 1973 by the representatives of eighty States [90]. It came into force two

---

[86]. See https://rsis.ramsar.org/ris-search/?solrsort=country_en_s%20asc&language=en&f[0]=montreuxListed_b%3Atrue&pagetab=1, accessed on 25 October 2023.
[87]. It came into force on 17 December 1975 and has 195 Parties (as of 10 October 2023).
[88]. Articles 1 and 2 of the Convention.
[89]. In 1911, a Swiss naturalist, Paul Sarasin, advocated the establishment of such restrictions. He tried to convince the Swiss Government to take measures to limit the export and import of bird feathers, as certain species were particularly affected by the fashion of feathered hats.
[90]. See Resolution 99-3 of the United Nations Conference on the Environment (Stockholm).

years later, in July 1975. It prohibits trade in endangered species (listed in Appendix I) and regulates trade in non-endangered species (listed in Appendix II), seeking to reconcile the imperative of their conservation with the need to preserve economic interests at stake, particularly in the exporting countries which for the most part are developing countries.

55. On 23 June 1979, the Bonn Convention on the Conservation of Migratory Species of Wild Animals was adopted[91]. This is an "umbrella" convention that has given rise to the adoption of a wide range of complementary instruments, including treaties such as the Agreement on the Conservation of Seals in the Wadden Sea (16 October 1990), the Agreement on the Conservation of European Bats (4 December 1991), the Agreement on the Conservation of African-Eurasian Migratory Waterbirds (16 June 1995), the Agreement on the Conservation of Small Cetaceans of the Baltic, North East Atlantic, Irish and North Seas (17 March 1992), the Agreement on the Conservation of Cetaceans of the Black Sea, Mediterranean Sea and Contiguous Atlantic Area (24 November 1996), the Agreement on the Conservation of Albatrosses and Petrels (19 June 2001), the Agreement on the Conservation of Gorillas and their Habitats (21 October 2007), or more flexible instruments like the Memorandum of Understanding concerning Conservation Measures for the Slender-billed Curlew (10 September 1994) or the Memorandum of Understanding concerning Conservation Measures for the West African Populations of the African Elephant *(Loxodonta africana)* of 22 November 2005, or even action plans (African-Eurasian Migratory Landbirds, Western Lowland Gorillas and Central Chimpanzees, White-headed Duck, Migratory Sharks, etc.). These are all legally separate instruments, although their links to the Bonn Convention are important, particularly from an institutional point of view. A State may be a party to an agreement because its territory is part of the "range" of the species in question, without necessarily being a party to the Bonn Convention. Article 5 of the Bonn Convention suggests "guidelines for agreements". These are relatively precise guidelines, but only optional as they are written in the conditional tense. Moreover, they are not binding on non-party States.

56. Under pressure from naturalist associations, after Africa (1933) and America (1940), the South Pacific also adopted a regional convention: the Apia Convention on Conservation of Nature in the

---

91. It came into force on 1 November 1983 and has 133 Parties (as of 10 October 2023).

South Pacific (12 June 1976). It was then Europe's turn with the Convention on the Conservation of European Wildlife and Natural Habitats. Signed in Bern, Switzerland, on 19 September 1979, under the auspices of the Council of Europe, and commonly referred to as the Bern Convention, it came into force on 1 June 1982. A few months earlier, the European Union had adopted its first major nature protection instrument, Directive 79/409 on the conservation of wild birds [92]. This was followed by the Benelux Convention on Nature Conservation and Landscape Protection (8 June 1982), the ASEAN Agreement on the Conservation of Nature and Natural Resources (9 July 1985) and, at a sub-regional level, the Protocol Agreement on the Conservation of Common Natural Resources (4 June 1982) signed by the Democratic Republic of Congo, Uganda and Sudan. Further regional co-operation was initiated, aimed at protecting regions that share a certain unity from an environmental standpoint, regardless of national borders. Among these are mountainous regions (the Alps with the Alpine Convention adopted in Salzburg on 7 November 1991 and later supplemented by a series of protocols; the Carpathian Mountains with the Carpathian Convention adopted in Kiev on 22 May 2003) and regional seas. Indeed, eighteen programmes on regional seas have been initiated by UNEP, involving more than 150 States. They have led to a dozen specific conventions, often supplemented by protocols, following the Barcelona Convention for the Protection of the Mediterranean Sea against Pollution (16 February 1976). Bilateral agreements have also been adopted, such as the 1986 China-Australia Migratory Bird Agreement [93].

57. This period also saw a proliferation of conventions on fisheries, with the creation of some fifty regional organisations, some of which cover the resources of a given area while others focus more on managing and conserving one or more species identified in one or more areas [94].

---

92. Directive 2009/147/EC of the European Parliament and of the Council of 30 November 2009 on the conservation of wild birds, *OJ* L 20, 26 January 2010, pp. 7-25.

93. Agreement between the Government of Australia and the Government of the People's Republic of China for the Protection of Migratory Birds and their Environment; Canberra, 20 October 1986; E. Hamman, "Bilateral Agreements for the Protection of Migratory Birdlife: The Implementation of the China-Australia Migratory Bird Agreement (CAMBA)", *Asia Pacific Journal of Environmental Law*, Vol. 22, No. 1, 2019, pp. 137-159.

94. S. Gambardella, *La gestion et la conservation des ressources halieutiques en droit international. L'exemple de la Méditerranée*, thèse pour le doctorat en droit, Aix-Marseille Université, 2013.

This period was also marked by the adoption of the United Nations Convention for the Law of the Sea (10 December 1982). The "Ocean's Constitution" contains many provisions aimed at protecting the marine environment, albeit with a very general approach.

58. As we can see, there were significant developments in international law during this second phase. Many conventions were adopted, some designed to be universal but with a sector-specific purpose, others regional, whether general or sector-specific, pursuing various approaches and involving certain States only [95]. This abundant and somewhat incoherent set of conventions was not enough to protect biodiversity and needed to be consolidated.

3) The consolidation phase (since 1992)

59. From 3 to 14 June 1992, echoing the first major UN conference on the environment held in Stockholm in 1972, Rio de Janeiro hosted the United Nations Conference on Environment and Development (UNCED), also known as the Earth Summit. This conference was a turning point in the perception of environmental issues. A programme of action for the twenty-first century was adopted, referred to as *Agenda 21* – whose Chapter 15 focused on the preservation of biological diversity – as well as the opening for signature of the Convention on Biological Diversity, at the same time as the United Nations Framework Convention on Climate Change (UNFCCC). The adoption of the Convention on Biological Diversity undoubtedly constituted a major milestone for the international law on biodiversity.

a) *The invention of biological diversity and the adoption of the Rio Convention on Biological Diversity*

60. At the end of the 1980s and beginning of the 1990s, environmental and economic reasons but also conservation, exploitation and use issues as well as the concerns of the North and South converged to establish biodiversity, very soon after its "invention", as a major issue in international relations. Because it was a global problem (even if this is not the only level at which it can be apprehended), biodiversity required international co-operation and the development of international law.

61. At the time, the idea of a global treaty on the conservation of species and ecosystems was not new. It had been introduced at an

---

95. V. Koester, "The Five Biodiversity-Related Conventions", *Environmental Policy and Law*, Vol. 31, No. 3, ICEL, Bonn, 2001, pp. 151-156.

international conference in Bern in 1913 and had resurfaced in 1949 at the United Nations Scientific Conference on the Conservation and Utilization of Resources held at Lake Success. In 1981, the 15th General Assembly of the International Union for the Conservation of Nature (IUCN), a very active NGO in the field of nature protection, called for the adoption, with regard to the conservation of biological resources, of an "international arrangement and rules to implement it"[96]. The IUCN Environmental Law Centre set about preparing a draft treaty, and convinced the WWF, Norway and UNEP of its relevance. The World Conservation Strategy adopted in 1980 by the International Union for the Conservation of Nature, with inputs from UNEP and WWF, was instrumental to the maturation of the project. This document already expressed the various objectives that would later be set by the Rio Convention: maintaining essential ecological processes and life-support systems, preserving genetic diversity and ensuring the sustainable use of species and ecosystems[97]. In turn, the World Charter for Nature, adopted in 1982 by the UN General Assembly, recognised the need to protect "genetic viability on Earth"[98]. In 1987, the conclusions of the Brundtland Report went in the same direction, drawing on the UN Convention on the Law of the Sea as a model[99]. UNEP then organised various expert meetings from which the key features of the future convention emerged. Negotiations formally began in 1988. Ten meetings were held between 1988 and 1992: three meetings of the *Ad Hoc* Group of Experts on Biological Diversity, two of the *Ad Hoc* Group of Legal and Technical Experts on Biological Diversity (slightly expanded) and five meetings of the Intergovernmental Negotiating Committee for a Convention on Biological Diversity. The Convention on Biological Diversity (CBD) was finally adopted on 22 May 1992 in Nairobi[100]. It was opened for signature at the Earth Summit in Rio

---

96. D. McGraw, "The Story of the Biodiversity Convention: From Negotiation to Implementation", in P. Leprestre (ed.), *Governing Global Biodiversity. The Evolution and Implementation of the Convention on Biological Diversity*, Ashgate, 2004, p. 12. See also for a personal account as a negotiator, F. McConnell, *The Biodiversity Convention: A Negotiating History: A Personal Account of Negotiating the United Nations Convention on Biological Diversity, and After*, Kluwer, 1996.

97. IUCN, World Conservation Strategy: Living Resource Conservation for Sustainable Development, 1980, p. VI, https://portals.iucn.org/library/node/6424, accessed on 25 October 2023.

98. UNGA, Resolution A/37/7 of 28 October 1982, *World Charter for Nature*.

99. World Commission on Environment and Development, *Our Common Future*, Oxford paperbacks, 1987, p. 187.

100. On the genesis of this convention, see A. Gillespie, *Conservation, Biodiversity and International Law*, Edward Elgar, 2012, p. 4 *et seq.*; D. M. McGraw, "The

de Janeiro the following month, where it received 157 signatures. It came into force the following year and now has 196 Parties [101], which makes it one of the most widely ratified international conventions in the world. However, there is one major absentee from the list of Parties, the United States, which signed the CBD in 1993 but never ratified it.

62. The content of the Convention reflects what proved to be a very delicate negotiation process. This process was initially supported by the Americans, who argued for a more global and coherent approach to biodiversity issues before feeling "overwhelmed" by issues of international equity and justice and of economic development [102]. Indeed, developing countries were in a strong position during these negotiations as they harbour four-fifths of the world's biodiversity. Under pressure from them, the project gradually evolved from a conservation convention – it originally came from scientists and environmental activists – to a more global convention with implications for economic development [103]. The countries of the South made their voices heard all the more strongly because they felt deeply "colonised" in the climate negotiations that were being held in parallel [104]. Some say negotiations were also made difficult by the fact that the most experienced negotiators had been sent to the climate negotiations [105]. At the time, biodiversity issues received less attention than climate change. Even today, although things have started to change recently, they still have a lower profile than climate change [106].

63. The United States would have wanted to postpone the negotiations until after Rio. They arrived in Nairobi for the last meeting with sixteen non-negotiable demands [107]. In order to complete the negotiations before the Rio summit, negotiators left out the most sensitive issues such as

---

Story of the Biodiversity Convention: From Negotiation to Implementation" (n. 96), pp. 7-38.

101. As of 14 December 2023.

102. D. McGraw, "The Story of the Biodiversity Convention: From Negotiation to Implementation" (n. 96), p. 12.

103. M.-A. Hermitte, "La Convention sur la diversité biologique", *Annuaire français de droit international*, 1992, Vol. 38, pp. 844-870.

104. V. Koester, "The Biodiversity Convention Negotiation Process and Some Comments on the Outcome", *Environmental Policy and Law*, 1997, 27, p. 175.

105. K. Rosendal, "Implications of the US 'No' in Rio", in V. Sanchez and C. Juma (eds.), *Biodiplomacy: Genetic Resources and International Relations*, African Centre for Technology Studies (ACTS) Press, Nairobi, p. 92.

106. D. McGraw, "The Story of the Biodiversity Convention: From Negotiation to Implementation" (n. 96), p. 16.

107. Spielman, "White House Has Serious Problems with UN Species-Saving Accord", Associated Press, 8 May 1992, quoted by D. McGraw, "The Story of the Biodiversity Convention: From Negotiation to Implementation" (n. 96), p. 35.

biotechnology, technology transfer and financing. A provision on the precautionary principle was transferred to the preamble with a more flexible wording. A provision on liability for damage to biodiversity, which provided that those responsible for damage should bear the costs of repairing it, was eventually withdrawn due to the reluctance of many States. One of the drafts had also included lists of areas or species to be adopted by the COP as in the World Heritage Convention, the Ramsar Convention or CITES, but in the end the selection and management of protected areas or species was left to the Parties' discretion [108]. Biodiversity was placed under the sovereignty of States [109] and was not declared a "common heritage of mankind", contrary to what some had wanted. States simply recognised that "the conservation of biological diversity is a common concern of humankind" [110]. Thus, far from the project originally imagined by IUCN and industrialised States, the CBD was eventually seen as a new type of convention, a "sustainable development" convention also touching on issues of intellectual property rights, trade, technology, health, culture, etc. [111]. This evolution resulted in a considerably more cumbersome and even more fragile Convention: "By bringing these 'non-traditional issues' into the bargain, the CBD becomes a courageous political document but a rather clumsy and cumbersome legal text" [112].

b) *A convention designed to be modern and scientifically based*

64. The Convention on Biological Diversity did not come into existence within a conventional vacuum. However, because it was intended to be universal, the Convention on Biological Diversity was the first convention to be so comprehensive in its treatment of biodiversity issues, covering areas, species and the relationships between them, wild and domestic biological diversity, *in situ* and *ex situ* conservation,

---

108. A. Boyle, "The Rio Convention on Biological Diversity", in M. Bowman and C. Redgwell, *International Law and the Conservation of Biological Diversity*, Kluwer Law International, 1996, p. 37.
109. See Article 15, para. 1, which states: "Recognizing the sovereign rights of States over their natural resources, the authority to determine access to genetic resources rests with the national governments and is subject to national legislation".
110. Preamble.
111. C. Tinker, "A 'New Breed' of Treaty: The United Nations Convention on Biological Diversity", *Pace Environmental Law Review*, Vol. 13, Issue 1, Fall, 1995, September 1995, pp. 191-218; M.-A. Hermitte, "La Convention sur la diversité biologique" (n. 103), pp. 844-870.
112. D. McGraw, "The Story of the Biodiversity Convention: From Negotiation to Implementation" (n. 96), p. 24.

planning, regulation, research, education and information activities, etc., while at the same time having a universal rather than regional scope. It represented a new approach, possibly even a paradigm shift, for the international law on biodiversity. It also marked a new stage in the international legislative process, designed to give more coherence to the sector-specific and regional agreements that had been previously adopted, although no formal link was established with them.

65. The CBD is designed to be modern and scientifically based, relying on scientific methods and concepts. Its definition of biological diversity, which focuses on the three levels of the biological hierarchy, is often quoted and serves as a reference [113]. The recommended methods also reflect the desire to provide a scientific basis for the Convention, with a constant focus on systematism and rationality and even the adoption of approaches that were new at the time, such as the approach based on "precaution" [114]. The term "scientific" itself is used twenty-four times in the Convention.

66. For all that, the Convention is not free of ambiguities, firstly because the concepts on which it is based are not themselves free of ambiguities. This is especially true for the concept of *biological diversity*, which, as we previously discussed, is eminently complex, shifting and in some respects elusive and controversial [115]. The very definition of the three levels of biodiversity, which is the basis of the Convention, requires further clarification and refinement [116]. If our knowledge of biodiversity is still partial and limited, what, then, of the ambition to "control", "manage" and "engineer" it? In these circumstances, it is hardly surprising that the translation of this concept into law is both delicate and imperfect.

c) *A threefold objective*

67. By moving from the more traditional categories that have long been used in political and legal discourse (nature, fauna, flora, species,

---

113. "Biological diversity: the variability among living organisms from all sources including, *inter alia*, terrestrial, marine and other aquatic ecosystems and the ecological complexes of which they are part: this includes diversity within species, between species and of ecosystems" (Art. 2).
114. The preamble notes that "where there is a threat of significant reduction or loss of biological diversity, lack of full scientific certainty should not be used as a reason for postponing measures to avoid or minimize such a threat" (para. 9). This is one of the first formulations of the precautionary approach or principle.
115. See above, Introduction, para. 6 *et seq.*
116. B. Chevassus-au-Louis, *La biodiversité, c'est maintenant*, Ed. de l'Aube, 2013, p. 40.

sites, etc.) to *biological diversity*, is there a desire to provide a better scientific basis for conservationist policies and thus make them more effective, or is there a discreet shift towards an instrument more focused on the exploitation of biological resources, and in particular genetic material? According to Article 1 of the Convention:

> "The objectives of this Convention, to be pursued in accordance with its relevant provisions, are the conservation of biological diversity, the sustainable use of its components and the fair and equitable sharing of the benefits arising out of the utilization of genetic resources, including by appropriate access to genetic resources and by appropriate transfer of relevant technologies, taking into account all rights over those resources and to technologies, and by appropriate funding."

Thus, the Convention sets out not one but three objectives. Linking conservation with sustainable use and benefit-sharing is not inconsistent in itself. But the conservation objective loses the central place it had in the first draft prepared by IUCN. Rather, the Convention seems to be the result of a convergence of major conservationist NGOs with interest groups whose economic activity depends on genetic resources, such as seed companies and agri-food and pharmaceutical industries, these different actors holding opposing views on the causes of the problem, the means to remedy it and even the objectives to be achieved [117].

68. It is also interesting to note that the Convention conceptually links cultural diversity and biological diversity, on the assumption that cultural diversity should be seen as guaranteeing biodiversity [118]. In this respect, the Convention is the result of an objective alliance between environmentalists and indigenists that popularised the idea that cultural diversity, expressed through diverse uses of natural resources, plays a major role in maintaining ecological balance [119]. In other words, "what

---

117. C. Aubertin, V. Boisvert and F.-D. Vivien, "La construction sociale de la question de la biodiversité", *Natures, Sciences, Sociétés*, Vol. 6, 1998, pp. 7-19. See also F.-D. Vivien, "De Rio à Johannesburg les négociations autour de la diversité biologique", *Ecologie & politique*, 2002/3, No. 26, pp. 35-53.

118. Unesco, *Diversité culturelle et biodiversité pour un développement durable : table ronde de haut niveau organisée conjointement par l'Unesco et le UNEP le 3 septembre 2002 à Johannesburg à l'occasion du Sommet mondial pour le développement durable*, Paris, Unesco, https://wedocs.unep.org/bitstream/handle/20.500.11822/13741/DiversiteCulturelleetBiodiversite.pdf?sequence=1&isAllowed=y, accessed on 25 October 2023.

119. F. Kohler, "Diversité culturelle et diversité biologique : une approche critique fondée sur l'exemple brésilien", *Natures Sciences Sociétés*, 2/2011, Vol. 19, pp. 113-124.

for some is 'nature' is the 'culture' of local peoples"[120]. In reality, it has been shown that the assumption that indigenous peoples are necessarily respectful of the environment should be qualified.

69. Beyond that, this also raises questions about the relationship between humans and biological diversity. Biological diversity and humans have not evolved in isolation, but have in fact co-evolved and co-adapted[121]. Humans have and continue to "make" biological diversity. Conserving biological diversity therefore often requires the pursuit of human activities such as agriculture, grazing, etc. This has implications for biodiversity protection initiatives themselves as they focus on species and environments that are already culturally and economically significant to those who live there, depend on them, and in many cases, have property rights over them[122].

70. Thus, a gradual shift has taken place, which was already foreseeable in 1992 given that the CBD expressed a rather utilitarian vision of biodiversity[123]. Initially, the institutions established within the CBD were equally – if not more – interested in the exploitation of genetic resources as they were in the conservation of biodiversity. Although it may be excessive to say that the Convention reduced biodiversity to a simple issue of genetic resources, from which the highest possible benefits should be derived[124], the subject matter and tone of the debates taking place within the Convention as well as the subject matter of the first three protocols, certainly do give that impression. For some, this international law instrument, which should have confirmed the creation of a global public good and set out the responsibilities of each party towards its sustainable use, can be viewed as essentially focused on laying down a legal framework guaranteeing the development of biotechnology[125]. The CBD, very general and with mild obligations, called for much more concrete action. The treaty institutions found themselves somewhat entangled in the initial, unresolved contradictions. As we shall see, the definition of strategic

---

120. M. Roué, "Entre cultures et natures", *Revue internationale des sciences sociales*, 2006/1, No. 187, p. 13 (our translation).
121. G. Rossi Georges and V. André, "La biodiversité: questions de perspectives", *Annales de géographie*, 2006/5, No. 651, pp. 468-484.
122. *Ibid.*
123. M.-A. Hermitte, "La Convention sur la diversité biologique" (n. 103), pp. 844-870.
124. J.-P. Maréchal, "Quand la biodiversité est assimilée à une marchandise", *Le Monde diplomatique*, July 1999, pp. 6-7.
125. C. Aubertin, V. Boisvert and F. D. Vivien, "La construction sociale de la question de la biodiversité" (n. 117).

conservation objectives did, however, provide the Convention with the opportunity to position itself, in a second phase, as a key instrument of biological diversity conservation.

d) *A framework convention supplemented by subsequent protocols*

71. As is often the case in the environmental field, the CBD is not an isolated instrument but a component of a much larger legal package, which includes other treaties – three protocols – and many other related instruments. Legally, the Convention is a framework convention; it is a minimum agreement, the first step in a regulatory *process* towards a more elaborate and restrictive regime that will take the form of additional *protocols*. By providing a normative and institutional framework, in particular through the creation of a Conference of the Parties or COP, this framework convention allows negotiations to continue in order to gradually reach a consensus that was not present at the time of its adoption. This is especially important as the obligations laid down in the CBD are very general and often even weakened by the addition of the expression "as far as possible and as appropriate".

72. The Convention on Biological Diversity was indeed supplemented by two protocols, one of which gave rise to a second protocol. Together with the decisions adopted by the Conference of the Parties to these various treaties, they form what political scientists refer to as an "international regime": a set of implicit and explicit principles, norms, rules and decision-making procedures around which the expectations of actors in a specific field converge and which help to guide behaviour in a certain direction [126].

- *The Cartagena Protocol*

73. The first protocol to the CBD is the Cartagena Protocol on Biosafety. Here, the framework convention technique proved particularly useful. Although *Agenda 21* advocated the development of international co-operation on biosafety as early as 1992 (para. 16.29), the Convention itself was rather laconic on the issue [127]. It took another seven

---

126. S. Krasner (ed.), *International Regimes*, Ithaca, Cornell University Press, 1983.
127. See Article 8 *(g)*, which called on States to adopt measures to manage the potential impacts of biotechnological risk on the conservation of biological diversity and human health. Article 19 (3) of the Convention referred to the need for an international protocol on the issue.

years for a consensus to painfully mature and for a protocol to be agreed. Adopted in January 2000, the Protocol focuses on biosafety, i.e. the assessment, prevention and management of environmental and health risks associated with biotechnology. The aim was both to harmonise the Parties' national laws, still disparate, sometimes even non-existent, and also to organise co-operation and prevent or even resolve possible inter-State conflicts, particular trade-related ones. It came into force in September 2003 and has 173 Parties. The Protocol has played an important role, including on a symbolic level, despite the WTO's force of attraction on these issues.

- *The Kuala Lumpur Protocol*

74. This Protocol was supplemented in 2010 by a Protocol . . . to the Protocol: the Kuala Lumpur Protocol [128]. During the negotiations on the Cartagena Protocol, no agreement could be reached on the issue of liability for damage caused by living modified organisms, even though this was an essential condition of their social acceptability [129]. As a compromise, Article 27 of the Cartagena Protocol left it to the first Meeting of the Parties to the Convention sitting as the Meeting of the Parties to the Protocol (COP-MOP) to initiate a process to devise appropriate rules and procedures on liability and redress. Negotiations were long and difficult. The new instrument, which is referred to as the Nagoya-Kuala Lumpur Supplementary Protocol on Liability and Redress to the Cartagena Protocol on Biosafety, was adopted more than ten years after the Cartagena Protocol. It lays down the beginnings of a liability and redress regime [130]. However, the Protocol is still timid and lags behind other international regimes dealing with liability.

- *The Nagoya Protocol*

75. The second Protocol to the Convention is the Nagoya Protocol on Access to Genetic Resources and the Fair and Equitable Sharing of Benefits. This Protocol addresses a long-standing demand for equity – already very much on the table in the 1992 Convention negotiations

---

128. The Protocol came into force in 2018 and currently has fifty-four Parties.
129. M.-A. Hermitte, S. Maljean-Dubois and E. Truilhé-Marengo, "Actualités de la Convention sur la diversité biologique : science et politique, équité, biosécurité", *Annuaire français de droit international*, 2011, p. 426 ss.
130. *Ibid.*

– by purporting to combat biopiracy and ensure a level playing field when accessing biological resources in the South [131].

e) *Defining a strategic framework: From the Aichi Targets to the Sustainable Development Goals and the post-2020 framework*

76. A few years after the adoption of the Convention on Biological Diversity, the COP to the CBD came to a rather negative conclusion regarding its implementation. The general impression was that the work of the Convention was going in too many directions. Despite attempts to refocus priorities, the dominant impression was that of a dispersion of efforts, which could only slow down the implementation of an already relatively fragile and isolated instrument. The situation became deadlocked as soon as it was necessary to step up and actually define, in specific sectors, concrete means of action, with associated funding and precise deadlines. Debates were structurally contentious, especially on issues relating to forests, access to genetic resources and invasive species.

77. From then on, the COP put the emphasis on a strategic approach that consisted in defining political objectives designed to be implemented at regional and national level and to guide and energise State action. The Ministerial Declaration of The Hague, adopted by the COP in 2002, recognised the "need for clear targets and timetables as follow-up to the adoption of the Strategic Plan and to put mechanisms in place to reach these targets and review progress in the implementation of the Convention's work programmes". It also featured an undertaking to "move from dialogue to action". Parties admitted that "[w]ith some honourable exceptions, our responses are too few, too little and too late" and reconfirmed "the commitment to have instruments in place to stop and reverse the current alarming biodiversity loss at the global, regional, sub-regional and national levels by the year 2010" [132]. This "strategic plan" set as its main objective "to achieve by 2010 a significant reduction of the current rate of biodiversity loss at the global, regional and national level as a contribution to poverty alleviation and to the benefit of all life on earth", to which it attached a series of strategic goals and objectives [133]. The Johannesburg World Summit on

---

131. It came into force in 2011 and has 140 Parties.
132. The Hague Ministerial Declaration of The Conference of Parties to the Convention on Biological Diversity, UNEP/CBD/COP/6/20, p. 365.
133. Decision VI/26, *Strategic Plan for the Convention on Biological Diversity*, UNEP/CBD/COP/6/20 (2002), p. 332.

Sustainable Development further built on these objectives [134], as did the Syracuse G8/20 [135].

78. In 2010, at COP X, in Nagoya, the Parties expressed concerns about the implementation of this Strategic Plan, and so the COP adopted a new Strategic Plan for the 2011-2020 period [136]. The objectives, which had until then been rather vague, were revised and clarified. The new plan set out five "strategic goals" comprised of the twenty Aichi Targets, which were essentially quantified objectives to be achieved by 2015 or 2020. In addition, Target 17 specifically laid down the following goal: "By 2015 each Party has developed, adopted as a policy instrument, and has commenced implementing an effective, participatory and updated national biodiversity strategy and action plan" (NBSAP). In turn, the COP decision "urged" the Parties to implement these international objectives, in particular through national biodiversity strategies and action plans (NBSAPs), which the Parties are required to develop under Article 6 of the Convention. The Parties were required to "review, and as appropriate update and revise, their national biodiversity strategies and action plans" using the set of indicators developed for the Strategic Plan "as a flexible framework". More attention was also given to the implementation of the new strategy. A monitoring system was put in place. Indeed, the Parties were required to "report to the Conference of the Parties through their fifth and sixth national reports and any other means to be decided by the Conference of the Parties" [137]. They were to

> "inform the Conference of the Parties of the national targets or commitments and policy instruments they adopt to implement the Strategic Plan, as well as any milestones towards these targets, and report on progress towards these targets and milestones, including through their fifth and sixth national reports".

The COP "will review the progress towards the Aichi Biodiversity Targets as set out in the Strategic Plan" and "make recommendations to overcome any obstacles encountered in meeting those targets". The

---

134. *Report of the World Summit on Sustainable Development*, Johannesburg, South Africa, 26 August-4 September 2002, A/CONF.199/20, 2002, para. 44.
135. "Carta di Siracusa" on Biodiversity (adopted 24 April 2009), Preamble, paras. II and VIII.
136. Decision X/2 (2010), *The Strategic Plan for Biodiversity 2011-2020 and the Aichi Biodiversity Targets*, UNEP/CBD/COP/DEC/X/2 (2010), p. 117.
137. Following guidance provided by Decision X/10, Part 3 of the report should present the national measures taken to implement the Convention that contribute to the achievement of the strategic goals and the Aichi Targets.

COP also asked for "predictable and timely" financial support from the Global Environment Facility.

79. However, ten years later, targets were far from being met, and implementation at the national level was still largely insufficient. The first global assessment of the IPBES reported a broad consensus among scientists on the seriousness of the threats to biodiversity [138]. Its findings coincided with the conclusions of the *Global Biodiversity Outlook Report* issued in 2020, which stated that at the global level, none of the twenty targets had been fully achieved, although six of them had been partially achieved [139]. Thus, the question was how to strengthen the global architecture and to improve the implementation of the Aichi Targets, both internationally and, more importantly, nationally, by each of the Parties to the CBD. The negotiation process towards a revised strategic framework was launched at COP 14 in 2018 [140]. Postponed because of the pandemic, the adoption of the new framework was finally reached at COP 15, in December 2022. The new plan, called the "Kunming-Montreal Global Biodiversity Framework", consists of four Goals for 2050 and twenty-three Targets to be achieved by 2030. More precise on many aspects and designed to be implemented more effectively, it has been presented as a major contribution to the achievement of the 2030 Agenda for Sustainable Development [141].

f) *The Convention on Biological Diversity in the international governance of biodiversity*

80. Since then, and outside the scope of the Rio Convention on Biological Diversity, the normative structure has only marginally evolved. However, there have been some regional developments worth mentioning here, with the adoption of new regional conventions in Central America (Convention for the Conservation of the Biodiversity

---

138. See above, Introduction, para. 26 *et seq*.
139. *5th Global Biodiversity Outlook Report*, 2020, https://www.cbd.int/gbo5, accessed on 25 October 2023.
140. COP Decision 14/34 (2018), *Comprehensive and Participatory Process for the Preparation of the Post-2020 Global Diversity Framework*. See also the decision of the COP-MOP to the Cartagena Protocol on Biosafety 9/7 (2018), *Preparation for the Follow-Up to the Strategic Plan for Biodiversity 2011-2020 and the Strategic Plan for the Cartagena Protocol on Biosafety 2011-2020*, and the decision adopted by the COP-MOP to the Nagoya Protocol, 3/15 (2018), *Preparation for the Follow-Up to the Strategic Plan for Biodiversity 2011-2020*.
141. Decision 15/4 (2022), *Kunming-Montreal Global Biodiversity Framework*, CBD/COP/DEC/15/4, 19 December 2022.

and the Protection of Wilderness in Central America, Managua, 5 June 1992; Inter-American Convention for the Protection and Conservation of Sea Turtles, Caracas, 1 December 1996), Europe (European Landscape Convention, 20 October 2000) and Central Asia (Framework Convention on Environmental Protection for Sustainable Development in Central Asia, Ashgabat, 22 November 2006). In Africa, the Maputo African Convention on the Conservation of Nature and Natural Resources (Revised Version) was adopted at the second session of the OAU Conference on 11 July 2003 [142]. It recently came into force and is to replace the Algiers Convention [143]. There is also the Protocol for the Implementation of the Alpine Convention in the Field of Nature Protection and Landscape Conservation (Chambéry, 20 December 1994), as well as numerous bilateral agreements concluded after the dissolution of the USSR between its former republics, or between them and former Soviet bloc countries [144]. The Bonn Convention on Migratory Species was supplemented by a number of more specific treaties on groups of migratory species [145]. Within the EU, the adoption of the Directive on the conservation of natural habitats and of wild fauna and flora (21 May 1992), at the same time as the adoption of the Rio Convention, represented an important milestone [146]. The EU itself is a party to several international conventions on biodiversity (including the Rio Convention). From the point of view of EU law, these conventions are mixed agreements, concluded by both the EU and its Member States.

---

142. This Convention, which came into force recently, provides for the adoption of a subsequent protocol on biodiversity (Article 13).

143. S. Maljean-Dubois, "La contribution de l'Union africaine à la protection de la nature en Afrique: de la Convention d'Alger à la Convention de Maputo", in *Liber Amicorum* Raymond Ranjeva, *L'Afrique et le droit international. Variations sur l'organisation internationale,* Pedone, Paris, 2013, pp. 205-218; *Revue Africaine de Droit de l'Environnement-African Journal of Environmental Law,* "Entrée en vigueur et mise en œuvre de la Convention de Maputo relative à la conservation de la nature et des ressources naturelles en Afrique", Special Issue, No. /2019.

144. Bilateral Agreement between the Lithuanian Department of Environment and the Ministry of Environmental Protection, *Nature* Conservation and Forestry of Poland (24 January 1992), Agreement between the Government of Uzbekistan and the Government of Kyrgyzstan on Cooperation in the Sphere of Environmental protection and Rationale Nature Management (25 December 1996), Agreement between the Government of Uzbekistan and the Government of Kazakhstan on Cooperation in the Sphere of Environment Protection and Rationale Nature Management (2 June 1997), Agreement between the Ministry of Environmental Protection of Ukraine and the Ministry of *Nature* and Environment of Mongolia on Cooperation in the Field of Environmental protection (8 December 2004), etc.

145. See above, para. 55.

146. Council Directive 92/43/EEC of 21 May 1992 on the conservation of natural habitats and of wild fauna and flora, *OJ* L 206, 22.7.1992, pp. 7-50.

81. In terms of universal instruments, the International Treaty on Plant Genetic Resources for Food and Agriculture (International Treaty) was adopted in Rome on 3 November 2001, under the auspices of the FAO. The 1982 United Nations Convention on the Law of the Sea was supplemented by the Agreement for the Implementation of the Provisions of the United Nations Convention on the Law of the Sea of 10 December 1982 relating to the Conservation and Management of Straddling Fish Stocks and Highly Migratory Fish Stocks (New York, 4 August 1995). More recently, international negotiations were launched at Rio+20, under the aegis of the UN, which first took place under the auspices of the Working Group to study issues relating to the conservation and sustainable use of marine biological diversity beyond areas of national jurisdiction [147]. The work of this *ad hoc* Working Group highlighted the magnitude of the issues at stake through the unprecedented loss of marine biodiversity, over-exploitation of resources, habitat destruction, pollution, ocean acidification and the effects of climate change [148]. The group recommended to the UN General Assembly that negotiations be conducted towards a new legally binding agreement under the United Nations Convention on the Law of the Sea [149]. The Agreement under the United Nations Convention on the Law of the Sea on the Conservation and Sustainable Use of Marine Biological Diversity of Areas Beyond National Jurisdiction (the BBNJ treaty) was finally adopted on 19 June 2023 and this new treaty fills an important gap [150]. Addressing other long-identified needs, other international conventions with a strong biodiversity dimension could be negotiated in the future. This could be the case for soils or forests, or the environmental impact of agricultural activities, which no international convention focuses on for now.

82. Thus, one cannot help but think that the construction of the international law on biodiversity has not been rational; in a way, it started at the end. As our understanding and knowledge evolved, States entered

---

147. Ad Hoc Open-ended Informal Working Group to study issues relating to the conservation and sustainable use of marine biological diversity beyond areas of national jurisdiction, established by paragraph 73 of UNGA Resolution 59/24.

148. Report of the Preparatory Committee established by General Assembly Resolution 69/292: Development of an international legally binding instrument under the United Nations Convention on the Law of the Sea on the conservation and sustainable use of marine biological diversity of areas beyond national jurisdiction, A/AC.287/2017/PC.4/2, 31 July 2017.

149. Letter dated 13 February 2015 from the Co-Chairs of the *Ad Hoc* Open-ended Informal Working Group to the President of the General Assembly, A/69/780.

150. UNGA 77/321, *Agreement under the United Nations Convention on the Law of the Sea on the Conservation and Sustainable Use of Marine Biological Diversity of Areas Beyond National Jurisdiction*, 1 August 2023.

into multiple conventions at the global and regional level, protecting certain species, certain groups of species, certain habitats, before finally adopting, in 1992, the Convention on Biological Diversity which in a way forms the base of this body of law. It is the only instrument that pertains to all species and all activities across the globe. This is why it has been described as an "omnibus" convention or a "convention for all life on Earth" [151]. It does in fact contain a provision linking it to pre-existing conventions in its Article 22, which states that

> "[t]he provisions of this Convention shall not affect the rights and obligations of any Contracting Party deriving from any existing international agreement, except where the exercise of those rights and obligations would cause a serious damage or threat to biological diversity."

83. Thus, the earlier conventions have not lost their *raison d'être*. Even supplemented by its protocols and the Aichi and Kunming-Montreal Targets, the content of the Convention on Biological Diversity is still very general. Other instruments adopted before or after the Convention therefore supplement it with more specific and more appropriate provisions due to their narrower scope, *ratione loci* and/or *materiae*. Some of the subsequent instruments are actually inspired by its provisions. Others use the Convention's definition of biological diversity [152]. Others expressly refer to it [153].

84. What already constitutes a conventional system is embedded in a reality that also goes beyond it: a "regime complex" [154] of which it forms the backbone but which also includes other specialised regimes,

---

151. D. McGraw, "The Story of the Biodiversity Convention: From Negotiation to Implementation" (n. 96), p. 24.
152. See, for example, Articles V, IX, XII or Annex II of the Maputo African Convention (2003); or Article 1 of the Framework Convention for the Protection of the Environment for Sustainable Development in Central Asia, Ashgabat, 2006.
153. I. Michallet, "La notion de diversité biologique en droit international" (n. 20), p. 78. See, in particular, the preamble of the AEWA which states that "migratory waterbirds constitute an important part of the global biological diversity which, in keeping with the spirit of the Convention on Biological Diversity, 1992, and Agenda 21 should be conserved for the benefit of present and future generations". See, along the same lines, the Agreement between the Government of Republic of Kazakhstan, Government of Kyrgyz Republic and Government of Republic of Uzbekistan on co-operation in the sphere of biological diversity conservation of West Tien Shan, Bishkek, 17 March 1998.
154. K. Raustiala and D. G. Victor, "The Regime Complex for Plant Genetic Resources", *International Organization*, No. 55, 2004, p. 280; R. O. Keohane and D. G. Victor, *The Regime Complex for Climate Change*, Discussion Paper 10-33, Harvard J.-F. Kennedy School of Government, 2010.

most of which were adopted earlier (CITES in 1973, the Ramsar Convention in 1971, the 1979 Bonn Convention and its agreements, etc.), public-private regulatory mechanisms (REDD+ projects for Reducing Emissions from Deforestation and Degradation under the auspices of the UN Framework Convention on Climate Change) or entirely private ones (forest certification), as well as regional nature protection and natural resource management regimes, most of which were established prior to the CBD (the 1940 Convention in America, the 1992 Convention in Central America, the 2003 Maputo Convention in Africa, the 1979 Bern Convention in Europe, the 1985 ASEAN Agreement in Southeast Asia, etc.).

85. Nor is this body of law unrelated to other conventions adopted in other fields, such as those protecting indigenous or aboriginal peoples and their relationship with their environment, in particular traditional knowledge (such as the Indigenous and Tribal Peoples Convention, 1989 [No. 169]).

86. Unlike other Rio Conventions, the UN Framework Convention on Climate Change or the United Nations Convention to Combat Desertification of 1994, the Convention on Biological Diversity arrived in a field that was already highly regulated, but the IUCN's idea was that the existing law was not enough to curb extinction and that a new tool was needed to foster co-operation and, above all, create a link between all the pre-existing systems. The role assigned to the Convention was also to raise the profile of biodiversity issues at the international level, including outside this regime complex devoted to biodiversity and its components, and even to define objectives, principles and standards that would become shared references at the international level and be taken into account across all the various actions and policies, including those outside the environmental field [155]. Indeed, the main drivers of biodiversity are dealt with outside this regime complex (climate, chemicals, urbanisation, transport, conflicts, trade, etc.). The regional and global IPBES reports in 2018 and 2019 have contributed to an increased recognition of the issue of biodiversity conservation and greater media coverage. Thus, in May 2019, the G7 that took place in Metz focused on this issue [156]. In March 2019, at the invitation of

---

155. L. Guay, "The Science and Policy of Global Biodiversity Protection", in P. Le Prestre (ed.), *Governing Global Biodiversity. The Evolution and Implementation of the Convention on Biological Diversity*, Routledge, 2002, p. 229.

156. See https://www.elysee.fr/admin/upload/default/0001/04/e69a15d02877b265 898bd98391adf06fa0bff386.pdf, accessed on 25 October 2023.

the CBD COP, the UN General Assembly proclaimed the 2021-2030 decade the United Nations Decade on Ecosystem Restoration [157], succeeding the United Nations Decade on Biodiversity (2011-2020) [158].

87. It should be added that the strategic plans adopted in 2010 (Aichi Targets) and 2022 (post-2020 framework) have been a true success at the international level. Their adoption was a real step forward, effectively allowing a strategic refocusing of convention-based activities around these targets. The subsequent COPs have shown that the definition of these targets did in fact structure and energise the work of the Conference of the Parties, which no longer avoids the most sensitive and controversial subjects (biofuels, geoengineering, etc.) and does not hesitate, if not to take over, at least to develop an assertive strategy that could enable it to make its voice heard more effectively in the years to come in a very competitive international landscape. The Convention, which until now had been rather marginalised in international governance, has been able to assert itself more [159]. The Aichi Targets eventually enabled the CBD to play the role of an umbrella convention on nature conservation, a role that it was initially intended to play but which it had struggled to fulfil until then. Indeed, UNEP supported the implementation of the targets as "an important global policy framework for reversing the ongoing decline in biodiversity and ecosystem services identified in GEO-5" [160]. The strategic framework was subsequently used by other conventions aimed at protecting biodiversity and ecosystems [161]. But this influence goes far beyond the "biodiversity cluster", as the Rio+20 Conference built on these targets [162] and they

---

157. UNGA Resolution 73/284, *United Nations Decade on Ecosystem Restoration (2021–2030)*, 1 March 2019.
158. UNGA Resolution 65/161, *Convention on Biological Diversity*, 20 December 2010, para. 19.
159. M.-A. Hermitte, S. Maljean-Dubois and E. Truilhé-Marengo, "Actualités de la Convention sur la diversité biologique : science et politique, équité, biosécurité" (n. 129), p. 436.
160. UNEP, Decision 27/11: State of the Environment and Contribution of the United Nations Environment Programme to Meeting Substantive Environment Challenges, UNEP/GC.27/17, 12 March 2013, p. 28.
161. G. Futhazar, "The Diffusion of the Strategic Plan for Biodiversity and Its Aichi Biodiversity Targets Within the Biodiversity Cluster: An Illustration of Current Trends in the Global Governance of Biodiversity and Ecosystems", *Yearbook of International Environmental Law*, Vol. 25, No. 1 (2015), p. 134. See, for instance, CITES, COP Decision 17.22 (2016). See also K. Rogalla von Bieberstein, E. Sattout, M. Christensen, P. Pisupati, N. D. Burgess, J. Harrison and J. Geldmann, "Improving Collaboration in the Implementation of Global Biodiversity Conventions", *Conservation Biology*, Vol. 33, No. 4, pp. 821-831.
162. UNGA Resolution 66/288, *The Future We Want*, 11 September 2012, para. 197 *et seq.*

were also largely included in the Sustainable Development Goals. The Aichi Targets have been a major inspiration for the UN's definition of the 17 Sustainable Development Goals, as part of the 2030 Agenda for Sustainable Development. Indeed, biodiversity and ecosystems have a key place in the SDGs and associated targets, in particular in SDG 14 (marine biodiversity) and 15 (terrestrial biodiversity), but also across most of the SDGs [163]. The new Kunming-Montreal Global Biodiversity Framework has been framed in order to consolidate this dynamic. This is an acknowledgement of the fundamental importance of biodiversity issues for human development and well-being. These developments reflect how far these issues have come in less than a century, from the protection of birds useful to agriculture to a global development agenda defined by the United Nations. And while the SGDs have been subject to some criticism [164], the transformational, game-changing role of these strategic goals has been widely recognised [165].

88. Yet the implementation of the Aichi Targets is far from perfect. As mentioned before, the latest *Global Biodiversity Outlook 5* shows that "at the global level none of the 20 targets have been fully achieved, though six targets have been partially achieved (Targets 9, 11, 16, 17, 19 and 20)". It adds that

> "national targets are generally poorly aligned with the Aichi Biodiversity Targets, in terms of scope and the level of ambition. Fewer than a quarter (23 percent) of the targets are well aligned with the Aichi Targets and only about a tenth of all national targets are both similar to the Aichi Biodiversity Targets, and on track to be met".

Lastly, "there have been gaps in both the level of ambition of the commitments of countries to address the Aichi Biodiversity Targets nationally, as well as in the actions to reach these commitments" [166]. The

---

163. CBD, Biodiversity and the 2030 Agenda for Sustainable Development, Technical Note, undated, https://www.cbd.int/development/doc/biodiversity-2030-agenda-technical-note-fr.pdf, accessed on 25 October 2023.

164. L. J. Kotzé, "The Sustainable Development Goals: An Existential Critique Alongside Three New-Millennial Analytical Paradigms", in D. French and L. J. Kotzé, *Sustainable Development Goals: Law, Theory and Implementation*, EE, 2018, p. 41; S. Mair *et al.*, "A Critical Review of the Role of Indicators in Implementing the Sustainable Development Goals", in W. Leal Filho (ed.), *Handbook of Sustainability Science and Research*, Springer, 2017, p. 42.

165. C. Brölmann, "Sustainable Development Goal 6 as a Game Changer for International Water Law", *ESIL Reflections* 7:5 (2018).

166. Secretariat of the Convention on Biological Diversity (2020) *Global Biodiversity Outlook 5 – Summary for Policy Makers*, Montreal, p. 4.

negotiations of the post-2020 framework were to clarify their content, improve monitoring mechanisms and support implementation. The idea was more to further develop and strengthen the Aichi Framework rather than to engage in a more coercive approach on which there was no consensus between States [167]. The new Kunming-Montreal Global Biodiversity Framework represents a step forward from this point of view [168].

89. This short history of biodiversity treaties shows how far we have come, from protecting the Rhine salmon or birds useful to agriculture, to placing biodiversity protection at the heart of the 2030 Agenda for Sustainable Development.

Section 2. The apprehension of biodiversity by international institutions

90. Biodiversity issues are dealt with by many intergovernmental organisations. They are also at the heart of the activities of treaty institutions created pursuant to international conventions. It is also important to highlight the growing role of non-State actors who are increasingly involved in the international governance of biodiversity.

1) The role of intergovernmental organisations

91. Intergovernmental organisations play an important role here and are entrusted with a wide range of missions. The creation of IPBES (Intergovernmental Science-Policy Platform for Biodiversity and Ecosystem Services) in particular could have far-reaching consequences on the apprehension of biodiversity by international institutions and international law.

a) *A major role*

92. In 1972, the Stockholm Declaration and more generally the Stockholm Conference contributed to raising awareness of the growing dangers threatening the planet, and marked the beginning of a sustained normative activity at the international level. The United Nations Environment Programme (UNEP) was created in 1972

---

167. For a view opposing this, see, with very ambitious and therefore unrealistic proposals, C. Klein, "New Leadership Needed: The Convention on Biological Diversity", *Emory International Law Review*, Vol. 31, 2016, pp. 135-165.
168. M. Daval, "Un nouveau 'cadre mondial pour la biodiversité': enjeux et perspectives", *Revue juridique de l'environnement*, 2023/2, Vol. 48, pp. 319-335.

following the Conference, the UN General Assembly declaring itself "aware of the urgent need for a permanent institutional arrangement within the United Nations system for the protection and improvement of the environment" [169]. Whether at a universal or regional level, the environmental issue has been addressed by most international organisations, each contributing in their own field of action to the development of international environmental law. Principle 25 of the Stockholm Declaration recognises the importance of their role: "States shall ensure that international organizations play a coordinated, efficient and dynamic role for the protection and improvement of the environment." Thanks to their permanent structures, international organisations provide indispensable support for multilateral co-operation. They are the best forum for this. After all, didn't the first international organisation, the 1815 Central Commission for the Navigation of the Rhine, respond to a need for co-operation on the use of a common resource [170]?

93. Biodiversity issues are no exception to the rule. They are even specifically promoted by international organisations, under pressure from influential non-governmental organisations, which are real catalysts of public opinion [171]. At the universal level, the work of the United Nations, through its various bodies and in particular UNEP, but also of the UN family institutions (especially UNESCO, FAO and IMO), has played a major role in raising awareness of these issues among States and the general public. Most regional organisations are also tackling biodiversity issues, including the European Union, Council of Europe, African Union, Organization of American States, Association of Southeast Asian Nations, etc.

b) *A wide range of missions*

94. Intergovernmental organisations have been given various missions:

– Scientific and technical assessment, whether of the state of biodiversity or of the various factors influencing it. They can perform

---

169. UNGA Resolution 27/2997, 15 December 1972, *Institutional and Financial Arrangements for International Environment Cooperation.*
170. P. Le Prestre, *Protection de l'environnement et relations internationales. Les défis de l'écopolitique mondiale*, Armand Colin, Paris, 2005, p. 64.
171. M. Dias Varella, "Le rôle des organisations non-gouvernementales dans le développement du droit international de l'environnement", *Journal du droit international*, 1/2005, pp. 41-76.

these missions themselves, internally, or provide financial support to external experts or organisations. Very often, they are simply a place for the centralisation and exchange of information. By fostering the exchange of information, or even by aggregating in reports the information collected at the national level (like the *Global Environmental Outlook* or GEO reports of the United Nations Environment Programme), they fulfil a fundamental mission. This role may go beyond the strictly scientific field to include economic and social aspects, including legal aspects (see, for instance, the works of the International Law Commission). In addition to reviewing information and generating knowledge, they also disseminate this knowledge. These assessment missions contribute to the mobilisation of both national and international stakeholders around the challenges of biodiversity conservation. The formation of a consensus on scientific knowledge is the essential prerequisite to the regulation phase. The creation of the IPBES, which is designed to play the same role as the IPCC for climate, is significant. We will return to this below.

– Regulation. This role is often confined to the enactment of soft law (resolutions and other instruments of uncertain legal status). They abound in the environmental field where they have and continue to play a real guiding role. Declarations such as the Stockholm or Rio Declaration, or even the World Charter for Nature, have contributed to the definition of international benchmarks and principles that have been widely disseminated across international treaties as well as national constitutions and legislation. As such, they have helped to crystallise customary norms. Resolutions have also established conservation programmes. One example is the label of the Council of Europe known as European Diploma for Protected Areas, which applies to certain natural sites of exceptional European interest for the conservation of biological, geological or landscape diversity and which are subject to exemplary management. The Council of Europe has a Committee for the activities of the Council of Europe in the field of biological and landscape diversity (CO-DBP). This programme, created in 1965 by a resolution of the Committee of Ministers of the Council of Europe [172], awards distinctions to remarkable sites and is designed to encourage their effective protection and management.

---

172. Committee of Ministers, Council of Europe, *Resolution (65) 6 Instituting the European Diploma, as amended by Resolution (98) 29 on the Regulations for the European Diploma for Protected Areas.*

Another example is the Man and Biosphere Programme (MAB), launched in 1970 by UNESCO and focused on the creation of a world network of protected areas known as "biosphere reserves" [173]. With certain regional extensions, such as the Latin American Network for Technical Cooperation on National Parks, other Protected Areas and Wild Flora and Fauna (REDPARQUES), these programmes operate under the aegis of two intergovernmental organisations without a treaty basis. Other UN initiatives include the proclamation by the UN General Assembly of the 2011-2020 "United Nations Decade on Biodiversity" [174], and of the 2021-2030 "United Nations Decade on Ecosystems Restauration" [175]. A very small number of organisations (the European Union, for example) have been given real regulatory power in environmental matters. However, one of the ways in which international organisations can exercise their regulatory power is by initiating, organising and hosting inter-State negotiations for the adoption of treaties. Most multilateral environmental treaties have thus been concluded under the auspices of an international organisation, whether universal (very often the United Nations) or regional (the Council of Europe or the African Union, for instance), which served as the negotiating forum. They play the important roles of mediation – referring to the ability to reconcile States' different definitions of their interests – and of matrix – the ability to provide the expertise, infrastructure and stimuli necessary for the development of co-operation in a given field [176].

– Monitoring the implementation of rules, capacity-building and sanctioning non-compliance. Normally, States are in charge of monitoring the implementation of internationally defined rules. However, in the environmental field, for several reasons related in particular to the nature of the obligations created, this monitoring has gradually become multilateral and is generally performed, at least in part, by international institutions. This is especially the case for the obligations laid down in the international conventions on environmental protection, whose implementation is monitored by the treaty bodies (see below). However, international organisations

---

173. See above, para. 51.
174. UNGA 65/161, 20 December 2010, *Convention on Biological Diversity*, para. 19.
175. UNGA 73/284, 1 March 2019, *United Nations Decade on Ecosystem Restoration* (2021-2030).
176. P. Le Prestre, *Protection de l'environnement et relations internationales* (n. 170), p. 68.

under whose auspices the biodiversity protection conventions were adopted often continue to play a role in their implementation, beyond the administrative roles generally performed (depositary, secretariat, etc.). For example, the Bern Convention of 1979 on the Conservation of European Wildlife and Natural Habitats, concluded under the auspices of the Council of Europe, established a Standing Committee that can be likened to a Conference of the Parties given its composition and statutes, but it also provides for the intervention of the Committee of Ministers of the Council of Europe in a number of instances.

95. With regard to capacity-building, mention can be made of the United Nations Development Programme (UNDP) or development banks, and in particular the World Bank. The Global Environment Facility, jointly managed by the World Bank, UNDP and UNEP, is the main international financing mechanism; it supports the implementation of international environmental protection conventions. Eligible projects include those aimed at preserving biological diversity and natural habitats [177].

c) *The creation of the Intergovernmental Science-Policy Platform for Biodiversity and Ecosystem Services*

96. The Intergovernmental Science-Policy Platform for Biodiversity and Ecosystem Services (IPBES) is often presented as the biodiversity equivalent of IPCC (Intergovernmental Panel on Climate Change). However, it differs in several ways, for at least two reasons. Firstly, the context is different for biodiversity, with a much more complex and fragmented legal and institutional landscape. Indeed, whereas the creation of IPCC in 1988 preceded (and prepared) the adoption of the 1992 United Nations Framework Convention on Climate Change, on the contrary, when IPBES was created in 2012, the field of biodiversity was already characterised by a multitude of universal, regional and even bilateral international conventions, general or sector-specific. Moreover, the creation of IPBES took place twenty-three years after the creation of IPCC. Negotiations therefore benefitted from the previous experience of establishing a science-policy interface on an international scale in the field of climate. It should be added that attitudes have

---

177. See below, para. 600 *et seq.*

changed considerably since 1988 with regard to the design of scientific and technical expert mechanisms. For all that, the creation of IPBES proved difficult. Even though the platform was officially created in 2012 and held its first meeting in early 2013, its status and "governance", as well as its procedures and operating methods, had not yet been fully defined.

- *A difficult start*

97. The design of this new institution resulted from a relatively long and arduous process of international negotiations. It started with an idea introduced in Paris in 2005 during an international conference on biodiversity and supported by French President Jacques Chirac. An international consultation process was then launched, led by the French Biodiversity Agency and with the support of the international programme DIVERSITAS. It was named IMoSEB for International Mechanism of Scientific Expertise on Biodiversity. A series of meetings were held between February 2006 and November 2007. It was then agreed to invite the UNEP Executive Director, in collaboration with governments and other partners, in order to organise an intergovernmental and multi-stakeholder meeting to explore the possibility of establishing an intergovernmental mechanism on biodiversity and ecosystem services.

98. In March 2008, UNEP produced a concept note concluding that an intergovernmental and multi-stakeholder platform on biodiversity and ecosystem services was needed. This note was circulated as an information document at the ninth meeting of the Conference of the Parties to the Convention on Biological Diversity, held in May 2008 [178]. UNEP then organised three special intergovernmental and multi-stakeholder meetings on an intergovernmental science-policy platform on biodiversity and ecosystem services. The first meeting, which took place in Malaysia in November 2008, was very contentious but nevertheless led to the adoption of a roadmap known as the "Putrajaya Roadmap" [179]. The second meeting was held in Nairobi in October 2009, at the launch of the 2010 Year of Biodiversity. To prepare this meeting, a very comprehensive study called the *Gap Analysis* was circulated,

---

178. CBD, An Intergovernmental and Multi-Stakeholder Approach to Strengthening the Science - Policy Interface on Biodiversity and Ecosystem Services, *Note by the Executive Secretary*, UNEP/CBD/COP/9/INF/37/Rev.1, 23 May 2008. The concept note is in the Annex.

179. *Report of the* Ad Hoc *Intergovernmental and Multi-Stakeholder Meeting on an Intergovernmental Science-Policy Platform on Biodiversity and Ecosystem Services*, UNEP/IPBES/1/6, 23 May 2008.

produced by UNEP and France but with input and comments from many governments, international organisations and NGOs [180]. It showed, first of all, that IPBES would not exist in a vacuum: on the contrary, there were many science-policy interfaces, owing to historical factors but also structurally to the complexity of the international governance of biodiversity. However, these many "interfaces" were underfunded and could not fulfil their mission, especially as collaboration between them was limited. Yet there was a clear need: knowledge in this area was still lacking, in particular on the complexity of human-ecosystem interactions, but also in terms of long-term observations and monitoring programmes. Lastly, scientific information and knowledge were not always transferred and communicated in the most effective way to decision-makers. During the meeting in Malaysia, positions were softened and a consensus emerged on the missions of IPBES. The platform was to conduct periodic assessments of the state of biodiversity, rely on the assessment of ecosystem services [181], but also serve as a network for the exchange of knowledge between countries in the North and South.

99. In June 2010, a third meeting was convened by UNEP in Busan, Republic of Korea [182]. This meeting came to the conclusion that IPBES should be created. It defined the missions of IPBES and agreed on a number of principles that would form the basis of the future structure [183]. The final document of the Busan meeting was well received by the Conference of the Parties to the Convention on Biological Diversity, at its tenth meeting held in Nagoya, Japan, in October 2010 [184]. Immediately after, it was also submitted for consideration to the UN General Assembly at its sixty-fifth session. The General Assembly adopted a resolution requesting UNEP to organise a plenary meeting to

---

180. *Gap Analysis for the Purpose of Facilitating the Discussions on How to Improve and Strengthen the Science-Policy Interface on Biodiversity and Ecosystem Services*, UNEP/IPBES/2/INF/1, 19 August 2009. See also *Interface entre la science et la politique dans le domaine de la biodiversité et des services écosystémiques : analyse des carences*, UNEP/IPBES/2/2, 9 August 2012.

181. See the work of The Economics of Ecosystems and Biodiversity, http://www.teebweb.org/, accessed on 25 October 2023.

182. *Report of the Third Ad Hoc Intergovernmental and Multi-Stakeholder Meeting on the Intergovernmental Science-Policy Platform on Biodiversity and Ecosystem Services*, UNEP/IPBES/3/3, 11 June 2010; Decision UNEP SS.XI/4, February 2010.

183. Busan Outcome, in *Intergovernmental Science-Policy Platform on Biodiversity and Ecosystem Services*, Report of the Executive Director, UNEP/GC.26/6, 7 December 2010, p. 7.

184. CBD, Decision X/11 (2010), *Science-Policy Interface on Biodiversity, Ecosystem Services and Human Wellbeing and Consideration of the Outcome of the Intergovernmental Meetings*.

fully operationalise the platform as soon as possible [185]. The resolution was taken into account in the decision adopted by the UNEP Governing Council at its twenty-sixth session, in February 2011, which decided,

> "without prejudice to the final institutional arrangements for the intergovernmental science-policy platform on biodiversity and ecosystem services and in consultation with all relevant organizations and bodies, in order fully to operationalize the platform, to convene a plenary meeting providing for the full and effective participation of all member States, in particular representatives from developing countries, to determine modalities and institutional arrangements for the platform at the earliest opportunity" [186].

100. UNEP then started working on preparing this first plenary meeting in co-operation with UNESCO, FAO, UNDP and other organisations. Many issues remained unresolved and several meetings were held in 2011 to try to resolve them beforehand. The plenary finally took place in two sessions, the first one in October 2011 in Nairobi and the second one in April 2012 in Panama City. It was during this second session that IPBES was created, by a resolution adopted on 21 April 2012 [187]. IPBES was created as "an independent intergovernmental body", which would later decide on its link with the United Nations system, with its headquarters located in Bonn [188]. When the resolution was adopted, the representatives of Bolivia, Egypt and Venezuela indicated that their governments should not be listed as supporting the resolution. They particularly regretted that IPBES was not given a "UN" status from its inception. At the end of January 2013, the first session of the platform's plenary finally took place.

- *Structure and composition of IPBES*

101. After an initial negotiation process largely open to "interested parties", was IPBES going to have a classic intergovernmental composition? Or was it going to be more "modern", participatory,

---

185. Resolution A/RES/65/162, UN General Assembly, 20 December 2010, *Report of the Governing Council of the United Nations Environment Programme on its 11th Special Session*, para. 17.
186. UNEP Governing Council, Decision 26/4, 24 February 2011, *Intergovernmental Science-Policy Platform on Biodiversity and Ecosystem Services*, UNEP/GC.26/19, p. 9.
187. See the text, https://akn.ipbes.net/un-ipbes/act/charter/2012/1/eng/resources/eng.html, accessed on 25 October 2023.
188. *Ibid.*

open to private actors, NGOs and scientists, even perhaps companies? From this point of view, the Busan document adopted a relatively classic inter-State conception, since plenary participants were to be the UN Member States and regional economic integration organisations: "Intergovernmental organizations and other relevant stakeholders should participate in the Plenary as observers" and would not take part in decision-making [189]. Indeed, demonstrating the political importance they attach to the issues at stake, many States expressed their preference for an intergovernmental structure. Of course, this does not preclude States from appointing experts to their delegations [190]. But these experts are not there *intuitu personae* and their independence is therefore very limited. Nor does it preclude the plenary from encouraging and taking into account contributions and suggestions from relevant stakeholders.

102. The Busan document had established that membership would be open to any UN Member State that expressed an interest in joining. It had also been agreed in Busan that the platform would be accessible to regional economic integration organisations, the European Union being the only one included in this "tailor-made" status, which it enjoys in a number of multilateral treaties and international organisations (such as the WTO). However, at the Panama meeting, the United States, the African group and the Latin American and Caribbean Group opposed full membership for the EU. In addition, the voting rules, but also the possibility for a representative of the Commission to hold elected office in the IPBES bodies, were causing internal tensions between the Commission and EU Member States. In the end, it was decided that the platform would be open to UN Member States who can become members by expressing their intention to join the platform. Thus, for now, the EU has a "simple" observer status, although this could change in the future [191]. This should be seen in the context of the EU having been granted observer status at the UN, thus creating a new category of – non-State – members of the UN, with a comfortable status which, although not equivalent to that of the Member States, has sparked much discussion [192]. The issue goes well beyond IPBES and is

---

189. Busan Outcome (n. 183), para. 6.
190. *Ibid.*, para. 6 *(a)*.
191. Article 2 of the Rules of Procedure (Decision IPBES/1/1 Rules of Procedure for the Plenary of the Platform, 31 January 2013) which specifies in brackets that "Issues of membership/participation of regional economic integration organizations remain under discussion with a view to resolution as soon as possible".
192. UNGA, Resolution A/RES/65/276, 3 May 2011, Participation of the European Union in the Work of the United Nations.

of particular concern to the European Commission as the conditions for EU participation in the platform could set a precedent in other fora where it is also being discussed.

103. The resolution of 21 April 2012 set out the general structure of the platform. It is an "independent intergovernmental body" (para. 1), composed of a Plenary, which is the decision-making body, and two subsidiary bodies: a Bureau composed of ten members and a Multidisciplinary Expert Panel (MEP) composed of twenty-five experts in the field of biodiversity and ecosystem services, with expertise in both natural and social sciences as well as traditional and local knowledge representing the different regions of the UN [193].

- *The missions of IPBES*

104. Like IPCC, IPBES does not conduct research itself. The Busan Outcome specified that

> "[t]he new platform should identify and prioritize key scientific information needed for policymakers at appropriate scales and catalyse efforts to generate new knowledge by engaging in dialogue with key scientific organizations, policymakers and funding organizations, but should not directly undertake new research" [194].

Similarly, IPBES

> "should perform regular and timely assessments of knowledge on biodiversity and ecosystem services and their interlinkages, which should include comprehensive global, regional and, as necessary, subregional assessments and thematic issues at appropriate scales and new topics identified by science and as decided upon by the plenary" [195].

The role of "catalysing" knowledge production is new compared to IPCC. It places IPBES at an intermediate level between IPCC – which presents the state of knowledge on climate change – and a body that would conduct research directly. Given the many potential demands and the fragmentation of biodiversity governance, one fundamental issue –

---

193. Decision IPBES-2/1, Amendments to the Rules of Procedure for the Plenary with Regard to Rules Governing the Multidisciplinary Expert Panel (IPBES-2/1).
194. Busan Outcome (n. 183), para. 6 *(b)*.
195. *Ibid.*, para. 6 *(c)*.

not found in the design of IPCC – is the prioritisation of requests [196]. The plenary was tasked with setting up a mechanism to receive and prioritise requests, contributions and suggestions [197]. Indeed, IPBES has many potential users, far beyond the institutions of the Convention on Biological Diversity [198].

105. Clearly designed to provide expertise for policy-makers, IPBES was assigned new and broader missions compared to IPCC, including capacity-building and the management of a Trust Fund. This is also a need that the IPCC did not initially address: the participation of developing countries, given the fears of countries in the South that unequal capacities would prevent access and benefit-sharing. Some of these countries are also the richest in biodiversity; it is therefore important for the effectiveness of the system to ensure that research can be carried out on their territory. However, this expertise for policy-makers must not be prescriptive; here, States are trying to protect their prerogatives. The platform should therefore provide policy-relevant information but not policy-prescriptive advice, bearing in mind the respective mandates of multilateral environmental agreements. In this respect, IPBES is similar to IPCC, whose mission is as follows:

> "To assess on a comprehensive, objective, open and transparent basis the scientific, technical and socio-economic information relevant to understanding the scientific basis of risk of human-induced climate change, its potential impacts and options for adaptation and mitigation. IPCC reports should be neutral with respect to policy, although they may need to deal objectively with scientific, technical and socio-economic factors relevant to the application of particular policies." [199]

The IPCC is therefore required to describe the different adaptation and mitigation strategies without ever taking a position on which strategies should be preferred.

---

196. *Ibid.*, para. 6 *(a)*.
197. See the aforementioned resolution of 21 April 2012.
198. IPBES, Note by the Secretariat, *Report on the Prioritization of Requests, Inputs and Suggestions on Short-Term Priorities and Longer-Term Strategic Needs for the Next Work Programme of the Platform*, IPBES/7/6/Add.1, 5 March 2019.
199. Principles Governing IPCC Work Approved at the Fourteenth Session, Vienna, 1-3 October 1998, on 1 October 1998, amended at the Twenty-First Session, Vienna, 3 and 6-7 November 2003, the Twenty-Fifth Session, Mauritius, 26-28 April 2006, the Thirty-Fifth Session, Geneva, 6-9 June 2012 and the Thirty-Seventh Session, Batumi, 14-18 October 2013.

- *Operating principles of IPBES*

106. The Busan Outcome envisaged a platform whose assessments should be "scientifically credible, independent and peer-reviewed, and must identify uncertainties. There should be a clear and transparent process for sharing and incorporating relevant data" [200]. It specified that IPBES should also:

> "*(b)* Be scientifically independent and ensure credibility, relevance and legitimacy through the peer review of its work and transparency in its decision-making processes;
>
> *(c)* Use clear, transparent and scientifically credible processes for the exchange, sharing and use of data, information and technologies from all relevant sources, including non-peer-reviewed literature, as appropriate." [201]

107. This wording was used in the resolution of 21 April 2012. In this respect, the development of IPBES must take into account existing mechanisms as well as the criticisms and suggestions made about IPCC during the assessment process carried out in 2010 at the request of the UN [202]. In terms of adopting decisions, consensus is the rule when it comes to substantive issues. However:

> "When considering reports, differing views are to be explained and, upon request, recorded. Differing views on matters of a scientific, technical, or socioeconomic nature are, as appropriate in the context, to be represented in the scientific, technical, or socioeconomic document concerned. Differences of views on matters of policy or procedure are, as appropriate in the context, to be recorded in the Report of the Session." [203]

108. Thus, the creation of this international science/policy, expert/decision-maker interface mechanism has not been without its challenges. The IPCC experience provided a very useful starting point, but paradoxically, the process of creating IPBES took longer and was trickier than the process leading to the creation of IPCC. It is true that

---

200. Busan Outcome (n. 183), para. 6 *(c)*.
201. *Ibid.*, para. 7.
202. Intergovernmental Science-Policy Platform on Biodiversity and Ecosystem Services, Report of the Executive Director, UNEP/GC.26/6, p. 6.
203. Decision IPBES/1/1, Rules of Procedure for Sessions of the Plenary of the Intergovernmental Science-Policy Platform on Biodiversity and Ecosystem Services, 31 January 2013.

International Biodiversity Law 85

the process was at the heart of significant political issues, particularly with regard to North-South relations, with the "disappointed promises" of Rio fuelling a certain mistrust on the part of the countries of the South. The creation of the platform was also disturbed by external issues and difficulties, such as the status of the European Union in multilateral agreements and institutions. In this sensitive context, it is hardly surprising that the resolution of 21 April 2012 was careful to specify that "[t]he present resolution and any future decisions of the Platform have a legally non-binding nature". However, this insistence on sovereignty does have its limits. Of course, it means a State can "exit" the platform as freely as it entered it. However, down the line, this resolution, like future decisions, has and will inevitably continue to have a "normative force" [204] and tangible, operational consequences as it will allow the geographical establishment of the platform and govern how it works [205].

109. Despite all these challenges, IPBES started producing work in 2016. So far, it has published a number of special assessment reports (on pollinators, land degradation, the methodological assessment of scenarios and models of biodiversity and ecosystem services, invasive alien species), a series of regional reports in the spring of 2018 (on Europe and Central Asia, Asia Pacific, Africa, the Americas) as well as its major global assessment in the spring of 2019, which received extensive media coverage [206].

2) The multifaceted institutionalisation of co-operation within the conventional framework

110. In addition to international organisations with a general purpose that gradually became involved in environmental issues and to this end often set up specialised bodies, there was a proliferation from the 1970s onwards of institutions created pursuant to various treaties, with an uncertain legal nature and very disparate composition, powers and resources. These institutions play a major role in the gradual

---

204. C. Thibierge, *La force normative. Naissance d'un concept*, LGDJ, Paris, 2009.
205. See along the same lines, J. Brunnée, "COPing with Consent: Law-Making under Multilateral Environmental Agreements", *Leiden Journal of International Law*, Vol. 15, 2002, pp. 1-52.
206. *Summary for Policymakers of the Global Assessment Report on Biodiversity and Ecosystem Services of the Intergovernmental Science-Policy Platform on Biodiversity and Ecosystem Services*, https://www.ipbes.net/event/ipbes-7-plenary, accessed on 25 October 2023.

construction of legal regimes. They modify (by revising) or complete (by adding annexes or by adopting additional protocols) the original provisions of conventions. More often still, they produce soft law: they interpret and clarify the original text and monitor its application through numerous declarations, resolutions, strategies, action plans, etc. Through this production of secondary law, they bring the initial commitments to "life" by gradually clarifying obligations that were often vague at first and adapting them to the evolution of knowledge and needs. Institutionalisation also provides a basis for the exchange of information between Parties and for co-operation, as well as for the provision of multilateral technical or financial assistance to some of them. Institutionalisation is also essential to implement effective multilateral monitoring of the Contracting States' performance of their treaty obligations. Thus, how well treaty institutions work is often even considered as an indicator of the effectiveness of the treaties in question [207].

111. In practice, these treaty-based structures are very diverse, depending partly on when they were established, on their regional or universal dimension and on their purpose. However, despite the proliferation of these structures, the way they are organised seems to converge towards an institutional model in the form of a triptych, with each new convention largely inspired by previous ones. Co-operation structures are generally made up of one or more political governing bodies (decision-making bodies), scientific structures (consultative bodies made up of experts) and administrative structures – in charge of secretariat roles – to which are sometimes added clearing-house mechanisms and/or financial mechanisms, or regional centres. The structure of these treaty institutions is generally similar to that of "micro" international organisations, although they do not all enjoy international legal personality and often only have the status of diplomatic conferences, the only permanent feature being the secretariat [208]. Still,

---

207. P Sand, *The Effectiveness of International Environmental Law. A Survey of Existing Legal Instruments*, Cambridge, Grotius Publications, 1992; P. M. Haas, R. O. Kehoane and M. A. Levy, *Institutions for the Earth, Sources of Effective International Environmental Protection*, Cambridge, MIT Press, 1994; R. Churchill and G. Ulfstein, "Autonomous Institutional Arrangements in Multilateral Environmental Agreements: A Little-Noticed Phenomenon in International Law", Vol. 94, *AJIL*, 2000, pp. 623-659.
208. R. R. Churchill and G. Ulfstein, "Autonomous Institutional Arrangements in Multilateral Environmental Agreements: A Little-Noticed Phenomenon in International Law" (n. 207), p. 623.

they play a major role in international environmental governance, each in their own field of activity.

112. The institutional arrangements stemming from the Convention on Biological Diversity are at the heart of the complex of regimes on biodiversity, but this complex is far broader. This seemingly fragmented institutional landscape raises questions about the relationship between the different regimes.

a) *The institutions created pursuant to the Convention on Biological Diversity*

113. The Convention on Biological Diversity creates, according to a classic triptych, a political body, the Conference of the Parties or COP (Art. 23), which meets every two years, an administrative body, the secretariat (Art. 24) as well as subsidiary bodies.

- *The political body*

114. In the case of the Convention on Biological Diversity, institutionalisation actually began before the treaty came into force. An intergovernmental body was put in place as soon as the Convention was adopted specifically to prepare its entry into force [209]. This body was able to hold two meetings, in October 1993 and in June 1994, before the first Conference of the Parties (COP) in November-December 1994, which was therefore able to prepare the adoption of a number of decisions, in particular institutional ones.

115. Like many other COPs, the Conference of the Parties is held every two years (unlike the climate change conference which is held annually). Fifteen ordinary Conferences of the Parties have taken place, as well as two extraordinary meetings of the Conference of the Parties. The first one, in two parts, in 1999 and 2000, led to the adoption of the Cartagena Protocol. The second one, in 2020 (as the Fifteenth meeting of the Conference of the Parties was postponed due to constraints arising from the COVID-19 pandemic), was convened to enable the continued operations of the bodies and processes of the Convention, including its secretariat and the meetings of the Conference of the Parties and its subsidiary bodies.

116. In addition to the Conference of the Parties to the Convention, the Meeting of the Parties to the Cartagena Protocol was established,

---

209. Intergovernmental Committee on the CBD (ICCBD).

which also serves as the Meeting of the Parties to the Nagoya-Kuala Lumpur Supplementary Protocol on Liability and Redress to the Cartagena Protocol on Biosafety (ten meetings so far) and the Meeting of the Parties to the Nagoya Protocol (four meetings so far). Thus, there is not one, but three Conferences of the Parties. They are held at the same time for a two-week session. As a rule, for practical reasons (as the agendas and the Parties differ between the three instruments) the meetings take place separately, one after the other. When the Conference of the Parties (COP) meets as the Meeting of the Parties (COP-MOP) to one of the Protocols, States that are a Party to the Convention but not to the Protocol in question attend as observers and do not take part in the vote, according to the following principle: "decisions under this Protocol shall be taken only by those that are Parties to it" [210]. To improve coherence and integration between the Convention and the Protocols, there have been attempts to organise concurrent meetings [211].

117. As a plenary political body, the COP to the Convention on Biological Diversity plays a key role. It adopts its own rules of procedure [212]. It "keeps under review" the implementation of the Convention and as such organises the international monitoring of the Convention's implementation, reviews "scientific, technical and technological advice on biological diversity" given by its scientific body, considers and adopts, as required, protocols, amendments to the Convention and its annexes, to any protocol, as well as to any annexes. It establishes subsidiary bodies, particularly to provide scientific and technical advice, "as are deemed necessary" for the implementation of the Convention. It contacts, through the secretariat, "the executive bodies of conventions dealing with matters covered by this Convention with a view to establishing appropriate forms of cooperation with them". Lastly, it must "consider and undertake any additional action that may be required for the achievement of the purposes of this Convention in the light of experience gained in its operation" [213]. In order to fulfil its missions, it has produced a wealth of secondary law over nearly thirty

---

210. Cartagena Protocol, Article 29, para. 2; Nagoya Protocol, Article 26 para. 2.
211. COP-MOP to the Cartagena Protocol (2018), Decision 9/8, *Review of Experience in Holding Concurrent Meetings of the Conference of the Parties to the Convention, the Conference of the Parties Serving as the Meeting of the Parties to the Cartagena Protocol, and the Conference of the Parties Serving as the Meeting of the Parties to the Nagoya Protocol.*
212. See CBD, Decision I/1, *Rules of Procedure of the Conference of the Parties* (1994).
213. Article 23, para. 4 *(a)* to *(i)*.

years, with almost 500 decisions over fifteen sessions. The significance of these "decisions" vary. Some of them interpret and clarify the content of the obligations defined in the Convention, setting out procedures, rules and standards or setting strategic objectives. In this respect, the decision of the Conference of the Parties defining the Aichi Targets is particularly worth mentioning: the 2010 X/2 Decision that adopted the Strategic Plan for Biodiversity 2011-2020 and the Aichi Biodiversity Targets; the 15/4 Decision that adopted the Kunming-Montreal Global Biodiversity Framework. These two decisions reflect an attempt to both refocus and energise international efforts in this area around ambitious, clear and quantified targets, in the manner of the Millennium Goals or the Sustainable Development Goals that were been adopted during the Rio+20 Conference.

118. Decisions are adopted solely by consensus. Indeed, when the COP adopted its rules of procedure at its first session, it provided for an exception, Article 40 (1), which deals with the decision-making process and on which no agreement has yet been reached. This article reads as follows:

"[1. The Parties shall make every effort to reach agreement on all matters of substance by consensus. If all efforts to reach consensus have been exhausted and no agreement reached, the decision, [except a decision under paragraph 1 or 2 of article 21 of the Convention] shall, as a last resort, be taken by a two-thirds majority vote of the Parties present and voting, unless otherwise provided by the Convention, the financial rules referred to in paragraph 3 of article 23 of the Convention, or the present rules of procedure. [Decisions of the Parties under paragraphs 1 and 2 of article 21 of the Convention shall be taken by consensus.]].[214]

In these conditions, consensus, this "passive unanimity, typical of situations of indifference"[215], is the only way to adopt a decision; there can be no threat of a vote. This has limited consequences, however, as according to UN practice, the adoption of a decision by vote rather than by consensus constitutes a failure and should be avoided. This consensus rule was however made more flexible and, in some circumstances, decisions have been adopted despite the reservations of one State or

---

214. Decision I/1, aforementioned, *Rules of Procedure of the Conference of the Parties* (1994).
215. G. Devin and M.-C. Smouts, *Les organisations internationales*, A. Colin, Paris, 2011, p. 91 (our translation).

another. When this happens, these reservations are recorded in the minutes of the Conference of the Parties [216].

- *The secretariat*

119. The secretariat of the Convention and of its protocols has been entrusted to UNEP (unlike the secretariat of the UN Framework Convention on Climate Change). It is based in Montreal, Canada. Its Executive Secretary is appointed by the UN Secretary-General in consultation with the COP through its Bureau. Since February 2023, David Cooper has been acting as the Executive Secretary. The secretariat is in charge of preparing the meetings of the Parties and of the various subsidiary bodies. It acts as a channel for the exchange of information between the Parties. It co-ordinates with other relevant international bodies, and in particular enters into "such administrative and contractual arrangements as may be required for the effective discharge of its functions" and performs "such other functions as may be determined by the Conference of the Parties" [217]. The team now includes around 110 people. It is funded by the General Trust Fund to which all Parties contribute [218].

- *The subsidiary bodies*

120. The COP to the Convention on Biological Diversity and the two COP-MOP meetings can rely on two subsidiary bodies: the Subsidiary Body for Implementation (SBI) and the Subsidiary Body on Scientific, Technical and Technological Advice (SBSTTA).

121. The SBSTTA was established by the Convention [219]. It is open to the participation of all Parties and is multidisciplinary. It "shall comprise government representatives competent in the relevant field of expertise" [220]. It provides "scientific and technical assessments of the status of biological diversity", prepares "scientific and technical assessments of the effects of types of measures taken in accordance

---

216. For example, in 2002, with formal objections from Turkey and Australia to two decisions; Report of the Sixth Meeting of the Conference of the Parties to the Convention on Biological Diversity, UNEP/CBD/COP/6/20*, 23 September 2002, para. 295 *et seq.*
217. Article 24 of the Convention.
218. CBD, Decision I/6, *Financing of and Budget for the Convention* (1994).
219. Article 25 of the Convention.
220. *Ibid.*

with the provisions of the Convention" and generally responds "to scientific, technical, technological and methodological questions that the Conference of the Parties and its subsidiary bodies may put to the body" [221]. The COP established its *modus operandi* in 2008 to streamline its work and ensure that "assessments are carried out in an objective and authoritative manner" [222]. It meets once or twice a year and can itself convene *ad hoc* expert groups.

122. One question that arises is the relationship between SBSTTA and IPBES, which was created outside the scope of the Convention on Biological Diversity. The Conference of the Parties to the Convention followed the IPBES negotiations very closely, but remained more of a spectator than a true player. Its very brief resolution X/11 [223] simply encouraged the UN General Assembly to explore the possibility of creating IPBES "at the earliest opportunity". The decision particularly stressed the need for IPBES to "be responsive to, *inter alia*, the needs of the Convention" and to thereby strengthen SBSTTA. It asked the Executive Secretary of the CBD, in collaboration with the Bureau of the SBSTTA, to examine how the CBD could make full and effective use of the platform, seeking complementarity and avoiding duplication [224]. The relationship between IPBES and the CBD's SBSTTA could resemble the relationship between IPCC and the UNFCCC's SBSTTA. In this case, in the spectrum between science and policy, the SBSTTA occupies a subtle intermediate position between IPCC and policy-makers: it considers scientific and technical issues, takes responsibility for the political expression of controversies that arise within the COPs regarding these issues, and acts as a link with governments [225]. It can even be considered as a "buffer" between IPCC and governments. Thus, it was able to temper the initial criticism of IPCC by encouraging developing countries to express their disagreements. According to Amy Dahan, the IPCC-SBSTTA pairing crystallises this co-production of science and policy, where the two seemingly contradictory paths of

---

221. *Ibid.*
222. CBD, Decision VIII/10, *Operations of the Convention* (2008).
223. CBD, Decision X/11, *Science-Policy Interface on Biodiversity, Ecosystem Services and Human Well-being and Consideration of the Outcome of the Intergovernmental Meetings*, 29 October 2010.
224. *Potential Relationships between the Intergovernmental Science-Policy Platform and Existing Institutions, Note by the Secretariat*, UNEP/IPBES/3/INF/11, 7 June 2010.
225. A. Dahan, S. Aykut, H. Guillemot and A. Korczak, *Les arènes climatiques: forums du futur ou foires aux palabres*, rapport de Recherche, February 2009, p. 4, https://docplayer.fr/6352460-Les-arenes-climatiques-forums-du-futur-ou-foires-aux-palabres.html, accessed on 25 October 2023.

political conflict and scientific consensus intertwine within a complex game of back-and-forth and competition [226].

123. As for the SBI, it was recently created by the COP [227], replacing the *Ad Hoc* Open-ended Working Group on the Review of Implementation of the Convention. It has held only three meetings, in 2016, 2018 and 2022. It plays a role in reviewing progress in the implementation of the Convention, in strategic plans to support effective implementation and in strengthening implementation mechanisms.

- *Proliferation*

124. Because of both the technical and controversial nature of the subject at hand, the COP and its subsidiary bodies have established a great number of bureaux, *ad hoc* expert groups, open-ended working groups on protected areas and on Article 8 *(j)*, workshops and so on. The result is that the calendar of meetings is full and negotiations are almost permanent. A clearing-house mechanism designed to promote scientific and technical co-operation has also been set up. The Convention has therefore become, from an institutional point of view, a "big machine", as shown by the following diagram.

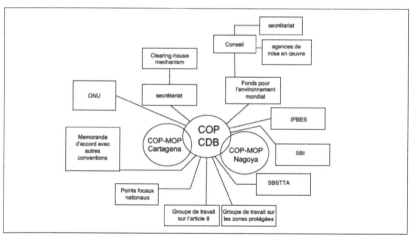

Institutional diagram of the Convention on Biological Diversity [228]

---

226. *Ibid.*, 136.
227. CBD, Decision XII/26, *Improving the Efficiency of Structures and Processes of the Convention: Subsidiary Body on Implementation* (2014). Terms of reference for the SBI in the Annex.
228. CBD, https://www.cbd.int/gbo1/chap-02.shtml, accessed on 25 October 2023.

b) *The profusion beyond the Convention on Biological Diversity*

125. Here, we have only presented the institutions created pursuant to the Convention on Biological Diversity, which is at the heart of the complex of regimes on biodiversity. But many other treaty institutions have been created at the regional or global level. They generally adopt the same triptych comprising a plenary political body, the COP, sometimes a smaller political body to liaise between two COPs, one or more expert bodies and a secretariat, which often is the only permanent element.

- *Conference of the Parties*

126. Since the 1970s, most conventions provide that their Contracting Parties will meet regularly. This is an almost unavoidable provision. Several conventions, for instance, the Convention on Wetlands of International Importance Especially as Waterfowl Habitat (Ramsar, 2 February 1971), have also been revised to include such provisions. Conventions concluded in the framework of international organisations use pre-existing structures, both for economic reasons and because these international organisations are keen to keep them in their fold. For example, the World Heritage Convention, adopted under the auspices of UNESCO, does not create a Conference of the Parties, but assigns certain functions to the General Conference of UNESCO. Other instruments rely on existing structures and also create new ones. For example, the Bern Convention on the Conservation of European Wildlife and Natural Habitats, concluded within the framework of the Council of Europe, provides, as we have seen, for the intervention of the Committee of Ministers of the Council of Europe in certain circumstances. But it also establishes a Standing Committee which, given its composition and statutes, can be compared to a Conference of the Parties, despite its name that is usually reserved for smaller political bodies. Indeed, according to Article 13 of the Convention, any Contracting Party may be represented on this body by one or more delegates. The Convention provides for meetings to be held at least every two years and whenever a majority of the Contracting Parties so request. In practice, they have been held on a regular basis, every year since the Convention entered into force.

127. Other conventions, which do not relate to any pre-existing international institution, create co-operation structures *ex nihilo*. Thus, the

Convention on International Trade in Endangered Species of Wild Fauna and Flora (CITES), signed in 1973, provides in its Article XI for the Conference of the Parties to meet regularly – at least once every two years – as well as for the possibility of extraordinary sessions, at the request of at least one-third of the Parties. It must "review the implementation" of the Convention. In particular, it reviews proposals for amendments to Appendices I and II of the Convention and adopts them where appropriate. It also adopts resolutions to clarify the interpretation of the Convention and "where appropriate", makes recommendations for improving the effectiveness of the present Convention.

128. Another example is the Canberra Commission, established by Article 7 of the Convention on the Conservation of Antarctic Marine Living Resources, which is composed of representatives of the original Contracting Parties, subsequent Parties and regional economic integration organisations that also joined later on [229]. The Commission is thus a permanent plenary body that serves as a Conference of the Parties [230].

129. As conventions adopted in the environmental field are very often "framework conventions", the Conferences of the Parties established by these conventions become intertwined with those created by their protocols, and the more protocols are involved, the more complex this process becomes. Framework conventions thus give rise to a plurality of Conferences of the Parties, although the States represented thereon are not necessarily the same. However, as in the case of the Convention on Biological Diversity, a grouping of meetings is generally provided for or set up for practical as well as economic reasons. In the same way, the Bonn Convention provides for the establishment of a Conference of the Parties, whose ordinary sessions are held "at intervals of not more than three years, unless the Conference decides otherwise" [231]. The widespread establishment of a Conference of the Parties specific to each of the agreements adopted under this Convention is in line with the guidelines for the conclusion of agreements set out in Article V of the Convention, which states: "Each Agreement should . . . establish, if necessary, appropriate machinery to assist in carrying out the aims

---

229. Provided, in the case of the latter two categories, that their participation has been accepted by the original Contracting Parties, who thereby reserve a certain right of control over the composition of the Commission.

230. It holds an annual session, and may also hold special sessions at the request of one-third of its members. It is based in Hobart, Tasmania, Australia.

231. See its Article VII. Extraordinary meetings can take place "at any time on the written request of at least one-third of the Parties".

of the Agreement, to monitor its effectiveness, and to prepare reports for the Conference of the Parties". This is the case, for example, with the Agreement on the Conservation of African-Eurasian Migratory Waterbirds, which establishes a Meeting of the Parties as a "decision-making body" and provides in its Article 6 that it will meet at regular intervals of less than three years, in conjunction with the Meeting of the Parties to the Bonn Convention so far as possible [232]. Similarly, the Geneva Protocol concerning Mediterranean Specially Protected Areas, which is a protocol to the Barcelona Convention for the Protection of the Mediterranean Sea against Pollution, provides for a Meeting of the Parties to meet every two years, in conjunction with the meetings of the Parties to the parent Convention [233]. In the same spirit of "economy", the Conference of the Contracting Parties to the Alpine Convention, known as the Alpine Conference, which meets regularly – generally every two years – serves as a Conference of the Parties for its various protocols [234].

130. In contrast to the Algiers Convention, which suffered from a real and detrimental deficit in this respect, the Maputo Convention makes provision for institutional arrangements, with the creation of a secretariat and a Conference of the Parties [235]. These provisions are fairly standard except that the Conference of the Parties meets at ministerial level, a sign of the importance that States wanted this body to have. Its mission is to examine and encourage the effective implementation of the Convention, and it may create subsidiary bodies if necessary. The secretariat itself is assigned a large mission, as it is asked, among other things, "to draw the attention of the Conference of the Parties to matters pertaining to the objectives of this Convention and its implementation" and therefore participate in monitoring its implementation. It was also essential to include a provision on financial resources. From this point of

---

232. On the written request of at least one-third of the Parties, the Agreement secretariat shall convene an extraordinary session of the Meeting of the Parties, Article VI.3.

233. Adopted on 3 April 1982, entered into force on 23 March 1986. The same applies to the *Protocol* concerning Specially Protected Areas and Wildlife to the Convention for the Protection and Development of the Marine Environment of the Wider Caribbean Region (Art. 23). However, this is not the case for the Protocol for the *Conservation* and Management of Protected Marine and Coastal Areas of the South-East Pacific (Art. 14), but even where this is not explicitly provided for, meetings may be joint in practice.

234. For example, Parties to the Alpine Convention that are not Parties to the *Protocol* for the Implementation of the Alpine Convention in the Field of Nature Protection and Landscape Conservation do not take part in the vote.

235. Articles XXVI and XXVII.

view, Article XXVIII envisages, among other things, the establishment of a conservation fund under the authority of the Conference of the Parties.

- *Smaller political bodies*

131. Institution of regular meetings of the Parties alone often does not suffice. These meetings are difficult and costly to organise and it is hard to imagine more than one meeting a year. However, in the meantime, once a convention is "up and running", decisions often have to be made. Very quickly, the need arose for a subsidiary body, composed of about eight to twenty members, in which the Parties would take turns. Generally kept small, these bodies are often referred to as "permanent" because their flexibility allows for frequent meetings. For example, under CITES, the Standing Committee, which has a general purpose, guides the implementation of the Convention, ensures its application in the interval between two meetings of the Parties, to which it reports on its activities. It also monitors budgetary expenditure and its preliminary approval is required before seeking external funds, which occurs more and more frequently and for increasingly large amounts [236].

132. When the provisions of the Convention do not contemplate such a committee, the Conference of the Parties often establishes it. For example, the Convention on the Conservation of Migratory Species of Wild Animals did not provide for the creation of a Standing Committee; the Conference of the Parties did so in its Resolution 1.1 [237]. This Standing Committee, which holds around one session a year, is composed of seven members appointed on the basis of equitable geographical representation and includes a representative of the Convention's depositary country – Germany – and of the host country of the following Conference. Adopted in 1971, the Convention on Wetlands of International Importance Especially as Waterfowl Habitat also did not provide for a smaller committee. But the need for such an institution was soon felt and at the Conference of the Parties held in Groningen in 1984, a working group was tasked with examining this issue and reporting to the following COP. At that following COP, in Regina in 1987, the

---

236. J.-M. Lavieille (ed.), *Conventions de protection de l'environnement. Secrétariats, Conférences des Parties, Comités d'experts*, PULIM, Limoges, 2000, p. 220. It may itself set up *ad hoc* working groups.

237. Resolution 1.1 (1985).

decision was made to establish a Standing Committee. Nine Contracting Parties, appointed by the COP, are represented on this committee. Seven of these members are elected according to the principle of equitable geographical distribution, "with due regard for a proper representation of developing countries" [238]. The other two members are the COP host and the host of the following COP. In addition, the two host Parties of the two sections of the Convention secretariat – the UK and Switzerland – as well as the Director General of IUCN and of another NGO, Wetlands International, participate as observers as part of their secretariat role for the Convention. The Contracting Parties that are not members of the Committee may also be granted observer status at these meetings, which take place at least once a year. Similarly, the Bern Convention on the Conservation of European Wildlife and Natural Habitats did not at first envisage a smaller body. The Standing Committee of this Convention is a plenary body, which is rather cumbersome in terms of organisation. To address this, the Standing Committee set up a Bureau in January 1991, at its tenth session. This Bureau is a troika consisting of the Chair of the Standing Committee, the Vice-Chair and the previous Chair, together with two additional Bureau members. The Bureau is in charge of making administrative and organisation decisions in between plenary meetings. It operates in a very flexible way, meeting at the request of its Chair.

133. There are however many conventions, especially the most recent ones, that make provision for an executive body from the outset. Thus, Article 9 of the Convention concerning the Protection of the World Cultural and Natural Heritage created the Intergovernmental Committee for the Protection of the World Cultural and Natural Heritage, composed of twenty-one States Parties to the Convention, elected at the sessions of the General Conference of UNESCO, according to the principle of equitable geographical representation of the different regions and cultures of the world, with one-third of members to be renewed each year. Similarly, Article 8 of the Alpine Convention establishes a Permanent Committee which also serves as the Permanent Committee for its Protocol on Nature Protection and Landscape Conservation [239]. Although this is an executive body, it is also a plenary forum given the small number of Parties to this Convention.

---

238. See the Resolution 3.3: Establishment of a Standing Committee, Third Meeting of the Conference of the Contracting Parties, Regina, Canada, 27 May-5 June 1987.
239. Article 8.

- *Expert bodies*

134. The desire to take advice from scientists is very clear in all recent conventions. Some instruments create one or more *ad hoc* scientific bodies, while others prefer to rely on existing international bodies or individual experts. Sometimes, both approaches are combined.

135. The solution of relying on pre-existing bodies or individual experts was adopted in the Convention concerning the Protection of the World Cultural and Natural Heritage. Thus, the Intergovernmental Committee for the Protection of the World Cultural and Natural Heritage may invite public or private bodies as well as private individuals to its meetings at any time in order to consult them on specific issues. With regard to nature conservation, the list of accepted observers includes a representative of IUCN. Lastly, it may create such advisory bodies as it deems necessary for the performance of its task [240]. Similarly, the Bern Convention on the Conservation of European Wildlife and Natural Habitats provides that "in order to discharge its functions, the Standing Committee may, on its own initiative, arrange for meetings of groups of experts" [241]. This provision is often used and the Parties have not found it necessary to create a general scientific body. The same approach is used in the Protocol for the Conservation and Management of Protected Marine and Coastal Areas of the Southeast Pacific [242] and the Alpine Convention [243].

136. By contrast, some instruments create *ad hoc* structures, generally called Scientific Panels, that bring together experts with recognised qualifications in their field and that meet regularly, once or twice a year. The creation of such structures is now very common and treaty systems now feature a growing number of them. However, they are not always independent bodies, often because of their composition and the rules governing the appointment of experts. Here as well, these structures were not envisaged in the earlier conventions and had to be set up by the Conferences of the Parties. For example, the Ramsar Convention originally provided in its Article 6 simply that the Conference of the Parties requests reports and statistics from "relevant international bodies". A series of working groups were set up under this article and the secretariat worked very closely with NGOs, in particular Wetlands

---

240. Article 10, para. 3.
241. Article 14, para. 2.
242. Article 12.
243. Article 6, para. 5.

International. After the Convention was given a financial regime, budgets always included a line for expert services. However, in 1991, in order to be able to focus on administrative matters, the Standing Committee of the Convention proposed that a scientific committee be established. It suggested that the Working Group on the Criteria of Wise Use of Wetlands, one of the most important expert groups created at the third meeting of the Parties, be transformed into a scientific committee [244]. The decision was adopted by the fifth meeting of the Parties to create a Scientific and Technical Review Panel (STRP) out of this Working Group [245]. The STRP is composed of seven members with relevant scientific and technical knowledge, appointed by the Conference of the Parties on an individual basis for a period of three years. It meets at least once a year and can itself seek advice from experts and scientists on specific issues [246].

137. Several technical committees have also been created under CITES [247]. The Animals and Plants Committees include scientists whose mission is essentially to advise and guide other treaty institutions on the treatment of wild species (assessment of their conservation status, review of biological and commercial data, proposed amendments to the Appendices). To this end, they perform a periodic review of the Appendices. An Identification Manual Committee was also created in order to co-ordinate the development of identification manuals for plant and animal species and to assist Parties in developing national or regional manuals. As for the Nomenclature Committee, it develops standardised reference lists for the nomenclature of animal and plant taxa, for sub-species and botanical varieties. It deals with the question of synonyms and proposes possible name changes in the interest of harmonisation and common interpretation of the Convention's Appendices. In addition, one of the secretariat's functions is to "undertake scientific and technical studies in accordance with programmes authorized by the

---

244. Proceedings of the Fourth Conference of the Parties, Montreux, Switzerland, 27 June to 4 July 1990, Gland, Recommendation 4.7: Mechanisms for Improved Application of the Ramsar Convention.
245. Resolution on the Establishment of a Scientific and Technical Review Panel, *Fifth Meeting of the Conference of the Contracting Parties, Kushiro, 9-16 June 1993*, Gland, p. 166.
246. Designation is made on the proposal of the Standing Committee, on the basis of lists submitted to the Convention secretariat by the Parties, and according to the principle of equitable geographical distribution. IUCN and Wetlands International are granted observer status.
247. See the Resolution Conf. 11.1 (Rev. CoP17), Annex 2, adopted in 1987 at the Ottawa COP.

Conference of the Parties as will contribute to the implementation of the present Convention"[248]. This mechanism also relies on the "national scientific authorities" designated by the Parties.

138. Very quickly, conventions started to make provision for the creation of scientific structures. Thus, the Bonn Convention on Migratory Species established from the outset a Scientific Council in its Article 8: "Any Party may appoint a qualified expert as a member of the Scientific Council". The Scientific Council also includes qualified experts selected and appointed by the Conference of the Parties, up to a maximum of eight. The Scientific Council meets at the invitation of the secretariat, whenever the Conference of the Parties so requests, on average once a year. The Agreement on the Conservation of African-Eurasian Migratory Waterbirds, adopted pursuant to the Bonn Convention, also contains provisions for the establishment of such a committee, the Technical Committee[249], composed of nine experts representing different regions of the Agreement area, with a balanced geographical distribution, one representative appointed by IUCN, Wetlands International and the International Council for Game and Wildlife Conservation (CIC) and one thematic expert from rural economics, game management, environmental law and communication, education and public awareness. The meeting of the Parties to the Agreement specified the rules governing the appointment of experts and of the Chair as well as the duration of their term of office[250].

139. Similarly, a scientific committee was created pursuant to the Canberra Convention, which meets as often as needed to perform its functions[251]. Each member of the Canberra Commission appoints a representative with appropriate scientific expertise, who may be accompanied by other experts and advisers as appropriate. It is an advisory body to the Commission and may, on an *ad hoc* basis, seek advice from other experts, and it may itself establish subsidiary bodies. Thus, it is currently supported by four Working Groups on Ecosystem Monitoring and Management (WG-EMM), Fish Stock Assessment (WG-FSA), Statistics, Assessments and Modelling (WG-SAM), Incidental Mortality Associated with Fishing (WG-IMAF), Survey and Analysis Methods (WG-ASAM).

---

248. Article 12.
249. Article VII.
250. AEWA, *Report of the First Session of the Meeting of the Parties, Cape Town, South Africa, 6-9 November 1999*, UNEP/AEWA/MOP1.
251. Article XIV.

140. These structures are intended to meet regularly, as the need arises, about once or twice a year, with increasing use of video conferencing. For cost-effective reasons, work also increasingly takes place via video conference.

141. Beyond the Convention on Biological Diversity, the creation of IPBES also raised the question of its relationship with many other multilateral environmental agreements. The bodies created under these agreements must position themselves with respect to IPBES, define working relationships and gradually build partnerships with it. Without these partnerships, IPBES will have failed to fulfil part of its functions [252].

- *Secretariats*

142. The administrative body is the third element of the institutional triptych. As soon as co-operation is institutionalised, the need arises for a secretariat, however modest. A Conference of the Parties means having a secretariat. The allocation of administrative tasks to permanent bodies is another characteristic feature of recent treaty regimes. These administrative structures, which are poorly funded, are usually very light, especially when the number of Parties is small.

143. The secretariat can thus be entrusted to the country holding the presidency of the Conference of the Parties. The 1991 Alpine Convention illustrates this approach, which is cost-effective for Contracting States while providing the secretariat with adequate resources. The downside of this approach is that all or part of the convention's "memory" is lost whenever the presidency changes. More often, Contracting States make use of existing international institutions, intergovernmental organisations and on rare occasions non-governmental organisations, and strengthen them so these additional needs can be met. For this reason, the Alpine Conference eventually established a permanent secretariat in 2002 at its seventh meeting.

144. UNEP plays an important role in providing intergovernmental support. A wide range of conventions have entrusted it with the role of

---

252. See, for example, Ramsar Resolution XI.6 adopted by the Eleventh Meeting of the Conference of the Parties to the Convention on Wetlands; Resolution 10.8 adopted by the Conference of the Parties at its Tenth Meeting on Cooperation between the Intergovernmental Science-Policy Platform on Biodiversity and Ecosystem Services (IPBES) and CMS; Decision SC 61 adopted by the Standing Committee of the Convention on International Trade in Endangered Species of Wild Fauna and Flora at its Sixty-First Meeting of the Standing Committee.

secretariat. There are several practical advantages to this approach, in particular in terms of financial security (application of United Nations financial management rules, internal audits, etc.). Thus, the CITES secretariat is run by UNEP (Art. 12). To this end, UNEP has set up an office based in Geneva, Switzerland, and is contractually assisted by IUCN in its mission. This secretariat is relatively well staffed with about fifty people. This is not excessive given the scope of the remit and the complexity of the issues it deals with. The secretariat of the Convention on the Conservation of Migratory Species of Wild Animals is also entrusted to UNEP[253], which also runs the secretariat for most conventions of the "Regional Seas Programme" adopted under its auspices, such as the one for the Barcelona Convention, set up in Athens.

145. There are other UN bodies and institutions of the UN family that have been given responsibilities in this area. One example is the United Nations Economic Commission for Europe, which runs the secretariat of the Convention on Environmental Impact Assessment in a Transboundary Context, adopted in 1991 in Espoo, Finland. Some regional organisations also perform these administrative tasks. This is the case for the Convention concerning the Protection of the World Cultural and Natural Heritage, whose secretariat has been performed by the UNESCO World Heritage Centre since 1992. Similarly, the Convention on the Conservation of European Wildlife and Natural Habitats has a small secretariat provided by the Council of Europe. In the same vein, the ASEAN acts as secretariat of the ASEAN Agreement on the Conservation of Nature and Natural Resources, while the Pacific Community performs these duties for the Apia Convention.

146. It is much less common for the secretariat role to be entrusted to an NGO. This is the case however with the Ramsar Convention on Wetlands of International Importance. From the start, it created a secretariat called the Bureau of the Convention and its Article 8 assigned these functions to IUCN, which was to "perform the continuing bureau duties under this Convention until such time as another organization or government is appointed by a majority of two-thirds of all Contracting Parties". In reality, to this day, IUCN still runs the Bureau, but its

---

253. See the *Memorandum of Understanding between the Standing Committee of the Conference of the Parties to the Convention in International Trade in Endangered Species of Wild Fauna and Flora and the Executive Director of the United Nations Environment Programme concerning Secretariat Services and Support of the Convention*, https://cites.org/sites/default/files/common/disc/sec/CITES-UNEP.pdf, accessed on 25 October 2023.

organisation was modified at the Conference of the Parties in Regina in 1987. Until then, IUCN had been performing these duties with the help of Wetlands International as a technical and scientific advisor. However, in the absence of financial provisions, IUCN, which was only receiving support from UNEP and WWF for this role, did not have the means to create a special secretariat for Ramsar. In 1980, amendments were called for by the Cagliari Conference of the Parties. In 1984, the Groningen Conference established a working group to examine the most effective means of providing a full secretariat service. It presented its findings in Regina in 1987: only the joint proposal of Wetlands International and IUCN to create administrative structures was selected and the Conference of the Parties adopted these recommendations. The secretariat of the Ramsar Convention has since been provided by IUCN, funded from the Convention's budget. The secretariat includes a General Secretary, appointed by the IUCN Director General, in consultation with and on the proposal of the Standing Committee, and other staff members, appointed by the IUCN Director General, on the recommendation of the Secretary-General. It is based at the IUCN headquarters in Gland, Switzerland.

147. Thus, there are many treaty institutions, confirming the impression of fragmented governance landscape.

c) *Institutional fragmentation and defragmentation*

148. The institutional landscape has been historically fragmented, but co-operation is developing significantly between the various institutions involved and in practice fosters some form of defragmentation. The question remains as to the relationship between the institutions acting for biodiversity and other institutions outside the field of biodiversity (for example, climate, desertification or chemicals) or more generally, outside the environmental field.

- *A fragmented institutional landscape*

149. The institutional framework for biodiversity appears to be fragmented between many different institutions – intergovernmental organisations but mostly treaty institutions. This fragmented landscape has real benefits in terms of flexibility, as issues can be dealt with by small or even micro-institutions, mostly regional or specialised (migratory species, wetlands, etc.), which are smaller than large insti-

tutions, focused on specific objectives and often closer to the "ground". This polycentric international governance can be seen not as an addition of multiple initiatives, a set of confused and competing enterprises, but rather as a means to gradually build trust between States. Thus, "[p]roceeding by small steps to build confidence and generate patterns of reciprocity is not a timid, second-best strategy", but is on the contrary more suited to the realities of international life than a single, overarching approach [254].

150. However, fragmentation is not without its challenges: a lack of coherence and a certain dispersal of efforts and means, duplication and deficits, a lack of co-ordination and sometimes even sterile competition between treaty systems. As noted in a 2018 UN Environment Programme report, "[t]he structure of international environmental governance is characterized by institutional fragmentation and a heterogeneous set of actors, revealing important coherence and coordination challenges" [255]. This conclusion, made in respect of international environmental governance in general, especially applies to biodiversity governance. Not to mention that participating in every meeting constitutes a heavy burden for States. Admittedly, the Convention on Biological Diversity, which has a global scope and a wide-ranging purpose, was designed to play the role of an "umbrella" convention and bring some coherence to this fragmented governance landscape. But the fact that it is one of the last building blocks of this conventional edifice made this difficult for both practical and psychological reasons. It was necessary to counter the local "feudal systems" that had arisen in this "fragmented realm" [256].

151. Pragmatism undoubtedly requires one to abandon the idea, at least in the medium-term, of a hierarchical and entirely rational governance structure. However, this should not mean giving up on the need to put some order into this fragmented landscape, as evidenced by Mireille Delmas-Marty [257]. A number of levers can be used to move towards "defragmentation", one of which is institutional co-operation at the level of the COPs or secretariats. This common-sense solution

---

254. R. O. Keohane and D. G. Victor, "Cooperation and Discord in Global Climate Policy", *Nature Climate Change*, 9 May 2016, p. 5.
255. UNEP, *Gaps in International Environmental Law and Environment-Related Instruments: Towards a Global Pact for the Environment Report of the Secretary-General*, A/73/419, 30 November 2018, p. 2.
256. H. Van Asselt, F. Sindico and M. A. Mehling, "Global Climate Change and the Fragmentation of International Law", *Law and Policy*, October 2008, Vol. 30, No. 4, p. 427.
257. M. Delmas-Marty, *Les forces imaginantes du droit*, Vol. II: Le pluralisme ordonné, Seuil, Paris, 2006.

does however encounter various forms of resistance: firstly, from the treaty bodies themselves, and secondly from States who fear that the secretariats will go too far and invoke the principle of speciality of international organisations to block any inter-treaty co-operation over which they would risk losing control. Thus, according to Australia, "[a]ll cooperation must respect the individual mandates and independent legal status of each convention" [258], fears that are in fact reflected in the recommendations of the *Ad Hoc* Working Group set up by the UN General Assembly to assess possible gaps in international environmental law and environment-related instruments in order to strengthen their implementation [259]. In this respect, Margaret Young pointed out the risks that co-operation between organisations might elude States and could lead to a managerial drift whereby decisions would be taken by invisible experts [260].

- *Strengthening co-operation between biodiversity conventions*

152. The objective of strengthening interinstitutional co-operation is not new and it goes beyond the field of biodiversity [261]. In 1998, as part of his reform plans, the UN Secretary-General set up a Task Force on Environment and Human Settlement, which completed its work in 1999. It focused mainly on the issue of interagency links, intergovernmental bodies, and the revitalisation of UNEP. Its recommendations were reviewed by the Governing Council of UNEP and adopted by the General Assembly in Resolution 53/242 [262]. An Environment Management Group was set up to consider the improvement of co-ordination between organisations and also between conventions. More generally, UNEP is working to strengthen co-ordination and synergies between international environmental conventions, bearing in mind the autono-

---

258. UNFCCC (SBSTA), *Views on the Paper on Options for Enhanced Cooperation among the Three Rio Conventions. Submissions from Parties*, FCCC/SBSTA/2006/MISC.4, 23 March 2016, p. 3 (Submission from Australia).
259. See UNGA Resolution A/RES/72/277, 10 May 2018, *Towards a Global Pact for the Environment*. See also the UNGA Resolution A/RES/73/333, *Follow-up to the Report of the* Ad Hoc *Open-ended Working Group Established Pursuant to General Assembly Resolution 72/277*, 30 August 2019.
260. M. Young, *Trading Fish, Saving Fish: The Interaction between Regimes in International Law*, CUP, Cambridge, 2011, p. 276.
261. See in 1997 UNGA Resolution S/19-2. *Programme for the Further Implementation of Agenda 21*, para. 46 *(h)*, and the *Report of the World Summit on Sustainable Development, Plan of Implementation*, A/CONF.199/20, para. 140.
262. UNGA Resolution A/RES/53/242, *Report of the Secretary-General on Environment and Human Settlements*, 28 July 1999.

mous decision-making power of the Conferences of the Parties to these agreements. However, the experience of the Joint Liaison Group (JLG), set up in 2001 to co-ordinate the actions of the Parties to the three "Rio Conventions" (climate, biodiversity, desertification), showed the limits of a co-ordination that was only formal because of a lack of means and commitment [263]. In 2009, the JLG noted that there was a disconnect between the roles and mandates assigned to the JLG by each convention and that this led to difficulties in implementing the envisaged activities. Indeed, the JLG can only implement activities mandated by all the governing bodies of the relevant conventions [264]. Its work has met with resistance from States and political opposition to the defragmentation of regimes, especially as the Parties differ from one regime to the next. For example, the United States is party to the 1992 Framework Convention on Climate Change but not to the Convention on Biological Diversity. As a result, the JLG has had only a limited impact on issues of common concern to several regimes [265].

153. With regard to co-operation between biodiversity conventions, at least at the universal level, the adoption of the Aichi and Kunming-Montreal Targets in 2010 and 2022 constituted a turning point. Indeed, while co-operation was for a long time merely wishful thinking, it has steadily increased since their adoption and is starting to bear fruit. Strongly encouraged by the Convention on Biological Diversity [266], supported by the UN General Assembly [267], co-operation is sometimes

---

263. R. O. Keohane and D. G. Victor, "Cooperation and Discord in Global Climate Policy" (n. 254), p. 5.

264. "There remains a disconnect between the roles and mandates given to the JLG by each convention with this disconnect resulting in limitations when considering the implementation of the requested activities. For example, only activities that are mandated by all the governing bodies of each convention could be effectively implemented by the JLG." H. Van Asselt, F. Sindico and M. A. Mehling, "Global Climate Change and the Fragmentation of International Law" (n. 256), p. 427.

265. UNFCCC (SBSTA), *Views on the Paper on Options for Enhanced Cooperation among the Three Rio Conventions. Submissions from Parties*, FCCC/SBSTA/2006/MISC.4, 23 March 2016, p. 3 (Submission from Australia).

266. See in particular its decisions XIII/24, XII/6, XI/6, X/20, X/5, IX/27 and VII/26; CITES COP Decision Conf. 16.4; CMS COP Decision 10.21; ITPGRFA Resolutions 10/2015, 5/2013 and 6/2013; Ramsar COP Decision XI/6, XI.1; and the World Heritage Committee WHC 40 COM 5A and WHC 33 COM 5C. See the Decision 15/4 (2022), *Kunming-Montreal Global Biodiversity Framework*, CBD/COP/DEC/15/4, 19 December 2022, and Decision 15/13 (2022), *Cooperation with Other Conventions and International Organizations*.

267. UN General Assembly, Resolution A/RES/65/161, *Convention on Biological Diversity*, 20 December 2010, para. 19. The UNGA recognised the importance of enhancing synergies among the biodiversity-related conventions, without prejudice to their specific objectives, and encouraged the Conferences of the Parties to the biodiversity-related multilateral environmental agreements to consider strengthening

even formalised, in particular at the level of the secretariats, for example, with the conclusion of many memoranda of understanding between two or more secretariats. At the initiative of the COP to the CBD, a Biodiversity Liaison Group was set up in 2004 [268]. It brings together the six universal conventions dealing specifically with biodiversity: the Convention on Biological Diversity, CITES, the Convention on Migratory Species, the International Treaty on Plant Genetic Resources for Food and Agriculture, the Convention on Wetlands of International Importance and the Convention concerning the Protection of the World Cultural and Natural Heritage. The International Plant Protection Convention is also sometimes included. This set of conventions is referred to as a biodiversity cluster. Such co-operation is crucial; this conclusion has led to a proposal for the creation of an atmospheric cluster between the climate and the ozone secretariats, which could in turn strengthen its links with the biodiversity cluster [269]. The discussions focus in particular on the possible harmonisation of reporting requirements in the various biodiversity conventions [270]. In this respect, a recent decision of the CBD's COP, "encourages Parties to collaborate, where appropriate, with other reporting processes, including the Sustainable Development Goals and relevant multilateral environment agreement reporting, including by using a modular data reporting tool, such as DART, on a voluntary basis" [271].

154. In 2006, a Memorandum of Cooperation between the agencies supporting the implementation of the CBD Strategic Plan was concluded by the CBD, CITES, the Bonn Convention (CMS) and the Convention of Ramsar, among others. This was followed by a new

---

efforts in this regard, taking into account relevant experiences and bearing in mind the respective independent legal status and mandates of these instruments.

268. See COP CBD, Decision VII/26, *Cooperation with Other Conventions and International Organizations and Initiatives.*

269. See in 1997 UNGA Resolution S/19-2. *Programme for the Further Implementation of Agenda 21,* para. 46 *(h),* and the *Report of the World Summit on Sustainable Development, Plan of Implementation,* A/CONF.199/20, para. 140.

Established in 2001 pursuant to Resolution A/RES/53/242, UNGA, Report of the Secretary-General on Environment and Human Settlements, 10 August 1999. See Coordination within the UN System, Including with the Environmental Management Group, Report of the Executive Director, UNEP/GC.27/15/Add.1, 17 January 2013.

270. See the *Digital Data Reporting Tool* (DaRT) developed by UNEP-InforMEA; Resolution 2/17 UN Environment Assembly, *Enhancing the Work of UNEP in Facilitating Cooperation, Collaboration and Synergies Among Biodiversity-Related Conventions,* 27 May 2016.

271. Decision 15/6 (2022), *Mechanisms for Planning, Monitoring, Reporting and Review,* para. 12.

agreement after the adoption of the Aichi Targets, which was signed by even more parties. Joint work programmes were adopted between the CBD and CITES, the CBD and the CMS, the CBD and the Convention of Ramsar, etc. For instance, in 2014, COP 11 of the Convention on the Conservation of Migratory Species adopted a 2015-2023 Strategic Plan for Migratory Species which is in keeping with the 2011-2020 Strategic Plan for Biodiversity and the Aichi Targets. This Strategic Plan for Migratory Species links migratory species priorities with the main Aichi Targets for biodiversity and enables the integration within NBSAPs of targets related to migratory species. A joint work plan between the CBD and CMS secretariats was adopted, which identifies activities that contribute to the achievement of the objectives of both conventions. The secretariats hold annual co-ordination meetings and regular teleconferences to exchange information on the implementation of the joint work plan [272].

155. The defragmentation movement has also impacted other institutions. Thus, with regard to fisheries, the Kobe Process was initiated voluntarily by five fisheries organisations in order to improve the effectiveness of their policies and activities. It has enabled a pooling of experiences, leading to both a strengthening and an improved coherence of management methods and standards. The process has facilitated the circulation of actors (networks of scientists, professional bodies...) from one system to another. It has been a vector of dialogue and an initiator of joint projects. According to Sophie Gambardella, the Kobe Process seems to have eroded institutional compartmentalisation in favour of a permeability of international fora, making it possible to envisage a mindset of mutual enrichment nourished by the circulation of actors and standards for the international management of tuna [273]. This is a case of integrated co-operation, but it is a flexible and non-permanent co-operation, which consists of meetings whose recurrence varies as needed.

---

272. CBD, Note by the Executive Secretary, *Cooperation with Other Conventions, International Organizations and Partnerships to Enhance the Implementation of the Strategic Plan for Biodiversity 2011-2020*, UNEP/CBD/COP/13/16, 6 October 2016, paras. 7-8. See https://www.cbd.int/cooperation/related-conventions/mandates.shtml#jwp, accessed on 25 October 2023.
273. S. Gambardella, "Le processus de Kobé : un vecteur de circulation des normes et des acteurs dans un contexte de gouvernance internationale fragmentée", in S. Maljean-Dubois (ed.), *Circulations de normes et réseaux d'acteurs dans la gouvernance internationale de l'environnement*, Confluence des droits, DICE, Aix-en-Provence, 2017.

156. For several years, UNEP has continuously been involved in fostering synergies between the biodiversity conventions [274] and the United Nations Environment Assembly has called for this process to be further developed in the coming years [275]. This fostering of synergies is not based solely on co-operation between institutions; it should also be an objective pursued by each institution in its own individual activities [276].

157. The disconnect with international organisations outside the environmental field is just as – if not more – problematic for the effectiveness of the international law on biodiversity.

• *The challenge of the disconnect with international organisations outside the environmental field*

158. The conventions on biological diversity, and especially the 1992 Convention, are competing with the many international organisations that have become involved in certain issues (World Trade Organisation, FAO, World Intellectual Property Organisation). The multiplicity of international fora where these issues are debated, the different ways in which they apprehend these issues and the inadequate co-ordination between these fora partly explain the mixed results in the implementation of the 1992 Convention [277]. The problem is particularly acute with regard to two issues: trade in GMOs and access and benefit-sharing, for which there is a disconnect in the way they are addressed by international law – the former by the WTO and the Cartagena Protocol [278], the latter by the WTO and the Nagoya

---

274. See in particular its decision SS.XII/2: Enhanced Coordination across the United Nations System, Including the Environment Management Group (Twelfth Special Session of the Governing Council/Global Ministerial Environment Forum, Nairobi, 20-22 February 2012, 2 March 2012.
275. See its Decision 2/17, Enhancing the Work of UNEP in Facilitating Cooperation, Collaboration and Synergies Among Biodiversity-Related Conventions, UNEP/EA.2/Res.17, 3 August 2016.
276. H. Van Asselt, "Managing the Fragmentation of International Environmental Law: Forests at the Intersection of the Climate and Biodiversity Regimes", *New York University Journal of International Law and Politics*, 2011-2012, Vol. 44, p. 1205.
277. C. Noiville, "La mise en œuvre de la Convention de Rio sur la conservation de la diversité biologique et ses relations avec l'accord de l'OMC sur les ADPIC. Analyse juridique de l'outil économique", in *L'outil économique en droit international et européen de l'environnement*, S. Maljean-Dubois (ed.), La Documentation française, Paris, 2002, pp. 281-303.
278. S. Maljean-Dubois, "Biodiversité, biotechnologies, biosécurité: le droit international désarticulé", *Journal du droit international*, No. 4, 2000, p. 955; S. Maljean-Dubois, "Le spectre de l'isolation clinique: quelle articulation entre les règles de l'OMC et les autres règles du droit international?", in *Revue européenne de droit de l'environnement*, No. 2/2008, pp. 159-176. WTO, *European Communities – Measures Affecting the Approval and Marketing of Biotech Products*, (DS 291/292/293), Report of the Panel, 29 September 2006.

Protocol [279]. It is also an issue in relation to forests, with regard to which the work of the conventions largely overlaps with the work of the United Nations Forum on Forests [280], and is in competition with REDD+ initiatives carried out under the auspices of the UN Framework Convention on Climate Change Reducing Emissions from Deforestation and Degradation [281]. On these issues, the framework of the biodiversity conventions seems both fragile and isolated.

3) Non-State actors

159. Given the magnitude of the environmental as well as economic and social issues at stake, the normative activity taking place in the framework of environmental conventions naturally interests advocacy groups as diverse as "conservationist" NGOs or business associations. These private actors enter the normative process, in which they intervene at different levels – solicited or of their own accord, on an occasional or regular basis – and with very variable effects – non-existent, marginal or real. There are thousands of people involved in the transnational governance of biodiversity, often in collaboration with governments [282]. They participate as observers in treaty institutions and engage in various forms of collaboration extending as far as institutional "action agendas".

a) *Non-State actors as observers in treaty institutions*

160. Non-State actors are increasingly present in these treaty institutions. This development is particularly noticeable and necessary in environmental matters [283]. They are generally given observer status in a liberal manner during the sessions of the political bodies. Often, observer delegations even outnumber those of the Contracting Parties. This was the case, for example, in 2018 at the Fourteenth Conference

---

279. J.-F. Morin et A. Orsini, "Policy Coherency and Regime Complexes: The Case of Genetic Resources", *Review of International Studies*, 40 (2), 2014, pp. 303-324.
280. CBD, *Forest Biological Diversity, Report of the Workshop on Forests and Biological Diversity, Accra, Ghana, 28-30 January 2002*, Note by the Executive Secretary, UNEP/CBD/COP/6/INF/7, 4 March 2002.
281. H. Van Asselt, "Managing the Fragmentation of International Environmental Law: Forests at the Intersection of the Climate and Biodiversity Regimes" (n. 276), p. 1205.
282. P. Pattberg and O. Widerberg, M. T. J. Kok, "Towards a Global Biodiversity Action Agenda", *Global Policy*, 2019, p. 2.
283. K. Von Moltke, "Governments and International Civil Society in Sustainable Development: A Framework", *International Environmental Agreements*, No. 2 (4), 2002, pp. 339-357.

of the Parties to the Convention on Biological Diversity, with over 400 observer delegations compared to 196 States Parties [284]. Contrary to certain misconception, the involvement of private actors is not noticeable solely in the COPs. It also takes place in more specialised meetings such as workshops. In contrast, the participation of private actors in smaller treaty bodies – bureaux, standing committees, etc. – is much more exceptional.

- *A wide variety of actors*

161. Behind the same observer status, there are organisations of very different sizes and means, defending sometimes contradictory interests: the large environmentalist NGOs rub shoulders with trade unions, charities, business associations, local authorities and, more recently, representatives of indigenous and local communities. For example, the non-governmental observers at the CBD COP 14 fell into four different categories:

- "academic and research institutions" (universities, research institutes and foundations, learned societies);
- "indigenous groups" (NGOs representing indigenous peoples at local, national or international level);
- "non-governmental organisations" in the strict sense (focusing on biodiversity or more generally on environment and sustainable development, at local, national or international level);
- "industry" (national and international companies and business associations).

162. Of course, NGO representation varies between conventions, depending on their purpose and scope of application. Only a few very large environmental NGOs have a broad enough mission and sufficient means to participate in almost all the treaty institutions. Lastly, NGOs from the "North" are over-represented, mainly because they have more resources. In this "nebula", not all organisations have the characteristics that traditionally define NGOs in the strict sense, in particular that of having a "non-profit-making aim of international utility" [285]. It is true

---

284. *Report of the Conference of the Parties to the Convention on Biological Diversity on its Fourteenth Meeting*, CBD/COP/14/14, 20 March 2019, p. 284 *et seq.*
285. See the European Convention on the Recognition of the Legal Personality of International Non-Governmental Organisations, Article 1. M.-O. Wiederkehr, "La Convention européenne sur la reconnaissance de la personnalité juridique des organisations internationales non gouvernementales du 24 avril 1986", *AFDI,* 1987, p. 749 ss.

that in the absence of a recognised international status, even minimal, what constitutes an NGO is not well defined [286]. The traditional definition has most likely "cracked" because of its narrowness, and broader definitions have been developed. This is reflected in the Directives concerning UNESCO's relations with international non-governmental organisations: any organisation that "has not been established by intergovernmental agreement, or by a government and that its purposes, functions, structure and operation are non-governmental, democratic and non-profit-making in character" [287]. It should be noted though that not all organisations that attend treaty structures have an international dimension. See, for example, the Federation of Industries of the State of Sao Paolo or the Coordinadoria Nacional de Pueblos Indígenas de Panamá present at COP 14 on biodiversity.

163. The "negative" expression (*non*-governmental organisation) clearly reflects a conceptually and linguistically poor definition. It is also a source of misunderstanding. At the same time, this "non-governmental" nature really is the only thing that these organisations have in common, since, as we have said, they differ greatly in terms of fields of activities (narrow, specialised, broad), levels of action (city, country, global), modalities of action (budget, staff) or members (whether they are from the "general public", representatives of socio-professional categories, political or religious circles, whether they are collective and/or individual members).

164. IUCN deserves a special mention here since it has such a special place in the institutional landscape. Created in 1948, it is the largest nature conservation NGO. It has an original structure made up of States, government bodies and non-governmental members (national and international NGOs). Nearly 140 nationalities are represented and all members have equal voting rights. It also includes specialised commissions involving some 15,000 volunteer experts chosen for their qualifications [288]. Many questions arise: what does IUCN have in common with a "small" local nature conservation organisation?

---

286. R. Ranjeva, "Les organisations non gouvernementales et la mise en œuvre du droit international", *Recueil des cours*, Vol. 270 (1997), p. 26.
287. UNESCO, *New Directives concerning UNESCO's Partnership with Non-Governmental Organizations*, Executive Board,187 EX 37.
288. C. de Klemm and J. Olivier, "Le rôle des ONG dans le droit de l'environnement: l'exemple de l'IUCN", in *Les Nations Unies et la protection de l'environnement: la promotion d'un développement durable*, Septièmes rencontres internationales d'Aix-en-Provence, S. Maljean-Dubois and R. Mehdi (eds.), Pedone, Paris, 1999, p. 177 ss.

Or with companies such as Yves Rocher or Sony Computer Science Laboratories present as observers at the COP 14 on biological diversity?

- *The observer status*

165. At the CITES Conference, observer status may be given to public and private institutions – "Any body or agency technically qualified in protection, conservation or management of wild fauna and flora" – provided that if they are national they must "have been approved for this purpose by the State in which they are located", and unless "at least one-third of the Parties present object" [289]. This provision was included and adapted in most subsequent conventions. Under the Convention on Biological Diversity, there are two categories of observers, as distinguished by the rules of procedure [290]:

– the United Nations, its specialised agencies and the International Atomic Energy Agency as well as any State not Party to the Convention (first category),
– any body or agency, whether governmental or non-governmental, qualified in fields relating to the conservation and sustainable use of biological diversity, which has informed the secretariat of its wish to be represented (second category). This definition is applied in a very liberal manner.

166. The former may "upon invitation of the President, participate without the right to vote in the proceedings of any meeting unless at least one third of the Parties present at the meeting object". The latter are informed by the Convention secretariat of meetings so that they can participate "as observers unless at least one third of the Parties present at the meeting object". Like the former, they participate "without the right to vote" in the proceedings of the meetings, but unlike the former, who participate in all meetings, they may only participate in meetings "of direct concern to the body or agency they represent unless at least one third of the Parties present at the meeting object" [291].

167. Observers present at the various Conferences of the Parties use their right to speak during the meetings, while sometimes considerably influencing the debates through active "corridor diplomacy". Their

---

289. Article XI.
290. Rules 6 and 7 of the Rules of Procedure, UNEP/CBD/COP/1/17, p. 82.
291. *Rules of Procedure for Meetings of the Conference of the Parties to the Convention on Biological Diversity*, see Annex to Decision I/1 and Decision V/20.

increasing involvement is not without causing a stir among "official" delegates. It is true that, through their extensive presence and frequent interventions, NGOs can hinder the debates and in particular contribute to making them last much longer. This may partly explain why some conventions deny them access to some of the bodies they establish. For example, while NGOs are largely accepted as observers during meetings of the Conference of the Parties to the Agreement on the Conservation of African-Eurasian Migratory Waterbirds (AEWA), their participation in the Technical Committee is limited by the terms of the Agreement: the Chair of this Committee may admit no more than four observers from specialised international governmental or non-governmental organisations [292].

168. On rarer occasions, the consultative status of a particular NGO is formalised from the start, in the convention itself. For example, IUCN has a consultative voice at meetings of the Intergovernmental Committee for the Protection of the World Cultural and Natural Heritage (Art. 8.3 of the Convention) and the rules of procedure of this Committee refer to IUCN very frequently [293].

169. The specific mention of NGOs in conventions marks the formal recognition of their roles and activities. However, observer status does not give NGOs the right to vote. NGOs are "gagged" by rules of procedures. Once their sparingly distributed right to speak has been exhausted, they are reduced to playing a simple role as a watchdog monitoring the behaviour of States within the intergovernmental body, a sort of "Jiminy Cricket" [294]. However, some solutions are being tested to mitigate these limitations. The rules of procedure of the Standing Committee of the Bern Convention, for example, allow NGOs to participate very actively. Although observers do not have a right to vote, they may, with the support of a State delegation or with the Chair's authorisation, make oral or written statements on the subjects being discussed. Proposals from observers can also be voted on if put forward by a delegation [295].

---

292. Article 7.1.
293. Document WHC-2015/5 July 2015, Articles 6, 9, 14, 43.
294. M. Bettati, "La contribution des ONG à la formation et à l'application des normes internationales. Rapport introductif", M. Bettati and P.-M. Dupuy (eds.), *Les ONG et le droit international*, Economica, Paris, 1986, p. 14.
295. Article 9 of the Rules of Procedure, of which a proposed amendment is under consideration. See Standing Committee, Convention on the Conservation of European Wildlife and Natural Habitat, *Proposed Amendments to the Rules of Procedure of the Standing Committee*, T-PVS/Inf(2021)44, 7 October 2021.

170. Another limitation is that NGOs cannot always take part in informal meetings and working groups, which are becoming increasingly significant. There is also an issue around access to information in between sessions. COPs are events; they only take place every year or even every two or three years. Solutions are being tested to ensure some continuity in access to information.

171. But NGOs do not participate solely through their status as observers. Firstly, NGOs, regardless of the observer status they may or may not have within political bodies, are sometimes included into scientific bodies. This is the case in the Technical Committee of the AEWA, which includes a representative of IUCN, of Wetlands International and of the CIC (International Council for Game and Wildlife Conservation), as well as, most interestingly, thematic experts in rural economics, game management, environmental law and communication, education and public awareness [296].

172. Sometimes – although it is quite rare – an NGO is entrusted with the secretariat duties of a convention. Thus, the Convention on Wetlands of International Importance entrusted its secretariat, known as the "Bureau" of the Convention, to IUCN [297]. For a while, IUCN also acted as the secretariat of CITES.

173. Lastly, since the 1990s, there has been a trend towards the creation of consultative bodies where NGOs find themselves on an equal footing with other actors. For example, the Mediterranean Commission on Sustainable Development (MCSD), established pursuant to the Barcelona Convention for the Protection of the Mediterranean Sea against Pollution and its Protocols, is a consultative body that includes representatives of the Contracting Parties and of "civil society" (NGOs, representative of socio-economic circles and local authorities).

174. In short, NGOs are not statutorily on the same level as States, but neither are they complete third parties [298]. The international governance of biodiversity reflects the existence of a public space outside the State in which NGOs can serve to encourage, relay, channel and express public opinion [299], despite the criticisms they may sometimes receive (irresponsibility, manipulation, opacity of structures and operating

---

296. AEWA, Article 7.
297. Rèsolution on secretariat matters (COP 4), 20 January 1990, as Annexed to Doc.C.4.15 (Rev.1).
298. R. Ranjeva, "Les organisations non gouvernementales et la mise en œuvre du droit international", *Recueil des cours*, tome 270 (1997), p. 43.
299. M. Bettati, "La contribution des ONG à la formation et à l'application des normes internationales. Rapport introductif" (n. 294), p. 7.

methods, even activism, looking for the spectacular, etc. [300]). A partnership is emerging in some areas, with NGOs contributing to the creation of law but above all to its implementation, and enjoying as a result a growth in terms of their reputation, their resources as well as their field of activity [301]. But this partnership does not entail a reciprocal recognition of equality, far from it. Save for some rare exceptions, NGOs are not yet true "transnational private powers", but rather "influencers of opinion" [302].

b) *Various forms of co-operation*

175. According to a UNEP study, collaboration between treaty bodies and civil society regularly consists of the following: provision of technical advice and information, assisting secretariats to communicate with non-parties, promotion of implementation, reviewing and communicating information as to possible non-compliance situations, implementation of national policies, putting pressure on governments to implement conventions, participation in the decision-making process, information and awareness-raising activities [303]. These extremely varied forms of involvement allow NGOs to act on both the content of rules as well as their implementation.

176. They influence the content of rules through intervention in the decision-making process, either in the gestation of norms and/or later during the normative process through the provision of expertise or lobbying. In terms of initiatives, the role of IUCN in nature conservation conventions particularly deserves to be highlighted. IUCN was asked by Germany to prepare the text of the Convention on the Conservation of Migratory Species of Wild Animals. It also took spontaneous initiatives, for which it then sought a sponsor. It was thus during a meeting of specialists on polar bears, organised by IUCN, that the possibility of establishing an agreement for the protection of this species was examined. Similarly, CITES was the focus of a resolution

---

300. R. Ranjeva, "Les organisations non gouvernementales et la mise en œuvre du droit international" (n. 298), p. 79, p. 91.
301. Y. Beigbeder, *Le rôle international des organisations non gouvernementales*, Bruylant, Bruxelles, 1992, p. 4.
302. According to C. Zorgbibe, "La diplomatie non gouvernementale", in *Les ONG et le droit international*, M. Bettati and P.-M. Dupuy (eds.), Economica, Paris, 1986, p. 36 (our translation).
303. Open-ended Intergovernmental Group of Ministers or their Representatives on International Environmental Governance, Second Meeting, Bonn, Germany, 17 July 2001, *International Environmental Governance: Multilateral Environmental Agreements (MEAs)*, UNEP/IGM/2/INF/3, 10 July 2001, p. V.

at the IUCN General Assembly as early as 1963, ten years before it was officially adopted. The Convention on Biological Diversity also stemmed from a resolution of the IUCN Assembly in 1981 [304]. Sometimes, NGOs intervene before even the creation of norms: in the identification of environmental "problems" and raising awareness of the issues at stake, or even in carrying out scientific studies which are a necessary prerequisite for conventional work. One example is the work of IUCN on threatened species regularly published in the *Red Data Books*, on which the negotiators of the Bern and Bonn Conventions based their lists of annexed species [305].

177. With regard to the negotiation process itself, NGOs now participate quite extensively in intergovernmental negotiating committees and then in diplomatic conferences that prepare and adopt conventions. They do not have the opportunity to negotiate *per se*, but they are generally allowed to make contributions [306].

178. In terms of the implementation of rules, NGOs intervene in various ways. Sometimes, these organisations are in a complementary relationship with States and treaty institutions, that go so far as to call on them for expert missions or the performance of operational activities. Other times, NGOs adopt a more critical, even accusatory stance. They can then become troublesome and disruptive for States. Ambivalence thus characterises these relations that are sometimes peaceful, sometimes tumultuous.

179. Treaty bodies rely heavily on the expertise of NGOs in the preparation of meetings. NGOs can contribute to the preparation of agendas, provide technical documents, various reports and minutes, or simply communicate information. For instance, the World Heritage Bureau receives information from civil society on the status of conservation of natural and cultural World Heritage properties. For the "natural sites" for example, IUCN reviews the nominations of sites to the World Heritage List [307]. When the Committee considers the

---

304. C. de Klemm and J. Olivier, "Le rôle des ONG dans le droit de l'environnement: l'exemple de l'IUCN" (n. 288), p. 178.
305. P. J. Sands, "The Role of Non-Governmental Organizations in Enforcing International Environmental Law", in *Control over Compliance with International Law*, W. E. Butler (ed.), Martinus Nijhoff Publishers, Netherlands, 1991, p. 62 ss.
306. P. Bombay, "The Role of Environmental NGOs in International Environmental Conferences and Agreements: Some Important Features", *European Environmental Law Review*, July 2001, p. 228.
307. Para. 57 *et seq.* of the Intergovernmental Committee for the Protection of the World Cultural and Natural Heritage, UNESCO, *Operational Guidelines for the Implementation of the World Heritage Convention*.

inscription of a property on this list, it may decide to send a mission of qualified observers from IUCN or other organisations to the site [308].

180. Another illustration: two NGOs play a major role in the implementation of CITES. First of all, IUCN is very involved in the administrative and scientific management of the Convention. Second, TRAFFIC, for Trade Records Analysis of Flora and Fauna in Commerce, is a federation of NGOs put in place by WWF and IUCN specifically for this purpose, and whose many offices form a global network in charge of monitoring international wildlife trade, co-operating with the CITES secretariat. It helps Parties in building their capacity to investigate the illegal wildlife trade and combat fraud by providing technical advice. It prepares many reports and provides the CITES secretariat with information on its research into illegal trade. Set up by IUCN, WWF and UNEP in Cambridge, the World Conservation Monitoring Centre (WCMC) is in charge of establishing a database, particularly on animal and plant species and their trade. After an initial period (1988-2000) during which the Centre was managed and financed jointly by these organisations, it became a unit of UNEP, of which it is the global centre for biodiversity information and assessment.

181. NGOs also sometimes act as mediators – or communication channels – between the national and international spheres, in particular when they provide expertise, information and education on the conventions, assessments of national legislation, and when they work on drafting implementing legislation; in short, when they participate in building and strengthening legal "capacity". The role played by IUCN in this respect can also be highlighted, as when the Environmental Law Centre produced a Guide to the Convention on Biological Diversity [309], commenting on each article of the Convention.

182. It is also common for NGOs to provide support through the performance of operational activities on the ground. For example, in the framework of the Ramsar Convention, IUCN and Wetlands International regularly organise joint meetings with other NGOs (WWF, BirdLife International) on programme development and project implementation. As another illustration, in 1997, TRAFFIC (the above-mentioned NGO federation) was mandated by the Conference of the Parties of CITES

---

308. *Ibid.*, paras. 82-83.
309. L. Glowka, F. Burhenne-Guilmin, H. Synge, J. A. McNeely and L. Gündling, *Guide de la Convention sur la diversité biologique*, IUCN, Environmental Policy and Law Paper No. 30, 1996, https://portals.iucn.org/library/efiles/documents/EPLP-030-Fr.pdf, accessed on 25 October 2023.

to monitor and enforce the decision of the COP to allow ivory trade in Botswana, Namibia and Zimbabwe, subject to a permit system. It was thus tasked with conducting a control of all declared ivory stocks and established the Elephant Trade Information System (ETIS).

183. Finally, NGOS play a role in monitoring the implementation by States of their obligations. They even provide increasing support in this respect by revealing, through their monitoring activities, the existence of implementation difficulties in some States. The main technique used for the international monitoring of the implementation of treaty obligations is the reporting system. It is obviously imperfect given that information is given by States themselves and therefore the person doing the monitoring is the same as the person being monitored. The involvement of NGOs can mitigate this downside. It is more or less developed depending on the treaty systems, sometimes official, sometimes unofficial. In the latter case, it is the result of relationships established with the secretariats of conventions, based on the mutual exchange of information.

c) *Public-private partnerships and the "Action Agenda"*

184. Egypt and China, in their respective capacities as host and future host of the CBD COP 14 and COP 15, announced in November 2018, at the COP 14, the launch of the "Sharm El-Sheikh to Beijing Action Agenda on Nature and People"[310]. A dedicated platform went live rather discreetly in March 2019[311] and this process is still very much a work in progress.

185. The idea of an *action agenda* for biodiversity reflects a long-standing trend to foster the mobilisation of non-State actors in and around international environmental policies. These initiatives have an important strategic dimension: they are designed to create, strengthen and maintain the ambition of multilateral discussions, but also to complement them, support their completion and even act as an intermediary. Such mobilisation can also have the merit of creating a virtuous pressure on the negotiation process, by signalling to political leaders that a large number of actors are ready to act in favour of

---

310. UN Biodiversity Conference 2018, Sharm El-Sheikh, Egypt Announcement: Sharm El-Sheikh to Beijing Action Agenda for Nature and People, https://www.cbd.int/cop/cop-14/annoucement/nature-action-agenda-egypt-to-china-en.pdf, accessed on 25 October 2023.

311. See https://www.cbd.int/action-agenda/. It lists 718 commitments as of 25 October 2023.

biodiversity, and are in fact waiting for an ambitious international framework that would create the conditions to encourage action and help steer it. An action agenda can also have a catalytic effect, strengthening existing coalitions [312] and/or launching new ones. At the same time, its proximity to the negotiating area can prevent the dispersal of these efforts and ensure that these initiatives best serve the achievement of global goals agreed in the multilateral framework.

186. Although action agenda had been created pursuant to the Johannesburg Type II Partnerships (2002), the Rio+20 voluntary commitments (2012), the Sendai Framework for Disaster Risk Reduction 2015-2030 (2015) or the Ocean Action Agenda (2017), here, inspiration was mainly found in the Climate Agenda, which constitutes as a reference in this field. Launched in Lima in 2014 by the Peruvian and French presidencies of UNFCCC COP 20 and COP 21, the primary aim of Lima-Paris Action Plan was to demonstrate that the commitments of non-State actors could contribute to achieving the temperature limitation objectives, in particular by helping close the ambition gap before 2020. Thanks to the strong involvement of these presidencies and the effective support of the UN Secretary-General and the UNFCCC secretariat, the Lima-Paris Action Plan made it possible to raise awareness among and mobilise various groups of actors (scientists, companies, financial institutions, local authorities, NGOs) through a series of events focused on sector-specific themes. These events enabled concrete initiatives to be formalised and given visibility through the registration of voluntary commitments on the online platform "NAZCA" (Non-State Actors Zone for Climate Action), which was set up by the UNFCCC secretariat (and which currently reports the participation of 32,517 actors [313]). The actors directly involved in the organisation of COP 21 regard the Lima-Paris Action Plan as a "driving force" in the negotiations leading up to Paris, enabling the "construction of alliances, multi-stakeholder coalitions that act, move forward, drive and influence States and vice versa" [314].

187. As defined during the CBD COP 14, the "Sharm El-Sheikh to Beijing Action Agenda on Nature and People" has three objectives:

---

312. There are already many initiatives and coalitions on biodiversity, such as the ICRI on corals, the Coalition of the Willing on Pollinators or even various coalitions and initiatives on forests.

313. On 27 October 2023.

314. T. Ourbak, *Analyse rétrospective de la COP 21 et de l'Accord de Paris : un exemple de diplomatie multilatérale exportable*, rapport d'expertise, MAEDI, 2017, p. 14 (our translation).

- to raise awareness among the general public of the urgent need to halt the loss of biodiversity and restore its health for the benefit of humanity and the global ecosystem;
- to inspire and help implement nature-based solutions to key global challenges;
- to catalyse co-operation initiatives across sectors and stakeholders in support of the Global Biodiversity Goals.

These objectives are very broad, which calls into question the concrete usefulness of such an Agenda, which is softly supported by the new Kunming-Montreal Global Biodiversity Framework adopted in 2022 [315].

---

315. See A. Rankovic, S. Maljean-Dubois, M. Wemaëre and Y. Laurans, *An Action Agenda for Biodiversity: Expectations and Issues in the Short and Medium Terms*, Policy brief, Iddri, p. 4, April 2018, https://www.iddri.org/en/publications-and-events/issue-brief/action-agenda-biodiversity-expectations-and-issues-short-and, accessed on 25 October 2023. Decision 15/4 (2022), *Kunming-Montreal Global Biodiversity Framework*, CBD/COP/DEC/15/4, 19 December 2022, para. 22.

CHAPTER II

THE STATUS OF BIODIVERSITY IN INTERNATIONAL LAW

188. Customary international law determines the bases on which sovereignty over resources is allocated among States. It places biodiversity under the full and complete jurisdiction of the territorial State. This status seems rather ill-suited to the needs of biodiversity protection, which is a global conservation issue that mostly ignores borders. From this point of view, there are clear contradictions between legal classifications and the most basic biological data [316]. The effects of this status are however tempered by a body of obligations aimed at protecting biodiversity, with a now well-established customary basis. In other, more exceptional cases, biodiversity is located and moves across areas that do not fall within the national jurisdiction of any State. In these situations, it has a specific status. As we shall see when we examine the values attributed to biodiversity by international law instruments, the elements of biodiversity and biodiversity itself are still largely equated to *resources* that must be protected because they are *useful* to humans.

Section 1. The legal regime of biodiversity in international law

1) Biodiversity within the States' territorial jurisdiction

189. Since in most cases biodiversity falls under the jurisdiction of the territorial sovereign, from the point of view of international law it is considered *res propria*. This does not affect the status that can be assigned to it internally by States' domestic laws. But *vis-à-vis* other States, each State can assert its own, exclusive rights over biodiversity. Here, because it is based on territorial title, the jurisdiction of the State is indeed extremely broad. It has even given rise to excessive claims. It is however limited by the prohibition of abuse of rights, from which the courts have inferred a set of due diligence obligations.

---

316. According to N. de Sadeleer, "De la protection à la sauvegarde de la biodiversité", *Ecologie politique*, No. 9, Spring 1994, p. 25.

a) *Territorial sovereignty over natural resources*

190. In international law, biodiversity is viewed as a *natural resource* over which each State exercises its sovereignty. The State's sovereignty over natural resources is the corollary of the sovereignty it exercises over its territory. As a result, the former is as long-standing and well established in positive law as the latter. Territory is therefore the essential legal basis of the State's jurisdiction, despite the fact that the environment – which is the fabric of the territory – is paradoxically made up of elements, such as birds or fish, whose intrinsic mobility means they are bound to ignore political borders [317]. These elements, which do not really lend themselves to the idea of appropriation, have nevertheless always been associated, by a sort of legal fiction, with the unshakeable stability of the territory [318].

191. Generally speaking, international law takes into account natural realities through the lens of human factors. This was expressed clearly by the arbitral tribunal that ruled on the *Lac Lanoux* case: "The unity of a basin is supported at the legal level only to the extent that it conforms to the realities of life" [319]. Thus, the allocation of natural resources depends on the spatial delimitation and allocation of sovereignty among States. Access to resources is therefore determined by the ways in which territory is acquired, the adoption of agreements, maritime delimitation, etc. [320]. A State's jurisdiction is exercised *ratione loci*, over all the areas under its jurisdiction, and exclusively over those areas [321]. Accordingly, like other natural resources including mineral resources, biodiversity is

---

317. P. M. Dupuy, "La frontière et l'environnement", in *La frontière*, SFDI, Pedone, Paris, 1980, p. 269.
318. *Ibid.* A comparison can be made here with the status of boundaries. See C. de Visscher, *Problèmes de confins en droit international public*, Pedone, Paris, 1969, p. 7: while "the border involves stability, boundaries remain an expression of movement" (our translation).
319. Award of 16 November 1957, Original French text in *Lac Lanoux*, RGDIP, 1958, p. 103, para. 8; United Nations, *Reports of International Arbitral Awards*, Vol. XII (Sales No. 63.V.3), p. 281 *et seq*. Partial English translation in A/CN.4/399 and Add.1 and 2, Second Report on the Law of the Non-Navigational Uses of International Watercourses, by Mr S. C. McCaffrey, Special Rapporteur, Yearbook of the International Law Commission, 1986, Vol. II (1), p. 117.
320. I. Brownlie, "Legal Status of Natural Resources in International Law. Some Aspects", *Recueil des cours*, tome 162 (1979), Vol. I, p. 253.
321. According to the International Court of Justice, "The basic legal concept of State sovereignty in customary international law, expressed in, *inter alia*, Article 2. paragraph 1, of the United Nations Charter, extends to the internal waters and territorial sea of every State and to the air space above its territory". *Military and Paramilitary Activities in and against Nicaragua (Nicaragua v. United States of America)*, Merits, Judgment, *ICJ Reports 1986*, p. 14, para. 212.

allocated among States according to the borders established to delimit their respective territories. Insofar as everything on land is placed under the jurisdiction of the sovereign State [322], and as airspace, the territorial sea and the exclusive economic zone located between the latter and the high seas are considered here as extensions of the territory, biodiversity is in most situations under the jurisdiction of the territorial sovereign.

192. As old as the State itself, its jurisdiction over its natural resources was of course taken into account in classical international law. But this "economic" aspect of sovereignty remained somewhat hidden until States started to experience difficulties in exercising it. Under pressure from decolonised countries – who relied on this principle of sovereignty to assert their right to exploit their national resources (oil in particular) against former colonising powers – the sovereignty of States over their natural resources was reaffirmed and reinforced, to be described as permanent, full and inalienable. The UN General Assembly echoed the demands of developing countries in favour of the principle of permanent sovereignty over natural resources. Several resolutions were passed in this context, including the Charter of Economic Rights and Duties of States adopted in 1974 [323]. Although not binding in and of themselves, these resolutions had a significant effect on the development of treaty law and more generally on State practice, and they sanctioned the emergence of a customary rule. They confirmed the exclusivity of the State's sovereign rights over its territory [324].

193. At first, countries of the South sought to protect themselves against the exploitation of their resources by foreign States or companies (especially mineral resources). However, as their demands pertained to all natural resources, they quickly spread to environmental matters. Developing countries relied on this principle of sovereignty to deny countries of the North the right to monitor their environmental policies. Asserted in this very specific context of demands for a New International Economic Order, this principle also came to be applied with regard to natural resources other than minerals, and therefore to biodiversity. It was even given new impetus in this respect, once again driven by developing countries who wanted to limit the industrialised countries' right to control their environmental and development policies. Thus,

---

322. The Antarctic is an exception in this respect. A. Kiss, *L'écologie et la loi: le statut juridique de l'environnement*, L'Harmattan, Paris, 1989, p. 172.
323. Resolution 3281/XXIX (1974). See also Resolutions 626/VII (1952), 1803 / XVII (1962), 2158/XXI (1966), 3201 /S-VI (1974).
324. A. Diaz, "Permanent Sovereignty over Natural Resources", *Environmental Policy and Law,* 24/4, June 1994, p. 157 *et seq.*

Principle 21 of the aforementioned Stockholm Declaration (1972) stated that "States have, in accordance with the Charter of the United Nations and the principles of international law, the sovereign right to exploit their own resources pursuant to their own environmental policies . . .". In 1982, with regard to the marine environment, Article 193 of the Montego Bay Convention on the Law of the Sea also provided that "States have the sovereign right to exploit their natural resources pursuant to their environmental policies". The principle was expressed in a very similar way in the 1992 Rio Declaration (Principe 2) [325] and in Article 3 of the Rio Convention on Biological Diversity [326]. As noted by N. de Sadeleer, this concept seems to have found a new lease of life in the context of the United Nations Conference on Environment and Development in Rio de Janeiro: the concept of sovereignty is now relied on primarily in the context of potential ecological disputes between, on the one hand, "rich" States concerned about environmental protection and, on the other hand, "poor" States concerned about catching up economically [327].

194. During the negotiations leading up to the Rio Conference and the adoption of the Convention on Biological Diversity in 1992, it was envisaged that biological diversity should be described as the common heritage of mankind. However, this proposal sparked heated debate and was resisted both by countries in the South (who feared interference in their environmental and development policies) and in the North (who feared potential financial implications). As a compromise, the Convention simply states that "the conservation of biological diversity is a common concern of humankind" [328]. This means that State sovereignty is neither unlimited nor absolute [329]. Note that the same expression was used in relation to climate change in UN General Assembly Resolution 43/53 in 1988, precisely to avoid the global climate being seen as a common heritage of humanity [330].

---

325. Rio Declaration on Environment and Development, Report of the United Nations Conference on Environment and Development, Rio de Janeiro, 3-14 June 1992, A/CONF.151/26, Vol. 1, p. 3.
326. "In accordance with the Charter of the United Nations and the principles of international law, the sovereign right to exploit their own resources pursuant to their own environmental policies..."
327. N. de Sadeleer, "De la protection à la sauvegarde de la biodiversité", Ecologie politique, No. 9, 1994, p. 43.
328. Preamble.
329. See Articles 6 to 9, which specify the States' obligations in terms of conservation and sustainable use.
330. UNGA, Resolution A/43/53, 6 December 1988, *Protection of Global Climate for Present and Future Generations of Mankind.*

195. Biodiversity is thus placed under the jurisdiction of the territorial sovereign. The jurisdiction arising from territorial sovereignty is the broadest jurisdiction recognised to the State by international law [331]. It is traditionally characterised as complete and full. *Complete,* because the powers of the State in this respect are extremely wide. It is true that a State's international commitments may restrict these powers, thus limiting its complete discretion. However, subject to customary rules, such limitation always requires the State's consent. Territorial sovereignty is also *full* because it implies the exclusive right to perform State activities. A State has the right to object to the activities of other States on its territory. Any incursion by another State or international organisation into its territory requires its prior consent. For example, with regard to hunting, reciprocal international arrangements were made in the nineteenth century to allow hunters from one State to retrieve game hunted and wounded in that State that had fled to or fallen on the territory of another State [332]. The State may thus freely destroy or allow the destruction of wild fauna or flora, or of natural sites. It may also prohibit the export of certain species of great economic importance [333]. The sovereignty that the State exercises over biodiversity within its jurisdiction is an *imperium.* This *imperium* exists on top of the appropriation or non-appropriation – *dominium* – by individuals, which is a matter of domestic law. Within the State's jurisdiction, wild animals are generally considered *res nullius.* This is the most common approach, although many States have made wild animals the property of the State [334]. The legal regime applicable to biodiversity thus depends on the territory on which it is found. Some species are sedentary, but

---

331. In the *Lac Lanoux* case, the arbitral tribunal expressed this in a now famous statement: "Territorial sovereignty acts as a presumption. It must yield to all international obligations, whatever their origin, but only to them". Award of 16 November 1957, *Lac Lanoux* (n. 319), p. 99. Commentary by F. Duléry, *RGDIP*, 1958, pp. 469-516; A. Gervais, *AFDI*, 1960, pp. 372-434. Partial English translation in A/CN.4/399 and Add.1 and 2, Second Report on the Law of the Non-Navigational Uses of International Watercourses, by Mr Stephen C. McCaffrey, Special Rapporteur, Yearbook of the International Law Commission, 1986, Vol. II (1), p. 117.

332. J. Barberis, *Los recursos naturales compartidos entre Estados*, ed. Tecnos, Madrid, 1979, p. 79, footnotes 4 and 5.

333. This was the case in China for bombyx mori eggs, in the Andean countries for chinchillas and vicuñas, etc. C. de Klemm, "Le patrimoine naturel de l'humanité", *L'avenir du droit international de l'environnement*, The Hague Academy of International Law, Martinus Nijhoff Publishers, 1984, p. 127.

334. This is the case in Brazil, Italy, many African States, some States in the United States and Australia and some Canadian provinces. C. de Klemm, "Des qualifications et des règles fondées sur l'appropriation permettent-elles de protéger l'environnement?", in *Le droit et l'environnement*, Actes des Journées de l'environnement du CNRS, 30 November-1 December 1988, PIREN, CNRS, Paris, 1989, p. 238.

migratory birds or fish, when crossing borders, are thereby subject to different jurisdictions [335]. In theory, each State through which they pass exercises sovereign rights over them. In a way, they experience an application of the principle of "successive ownership" [336].

b) *Excessive claims*

196. While the doctrine of *absolute* territorial sovereignty is now viewed as obsolete, it did historically have some supporters. At the end of the nineteenth century, Judson Harmon, the Attorney General of the United States, attempted to justify the United States' use of the waters of the Rio Grande to the detriment of Mexico, with what became known as the *Harmon Doctrine*. In an 1895 opinion regarding the dispute between the two countries, he argued that the Mexican Government was not in a position to protest against water intakes from the border river Rio Grande carried out on American territory, even though they caused a reduction in the amount of water received by Mexico, and thereby harmed Mexican farmers. Harmon told the US State Department that international law imposed no obligation or responsibility on the US, on the grounds that assuming the existence of such a duty would be incompatible with the sovereign jurisdiction of the US over its national domain [337]. In doing so, the Attorney General viewed the border as the boundary of an enclosure within which the State was free to exercise its sovereignty, without any concern for the consequences that such licence may have on its neighbour [338]. This doctrine resurfaces from time to time, for instance, to some extent, when Brazilian President Bolsonaro asserted at the UN General Assembly the absolute sovereignty of his country over the Amazon [339].

---

335. If the migration is within the jurisdiction of a State, then the status is the same along the entire migration route. The establishment of the exclusive economic zone leads to the inclusion in this category of a large number of marine migratory species, including many seabirds, which used to cross the boundary between the territorial sea and the high seas on a regular basis and now no longer reach the high seas. According to C. de Klemm, "Migratory Species in International Law", *Natural Resources Journal*, Vol. 29, 1989, pp. 936-937.
336. C. de Klemm, "The Conservation of Migratory Species Through International Law", *Natural Resources Journal*, 1972, p. 272.
337. J. Andrassy, "Les relations internationales de voisinage", *Recueil des cours*, 1951, Vol. II, p. 88.
338. P.-M. Dupuy, "La frontière et l'environnement" (n. 317), p. 269; A. L. Springer, "United States and International Law: Stockholm Principle 21 Revisited", in *International Environmental Diplomacy; The Management and Resolution of Transfrontier Environmental Conflicts*, J. E. Caroll (ed.), CUP, Cambridge, 1988, p. 47.
339. Speech on 23 September 2019, 74th Session of the UN General Assembly.

197. Excessive, this argument is bound to fail. Symmetrically, it clashes with the doctrine of absolute territorial integrity defended by other authors [340]. The latter also claims to hermetically seal the border, but in order to protect the national territory from any external damage [341]. The dogmatism of these two attitudes means they cannot be reconciled. Neither of them can be sustained in the long-term. Indeed, legal academics and practitioners are almost unanimous in condemning these unilateral ways of resolving inter-State disputes [342]. In fact, as Pierre-Marie Dupuy points out:

> "No State is immune to the following two logics: the first one stems from the natural inclination of sovereignties and leads to the predatory monopolisation of resources, caught up in the trap of territory and confined within its borders; the second logic, on the contrary, stems from the lucid realisation that the first tendency leads to failure, and generates not the dynamic of monopolisation, but that of cooperation and international coordination as to the use of the environment, perceived here as a collective asset." [343]

198. Although the first logic has not disappeared from international life, the latter has prevailed.

c) *The prohibition of abuse of rights and the principle of damage prevention*

199. Indeed, the rights of the territorial sovereign are neither unlimited nor absolute. They must be reconciled with the rights of other States over their own natural resources. In various instruments, the principle of the sovereignty of States over their natural resources is systematically counterbalanced by an obligation to prevent damage. Thus, in return for their sovereign rights over their own resources, the Stockholm Declaration adds that States have "the responsibility to ensure that activities within their jurisdiction or control do not cause damage to the environment of other States or of areas beyond the limits of national jurisdiction" [344]. With regard to the marine environment,

---

340. P. M. Dupuy, "La frontière et l'environnement" (n. 317), p. 269.
341. *Ibid.*
342. J. Andrassy, "Les relations internationales de voisinage" (n. 337), p. 87 *et seq.*
343. P. M. Dupuy, "Le droit international et la souveraineté des États. Bilan et perspectives", in *L'avenir du droit international de l'environnement*, The Hague Academy of International Law, Colloques – Workshop Series, 1985, p. 29 (our translation).
344. Stockholm Declaration, *Report of the United Nations Conference on the Human Environment, Stockholm 5-16 June 1972*, A/CONF.48/14/Rev/1, p. 3.

Article 193 of the Montego Bay Convention on the Law of the Sea provides that "States have the sovereign right to exploit their natural resources pursuant to their environmental policies *and in accordance with their duty to protect and preserve the marine environment*"[345]. As for the 1992 Rio Declaration, its Principle 2 provides the following:

> "States have, in accordance with the Charter of the United Nations and the principles of international law, the sovereign right to exploit their own resources pursuant to their own environmental and developmental policies, and the responsibility to ensure that activities within their jurisdiction or control do not cause damage to the environment of other States or of areas beyond the limits of national jurisdiction."[346]

Article 3 of the Rio Convention on Biological Diversity includes an almost identical statement[347].

200. This "duty", which ultimately stems from the need for territorial sovereignties to co-exist in good neighbourly relations, has been very clearly recognised as a customary obligation by various court decisions. The judgment of the International Court in 2010 in the Pulp Mills on the River Uruguay is interesting in this respect[348], as well as the 2015 judgment in the cases opposing Costa Rica and Nicaragua regarding activities carried out along the River San Juan[349]. The ITLOS Seabed Disputes Chamber Advisory Opinion (2011)[350], and the award

---

345. Emphasis added.
346. Rio Declaration, aforementioned.
347. "States have, in accordance with the Charter of the United Nations and the principles of international law, the sovereign right to exploit their own resources pursuant to their own environmental policies, and the responsibility to ensure that activities within their jurisdiction or control do not cause damage to the environment of other States or of areas beyond the limits of national jurisdiction." See also the Southern African Development Community Protocol on Wildlife Conservation and Law Enforcement (18 August 1999): "Each State Party shall ensure the conservation and sustainable use of wildlife resources under its jurisdiction. Each State Party shall ensure that activities within its jurisdiction or control do not cause damage to the wildlife resources of other states or in areas beyond the limits of national jurisdiction" (Art. 3, para. 1).
348. *Pulp Mills on the River Uruguay (Argentina v. Uruguay)*, Judgment, *ICJ Reports 2010*, p. 14. This was already outlined in the *Danube Dam.* case, decided in 1997: *Gabcikovo-Nagymaros Project (Hungary/Slovakia)*, Judgment, *ICJ Reports 1997*, p. 38.
349. *Certain Activities Carried Out by Nicaragua in the Border Area (Costa Rica v. Nicaragua)* and *Construction of a Road in Costa Rica along the San Juan River (Nicaragua v. Costa Rica)*, Judgment, *ICJ Reports 2015*, p. 665.
350. *Responsibilities and Obligations of States with respect to Activities in the Area*, Advisory Opinion, 1 February 2011, *ITLOS Reports 2011*, p. 10.

in The South China Sea Arbitration case (2016)[351] are also instructive on this point[352].

201. In the Pulp Mills case, the Court points out "that the principle of prevention, as a customary rule, has its origins in the due diligence that is required of a State in its territory". It is "every State's obligation not to allow knowingly its territory to be used for acts contrary to the rights of other States" (Corfu PULP MILLS (JUDGMENT) 55 45 Channel (*United Kingdom* v. *Albania*), Merits, Judgment, *ICJ Reports 1949*, p. 22)[353]. In doing so, the Court equates due diligence with a prohibition on the State to allow knowingly its territory to be used for acts contrary to the rights of other States *(sic utere tuo ut alienum non laedas)*, which is a fundamental principle of good-neighbourliness and co-existence, of respect for territorial sovereignties which are indeed exclusive but not absolute. It is precisely because it is fundamental for the co-existence of sovereignties that the customary nature of the principle of prevention is so readily recognised. Thus, the principle of prevention is – "as a customary rule" – an extension or application of the due diligence that States must more generally exercise in their international relations.

202. With regard to biodiversity, a basis for general prevention obligations can also be found in the previously mentioned statement that "the conservation of biological diversity is a common concern of humankind"[354]. As noted by Pascale Ricard, this notion reflects the fact that it is no longer simply a question of profiting from a resource that can be exploited in the common interest. The issue here is to address a particular concern that can only be apprehended through co-operation between States and their mutual recognition of the reality of the problem[355].

---

351. *PCA Case No. 2013-19 in the matter of the South China Sea Arbitration before an Arbitral Tribunal Constituted under Annex VII to the 1982 United Nations Convention on the Law of the Sea, between the Republic of the Philippines and the People's Republic of China*, Award of 12 July 2016, pt. 941 et 948.

352. See also Corte interamericana de derechos humanos, Opinión consultativa OC-23/17 de 15 de noviembre de 2017 solicitada por la Republica de Colombia, *Medio Ambiente y derechos humanos (Obligaciones estatales en relacion con el medio ambiente en el marco de la protecion y garantia de los derechos a la vida y a la integridad personal – interpretacion y alcance de los articulos 4.1 y 5.1, en relacion con los articulos 1.1 y 2 de la convencion americana sobre derechos humanos)*, in particular para. 102.

353. Judgment of 20 April 2010, para. 101.

354. See above, para. 194.

355. P. Ricard, *La conservation de la biodiversité dans les espaces maritimes internationaux. Un défi pour le droit international*, Pedone, Paris, 2019, p. 330.

203. Case law has specified the content of these due diligence obligations, viewing them as a set of positive obligations that can be seen as forming the basis of international environmental law in general and of the international law on biodiversity in particular. This foundation is all the more valuable because it is customary and therefore binding on everyone at all times, even in the absence of more specific treaty rules. It is the foundation on which treaty obligations are built, and it is also the foundation on which national regulations should be built, or at the very least a foundation that they should most definitely take into account [356].

d) *Shared natural resources*

204. Pursuant to Resolution 3129/XXVIII of the United Nations General Assembly [357], UNEP set up a Working Group of Experts on Natural Resources Shared by Two or More States, which at its last session, attended by twenty-six States, adopted the *Draft Principles of Conduct for the Guidance of States in the Conservation and Harmonious Exploitation of Natural Resources Shared by Two or More States* [358]. The Principles were approved by consensus by the UNEP Governing Council in its decision 6/14 of 19 May 1978 [359]. Without referring to these Principles themselves, the International Court of Justice has repeatedly referred to this notion of shared natural resources, from which it has inferred practical consequences. While shared natural resources remain under territorial sovereignty, the fact that they are shared seems to imply stronger due diligence obligations. In 1997, the International Court of Justice thus clearly established as customary the principle of equitable use of shared natural resources:

"The Court considers that Czechoslovakia, by unilaterally assuming control of a shared resource, and thereby depriving

---

356. On the content of due diligence obligations, see Chapter 3 below.
357. UNGA, Resolution 3129/XXVIII, 13 December 1973, *Co-operation in the Field of the Environment concerning Natural Resources Shared by Two or More States*.
358. Draft Principles of Conduct for the Guidance of States in the Conservation and Harmonious Exploitation of Natural Resources Shared by Two or More States: Report of the Intergovernmental Working Group of Experts on Natural Resources Shared by Two or More States on the Work of its Third Session held in Nairobi from 10 to 21 January 1977: Note by the Executive Director, Nairobi: UNEP, 25 February 1977, 24 p. It includes the report of the Intergovernmental Working Group of Experts on Natural Resources Shared by Two or More States on the Work of its Third Session, held at Nairobi from 10 to 21 January 1997 (UNEP/IG.7/3).
359. Doc. UNEP GC1/L.6/ Add.5 22 May 1978.

Hungary of its right to an equitable and reasonable share of the natural resources of the Danube – with the continuing effects of the diversion of these waters on the ecology of the riparian area of the Szigetkoz – failed to respect the proportionality which is required by international law." [360]

In 2006, in its order in response to Argentina's request for provisional measures in the Pulp Mills case, the Court stated:

> "The present case highlights the importance of the need to ensure environmental protection of shared natural resources while allowing for sustainable economic development; whereas it is in particular necessary to bear in mind the reliance of the Parties on the quality of the water of the River Uruguay for their livelihood and economic development; whereas from this point of view account must be taken of the need to safeguard the continued conservation of the river environment and the rights of economic development of the riparian States." [361]

205. The corollary of the obligations of prevention is a general obligation to co-operate in the management of these resources. This principle already existed in an entirely different context in the Charter of Economic Rights and Duties of States:

> "In the exploitation of natural resources shared by two or more countries, each State must co-operate on the basis of a system of information and prior consultations in order to achieve optimum use of such resources without causing damage to the legitimate interest of others." [362]

This principle is also reflected in the UNEP Draft Principles [363]. In the Pulp Mills on the River Uruguay case, the Court linked the obligation to prevent damage to the obligation to co-operate, at least in that specific treaty context:

---

360. *Gabcikovo-Nagymaros Project (Hungary/Slovakia)*, Judgment, *ICJ Reports 1997*, p. 7, see paras. 78, 85 and 150, pp. 54, 56 and 77.
361. *Pulp Mills on the River Uruguay (Argentina v. Uruguay)*, Provisional Measures, Order of 13 July 2006, *ICJ Reports 2006*, p. 113, para. 80.
362. UN General Assembly, Resolution 3281/XXIX, 12 December 1974, Article 3.
363. Draft Principles of Conduct for the Guidance of States in the Conservation and Harmonious Exploitation of Natural Resources Shared by Two or More States: Report of the Intergovernmental Working Group of Experts on Natural Resources Shared by Two or More States on the Work of its Third Session held in Nairobi from 10 to 21 January 1977, aforementioned.

"... co-operation between the Parties which is necessary in order to fulfil the obligation of prevention. This first procedural stage results in the 1975 Statute not being applied to activities which would appear to cause damage only to the State in whose territory they are carried out"[364].

As the Court explained, co-operation is "all the more vital when a shared resource is at issue, as in the case of the River Uruguay, which can only be protected through close and continuous co-operation between the riparian States"[365].

206. The topic of shared natural resources was put on the agenda of the International Law Commission in 2002, which adopted a first set of draft articles on the law of transboundary aquifers. Comments on the draft articles included the following:

"Draft article 7 sets out the principle of a general obligation of the aquifer States to cooperate with each other and contemplates procedures for such cooperation. Cooperation among aquifer States is a prerequisite for shared natural resources, and the draft article serves to provide a background context for the application of the provisions on specific forms of cooperation, such as regular exchange of data and information, as well as protection, preservation and management."[366]

Prevention and co-operation obligations with respect to international watercourses can also be found in the Convention on the Law of the Non-Navigational Uses of International Watercourses[367].

207. Provisions on co-operation as to natural resources are frequently included in international conventions on biodiversity. For instance, Article 5 of the Ramsar Convention provides as follows:

"The Contracting Parties shall consult with each other about implementing obligations arising from the Convention especially in the case of a wetland extending over the territories of more than one Contracting Party or where a water system is shared by Contracting Parties."

---

364. Judgment cited above, para. 102.
365. Judgment cited above, para. 81.
366. ILC, *Draft Articles on the Law of Transboundary Aquifers, with Commentaries* (2008), Yearbook of the International Law Commission, 2008, Vol. II, Part Two.
367. See Articles 7 and 8. The ILC eventually dropped the delicate issue of gas and oil.

By way of example, the Democratic Republic of Laos, Thailand and Vietnam have been jointly managing the wetlands of the Lower Mekong Basin since 1990 [368].

2) Biodiversity outside territorial jurisdiction

208. Biodiversity can escape territorial sovereignty. This is true of species that live in or pass through during their migration – whether in the water, in the air or on land – the international spaces of the high seas or of the Antarctic continent. In these two cases, the classification and resulting legal regime differ, but both reflect a relative internationalisation [369].

a) *Marine biodiversity beyond national jurisdiction*

209. The original status of biodiversity as *res nullius* has gradually evolved to take into account the necessary co-existence between States. This is an important issue, because the deep seabed, the Area and the water column above it harbour exceptional, highly specific ecosystems, including many endemic species that are still mostly unknown. The major environmental implications of their conservation are especially important at a time when prospection has begun in the very specific legal and institutional context of the Area.

- *An initial status of* res nullius

210. In theory, as a corollary of the principle of freedom of the high seas, all States may enjoy the biological resources that are found there, whether marine flora or fauna, including avifauna [370]. This also applies to genetic resources [371]. While they cannot appropriate the high seas

---

368. Ramsar Handbook, Ramsar Handbook for the Wise Use of Wetlands, 4th ed., 2010, p. 23.
369. A. Mahiou, "Procédures de décision et droit international", *Revue Tiers Monde*, tome XXXIII, No. 130, April-June 1992, p. 430.
370. This is a secondary issue with regard to birds, since migratory land birds, which have to cross the high seas during their migrations, usually do so in one go. On the other hand, although seabirds have sometimes been hunted outside territorial limits, this is not the greatest danger to them. Pollution of the sea by oil spills, for example, has a much more important impact. C. de Klemm, "Principes juridiques applicables aux espèces migratrices", in *EPL*, 1976, Vol. 2, p. 18.
371. However, despite their biological interconnectedness, the status of genetic resources located not in the water column but on the seabed beyond national jurisdictions continues to be debated. D. Tladi, "L'exploitation des ressources biologiques non halieutiques", in M. Forteau and J.-M. Thouvenin (eds.), *Traité de droit international de la mer*, Pedone, Paris, 2017, p. 749 *et seq.*

themselves, which are considered *res communis*, States (directly or via private operators) can however appropriate these same resources, initially seen as *res nullius*. Indeed, for a long time, there were no restrictions on accessing these resources. Any State was in theory free to exploit them as it pleased, or even to destroy them if it was in its interest [372]. In the absence of an organised framework, the right of first occupant remained the rule, as in the time of the "conquistadors" [373]. In other words: first come, first served [374]. Users or operators were accountable to no one except the State to which they belonged: the law of nationality and the law of the flag were the only bases for the exercise of any jurisdiction [375]. The inadequacy of this status becomes clear as soon as one realises the increasing scarcity of resources, or more generally the fact that they are not inexhaustible, and the potential that genetic resources represent. Moreover, this freedom of exploitation is also restricted by the fact that the rights of other users or exploiters must be respected.

- *Extending due diligence obligations to biodiversity on the high seas*

211. As early as 1893, the award between the United States and the United Kingdom relating to the Rights of Jurisdiction of the United States in the Bering's Sea and the Preservation of Fur Seals confirmed this point of view [376]. Sea lions were breeding on the Pribilof Islands, which belonged to the United States since its purchase of Alaska from Russia. Deep-sea exploitation by British ships were driving the species to the brink of extinction. The United States declared that the resources were its property and that deep-sea exploitation should stop. It seized the British ships. The British argued that sea lions were *res nullius* on

---

372. C. de Klemm, "L'évolution de la protection de la faune et de la flore marines dans les conventions internationales", in *Droit de l'environnement marin, développements récents,* Colloque de la Société française de droit de l'environnement, Economica, Paris, 1988, p. 25.
373. M. Rémond-Gouilloud, "Ressources naturelles et choses sans maître", in *L'homme, la nature et le droit,* B. Edelman and M. A. Hermitte (eds.), Bourgois, Paris, 1988, p. 224.
374. R.-J. Dupuy, *L'humanité dans l'imaginaire des nations,* Julliard, Paris, 1991, p. 228.
375. A. Mahiou, "Procédures de décision et droit international" (n. 369), p. 433.
376. Award between the United States and the United Kingdom relating to the Rights of Jurisdiction of the United States in the Bering's Sea and the Preservation of Fur Seals, 15 August 1893, *Reports of International Arbitral Awards,* UN, Vol. XXVIII, pp. 263-276.

the high seas. The arbitral tribunal found that no one had exclusive rights of protection or property over these resources and that no State could prevent another from exploiting them. Although it did not find in favour of the US, it did consider that the extinction of a species was *contra bonos mores*, in other words, an infringement of international public policy [377]. It also invited the Parties to conclude a co-operation agreement to organise the joint management of sea lion herds on a rational basis.

212. More recently, another interesting case dealt with the conservation of migratory marine species. When commercial fishing of Atlantic salmon increased significantly from the early 1970s onwards, the States from which the fish originated claimed an exclusive right to these animals on the high seas, i.e. sole ownership of these animals [378]. They did obtain a reduction in fishing efforts from the main exploiting countries, but not on the basis of this theory of the State of origin. Indeed, this theory is unfair to countries that traditionally fish these animals and is also impossible to apply, as the State of origin of animals cannot be identified once on the high seas [379].

213. As for the International Court of Justice, it has specified, when dealing with inter-State conflicts over fisheries, the content of the reciprocal rights and obligations of States over resources referred to as common. In 1974, in the *Fisheries Jurisdiction* case [380], the Court invited the disputing States to start negotiations, the main purpose of which was to ensure the conservation of these resources in the maritime zone where Iceland, a coastal State, could invoke only preferential rights. These negotiations were also required to take into account the interests of other States in the protection of animal species. This decision attests to the existence of a customary obligation of equitable use of these resources.

214. As previously mentioned, the 1982 Law of the Sea Convention makes it clear that "States have the obligation to protect and preserve the marine environment" [381]. Here as well, rights and obligations go

---

377. C. de Klemm, "Principes juridiques applicables aux espèces migratrices", *Environmental Policy and Law*, 1976, Vol. 2, p. 18.

378. The issue had also arisen because of the Japanese exploitation of Alaskan salmon on the high seas. It was resolved in 1952 with the signing of the North Pacific Fisheries Convention. *Ibid.*

379. *Ibid.*

380. *Fisheries Jurisdiction (United Kingdom v. Iceland)*, Merits, Judgment, *ICJ Reports 1974*, p. 3.

381. Article 192.

hand in hand, obligations counterbalancing rights. The same balancing approach is found in Principle 2 of the Rio Declaration [382] and in Article 3 of the Rio Convention on Biological Diversity, which are careful to extend the States' duty of prevention to areas beyond national jurisdiction, which is particularly relevant to biodiversity on the high seas. The impact of these provisions is however limited given the expansion of States' exclusive economic zones [383]. States have the same duties of care on the high seas as on the territory of other States. States' obligations are exercised "over entities of their nationality and under their control" [384]. Article 194 (2) of the United Nations Convention on the Law of the Sea specifies that "States shall take all measures necessary to ensure that activities under their jurisdiction or control are so conducted as not to cause damage by pollution to other States and their environment. . ." [385]. Pointing in the same direction, reference can be made to the aforementioned opinion of the Chamber of the International Tribunal for the Law of the Sea of 2011 [386] as well as the opinion of the same Tribunal of 2015 regarding illegal, undeclared and unregulated fishing activities, which are by definition delicate to apprehend legally. Thus, to prevent such activities, "the flag State is under an obligation to exercise effectively its jurisdiction and control in administrative matters over fishing vessels flying its flag, by ensuring, in particular, that such vessels are properly marked" [387]. These are *erga omnes* obligations.

215. This is confirmed by the new Agreement under the United Nations Convention on the Law of the Sea on the Conservation and Sustainable Use of Marine Biological Diversity of Areas Beyond National Jurisdiction (the BBNJ treaty) [388], which is "[r]especting the sovereignty, territorial integrity and political independence of all States".

---

382. Rio Declaration, aforementioned.
383. P. Ricard, *La conservation de la biodiversité dans les espaces maritimes internationaux. Un défi pour le droit international* (n. 355), p. 41 *et seq.*
384. *Responsibilities and Obligations of States with respect to Activities in the Area*, Advisory Opinion, 1 February 2011, ITLOS Reports 2011, p. 10, in particular at para. 126.
385. See, in the same vein, Article 206 of the Convention.
386. *Responsibilities and Obligations of States with respect to Activities in the Area*, Advisory Opinion, 1 February 2011, ITLOS Reports 2011, p. 10.
387. *Request for Advisory Opinion Submitted by the Sub-Regional Fisheries Commission*, Advisory Opinion, 2 April 2015, ITLOS Reports 2015, p. 4, in particular para. 137.
388. UNGA 77/321, *Agreement under the United Nations Convention on the Law of the Sea on the Conservation and Sustainable Use of Marine Biological Diversity of Areas Beyond National Jurisdiction*, 1 August 2023.

It does not state that marine genetic resources are part of the common heritage of humankind, but it recognises the "needs of humankind as a whole" and mentions, among general principles and approaches, "[t]he principle of the common heritage of humankind which is set out in the Convention" [389].

b) *Biodiversity in the Antarctic*

216. In the Antarctic Convergence Zone [390], biodiversity also enjoys an internationalised status [391]. The treaty regime has an *erga omnes* value that is especially indisputable as it has contributed to the establishment of customary rules [392]. For the "possessor" States, it constitutes a freely consented restriction on the exercise of their sovereignty. For "non-possessor" States, it is a new status, applicable to lands over which no sovereignty is therefore recognised [393].

217. Because of its geographic location and the political context, and following the experience of scientific co-operation during the International Geophysical Year in 1957-1958 [394], the Antarctic became internationalised, as evidenced by the Washington Treaty of 1 December 1959, the various related measures and recommendations and the subsequent conventions and protocols adopted pursuant to this initial agreement. Although the Antarctic "model" remained somewhat oligarchic (as control was reserved to a small number of States that had demonstrated their technological capabilities [395]), the practice

---

389. Preamble; Article 7.
390. *Ratione loci*, the Washington Treaty applies to a specific geographical area south of the sixtieth parallel. However, the Antarctic marine ecosystem is broader, as it also includes what is referred to as a convergence zone, where cold waters from the Antarctic continent, rising well above this latitude, sink beneath warm waters from the north. The Canberra Convention applies not only south of the sixtieth parallel, but also between this latitude and the Antarctic Convergence Zone. See G. Guillaume, "Le statut juridique de l'Antarctique", in *Les grandes crises du droit*, ed. du Seuil, Paris, 1994, pp. 137-138. However, the Convention does not affect the sovereign rights of the French Republic over the Kerguelen and Crozet Archipelago, which falls within its scope.
391. The situation for biodiversity in the Arctic is quite different, as there is no international status. However, international marine areas have recently been subject to specific conservation measures. See P. Ricard, *La conservation de la biodiversité dans les espaces maritimes internationaux. Un défi pour le droit international* (n. 355), p. 123 *et seq*.
392. Thus, it is the universal value of this regime and the fact that it is common law that leads us to present it here.
393. G. Guillaume, "Le statut juridique de l'Antarctique" (n. 390), p. 132.
394. R.-J. Dupuy, "L'Année géophysique internationale a eu pour effet de substituer une internationalisation de fait à un partage théorique de l'Antarctique"; "Le statut de l'Antarctique", in *AFDI*, 1958, p. 197.
395. R.-J. Dupuy, *L'humanité dans l'imaginaire des nations* (n. 374), p. 227.

of this "executive board", as it is sometimes called, did reflect an internationalisation. But this internationalisation did not result in the continent being considered as part of the common heritage of mankind [396]. Indeed, this approach was rejected by the signatories of the Washington Treaty, despite the strong push by developing countries of the UN, led by Malaysia in particular [397].

218. Nonetheless, even in 1959, the Contracting Parties were aware that theirs were not the only interests at stake. The "collective management" regime adopted was inspired by the "interest of all mankind", as stated in the preamble to the Treaty. Various measures were adopted to protect Antarctic marine fauna and flora [398]. Although it did not classify Antarctic biodiversity as a common heritage, the 1980 Convention on the Conservation of Antarctic Marine Living Resources (CAMLR Convention) did recognise the following:

> "Prime responsibilities of the Antarctic Treaty Consultative Parties for the protection and preservation of the Antarctic environment and, in particular, their responsibilities under Article IX, paragraph 1 *(f)* of the Antarctic Treaty in respect of the preservation and conservation of living resources in Antarctica." [399]

In 1991, the Protocol on Environmental Protection to the Antarctic Treaty went even further. It designated the continent as a natural reserve, dedicated to peace and science, and stated that the signatory States were "[c]onvinced that the development of a comprehensive regime for the protection of the Antarctic environment and dependent and associated ecosystems is in the interest of mankind as a whole" [400]. Despite this, the Antarctic and the biodiversity it harbours are still not considered as a common heritage of mankind. But the fact remains that there is a customary basis underpinning these treaty obligations: the obligation – identical to the one that applies on the high seas – not to cause damage to the environment in areas beyond national jurisdiction.

---

396. On the application of this concept to the Antarctic, see J. Verhoeven *et al.*, *The Antarctic Environment and International Law*, Graham and Trotman/Martinus Nijhoff Publishers, Boston, London, Dordrecht, 1992, p. 89 *et seq.*

397. G. Guillaume, "Le statut juridique de l'Antarctique" (n. 390), p. 150.

398. See above, Chapter 1, para. 51.

399. This provision provides for the adoption by the Parties to the Treaty of Measures relating to the Protection and Conservation of Antarctic Fauna and Flora.

400. Preamble. See A. C. Kiss, "La notion de patrimoine commun de l'humanité", *Recueil des cours*, 2 (175), p. 136 *et seq.*

Section 2. The values of biodiversity in international law

219. By definition, legal rules tend to focus on the protection of human interests, whether moral or material. Environmental law itself – as we know it – is structured around the objective of protecting the environment, the latter being defined as everything that surrounds . . . humans. The approach is mostly anthropocentric. The environment is protected insofar as it meets human needs. For instance, this is how the International Court of Justice sees it when it "also recognizes that the environment is not an abstraction but represents the living space, the quality of life and the very health of human beings, including generations unborn"[401]. But while this position is predominant at the international level, it is not unanimously shared. Biocentrism, which places all sentient beings at the centre, whether human or not, or the even more radical ecocentrism, that also wishes to protect biotic communities, reflect other cosmogonies. In reality, conceptions of the value of biodiversity vary in time and space.

220. Discussing and clarifying the values of biodiversity is a prerequisite for the law's apprehension of biodiversity. Legal rules reflect these values and thus make it possible to bring them to light. The aim is to convince people of the value, of the need even, to protect biodiversity. The greater the values, the stronger the incentives to conserve nature [402]. By enshrining these values in law, legal rules also help to produce them. The law has a performative function here. As has been highlighted:

> "Such statements of values, which often stem from a reaction to threats perceived at a given moment in society, but which are not necessarily consensual, point to the performative function of the law, which is not solely the reflection of what is. It also instantiates what one would like reality to be, what one thinks should happen, as described by François Ost, for whom 'the main function of the law is performative: it consists in making a certain representation, that is valued by the author of the norm, become reality'."[403]

---

401. *Legality of the Threat or Use of Nuclear Weapons*, Advisory Opinion, *ICJ Reports 1996*, p. 226, para. 29.

402. V. Maris, V. Devictor, I. Doussan and A. Roche *et al.* (eds.), *Valeurs de la biodiversité et services écosystémiques*, ed. Quæ, 2016, p. 22 (our translation).

403. F. Ost, 1995, quoted by V. Maris, V. Devictor, I. Doussan and A. Béchet, "Les valeurs en question", *Valeurs de la biodiversité et services écosystémiques*, ed. Quæ, 2016, p. 33 (our translation).

From this point of view, international instruments are interesting to analyse for two reasons. On the one hand, international law provides a useful indication of the values attributed to biodiversity as the instruments adopted are the result of a consensus between States, whether at the international or regional level. On the other hand, international law guides and influences national policies and legislation. It contributes to the construction of shared global reference systems.

221. At the international level, the recognition of the value of biodiversity has led States to acknowledge their responsibility with regard to biodiversity conservation. It is because biodiversity has a value – perhaps even values – that its conservation is necessary and that States must seek to protect it. The preambles of international conventions are very interesting in this respect as they provide a wealth of information on the inspiration that motivated signatory States. They faithfully reflect how conceptions evolve. The historical analysis of international instruments reveals a shift from a conception based on the strict usefulness of biodiversity (with a short-term perspective) to the expression of a responsibility with regard to the conservation of a heritage that not only has a value for present and future generations, but also and above all an intrinsic value. However, in the 2000s, in the wake of the UN report on the evaluation of ecosystems [404], there was a new evolution: a return to an instrumental and pragmatic approach focused on the objective of maintaining the services provided by ecosystems.

222. The values conferred on biodiversity are thus manifold. Biodiversity is recognised, in turn – and sometimes simultaneously – as having *(a)* instrumental, *(b)* heritage and *(c)* intrinsic value [405]. The ecosystem services approach marked a return to *(d)* an instrumental approach, which currently prevails.

1) The instrumental value of biodiversity

223. Historically, and to this day still, "nature" has been protected because of its usefulness to humans. The first, strictly utilitarian conceptions were followed by approaches still dominated by usefulness but with a broader meaning.

---

404. Ecosystems and Human Well-being: General Synthesis (n. 37).
405. Using the distinction made in Fondation pour la recherche sur la biodiversité, *Les valeurs de la biodiversité. Reflets des relations multiples des hommes à la nature*, Fiche clé No. 3, May 2013.

a) *Strictly utilitarian approaches*

224. Initially, a strictly utilitarian approach prevailed. The Convention for the Preservation of Wild Animals, Birds and Fish in Africa (1900) clearly reflected this. It was primarily to protect their interests that European countries sought to harmonise the regime applicable to their African possessions. For instance, they wanted to ensure the sustainability of the ostrich feather trade [406].

225. The utilitarian approach was even clearer in the Paris Convention for the Protection of Birds *Useful* to Agriculture [407], apparent in its very title. This Convention expressly reflected the utilitarian, short-term perspective of those times. It purported to protect "useful" birds, mainly insectivores, and classified as "harmful" species most diurnal raptors, including eagles and falcons, species that are now strictly protected. The Convention thereby denied the fundamental role of these birds in how ecosystems function [408].

226. Later on, through the first bilateral agreements on birds, States mainly sought to maintain hunting resources and share them out fairly. This is also true of the Whaling Convention. While it is now seen by many as an agreement designed to protect emblematic species, on closer examination, the provisions of this 1946 instrument show that the intention at the time was to organise the sustainable hunting of these species, including for future generations. This long extract from the Convention reflects this:

> "Recognizing the interest of the nations of the world in safeguarding for future generations the great natural resources represented by the whale stocks;
>
> Considering that the history of whaling has seen overfishing of one area after another and of one species of whale after another to such a degree that it is essential to protect all species of whales from further over-fishing;
>
> Recognizing that the whale stocks are susceptible of natural increases if whaling is properly regulated, and that increases in the size of whale stocks will permit increases in the number of whales which may be captured without endangering these natural resources;

---

406. P. Fauchille, "Protection des animaux en Afrique. Convention de Londres du 19 mai 1900", Chronique des faits internationaux, in *RGDIP,* 1900, p. 521.
407. Emphasis added.
408. J.-P. Beurier, *Droit international de l'environnement*, Pedone, Paris, 2017.

Recognizing that it is in the common interest to achieve the optimum level of whale stocks as rapidly as possible without causing widespread economic and nutritional distress;

Recognizing that in the course of achieving these objectives, whaling operations should be confined to those species best able to sustain exploitation in order to give an interval for recovery to certain species of whales now depleted in numbers."

227. These strictly utilitarian approaches lead to a dead end. The progress of scientific knowledge quickly convinced States that such an approach alone could not be a valid basis for an adequate conservation policy. This is why it quickly became outdated and gave way to a broader utilitarian approach.

b) *Broader utilitarian approaches*

228. In a second phase, international instruments were still imbued with a utilitarian approach, but a much looser one. Conservation was still contemplated because it was useful for humans, therefore from an anthropocentric perspective. But this usefulness was understood more broadly, focusing not only economic, social and recreational benefits, but also scientific usefulness, viewed both as the role played in ecosystems and the importance for scientific work. This approach thus provided a basis for the preservation of all species, all of which may be useful in this way.

229. This shift can be seen in the preambles of international treaties but also in the major soft law instruments of international environmental law.

230. Already in 1950, in the International Convention for the Protection of Birds, States Parties declared that they were "realizing the danger of extermination which threatens certain species of birds and the concerned about the numerical decrease in other species, particularly migratory species".

231. In 1968, in the preamble to the African Convention on the Conservation of Nature and Natural Resources, signed in Algiers, States Parties declared that they were "fully conscious of the ever-growing importance of natural resources from an economic, nutritional, scientific, educational, cultural and aesthetic point of view".

232. In the preamble to the 1970 Benelux Convention on the Hunting and Protection of Birds, the three signatories expressed that they were "desirous of harmonizing the principles governing their laws

and regulations on the subject of hunting and the protection of birds in the wild state, which were established in the interests of land-holders, agriculture and the efficient protection of nature".

233. The Convention on Wetlands of International Importance also focused on the value of wetlands as being "of international importance", considering their "fundamental ecological functions of wetlands as regulations of water regimes and as habitats supporting a characteristic flora and fauna, especially waterfowl" [409]. The preamble recognised their "great economic, cultural, scientific and recreational value", and specified that from that point of view their "loss . . . would be irreparable".

234. The following year, in the Stockholm Declaration, members of the UN declared the following:

> "1. Man is both creature and moulder of his environment, which gives him physical sustenance and affords him the opportunity for intellectual, moral, social and spiritual growth. In the long and tortuous evolution of the human race on this planet a stage has been reached when, through the rapid acceleration of science and technology, man has acquired the power to transform his environment in countless ways and on an unprecedented scale. Both aspects of man's environment, the natural and the man-made, are essential to his well-being and to the enjoyment of basic human rights the right to life itself. . . . The protection and improvement of the human environment is a major issue which affects the well-being of peoples and economic development throughout the world; it is the urgent desire of the peoples of the whole world and the duty of all Governments." [410]

However, it was further stated that "[o]f all things in the world, people are the most precious" [411].

235. Similarly, in the preamble to the Washington Convention on International Trade in Endangered Species of Wild Fauna and Flora, signed in Washington in March 1973, the States declared that they were "[c]onscious of the ever-growing value of wild fauna and flora from aesthetic, scientific, cultural, recreational and economic points of view". They recognised that "[w]ild fauna and flora in their many beautiful

---

409. Article 22 of the Convention.
410. Preamble, paras. 1-2.
411. *Ibid.*, para. 5.

and varied forms are an irreplaceable part of the natural systems of the earth which must be protected for this and the generations to come".

236. In 1976, in the preamble to the Apia Convention on Conservation of Nature in the South Pacific, the signatories declared that they were conscious of "the importance of natural resources from a nutritional, scientific, educational, cultural and aesthetic point of view".

237. In the preamble to the 1976 US-Soviet Treaty on the Conservation of Migratory Birds and their Environment, both Parties viewed migratory birds as "a natural resource of great scientific, economic, aesthetic, cultural, educational, recreational and ecological value". In 1979, in the Convention on the Conservation of Migratory Species of Wild Animals, States referred to the "ever-growing value" of wild fauna. This value was understood broadly: "from environmental, ecological, genetic, scientific, aesthetic, recreational, cultural, educational, social and economic points of view". This approach also dominated the preamble to the Agreement on the Conservation of African-Eurasian Migratory Waterbirds, in which the Contracting Parties declared that they were "aware of the economic, social, cultural and recreational benefits accruing from the taking of certain species of migratory waterbirds and of the environmental, ecological, genetic, scientific, aesthetic, recreational, cultural, educational, social and economic values of waterbirds in general", of their vulnerability, as they migrate over long distances and are dependent on wetland systems that are diminishing in size and are being degraded by unsustainable human activities. The Parties therefore recognised the need to take immediate action to halt their decline in the regions concerned.

2) The heritage value of biodiversity

238. The recognition of biodiversity as having a heritage value was less straightforward at the international level than in many national legislations. Indeed, States feared being stripped of the attributes of their territorial sovereignty, and instead stuck to their rights, defending the permanent sovereignty of States over their natural resources [412]. Recognising biodiversity as a common heritage of all States or even of humanity would by definition lead to limiting the rights of sovereign States. Instead, several conventions recognise the protection of biodiversity as a "common interest" or a "common concern of

---

412. See above, para. 196.

humankind"[413]. In the Agreement on the Conservation of Gorillas and their Habitats of 2007 (referred to as the Gorilla Accord), the Parties declared that they were "aware of the exceptional significance of great apes for the natural and cultural heritage of humankind". Very few conventions go so far as to recognise that biodiversity is a common heritage. At the global level, the Convention concerning the Protection of the World Cultural and Natural Heritage takes this approach but it balances this recognition with a vehement reaffirmation of the sovereign rights of States. Thus, the Convention states as follows:

> "Each State Party to this Convention recognizes that the duty of ensuring the identification, protection, conservation, presentation and transmission to future generations of the cultural and natural heritage referred to in Articles 1 and 2 and situated on its territory, *belongs primarily to that State.*"[414]

It also states the following:

> "Whilst fully respecting the sovereignty of the States on whose territory the cultural and natural heritage mentioned in Articles 1 and 2 is situated, and without prejudice to property right provided by national legislation, the States Parties to this Convention recognize that such heritage constitutes a world heritage for whose protection it is the duty of the international community as a whole to co-operate."[415]

239. The heritage value of biodiversity is also found in the non-binding 1983 International Undertaking on Plant Genetic Resources, adopted by Resolution 8/83 of the FAO Conference, which states in its objectives that it is "based on the universally accepted principle that plant genetic resources are a heritage of mankind and consequently should be available without restriction"[416]. On the other hand, it is absent from the International Treaty on Plant Genetic Resources for Food and Agriculture adopted within the same framework in 2001 and which refers neither to heritage nor to humanity, although the Parties do declare that they are "cognizant that plant genetic resources for food and agriculture are a common concern of all countries, in that all countries depend very largely on plant genetic resources for food

---

413. Expression used in the Rio Convention on Biological Diversity (1992).
414. Article 4, emphasis added.
415. Article 6, para. 1.
416. Article 1.

and agriculture that originated elsewhere". At the same time, the Treaty recalls the States' "sovereign rights over their plant genetic resources". As for the United Nations Convention on the Law of the Sea (Montego Bay, 1982), while it famously states that "[t]he Area and its resources are the common heritage of mankind"[417], the resources in question are not biological resources but only mineral resources[418]. With regard to biological resources, negotiations are ongoing and have not yet been concluded. The status of these resources is precisely one of the points on which States disagree[419].

240. At the regional level, it should be noted that the preamble to the Bern Convention on the Conservation of European Wildlife and Natural Habitats (1979), without referring to a common heritage, does nevertheless recognise that "[w]ild flora and fauna constitute a natural heritage of aesthetic, scientific, cultural, recreational, economic and intrinsic value that needs to be preserved and handed on to future generations". In European Union law, birds were recognised very early on as a common heritage of the European Member States[420]. This recognition was extended in 1992 to natural habitats and threatened species:

> "In the European territory of the Member States, natural habitats are continuing to deteriorate and an increasing number of wild species are seriously threatened; whereas given that the threatened habitats and species form part of the Community's natural heritage and the threats to them are often of a transboundary nature, it is necessary to take measures at Community level in order to conserve them."[421]

The Court of Justice has drawn concrete consequences from this in its interpretation of EU law[422].

---

417. Article 136.
418. See Article 133 *(a)* according to which "'resources' means all solid, liquid or gaseous mineral resources *in situ* in the Area at or beneath the seabed, including polymetallic nodules". M.-P. Lanfranchi, "Gestion durable des ressources minérales marines et droit international", *Journal du droit international*, 2019, pp. 717-738.
419. See above, para. 211.
420. Directive 2009/147/EC of the European Parliament and of the Council of 30 November 2009 on the conservation of wild birds *OJ L 20*, 26.1.2010, pp. 7-25 (Codified Version of the Directive 79/409/EEC of 2 April 1979).
421. Council Directive 92/43/EEC of 21 May 1992 on the conservation of natural habitats and of wild fauna and flora *OJ L 206*, 22 July 1992, pp. 7-50.
422. According to the Court, "faithful transposition is particularly important in the case of the Directive where management of the common heritage is entrusted to the Member States in their respective territories" (Judgment of the Court, 12 July 2007, Commission/Republic of Austria, C507/04, Rec. p. I5939, at para. 92).

3) The intrinsic value of biodiversity

241. In some instruments, utilitarian conceptions have given way to the recognition of an intrinsic value of wild fauna and flora, and even of biodiversity. Despite appearances, this might not constitute the beginning of a shift from anthropocentrism towards eco- or biocentrism. Indeed, States do not draw all the legal consequences therefrom. This recognition is conceived more as a way to declare that a higher motivation is being pursued, rather than the justification of a legal revolution leading, for example, to the recognition of a legal personality for nature. In this respect, the recognition of an intrinsic value, however justified it may appear from an ethical point of view, does not seem to be necessary. Awareness of wildlife's usefulness – meant in the broadest sense – can in itself be a valid basis for conservation policy.

242. The recognition of an intrinsic value is still exceptional. At the regional level, the preamble to the Bern Convention on the Conservation of European Wildlife and Natural Habitats recognised in 1979 the "aesthetic, scientific, cultural, recreational, economic" but also the "intrinsic" value of "natural heritage" as well as "the essential role played by wild flora and fauna in maintaining biological balances". Recognition of an intrinsic value can also be found in the preamble to the 1982 World Charter for Nature [423], which solemnly proclaims that "[e]very form of life is unique, warranting respect regardless of its worth for man". This recognition was not explicitly challenged during negotiations, but certain positions nevertheless revealed some resistance, such as the following statement from Brazil:

> "The Preamble contains philosophical and doctrinal principles which do not enjoy unanimous support, since from different points of view they are and will be considered heterodox, unfounded or simply irrelevant. They are therefore not likely to contribute to the protection of nature, which can only be founded on pragmatism if it is to have any real or practical effect." [424]

This terminology was used in the draft international covenant on the environment and development initiated by IUCN [425], which proclaimed

---

423. UNGA, Resolution A/RES/37/7, 28 October 1982, *World Charter for Nature*.
424. M. Bowman, "The Nature, Development and Philosophical Foundations of the Biodiversity Concept in International Law", in M. Bowman and C. Redgwell, *International Law and the Conservation of Biological Diversity*, Kluwer Law International, 1996, p. 19.
425. See International Covenant on Environment and Development, Draft, Commission on Environmental Law of IUCN.

among its fundamental principles that nature as a whole and all life forms warrant respect and are to be safeguarded, and that the integrity of the Earth's ecological systems shall be maintained and where necessary restored [426]. The work of IUCN, which is also behind the World Charter for Nature, most likely influenced the drafting of the Rio Convention on Biological Diversity: in its preamble, the Contracting Parties declare that they are "[c]onscious of the intrinsic value of biological diversity and of the ecological, genetic, social, economic, scientific, educational, cultural, recreational and aesthetic values of biological diversity" and "[c]onscious also of the importance of biological diversity for evolution and for maintaining life sustaining systems of the biosphere" [427]. In the 2015 Paris Agreement on Climate Change, a different wording was used. The Parties highlighted "the importance of ensuring the integrity of all ecosystems, including oceans, and the protection of biodiversity, recognized by some cultures as Mother Earth, and noting the importance for some of the concept of 'climate justice', when taking action to address climate change" [428]. The Agreement thereby alludes to Latin American cosmogonies, especially Andean ones, that view Mother Earth or *pachamama* as the goddess at the origin of everything and who deserves the utmost respect.

243. Thus, the recognition of this intrinsic value is still rare. In international law, fauna, flora and biodiversity are mainly perceived as *resources*, like in the Agreement under the United Nations Convention on the Law of the Sea on the Conservation and Sustainable Use of Marine Biological Diversity of Areas Beyond National Jurisdiction that regulates the utilization of "marine genetic resources".

244. Furthermore, contrary to many domestic legislations, international law has not gone so far as to recognise animal rights. International law on biodiversity has very little do to with animal welfare, which arises mainly as an incidental issue in matters of transport and trade [429]. In the *Seals* case, the WTO Appellate Body did however uphold the finding of the Panel that the protection of public moral concerns regarding animal welfare is "an important value or interest" [430]. At the regional level, and

---

426. Article 2.
427. First and second paragraphs.
428. Paris Agreement, https://unfccc.int/files/meetings/paris_nov_2015/application/pdf/paris_agreement_english_.pdf, accessed on 20 December 2023.
429. W. Scholtz (ed.), *Animal Welfare and International Environmental Law. From Conservation to Compassion*, Edward Elgar, 2019.
430. WTO, European Communities – Measures Prohibiting the Importation and Marketing of Seal Products, AB-2014-1 – AB-2014-2 – Report of the Appellate Body, WT/DS400/AB/R, WT/DS401/AB/R, 22 May 2014, p. 160.

in particular at the European level, there have been more significant developments. Thus, the European Convention for the Protection of Animals during International Transport (revised), adopted in Chisinau on 6 November 2003, lays down a fundamental principle according to which "[a]nimals shall be transported in a way which safeguards their welfare, including health"[431]. The Treaty on the Functioning of the European Union also features a clause on the inclusion of animal welfare requirements into EU policies:

> "In formulating and implementing the Union's agriculture, fisheries, transport, internal market, research and technological development and space policies, the Union and the Member States shall, since animals are sentient beings, pay full regard to the welfare requirements of animals, while respecting the legislative or administrative provisions and customs of the Member States relating in particular to religious rites, cultural traditions and regional heritage."[432]

4) From the value of biodiversity to ecosystem services: The return to an instrumental approach

245. It was the United Nations report on ecosystem assessment that truly promoted and publicised the concept of ecosystem services[433]. This report was the result of a process initiated by the Secretary-General of the UN that lasted from 2001 to 2005. The idea was for the Millennium Ecosystem Assessment to play a role similar to the IPCC reports:

> "The MA responds to requests for information received through the Convention on Biological Diversity and other international conventions (the United Nations Convention to Combat Desertification, the Ramsar Convention on Wetlands, and the Convention on Migratory Species) and is also designed to meet the needs of other stakeholders, including business, civil society, and indigenous peoples."

---

431. Article 4, para. 1.
432. Consolidated Version of the Treaty on the Functioning of the European Union, *OJ* C 326, 26 October 2012, Article 13.
433. UN, Millennium Ecosystem Assessment, *Ecosystems and Human Well-being: Biodiversity Synthesis* (n. 37).

It was designed to provide an overview of scientific knowledge for these users [434]. The objective was therefore clearly for this report to become a decision support tool.

246. The assessment linked together a functional approach to biodiversity and the notion of services rendered, which represent the benefits that humans derive from ecosystem functions and processes [435]. It has had a significant impact on the direction of ecological research, but also on public policy, especially at a global level. The monetary valuation of biodiversity and ecosystem services is thus a powerful argument in favour of conservation [436]. However, this movement also paves the way for the promotion of market instruments for the protection of biodiversity, and in particular for offsetting and payments for environmental services.

247. Despite the recognition of the intrinsic value of biological diversity in the Convention on Biological Diversity, this shift back to an instrumental approach was already in the making in the products of the 1992 Rio Summit. The Rio Declaration on Environment and Development gave no indication of the value of biodiversity or even of the environment. Although they were adopted at the same time, the Forest Principles moved away from the intrinsic view, although they gave biodiversity a broader instrumental value: "Forest resources and forest lands should be sustainably managed to meet the social, economic, ecological, cultural and spiritual needs of present and future generations." [437] Similarly, Agenda 21 insisted on the need to assess the value of biodiversity: "Biological resources constitute a capital asset with great potential for yielding sustainable benefits". In particular, governments should "ascribe values to biological and genetic resources", and "undertake long-term research into the importance of biodiversity for the functioning of ecosystems and the role of ecosystems in producing goods, environmental services and other values supporting sustainable development" [438]. The notion of "services" rendered was already present:

---

434. *Ibid.*
435. I. Doussan, "Nature à vendre", *Etudes foncières*, No. 154, 2011, p. 10.
436. V. Marris, V. Devictor, I. Doussan and A. Roche *et al.* (eds.), *Valeurs de la biodiversité et services écosystémiques* (n. 403), p. 22. V. Maris, *La part sauvage du monde. Penser la nature dans l'anthropocène*, Seuil, Paris, 2018.
437. *Non-Legally Binding Authoritative Statement of Principles for a Global Consensus on the Management, Conservation and Sustainable Development of All Types of Forests*, General Assembly, UN, 14 August 1992, 2 *(b)*.
438. *Agenda 21*, para. 15.5, https://sustainabledevelopment.un.org/content/documents/Agenda21.pdf, accessed on 20 December 2023, paras. 15.3 and 15.5.

"Our planet's essential goods and services depend on the variety and variability of genes, species, populations and ecosystems. Biological resources feed and clothe us and provide housing, medicines and spiritual nourishment. The natural ecosystems of forests, savannahs, pastures and rangelands, deserts, tundra, rivers, lakes and seas contain most of the Earth's biodiversity. Farmers' fields and gardens are also of great importance as repositories, while gene banks, botanical gardens, zoos and other germplasm repositories make a small but significant contribution. The current decline in biodiversity is largely the result of human activity and represents a serious threat to human development." [439]

248. The Parties to the Convention on Biological Diversity have embraced this new approach [440]. The Strategic Plan adopted in Nagoya in 2010 for the 2011-2020 period clarified the "vision" of "living in harmony with nature": "by 2050, biodiversity is *valued,* conserved, restored and wisely used, *maintaining ecosystem services,* sustaining a healthy planet and *delivering benefits essential for all people*". Adopted at the same time, the Nagoya Protocol echoes this vision when, in the name of pragmatism, it "values" biodiversity economically in order to better protect it. This motivation is apparent in its preamble, in which the signatory Parties recognise that:

"[P]ublic awareness of the economic value of ecosystems and biodiversity and the fair and equitable sharing of this economic value with the custodians of biodiversity are key incentives for the conservation of biological diversity and the sustainable use of its components."

249. The twenty major strategic objectives known as the "Aichi Targets" are directly inspired by this approach. For example, the creation of protected areas must focus mainly on areas that are important for the conservation of biodiversity and of "ecosystem services". Indeed, Target 11 states:

"By 2020, at least 17 per cent of terrestrial and inland water areas, and 10 per cent of coastal and marine areas, especially

---

439. *Ibid.*, para. 15.2.
440. See, for instance, NEP-WCMC, *Developing Ecosystem Service Indicators: Experiences and Lessons Learned from Sub-Global Assessments and Other Initiatives. Secretariat of the Convention on Biological Diversity*, Montreal, Canada. Technical Series No. 58, 2011.

areas of particular importance for biodiversity and ecosystem services, are conserved through effectively and equitably managed, ecologically representative and well connected systems of protected areas and other effective area-based conservation measures, and integrated into the wider landscapes and seascapes."

Furthermore, Target 14 states:

"By 2020, ecosystems that provide essential services, including services related to water, and contribute to health, livelihoods and well-being, are restored and safeguarded, taking into account the needs of women, indigenous and local communities, and the poor and vulnerable",

and Target 15 provides as follows:

"By 2020, ecosystem resilience and the contribution of biodiversity to carbon stocks has been enhanced, through conservation and restoration, including restoration of at least 15 per cent of degraded ecosystems, thereby contributing to climate change mitigation and adaptation and to combating desertification."

250. This approach was reiterated, as could be expected, in the Declaration adopted at the 2012 "Rio+20" Conference entitled "The Future We Want". The UN members made the following declaration:

"We reaffirm the intrinsic value of biological diversity, as well as the ecological, genetic, social, economic, scientific, educational, cultural, recreational and aesthetic values of biological diversity and *its critical role in maintaining ecosystems that provide essential services, which are critical foundations for sustainable development and human well-being.* We recognize the severity of the global loss of biodiversity and the degradation of ecosystems, and emphasize that these undermine global development, affecting food security and nutrition, the provision of and access to water and the health of the rural poor and of people worldwide, including present and future generations. This highlights the importance of the conservation of biodiversity, enhancing habitat connectivity and building ecosystem resilience." [441]

---

441. UNGA Resolution A/RES/66/288, 27 July 2012, *The Future We Want*, para. 197. Emphasis added.

251. In this respect, it is quite significant that the "IPCC of biodiversity", also created in 2012, is called the Intergovernmental Science-Policy Platform for Biodiversity and Ecosystem Services [442].

252. Here, the ecologists' interests came up against more materialistic, economistic and financial interests. This is a very Western approach, far removed from the Andean *pachamama*. However, it has been accepted by the countries of the South, who hope to be able to financially value their rich biodiversity.

253. This convergence of interests, both between the environment and the economy, and between North and South, explains in part the political success of this approach. Yet, as they spread like a flash in the pan in the international governance arena [443], these new directions have perhaps been insufficiently debated, insufficiently discussed, despite the fact that they are highly debatable. They are attractive to ecologists and financial donors alike, but also reassuring for decision-makers because they lead to a concrete methodology. The value of ecosystem services can be measured and even quantified. This quantification provides decision-makers with a decision-making aid, making it possible to rank and prioritise the services, objects or areas to be protected almost mathematically. But isn't the "rational" choice promised by economists just an illusion?

254. Basing a biodiversity policy on the economic measurement of the – by and large immeasurable – value of biodiversity that is still largely unknown is by definition risky. Such an approach is somewhat dangerous if it overlooks the complexity of the natural and social systems involved and leads to the belief that simple mechanisms at the end of the chain are enough to ensure their sustainability [444]. In doing so, there is also a risk of failing to include the long-term dimension and the need for precaution: do we know today what will be useful to humans tomorrow? Or simply even important to them? By trying to protect biodiversity in and of itself, and therefore all its potential, wouldn't we be avoiding this risk? Lastly, such an approach may encourage

---

442. D. Pesche, M. Oubenal, J.-C. Vandevelde and M. Hrabanski, "Le 'consensus d'Antalya': les avancées de la Plateforme intergouvernementale scientifique et politique sur la biodiversité et les services écosystémiques (IPBES)", *Natures Sciences Sociétés*, 22 (2014), pp. 240-246.

443. E. Lugo, "Ecosystem Services, the Millennium Ecosystem Assessment, and the Conceptual Difference between Benefits Provided by Ecosystems and Benefits Provided by People", *Journal of Land Use*, 23 (2), 2008, pp. 243-262.

444. J.-P. Chassany and J.-M. Salles, "Potentiels et limites des paiements pour services environnementaux dans les programmes de lutte contre la désertification", *Sécheresse* 23, 2012, p. 178.

the pure and simple commodification of biodiversity, leading to the generalisation of offsetting and payments for environmental services, without resolving all the ethical and practical questions that this raises. How to assess equivalence? Is there an equivalent compensation for everything [445]? These risks should be weighed up more carefully, otherwise neither biodiversity nor indeed ecosystem services will be preserved.

255. At the same time, major instruments of international law reveal that States very often refuse to choose, and even more so to rank, the various values of biodiversity. International law therefore struggles to play the role it should play in reconciling these values. The enumeration of these values in the preambles of several treaties, as well as the three objectives of the Convention on Biological Diversity, which are difficult to reconcile, reflect this very clearly. This is reflected in the new biodiversity framework post-2020, the Kunming-Montreal Global Biodiversity Framework, adopted in December 2022 at the nineteenth meeting of the Conference of the Parties to the Convention on Biological Diversity. This new strategic plan prefers not to choose between different value systems, but to recognize and accept them all:

> "Nature embodies different concepts for different people, including biodiversity, ecosystems, Mother Earth, and systems of life. Nature's contributions to people also embody different concepts, such as ecosystem goods and services and nature's gifts. Both nature and nature's contributions to people are vital for human existence and good quality of life, including human wellbeing, living in harmony with nature, and living well in balance and harmony with Mother Earth. The Framework recognizes and considers these diverse value systems and concepts, including, for those countries that recognize them, rights of nature and rights of Mother Earth, as being an integral part of its successful implementation."

256. To conclude, the values attributed to biodiversity in international law are often manifold and have evolved over time. After the first instruments marked by utilitarianism, the recognition of the intrinsic value of biodiversity was promoted by environmentalists in order to strengthen environmental policy, albeit without much success.

---

445. I. Doussan, "Les services écologiques: un nouveau concept pour le droit de l'environnement?", in *La responsabilité environnementale, prévention, imputation, réparation*, C. Cans (ed.), Dalloz, Paris, 2009, pp. 125-141.

Their pragmatism then led them to support the economic valuation of biodiversity through the valuation of ecosystem services [446], but different ways of thinking are also increasingly recognised, as illustrated by the Paris Agreement or the Kunming-Montreal Global Biodiversity Framework.

---

446. M. Antona and M. Bonnin, *Généalogie scientifique et mise en politique des SE (Services environnementaux et services écosystémiques)*, note de synthèse de revue bibliographique et d'entretiens, WP1, Programme SERENA, document de travail, No. 2010-0; M. Bonnin, *Genèse des services environnementaux dans le droit. 1: L'apparition récente et emmêlée des services environnementaux dans le droit international de l'environnement*, Programme SERENA, Note de synthèse, No. 2010-05.

CHAPTER III

INTERNATIONAL LAW
AND BIODIVERSITY CONSERVATION

257. Biodiversity conservation and the measures related to this objective occupy a central place in the international law on biodiversity. Before presenting the how (what actions, what policies, what instruments), it is important to identify the what: what exactly does conservation focus on? We will conclude this chapter by discussing new legal approaches and developments.

Section 1. The focus of conservation

258. On this topic, approaches can be either global or targeted. But one does not preclude the other, as targeted approaches can be part of global approaches.

1) Global approaches

259. Global approaches have been based on three concepts: nature, wildlife and biological diversity, the latter placing more emphasis on the functionality of environments.

a) *Nature*

260. Nature is the focus of the World Charter for Nature adopted by the UN General Assembly in 1982, which provides that "[n]ature shall be respected and its essential processes shall not be impaired" [447]. A number of regional treaties also deal with the conservation of nature, or of fauna and flora in general, rather than the conservation of individual species and/or habitats or types of habitats. The Washington Convention on International Trade in Endangered Species of Wild Fauna and Flora thus purports to protect and preserve fauna and flora. The same is true of the 1968 African Convention on the Conservation of Nature and

---

447. UNGA, Resolution A/RES/37/7, 28 October 1982, *World Charter for Nature*, I), para. 1.

Natural Resources (or Algiers Convention), which sets out measures to conserve "all" species of flora and fauna in general [448], and of the Apia Convention on Conservation of Nature in the South Pacific (1976) [449].

261. The Bern Convention on the Conservation of European Wildlife and Natural Habitats (1979) also provides a good illustration of this approach. Following the first European instruments that dealt mainly with birds, the committee of experts that drafted this Convention was tasked with defining a coherent policy for the protection of wildlife. Indeed, the Bern Convention focuses on both fauna and flora, and especially on their habitats. It promotes the conservation of all plant and animal species as well as their habitats. In this respect, it is the first European instrument to introduce a global nature protection policy. Widely ratified, it now includes 50 States, spanning Europe from East to West and beyond, the Western Mediterranean and Macaronesia region (the Azores, Madeira, the Canary Islands and Cape Verde) as well as the East Atlantic migratory route to Senegal. Furthermore, the European Union itself – the European Economic Community at the time – has been a party to it since 1981. Even though it was adopted earlier, the Convention is now a tool for the regional implementation of the 1992 Rio Convention on Biological Diversity. It also largely inspired the wording of the 1992 European "Natura 2000" directive, which is a much more comprehensive and prescriptive instrument [450]. But this does not mean that the Bern Convention has become irrelevant. By involving fifty States and not just the twenty-eight countries of the European Union, it continues to be the only regional nature protection instrument pertaining to wider Europe. Similar but with different scopes, mention can be made of the Benelux Convention on Nature Conservation and Landscape Protection (8 June 1982), and of the Protocol for the Implementation of the Alpine Convention in the Field of Nature Protection and Landscape Conservation (Chambéry, 20 December 1994) which states that "each Contracting Party undertakes to take the necessary measures to ensure the protection, management and, where necessary, restoration of nature and landscapes in the Alpine region" [451].

---

448. Articles VI, VII and X.
449. Article 5.
450. Council Directive 92/43/EEC of 21 May 1992 on the conservation of natural habitats and of wild fauna and flora *OJ L 206,* 22 July 1992, pp. 7-50.
451. Article 2 (our translation).

b) *Wildlife*

262. Focusing on wildlife means prioritising the wild part of biodiversity, i.e. excluding domestic animals and cultivated plants. But in reality, conventions based on this approach do not necessarily vary much in substance from those aimed at protecting nature or biodiversity, especially since the boundary between what is wild and what is domesticated is becoming increasingly blurred, as previously discussed.

263. For the most part, the protection of wildlife is the subject of relatively old instruments. Thus, the Washington Convention on Nature Protection and Wild Life Preservation in the Western Hemisphere provides for the creation of *strict wilderness reserves*. This refers to "[a] region under public control characterized by primitive conditions of flora, fauna, transportation and habitation wherein there is no provision for the passage of motorized transportation and all commercial developments are excluded"[452]. The 1973 Convention on International Trade in Endangered Species of Wild Fauna and Flora (CITES) refers to wildlife in its title, as does the 1979 Convention on the Conservation of European Wildlife and Natural Habitats. Other examples include the Agreement for Cooperation and Consultation between the Central African States for the Conservation of Wild Fauna (1983), the Protocol concerning Protected Areas and Wild Fauna and Flora in the Eastern African Region (1985) and the Southern African Development Community Protocol on Wildlife Conservation and Law Enforcement (1999).

264. Interestingly, on the occasion of the fortieth anniversary of CITES in 2013, the UN General Assembly proclaimed 3 March as "World Wildlife Day". It reaffirmed the intrinsic value of wild species and their various contributions to sustainable development and human well-being, including from an ecological, genetic, social, economic, scientific, educational, cultural, recreational and aesthetic point of view[453]. Wilderness, which is not always well defined in treaties and which for a time seemed overshadowed by the notion of biodiversity, is currently the focus of a renewed interest, with projects – still hypothetical – to reclaim wilderness, in other words, rewilding. In 2016, a long-awaited book was published in the United States by Edward O. Wilson, *Half-Earth: Our Planet's Fight for Life*, which

---
452. Article I.
453. UNGA Resolution 68/205, 20 December 2013, *World Wildlife Day*.

details a rewilding initiative that proposes to devote half of the Earth's surface to preserving biodiversity [454]. This approach is the opposite of de-wilding, which on the contrary proposes to do away with nature and replace it with a more anthropo-compatible vision [455].

c) *Biological diversity*

265. Even before the adoption of the Rio Convention on Biological Diversity, the ASEAN Agreement on the Conservation of Nature and Natural Resources (9 July 1985) reflected a more modern and functional global approach by specifying that:

> "The Contracting Parties... undertake to adopt... the measures necessary to maintain essential ecological processes and life-support systems, to preserve genetic diversity, and to ensure the sustainable utilization of harvested natural resources under their jurisdiction in accordance with scientific principles and with a view to attaining the goal of sustainable development." [456]

In 1992, the Rio Convention on Biological Diversity went even further than this precursor agreement. Indeed, it explicitly refers to the "conservation of biological diversity" as one of its objectives, a diversity defined as "variability among living organisms from all sources including, *inter alia*, terrestrial, marine and other aquatic ecosystems and the ecological complexes of which they are part: this includes diversity within species, between species and of ecosystems" [457]. In this respect, it inspired the African Maputo Convention (2003), which includes the concepts of biological and genetic diversity and contains very detailed provisions directly inspired by the Rio Convention and aimed at *in situ* as well as *ex situ* conservation [458]. The Convention does not provide a list of protected species, contrary to the Algiers Convention (1968) whose list needed updating. The production of such a list has been left to national legislation, but it could be adopted at a later stage as an annex to the Convention [459].

---

454. W. Lynn, "Réensauvager la moitié de la Terre : la dimension éthique d'un projet spectaculaire", *The Conversation*, 20 September 2015.
455. V. Devictor, *Nature en crise. Penser la biodiversité* (n. 2), p. 253.
456. Article 1 (1).
457. Article 2.
458. Articles IX and X, and Annex 1.
459. Article X (2).

266. The Protocol concerning Specially Protected Areas and Biological Diversity in the Mediterranean (1995) is not as all-inclusive as its title seems to suggest, as it focuses mainly on the "components of biological diversity important for its conservation and sustainable use" or "areas of particular natural or cultural value". Thus, it provides that protected areas should promote the conservation of:

> "*(a)* representative types of coastal and marine ecosystems of adequate size to ensure their long-term viability and to maintain their biological diversity;
>
> *(b)* habitats which are in danger of disappearing in their natural area of distribution in the Mediterranean or which have a reduced natural area of distribution as a consequence of their regression or on account of their intrinsically restricted area;
>
> *(c)* habitats critical to the survival, reproduction and recovery of endangered, threatened or endemic species of flora or fauna;
>
> *(d)* sites of particular importance because of their scientific, aesthetic, cultural or educational interest." [460]

267. As for the Protocol on Conservation and Sustainable Use of Biological and Landscape Diversity to the Framework Convention on the Protection and Sustainable Development of the Carpathians (22 May 2003) [461] and the Protocol concerning the Conservation of Biological Diversity and the Establishment of Network of Protected Areas in the Red Sea and Gulf of Aden (12 December 2005) [462], they reflect a very comprehensive approach to biodiversity. Other examples include the Convention on the Sustainable Management of the Lake Tanganyika (23 August 2005), the International Treaty on Plant Genetic Resources for Food and Agriculture (3 November 2001), the International Agreement on the Creation of a Marine Mammal Sanctuary in the Mediterranean (21 February 2002), the UNECE Convention on Access to Information, Public Participation in Decision-Making and Access to Justice in Environmental Matters (Aarhus Convention) (25 June 1998), which all refer to biological diversity.

268. Protecting biological diversity means looking at the functionality of environments, rather than at individual species in and of

---

460. Article 4.
461. Article 4: "Each Party shall develop and implement policies and strategies in its national territory aiming at the conservation, restoration and sustainable use of biological and landscape diversity of the Carpathians while taking into consideration policies and strategies developed and implemented by other Parties".
462. Article 4 (1).

themselves. The Convention on Biological Diversity contains a very important general provision which states:

> "Each Contracting Party shall, in accordance with its particular conditions and capabilities: *(a)* Develop national strategies, plans or programmes for the conservation and sustainable use of biological diversity or adapt for this purpose existing strategies, plans or programmes which shall reflect, *inter alia*, the measures set out in this Convention relevant to the Contracting Party concerned." [463]

The COP has paid much attention to this provision, insisting on its importance. Thus, according to Aichi Target 17, "[b]y 2015 each Party has developed, adopted as a policy instrument, and has commenced implementing an effective, participatory and updated national biodiversity strategy and action plan" [464]. NBSAPs are indeed the main tool for implementing the Convention and the Aichi Targets in national legislations [465]. They are also a way to strengthen the co-ordination of national responses to the various biodiversity conventions [466]. Nevertheless, the COP was forced to recognise that "[o]nly a limited number of Parties have adopted their national biodiversity strategies and action plans as whole-of-government policy instruments" [467]. The Kunming-Montreal Global Biodiversity Framework adopted in 2022 places NBSAPs at its heart and tries to provide better guidance, specifying that:

> "National biodiversity strategies and action plans, revised or updated in alignment with the Framework and its goals and targets as the main vehicle for implementation of the Framework, *including national targets communicated in a standardized format.*" [468]

---

463. Article 6.
464. See Decision X/2 (2010), *The Strategic Plan for Biodiversity 2011-2020 and the Aichi Biodiversity Targets*, UNEP/CBD/COP/DEC/X/2 (2010), p. 117.
465. P. Herkenrath, "The Implementation of the Convention on Biological Diversity – A Non-Government Perspective Ten Years on", *Review of European, Comparative and International Environmental Law*, 2002, Vol. 11, pp. 29-37.
466. K. Rogalla von Bieberstein, E. Sattout, M. Christensen, B. Pisupati, N. D. Burgess, J. Harrison and J. Geldmann, "Improving Collaboration in the Implementation of Global Biodiversity Conventions", *Conservation Biology*, Vol. 33, No. 4,- pp. 821-831.
467. CBD, Decision 14/1 (2018), *Updated Assessment of Progress Towards Selected Aichi Biodiversity Targets and Options to Accelerate Progress*.
468. Decision 15/4 (2022), *Kunming-Montreal Global Biodiversity Framework*, CBD/COP/DEC/15/4, 19 December 2022. Emphasis added.

269. The Convention requires Parties to identify the components of biological diversity that are important for its conservation and sustainable use [469] since, in practice, protection measures will target these components: certain species – because they are threatened, rare, endemic, representative, etc. – and certain areas – because they are rich in biodiversity, rare, home to threatened species, representative of certain types of ecosystems, etc. However, as essential as it may be, the creation of protected areas cannot suffice to "maintain the integrity of genetic resources if the areas so set aside are nothing more than islands surrounded by an artificial environment from which all nature has been excluded" [470]. This is why conservation methods have subsequently been directed towards protecting nature outside of protected areas, moving beyond the concept of "nature as a sanctuary". Thus, the COP of the Convention on Biological Diversity found in 2004 that:

> "While the number and extent of protected areas has been increasing in the past decades, so that around 11 per cent of the world's land surface is currently in protected status, existing systems of protected areas are neither representative of the world's ecosystems, nor do they adequately address conservation of critical habitat types, biomes and threatened species, and, with marine areas particularly under-represented actions need to be taken to fill these gaps." [471]

In 2010, the COP called on States to:

> "Enhance the coverage and quality, representativeness and, if appropriate, connectivity of protected areas as a contribution to the development of representative systems of protected areas and coherent ecological networks that include all relevant biomes, ecoregions, or ecosystems." [472]

270. Habitat protection regulations are an essential complement to, and even an actual element of, species protection and make it possible to implement what C. de Klemm called the ecological management of wildlife. This ecological management requires taking into account all factors besides harvesting that may adversely affect the conservation

---

469. Article 7 *(a)*.
470. C. de Klemm, "Le patrimoine naturel de l'humanité", *L'avenir du droit international de l'environnement*, P. M. Dupuy (ed.), Colloque de l'Académie de droit international de La Haye, Martinus Nijhoff Publishers, 1984, p. 12 (our translation).
471. CBD, Decision VII/28 (2004), *Protected Areas (Arts. 8* (a) *to* (e)*)*.
472. CBD, Decision X/31 (2010), *Protected Areas*.

status of a species [473]. These factors can be many and varied: destruction or alteration of habitats, pollution, introduction of alien species and, in general, all processes of human or even natural origin that may affect the reproduction, feeding, migration, moulting and any other aspect of the biology of species and thus their conservation status. Accordingly, protecting the habitat of species entails the implementation of a wide variety of methods. The delimitation of protected areas is certainly a preferred technique and one of the first to be put in place. However, it is only one of many possible methods. Attention must also be paid to biodiversity outside protected areas, to ordinary biodiversity and the factors and processes that influence its conservation status.

271. In this respect, the COP of the Convention on Biological Diversity promotes an ecosystem approach [474]. It is inspired by numerous scientific publications which, since the early 1990s, have highlighted the inefficiency of biodiversity conservation policies and proposed a new, holistic approach known as the *ecosystem approach* or EcAp. This means that ecosystems must be considered as a whole, instead of focusing on isolated elements (such and such species or habitat). The approach must be coherent and capable of evolving in order to adapt to changes and take into account the evolution of knowledge [475].

272. This principle was given legal recognition quite early on. The Convention on the Conservation of Antarctic Marine Living Resources (Canberra, 1980) was one of the first instruments to promote an ecosystem approach. This Convention was a response to the decline in krill stocks caused by increased fishing activity in the region. Krill play a central role in the Antarctic marine ecosystem's food chain. Their disappearance therefore threatens the entire ecosystem. Without referring to it explicitly, the Convention implemented the ecosystem approach, not only through an appropriate geographical scope (the Antarctic marine ecosystem), but also through its provisions which do

---

473. C. de Klemm and S. Maljean-Dubois, "L'Accord du 16 juin 1995 relatif à la conservation des oiseaux d'eau migrateurs d'Afrique-Eurasie", *Revue juridique de l'environnement*, No. 1/1998, pp. 5-30.

474. In this respect, the Kunming-Montreal Global Biodiversity Framework is "to be implemented based on the ecosystem approach of the Convention". See Decision 15/4 (2022), Kunming-Montreal Global Biodiversity Framework, CBD/COP/DEC/15/4, 19 December 2022, para. 7, *f*).

475. G. Futhazar, *L'évolution du droit international de l'environnement en Méditerranée: quelle influence de l'IPBES?*, Confluence des droits, Aix-en-Provence, 2020, p. 367 *et seq.*, https://books.openedition.org/dice/14388, accessed on 16 October 2023.

not focus on any particular species. On the contrary, Article II requires the Parties to comply with the following principles:

"Maintenance of the ecological relationships between harvested, dependent and related populations of Antarctic marine living resources and the restoration of depleted populations to the levels defined in sub-paragraph *(a)* above; and ... prevention of changes or minimization of the risk of changes in the marine ecosystem which are not potentially reversible over two or three decades, taking into account the state of available knowledge of the direct and indirect impact of harvesting, the effect of the introduction of alien species, the effects of associated activities on the marine ecosystem and of the effects of environmental changes, with the aim of making possible the sustained conservation of Antarctic marine living resources." [476]

273. The COP to the Ramsar Convention also promotes an ecosystem approach without saying so when it defines wise use of wetlands as "sustainable utilization for the benefit of humankind in a way compatible with the maintenance of the natural properties of the ecosystem" and specifies that "[n]atural properties of the ecosystem are defined as 'those physical, biological or chemical components, such as soil, water, plants, animals and nutrients, and the interactions between them'" [477]. But it was the COP to the Convention on Biological Diversity that developed the conceptual framework of the ecosystem approach, by adopting in 2000 a decision entitled "Ecosystem Approach" which defined the latter as a "strategy for the integrated management of land, water and living resources that promotes conservation and sustainable use in an equitable way" [478]. The COP also specified the principles governing its application. As a result, the principle was disseminated in many regimes aimed at fisheries management and biodiversity conservation, and even in the Global Environmental Facility (GEF),

---

476. Article II.
477. Recommendation 3.3: Wise Use of Wetlands (1987). G. Futhazar, *L'évolution du droit international de l'environnement en Méditerranée : quelle influence de l'IPBES?* (n. 475), p. 371. D. Farrier and L. Tucker, "Wise Use of Wetlands under the Ramsar Convention: A Challenge for Meaningful Implementation of International Law", *Journal of Environmental Law*, Vol. 1, No. 1, 2000, p. 26; N. Davidson and D. Coates, "The Ramsar Convention and Synergies for Operationalizing the Convention on Biological Diversity's Ecosystem Approach for Wetlands Conservation and Wise Use", *Journal of International Wildlife Law and Policy*, Vol. 14, No. 3, 2011, pp. 199-205.
478. Decision CBD V/6 (2000), *Ecosystem Approach*; Decision CBD VII/11 (2004), *Ecosystem Approach*.

which has made it a crucial element of its funding strategies [479]. Very recently, the UN General Assembly itself referred to it, "[s]tressing the importance of the ecosystem approach for the integrated management of land, water and living resources" [480]. However, the implementation of this approach remains difficult, with many obstacles to overcome [481].

2) *Targeted approaches*

274. Some instruments focus on particular species or areas that enjoy specific protection, either exclusively or in addition to a more general approach.

a) *Specific species*

275. The protection of certain species [482] often relates to threatened species. Such a choice is justified, but it is part of a reactive rather than preventive approach. The protection of specific species must therefore go beyond endangered species. In practice, in addition to the latter, treaties also focus on emblematic, aesthetic, rare, threatened, endemic, migratory, cultivated, exploited and even over-exploited species. The identification of species in need of enhanced protection has evolved considerably over time, as scientific knowledge has become more refined. From this point of view, there is a significant gap between the Paris Convention for the Protection of Birds Useful to Agriculture (1902) and the most recent conventions [483]. But such identification is also strongly influenced by human perceptions. It reflects the evolution that has led from the recognition of the usefulness of certain species (such as insectivorous birds, fur seals or whales) to that of their ecological or even intrinsic value.

276. The definition of categories, but also of what falls into these categories (which criteria, which species) is based, in part at least, on sometimes complex and often evolving scientific data. States need to

---

479. G. Futhazar, *L'évolution du droit international de l'environnement en Méditerranée : quelle influence de l'IPBES?* (n. 475), p. 375.
480. UGA, Resolution A/RES/73/284, *United Nations Decade on Ecosystem Restoration (2021-2030)*, 1 March 2019.
481. G. Futhazar, *L'évolution du droit international de l'environnement en Méditerranée : quelle influence de l'IPBES?* (n. 475), p. 377.
482. This is generally understood to mean "any species, sub species, or geographically separate population thereof" (Art. V, Maputo African Convention).
483. This 1902 Convention confers "absolute protection" on birds useful for agriculture, representing more than 150 species listed in Schedule I of the Convention – a list that may be added to by national laws.

rely on their scientific bodies or on external support to make informed decisions. That being said, the criteria used to determine which species should enjoy enhanced protection are not based solely on objective biological data, but rather on the interpretation of such data, and more broadly on general conceptions of the place and role of wildlife. In practice, the experts' data is scrutinised by political bodies, which do not automatically translate it into law.

277. Many instruments use the technique known as listing. They identify the species that should enjoy enhanced protection (positive listing) or, in order to avoid very long positive lists, the species that do not enjoy enhanced protection (negative listing). These lists must be revised regularly, depending on the inclusion of new States, scientific knowledge and the conservation status of species. This is why these lists are generally annexed to conventions: revision procedures are simpler than for the text of the convention itself, which is necessarily more rigid [484]. Once established, the definition of an international list restricts the States Parties' room for manoeuvre. Without seeking to be exhaustive, we will simply give a few examples of the way the issue is dealt with in various instruments from different eras and pursuing different objectives.

278. Within biological diversity, the Rio Convention on Biological Diversity focuses specifically on threatened species. Each Party must provide for their recovery and must "[d]evelop or maintain necessary legislation and/or other regulatory provisions for the protection of threatened species and populations", including through reintroduction into their natural habitat [485]. Aichi Target 12 provides that "[b]y 2020 the extinction of known threatened species has been prevented and their conservation status, particularly of those most in decline, has been improved and sustained". Kunming-Montreal Target 4 is even more accurate, stating that Parties should

> "[e]nsure urgent management actions to halt human induced extinction of known threatened species and for the recovery and conservation of species, in particular threatened species, to significantly reduce extinction risk, as well as to maintain and restore the genetic diversity within and between populations of native, wild and domesticated species to maintain their adaptive

---

484. C. de Klemm and C. Shine, *Biological Diversity Conservation and the Law*, IUCN, Environmental paper No. 19, Gland, 1993, p. 44.
485. Article 8.

potential, including through *in situ* and *ex situ* conservation and sustainable management practices, and effectively manage human-wildlife interactions to minimize human-wildlife conflict for coexistence" [486].

But the Convention does not contain a list. In reality, threatened species are not at the heart of the Convention, nor of the Convention's work, contrary to other global or regional conventions.

279. For example, CITES focuses on "all species threatened with extinction which are or may be affected by trade"; these species are listed in Appendix I [487]. Appendix II, on the other hand, includes "all species which although not necessarily now threatened with extinction may become so unless trade in specimens of such species is subject to strict regulation in order to avoid utilization incompatible with their survival" [488]. To adjust these lists, which are by definition bound to change, the COP of CITES first relies on the work of IUCN, whose regularly updated Red Lists are an authority on the subject and are regularly used in the context of international conventions to determine the conservation status of species [489]. But the COP also set up two committees in 1987: the Animals Committee and the Plants Committee. They undertake periodic reviews of the animal or plant species listed in the Appendices [490]. Proposals to amend the Appendices must in any case be supported by sound scientific data [491]. For some species, because of the economic stakes involved, such proposals can give rise to heated debate. Recent examples include rosewood, bluefin tuna, great whales, African elephants, rhinoceroses and pangolins. It should be noted that the lists defined by CITES enjoy a certain authority outside CITES, including in litigation proceedings. Thus, for example, the WTO Appellate Body referred to them in the *Shrimp-Turtle* case to determine the endangered status of the marine turtles in question. It stated the following:

---

486. Decision 15/4 (2022), *Kunming-Montreal Global Biodiversity Framework*, CBD/COP/DEC/15/4, 19 December 2022, para. 13.
487. Article II (1).
488. Article II (2).
489. See the dedicated IUCN website, https://www.iucnredlist.org, accessed on 25 October 2023.
490. Resolution CITES Conf. 14.8 (Rev. CoP17), *Periodic Review of Species Included in Appendices I and II*.
491. T. Deleuil, "La CITES et la protection internationale de la biodiversité", *Revue juridique de l'environnement*, 2011/5 (Special Issue), pp. 45-62.

"The exhaustibility of sea turtles would in fact have been very difficult to controvert since all of the seven recognised species of sea turtles are today listed in Appendix 1 of the Convention on International Trade in Endangered Species of Wild Fauna and Flora (CITES). The list in Appendix 1 includes 'all species threatened with extinction which are or may be affected by trade'." [492]

Similarly, in the South China Sea case, the Arbitral Tribunal stated:

"All of the sea turtles *(Cheloniidae)* found on board Chinese fishing vessels are listed under Appendix I to the CITES Convention as species threatened with extinction and subject to the strictest level of international controls on trade. CITES is the subject of nearly universal adherence, including by the Philippines and China, and in the Tribunal's view *forms part of the general corpus of international law that informs the content of Article 192 and 194 (5) of the Convention.*" [493]

280. The Convention on the Conservation of Migratory Species of Wild Animals distinguishes between endangered migratory species – listed in Appendix I – and migratory species whose conservation status is unfavourable and which require international agreements for their conservation and management – listed in Appendix II. A species is deemed "endangered" if it is "in danger of extinction throughout all or a significant portion of its range" [494]. The Convention reflects a desire to take into account the most advanced scientific knowledge when it specifies that "[a] migratory species may be listed in Appendix I provided that reliable evidence, including the best scientific evidence available, indicates that the species is endangered" [495]. Up until now, the Scientific Council of the Convention has also been guided by the work of IUCN, although there have been discussions on this issue. On the other hand, Appendix II to the Convention lists the species "to be the subject of Agreements", which are those

---

492. Report of the Appellate Body, *United States – Import Prohibition of Certain Shrimp and Shrimp Products*, AB-1998-4, WT/DS58/AB/R, para. 132, p. 50.
493. About the United Nations Convention on the Law of the Sea. See *PCA Case No. 2013-19 in the matter of the South China Sea Arbitration before an Arbitral Tribunal Constituted under Annex VII to the 1982 United Nations Convention on the Law of the Sea, between the Republic of the Philippines and the People's Republic of China*, Award of 12 July 2016, para. 956. Emphasis added.
494. Article I (1) *(e)*.
495. Article III (2).

"which have an unfavourable conservation status and which require international agreements for their conservation and management, as well as those which have a conservation status which would significantly benefit from the international co-operation that could be achieved by an international agreement".

There are four conditions for determining whether the conservation status of a species is favourable. If one of them is not met, the conservation status is deemed unfavourable:

"(1) population dynamics data indicate that the migratory species is maintaining itself on a long-term basis as a viable component of its ecosystems;

(2) the range of the migratory species is neither currently being reduced, nor is likely to be reduced, on a long-term basis;

(3) there is, and will be in the foreseeable future, sufficient habitat to maintain the population of the migratory species on a long-term basis; and

(4) the distribution and abundance of the migratory species approach historic coverage and levels to the extent that potentially suitable ecosystems exist and to the extent consistent with wise wildlife management." [496]

281. In keeping with this provision, the Agreement on the Conservation of African-Eurasian Migratory Waterbirds, in its Article III.1, requires Parties to take measures to conserve migratory waterbirds, "giving special attention to endangered species as well as to those with an unfavourable conservation status". The action plan, which is appended to the Agreement and as such has a binding effect, identifies in its Table 1 the species that should benefit from special measures across the Agreement area or for some of their populations only. Populations listed in column A of the table are referred to as "priority species", which means that Parties give them priority, where appropriate, in their implementation of the Agreement. A classification by columns and numbers actually makes it possible to differentiate six categories of migratory bird populations according to their conservation status [497]. The Agreement thus goes a long way towards differentiation, which is explained by the fact that scientists played a very important role in its design.

---

496. Article I (1) *(c)*.
497. See this table in Annex 3 of the Agreement.

282. At the regional level, the Maputo African Convention on the Conservation of Nature and Natural Resources (Revised Version) defines the notion of "threatened species" as follows:

> "Any species of fauna or flora which is considered critically endangered, endangered, or vulnerable, for which definitions are contained in Annex 1 to this Convention, and for which criteria may be adopted and from time to time reviewed by the Conference of the Parties, taking into consideration the work of competent international organisations in this field." [498]

From "Vulnerable" to "Critically Endangered" to "Endangered", Annex 1 distinguishes three categories of threatened species according to whether the risk of extinction is high, very high or extremely high. The COP of this Convention, which has just come into force, will therefore have to adopt criteria to define the boundaries of these categories. These criteria will be subject to evolution, as it is provided that the COP will be able to revise them "from time to time". The Convention also reflects a desire to streamline efforts and ensure coherence as it provides that the COP may take into consideration "the work of competent international organisations in this field". Here as well, the work of IUCN comes to mind. This work is evidently widely used by treaty institutions as a basis for their classifications and lists, even if they are adapted to the purpose of each convention. This has the advantage of allowing the *de facto* harmonisation of categories between conventions, since most of them rely on the same method [499].

283. The first identified threat to wildlife was over-exploitation through hunting, fishing and trade. At first, protection methods therefore consisted in prohibiting or limiting the taking of threatened, rare or vulnerable species and regulating the taking of other species, without concern for the preservation of their habitats. However, when the combined effect of over-exploitation and the accelerated destruction of habitats became very worrying, nature conservation methods turned to the protection of specific areas: the habitats of wild fauna and flora.

---

498. Article V.
499. Report of the Fifth Meeting of the Scientific Council, Nairobi, Kenya, 4-5 June 1994, Convention on the Conservation of Migratory Species of Wild Animals, *Proceedings of the Fourth Meeting of the Conference of the Parties, Nairobi, Kenya*, 7-11 June 1994, UNEP/CMS/Conf.4.16, p. 121.

b) *Specific areas*

284. The establishment of protected areas has been identified as a necessary – but not sufficient – condition for sustaining wildlife.

- *Protected areas*

285. A protected area is a defined area that enjoys a legal protection regime and is managed with the aim of conserving fauna, flora and/or biodiversity. The term covers a variety of institutions with very different degrees of protection [500].

286. Many international instruments thus lay down an obligation to protect certain sites that provide the necessary living conditions for a species or group of species, or representative of a particular ecosystem. They further specify the obligations relating to their designation. Thus, the wish of the signatories of the Washington Convention of 12 October 1940 on Nature Protection and Wild Life Preservation in the Western Hemisphere was to

> "protect and preserve in their natural habitat representatives of all species and genera of their native flora and fauna, including migratory birds, in sufficient numbers and over areas extensive enough to assure them from becoming extinct through any agency within man's control" [501].

To this end, the Convention requires States Parties to establish "national parks", "national reserves", "nature monuments", "wilderness reserves" [502]. In the same vein, the Bern Convention (1979) purports to "conserve wild flora and fauna and their natural habitats, especially those species and habitats whose conservation requires the co-operation of several States, and to promote such co-operation" [503]. In this regard, "[p]articular emphasis is given to endangered and vulnerable species, including endangered and vulnerable migratory species" [504]. They must ensure the protection of the habitats of wild species of flora and fauna, "especially those specified in the Appendices I and II, and the conservation of endangered natural habitats" [505]. The same applies to the

---

500. For an overview of the issue, the theory and practice of protected areas, the existing categories and the related legal regimes, see C. de Klemm and C. Shine, *Biological Diversity Conservation and the Law* (n. 484) pp. 165-228.
501. Preamble.
502. Article II.
503. Article 1.
504. Article 3.
505. Article 4.

Convention on the Conservation of Migratory Species of Wild Animals (1979), which provides for the protection of the habitats of migratory species, which are defined as "any area in the range of a migratory species which contains suitable living conditions for that species" [506].

287. The Convention concerning the Protection of the World Cultural and Natural Heritage goes further by including in its definition of World Heritage the natural heritage defined as follows:

– natural features consisting of physical and biological formations or groups of such formations, which are of outstanding universal value from the aesthetic or scientific point of view;
– geological and physiographical formations and precisely delineated areas which constitute the habitat of threatened species of animals and plants of outstanding universal value from the point of view of science or conservation;
– natural sites or precisely delineated natural areas of outstanding universal value from the point of view of science, conservation or natural beauty [507].

288. This definition means that the Convention only has a limited impact on the protection of natural heritage, since it only concerns natural sites of outstanding universal value, defined as "cultural and/or natural significance which is so exceptional as to transcend national boundaries and to be of common importance for present and future generations of all humanity" [508]. Indeed, out of a total of 1,199 properties, the list contains 227 natural sites and 39 "mixed" natural and cultural sites, which is not much on a global scale [509]. The Committee has gradually clarified the criteria for inclusion of the World Heritage List, to the point of including the protection of biological diversity [510]. Thus, designated properties may "be outstanding examples representing significant on-going ecological and biological processes in the evolution and development of terrestrial, fresh water, coastal and marine ecosystems and communities of plants and animals" or "contain the most important

---

506. Article I.
507. Article 2.
508. Intergovernmental Committee for the Protection of the World Cultural and Natural Heritage, UNESCO, *Operational Guidelines for the Implementation of the World Heritage Convention*, 2017, para. 45.
509. As of 18 December 2023.
510. See Intergovernmental Committee for the Protection of the World Cultural and Natural Heritage, UNESCO, *Operational Guidelines for the Implementation of the World Heritage Convention,* 2017, para. 77 *et seq.* IUCN, through its international network of specialists, provides important support to the Committee in this selection.

and significant natural habitats for *in situ* conservation of biological diversity, including those containing threatened species of Outstanding Universal Value from the point of view of science or conservation" [511]. A second list is maintained, of properties in danger, at the instigation of the Committee for the Protection of the World Heritage [512]. A natural property may appear on this list for several reasons. It can be considered in "potential danger" if "[t]he property is faced with major threats which could have deleterious effects on its inherent characteristics", such as a modification of the legal protective status of the area; planned resettlement or development projects within the property or so situated that the impacts threaten the property; outbreak or threat of armed conflict, etc. A natural property can be considered in "ascertained danger" if it "is faced with specific and proven imminent danger", such as a serious decline in the population of the endangered species or the other species of "Outstanding Universal Value" for which the property was legally established to protect, either by natural factors such as disease or by human-made factors such as poaching, severe deterioration of the natural beauty or scientific value of the property, as by human settlement, construction of reservoirs which flood important parts of the property, industrial and agricultural development including use of pesticides and fertilizers, major public works, mining, pollution, logging, firewood collection, etc.

289. The Convention on Wetlands of International Importance (Ramsar, 1971) focuses exclusively on wetlands because of their "fundamental ecological functions . . . as regulations of water regimes and as habitats supporting a characteristic flora and fauna, especially waterfowl". It goes beyond the protection of the habitat of a particular species and focuses on a certain category of ecosystems. When joining the Ramsar Convention, States must include at least one site in the List of Wetlands of International Importance. However, there is no obligation in the Convention to include all sites of international importance. Afterwards, States can add new wetlands or extend the area of those already included in the list [513]. They must indicate the precise boundaries of the site [514], its size in hectares, its geographical location and attach a map and description of the area.

---

511. *Ibid.*, para. 77.
512. See paras. 179-180 of the aforementioned *Operational Guidelines*.
513. Article 2.5.
514. Article 2.1

290. The Convention specifies that, for the purpose of its implementation, wetlands "are areas of marsh, fen, peatland or water, whether natural or artificial, permanent or temporary, with water that is static or flowing, fresh, brackish or salt, including areas of marine water the depth of which at low tide does not exceed six metres"[515]. They "may incorporate riparian and coastal zones adjacent to the wetlands, and islands or bodies of marine water deeper than six metres at low tide lying within the wetlands, especially where these have importance as waterfowl habitat"[516]. The Convention adds that "[w]etlands should be elected for the List on account of their international significance in terms of ecology, botany, zoology, limnology or hydrology. In the first instance wetlands of international importance to waterfowl at any season should be included"[517].

291. In 1974, even before the Convention came into force, a conference of experts endeavoured to specify the criteria for selecting wetlands "of international importance" and the first Conference of the Parties, held in Italy in 1980, adopted the *Criteria for Identifying Wetlands of International Importance*[518]. These criteria are both quantitative and qualitative. Thus, a wetland should be considered internationally important if it regularly supports 1 per cent of the individuals in a population of one species or sub-species of waterbird. In addition, it has been accepted that a wetland should be considered internationally important if it regularly supports 20,000 or more waterbirds. Other criteria concern fish "a significant proportion of indigenous fish subspecies, species or families, life-history stages, species interactions and/or populations that are representative of wetland benefits and/or values and thereby contributes to global biological diversity" or are even more general "A wetland should be considered internationally important if it supports vulnerable, endangered, or critically endangered species or threatened ecological communities"[519].

292. The Bureau of the Convention has a right to review the sites listed. It controls the designation and checks that sites actually meet

---

515. Article 1.1.
516. Article 2.1.
517. Article 2.2.
518. The Ramsar Sites Criteria, *The Nine Criteria for Identifying Wetlands of International Importance*, https://www.ramsar.org/sites/default/files/documents/library/ramsarsites_criteria_eng.pdf, accessed on 28 October 2023.
519. *Ibid.*

the criteria [520]. States Parties have included 2,433 wetlands in the Convention's register, varying in size but representing over 254,000 hectares, and representative of the diversity of these environments.

293. As for the Rio Convention on Biological Diversity, it focuses on the *in situ* conservation of biological diversity, the latter being defined as "variability among living organisms from all sources including, *inter alia*, terrestrial, marine and other aquatic ecosystems and the ecological complexes of which they are part: this includes diversity within species, between species and of ecosystems" [521]. In particular, the Parties must "establish a system of protected areas or areas where special measures need to be taken to conserve biological diversity" [522]. Once again, the goal is not to protect the habitat of a particular species, but to conserve a diversity of ecosystems, the latter referring to the basic ecological units formed by the environment (known as the biotope) and the organisms living there (known as the biocoenosis) [523]. The Parties have set themselves a quantified objective here, since Aichi Target 11 provides as follows:

> "By 2020, at least 17 per cent of terrestrial and inland water areas, and 10 per cent of coastal and marine areas, especially areas of particular importance for biodiversity and ecosystem services, are conserved through effectively and equitably managed, ecologically representative and well connected systems of protected areas and other effective area-based conservation measures, and integrated into the wider landscapes and seascapes." [524]

The Kunming-Montreal new target has been carefully negotiated. Setting a more ambitious percentage and recognising the rights of indigenous peoples and local communities, it states:

> "Ensure and enable that *by 2030 at least 30 per cent* of terrestrial and inland water areas, and of marine and coastal areas, especially areas of particular importance for biodiversity and ecosystem functions and services, are effectively conserved and managed through ecologically representative, well-connected and

---

520. Ramsar Fifth COP, Resolution 5.4: The record of Ramsar Sites where changes in ecological character have occurred, are occurring, or are likely to occur ("Montreux Record").
521. Article 2.
522. Article 8.
523. Article 3.
524. CBD, Decision X/2 (2010), *The Strategic Plan for Biodiversity 2011-2020 and the Aichi Biodiversity Targets*, UNEP/CBD/COP/DEC/X/2 (2010), p. 117.

equitably governed systems of protected areas and other effective area-based conservation measures, recognizing indigenous and traditional territories, where applicable, and integrated into wider landscapes, seascapes and the ocean, while ensuring that any sustainable use, where appropriate in such areas, is fully consistent with conservation outcomes, recognizing and respecting the rights of indigenous peoples and local communities, including over their traditional territories." [525]

Here, as in many other matters, the Convention on Biological Diversity needs the support of other international biodiversity conventions that have more specific and concrete provisions.

294. As is the case for protected species, there is a progressive convergence of the criteria for protected areas, as evidenced by this decision of the COP to the Convention on Biological Diversity, which calls on the Parties to consider

"standard criteria for the identification of sites of global biodiversity conservation significance, when developing protected-area systems drawing on the IUCN Red List of Threatened Species, established criteria in other relevant processes including those of the UNESCO Man and Biosphere Programme, the World Heritage Convention, the Ramsar Convention on Wetlands, threatened ecosystem assessments, gap analysis, Key Biodiversity Areas and Important Bird Areas, and other relevant information" [526].

- *Buffer zones*

295. The definition of protected areas was a first step towards biodiversity protection. Scientists recommended to go beyond this by establishing so-called "buffer" zones. Because protected areas are sensitive to the effects of activities outside their perimeter, it is useful to define buffer zones, which are adjacent to the protected areas and subject to a less stringent protection regime, but nevertheless subject to the regulation and control of activities that could cause damage to the protected areas themselves. It is therefore a complementary technique to the establishment of protected areas, which contributes to the achievement of the latter's objectives.

---

525. Decision 15/4 (2022), *Kunming-Montreal Global Biodiversity Framework*, CBD/COP/DEC/15/4, 19 December 2022. Emphasis added.
526. CBD, X/31 (2010), *Protected Areas*.

296. The creation of "buffer" zones around nature reserves was contemplated as early as 1933 by the London Convention. It was then mentioned in most instruments aimed at protecting habitats, whether the establishment of these zones was encouraged or mandatory. For example, Article 8 *(e)* of the Rio Convention now encourages their establishment on a global scale, requiring the Parties "as far as possible and as appropriate" to "promote environmentally sound and sustainable development in areas adjacent to protected areas with a view to furthering protection of these areas". By way of example, buffer zones are one of the key features of the UNESCO World Network of Biosphere Reserve. In theory, the core protected areas of these reserves should be surrounded by precisely defined buffer zones where research, education, tourism and recreation activities can be carried out, as long as this does not affect the core areas. In addition, there is a transition area to allow for the wise use of the region's resources.

- *Ecological corridors*

297. The protection of ecological corridors pursues the same objective of strengthening of the effectiveness of protected areas. The fragmentation of landscapes due to the development of road and rail links results in compartmentalisation, and animal populations find themselves confined to small areas that are not connected to each other. This can compromise the survival of these populations and disrupt their genetic adaptability. The protection of ecological corridors makes it possible to protect species whose conservation cannot be guaranteed by the creation of protected areas alone. Even though it is well known to biologists, this concept was only recently expressed in legal terms. As explained by C. de Klemm, the dispersal capacity of species is of considerable importance as wild populations of animals and plants are becoming increasingly fragmented because of economic development. A fragmented population (referred to as a metapopulation by biologists) can only survive if genetic exchange between its different fragments is maintained and if inevitable local extinctions are compensated by recolonisation from the surviving populations. It is therefore essential to maintain the dispersal capacity of living organisms through continuous ecological corridors or links formed by protected natural elements (such as ponds or small wooded areas) as close together as necessary [527].

---

527. C. de Klemm, "Des 'Red Data Books' à la diversité biologique", in *A Law for the Environment*, IUCN, Gland, 1994, p. 177.

298. In the light of the progress of scientific knowledge, general conservation obligations laid down in a series of instruments can be interpreted as requiring the adoption of such measures. This is especially important as most instruments do not mention ecological corridors. Several treaties adopt a functional approach to conservation, particularly that of migratory species, which underlies the protection of ecological corridors. Some agreements explicitly refer to them, such as the Cooperative Agreement for the Conservation of Sea Turtles of the Caribbean Coast of Costa Rica, Nicaragua and Panama (8 May 1998) as regards the Mesoamerican migration corridor, or the Alpine Convention [528].

299. As for the Convention on Biological Diversity, Article 8 speaks of a "system of protected areas or areas where special measures need to be taken to conserve biological diversity", the notion of "system" referring to a functional approach. It also provides that each Party must "regulate or manage biological resources important for the conservation of biological diversity whether within or outside protected areas, with a view to ensuring their conservation and sustainable use" [529]. Although this provision is vague, it has been clarified by various COP decisions, promoting in particular the integration of protected areas as "the process of ensuring that the design and management of protected areas, corridors and the surrounding matrix fosters a connected, functional ecological network", specifying that it is a question of "integration of the values, impacts and dependencies of the biodiversity and ecosystem functions and services provided by protected areas into key sectors, such as agriculture, fisheries, forestry, mining, energy, tourism, transportation, education and health" [530].

300. Having attempted to discern what is protected by the international law on biodiversity, we will now discuss what such protection entails.

Section 2. The substance of protection measures

301. Biodiversity conservation policies, activities and instruments pursue various goals. Building on core general prevention obligations, they include the protection of species against exploitation, the protection of the environment itself and *ex situ* conservation.

---

528. Articles 11 and 12.
529. Article 8 *(c)*.
530. CBD, Decision 14/8 (2018), *Protected Areas and Other Effective Area-Based Conservation Measures*.

1) General prevention obligations

302. The general prevention obligations mentioned in the previous chapter provide a foundation for the development of more specific obligations. Stemming from both customary and treaty law, the obligation to take all appropriate measures to prevent damage to the environment in general, and to biodiversity in particular, extends to the obligation to follow a precautionary approach.

a) *The obligation to take all appropriate measure to prevent damage*

303. These are broad and exacting positive obligations. Legal scholars have long referred to an obligation not to cause/to prevent damage to the environment of other States, known as the *no harm rule*. In reality, the obligation of prevention is more an obligation of means than of result. The International Law Commission (ILC) stated in its *Draft Articles on Responsibility of States for Internationally Wrongful Acts (2001)*, that "[o]bligations of prevention are usually construed as best efforts obligations, requiring States to take all reasonable or necessary measures to prevent a given event from occurring, but *without warranting that the event will not occur*" [531].

304. According to the International Court of Justice, "[a] State is thus obliged to use all the means at its disposal in order to avoid activities which take place in its territory, or in any area under its jurisdiction, causing significant damage to the environment of another State" [532]. It is therefore not a vague obligation to abstain or to keep a distant watch, but rather an obligation to take appropriate, effective measures to avoid causing significant harm to the environment. The International Tribunal for the Law of the Sea, in its 2011 opinion, spoke similarly of "an obligation to deploy adequate means, to exercise best possible efforts, to do the utmost, to obtain this result" [533]. Relying on the case law of the ICJ, the Seabed Disputes Chamber made the following, very exacting statement:

> "It is an obligation which entails not only the adoption of appropriate rules and measures, but also a certain level of vigilance in their enforcement and the exercise of administrative control

---

[531]. *Yearbook of the International Law Commission*, 2001, Vol. II, Part Two, emphasis added.
[532]. Judgment of 20 April 2010, aforementioned, para. 101.
[533]. *Responsibilities and Obligations of States with respect to Activities in the Area*, Advisory Opinion, 1 February 2011, ITLOS Reports 2011, aforementioned, para. 110.

applicable to public and private operators, such as the monitoring of activities undertaken by such operators."[534]

The International Tribunal for the Law of the Sea confirmed this in its 2015 opinion, even though it was dealing with illegal, unreported and unregulated fishing activities, which by definition are difficult to apprehend legally. However, even in this case, the "flag State is under an obligation to exercise *effectively* its jurisdiction and control in administrative matters over fishing vessels flying its flag"[535]. Furthermore, the flag State

> "has the obligation to include in them enforcement mechanisms to monitor and secure compliance with these laws and regulations. Sanctions applicable to involvement in IUU fishing activities must be *sufficient to deter violations and to deprive offenders of the benefits accruing from their IUU fishing activities*"[536].

305. Although it is rarely referred to in the international arena, such an obligation is fundamental to the international law on biodiversity. As a core obligation, it is combined with treaty obligations. Customary obligations of due diligence and treaty obligations are in fact sometimes so inextricably intertwined that it becomes difficult to determine in the reasoning of a judge – who sometimes deliberately keeps things vague – what falls under one and what falls under the other. For instance, in the case of the Pulp Mills on the River Uruguay, when the Court declared that a State is "obliged to use all the means at its disposal in order to avoid activities which take place in its territory, or in any area under its jurisdiction, causing significant damage to the environment of another State"[537], it elaborated on the customary obligation by referring to "significant transboundary harm", a new element in its case law. But here the treaty obligation – Article 7 of the Statute of the River Uruguay, which the Court was interpreting – refers to "significant" harm. Thus, the customary obligation and the treaty obligation are intertwined. The award on the South China Sea also perfectly reflects the catalysis, indeed perhaps the symbiosis, between the two. For example, the Arbitral Tribunal found that the content of Article 192 of the United Nations Convention on the Law of the Sea is

---

534. Judgment of 20 April 2010, aforementioned, para. 197.
535. ITLOS Advisory Opinion, 1 April 2015, aforementioned, para. 137, emphasis added.
536. *Ibid.*, para. 138, emphasis added.
537. Judgment of 20 April 2010, aforementioned, para. 101.

informed by other provisions of Part XII of the Convention, but also by other applicable rules of international law, and in particular the "duty to prevent, or at least 'mitigate' significant harm to the environment when pursuing large-scale construction activities" [538]. It also stated the following:

> "The general obligation to 'protect and preserve the marine environment' in Article 192 includes a due diligence obligation to prevent the harvesting of species that are recognized internationally as being at risk of extinction and requiring international protection." [539]

This obligation most likely applies beyond the marine environment.

306. In this respect, treaty obligations complement or even hybridise with customary obligations. This is the case in the Rio Convention when it states that each Party must "regulate or manage biological resources important for the conservation of biological diversity whether within or outside protected areas, with a view to ensuring their conservation and sustainable use" or "promote the protection of ecosystems, natural habitats and the maintenance of viable populations of species in natural surroundings" [540]. Regional or sector-specific conventions go further. For example, the Bern Convention on the Conservation of European Wildlife and Natural Habitats (1979) provides as follows:

> "Each Contracting Party shall take appropriate and necessary legislative and administrative measures to ensure the special protection of the wild fauna species specified in Appendix II. The following will in particular be prohibited for these species:
>
> *a)* all forms of deliberate capture and keeping and deliberate killing;
>
> *b)* the deliberate damage to or destruction of breeding or resting sites;
>
> *c)* the deliberate disturbance of wild fauna, particularly during the period of breeding, rearing and hibernation, insofar as

---

538. Award, aforementioned, para. 941. The Tribunal is inspired here by two previous arbitration awards. *Indus Waters Kishenganga Arbitration (Pakistan v. India)*, Partial Award, 18 February 2013, PCA Award Series (2014), para. 451, quoting *Arbitration regarding the Iron Rhine ("IJzeren Rijn") Railway between the Kingdom of Belgium and the Kingdom of the Netherlands*, Award of 24 May 2005, PCA Award Series (2007), RIAA Vol. XXVII p. 35, see pp. 66-67, para. 59.

539. Award, aforementioned, para. 956.

540. Article 8 *(c)* and *(d)*.

disturbance would be significant in relation to the objectives of this Convention;

d) the deliberate destruction or taking of eggs from the wild or keeping these eggs even if empty;

e) the possession of and internal trade in these animals, alive or dead, including stuffed animals and any readily recognizable part or derivative thereof, where this would contribute to the effectiveness of the provisions of this Article." [541]

307. Here, the treaty obligation – to take appropriate and necessary legislative and administrative measures – expands and clarifies the customary duty of care. Many other conventions contain similar provisions.

b) *The precautionary approach*

308. For some, precaution is quite different from prevention, the former being relevant in the context of uncertainty but in the case of "threats of serious or irreversible damage" [542], the latter applying in the context of a proven risk. For others, precaution is an extension of prevention, and as such is part of the duty of care. This was the reasoning of the Seabed Disputes Chamber of the International Tribunal for the Law of the Sea in 2011. Indeed, for the Chamber, "[i]t is appropriate to point out that the precautionary approach is also an integral part of the general obligation of due diligence of sponsoring States, which is applicable even outside the scope of the Regulations" [543]. The precautionary approach is part of due diligence, which is an obligation, therefore the precautionary approach is mandatory even outside the scope of the two regulations in question. Thus, "[t]he due diligence obligation of the sponsoring States requires them to take all appropriate measures to prevent damage that might result from the activities of contractors that they sponsor", including "in situations where scientific evidence concerning the scope and potential negative impact of the activity in question is insufficient but where there are plausible indications of potential risks" [544]. The Chamber drew concrete consequences from this and provided that States must implement this precautionary approach and anticipate even

---

541. Article 6.
542. Rio Declaration, aforementioned, Principle 15.
543. Advisory Opinion, aforementioned, para. 131.
544. *Ibid.*, para. 131.

uncertain risks: "[t]he sponsoring State has to take measures within the framework of its own legal system in order to oblige sponsored entities to adopt such an approach"[545]. If one accepts the premise of the ITLOS Chamber's reasoning, one can apply its conclusions outside the field of the marine environment and the very specific zone that is the Area. This is particularly true for biodiversity, and in particular for endangered species. Indeed, the extinction of a species is the archetype of irreversible – and therefore serious – damage. But a precautionary approach or precautionary measures must also be applied beyond that, where there is a threat of significant reduction or loss of biological diversity. Even if States were unable to agree on its inclusion in the Convention's operative provisions, the preamble to the Convention on Biological Diversity very clearly states that "where there is a threat of significant reduction or loss of biological diversity, lack of full scientific certainty should not be used as a reason for postponing measures to avoid or minimize such a threat". On many occasions, the COP has called on the Parties to adopt a precautionary approach, for example, in relation to the development of climate geoengineering[546] or, more recently, synthetic biology[547]. In addition to the Cartagena Protocol on Biosafety to the Convention on Biological Diversity, in which this principle takes on an operational dimension with regard to the regulation of international GMO trade, several conventions refer to the precautionary principle or approach in their provisions[548].

2) Protection against exploitation

309. The protection of species against exploitation concerns hunting and fishing activities as well as trade and transport.

a) *Hunting and fishing*

310. Regulating or banning hunting and fishing reduces the pressure on the species in question. It also has positive consequences for species

---

545. *Ibid.*, para. 134.
546. Decision COP XI/20 (2012), *Climate-Related Geoengineering*.
547. Decision COP 14/19 (2018), *Synthetic Biology*.
548. See, for instance, the 1992 Convention on the Protection of the Marine Environment of the Baltic Sea Area (Art. 3), the 2007 Agreement on the Conservation of Gorillas and their Habitats (Art. II), the Convention de 2003 sur la gestion durable du lac Tanaganyika (no English version) (Art. 5), the 2003 African Convention on the Conservation of Nature and Natural Resources (Revised Version) (Art. IV), the Charte de l'eau du Bassin du Niger de 2008 (no English version) (Art. 6). On the Cartagena Protocol, see below.

that are not hunted or fished but are disturbed by these activities, which may be rare or endangered species. This has long been a method used to protect biodiversity.

- *The guiding principle of rational use*

311. *Rational or sustainable use* is a guiding principle for regulating the taking of exploited species. Implicit in a number of treaties, explicitly stated in others, this principle is widely accepted as the basis for the legal rules applicable to the exploitation of renewable natural resources. However, these instruments simply lay down this principle, and in most cases, it is not easy to define in practical terms the levels of sustainable use, for lack of sufficiently precise information. Indeed, rational or sustainable use means that the taking of a species is adjusted so that the conservation status of such species remains favourable at all times or, if it is no longer favourable, so that it becomes so as soon as possible. Applying this principle requires the establishment of a mechanism to regularly assess whether the level of taking is compatible with the maintenance of the species' favourable conservation status and, if not, to take the necessary measures to limit the number of animals taken. But assessing what constitutes the maximum level of taking requires the annual national collection of very precise data, for each such species, on mortality rates due to natural causes or caused by the taking of such species, reproductive rates, etc., and then the consolidation of such data at the international level. For most species, this information is still lacking and fragmented [549]. A whole range of measures can then be taken to ensure that the maximum level of taking is not exceeded. Some of them are empirical, i.e. they simply aim to limit such taking. Others, more specific, establish a rationing of the resource by defining an individual or global cap on the number of authorised catches.

312. The first bilateral treaties on migratory birds already referred to rational use. For example, the 1936 Convention between the United States and Mexico for the Protection of Migratory Birds and Game Mammals contains a reference to this principle in its preamble: ". . . it is necessary to employ adequate measures which will permit a rational utilization of migratory birds for the purposes of sport as well as for food, commerce and industry". Similarly, Article VII of the

---

549. See "Wise Use of Waterfowl Populations", J. H. Mooij *et al.*, in *Convention on Wetlands of International Importance Especially as Waterfowl Habitat, Proceedings of the Fifth Meeting of the Conference of the Contracting Parties Kushiro*, Japan, 9-16 June 1993, p. 177 *et seq.*

1940 Convention on Nature Protection and Wild Life Preservation in the Western Hemisphere provides as follows:

> "Adequate measures shall be adopted which will permit, in so far as the respective governments may see fit, a rational utilization of migratory birds for the purpose of sports as well as for food, commerce, and industry, and for scientific study and investigation."

Later on, rational use was referred to as a "fundamental principle", and set out in Article II of the 1968 African Convention on the Conservation of Nature and Natural Resources as follows: "The Contracting States shall undertake to adopt the measures to ensure conservation, utilization and development of soil, water, flora and faunal resources in accordance with scientific principles and with due regard to the best interests of the people" [550]. According to Article II of the Canberra Convention, the term "conservation" includes the notion of rational use, specified for species as the principle of "prevention of decrease in the size of any harvested population to levels below those which ensure its stable recruitment. For this purpose, its size should not be allowed to fall below a level close to that which ensures the greatest net annual increment . . .". The Protocol concerning Protected Areas and Wild Fauna and Flora in the Eastern African Region provides that any exploitation shall be regulated so as to restore and maintain populations at optimum levels. Article 2 of the Bern Convention provides as follows:

> "The Contracting Parties shall take requisite measures to maintain the population of wild flora and fauna at, or adapt it to, a level which corresponds in particular to ecological scientific and cultural requirements, while taking account of economic and recreational requirements and the needs of sub-species, varieties or forms at risk locally."

This ambiguous provision seems to view economic and recreational requirements as a less important consideration than the maintenance of populations [551]. In addition, the Bern Convention does not specify

---

550. Furthermore, Article VII of the Convention requires States to "manage wildlife populations inside designated areas according to the objectives of such areas and also manage exploitable wildlife populations outside such areas for an optimum sustained yield compatible with the complementary to other land uses". It adds that "with a view to as rational use as possible of game meat, the abandonment by hunters of carcasses of animals, which represent a food resource, is prohibited".

551. This is the analysis of S. Lyster who notes that it would have been easy to put ecological requirements on the same level as economic and recreational requirements.

what is meant by "economic and recreational requirements". On the other hand, although the principle of sustainable use is not explicitly mentioned in the Bonn Convention, the Agreement on the Conservation of African-Eurasian Migratory Waterbirds refers to it several times. In its preamble, the Parties express their belief "that any taking of migratory waterbirds must be conducted on a sustainable basis, taking into account the conservation status of the species concerned over their entire range as well as their biological characteristics". According to Article III, the Parties must "ensure that any use of migratory waterbirds is based on an assessment of the best available knowledge of their ecology and is sustainable for the species as well as for the ecological systems that support them". The action plan provides that the Parties must co-operate on hunting to ensure that their legislation implements the principle of sustainable use, taking into account the full geographical range of the waterbird populations concerned and their life history characteristics [552]. Parties must endeavour to undertake studies on the impact of hunting and trade on the populations listed in Table 1 and on the importance of these forms of "utilization" for the local and national economy [553].

313. Lastly, on a global level, Article 2 of the Convention on Biological Diversity defines sustainable use as "the use of components of biological diversity in a way and at a rate that does not lead to the long-term decline of biological diversity, thereby maintaining its potential to meet the needs and aspirations of present and future generations". It requires the Parties "as far as possible and as appropriate" to promote the maintenance of viable populations of species in their natural environment [554], to "endeavour to provide the conditions needed for compatibility between present uses and the conservation of biological diversity and the sustainable use of its components" [555]. Also "as far as possible and as appropriate", the Parties must "regulate or manage biological resources important for the conservation of biological diversity whether within or outside protected areas, with a view to ensuring their conservation and sustainable use" [556].

See S. Lyster, *International wildlife law. An Analysis of International Treaties concerned with the Conservation of Wildlife,* 1st ed. 1985, CUP, 2012, p. 68.
552. Para. 4 (1) (1) of the Action Plan.
553. Para. 5 (6) of the Action Plan.
554. Article 8 *(d)*.
555. Article 8 *(i)*.
556. Article 8 *(c)*.

- *Hunting regulations*

314. Many treaties regulate hunting, understood broadly here as the search for, pursuit of and capture or killing of animals living in the wild [557], but excluding the capture for scientific purposes, which is dealt with separately in treaties. International law has influenced most aspects covered by domestic hunting regulations. It therefore leads or should lead to significant restrictions on hunting activities for game species, in particular birds, whales, fur seals and polar bears.

– *Prohibitions*

315. Some treaties prohibit hunting altogether, sometimes even all taking. This is the case with the Polar Bear Agreement (1973), which in theory prohibits the "hunting, killing and capturing" of polar bears, although it does make exceptions, for example, for aboriginal hunting. The Convention for the Conservation of Antarctic Seals prohibits any killing or capture of the populations of the six species listed in its Article 1 [558]. In the same spirit, a moratorium on the commercial hunting of all whale populations was decided by the International Whaling Commission (IWC) in 1982 and came into force in 1986. This moratorium was challenged by several "whaling" countries. Norway filed an objection. Iceland did not object but withdrew from the IWC in 1992. It rejoined in 2002 with a retroactive objection to the moratorium and resumed its whaling programme in 2006. Japan filed an objection, and then withdrew it. After the ICJ ruling on 31 March 2014 [559], in which the Court ordered Japan to revoke all permits to kill, capture or process whales under its programme, and to refrain from granting new ones, Japan continued its scientific programme and eventually decided to withdraw from the Whaling Convention to get out of the moratorium.

– *Identifying game species*

316. International instruments may also identify huntable species using the listing technique, whether positive (list of all huntable

---

557. F. Colas-Belcour and J. Guilbaud, *La chasse et le droit,* Litec, Paris, 1999, 15th ed., p. 7.
558. Article 2.
559. *Whaling in the Antarctic (Australia v. Japan: New Zealand intervening),* Judgment, *ICJ Reports 2014*, p. 226.

species) or negative (list of protected species that may not be hunted). For example, the Bern Convention on the Conservation of European Wildlife and Natural Habitats (1979) distinguishes between strictly protected fauna species (listed in Appendix II), for which "all forms of deliberate capture and keeping and deliberate killing" are prohibited, and protected fauna species (Appendix III). For the latter, exploitation is possible, but "shall be regulated in order to keep the populations out of danger" by measures that shall include "the temporary or local prohibition of exploitation, as appropriate, in order to restore satisfactory population levels"[560].

– *Defining hunting seasons*

317. International law also deals with hunting seasons. The establishment of annual hunting seasons has long been a method of protecting game during the times of the year when it is most vulnerable. For instance, in the case of birds, spring hunting should be prohibited because it affects potential breeding birds. In Europe, from April to June, most species build their nests, lay their eggs and raise their young. However, for some species, this breeding and dependency phase starts earlier, in February or March, and/or continues later, until July or August, sometimes even September. In addition, there is the special case of migratory species which must also be protected during their return journey to their breeding grounds, a period when harvesting directly affects the breeding population after all the winter losses, therefore at a time when winter compensatory mechanisms no longer come into play. Some of these species form pairs and return to their nesting grounds in February and March.

318. Establishing opening and closing dates for hunting can have a significant impact on bird populations. Cooperation is particularly important in this area, at least for migratory species, since the strict legislation of one State may not have the desired effect if other range States adopt very different dates. International law seeks to promote the harmonisation of legislation. However, it faces many difficulties in this area, amid scientific controversy. The variability of behaviour between species, within a species, within the same year and from one year to the next, often makes it difficult to determine the exact timing of the hunting season.

---

560. Article 7.

319. International instruments sometimes simply encourage co-operation in this area. For example, Article 2 of the Benelux Convention on the Hunting and Protection of Birds (1970) provides that the Parties shall consult each other regarding the opening and closing dates of the hunting season. Instruments may also indicate the criteria according to which the hunting season is to be determined each year. This is the case in the bilateral treaties between Japan and the United States, Japan and the USSR, and Japan and Australia. For example, Article 2 (2) of the USSR-Japan Treaty provides that each Party shall determine hunting seasons on its territory by taking into account the breeding period of migratory birds during their annual cycle. The United States-USSR Convention provides that the hunting season shall be determined so as to allow the preservation and maintenance of stocks of migratory bird populations. Similarly, the Bern Convention is not very precise with regard to hunting seasons. Among the legislative and administrative measures to be taken to protect the fauna species listed in Appendix III (exploitable species), it requires "closed seasons and/or other procedures regulating the exploitation" without specifying the extent of the closed season or any conditions to which it must conform (Art. 7 (3) *(a)*). Disturbance during the breeding or rearing period is only prohibited for strictly protected fauna species (Appendix II), but not for protected fauna species (Appendix III). The Parties must however ensure that the closed seasons "are adequate and approximately disposed to meet the requirements of the migratory species specified in Appendix III"[561]. Should this provision be understood as prohibiting the hunting of these species during their return journey to their breeding grounds? The Convention is rather vague on this point. This open-ended provision therefore leaves the determination of the hunting season to the States' discretion.

320. Other instruments set dates or durations. For example, the Paris Convention for the Protection of Birds Useful to Agriculture (1902) imposes, from 1 March to 15 September each year, a ban on the taking and killing of the "useful" birds listed in the schedule to the Convention[562]. It therefore authorises the late closing of the waterfowl hunting season. In addition, an important concession was made to the countries of Northern Europe, which are – in very vague terms – authorised to modify the duration of the ban. The 1916 Convention

---

561. Article 10 (2).
562. To reinforce the ban, the sale and offering for sale is also prohibited during this period, as well as the entry, delivery and transport of these birds.

signed by Canada and the United States is more restrictive, stipulating that the hunting season may not exceed three and a half months for migratory game birds [563]. As for the 1936 Convention between the US and Mexico, it provides for a maximum hunting season of four months and specifies that the hunting of wild ducks is prohibited from 10 March to 1 September.

321. Although it was adopted in 1950, the International Convention for the Protection of Birds was relatively strict for that time in determining the hunting season. Indeed, it prohibits the exploitation of birds at least during their breeding season. For migratory birds, protection must also cover the period of "their return flight to their nesting ground, particularly in March, April, May, June and July". This "particularly" does not preclude, quite the contrary, the prohibition of hunting in February or August. This provision was widely opposed among the signatory States and stopped several of them from ratifying this convention [564].

322. The Agreement on the Conservation of African-Eurasian Migratory Waterbirds prohibits in its action plan the taking of game birds "during their various stages of reproduction and rearing and during their return to their breeding grounds if the taking has an unfavourable impact on the conservation status of the population concerned" [565]. Compared to the 1950 Convention, it also includes the rearing period of young birds. However, unlike the 1950 Convention, it introduces an element of relativity in the last part of the provision. This leaves much discretion to States, especially as it does not specify a date.

– *Specifying the means of hunting*

323. As for the means of hunting, international regulations primarily seek to prohibit massive and non-selective methods of capture and killing, which are likely to excessively disrupt hunting balances. Moreover, their non-selective nature can lead to the destruction of protected species. Here as well, international instruments come up against certain hunting traditions.

---

563. Article II.
564. In France especially. See M. Heuvet, *Rapport fait au nom de la Commission de la production et des échanges sur le projet de loi (n° 942) autorisant l'approbation de la convention internationale pour la protection des oiseaux*, Paris, 18 octobre 1950, Doc. AN No. 999, 2ᵉ session ordinaire, 1963-1964.
565. Para. 2 (1) (2) *(a)* of the Action Plan.

324. Thus, the Bern Convention prohibits in its Article 8 "the use of all indiscriminate means of capture and killing and the use of all means capable of causing local disappearance of, or serious disturbance to populations of a species, and in particular, the means specified in Appendix IV". For birds, Appendix IV prohibits in particular limes, hooks, live birds used as decoys which are blind or mutilated, tape recorders, electrical devices capable of killing and stunning, artificial light sources, mirrors and other dazzling devices, devices for illuminating targets, lighting devices for night shooting comprising an electronic image, magnifier or image converter, explosives, nets, traps, poison and poisoned or anaesthetic bait, semi-automatic or automatic weapons with a magazine capable of holding more than two rounds of ammunition, aircraft, motor vehicles in motion, etc. These means and methods are prohibited only for Appendix III species (protected but exploitable species) and for Appendix II species (strictly protected species), however, for the latter there may be exceptions as authorised by Article 9. Only the eleven species that are not listed in either Appendix II or Appendix III may be destroyed by these means. Thus, traditional hunting of ortolans, thrushes and larks is prohibited [566].

325. Another example is the 1932 arrangement between Denmark and Sweden, which prohibits the use of nets to catch seabirds in its Article 2. It goes on to prohibit the use of rifles of a calibre greater than twelve and automatic shotguns for hunting [567]. It also prohibits hunting with motorboats and other mechanically propelled boats in certain places and at certain times of the year [568]. Finally, it prohibits the use of punt guns [569].

326. Multilateral instruments also include the 1950 International Convention for the Protection of Birds, which provides for the prohibition of means of hunting "of such a nature as to result in the mass killing or capture of birds or to cause them unnecessary suffering". A fairly comprehensive list of such means is set out in Article 5. It includes, for example, snares, lime twigs, traps, hooks, nets, poisoned bait, stupefying agents, blinded decoy-birds, decoy-ponds with nets, mirrors, torches, and other artificial lights, fishing nets or tackle for the capture of aquatic birds, magazine or automatic sporting-guns holding

---

[566]. R. Romi, "Convention-révolution ou convention inutile? Premières réflexions sur les conséquences de l'introduction dans le droit interne de la convention de Berne", in *Les Petites Affiches,* No. 130, 29 octobre 1990, p. 16.
[567]. Article 3.
[568]. Article 4.
[569]. Article 5.

more than two cartridges, etc. The list is not exhaustive as paragraph *(k)* prohibits "all other methods designed for the mass capture or killing of birds".

327. As for the Benelux Convention on the Hunting and Protection of Birds (1970), its Article 4 originally provided that the three signatory governments "shall consult each other concerning the arms, ammunition, projectiles, tackle, apparatus, procedures and methods permitted for hunting" [570]. Deeming this provision too vague, the signatories decided in 1977 to further clarify it. An amendment to the Convention was made to that end [571]. It is now the Benelux Committee of Ministers that determines the weapons, ammunition, projectiles, devices and methods of hunting, taking into account the hunting requirements of each country or part of a country [572]. Following the 1977 amendment, hunting with firearms is also prohibited, at least between one hour after sunset and one hour before sunrise [573].

328. Finally, the Agreement on the Conservation of African-Eurasian Migratory Waterbirds does not specify the hunting and capture methods to be prohibited. It leaves it to the Parties to choose the measures to be adopted in order to comply with the obligation of result it establishes. Thus, its action plan provides that the Parties shall regulate the modes of taking for the exploitable species listed in column B of Table 1 [574]. "The object of such legal measures shall be to maintain or contribute to the restoration of those populations to a favourable conservation status and to ensure, on the basis of the best available knowledge of population dynamics, that any taking or other use is sustainable." Furthermore, its action plan requires Parties to strive to eliminate the use of poisoned bait [575].

– *Quotas*

329. Another method to manage hunting is the quota system: the prior determination of the number of specimens that may be taken

---

570. By its decision M (76) 15 of 24 May 1976, the Benelux Committee of Ministers prohibited, on the basis of this provision, the possession, transport, sale, offer for sale and purchase of certain types of nets traditionally used for hunting birds.
571. See the Protocol amending the Benelux Convention on the Hunting and Protection of Birds, 20 June 1977, entry into force on 2 January 1983.
572. In its Decision M (83) 17 of 24 September 1984, the Committee drew up a restrictive list of rifles and ammunition to be used for hunting the various game species.
573. New Article 4, para. 1.
574. Para. 2 (1) (2) *(b)* of the Action Plan.
575. Para. 4 (1) (5) of the Action Plan.

and the allocation of this quantity among operators at the international level. The first applications of the quota method date back to 1911 but more recent instruments rely on it for whales and seals [576]. This rather cumbersome method seems difficult to apply to birdlife on an international level [577]. However, through ringing systems and/or an adjustment of the hunting season, it would probably be possible to calculate a "rational" level of exploitation for each species each year and to divide this global quota between the relevant States. Indeed, such methods are used in North America, through the North American Waterfowl Management Plan concluded between the United States, Canada and Mexico [578]. The plan aims to prepare and implement a global strategy for the conservation of migratory waterfowl and their habitats and to restore the populations of these birds to their levels of the early 1970s, following the sharp declines in numbers observed after that date, no doubt caused by the reduction in the area of wetlands available for these birds. Each year, it sets the close season for hunting (generally two to three months), the hours during which hunting can take place and hunting quotas by province in Canada and by State in the United States. Quotas are defined per hunter and per day, for a species or a group of species. In some US States, there is a point system for ducks: each species is allocated a number of points, which may vary depending on whether it is a male or female. Species that need to be taken less have a high point value; some values are even equal to the daily maximum. A hunter has a given number of points per day and modulates his or her harvest within this limit. In Mexico, the federal government establishes, by annual regulation, State by State, the dates of the hunting season and the maximum daily quota. Thus, within an informal management framework based on a ministerial agreement, a very elaborate management regime has been put in place.

– *Co-operation*

330. Hunting regulations may also take the form of bilateral or regional co-operation, for example, in the fight against poaching (see the 1984 anti-poaching agreement between Benin and Burkina Faso),

---

576. A. Kiss, "La protection internationale de la vie sauvage", in *AFDI*, 1980, p. 683.
577. C. de Klemm, "The Problem of Migratory Species in International Law", in *Green Globe Yearbook*, 1994, p. 75.
578. North American Waterfowl Management Plan, signed in 1986, https://nawmp.org, accessed on 25 October 2023.

and go even further by including the exchange of information, the organisation of joint training courses, etc. (see the 1983 Agreement for Cooperation and Consultation between the Central African States for the Conservation of Wild Fauna between Gabon, Congo, Sudan and Cameroon, or the 1997 Protocol between the Russian Federation and Peoples Republic of China on Protection of Tiger).

- *Fishing regulations*

331. International law also deals with fishing activities, both at sea and in fresh water.

– *Sea fishing*

332. Fishing at sea is a real issue for biodiversity. Naturally, it has an impact on the species fished. As a result of the intensification of fishing, one-third of fish stocks are now overfished, which means that catches exceed reproductive capacity. The FAO tells us that over 33 per cent of fish stocks are exploited at a biologically unsustainable level, and nearly 60 per cent of stocks are exploited at the maximum sustainable level [579]. But fishing activities also have consequences for marine biodiversity and balances that go far beyond the species fished. Indeed, fishing is largely industrialised and the methods used are not always selective. In addition to disrupting ecological balances, they can have a destructive influence on deep waters and the seabed.

333. For a long time, customary international law developed after the adoption of the Convention on Fishing and Conservation of the Living Resources of the High Seas (1958) to the point of becoming very abundant. Indeed, the challenges vary according to species and geographical areas. This is why a multitude of treaties apply separately to certain fishing areas on the one hand and to certain species on the other, for the latter on a universal or regional scale. Agreements regulate fishing conditions and often also set quotas for the Parties. They create standing committees, the fisheries commissions, that play an important role in adapting measures to the evolution of stocks and of scientific and technical knowledge [580]. Even supplemented by the Agreement for the

---

579. FAO, *The State of World Fisheries and Aquaculture 2020*, 2020, http://www.fao.org/state-of-fisheries-aquaculture/fr/, accessed on 25 October 2023.
580. J. Beer-Gabel and V. Lestang, *Les commissions de pêche et leur droit : la conservation et la gestion des ressources marines vivantes*, Bruylant, Brussels, 2003.

Implementation of the Provisions of the United Nations Convention on the Law of the Sea of 10 December 1982 relating to the Conservation and Management of Straddling Fish Stocks and Highly Migratory Fish Stocks [581] and despite the Agreement to Promote Compliance with International Conservation and Management Measures by Fishing Vessels on the High Seas [582], the UN Convention on the Law of the Sea only sets out a very general framework and does not ensure co-ordination between the various specialised or regional fishing organisations. The new "law of the sea" has been powerless to stop overfishing [583]. In addition to an imperfect legal framework, which suffers from its fragmentation, the States' lack of commitment is blatant. They are not fulfilling their obligations properly, and IUU (illegal, unreported and unregulated) fishing is further undermining efforts, despite attempts to curb it [584]. Sustainable Development Goal 14 sets out the following for States:

> "By 2020, effectively regulate harvesting and end overfishing, illegal, unreported and unregulated fishing and destructive fishing practices and implement science-based management plans, in order to restore fish stocks in the shortest time feasible, at least to levels that can produce maximum sustainable yield as determined by their biological characteristics."

But States are nowhere near achieving this, as illegal and unregulated fishing is estimated to account for 12 to 28 per cent of fishing worldwide [585]. The International Tribunal for the Law of the Sea has clarified the general due diligence obligations of coastal States, but also of the flag States of vessels fishing in the exclusive economic zones of non-Member States with regard to the prevention and elimination of IUU fishing [586].

---

581. Agreement for the Implementation of the Provisions of the United Nations Convention on the Law of the Sea of 10 December 1982 relating to the Conservation and Management of Straddling Fish Stocks and Highly Migratory Fish Stocks, 4 December 1995.
582. Approved on 24 November 1993 by Resolution 15/93 of the 27th Session of the FAO Conference.
583. J. Bouloy, "L'exploitation des ressources halieutiques (la pêche)", in M. Forteau and J.-M.Thouvenin (eds.), *Traité de droit international de la mer*, Pedone, Paris, 2017, p. 705.
584. See, for example, the adoption of the FAO Agreement on Port State Measures to Prevent, Deter and Eliminate Illegal, Unreported and Unregulated Fishing (2009).
585. S. Gambardella, "Le rôle des organisations régionales de gestion des pêches dans la lutte contre la pêche illicite, non déclarée et non règlementée", *AFDI*, Vol. LXIV, 2018, p. 577.
586. *Request for Advisory Opinion Submitted by the Sub-Regional Fisheries Commission*, Advisory Opinion, 2 April 2015, ITLOS Reports 2015, p. 4.

– *Freshwater fishing*

334. With regard to lakes and rivers, fishing can also be an important issue for biodiversity. In addition to the general prevention obligations that apply to international rivers and lakes, and also to shared resources (migratory fish), codified by the 1997 Convention on the Law of the Non-Navigational Uses of International Watercourses [587], many treaties go further by specifying fishing methods, periods and quotas for certain species and/or certain lakes or rivers, and have done so for a long time. We have already mentioned the 1885 Treaty concerning the Regulation of Salmon Fishery in the Rhine River Basin. Concluded by Germany, Switzerland, the Netherlands and Luxembourg, this treaty prohibits the use of certain fishing methods, defines yearly and weekly fishing periods, and the minimum size of fish that can be caught. Other treaties include the Great Lakes Fisheries Convention (1954) between Canada and the United States, the Convention concerning Fishing in the Waters of the Danube (1958) with an annex containing regulations for fishing in the Danube River, and the Agreement between the Government of the French Republic and the Swiss Federal Council regarding Fishing in Lake Geneva (1982). The latter contains very detailed provisions that even include the protection of fish habitat and the fauna on which it feeds [588]. It also deals with the monitoring and sanctioning of violations [589]. Other examples include the Agreement between the Government of the Russian Federation and the Government of the Republic of Belarus regarding Cooperation in the Sphere of Fisheries (2002), the International Agreement between the Government of the Russian Federation and the Government of Peoples Republic of China regarding Cooperation in the Sphere of Protection, Regulation and Stock Enhancement of Live Aquatic Biodiversity in the Boundary Waters of the Rivers of Amur and Ussuri (1994), the Acuerdo entre el Gobierno de la República del Paraguay y el Gobierno de la República Federativa del Brasil para la conservación de la fauna acuática en los cursos de los ríos limítrofes (1994). Provisions on fishing are especially interesting when they are integrated into a broader framework for cooperation, as is the case with the Agreement on the Preparation of a Tripartite Environmental Management Programme for Lake Victoria (1994) between Kenya, Tanzania and Uganda, which is accompanied

---

587. Articles 7 and 8.
588. Article 6.
589. Article 11 *et seq.*

by a Protocol for Sustainable Development of Lake Victoria Basin (2003) that sets out measures aimed at the protection of biodiversity well beyond fishery resources [590].

b) *Trade and transport*

335. On the trade and transport of wildlife specimens, the Convention on Biological Diversity is silent. However, all instruments that prohibit or regulate the taking of a species or group of species contain additional provisions prohibiting or regulating their transport and trade, within a State and/or internationally.

• *National trade regulations*

336. These regulations are mainly aimed at excluding protected species from all transactions during the protection period, either all year round for strictly protected species, or during the close season for game species. In practice, instruments vary in their level of precision and requirements. Thus, in Europe, as early as 1902, the Paris Convention prohibited the transport, hawking, putting up to sale, sale and purchase of nests, eggs and nestlings of the protected bird species listed in Schedule I. The sale and putting up for sale of specimens of these birds are prohibited throughout the year, and the sale and putting up for sale of birds regarded as game are prohibited during the close season. The 1950 Paris Convention prohibits "the import, export, transport, sale, offer for sale, giving or possession of any live or dead bird or any part of a bird killed or captured in contravention of the provisions of this Convention, during the season in which the species concerned" [591]. At the time, the fashion for feathered hats led to the exclusion of feathers from this prohibition, which can be traded in any season. The same prohibition does however apply to eggs, their shells and broods of young birds [592]. The regulation of the capture of birds for their sale, transport for sale and captivity is left to the discretion of States, which must "regulate trade in the birds protected by this Convention and take all necessary measures to limit the expansion of such trade" [593].

---

590. See in particular its Article 6, Protection and Conservation of the Basin and its Ecosystem.
591. Article 3.
592. Article 4.
593. Article 9.

Also relating to birds, the Agreement on the Conservation of African-Eurasian Migratory Waterbirds provides that the possession, use and trade in birds and their eggs, and any parts thereof, which have been taken in contravention of its provisions, shall be prohibited by the Parties [594].

337. As for the Bern Convention, it prohibits the possession of and internal trade of animals listed in Appendix II, alive or dead, including stuffed animals and any readily recognisable part or derivative thereof "where this would contribute to the effectiveness of the provisions of this Article" [595]. In the European Union, it is supplemented by instruments governing intra-Community trade in fauna and flora, in particular the Birds [596] and Habitats Directives [597], but also in seal products [598].

338. On the African continent, after the 1933 London Convention [599] and the 1968 Algiers Convention [600], the Maputo African Convention on the Conservation of Nature and Natural Resources (Revised Version) provides that Parties shall "regulate the domestic trade in, as well as the transport and possession of specimens and products to ensure that such specimens and products have been taken or obtained in conformity with domestic law and international obligations related to trade in species" and to this end "provide for appropriate penal sanctions, including confiscation measures". It also specifies that Parties "where appropriate" "cooperate through bilateral or sub-regional agreements with a view to reducing and ultimately eliminating illegal trade in wild fauna and flora or their specimens or products" [601].

339. As for the ASEAN Agreement on the Conservation of Nature and Natural Resources, it provides that Parties shall regulate trade in and possession of specimens and products of species that they have – unilaterally – recognised as threatened [602]. Apart from this restriction, trade is allowed.

340. The regulation of international trade is the indispensable supplement to the principles laid down with regard to internal trade.

---

594. Para. 2 (1) (1) and 2 (1) (2) of the Action Plan.
595. Article 6 *(d)*.
596. Article 6.
597. Articles 12 and 13.
598. Regulation (EC) No. 1007/2009 of the European Parliament and of the Council of 16 September 2009 on trade in seal products, OJ L 286, 31 October 2009, pp. 36-39.
599. Article 9.
600. Article IX.
601. Article XI.
602. Article 5 *(b)*.

On this matter, international regulation is necessary as purely national policies are unable to resolve these types of issues.

- *Regulating international trade*

341. The regulation of international trade is at the heart of the CITES Convention, which has the specific mandate to ensure the sustainability of the trade in wild fauna and flora. While this is the stated objective, achieving it requires a detailed analysis of the conservation status of the species in question and the threats posed by trade. Given that thousands of species are impacted, this is an enormous task and treaty institutions do not have the means to tackle it on their own.

342. The Convention generally prohibits trade in endangered species. It seeks to regulate trade in other species to ensure sustainability. To legally translate this scientific differentiation between the two categories of species, CITES relies on the listing technique. It was one of the first environmental conventions to use this technique. More specifically, the Convention contains three lists in its appendix.

343. Appendix I covers all endangered species that are or could be affected by trade. Trade in these species is prohibited, subject to a limited number of exemptions. Under certain conditions, trade may take place for non-commercial purposes, for example, to museums or zoos. An export permit must be issued, and this can only be done on presentation of an import permit. Both permits must meet specific requirements and be endorsed by the scientific authority of the countries involved, certifying among other things that the operation will not be detrimental to the survival of the species [603]. A double control mechanism is therefore established and this is one of the key provisions of the Convention. The responsibility for control is shared, in a way, between importers and exporters.

344. Vulnerable species are listed in Appendix II. Their trade is allowed, but subject to certain conditions and also limited through a permit system. The import of a species listed in Appendix II requires the presentation of an export or re-export permit, certifying that the operation will not be detrimental to the survival of the species. However, unlike the provisions for Appendix I species, an import permit is not required and import for commercial purposes is permitted.

---

603. See Article III of the Convention. However, these principles only apply to wild species; artificially propagated or captive-bred species are subject to the Annex II regime.

Therefore, international trade in Appendix II species is legal as long as the conditions for issuing an export permit are met [604].

345. Appendix III includes species which a Party declares to be subject, within its jurisdiction, to regulations designed to prevent or restrict their exploitation and requiring co-operation from other Parties to control trade. However, conditions are not as strict as for species listed in Appendices I and II [605].

346. Each Conference makes changes to the Appendices: adding species, moving them from Appendix I to Appendix II and *vice versa*. This usually sparks bitter discussions. Political and diplomatic considerations come into play with regard to these changes; the technical aspect of these decisions should not make us forget the underlying economic stakes. Sometimes, the treatment of certain emblematic species actually receives a lot of media attention. For example, the partial lifting of the ivory ban in 1997 – the elephant had been listed in Appendix I in 1990 – caused quite a stir.

347. However, as meetings are prepared particularly thoroughly and rigorously, in most cases, scientific aspects are not underestimated. The States' proposals must be scientifically justified. They are then examined in turn by the Animals and Plants Committees and by the secretariat. Partner NGOs (IUCN, TRAFFIC) prepare their own scientific assessments and circulate them widely, including on their websites, to which the official CITES website itself refers.

348. Currently, some 5,800 animal species and 30,000 plant species are protected by CITES from over-exploitation designed to supply international trade. Just over 1,000 species are listed in Appendix I, just over 35,000 in Appendix II. Plant species outnumber animal species seven to one. In particular, entire families of plants which are particularly sought after, such as cacti or orchids, are listed in Appendix II. On the other hand, and although it is an interesting option, the ability to include a species in Appendix III has barely been used by the Parties so far [606]. The appendices were "cleaned up" in the early years. Indeed, in 1973, there was no obligation for States to provide detailed biological data to justify listing. Many species were listed simply because they were protected by national legislation; there were not necessarily traded. Much work is also being done on nomenclature.

---

604. Article IV.
605. Article V.
606. The States that have made use of this possibility are mainly developing countries from the African, American and Asian continents. 217 species are listed.

349. It should be added that the Conference of the Parties has allowed Parties to establish quota systems, even though this was not contemplated by the Convention [607]. Indeed, if quotas are well defined, they are an effective tool for the rational management of species. Setting an export quota can allow Parties to determine the maximum number of specimens that can be exported in a given year without adversely affecting the survival of the species concerned. This option is widely used. A Party choosing this option must inform the secretariat, which informs the other Parties. The Conference of the Parties can also set quotas, which can therefore be national or international.

350. The Convention is rather flexible, allowing States to modulate their commitment. Pursuant to Article XIV, States may, by virtue of their national legislation or other international commitments, adopt stricter measures than those set out in the Convention. Indeed, several African States have adopted very restrictive laws, prohibiting, for example, the export of all vertebrate animals or of all animals except fish, or even all animals and plants. Some countries, such as Switzerland, apply strict import controls, requiring, for example, a permit for all birds, mammals, reptiles and amphibians. Others, such as the United States, require as a condition of import that the species involved be included in an effective conservation programme in their country of origin [608]. Lastly, in EU law, the Convention was transposed by a specific Regulation in 1982 [609]. This Regulation, which was amended several times and largely consolidated in 1996 [610], transposes the Convention into the European Union legal system, while going further in many respects [611].

---

607. See Resolution Conf. 14.7 (Rev. CoP15), *Management of Nationally Established Export Quotas*, adopted in 2007.
608. *Ibid.*, p. 116.
609. Even though the Community was not then a Party to the Convention. Indeed, the text of CITES did not allow the European Community to accede as such, reserving this option to States only. An amendment to that end was adopted in 1983 by the Conference of the Parties in Gaborone, but it was slow to come into force. The European Union finally became a Party on 8 July 2015.
610. Council Regulation (EC) No 338/97 of 9 December 1996 on the protection of species of wild fauna and flora by regulating trade therein, OJ L 61, 3.3.1997, pp. 1-69. Consolidated Version, https://eur-lex.europa.eu/legal-content/EN/TXT/?uri=CELEX%3A01997R0338-20200101, accessed on 25 October 2023.
611. Under Article XIV of the Convention, which allows for the adoption of more stringent measures and provides as follows: "The provisions of the present Convention shall in no way affect the provisions of, or the obligations deriving from, any treaty, convention or international agreement concluded or which may be concluded between States creating a union or regional trade agreement establishing or maintaining a common external customs control and removing customs controls between the parties thereto insofar as they relate to trade among the States members of that union or agreement".

It contains provisions aimed at uniform application throughout the Union, in particular through the principle of mutual recognition of permits and certificates in the Community. It also reinforces CITES protection measures, by providing, for example, for the application of the Appendix I regime to species listed in Appendices II or III of the Convention or by requiring the presentation of an import permit for all species covered by the Convention, and not only those in Appendix I. In Europe, another Convention, this time adopted under the aegis of the Council of Europe, focuses on the protection of animals (including wild ones) during international transport, not to prohibit or restrict it, but this time to ensure their welfare [612].

351. Under CITES, States are required to establish criminal sanctions for trade and/or possession of specimens, and to require confiscation or return to the State of export of such specimens [613]. However, fraud is very frequent and occurs in many different ways. Many studies highlight the global extent of illegal trade. According to a recent report by the World Bank, it is worth between 5 and 23 billion US dollars per year [614]. National laws are not always adequate; in many cases, the sanctions imposed are not dissuasive enough. Enforcing the Convention at the national level is particularly burdensome and costly; not all States have the means to do it effectively. In developing countries, but not only, poaching and illegal export are common despite the great efforts made by some to reduce these practices. The difference between the number of pangolins seized between 2007 and 2013 (107,060) and those legally traded (1,467) illustrates the extent of the illegal trade compared to the legal trade. While the difference is not always so significant, it is estimated that around 25 per cent of the trade in Appendix II species is illegal [615].

352. In this respect, the improvement of international co-operation on criminal matters is absolutely key. Various instruments support the action of CITES in this regard, such as, in Africa, the aforementioned Article XI of the Maputo African Convention on the Conservation of Nature and Natural Resources (Revised Version). Concluded between

---

612. Convention adopted in Chisinau on 6 November 2003, revising an earlier convention (13 December 1968). It came into force on 14 March 2006.
613. See Article VIII.
614. World Bank, *Illegal Logging, Fishing and Wildlife Trade. The Costs and How to Combat It*, World Bank, 2019, p. 9; UNODC, *World Wildlife Crime Report*, United Nations Office on Drugs and Crime, Vienna, 2016.
615. UNODC, *World Wildlife Crime Report* (n. 614), p. 17. World Bank, *Illegal Logging, Fishing and Wildlife Trade. The Costs and How to Combat It* (n. 614), p. 9.

ten African States, the Lusaka Agreement on Co-operative Enforcement Operations Directed at Illegal Trade in Wild Fauna and Flora (1994) goes in the same direction. It supports CITES by attempting to "reduce and ultimately eliminate illegal trade"[616]. There is a sub-group on wildlife crime within ICPO-Interpol; there is also a CITES anti-corruption working group within the World Customs Organisation. Parties are not satisfactorily represented, especially for Asia and South America. This CITES Secretariat itself is collaborating with Interpol and the World Customs Organisation to set up a new computerised system to curb illegal trade[617]. There is also a now well-established practice of signing memoranda between the secretariat and various national enforcement agencies. An "International Consortium on Combating Wildlife Crime" has been set up, involving the CITES secretariat, INTERPOL, the United Nations Office on Drugs and Crime, the World Bank and the World Customs Organisation. It provides technical assistance to Member States.

353. The UN General Assembly has sought to address this issue on several occasions. To "[t]ake urgent action to end poaching and trafficking of protected species of flora and fauna and address both demand and supply of illegal wildlife products" is now Target 7 of the SDG 15. The General Assembly urged Member States to "take decisive steps at the national level to prevent, combat and eradicate the illegal trade in wildlife, on both the supply and demand sides" and called on them to make illicit trafficking in protected species of wild fauna and flora involving organised criminal groups a serious crime, in accordance with their national legislation and Article 2 *(b)* of the United Nations Convention against Transnational Organized Crime[618].

354. An issue that has arisen is the compatibility of CITES with WTO law. CITES has been among the environmental conventions scrutinised by the WTO secretariat precisely to examine this issue[619].

---

616. See Article 4 *et seq.* The Agreement was concluded on 9 September 1994, under the auspices of UNEP, by six African states: Kenya, South Africa, Swaziland, Tanzania, Uganda and Zambia. It came into force on 10 December 1996.

617. See also the Lusaka Agreement of 8 September 1994: Lusaka Agreement on Co-operative Enforcement Operations Directed at Illegal Trade in Wild Fauna and Flora.

618. UNGA Resolutions 69/314, 30 July 2015, 70/301, 9 September 2016 and 71/326, 11 September 2017, and more recently 73/343 of 16 September 2019, Tackling Illicit Trafficking in Wildlife. These resolutions echo Resolution 1/3 of 27 June 2014 adopted by the United Nations Environment Programme's United Nations Environment Assembly and also addressing the illegal trade in wildlife species.

619. WTO Secretariat, Matrix on Trade Measures Pursuant to Multilateral Trade Agreements, WT/CTE/W/160/Rev3TN/TE/S/5/Rev1, 16 February 2005.

The risk is very real as, in addition to regulating the import-export of endangered wildlife species, the Convention allows parties to adopt stricter trade measures, including a complete ban on trade in certain species. Recognising this risk, the COP called for mutual supportiveness of the decision-making processes between these bodies [620]. No panel has yet been called upon to resolve this issue, which therefore remains outstanding.

355. There is also a risk that the implementation of CITES might clash with the Whaling Convention, especially as collaboration between the two institutions is still limited [621]. Indeed, the vast majority of the great whales species affected by hunting are listed in Appendix I of CITES, which means that specimens of these species may under no circumstances be traded commercially and that non-commercial trade should only be authorised in exceptional circumstances [622]. Under the Whaling Convention, the commercial hunting of large whales has been fully prohibited since the entry into force in 1986 of the moratorium on commercial hunting adopted in 1982, which has been renewed several times. However, some States are threatening this moratorium. Norway and Iceland have rejected it, using their right to object. Iceland also conducts hunting campaigns for scientific purposes, under Article VIII of the Convention, as does Japan. All three countries have also filed reservations to the Convention with regard to the species they hunt. They also regularly lobby for the species they hunt to be moved from Appendix I to Appendix II, which would allow them to expand trade in whale products when the whales have been hunted for scientific purposes. However, co-operation between the two conventions has so far ensured that coherence is maintained [623]. For some, CITES wrongly focuses on politically explosive but environmentally secondary issues, making it "tragically impotent" [624]. For example, it failed to get the polar bear listed in Appendix I in 2009 or the bluefin tuna in 2010 [625].

---

620. T. Deleuil, "La CITES et la protection internationale de la biodiversité", *Revue juridique de l'environnement*, 2011, 36 (1), p. 49.
621. R. Caddel, "Inter-Treaty Cooperation, Biodiversity Conservation and the Trade in Endangered Species", *RECIEL* 22 (3) 2013, p. 269.
622. T. Deleuil, "La CITES et la protection internationale de la biodiversité" (n. 620), p. 52.
623. *Ibid.*, p. 56.
624. J. M. Chen, "The Fragile Menagerie: Biodiversity Loss, Climate Change, and the Law", *Indiana Law Journal*, Vol. 93, Issue 2 (Spring 2018), p. 316.
625. Although in this case it was useful because it allowed the International Commission for the Conservation of the Atlantic Tunas (ICCAT) to become more involved in bluefin tuna conservation. S. Gambardella, *La gestion et la conservation*

3) Protecting environments

356. The protection of environments is achieved either through the protection of specific areas or through protection against damaging activities in and outside these specific areas.

a) *The protection of specific areas*

357. The type of protection necessarily varies depending on the characteristics of the site in question, its size, its ecological character, the species present and their needs and the threats to its conservation. However, at the international level, obligations on the establishment of a protected area can only be set out in very general terms. It is understandable that instruments include obligations of result rather than very specific and detailed obligations of means. In general, international law is not very prescriptive and leaves it to States to determine the legal regime applicable to protected areas. However, two different directions can be identified, relating to the two main categories of protected areas. A distinction is generally made between strict protection regimes and regimes allowing exploitation which offer a compromise solution aimed at maintaining a level of economic activity according to specifications that guarantee the protection of the site. This solution, which seems to be ideal as it reconciles environmental protection and human activities, often turns out to be ineffective. It can even be counterproductive as it gives the illusion of protection even though it is not actually being achieved. A recent study published in the journal *Science* shows that one-third of the world's protected areas are heavily affected by human activities. Since 1992, the area of land devoted to nature conservation has almost doubled to cover nearly 19 million square kilometres (areas smaller than 5 square kilometres are not counted), almost 15 per cent of the Earth's surface. But 32.8 per cent of these enclaves are subject to intense human pressure, whether from construction, agriculture, grazing, human occupation, roads, railways, waterways or night-time lighting [626]. Here as well, the work of IUCN is very useful. Its World Commission on Protected Areas regularly reports on the issue in its *Planet Protected Report* [627].

---

des ressources halieutiques en droit international. L'exemple de la Méditerranée (n. 94), p. 296.

[626]. K. R. Jones *et al.*, "One-Third of Global Protected Land is under Intense Human Pressure", *Science*, 18 May 2018, Vol. 360, Issue 6390, pp. 788-791.

[627]. See the 2018 Report, https://livereport.protectedplanet.net/pdf/ProtectedPlanet Report2018.pdf, accessed on 25 October 2023.

358. Most international conventions aimed at protecting biodiversity promote the establishment of protected areas, but they are mostly very flexible and place only very "soft" obligations on States.

- *On a universal scale*

359. According to the Convention on Biological Diversity, Parties must "as far as possible and as appropriate" develop guidelines for the management of protected areas, regulate or manage biological resources important for the conservation of biodiversity in those areas "with a view to ensuring their conservation and sustainable use", rehabilitate and restore degraded ecosystems and promote the recovery of threatened species[628]. The Convention's obligations remain very general and are also greatly watered down by the addition of the words "as far as possible and as appropriate". However, the Convention has played a catalytic role at the international level, through the aforementioned Aichi Target 11, according to which:

> "By 2020, at least 17 percent of terrestrial and inland water areas, and 10 per cent of coastal and marine areas, especially areas of particular importance for biodiversity and ecosystem services, are conserved through effectively and equitably managed, ecologically representative and well connected systems of protected areas and other effective area-based conservation measures, and integrated into the wider landscapes and seascapes." [629]

The aforementioned Kunming-Montreal Target 3 has now taken over, with an objective of 30 per cent by 2030, and the requirement to recognise and respect the rights of indigenous peoples and local communities, including over their traditional territories[630]. The Convention's COP regularly urges better co-operation in these matters, for example, when it:

> "invites the Ramsar Convention on Wetlands, the Man and the Biosphere Programme of the United Nations Educational, Scientific and Cultural Organization (UNESCO), and the World Heritage Convention, along with other relevant partners, regional

---

628. See its Article 8, Conservation *in situ*.
629. CBD, Decision X/2, *The Strategic Plan for Biodiversity 2011-2020 and the Aichi Biodiversity Targets*.
630. Decision 15/4 (2022), *Kunming-Montreal Global Biodiversity Framework*, CBD/COP/DEC/15/4, 19 December 2022, para. 13.

agencies, bilateral and multilateral funding agencies, private foundations, the private sector and conservation organizations, to create synergies and partnerships, including with indigenous and local communities, and to consider aligning their activities towards supporting implementation of national action plans for the programme of work on protected areas" [631].

360. Indeed, many conventions further specify the States' obligations, each in its own field or at its own level. Thus, according to Article 4 (1) of the Ramsar Convention, the Parties must promote the establishment of nature reserves in wetlands, whether or not they are included in the Ramsar List, and adequately ensure their wardening. In practice, a wide variety of legal regimes, and therefore degrees of protection, apply to wetlands in the territory of the Parties. States have much discretion in determining the legal status and protection measures to be adopted for each designated area. A wetland may be fully or partially protected, or not protected at all. It may be publicly or privately owned. At least for those wetlands included in the List of Wetlands of International Importance, the conservation obligation is implicit in Article 4 (2), which states as follows:

> "Where a Contracting Party in its urgent national interest, deletes or restricts the boundaries of a wetland included in the List, it should as far as possible compensate for any loss of wetland resources, and in particular it should create additional nature reserves for waterfowl and for the protection, either in the same area or elsewhere, of an adequate portion of the original habitat."

Article 3 (1) of the Convention specifies that: "[t]he Contracting Parties shall formulate and implement their planning so as to promote the conservation of the wetlands included in the List, and as far as possible the wise use of wetlands in their territory." Resolutions 5.7 and VIII.14 called for the establishment of management planning for all Ramsar Sites – with appropriate support and funding for implementation and staff training – complemented by a monitoring programme with indicators on the ecological character of the site [632]. Effective conservation and

---

631. CBD, Decision XI/24, *Protected Areas*.
632. Resolution 5.7 (1993), *Management Planning for Ramsar Sites and Other Wetlands*; Resolution VIII.14 (2002), *New Guidelines for Management Planning for Ramsar Sites and Other Wetlands*.

management of the network of Ramsar Sites is one of the three strategic objectives of the Fourth Ramsar Strategic Plan 2016-2024.[633] The Plan also emphasises the need to involve all stakeholders, including indigenous peoples and local communities. In addition, the Parties must inform the Convention secretariat "if the ecological character of any wetland in its territory and included in the List has changed, is changing or is likely to change as a result of technological developments, pollution or other human interference" [634]. This suggests that such activities are not prohibited [635]. The degradation of certain sites has led to the creation of a procedure known as Wetlands Monitoring [636].

361. The vagueness of obligations is accentuated by the possibility for States to withdraw or reduce the extent of sites "because of its urgent national interests", even if they must compensate for withdrawals or reductions in area as much as possible [637]. The secretariat simply needs to be informed. While no sites have been withdrawn since their inscription, a number of them have undergone changes that have led to their degradation. Others have been reduced in size. This can only contribute to weakening the value of the list, even if in practice the Parties do compensate by adding equal or greater areas.

362. In fact, the main obligation of States is to promote the conservation of sites with the aim of preventing changes in their ecological character. In many respects, the ambition of the Ramsar Convention seems very limited and the Convention has received rather harsh criticism for this [638]. Some commentators have gone so far as to say that the obligation to conserve wetlands in the Ramsar Convention is so weak that it can hardly be viewed as an obligation [639]. More generally, and not least, the Convention has and continues to promote changes in the perception of wetlands. In many countries, the Convention has encouraged national wetland inventories and assessments. Other

---

633. Ramsar Convention, Fourth Strategic Plan 2016-2024, adopted by the Twelfth Meeting of the Conference of the Parties in Punta del Este, Uruguay, 1-9 June 2015, by Resolution XII.2.
634. Article 3 (2).
635. The Convention Bureau also maintains a register of sites that are likely to undergo changes in their ecological character. This register is known as the Montreux Record.
636. See below, Chapter 5.
637. Article 4 (2).
638. R. Romi, *Les espaces humides. Le droit entre protection et exploitation des terres,* L'Harmattan, Paris, 1992, p. 50.
639. C. de Klemm, "La protection des zones d'intérêt écologique", in *Tendances actuelles de la politique et du droit de l'environnement,* M. Bothe (ed.), IUCN, Gland, 1981, p. 191.

countries have developed national wetland policies. However, wetlands continue to decline both in terms of area and quality. It is estimated that during the twentieth century, the global extent of wetlands fell between 64 and 71 per cent [640]. With regard to Ramsar Sites, there are mixed results, reflecting the fact that the mere inscription of a site on the Ramsar List is far from sufficient to ensure the conservation of the natural wetland habitats it harbours.

363. The idea behind the Ramsar Convention was that the inscription of a site could be used by site managers to support requests for public funding, or by conservation groups to oppose certain development projects, etc. Similarly, the immediate advantage of the Convention concerning the Protection of the World Cultural and Natural Heritage is to strengthen the position of those who are responsible for protecting or enhancing a site (local national administrations, private individuals, etc.). Furthermore, in 1983, the High Court of Australia ruled that the Convention imposes a legal obligation to protect World Heritage sites. The State of Tasmania had challenged the constitutionality of Australian federal legislation adopted pursuant to the Convention that made it illegal to build a dam in the Tasmanian Wilderness. It had argued that the Convention was merely a political statement of intent with no legal effect. The dam project was eventually dropped [641].

- *On a regional scale*

364. On a regional scale, in Africa, Article 7 of the Convention relative to the Preservation of Fauna and Flora in their Natural State (1933) provided that States should set aside hunting reserves and

> "[c]onsider the possibility of establishing in each of their territories special reserves for the preservation of species of fauna and flora which it is desired to preserve, but which are not otherwise adequately protected, with special reference to species mentioned in the annex to the present Convention" [642].

---

640. Ramsar Convention, *Ramsar Briefing Note 7 – State of the World's Wetlands and their Services to People: A Compilation of Recent Analyses*, March 2015, https://www.ramsar.org/sites/default/files/documents/library/cop12_info_docs_pdf_e.pdf, accessed on 25 October 2023.

641. L. Sagne, *Les accords internationaux dans le domaine de la protection des habitats, Rapport de stage d'études au ministère de l'Environnement*, France, août 1992, M. Bigan (ed.), p. 7.

642. See also its Article 10.

The Algiers Convention which succeeded it in 1968 contained similar provisions. The Contracting Parties undertook to maintain or, if necessary, extend existing reserves and national parks and also consider the possibility of creating new natural areas in order to protect the most representative ecosystems and ensure the conservation of all the species inhabiting these ecosystems. The Convention thus guarantees the maintenance of the important network of national parks created by colonial powers across the African continent under the London Convention [643]. In the Maputo Convention, the provisions relating to conservation areas are more detailed, specifying the different management categories to be put in place based on the six main protected area categories established in the *Guidelines for Applying Protected Area Management Categories* published by IUCN in 1994 [644].

365. In America, the Convention on Nature Protection and Wild Life Preservation in the Western Hemisphere (1940) distinguishes four categories of natural areas to be protected: national parks, national reserves, nature monuments and wilderness reserves. It sets out conservation measures for each of these categories, which are identical to those of the London Convention [645]. Mention should be made of the existence, at a more technical level, of a Latin American Network for Technical Cooperation on National Parks, other Protected Areas and Wild Flora and Fauna, known as REDPARQUES. As for the Apia Convention on Conservation of Nature in South Pacific, it provides that protected areas may take the form of nature parks or national reserves. A nature park is defined in Article I as follows:

> "an area established for the protection and conservation of ecosystems containing animal and plant species, geomorphological sites and habitats of special scientific, educative and recreational interest or a natural landscape of great beauty, which is under the

---

643. N. de Sadeleer, "De la protection à la sauvegarde de la biodiversité", Ecologie politique, No. 9, 1994, p. 34.
644. See its Article XII and Annex 2. The guidelines were reissued by IUCN in 2008, https://portals.iucn.org/library/sites/library/files/documents/PAG-021.pdf, accessed on 25 October 2023.
645. C. de Klemm and C. Shine, *Biological Diversity Conservation and the Law* (n. 484), p. 141. In national parks, States must ensure that the resources exploited are not used for commercial purposes. They undertake to prohibit the hunting, killing or capturing of any part of the natural fauna (exclusive of fish), save by the permission, given for scientific or administrative purposes in exceptional cases by the authorities of the territory or by the central authorities under whom the reserves are placed, or *(b)* for the protection of life and property (Arts. 3 and 7). They must control "all white or native settlements in national parks with a view to ensuring that as little disturbance as possible is occasioned to the natural fauna and flora" (Art. 4).

control of the appropriate public authority and open to visits by the public",

the boundaries of which may not be altered so as to reduce their area and no part of which may be alienated except after very careful consideration [646]. Similarly, their resources may only be exploited for commercial purposes after a very thorough examination [647]. Harvesting is prohibited [648]. Use and access "under appropriate conditions, for inspirational, educative, cultural and recreative purposes" is permitted but must be regulated [649]. National reserves, which include bird sanctuaries, are aimed at the protection and conservation of nature. They "shall be maintained inviolate, as far as practicable", keeping in mind that, in addition to activities compatible with the objectives for which they were established, activities for scientific research purposes may also be permitted [650].

366. In Europe, pursuant to Article 4 (1) of the Bern Convention, States undertake to adopt "appropriate and necessary legislative and administrative measures" to protect the habitats of wild species of fauna and flora, in particular those listed in Appendix I (flora) and II (fauna). This is an obligation of result; the Contracting Parties remain free to decide on the means to use. According to the interpretation of the Standing Committee of the Convention, "appropriate measures" are those necessary and able to ensure the conservation of the habitats of species identified by the Committee as requiring specific habitat conservation measures, and more specifically of those parts of their geographical areas that are essential to their conservation, the critical sites. The term "conservation" means the maintenance and, where appropriate, restoration or improvement of the abiotic and biotic features that constitute habitats. This may require the control of activities that could indirectly result in the deterioration of these habitats. In addition, the obligation also applies to areas of importance outside the jurisdiction

---

646. Article III (1).
647. Article III (2).
648. Article III (3).
649. Article III (4).
650. Article IV. See also the Noumea Convention for the Protection of the Natural Resources and Environment of the South Pacific Region (1986), Article 14. More recent than the Apia and Kuala Lumpur treaties, this convention nevertheless contains many more escape clauses than the older conventions. C. de Klemm, "La protection des zones d'intérêt écologique" (n. 639), p. 191. The ASEAN Agreement requires the Parties to "take all measures possible in their power to preserve those areas"; "Contracting Parties shall, wherever possible, prohibit within such protected areas activities which are inconsistent with such objectives" (Art. 13).

of the Parties, which means, for example, that they must not encourage such deterioration there by providing financial aid, and that they must instead promote their conservation, by means of scientific, technical, legal or financial assistance.

367. Pursuant to the Convention, a network of sites called the Emerald Network was put in place. It was Recommendation No. 16 (1989) of the Standing Committee on Areas of Special Conservation Interest that launched the network, based on Article 4 of the Convention, with the dual objective of establishing common criteria for the identification of areas to be conserved and ensuring that the conservation and management of such areas have regard to certain minimum requirements. States are invited to establish areas of special conservation interest and to adopt "necessary and appropriate conservation measures". The idea is to target areas that are important for the survival of threatened or endemic species, or that support "significant numbers of species in an area of high species diversity" or "important populations of one or more species", contain "an important and/or representative sample of endangered habitat types", or contain "an outstanding example of a particular habitat type or a mosaic of different habitat types"[651]. Proposed sites are assessed before being formally included in the network. The effectiveness of the measures put in place is regularly reviewed. Parties must inform the secretariat of any significant changes that could substantially alter the ecological character of Emerald Network sites[652]. The network is very useful as it expands the Natura 2000 network that was established within the European Union[653]. Indeed, Natura 2000 sites are considered as a contribution of the EU Member States to the Emerald Network. Sites proposed by non-EU Member States are also added to the network.

368. With regard to birds, the Emerald Network also ties in with protected areas under the Agreement on the Conservation of African-Eurasian Migratory Waterbirds. Parties to this instrument encourage the protection, management, rehabilitation and restoration of protected sites, in liaison with other international or regional conventions

---

[651]. See this Resolution, para. 1, for the full list of criteria. See also Resolution No. 4 (1996) and Resolution No. 6 (1998).
[652]. Resolution No. 5 (1998); Council of Europe, Guidance on detecting, reporting, assessing and responding to changes in the ecological character of Emerald Network sites, T-PVS/PA (2018) 13, 14 January 2019.
[653]. For the purposes of the Council Directive 92/43/EEC of 21 May 1992 on the conservation of natural habitats and of wild fauna and flora *OJ* L 206, 22.7.1992, pp. 7-50.

specialising in habitat conservation [654]. They investigate the issues that arise or are likely to arise as a result of human activities and endeavour to implement remedial measures, including habitat restoration and rehabilitation measures, and compensatory measures for loss of habitat [655]. The action plan states that Parties must endeavour to develop strategies for the conservation of the habitats of all populations listed in Table 1, including the habitats of populations that are dispersed [656]. They must also endeavour, wherever possible, to rehabilitate and restore areas that were previously important for populations listed in Table 1 [657]. They must encourage, in protected areas, the development of co-operative programmes between all concerned to develop sensitive and appropriate ecotourism. Parties should however endeavour to assess the costs, benefits and other consequences that may arise from ecotourism in certain wetlands. In addition, where human disturbance threatens the conservation status of waterbird populations listed in Table 1, Parties must endeavour to take measures to reduce such impact. Appropriate measures may include, *inter alia*, the establishment of zones within protected areas where disturbance and public access are prohibited [658].

369. The protocols on marine and coastal protected areas established under the Regional Seas Conventions do not define categories of protected areas, but specify the obligations relating to designation. For example, Article 7 of the Protocol concerning Specially Protected Areas and Biological Diversity in the Mediterranean (1995), which pertains to marine and coastal areas, precisely defines protection, planning and management measures [659]. The Kingston Protocol, for the Caribbean region, sets out a general obligation to protect, preserve and manage in a sustainable manner those areas that need protection in order to maintain their special value. Parties must regulate or, where necessary, prohibit activities that are harmful to threatened species or their habitats [660]. In particular, they must adopt co-operative measures to ensure the protection of threatened species listed in the annexes to the Protocol [661].

---

654. Article III (2) *(c)*.
655. Article III (2) *(e)*.
656. Para. 3 (2) (4) of the Action Plan.
657. Para. 3 (3) of the Action Plan.
658. Para. 4 (3) (6) of the Action Plan.
659. Articles 6 and 7.
660. Article 10.
661. Article 11.

370. In the Antarctic, protected areas were first established under the Agreed Measures for the Conservation of Antarctic Fauna and Flora adopted in 1964 [662]. They protect a number of sites of special ecological value [663] as well as areas of scientific interest, dedicated to research, and prohibit further human interference. The Madrid Protocol was added on top of the agreed measures, but did not replace them. It did not prescribe any zoning but established the entire continent and its dependent and associated ecosystems as a "natural reserve, devoted to peace and science", in which the Parties generally "commit themselves to the comprehensive protection of the Antarctic environment and dependent and associated ecosystem" [664]. The Protocol provides that "activities in the Antarctic Treaty area shall be planned and conducted so as to limit adverse impacts on the Antarctic environment and dependent and associated ecosystems" and in particular

> "detrimental changes in the distribution, abundance or productivity of species or populations of species of fauna and flora; ... further jeopardy to endangered or threatened species or populations of such species; or ... degradation of, or substantial risk to, areas of biological, scientific, historic, aesthetic or wilderness significance" [665].

The Protocol prohibits any activity relating to mineral resources other than scientific research [666]. In addition, the conduct of other human activities is subject to conditions.

b) *General protection against harmful activities*

371. The creation of protected areas, as essential as it may be, does not suffice. Some species reproduce and live throughout their annual cycle in well-defined and circumscribed areas. Others, on the other hand, occupy very large habitats. In fact, the larger the "natural" areas in a country, the more widely most species spread over large regions. Some species, such as raptors, would require the establishment of extremely large protected areas; this is often difficult to achieve in

---

662. The Agreed Measures came into force on 1 November 1982 and are legally binding.
663. C. de Klemm and C. Shine, *Biological Diversity Conservation and the Law* (n. 484), p. 162.
664. Article 2.
665. Article 3 (2).
666. Article 7.

practice, especially in densely populated areas. Furthermore, the number of protected areas cannot be increased indefinitely: "You can't put everything under a bell jar." [667] And even if these areas were numerous enough to cover all the sites that meet the needs of wild species, they would not be ecologically cut off from the rest of the territory – they cannot be. On the one hand, human activities outside protected areas influence their ecological character. On the other hand, if parks and reserves are merely islands of natural habitat in an otherwise completely anthropised environment, we now know that they will necessarily lose many of their species and will therefore not be able to fully play their protective role [668]. Putting these principles into practice in recent years, international law has been trying to guide States towards a more general protection of the environment, experimenting with new techniques and methods.

372. The "globalisation" of protection can be achieved through a range of techniques and methods aimed at the protection of ecosystems, in addition to the establishment of protected areas. On the one hand, some of them are complementary to the institution of protected areas and contribute to the achievement of the latter's objectives. On the other hand, this globalisation includes the control of activities and processes that are harmful to biodiversity, regardless of any "zoning" of the territory. Because of the implications of this type of regulation, States are reluctant to commit and international law remains very hesitant. It is also clear that international law is more concerned with setting objectives, through obligations of result, than with detailing all the measures that States must take. Indeed, such measures vary greatly depending on local situations and needs, in addition to the fact that they are potentially unlimited.

- *The development of instruments complementary to the institution of protected areas*

373. Because protected areas are sensitive to the effects of activities outside their perimeter, we have seen that it is appropriate to define buffer zones, adjacent to the former and subject to a less restrictive protection regime, but nevertheless subject to regulation and control of activities likely to cause damage to the protected areas themselves.

---

667. C. de Klemm, "Des 'Red Data Books' à la diversité biologique" (n. 527), p. 176 (our translation).
668. *Ibid.*

The protection of ecological corridors pursues the same objective of strengthening the effectiveness of protected areas. Thus, for example, on the basis of Article 4 (1) of the Bern Convention,

> "[e]ach Contracting Party shall take appropriate and necessary legislative and administrative measures to ensure the conservation of the habitats of the wild flora and fauna species, especially those specified in the Appendices I and II, and the conservation of endangered natural habitats."

Recommendation No. 25 of the Standing Committee of the Convention on the Conservation of Natural Areas outside Protected Areas Proper focuses, in its third item, on ecological corridors and proposes in the annex a series of measures to be taken in this respect [669]. The relatively recent European Directive on the Conservation of Natural Habitats and of Wild Fauna and Flora includes the protection of ecological corridors. Article 10 provides that Member States must encourage the management of features of the landscape which are of major importance for wild fauna and flora. Member States must prevent the isolation of special areas of conservation, by granting protection to intermediate areas, to features

> "which, by virtue of their linear and continuous structure (such as rivers with their banks or the traditional systems for marking field boundaries) or their function as stepping stones (such as ponds or small woods), are essential for the migration, dispersal and genetic exchange of wild species".

Ecological corridors should enable exchanges and thus interactions between network areas. Even if this is not a strict obligation, it is one of the most interesting features of the directive. It seeks to put an end to the dismemberment that increases the vulnerability of nature. As pointed out by the rapporteur in the European Parliament with regard to the Commission's proposal for a Council Directive, in practice this can mean, among other things, expanding available areas and creating buffer zones around core areas. Continuity between habitats can be achieved by expanding them and by the appropriate management of intermediate areas, involving, for example, the widening, maintenance or development of wooded banks and forest areas, extensification, taking agricultural land out of production and a more appropriate

---

669. Adopted on 6 December 1991.

conception of land use, whether in terms of town development or unavoidable obstacles (motorways, etc.) [670].

374. Another important avenue is transboundary co-operation to manage shared ecosystems. This can be based on conventions (such as the Regional Seas or Mountain Conventions), but can also be developed alongside, or to implement, treaty obligations through transnational projects. An example is the WWF Heart of Borneo (HoB) initiative involving three ASEAN countries, Malaysia, Indonesia and Brunei, which have committed to co-operating on forest resource management and the conservation of a network of protected areas [671].

- *Controlling activities and processes that damage biodiversity*

375. The response to the biodiversity crisis should be multifaceted and thorough. It calls for a transformation of our methods of production, development and consumption: soil-friendly agricultural practices, fewer chemical inputs, control of urban sprawl and soil artificialisation, changes in the consumption of food and industrialised products, etc. Thus, conservation methods must also focus on limiting processes and activities that are potentially harmful to biodiversity. These processes and activities, which are almost always anthropogenic, must first be identified. As they are not yet well known, this requires an intensification of scientific research. The next step is not to prohibit them, but to maintain them at a level compatible with the conservation of wildlife and, more generally, of biological diversity [672]. This concept has very broad implications. Protection instruments can only impose general obligations in this respect. Building on the core due diligence obligations, the control of potentially damaging activities and processes relies on a multiplicity of sector-specific regulations, supplemented by cross-sectoral regulations.

---

670. J. Muntingh, *Second Report by the Committee on the Environment, Public Health and Consumer Protection on the Proposal from the Commission to the Council for a Directive on the Protection of Natural and Semi-Natural Habitats and of Wild Fauna and Flora*, 18 October 1990, Doc. A3-0254/90, p. 73..

671. M Lim, "Strengthening the Legal and Institutional Effectiveness of Transboundary Biodiversity Conservation in the 'Heart of Borneo'", *Asia Pacific Journal of Environmental Law*, 2014, Vol. 17, pp. 65-89.

672. C. de Klemm, "L'application et le suivi de la Convention de Berne et la nécessité d'intégrer la prise en compte des processus de destruction de la diversité biologique", in *Convention relative à la conservation de la vie sauvage et du milieu naturel de l'Europe*, Comité permanent, Quatorzième réunion, *Symposium sur la "Conférence des Nations Unies sur l'environnement et le développement, la Convention sur la diversité biologique et la convention de Berne : les prochaines étapes"*, T-PVS (94)14, p. 59.

376. For a long time, only specific activities or sources of pollution were addressed, and only extremely general obligations were laid down. For example, Article 3 (2) of the Bern Convention requires Parties to undertake in their planning and development policies and in their measures against pollution "to have regard to the conservation of wild flora and fauna". This is only an obligation of means. The provision can however be viewed in conjunction with Article 4 (1) of the Convention, according to which "[e]ach Contracting Party shall take appropriate and necessary legislative and administrative measures to ensure the conservation of the habitats of the wild flora and fauna species, especially those specified in the Appendices I and II". "Appropriate" measures presumably extend much further than the establishment of protected areas. Furthermore, the Convention must now be read in conjunction with Recommendation No. 25 of its Standing Committee on the Conservation of Natural Areas outside Protected Areas Proper, which includes in its annex a series of measures to be taken [673].

377. The Convention on the Conservation of Migratory Species of Wild Animals calls for, on the one hand, the "elimination of, to the maximum extent possible, or compensation for activities and obstacles which hinder or impede migration" and, on the other hand, the "prevention, reduction or control of the release into the habitat of the migratory species of substances harmful to that migratory species" [674]. The establishment of protected areas is only one of the ways to meet these obligations. The action plan of the Agreement on the Conservation of African-Eurasian Migratory Waterbirds further clarifies the Bonn Convention. Although the Agreement is binding, its provisions are not very prescriptive: it simply uses the phrase "shall endeavour". Thus, the Parties to the Agreement must endeavour to give special protection to those wetlands which meet internationally accepted criteria of international importance. They

> "shall endeavour to make wise and sustainable use of all of the wetlands in their territory. In particular, they shall endeavour to avoid degradation and loss of habitats that support populations listed in Table 1 through the introduction of appropriate regulations or standards and control measures".

To this end, they must

---

673. Adopted on 6 December 1991.
674. Article V.

"ensure, where practicable, that adequate statutory controls are in place, relating to the use of agricultural chemicals, pest control procedures and the disposal of waste water, which are in accordance with international norms, for the purpose of minimizing their adverse impacts on the populations listed in Table 1" [675].

In addition, in the event that human disturbance threatens the conservation status of waterbird populations listed in Table 1, Parties should consider measures to minimise the impact of existing structures [676]. In a novel way, the Agreement also contains provisions for "emergency situations". This expression can be seen as covering in particular major accidental pollution, such as oil spills or massive river pollution, but also natural disasters, such as prolonged periods of drought or very harsh winters. The Agreement thus overlaps and ties in with various instruments governing, for example, "critical situations" of maritime pollution. It organises co-operation between Parties, both in preventing such situations and in minimising their effects. According to Article III (2) *(f)* of the AEWA Agreement, Parties must co-operate in emergency situations that require international concerted action, and in identifying the migratory waterbird species that are most vulnerable to such situations. They must also co-operate in the development of appropriate emergency procedures to give greater protection to such species in these situations and in the preparation of guidelines to assist each of the Parties concerned in dealing with such situations [677]. When an emergency situation arises, the Technical Committee, in order to avoid deterioration in the conservation status of one or more species of migratory waterbirds, may ask the secretariat to convene an emergency meeting of the Parties concerned. The Parties concerned must meet as soon as possible in order to quickly establish a mechanism to give protection to species identified as being under particularly adverse threat. When a recommendation has been adopted at an emergency meeting, the Parties concerned must inform each other and the Agreement secretariat of the steps they have taken to implement it, or of the reasons why it was not implemented [678]. Protection includes emergency measures that the Parties must develop and implement for the populations listed in

---

675. Para. 3 (2) (3) of the Action Plan.
676. Para. 4 (3) (4) of the Action Plan.
677. The Conference of the Parties has to adopt criteria to define emergency situations which require urgent conservation measures and determine the modalities for assigning responsibility for action to be taken (Art. VI (7) *(e)*).
678. Article VII (4).

Table 1 of the Action Plan when exceptionally adverse or dangerous conditions occur anywhere in the Agreement Area, in co-operation with each other whenever possible and appropriate.

378. The Rio Convention on Biological Diversity requires Parties "as far as possible and as appropriate" to identify processes and categories of activities that have or are likely to have significant adverse impacts on the conservation and sustainable use of biological diversity and to monitor their effects [679]. Also "as far as possible and as appropriate", where a significant adverse effect on biological diversity has been determined, they "regulate or manage the relevant processes and categories of activities" [680]. This is a key provision of the Convention, complemented by Principle 3 of the *Addis Ababa Principles and Guidelines for the Sustainable Use of Biodiversity*, which provide as follows:

> "International, national policies, laws and regulations that distort markets which contribute to habitat degradation or otherwise generate perverse incentives that undermine conservation and sustainable use of biodiversity, should be identified and removed or mitigated." [681]

The content of the post-2020 Global Biodiversity Framework is worth noting from this point of view. Its Target 7 on pollution aims to reduce "pollution risks and the negative impact of pollution from all sources by 2030, to levels that are not harmful to biodiversity and ecosystem functions and services, considering cumulative effects", and the "overall risk from pesticides and highly hazardous chemicals by at least half" by 2030 [682].

379. According to the Protocol concerning Specially Protected Areas and Biological Diversity in the Mediterranean:

> "The Parties shall monitor the components of biological diversity referred to in paragraph 3 of this Article and shall identify processes and categories of activities which have or are likely to have a significant adverse impact on the conservation and

---

679. Article 7 *(c)*.
680. Article 8 *(l)*.
681. Secretariat of the Convention on Biological Diversity, *Addis Ababa Principles and Guidelines for the Sustainable Use of Biodiversity (CBD Guidelines)*, Montreal, Secretariat of the Convention on Biological Diversity, 2004.
682. Decision 15/4 (2022), *Kunming-Montreal Global Biodiversity Framework*, CBD/COP/DEC/15/4, 19 December 2022.

sustainable use of biological diversity, and monitor their effects." [683]

The Parties must take a series of explicitly listed protective measures, and ultimately "any other measure aimed at safeguarding ecological and biological processes and the landscape" [684].

380. The new African Convention on the Conservation of Nature and Natural Resources (2003), in its long and rather innovative Article XIII, focuses on processes and activities affecting the environment and natural resources. It provides as follows:

"1. The Parties shall, individually or jointly, and in collaboration with the competent international organizations concerned, take all appropriate measures to prevent, mitigate and eliminate to the maximum extent possible, detrimental effects on the environment, in particular from radioactive, toxic, and other hazardous substances and wastes. For this purpose, they shall use the best practicable means and shall endeavour to harmonize their policies, in particular within the framework of relevant conventions to which they are Parties.

2. To that effect, Parties shall

a) establish, strengthen and implement specific national standards, including for ambient environmental quality, emission and discharge limits as well as process and production methods and product quality;

b) provide for economic incentives and disincentives, with a view to preventing or abating harm to the environment, restoring or enhancing environmental quality, and implementing international obligations in these regards; and

c) adopt measures necessary to ensure that raw materials, non-renewable resources, and energy, are conserved and used as efficiently as possible, and that used materials are reused and recycled to the maximum extent possible while nondegradable materials are disposed of in the most effective and safe way."

381. Also, worth mentioning here is Chapter 3 of the ASEAN Agreement on the Conservation of Nature and Natural Resources. It focuses on the conservation of ecological processes and is indeed rather ambitious and comprehensive. The Parties undertake to prevent, reduce and

---

683. Article 3, para. 5.
684. Article 6 *(i)*.

control, as far as possible, the degradation of the natural environment, in addition to specific measures such as the promotion of adequate economic or fiscal incentives, and "to promote environmentally sound agricultural practice", as well as

> "to pay particular attention to the regulation of activities which may have adverse effects on processes which are ecologically essential or on areas which are particularly important or sensitive from an ecological point of view, such as the breeding and feeding grounds of harvested species" [685].

- *Regulating the introduction of alien species*

382. We refer here to the voluntary or accidental release, in a given territory, of a species that has never been present there [686]. The harmful impact of such introductions in natural environments is well known to scientists. Introductions, whether deliberate or accidental, often lead to the disappearance of indigenous species because of ethological incompatibilities, hybridisation phenomena, epizootics, the introduction of alien parasites, increased pressure on indigenous predators, etc. As a matter of fact, according to the first global assessment of IPBES, it is the fifth cause of biodiversity loss [687]. Control is further complicated by the many different routes of introduction. It requires a wide range of measures such as border controls and quarantines, prior authorisation for the intentional introduction of alien species, early detection and eradication of newly introduced species [688].

383. A review of the relevant instruments reveals that the introduction of alien species is almost systematically addressed, at least from the second half of the twentieth century onwards. Sometimes, States are asked to control voluntary introductions, for example, by means of prior authorisation procedures, such authorisations to be based on environmental impact assessments. Other times, they must

---

685. Article 10.
686. C. de Klemm, "Les introductions d'organismes naturels non indigènes dans le milieu naturel", in *Convention relative à la conservation de la vie sauvage et du milieu naturel de l'Europe*, Comité permanent, *Quatorzième réunion*, doc. T-PVS(95)17, p. 3.
687. IPBES, *Summary for Policymakers of the Global Assessment Report on Biodiversity and Ecosystem Services of the Intergovernmental Science-Policy Platform on Biodiversity and Ecosystem Services* (n. 38).
688. S. Lavallée, *Guide des négociations. Convention sur la diversité biologique. 14e session de la Conférence des Parties (CdP14, CdP/RdP9 et CdP/RdP3) du 17 au 29 novembre 2018, Charm El-cheikh, Egypte*, Institut de la Francophonie pour le développement durable, Montréal, 2018, p. 65.

prohibit them altogether. Generally, the more recent the instruments, the stricter they are in this respect. When it comes to preventing accidental introductions, legal instruments are by definition less effective. They can only require due diligence. The same is true of the control or eradication of alien species, which are by definition difficult to implement.

384. At the global level, the Rio Convention on Biological Diversity contains a rather weak provision in Article 8 *(h)*, according to which "[e]ach Contracting Party shall, as far as possible and as appropriate: . . . Prevent the introduction of, control or eradicate those alien species which threaten ecosystems, habitats or species"[689]. This has long been a concern of the COP, which has adopted guidelines on the prevention, introduction and mitigation of the impacts of alien species that threaten ecosystems, habitats or species: the *Supplementary Voluntary Guidance for Avoiding Unintentional Introductions of Invasive Alien Species Associated with Trade in Live Organisms*[690]. It also commissioned the secretariat to prepare a practical, non-binding information package for the Parties on the implementation of existing international standards, guidelines and recommendations. This now falls under Kunming-Montreal Target 6, according to which Parties have to

> "[e]liminate, minimize, reduce and or mitigate the impacts of invasive alien species on biodiversity and ecosystem services by identifying and managing pathways of the introduction of alien species, preventing the introduction and establishment of priority invasive alien species, reducing the rates of introduction and establishment of other known or potential invasive alien species by at least 50 percent by 2030, and eradicating or controlling invasive alien species, especially in priority sites, such as islands."

385. As for the Bonn Convention, it provides that, where feasible and appropriate, Parties that are Range States with regard to a migratory species listed in Appendix I must prevent, reduce or control "factors that are endangering or are likely to further endanger the species, including

---

[689]. The Convention also regulates the release of genetically modified organisms (Art. 8 *(g)*). See below, its Cartagena Protocol on this issue. It is supplemented on this point by Article 18 of the Protocol on Nature Protection and Landscape Preservation in Implementation of the Alpine Convention of 1991, which deals with the intentional or accidental introduction of genetically modified organisms.

[690]. Decision adopted by the Conference of the Parties to the Convention on Biological Diversity 14/11 (2018), *Invasive Alien Species*.

strictly controlling the introduction of, or controlling or eliminating, already introduced exotic species" [691].

386. Furthermore, in its guidelines on the conclusion of agreements relating to species listed in Appendix II, the Convention provides the following:

> "Where appropriate and feasible, each Agreement should provide for, but not be limited to . . . conservation and, where required and feasible, restoration of the habitats of importance in maintaining a favourable conservation status, and protection of such habitats from disturbances, including strict control of the introduction of, or control of already introduced, exotic species detrimental to the migratory species." [692]

The Agreement on the Conservation of African-Eurasian Migratory Waterbirds is indeed a very comprehensive and thorough instrument, as it addresses the voluntary introduction of bird species and more generally species of wild fauna and flora as well as the prevention of accidental introductions and provides for restoration measures. According to Article III (2) *(g)*, Parties must prohibit the deliberate introduction into the environment of non-native species of waterbirds, and must take all appropriate measures to prevent the accidental release of such species if such introduction or release is detrimental to the conservation status of wild flora and fauna. When non-native species of waterbirds have already been introduced, Parties must take all appropriate measures to prevent them from becoming a potential threat to native species. The action plan provides that Parties must, if they consider it necessary, prohibit the introduction of non-native species of animals and plants likely to adversely affect populations of non-migratory birds listed in Table 1. Similarly, they must ensure that appropriate precautions are taken to prevent the accidental escape of captive birds of non-native species. Lastly, as far as possible and if appropriate, when non-native species or hybrids thereof have already been introduced into their territory, States must ensure that such species or hybrids do not constitute a potential hazard to the populations listed in Table 1.

387. As for the Bern Convention, it requires States to "strictly control the introduction of non-native species" [693]. In addition, Recom-

---

691. Article III (4) *(c)*.
692. Article V (5) *(e)*.
693. Article 11 (2) *(b)*.

mendation (84)14 of the Committee of Ministers of the Council of Europe asks that Member States prohibit all introductions of alien species into the natural environment (subject to potential exceptions) and prevent accidental introductions. In 1992, the Standing Committee of the Convention established a Group of Experts on Invasive Alien Species. This Group analysed different national laws dealing with invasive species and submitted proposals to harmonise national regulations on the introduction of species, in particular with regard to definitions, territorial scope of regulation, the listing of species whose introduction is undesirable, identification of authorities in charge of issuing permits, conditions for issuing such permits, controls, etc. It defined the European Strategy on Invasive Alien Species, whose implementation it monitors on a regular basis. Since 2009, it has been working on identifying pathways of invasion and preparing a series of specific – non-binding – codes of conduct to deal with them. It has already endorsed such codes of conduct for activities such as horticulture, zoos and aquaria, botanical gardens, hunting, pets and recreational fishing.

388. The Apia Convention requires Contracting Parties to consider the consequences of introducing into an ecosystem species that have not previously been present there [694]. The Kuala Lumpur Convention contains similar provisions, while the Protocol concerning Protected Areas and Wild Fauna and Flora in the Eastern African Region provides in Article 7 that "[t]he Contracting Parties shall take all appropriate measures to prohibit the intentional or accidental introduction of alien or new species which may cause significant or harmful changes to the Eastern African Region" [695]. Article 12 of the Protocol concerning Specially Protected Areas and Wildlife to the Convention for the Protection and Development of the Marine Environment of the Wider Caribbean Region requires Parties to "take all appropriate measures to regulate or prohibit intentional or accidental introduction of non-indigenous or genetically altered species to the wild that may cause harmful impacts to the natural flora, fauna or other features of the Wider Caribbean Region". The Protocol for the Implementation of the Alpine Convention in the Field of Nature Protection and Landscape Conservation provides, in Article 17, that "[L]es Parties contractantes garantissent que des espèces de faune et de flore sauvages qui n'ont jamais

---

694. Article V (4).
695. In accordance with Article 196.1 of the 1982 United Nations Convention on the Law of the Sea.

été indigènes dans une région dans le passé connu, n'y soient pas introduites". In Africa, the Maputo African Convention on the Conservation of Nature and Natural Resources (Revised Version) provides that Parties should

> "strictly control the intentional and, in as far as possible, accidental introduction, in any area, of species which are not native to that area, including modified organisms, and endeavour to eradicate those already introduced where the consequences are detrimental to native species or to the environment in general" [696].

Lastly, for the Antarctic, the Madrid Protocol sets out extremely strict rules in this respect [697].

389. However, it is clear that these numerous provisions do little to curb the invasion of alien species, the impacts of which extend far beyond the international law on biodiversity [698].

- *Taking into account biodiversity in planning and development policies*

390. International law has made a tentative start in this respect. It is a principle of mainstreaming that requires that biodiversity protection be taken into account in decision-making and land-use planning processes.

391. Thus, the Rio Convention, which has the most general scope of application, provides that each Contracting Party

> "shall, in accordance with its particular conditions and capabilities:
>
> *(a)* Develop national strategies, plans or programmes for the conservation and sustainable use of biological diversity or adapt for this purpose existing strategies, plans or programmes which shall reflect, *inter alia*, the measures set out in this Convention relevant to the Contracting Party concerned; and
>
> *(b)* Integrate, as far as possible and as appropriate, the conservation and sustainable use of biological diversity into relevant sectoral or cross-sectoral plans, programmes and policies" [699].

---

696. Article IX.
697. See Article 4 of Annex II to the Protocol on Fauna and Flora.
698. P. Stoett, "Framing Bioinvasion: Biodiversity, Climate Change, Security, Trade, and Global Governance", *Global Governance* 103 (2010), Vol. 16, Issue 1, pp. 103-120.
699. Article 6.

392. Similarly, each Party "shall, as far as possible and as appropriate . . . integrate consideration of the conservation and sustainable use of biological resources into national decision-making" [700]. The COP has adopted several decisions on this subject, such as the recent 2018 decision entitled *Mainstreaming of Biodiversity in the Energy and Mining, Infrastructure, Manufacturing and Processing Sectors*, which established an Informal Advisory Group on Mainstreaming of Biodiversity [701]. Mainstreaming is addressed specifically in multiple Kunming-Montreal Targets, including in particular Target 14 which provides as follows:

> "Ensure the full integration of biodiversity and its multiple values into policies, regulations, planning and development processes, poverty eradication strategies, strategic environmental assessments, environmental impact assessments and, as appropriate, national accounting, within and across all levels of government and across all sectors, in particular those with significant impacts on biodiversity, progressively aligning all relevant public and private activities, and fiscal and financial flows with the goals and targets of this framework." [702]

393. At the regional level, in Africa, for example, the Maputo Convention takes into account all the elements of the environment, not from the narrow perspective of a nature protection convention, but from that of a relatively comprehensive instrument that seeks to take into account the environment in all its dimensions, with a view to promoting sustainable development, with both sector-specific and cross-cutting provisions. The Convention adopts a broad conception of sustainable development, which must be seen in conjunction with the Constitutive Act of the African Union (1999). The latter does not mention the environment in its preamble, but includes among the Union's objectives the goal to "promote sustainable development at the economic, social and cultural levels" [703]. This definition of sustainable development is unusual as environmental protection is generally considered to be one of the pillars of sustainable development. For example, according to

---

700. Article 10 *(a)*.
701. Decision 14/3 (2018), *Mainstreaming of Biodiversity in the Energy and Mining, Infrastructure, Manufacturing and Processing Sectors*.
702. Decision 15/4 (2022), *Kunming-Montreal Global Biodiversity Framework*, CBD/COP/DEC/15/4, 19 December 2022.
703. However, the protection of the environment is explicitly included in the remit of the Executive Council of the African Union (Art. 13).

the Johannesburg Declaration on Sustainable Development, "economic development, social development and environmental protection" are "the interdependent and mutually reinforcing pillars of sustainable development" [704]. We may also recall Principle 4 of the Rio Declaration on Environment and Development, which states that "[i]n order to achieve sustainable development, environmental protection shall constitute an integral part of the development process and cannot be considered in isolation from it" [705]. Setting aside the environmental pillar in this way is however only anecdotal, as on many occasions the Maputo Convention does, on the contrary, connect the three pillars and the cultural component, as when the preamble affirms the "ever-growing importance of natural resources from economic, social, cultural and environmental points of view". The wording is simplified compared to the Algiers Convention of 1968, which also referred to the nutritional, scientific, educational and aesthetic points of view. This link between the four dimensions of sustainable development is reaffirmed in Article XIV of the Convention, which deals specifically with "sustainable development and natural resources". According to this provision:

"The Parties shall ensure that *a)* conservation and management of natural resources are treated as an integral part of national and/or local development plans; *b)* in the formulation of all development plans, full consideration is given to ecological, as well as to economic, cultural and social factors in order to promote sustainable development."

It should be added that, in keeping with this emphasis on cultural aspects, the Convention refers several times to the traditional rights of local communities and indigenous knowledge, to which it devotes a specific article [706].

- *The obligation to carry out an impact assessment*

394. This is an obligation to carry out an impact assessment before authorising an activity that could cause significant harm to biodiversity. It is a key tool to implement the principle of prevention of environmental damage. It was introduced in national legislations at the end of the

---

704. This Declaration, World Summit on Sustainable Development, Johannesburg, South Africa, 26 August-4 September 2002.
705. This Declaration, Earth Summit, United Nations Conference on Environment and Development, Rio de Janeiro, Brazil, 3-14 June 1992.
706. Article XVII, see below.

1960s, with the American National Environmental Policy Act of 1969, the French law on nature protection of 1976 and the Quebec law of 1978 on environmental quality [707]. It has now become standard practice and has been included in many national legislations. However, these assessments are too often used to give projects a "formal legitimacy". Moreover, biodiversity should be given greater attention; it is too often the "forgotten aspect" of impact assessments [708]. What role does international law play in this respect?

395. Where the activity is potentially harmful to another State or in areas beyond national jurisdiction, the obligation is customary. It is part of the due diligence obligations previously discussed. The customary nature of this obligation was clearly recognised by the International Court of Justice in its 2010 and 2015 decisions. Indeed, as a result of the due diligence obligation, a "State must, before embarking on an activity having the potential adversely to affect the environment another State, ascertain if there is a risk of significant transboundary harm, which would trigger the requirement to carry out an environmental impact assessment" [709]. In other words, a State is required to do so "in order to fulfil its obligation to exercise due diligence in preventing significant transboundary harm" [710]. The customary nature of this obligation was confirmed by the International Tribunal for the Law of the Sea, as well as in the South China Sea Arbitration Award [711]. However, according to the International Court of Justice, general international law does not specify the scope and content of environmental impact assessments. Therefore:

> "It is for each State to determine in its domestic legislation or in the authorization process for the project, the specific content of the environmental impact assessment required in each case, having regard to the nature and magnitude of the proposed

---

707. M. Prieur, "Instruments internationaux et évaluation environnementale de la biodiversité: enjeux et obstacles", *Revue juridique de l'environnement* 36 (1), p. 7.
708. *Ibid.* (our translation).
709. *Certain Activities Carried Out by Nicaragua in the Border Area (Costa Rica v. Nicaragua)* and *Construction of a Road in Costa Rica along the San Juan River (Nicaragua v. Costa Rica)*, Judgment, *ICJ Reports 2015*, p. 665, at para. 104.
710. *Ibid.*, para. 108.
711. *Responsibilities and Obligations of States with respect to Activities in the Area*, Advisory Opinion, 1 February 2011, ITLOS Reports 2011, p. 50, para. 145; *PCA Case No. 2013-19 in the matter of the South China Sea Arbitration before an Arbitral Tribunal Constituted under Annex VII to the 1982 United Nations Convention on the Law of the Sea, between the Republic of the Philippines and the People's Republic of China*, Award of 12 July 2016, para. 947 *et seq.*

development and its likely adverse impact on the environment as well as to the need to exercise due diligence in conducting such an assessment." [712]

The only requirement set by the Court is that the assessment should be carried out before the project's implementation, a more than minimal requirement as this is the very essence of impact assessments.

396. Another weakness lies in the fact that although Principle 17 of the Rio Declaration sets out this obligation even outside of any risk of transboundary harm [713], this wider customary obligation has not yet been established.

397. In both respects, treaty law provides a necessary extension of the customary obligation. It clarifies the content and modalities of the obligation, and extends it to cases of potential damage within the territory of a State. Indeed, international conventions play a key role in promoting best practices and the emergence of minimum standards in this respect [714].

398. At the universal level, the World Charter for Nature (1982) already included the following in paragraph 11 *(c)*:

> "Activities which may disturb nature shall be preceded by assessment of their consequences, and environmental impact studies of development projects shall be conducted sufficiently in advance, and if they are to be undertaken, such activities shall be planned and carried out so as to minimize potential adverse effects."

Ten years later, the Rio Convention provided in Article 14 that Parties must adopt "as far as possible and as appropriate"

---

712. *Pulp Mills on the River Uruguay (Argentine v. Uruguay)*, Judgment, *ICJ Reports 2010*, p. 14, para. 205.

713. The legal principles set out by the World Commission on Environment and Development's Panel of Experts include an Article 5, which requires States to prepare or require a prior assessment of the impacts of an activity that may significantly affect a natural resource or the environment before initiating or authorising it. Article 16 (2) sets out a similar obligation in relation to activities that may have a transboundary impact. *Environmental Protection and Sustainable Development. Legal Principles and Recommendations*, Experts Group on Environmental Law of the World Commission on Environment and Development, June 1986, Graham and Trotman, Martinus Nijhoff, London, Dordrecht, Boston, 1987, p. 45.

714. D. Pritchard, "International Biodiversity-Related Treaties and Impact Assessment – How Can They Help Each Other?", *Impact Assessment and Project Appraisal*, 2005, Vol. 23, No. 1, p. 13.

"appropriate procedures requiring environmental impact assessment of its proposed projects that are likely to have significant adverse effects on biological diversity with a view to avoiding or minimizing such effects and, where appropriate, allow for public participation in such procedures".

They must take the results of this assessment into consideration in the decision-making process. Where such activities are undertaken, adverse effects should be avoided or minimised and such effects should be monitored so that they can be remedied. With this admittedly vague wording, Article 14 also seeks to impose inter-State co-operation based on the exchange of information regarding activities in one State that may affect the biological diversity of other States or areas beyond national jurisdiction [715]. The COP has adopted several decisions to clarify Article 14, including *Voluntary Guidelines on Biodiversity-Inclusive Impact Assessment* [716]. This document is not binding but its content encourages the inclusion of biodiversity in environmental impact assessments.

399. In this regard, other conventions complement the CBD with more specific provisions. The Ramsar Convention is relatively old and did not include a provision on impact assessment. However, the Conference of the Parties has stated that Article 3 of the Convention implies that impact assessments should be carried out and has adopted several resolutions to that end [717]. Such obligation has also been regarded as resulting from Article 5 of the UNESCO Convention, or Articles I, II and III of the Bonn Convention [718]. As for the Agreement on the Conservation of African-Eurasian Migratory Waterbirds, it states that Parties "shall assess the impact of proposed projects which are likely to lead to conflicts between populations listed in Table 1 ... and human interests, and shall make the results of the assessment publicly available" [719]. The Agreement also adds that, in implementing the specific measures set out in the Action Plan, "Parties should take into account the precautionary principle" [720]. In fact, it is interesting to note

---

715. Article 14 *(c)* and *(d)*.
716. Decision VIII/28 (Curitiba, 2006), *Impact Assessment: Voluntary Guidelines on Biodiversity-Inclusive Impact Assessment.*
717. Resolution VII.16 (1999), *The Ramsar Convention and Impact Assessment: Strategic, Environmental and Social.*
718. See, for instance, *Resolution 7.2 Impact Assessment and Migratory Species, Adopted by the Conference of the Parties at its Seventh Meeting (Bonn, 18-24 September 2002).* This resolution refers extensively to the work carried out in the framework of the CBD.
719. Para. 4 (3) (1) of the Action Plan, in Annex 3 of the Agreement.
720. Article II (2).

that the subject of impact assessments has given rise to collaboration between the conventions in the *biodiversity cluster*, including pursuant to capacity-building projects [721]. As noted by Michel Prieur, it was on the basis of the joint work of the three secretariats assisted by IUCN and the International Association for Impact Assessment that guidelines were adopted for the integration of biodiversity-related issues into environmental-impact-assessment legislation or processes and in strategic impact assessment, which were endorsed by the COPs of the Ramsar Convention and the Convention on Biological Diversity. The Ramsar secretariat even turned these guidelines into a manual on impact assessment published in 2004 [722].

400. Some instruments focus on specific areas, such as mountain ranges [723], the marine environment in general or regional seas [724]. The United Nations Convention on the Law of the Sea is very detailed [725]. The Madrid Protocol contains relatively stringent provisions and provides for an international control of the content of assessments by the Committee for Environmental Protection, and subsequently by the Antarctic Treaty Consultative Meetings [726]. European international law is also well developed. A Convention on Environmental Impact Assessment in a Transboundary Context was adopted within the framework of the United Nations Economic Commission for Europe (UNECE) in 1991 in Espoo, Finland. The Convention came into force in 1997 and has forty-five Parties, which are European countries and Canada [727].

---

721. D. Pritchard, "International Biodiversity-Related Treaties and Impact Assessment – How Can They Help Each Other?" (n. 714), p. 10.

722. Third edition, 2007. M. Prieur, "Instruments internationaux et évaluation environnementale de la biodiversité: enjeux et obstacles" (n. 707), pp. 7-28.

723. See, for instance, the 1994 Protocol for the Implementation of the Alpine Convention in the Field of Nature Protection and Landscape Conservation (Art. 9) or the 2003 Protocol on Conservation and Sustainable Use of Biological and Landscape Diversity to the Framework Convention on the Protection and Sustainable Development of the Carpathians done in (Art. 22, para. 1).

724. See, for instance, the 1986 Convention for the Protection of the Natural Resources and Environment of the South Pacific Region (Art. 16), the 1990 Protocol concerning Specially Protected Areas and Wildlife to the Convention for the Protection and Development of the Marine Environment of the Wider Caribbean Region (Art. 13), the 2003 Black Sea Biodiversity and Landscape Conservation Protocol to the Convention on the Protection of the Black Sea Against Pollution (Art. 6) or the 2008 Protocol on Integrated Coastal Zone Management in the Mediterranean (Art. 19).

725. Article 206. See also, before that, the Kuwait Regional Convention for Co-operation on the Protection of the Marine Environment from Pollution (Art. XI).

726. M. Prieur, "Instruments internationaux et évaluation environnementale de la biodiversité: enjeux et obstacles" (n. 707), pp. 7-28.

727. By 15 December 2020. The United States signed the Convention but never ratified it. Since an amendment entered into force in 2014, the Convention is open

A key principle of the Convention is that States must ensure that an environmental impact assessment is undertaken prior to a decision to authorise or undertake a proposed activity that is likely to cause a significant adverse transboundary impact. Projects that only affect the territory of one Party do not fall within the scope of this provision. The Convention was supplemented on 21 May 2003 by the Kiev Protocol on Strategic Environmental Assessment. It came into force in 2010 and has thirty-three Parties [728]. Lastly, EU law, which has been tackling this issue since 1985, is particularly demanding with regard to the environmental impact assessment of projects and plans and programmes [729]. The European Court of Human Rights has stepped in to support environmental instruments. It takes into account the decision-making process causing environmental damage [730] and requires it to include the conduct of appropriate investigations and assessments so as to prevent and assess in advance the effects of activities that may damage the environment and the rights of individuals. It also stresses the importance of public access to the conclusions of impact assessments [731].

401. On the African continent, according to the Maputo Convention, Parties must

> "ensure that policies, plans, programmes, strategies, projects and activities likely to affect natural resources, ecosystems and the environment in general are the subject of adequate impact assessment at the earliest possible stage and that regular environmental monitoring and audit are conducted"

and must "monitor the state of their natural resources as well as the impact of development activities and projects upon such resources" [732]. This new provision is very interesting, especially as it takes into account recent legal developments on impact assessments, making them compulsory as early as possible in the planning stage of projects, under the influence of EU and international law. The Convention's

---

for ratification by all UN Member States, not just the members of the UN Economic Commission for Europe.

728. As of 15 December 2023.

729. See the Directive 2011/92/EU of the European Parliament and of the Council of 13 December 2011 on the assessment of the effects of certain public and private projects on the environment, *OJ* L 26, 28 January 2012, pp. 1-21.

730. ECHR, 10 November 2004, *Taskin* v. *Russia*; 12 July 2005, *Okyay* v. *Turkey*; 2 November 2006, *Giacomelli* v. *Italy*; 5 September 2007, *Lemke* v. *Turkey*; 27 January 2009, *Tatar* v. *Romania*.

731. *Tatar* v. *Romania*, 27 January 2009, para. 113.

732. Article XIV, para. 2.

provisions on impact assessment are supplemented by those on the *ex post* assessment of the effects of projects and policies [733].

- *Climate change and biodiversity*

402. We have seen that IPBES ranks climate change as the third greatest threat to biodiversity and considers that this threat is going to increase. Climate change requires adaptation action, which according to scientific literature includes promoting movements of species through the absence of obstacles and the protection of ecological corridors, increasing the availability of habitats and reducing other stressors [734]. Spontaneous adaptation will not be possible everywhere and especially not for the most vulnerable species or ecosystems. So far, the issue has hardly been taken into account in international climate law, which has sometimes even encouraged the destruction of biodiversity, while the institutions of the Convention on Biological Diversity have long sought to improve the interactions between the two conventional spaces [735]. Such an immense challenge requires going much further. According to A. Trouwborst,

> "[w]hereas traditionally international nature conservation law has precisely focused on conserving species and habitats in their places of origin, it must now become a 'moving company', accompanying species and ecosystems on their journeys to higher latitudes and more suitable areas." [736]

This author calls for a protocol to the Convention on Biological Diversity designed to promote the adaptation of flora and fauna to this new situation. This is an interesting idea, especially since forecasts are very pessimistic and the aggravation of climate change could lead to the use of geoengineering techniques (such as ocean fertilisation), which could have dramatic consequences for biodiversity. Nature-

---

733. Article XIV, para. 3.
734. A. Trouwborst, "International Nature Conservation Law and the Adaptation of Biodiversity to Climate Change: A Mismatch?", *Journal of Environmental Law*, 21:3, 2009, p. 428.
735. S. Maljean-Dubois and M. Wemaëre, "Climate Change and Biodiversity", in *Encyclopedia of Environmental Law – Biodiversity and Nature Protection Law*, Edward Elgar Publishing, Jona Razzaque, E. Morgera (eds.), 2016, pp. 295-308. Decisions have also been taken by other COPs, such as the Bonn Convention on Migratory Species or the African-Eurasian Waterbird Agreement.
736. A. Trouwborst, "International Nature Conservation Law and the Adaptation of Biodiversity to Climate Change: A Mismatch?" (n. 734), p. 442.

based solutions to climate change provide an interesting response as they relay on the way ecosystems work to solve the climate problem. IUCN defines them as actions to protect, sustainably manage and restore natural and modified ecosystems that address societal challenges effectively and adaptively, simultaneously providing human well-being and biodiversity benefits [737]. Reforestation, soil restoration or increasing the role of oceans in climate strategies are very good examples. Nature-based solutions were at the heart of the UN Secretary-General's Climate Action Summit in September 2019. Research continues to make progress in this matter [738]. This is a way to link the implementation of the Paris Agreement and that of the Convention on Biological Diversity, if only by ensuring that nationally determined contributions take into account the Aichi Targets, even perhaps the targets set by the Paris Convention on Desertification [739]. The COP of the Convention on Biological Diversity has been particularly committed to this approach, encouraging Parties:

> "[t]o foster a coherent, integrated and co-beneficial implementation of the actions under the United Nations Framework Convention on Climate Change and its Paris Agreement, the 2030 Agenda for Sustainable Development, the Convention on Biological Diversity, including the Strategic Plan for Biodiversity 2011-2020 and the future post-2020 global biodiversity framework, the United Nations Convention to Combat Desertification, and other relevant international frameworks, such as the Sendai Framework for Disaster Risk Reduction 2015-2030".

In particular, the COP adopted very detailed voluntary guidelines for the design and effective implementation of ecosystem-based approaches to climate change adaptation and disaster risk reduction [740]. Nature-based solutions are also promoted by the Paris Agreement COP on climate change. In this respect, a recent decision:

---

737. See https://www.iucn.org/theme/nature-based-solutions, accessed on 25 October 2023.
738. See, for instance, R. Chami, T. Cosimano, C. Fullenkamp and S. Oztosun, "Nature's Solution to Climate Change. A Strategy to Protect Whales Can Limit Greenhouse Gases and Global Warming", *Finance and Development*, December 2019, pp. 34-38.
739. N. Seddon, S. Sengupta, M. García-Espinosa, I. Hauler, D. Herr and A. Raza Rizvi, *Nature-Based Solutions in Nationally Determined Contributions*, IUCN, University of Oxford, Gland, 2019.
740. Decision 14/5 (2018), *Biodiversity and Climate Change*.

"*Encourages* the implementation of integrated, multi-sectoral solutions, such as land-use management, sustainable agriculture, resilient food systems, nature-based solutions and ecosystem-based approaches, and protecting, conserving and restoring nature and ecosystems, including forests, mountains and other terrestrial and marine and coastal ecosystems, which may offer economic, social and environmental benefits such as improved resilience and well-being, and that adaptation can contribute to mitigating impacts and losses, as part of a country-driven gender-responsive and participatory approach, building on the best available science as well as Indigenous Peoples' knowledge and local knowledge systems." [741]

4) Ex situ conservation

403. As stated in the preamble to the Rio Convention on Biological Diversity, "[t]he fundamental requirement for the conservation of biological diversity is the *in situ* conservation of ecosystems and natural habitats and the maintenance and recovery of viable populations of species in their natural surroundings", but "*Ex situ* measures, preferably in the country of origin, also have an important role to play". Thus, they are secondary to *in situ* conservation. The Convention defines *ex situ* conservation as the conservation of components of biological diversity "outside their natural habitats" [742]. Article 9 of the Convention provides as follows:

404. "Each Contracting Party shall, as far as possible and as appropriate, and predominantly for the purpose of complementing *in situ* measures:

(a) Adopt measures for the *ex situ* conservation of components of biological diversity, preferably in the country of origin of such components;

(b) Establish and maintain facilities for *ex situ* conservation of and research on plants, animals and micro-organisms, preferably in the country of origin of genetic resources;

(c) Adopt measures for the recovery and rehabilitation of threatened species and for their reintroduction into their natural habitats under appropriate conditions;

---

741. Draft Decision -/CMA.5 (2023), *Outcome of the First Global Stocktake*, FCCC/PA/CMA/2023/L.17.
742. Article 2.

(d) Regulate and manage collection of biological resources from natural habitats for *ex situ* conservation purposes so as not to threaten ecosystems and *in-situ* populations of species, except where special temporary *ex situ* measures are required under subparagraph *(c)* above; and

(e) Cooperate in providing financial and other support for *ex situ* conservation outlined in subparagraphs *(a)* to *(d)* above and in the establishment and maintenance of *ex situ* conservation facilities in developing countries."

405. With regard to agricultural biodiversity, the Convention is supplemented by the International Treaty on Plant Genetic Resources for Food and Agriculture, which also provides for both *in situ* and *ex situ* conservation measures. The Parties undertake "as appropriate" to

"cooperate to promote the development of an efficient and sustainable system of *ex situ* conservation, giving due attention to the need for adequate documentation, characterization, regeneration and evaluation, and promote the development and transfer of appropriate technologies for this purpose with a view to improving the sustainable use of plant genetic resources for food and agriculture" [743].

The Parties acknowledge the importance for food of *ex situ* collections of plant genetic resources maintained outside their natural habitat [744].

406. Apart from this treaty, there are few provisions on this issue. One can however mention the Convention for the Conservation of the Biodiversity and the Protection of Priority Wilderness Areas in Central America, which was adopted at the same time and is largely influenced by the Convention on Biological Diversity [745]. The Protocol concerning Specially Protected Areas and Biological Diversity in the Mediterranean (1995) provides that "[t]he Parties shall formulate and adopt measures and plans with regard to *ex situ* reproduction, in particular captive breeding, of protected fauna and propagation of protected flora" [746]. In the Maputo African Convention (2003), it is provided that the Parties "establish and/or strengthen existing facilities for *ex situ* conservation to perpetuate animal or plant species of particular interest" [747].

---

743. Article 5.
744. Article 15.
745. Article XXVII.
746. Article 11 (6).
747. Article XI.

407. *Ex situ* conservation allows research to be carried out, but also plays a role in raising awareness and educating the public. It usually takes place in zoos, animal parks, aquaria, botanical gardens, arboretums, etc. It can also be based on collections of *in vitro* plant tissue and microbial cultures. It also includes seed, sperm and egg banks and, more recently, gene banks. The latter contain genetic material (plant cuttings, seeds, sperm, eggs, etc.). DNA sequence banks have also started to develop, such as GenBank in the United States, which collects and stores all publicly available nucleotide sequences and their translation into proteins. New sequencing techniques – high throughput sequencing or HTS – allow for DNA-only sequencing without the need for the original genetic material. There are many applications in the medical, pharmaceutical and agricultural fields. This is especially problematic as not all banks are public; some are privately-owned. The discussions within the Convention on Biological Diversity have been fierce on this subject, about the possible consequences of this phenomenon in terms of sharing and accessing information. The COP has launched a reflection process that resulted in the definition of Kunming-Montreal Target 13 adopted at the COP 15 in 2022 [748].

Section 3. New perspectives

408. Among the new avenues open to biodiversity conservation, we will briefly mention two that are in essence very different: offsetting and rights-based approaches.

1) Offsetting

409. The objective of ecological compensation (or compensatory measures) is to offset or counterbalance the effects leading to biodiversity loss of a development or the implementation of a project relating to construction, development, new infrastructures, a business park, etc. Offsetting plays a role when the negative impacts of such

---

748. CBD, Decision 14/20 (2018), *Digital Sequence Information on Genetic Resources*. According to Target 13, Parties "[t]ake effective legal, policy, administrative and capacity-building measures at all levels, as appropriate, to ensure the fair and equitable sharing of benefits that arise from the utilization of genetic resources and from digital sequence information on genetic resources, as well as traditional knowledge associated with genetic resources, and facilitating appropriate access to genetic resources, and by 2030, facilitating a significant increase of the benefits shared, in accordance with applicable international access and benefit-sharing instruments". See Decision 15/4 (2022), *Kunming-Montreal Global Biodiversity Framework*, CBD/COP/DEC/15/4, 19 December 2022.

project have not been avoided or mitigated beforehand (the *avoid-reduce-compensate* sequence). It can consist, for example, of initiatives to create new protected areas or to restore environments or species, such as the reintroduction or consolidation of a population, even in very remote locations. The aim is to re-establish an overall quality of the environment equivalent to the previous situation or, in other words, to ensure *"no net loss"* of biodiversity. The approach was developed in the United States in the 1980s for wetlands and gave rise to an offsetting market with *mitigation banks,* from which developers can if necessary purchase credits representing the advanced implementation of actions beneficial to biodiversity [749]. Offsetting can be mandatory or voluntary. It can be based on an ecosystem services approach, in which case it is based on the compensation of a lost ecosystem service by equivalent services.

410. From a conservation perspective, the approach is interesting as it imposes the repair of damage where previously nothing was planned. It is nonetheless risky. Indeed, it is only appropriate insofar as the destruction of biodiversity is not made easier as a result and if offsetting is only a last resort when the damage cannot be avoided and attempts have been made to minimise it. The approach can also be criticised because it is based on the idea that it is possible to calculate the value of units of biodiversity and offset their losses with actions of equal value [750]. It assumes that it is possible to define biodiversity units that are equivalent to each other. However, fungibility, whether of ecosystems, species or ecosystem services, is difficult to establish and by definition subjective. This leads to the monetary valuation of ecosystem services, which requires simplifying, reducing or even homogenising the components of biodiversity by turning units of biodiversity, which are essentially non-fungible, into fungible elements [751]. These are not only reductionist, but also purely instrumental approaches, reflecting a strictly utilitarian vision of biodiversity. Besides, not everything can be offset, whether it is a rare or very old ecosystem or a species threatened

---

749. C.-H. Born, "Le diable dans les détails: les défis de la régulation des marchés d'unités de biodiversité: l'exemple du conservation banking dans le cadre de l'Endangered Species Act (Etats-Unis)", *Revue internationale de droit économique,* 2015, Vol. 29, No. 2, pp. 151-181.

750. C. Granjou and I. Mauz, "Gouverner par les scénarios? Comment les institutions environnementales anticipent l'avenir de la biodiversité", *Quaderni,* 2011/3 (No. 76), p. 8.

751. V. Maris, *Philosophie de la biodiversité. Petite éthique pour une nature en péril,* Buchet Chastel, La Verte, 2nd ed., 2016, p. 19.

with extinction. By ignoring both the complexity and the intrinsic value of biodiversity, offsetting thus brings to light "a scientific abyss and a major ethical flaw" [752].

411. Despite these weaknesses, offsetting has spread to many countries, even if neither the concept nor the practice is yet stabilised [753]. Its dissemination was boosted by its promotion at the international level [754]. In France, for example, offsetting was initially envisaged by the Nature Protection Act of 10 July 1976 as one of the items of environmental impact assessments, and was then implemented across various specific administrative police regulations (forests, water and aquatic environments, protected species, "green and blue infrastructures", etc.). The 2016 law for the recovery of biodiversity, nature and landscapes provides a common framework while attempting to improve its implementation [755]. Many countries have introduced legislation, as has the European Union [756]. It is estimated that there are over 1,100 mitigation banks worldwide [757]. The attraction of offsetting has given rise to the creation of structured international coalitions, bringing together NGOs, States and financial institutions, such as the Business and Biodiversity Offsets Programme (BBOP) [758].

412. Offsetting is also made compulsory by the *Equator Principles*, which are based on the performance standards of the International Finance Corporation and have been adopted by many national financial institutions [759]. It is therefore mandatory for companies wishing to have their project financed by these institutions.

---

752. V. Devictor, *Nature en crise* (n. 2), p. 314 (our translation).
753. *Ibid.*, p. 311.
754. Decision XII/3 (2014) of the CBD COP, *Resource Mobilization*, paras. 37-38; see also the above-mentioned Article 4 of the Ramsar Convention.
755. Loi No. 2016-1087 du 8 août 2016 pour la reconquête de la biodiversité, de la nature et des paysages (*JORF* of 9 August 2016). V. Dupont and M. Lucas, "La loi pour la reconquête de la biodiversité : vers un renforcement du régime juridique de la compensation écologique?", *Cahiers droit, sciences et technologies*, Vol. 7, 2017, pp. 143-165.
756. See, in particular, Directive 2004/35/CE of the European Parliament and of the Council of 21 April 2004 on environmental liability with regard to the prevention and remedying of environmental damage, *OJ* L 143, 30.4.2004, pp. 56-75. N. Doswald, H. M. Barcellos and M. Jones *et al.*, *Biodiversity Offsets: Voluntary and Compliance Regimes. A Review of Existing Schemes, Initiatives and Guidance for Financial Institutions*, UNEP-WCMC, Cambridge, UK, UNEP FI, Geneva, Switzerland, 2012.
757. V. Devictor, *Nature en crise* (n. 2), p. 312.
758. J. Penca, "Biodiversity Offsetting in Transnational Governance", *RECIEL*, 2015, Vol. 24, Issue 1, pp. 93-102.
759. See Performance Standard 6 (PS6) on Biodiversity, which is aligned with the principles of the Business and Biodiversity Offsets Program (BBOP); *The Ecuador Principles, IV. A Financial Industry Benchmark for Determining, Assessing and Manag-*

413. Offsetting can however be used in a more positive way, as financial compensation for preserved or restored ecosystem services *(result based)*. This is known as payment for ecosystem services, a tool that is also increasingly common [760]. This is, for example, the ambition of the REDD+ mechanisms (for *Reducing emissions from deforestation and forest degradation in developing countries*) under the United Nations Framework Convention on Climate Change [761]. These mechanisms aim to financially compensate countries that reduce CO_2 emissions due to deforestation and forest degradation, and they can be applied at different levels. For example, the Central African Forest Initiative (CAFI), a coalition of financial donors largely funded by Norway, recently announced that Gabon was potentially going to receive up to 150 million US dollars as a "results-based payment" for conserving the carbon stock in its forests by maintaining a high forest cover and low deforestation rates [762].

2) Rights-based approaches

414. The rights-based approach is based on human rights but also, more recently and in a novel way, on recognising the rights of nature.

a) *Human rights*

415. In addition to the legal framework developed to protect biological diversity, the safeguard of human rights can potentially play an interesting role, in the same way that it supports environmental protection more generally. According to a joint statement by UN experts and rapporteurs at the time of the publication of the 2019 IPBES report, the erosion of nature, the extinction of species and the loss of biological diversity constitute an unprecedented threat to the human rights of present and future generations. In these circumstances,

---

ing *Environmental and Social Risk in Projects*, Version 4, November 2019; Business and Biodiversity Offsets Program (BBOP), *Standard on Biodiversity Offsets, BBOP*, Washington, DC, 2012.

760. C. T. Reid and W. Nsoh, *The Privatization of Biodiversity? New Approaches to Conservation Law*, Edward Elgar, Cheltenham, 2016.

761. UNFCCC, Decision 14/CP.19 (2013), *Modalities for Measuring, Reporting and Verifying*; Decision 9/CP.19 (2013), *Work Programme on Results-Based Finance to Progress the Full Implementation of the Activities Referred to in Decision 1/CP.16*, paragraph 70.

762. A. Karsenty, "REDD+: les bases ambiguës du 'paiement aux résultats' obtenu par le Gabon", *WillAgri*, 7 October 2019.

failure to protect biodiversity may constitute a violation of the right to a healthy environment [763]. In the same way, UN Special Rapporteur John H. Knox has highlighted the importance of biodiversity and ecosystem services for the full enjoyment of human rights and specified how human rights obligations apply to biodiversity-related measures. According to him:

> "States have obligations to protect against environmental harm that interferes with the enjoyment of human rights, and the obligations apply to biodiversity as an integral part of the environment. As the Special Rapporteur emphasized last year in relation to climate change, these obligations continue to be studied and clarified, and the present report should not be taken as the final word on their content. In particular, it does not substitute for the more detailed analysis of particular human rights by mandate holders, treaty bodies, regional human rights tribunals or others." [764]

The human right to a healthy environment is recognised and protected by 155 States [765].

416. The *Kyrtatos* case before the European Court of Human Rights revealed the Court's reluctance and showed that human rights protection is not always the most appropriate tool to rely on [766]. In this case, the applicants complained that urban development had destroyed the swamp adjacent to their property and that the site where their home was located had lost its beauty. They claimed that Article 8 of the European Convention on Human Rights had been violated. As the Court first recalled,

> "according to its established case-law, severe environmental pollution may affect individuals' well-being and prevent them from enjoying their homes in such a way as to affect their private and family life adversely, without, however, seriously endangering

---

763. See this Declaration, https://www.ohchr.org/EN/NewsEvents/Pages/DisplayNews.aspx?NewsID=24738&LangID=E, accessed on 25 October 2023.
764. Human Rights Council, *Report of the Special Rapporteur on the Issue of Human Rights Obligations relating to the Enjoyment of a Safe, Clean, Healthy and Sustainable Environment, Note by the Secretariat*, A/HRC/34/49, 19 January 2017, para. 26, p. 11.
765. D. Boyd, "Les droits comme réponse à l'apocalypse écologique", *OpenGlobalRights*, 25 March 2019.
766. I. Michallet, "Cour Européenne des droits de l'homme et biodiversité", in *L'environnement et la Convention européenne des droits de l'homme*, L. Robert (ed.), Bruylant, Brussels, 2013, pp. 91-102.

their health (see *Lopez Ostra* v. *Spain*, Judgment of 9 December 1994, Series A No. 303-C, p. 54, para. 51)".

However, the Court added the following:

"The crucial element which must be present in determining whether, in the circumstances of a case, environmental pollution has adversely affected one of the rights safeguarded by paragraph 1 of Article 8 is the existence of a harmful effect on a person's private or family sphere and not simply the general deterioration of the environment. Neither Article 8 nor any of the other Articles of the Convention are specifically designed to provide general protection of the environment as such; to that effect, *other international instruments and domestic legislation are more pertinent in dealing with this particular aspect.*" [767]

In this instance,

"even assuming that the environment has been severely damaged by the urban development of the area, the applicants have not brought forward any convincing arguments showing that the alleged damage to the birds and other protected species living in the swamp was of such a nature as to directly affect their own rights under Article 8 para. 1 of the Convention. It might have been otherwise if, for instance, the environmental deterioration complained of had consisted in the destruction of a forest area in the vicinity of the applicants' house, a situation which could have affected more directly the applicants' own well-being. To conclude, the Court cannot accept that the interference with the conditions of animal life in the swamp constitutes an attack on the private or family life of the applicants" [768].

Judge Zagrebelsky did however append a partly dissenting opinion to the judgment. According to him, it was clear that Article 8 had been violated:

"In the present case it is clear that there was a deterioration in the quality of the environment in which the applicants' house was situated. In particular, it is indisputable that the new urban development has caused damage to the habitat of the fauna which

---

767. Judgment of 22 May 2003, *Kyrtatos* v. *Geece, No. 41666/98,* para. 52. Emphasis added.
768. *Ibid.*, para. 53.

made the swamp area next to the applicants' property near the coast of Ayios Yiannis, exceptionally interesting and agreeable. In my view, it could hardly be said that the deterioration of the environment did not lead to a corresponding deterioration in the quality of the applicants' life, even without taking into account their special interest in the study of the swamp fauna." [769]

417. Although his appreciation of the facts was different, the judge confirmed that the Convention is a tool for protecting human rights, not biodiversity. As the Court pointed out, it is therefore not necessarily the most suitable tool for protecting biodiversity. That said, provided that the infringement of biodiversity constitutes an infringement of a protected right, the Convention and its interpretation by the Court can promote the protection of biodiversity. This was the case, for example, in the *Herrmann v. Germany* ruling. Mr Herrmann alleged that the requirement that he join a hunting association and the obligation to tolerate hunting on his property violated his rights under Article 1 of Protocol No.1 to the Convention (protection of property) and Article 9 of the Convention (freedom of thought, conscience and religion), both taken alone and in conjunction with Article 14 of the Convention (prohibition of discrimination), and under Article 11 of the Convention (freedom of assembly and association). The Court did indeed conclude that "the obligation to tolerate hunting on their property imposes a disproportionate burden on landowners who, like the applicant in the present case, are opposed to hunting for ethical reasons" [770]. In the opinion he appended to the judgment, partly concurring and partly dissenting, Judge Albuquerque stated the following:

> "Wild, abandoned or stray animals are also protected by the Convention as a part of a healthy, balanced and sustainable environment. Article 8 provides for an obligation on the State to avoid acts and activities that could have detrimental consequences for public health and the environment, and more specifically an obligation on the State to ensure and promote public health regarding the control of wild, abandoned and stray animals, ill animals and domestic animals."

According to him:

---
769. *Ibid.*
770. ECHR, 26 June 2012, *Herrmann v. Germany*, No. 9300/07, para. 93.

> "As one of the hallmarks of international and European law in contemporary times, the protection of animal life and welfare has also been upheld under the Convention, although this protection is still viewed as a derivative effect of a human right to property or to a healthy, balanced and sustainable environment."

Here, the judge referred to various international instruments, including the Convention on Biological Diversity.

418. The approach of the Inter-American Court of Human Rights seems to be much more open. In its 2017 advisory opinion, it stated that it must take into account the norms of international environmental law when interpreting the Inter-American Convention, and referred in particular to the Convention on Biological Diversity [771]. It found that the right to a healthy environment protects, unlike other rights, the components of the environment such as forests or rivers in and of themselves. According to the Court:

> "Se trata de proteger la naturaleza y el medio ambiente no solamente por su conexidad con una utilidad para el ser humano o por los efectos que su degradación podría causar en otros derechos de las personas, como la salud, la vida o la integridad personal, sino por su importancia para los demás organismos vivos con quienes se comparte el planeta, también merecedores de protección en sí mismos." [772]

But some Parties to the Convention on Biological Diversity are still very wary of an interpretation that implies mutual support between the CBD and international human rights instruments. For this reason, the COP had so far never engaged in human rights language, but had nevertheless made it possible through various decisions to operationalise human rights in connection with biodiversity conservation and the use of natural resources [773]. The new Global Biodiversity Framework post-2020 makes a decisive point here. A few months after the adoption

---

771. Corte interamericana de derechos humanos, Opinion consultativa OC-23/17 de 15 de noviembre de 2017 solicitada por la Republica de Colombia, *Medio Ambiente y derechos humanos (Obligaciones estatales en relacion con el medio ambiente en el marco de la protecion y garantia de los derechos a la vida y a la integridad personal – interpretacion y alcance de los articulos 4.1 y 5.1, en relacion con los articulos 1.1 y 2 de la convencion americana sobre derechos humanos)*, para. 44.

772. *Ibid.*, para. 63.

773. E. Morgera, "Dawn of a New Day: The Evolving Relationship between the Convention on Biological Diversity and International Human Rights Law", *Wake Forest Law Review*, 2018, Vol. 53, No. 4, 2018, p. 710.

International Biodiversity Law 247

of the UNGA Resolution affirming a clean, healthy and sustainable environment as a human right [774], the CBD COP stated that "[t]he implementation of the Framework should follow a human rights-based approach, respecting, protecting, promoting and fulfilling human rights. The Framework acknowledges the human right to a clean, healthy and sustainable environment" [775]. Furthermore, the global framework is much more protective of the rights of indigenous populations [776].

419. From this point of view, protecting the rights of indigenous peoples is key [777]. The Convention on Biological Diversity acknowledges this by stating in Article 8 *(j)* the following:

> "Each Contracting Party shall, as far as possible and as appropriate... Subject to its national legislation, respect, preserve and maintain knowledge, innovations and practices of indigenous and local communities embodying traditional lifestyles relevant for the conservation and sustainable use of biological diversity and promote their wider application with the approval and involvement of the holders of such knowledge, innovations and practices and encourage the equitable sharing of the benefits arising from the utilization of such knowledge, innovations and practices."

The COP set up a working group on this provision in 1998, which is still active. For example, based on its work, the COP adopted the *Akwé: Kon Voluntary Guidelines for the Conduct of Cultural, Environmental and Social Impact Assessment regarding Developments Proposed to Take Place on, or Which Are Likely to Impact on, Sacred Sites and on Lands and Waters Traditionally Occupied or Used by Indigenous and Local Communities* [778]. These guidelines have been used by national focal points to interpret the *OECD Guidelines for Multinational Enterprises*, while the Special Report of UN Special Rapporteur Knox recommended that private companies take them into account [779].

---

774. UNGA Resolution 73/300, 28 July 2022, *The Human Right to a Clean, Healthy and Sustainable Environment*.
775. Decision 15/4 (2022), *Kunming-Montreal Global Biodiversity Framework*, CBD/COP/DEC/15/4, 19 December 2022.
776. M. Daval, "Un nouveau 'cadre mondial pour la biodiversité': enjeux et perspectives", *Revue juridique de l'environnement*, 2/2023, p. 323.
777. F. Francioni, "Natural Resources and Human Rights", *Research Handbook on International law and Natural Resources*, Elgar, 2016, E. Morgera and K. Kulovesi (eds.), p. 72 et seq.
778. In the Annex to Decision VII/16 (2004), *Article 8* (j) *and related provisions*.
779. E. Morgera, "Dawn of a New Day: The Evolving Relationship between the Convention on Biological Diversity and International Human Rights Law" (n. 773),

420. The COP was also able to affirm the following:

> "The establishment, management and monitoring of protected areas should take place with the full and effective participation of, and full respect for the rights of, indigenous and local communities consistent with national law and applicable international obligations." [780]

The COP adopted in 2022 the Kunming-Montreal Global Biodiversity Framework, which represents a step forward in the recognition of the importance of indigenous peoples and local communities for the protection of biodiversity, and the need to respect their rights. It mentions eighteen times indigenous peoples. In particular, it asks Parties to

> "[e]nsure the full, equitable, inclusive, effective and gender-responsive representation and participation in decision-making, and access to justice and information related to biodiversity by indigenous peoples and local communities, respecting their cultures and their rights over lands, territories, resources, and traditional knowledge, as well as by women and girls, children and youth, and persons with disabilities and ensure the full protection of environmental human rights defenders" [781].

Here, the Convention implements Principle 22 of the Rio Declaration on Environment and Development, which states:

> "Indigenous people and their communities and other local communities have a vital role in environmental management and development because of their knowledge and traditional practices. States should recognize and duly support their identity, culture and interests and enable their effective participation in the achievement of sustainable development." [782]

Similarly, Article 29 (1) of the United Nations Declaration on the Rights of Indigenous Peoples provides the following:

---

pp. 691-712. See also CBD, Decision 14/12 (2018), *The Rutzolijirisaxik Voluntary Guidelines for the Repatriation of Traditional Knowledge Relevant for the Conservation and Sustainable Use of Biological Diversity.*
780. CBD, Decision VII/28 (2004), VII/28, *Protected Areas (Arts. 8 (a) to (e))*, para. 22.
781. Decision 15/4 (2022), *Kunming-Montreal Global Biodiversity Framework*, CBD/COP/DEC/15/4, 19 December 2022.
782. E. Morgera, "Dawn of a New Day: The Evolving Relationship between the Convention on Biological Diversity and International Human Rights Law" (n. 773), p. 703.

"Indigenous peoples have the right to the conservation and protection of the environment and the productive capacity of their lands or territories and resources. States shall establish and implement assistance programmes for indigenous peoples for such conservation and protection, without discrimination." [783]

421. Environmental policies may conflict with the rights of indigenous peoples. Dealing with this situation, the African Commission on Human and Peoples' Rights found that the territory of an indigenous people transformed into a reserve should be returned to them given that in the pursuit of creating a Game Reserve, the Respondent State had unlawfully evicted the Endorois from their ancestral land and destroyed their possessions. It was of the view that the upheaval and displacement of the Endorois from the land they call home and the denial of their property rights over their ancestral land was disproportionate to any public need served by the Game Reserve [784]. Similarly, the African Court found in 2017 that the eviction of the Ogieks from their traditional land in the Maun Forest, which Kenya had justified by invoking a need to preserve the forest in question, was a violation of several articles of the African Charter, such as the rights to culture, religion, property, natural resources and development [785]. The Inter-American Court of Human Rights followed a similar approach in a case where the collective property of an indigenous people conflicted with the creation of a private nature reserve by the State, for which it had not taken into account the claims of the indigenous people or carried out prior consultation. The Court held that the right of the people in question prevailed, particularly in the name of the continuity of their traditional activities [786].

422. The Inter-American Court has relied on these various instruments to protect the rights of indigenous peoples in connection with biodiversity conservation issues. It was thus able to state the following:

---

783. UNGA, 13 September 2007, Resolution No. 61/295, United Nations Declaration on the Rights of Indigenous Peoples.
784. African Com. Human Rights, 25 November 2009, *Centre for Minority Rights Development (Kenya) and Minority Rights Group (on behalf of Endorois Welfare Council)* v. *Kenya*, No. 276/03, para. 214.
785. African Com. Human Rights, 26 May 2017, *Ogiek* v. *Kenya*.
786. Inter-American Court of Human Rights, 24 August 2010, *Case of the Xákmok Kásek Indigenous Community* v. *Paraguay*, Judgment of August 24, 2010 (Merits, Reparations, and Costs), para. 169. C. Perruso, *Le droit à un environnement sain en droit international*, Thèse pour le doctorat en droit, Université Paris 1 Panthéon Sorbonne, Université de Sao Paulo, 2019, p. 200.

"Thus, the criteria of *a)* effective participation, *b)* access and use of their traditional territories, and *c)* the possibility of receiving benefits from conservation – all of the foregoing provided that they are compatible with protection and sustainable use . . . – are essential elements . . . Consequently, the State must have adequate mechanisms to implement these criteria as a means of guaranteeing the right to a dignified life and to cultural identity to the indigenous and tribal peoples in relation to the protection of the natural resources that are in their traditional territories." [787]

In the same way the institutions of the Convention on Biological Diversity rely on the work of the United Nations, and in particular that of the United Nations Permanent Forum on Indigenous Issues [788], the Inter-American Court has been contributing to the hybridisation of the rights of indigenous peoples and biodiversity law.

b) *The rights of nature*

423. Viewing non-humans as legal subjects is not something new: "The legal subject, an abstract category and the primary instrument of the law, does not change over time, but its substance is modified." [789] In fact, not all humans have always been considered legal subjects, as slaves were excluded for thousands of years, and legal persons were only added in the nineteenth century [790]. The idea of recognising rights for nature or its elements in order to better protect them, and enhance the effectiveness of environmental law, has seduced many environmentalists who see it as a solution to many of the challenges raised by the implementation of environmental law.

424. Very controversial at first [791], this idea is starting to be included in positive law with the recognition of the rights of non-human living

---

787. *Caso Pueblos Kaliña y Lokono v. Surinam. Fondo, Reparaciones y Costas.* Sentencia de 25 de noviembre de 2015. Serie C No. 309, para. 181, see also paras. 177-170.

788. Recommendations from the United Nations Permanent Forum on Indigenous Issues to the Convention on Biological Diversity, CBD/WG8J/11/L.3, 22 November 2019.

789. R. Demogue, "Le sujet de droit", *Revue trimestrielle de droit civil*, 1909, p. 611 (our translation); and even more importantly, D. Christopher, "Towards legal rights for natural objects", 45 *South California Law Review* 450 (1972).

790. M.-A. Hermitte, "Artificialisation de la nature et droit(s) du vivant", in *Les Natures en question*, Colloque de rentrée du Collège de France 2017, P. Descola (ed.), Odile Jacob, Paris, 2019.

791. C. D. Stone, "Should Trees Have Standing? Towards Legal Rights for Natural Objects", *Southern California Law Review*, 45 (1972), pp. 450-501.

entities, individually (an animal) or more often collectively (an ecosystem)[792]. Thus, to give just a few examples, in 1992, Switzerland recognised in its federal constitution the dignity of animals, which can be relied on against abuses in the field of genetic engineering[793]. The 2008 Ecuadorian Constitution devotes a chapter to the "Rights of Nature", which are essential in order to achieve the "good way of living" (*Buen Vivir* in Spanish)[794]. In 2009, Bolivia introduced similar provisions in its Constitution and adopted in 2010 the Law of Mother Earth, which includes the right to life and existence, the right to continue vital cycles and processes free from human alteration, the right to pure water and clean air, the right not to be polluted and the right not to have a modified or genetically modified cell structure[795]. Several Colombian rivers have been recognised by court decisions as legal subjects, such as the Rio Atrato in the Colombian Constitutional Court ruling of 10 November 2016[796] or the Amazon River in a decision of 5 April 2018[797]. In 2014, the New Zealand Parliament granted former national park Te Urewera the same legal rights as a person[798]. In 2017, it extended these rights to the Whanganui River and then to the sacred mountain Mount Taranaki, and appointed guardians (the Maori indigenous peoples and the government)[799]. In 2017, in two decisions, the High Court of the Himalayan State of Uttarakhand (India) held that the Ganges and one of its tributaries, the Yamuna, were now living entities with the status and related rights of a legal person. The court exercised the *parens patriae* jurisdiction, a royal prerogative in common law countries whereby the Crown can act on behalf of those who are incapable of acting for themselves (or to settle disputes over access to water). "This technical

---

792. D. R. Boyd, *The Rights of Nature: A Legal Revolution That Could Save the World*, ECW Press, Canada, 2017.
793. O. Le Bot, "Les grandes évolutions du régime juridique de l'animal en Europe: constitutionnalisation et déréification", *Revue québécoise de droit international*, 2011, Vol. 24-1, p. 251.
794. D. Victor, "La lente consécration de la nature, sujet de droit: le monde est-il enfin Stone?", *Revue juridique de l'environnement*, 2012, 3, p. 479.
795. P. Villavicencio Calzadilla and L. J. Kotzé, "Living in Harmony with Nature? A Critical Appraisal of the Rights of Mother Earth in Bolivia", *Transnational Environmental Law*, 2018, pp. 1-28; D. Victor, "La lente consécration de la nature, sujet de droit: le monde est-il enfin Stone?" (n. 794), p. 479.
796. Corte constitucional, Républica de Colombia, Sala Sexta de Revision, T-622, 10 November 2016.
797. Corte Suprema de Justicia, Sala de Casacion Civil, STC 4360-2018, Radicacion No. 1101-22-03-000-2018-00319-01, Bogota, 5 April 2018.
798. C. J. Iorns Magallanes, "Nature as an Ancestor: Two Examples of Legal Personality for Nature in New Zealand", *Vertigo*, Vol. 22, Sept. 2015 [online].
799. *Ibid.*

choice is important because it refers to the state of abandonment of a vulnerable person, which justifies removing relatives and placing the person under the protection of the law." [800] The High Court held that these entities have all the rights, duties and liabilities necessary to preserve them, and appointed individuals who will have to act *in loco parentis*. They will be the human face of the protection of rivers and their tributaries, with a duty to promote their health and well-being [801]. This status was later extended to the Gangotri and Yamunotri glaciers; the judge ordered the State and central governments to do everything possible to preserve their health and well-being, and the Chief Secretary of Uttarakhand was ordered to appoint representatives to ensure that industries, hotels, ashrams, etc. do not discharge anything into the rivers [802]. These constructions were overturned by the Supreme Court of India; it found this status to be legally unsustainable. In May 2017, after recognising the *Atrato River* (which had been polluted by a mining operation) as a legal subject, the Colombian Constitutional Court justified the obligation to designate a legal representative for it, who, in conjunction with the inhabitants, would ensure its protection, conservation and restoration. It ordered the Government to act by designating such a guardian to take the necessary actions against this illegal mine using toxic substances such as mercury [803]. In 2018, the Colombian Supreme Court recognised the Amazon River as a legal subject [804]. In 2019, in the United States, following a referendum, Lake Erie was granted the legal right to exist and thrive naturally and as a result, the people of Toledo can sue polluters on behalf of the Lake [805].

425. In its aforementioned 2017 opinion, the Inter-American Court of Human Rights took note of the current trend of recognising a legal personality and rights for nature, not only in court decisions but also in constitutional provisions [806].

---

800. M.-A. Hermitte, "Artificialisation de la nature et droit(s) du vivant" (n. 790) (our translation).
801. *Ibid.*
802. V. David, "La personnalité juridique reconnue aux fleuves Whanganui, Gange et Yamuna", *Revue juridique de l'environnement*, 2017-3 p. 421.
803. M.-A. Hermitte, "Artificialisation de la nature et droit(s) du vivant" (n. 790).
804. M. Brilman, "Environmental Rights and the Legal Personality of the Amazon Region", EJIL: Talk, Blog of the European Society of International Law, 24 April 2018.
805. P. Bouvier, "Aux Etats-Unis, le lac Erié a désormais le droit légal 'd'exister et de prospérer naturellement'", *Le Monde*, 22 February 2019.
806. "En este sentido, la Corte advierte una tendencia a reconocer personería jurídica y, por ende, derechos a la naturaleza no solo en sentencias judiciales sino incluso en ordenamientos constitucionales." Corte interamericana de derechos humanos, Opinion consultativa OC-23/17 de 15 de noviembre de 2017 solicitada por la Republica de

426. Marie-Angèle Hermitte proposes to go further and to consider fundamental rights for all living things [807]. However, while this movement is presented as a panacea, most of the issues that the rights of nature or of living beings are supposed to remedy are likely to resurface if they are not properly addressed within the framework of this new paradigm [808]. The fact remains that, while international law has generally been ahead of national law in protecting human rights, here it is more of a spectator. These developments are emerging in national laws and spread horizontally from one State to another without international law promoting or encouraging them. However, the Kunming-Montreal Global Biodiversity Framework, adopted by the CBD COP in 2022 shows at least an interesting recognition of a plurality of values and ways of considering and protecting biodiversity:

> "Nature embodies different concepts for different people, including biodiversity, ecosystems, Mother Earth, and systems of life. Nature's contributions to people also embody different concepts, such as ecosystem goods and services and nature's gifts. Both nature and nature's contributions to people are vital for human existence and good quality of life, including human well-being, living in harmony with nature, and living well in balance and harmony with Mother Earth. The Framework recognizes and considers these diverse value systems and concepts, *including, for those countries that recognize them, rights of nature and rights of Mother Earth*, as being an integral part of its successful implementation." [809]

427. The same goes for animal rights. As mentioned above, the international law on biodiversity is still very marginally concerned with animal welfare, mainly as a side issue to transport and trade matters [810]. Yet there are many arguments to support international law-

---

Colombia, *Medio Ambiente y derechos humanos (Obligaciones estatales en relacion con el medio ambiente en el marco de la protecion y garantia de los derechos a la vida y a la integridad personal – interpretacion y alcance de los articulos 4.1 y 5.1, en relacion con los articulos 1.1 y 2 de la convencion americana sobre derechos humanos)*, para. 62.

807. M.-A. Hermitte, "Artificialisation de la nature et droit(s) du vivant" (n. 790).
808. J. Bétaille, "Rights of Nature: Why It Might Not Save the Entire World", *Journal for European Environmental & Planning Law*, 16 (2019), p. 59 *et seq.*
809. Decision 15/4 (2022), *Kunming-Montreal Global Biodiversity Framework*, CBD/COP/DEC/15/4, 19 December 2022.
810. W. Scholtz (ed.), *Animal Welfare and International Environmental Law. From Conservation to Compassion*, Elgar, 2019.

making headway on this issue. Bringing animals within the scope of international and European law would raise their protection to a higher level because of the strategic influence of international law and would give them greater protection. Removing animals from the category of "things" where they are traditionally confined could follow from this upward aspiration [811]. As noted by Anne Peters, beyond the risks and accusations of cultural imperialism, there are at least three arguments in favour of internationalising the status of animals:

> "Firstly, from the perspective of fairness and justice, such rights ... are incumbent on animals independently of their place of birth and abode. Secondly, international rights would serve as a benchmark for domestic law. International instruments would potentially allow for some monitoring of, or at least facilitate the formulation of criticism against domestic practices which do not satisfy the international standard. Thirdly, the endorsement of animal rights in only one state would probably lead to the outsourcing of the relevant industry." [812]

Our growing knowledge of the intelligence of animals, of their sensitivity and even their wisdom, not to mention the intelligence of plants, is gradually eroding the socially constructed boundary that separates humans from animals [813] and calls for our legal systems to evolve.

---

811. O. Dubos and J.-P. Marguénaud, "La protection internationale et européenne des animaux", *Pouvoirs,* 2009, No. 4, Vol. 131, pp. 113-126.
812. A Peters, "Liberté, Égalité, Animalité: Human – Animal Comparisons in Law", *Transnational Environmental Law*, 2016, p. 27.
813. See, for example, Y. De La Bigne *et al.*, *L'animal est-il l'avenir de l'homme?*, Larousse, Paris, 2017.

CHAPTER IV

INTERNATIONAL LAW AND BIOSAFETY

428. *Biotechnology* is defined in the Convention on Biological Diversity as "any technological application that uses biological systems, living organisms, or derivatives thereof, to make or modify products or processes for specific use" [814]. It covers a range of techniques aimed at the industrial exploitation of micro-organisms, animal and plant cells and their components. Made possible by the discovery in the 1950s of the role of deoxyribonucleic acid (DNA) and the genes it contains, and tested from the 1970s onwards, "genetic engineering" techniques produced marketable results from the 1990s onwards and developed quickly thereafter. Revolutionary in many respects, they enable the direct manipulation of the genetic code of living beings [815]. As they allow the barrier between species and between kingdoms to be crossed, they open up endless possibilities of combination. Isolated genes can be read, copied, modified, combined in different ways and transferred from one living being to another.

429. Genetic engineering is used to create genetically modified organisms (GMOs), through the technique of transgenesis, by isolating genes and then introducing modified genes into cells or whole organisms in order to change their biological properties. In addition to the creation of GMOs, these techniques also enable the genetic characterisation of individuals in order to diagnose genetic diseases, as well as gene therapy. Genetic engineering techniques can therefore have a wide range of applications, particularly in the agri-food, industrial, pharmaceutical and medical fields. A distinction is made between *transgenesis* and *mutagenesis*. Transgenesis is the insertion of a new DNA sequence. Mutagenesis, on the other hand, is the modification of information at the level of a gene; it does not involve the insertion of a DNA sequence into the genome.

430. Since the end of the 1990s, new genome engineering technologies have been developed, which make it possible to target a speci-

---

814. Article 2.
815. In this respect, they can hardly be compared with the classical breeding and hybridisation methods that have been tried out for several decades, which are merely an acceleration of natural phenomena.

fic DNA area to increase the precision of the correction or insertion performed, thus preventing cellular toxicities and ensuring reliable reproducibility of the intervention [816]. These new mutagenesis technologies, referred to as "directed" or "targeted" mutagenesis, are currently seen as very promising in terms of applied biological research and industrial innovation. Genetic engineering techniques have recently taken another leap forward with the development of the CRISPR-Cas9 technology, which marked the transition from very expensive techniques to a fast, efficient and cost-effective process. It allows a DNA sequence to be "cut" with "molecular scissors" in a relatively simple way and to be replaced by another sequence. This is the technique that was used in China to "engineer" the twin daughters of an HIV-positive man, making them resistant to the HIV virus [817]. Another avenue of development for genetic engineering is synthetic biology or synthetic genomics, which enables the production of new organisms from an entirely artificial genome. Synthetic biology makes genetic engineering simpler, faster and more cost-effective.

431. After biodiversity and biotechnology, the need to assess, prevent and manage the risks associated with the development of biotechnology has given rise to a third neologism: *biosafety*. Scientists are looking at the environmental risk that could take the form of genetic pollution with potentially irreversible consequences. There is also a debate around the risks faced by humans or animals ingesting GMOs, in terms of food safety and health, as these substances may be toxic or more allergenic. The complexity of assessing these risks lies in the diversity of GMOs, which means that they have to be assessed on a case-by-case basis and over time. For example, the environmental and health benefits of Roundup Ready soya or maize are far from what was initially promised. It causes herbicide resistance in a growing number of weeds and does not actually limit the use of herbicides, especially glyphosate, which is classified as a carcinogen by the WHO and is at the heart of much controversy.

---

816. The Court of Justice of the European Union has ruled that organisms derived from mutagenesis are GMOs and as such are covered by the European GMO Regulation. CJEU, Judgment of the Court (Grand Chamber) of 25 July 2018. *Confédération paysanne* et al. v. *Premier ministre et Ministre de l'agriculture, de l'agroalimentaire et de la forêt*, Request for a preliminary ruling from the Conseil d'État, ECLI:EU:C:2018:583.

817. J. Gabbatiss, "World's First Genetically Altered Babies Born in China, Scientist Claims. Leading Scientists Described the Work as 'Monstrous' and 'Far Too Premature'", *The Independent*, 6 November 2018.

432. Biotechnological development brings up important economic and social issues. It raises the prospect of major changes in agricultural technique and in the status of farmers, increasingly dependent on the multinational companies that market these products. The Monsanto Company has abandoned the development of its "Terminator" technology, which introduced a sterility gene into its seeds and was designed to prevent farmers from replanting part of their harvest [818]. But Monsanto, which was acquired by Bayer in 2018, continues to deny farmers what is referred to as the "farmers' privilege". Moreover, the bundle sale of certain herbicide-resistant seed and the herbicide in question – as in the case of Roundup Ready soya or maize – effectively makes farmers dependent. The reduction in the diversity of cultivated species on a global scale, underpinned by the development of biotechnology, can also be dangerous including with regard to the objective of food security.

433. This development also raises ethical questions. The patentability of living organisms, which is now recognised, allows for the appropriation of nature, which offends certain philosophical or religious convictions. The creation of a "bio-industrial" fauna and flora – what P. Roqueplo refers to as a "Technonature" [819] – changes our relationship with nature. With Chinese GMO babies, even the human species is affected. The prospect is looming of a standardised and industrialised world, of humans cut off from their roots and their environment [820], of improved and "augmented" humans [821]. As they resonate with strong cultural and symbolic values, GMOs elicit rejection and even anguish that are not always rational.

434. In this context, scientific controversies are intense and widely amplified by the media. In many countries, especially in Europe, uncertainties are fuelling the concerns of consumers and citizens who have already been alarmed by mad cows, dioxin-infested chickens, adulterated milk, hormone-fed beef, etc. There was a first wave of opposition in the mid-1970s to genetically modified bacteria used by research laboratories, particularly for the production of medicine. In the

---

818. GURT Technology, for Genetic Use Restriction Technology. The COP of the Convention on Biological Diversity adopted a *de facto* moratorium on these technologies in 2000, which it reinforced and extended in 2006, even excluding field trials. See its decisions V/5 (2000) and VIII/23 (2006).
819. P. Roqueplo, *Entre savoir et décision, l'expertise scientifique*, INRA ed., 1997.
820. J. Rifkin, *The Biotech Century*, Tarcher, Putnam, 1998.
821. T. Magnin, *Penser l'humain au temps de l'homme augmenté*, Albin Michel, Paris, 2017.

mid-1980s, the prospect of large-scale exploitation of transgenic plants led to a new wave of controversy. Europe and the United States took different approaches. While the US Congress gave the green light to the exploitation of GMOs in 1984, the European Community sought to strictly control GMO research and more generally the spread of GMOs. As a result, GMOs developed mainly outside the European continent, in particular in the United States. The export of GMOs to European countries for food and feed use or for cultivation, from 1996 onwards, once again sparked heated controversy. In Europe, opposition to GMOs brought together environmentalists and consumer associations as well as farmers. The cultivation and/or marketing authorisations issued in several European countries were challenged. In December 1998, the French Conseil d'État suspended the authorisation that had been granted for the cultivation of Novartis maize [822]. The following summer, the EU adopted a moratorium on new authorisations, pending the adaptation of Community law on the subject, with a view to organising the labelling and traceability of GMOs. These is also growing reticence outside Europe.

435. Although it did not explode as one might have expected, GMO cultivation nevertheless gradually increased to reach around 190 million hectares worldwide. The five main GMO producers are the US, Brazil, Argentina, Canada and India [823]. In 2019, 17 million farmers were growing GMO crops in twenty-four developing countries and five industrialised countries. The surface area of land cultivated with GMOs continues to grow, mainly in developing countries. The area cultivated with GMOs in these countries is now even greater than in industrialised countries. In terms of cultivation, the main crops are soya, maize, cotton and rapeseed, which account for 99 per cent of the cultivated surface area. The rest is divided between sugar beet, papaya, squash, aubergine and potato [824]. The vast majority of these plants, thanks to genetic modification, contain or accumulate pesticides in their tissues, either because they produce the pesticide themselves (as in the case of Bt maize, which produces insecticidal toxin *Bacillus thuringiensis* that protects it from corn borers) or because they can absorb it without dying (as in the case of Roundup-resistant soya or maize).

---

822. French Conseil d'Etat, 11 December 1998, *Association Greenpeace France et autres*, No. 194348.
823. J. Clive, *Global Status of Commercialized Biotech/GM Crops*, 2019, ISAAA Brief No. 54.
824. *Ibid.*

436. But the development of biotechnology is a matter of concern for many developing countries, which do not always have the capacity to effectively assess and manage the risks associated with GMOs. GMO research does not take into account their actual needs. Most GMO field trials and commercial releases focus on herbicide- and disease-resistant crops rather than on developments that could have a real impact on the food production of these developing countries, such as improved drought resistance. The industry is more interested in high-yielding crops for export sales than in food crops. GMOs are not well suited to traditional agricultural practices and there is also a risk that they will replace staple products exported by the South. Lastly, developing countries are protesting against the "biopiracy" that results from "bioprospecting" on their territory.

437. Broadly speaking, the North/South conflict – over access to genetic resources – is further complicated by a transatlantic conflict between the European Union and the United States over the principles governing GMO trade. The demands for environmental and health protection, for development in the countries of the South and for international trade and free trade are conflicting in many respects [825]. In order to objectify and resolve these conflicts, the need for an appropriate and coherent legal framework was quickly felt. Trade, commerce, biopiracy, accidental leakage: genetic resources and GMOs cross national borders. Accordingly, international law has been called upon to play a particularly important role, both to harmonise national laws that are still disparate (sometimes even non-existent) and to organise co-operation and conflict resolution between States. But in this "controversial universe" [826], where the financial stakes are huge, regulatory progress has been particularly slow.

438. The Rio Convention on Biological Diversity has been a key part of this international regulatory process. Its first protocol, adopted in 2010, deals with biotechnological risks and seeks in particular to enable "safe" international trade in GMOs. It was supplemented in 2010 by a protocol to the Protocol on Liability and Redress.

---

825. As noted in C. Noiville, *Ressources génétiques et droit,* Pedone, Paris, 1997, p. 6.
826. According to the words of Olivier Godard, "Stratégies industrielles et conventions d'environnement: de l'univers stabilisé aux univers controversés", *Environnement, Economie*, INSEE méthodes, Nos. 39-40, pp. 145-174 (our translation).

Section 1. The Cartagena Protocol on Biosafety to the Convention on Biological Diversity

439. Torn between the conflicting logics of environmental and health protection on the one hand, and free international trade on the other hand, the provisions of the Cartagena Protocol on Biosafety reflect a compromise between exporting countries concerned about finding outlets for their production (especially the US) and importing countries (including the European Union and developing countries) worried about the risks posed by GMOs to health, the environment or their economic and social systems. The Protocol's approach is progressive, but its implementation faces real challenges. Because of the many different international fora in which these issues are debated, and the different ways they are apprehended, international law hardly appears as a homogeneous and coherent body of rules; indeed, it seems to be somewhat disjointed.

1) Two conflicting logics

440. The treatment of GMO trade is caught between the conflicting logics of protection against risks on the one hand, and free international trade on the other hand. This conflict explains why negotiations leading to the adoption of the Cartagena Protocol were slow and difficult.

a) *The Protocol's ties with the Rio Convention and international environmental law*

441. Materially and institutionally tied to the Rio Convention, the Protocol adds to the corpus of international environmental law, which had until then been rather wanting and incomplete on this matter.

- *The first protocol to the Convention on Biological Diversity*

442. The instrument adopted in January 2000 is the first protocol of the Rio Convention. Already in 1992, at the United Nations Conference on Environment and Development in Rio, the issue of biosafety had received attention. Adopted at that time, *Agenda 21* had called for the strengthening of biosafety and the development of international co-operation mechanisms, stating that only when adequate and transparent safety and border-control procedures were put in place would the whole community be able to derive maximum benefit from biotechnology and be in the best position to accept the potential

benefits and risks thereof[827]. The Convention on Biological Diversity, rather laconic on the issue, mostly called for more concrete action by its Conference of the Parties. Article 19 (3) explicitly refers to the possible adoption of a protocol and outlines its content. In reality, what happened in 1992 was that the difficulty was postponed because there was not enough time to achieve a consensus on this point. Indeed, it took another seven years for the instrument to be adopted.

- *The Protocol and international environmental law*

443. Prior to the adoption of the Protocol, several instruments dealt with the international aspects of "biosafety", but most of them were sector-specific and/or non-binding. This was true of the 1995 *International Technical Guidelines for Safety in Biotechnology* produced by UNEP. These guidelines, which were relatively detailed and included an implementation plan, were designed to bridge a gap pending the adoption of the Protocol. They also provided a concrete basis for international co-operation in this area, but had the downside of being only an incentive. On a regional level, the OECD, which had been dealing with biosafety since the early 1980s, had also adopted recommendations on prior assessment and issued guidelines, the impact of which had been quite significant[828]. An instrument such as the 1951 International Plan Protection Convention could have been viewed as applicable to GMOs insofar as they pose a threat to plant life – thus contributing to biosafety – but no agreement had been reached between the Parties on this point[829].

444. Ultimately, the only binding instrument of general scope in the field of biosafety had been produced by EU law, with Directives 90/219/EEC on contained use of genetically modified micro-organism and 90/220/EEC on the deliberate release of GMOs into the environment[830]. The compatibility of these two instruments with the

---

827. See paragraph 16.29 of Agenda 21.
828. C. Noiville, *Ressources génétiques et droit* (n. 825), p. 53 *et seq.*
829. See its Article II, para. 2.
830. Directive 90/219/EEC amended by Directive 98/81/EC of the Council of 26 October 1998, *OJ* L 330, 5 December 1998, p. 13; Directive 90/220/CEE of the Council of 23 April 1990, *OJ* L74, 8 May 1990, p. 32. Directive 90/219 and its successive amendments were repealed and consolidated into a single act by Directive 2009/41/EC of the European Parliament and Council of 6 May 2009, *OJ* L 125, 21 May 2009, pp. 75-97. Directive 90/220 was repealed by Directive 2001/18/EC of the European Parliament and of the Council of 12 March 2001 on the deliberate release into the environment of genetically modified organisms and repealing Council Directive 90/220/EEC, OJ L 106, 17 April 2001, pp. 1-39.

Protocol does not raise any issues, as the latter recognises the legitimacy of "bilateral, regional and multilateral agreements and arrangements" on GMOs, whether they predate or post-date it (Art. 14). Provided that they "do not result in a lower level of protection than that provided for in the Protocol", "the provisions of the Protocol shall not affect intentional transboundary movements that take place pursuant to such agreements or arrangements between the parties to those agreements or arrangements". EU law is easily compatible as the Protocol does not require strict compliance, but leaves much room for manoeuvre.

445. Thus, until the adoption of the Protocol and leaving aside EU regulations, international environmental law had left the field clear to WTO, as far as international trade was concerned.

b) *WTO law and biosafety*

446. The issue of the relationship between the Protocol and WTO law was tricky. It plagued negotiations up until the last minute. Concerned about the outcome, the WTO had requested observer status at the extraordinary Conference of the Parties in charge of adopting the Protocol.

447. The question was part of a broader context, as other multilateral environmental agreements include trade restrictions either on a primary basis (CITES, Basel Convention on the Control of Transboundary Movements of Hazardous Wastes and their Disposal) or on a subsidiary basis (Montreal Protocol on Substances that Deplete the Ozone Layer). The WTO's Committee on Trade and Environment, created in 1994 following the Marrakech Conference, looked closely at the question of their compliance with WTO rules [831].

448. During the negotiations, there was mostly opposition between, on the one hand, the United States, and on the other hand, the EU and developing countries. The argument of the US was that the WTO should treat GMOs as "conventional" agricultural products and apply the same rules to them. The US did not want this issue to be included in the WTO negotiating agenda as such and preferred a bilateral discussion with the Europeans. On the contrary, the Europeans supported a multilateral approach and preferred to deal with the issue within the framework of the Rio Convention and the adoption of a specific protocol, which would generalise the case-by-case authorisation procedure adopted by

---

831. WTO, *Trade and Environment Bulletin*, TE/029, 30 July 1999.

the European Union. The EU also called for WTO recognition of the precautionary principle and for the clarification of labelling rules. In the end, the reluctance of the US did not prevent the Protocol from being adopted.

449. The latter contains rather ambiguous provisions as to its relationship with WTO law. During the negotiations, it was sometimes stated that it would be subordinated to international trade rules – a claim made by GMO exporters – and sometimes that the two regimes would be mutually supportive. The EU refused to subordinate the Protocol to WTO law and wanted it to be possible to rely on other obligations in the context of WTO dispute settlement procedures [832]. In the end, three provisions were included at the end of the preamble:

> "*Recognizing* that trade and environment agreements should be mutually supportive with a view to achieving sustainable development,
>
> *Emphasizing* that this Protocol shall not be interpreted as implying a change in the rights and obligations of a Party under any existing international agreements,
>
> *Understanding* that the above recital is not intended to subordinate this Protocol to other international agreements."

450. This ambiguous section is the result of a difficult balancing act and perhaps the least worst solution [833]. It refuses to establish a hierarchy between the two legal systems; however, it fails to resolve the practical difficulties that their co-existence might cause.

c) *Lengthy and difficult negotiations*

451. After preparatory work began in 1993, the Conference of the Parties established an *Ad Hoc* Group of Experts on Biosafety (hereinafter AHGEB) to prepare a draft protocol [834]. The AHGEB held six formal negotiating sessions. The last one, in February 1999 in Cartagena, Colombia, immediately preceded the extraordinary Conference of the Parties convened to adopt the Protocol [835]. There were not many

---

832. European Parliament Resolution on the Communication from the Commission to the Council and the European Parliament on the EU approach to the WTO Millennium Round (COM(1999) 331 "C5-0155/1999" 1999/2149(COS)).
833. F. Burhenne-Guilmin, "The Biosafety Protocol is Adopted in Montreal", *EPL*, 2000, Vol. 30, Nos. 1-2, p. 48.
834. COP Decision II/5. See also Decision I/9.
835. COP Decision IV/5.

controversial provisions, but at the time they elicited seemingly irreconcilable disagreements. Despite prolonged negotiations, the Conference failed to adopt the Protocol and had to be suspended.

452. Negotiations were marked by the formation of five geographical or affinity groups of States:

- the Miami Group (including Canada, Australia, Argentina, Chile and Uruguay) brought together the main GMO exporting countries;
- the like-minded countries group comprised the Group of 77 plus China, minus Chile, Uruguay and Argentina;
- the European Union;
- the CEECs;
- a Compromise Group, comprising Japan, Mexico, Norway, South Korea, Switzerland and Singapore.

453. Broadly speaking, negotiations pitted the first group against the following three, while the fifth group adopted more intermediate views. The United States only had observer status, as it had not ratified the Rio Convention on Biological Diversity. It could not take part in the discussions with voting rights. However, it had a considerable influence on the outcome of the negotiations, lending strong support to the Miami Group.

454. Another characteristic of this negotiation process was that the North-South divide – a usual feature in discussions under the Rio Convention on Biological Diversity – did not clearly emerge here. The European Union and most developing countries took a fairly protective stance. The Group of 77 supported the possibility for a country to refuse to import GMOs. Fearing for their local production systems, the G77 countries left to the Miami Group their traditional argument that environmental protection rules are a pretext for disguised protectionism.

455. Lastly, during the extraordinary COP session, environmental NGOs and even more so industry representatives also participated in the debates, as well as journalists, whose massive presence was the result of the Chair's desire to publicise the discussions.

456. Negotiations were difficult, even though the COP had repeatedly stressed the urgency of the matter. The method was somewhat chaotic. Contact groups and informal committees proliferated, dealing in reality with related subjects. The clusters analysis [836], another form of *package deal* negotiations, was also relied on. Much progress was

---

836. See Note from the Secretariat, UNEP/CBD/BSWG/6/3, 19 November 1998.

made in the Friends of the Chair group, with negotiators working on a single "package". After several months of intense, mostly informal negotiations, the Cartagena Protocol was finally adopted – in Montreal – on 29 January 2000, almost a year after the Cartagena failure [837]. A compromise was reached after a final night of negotiations between the European Union and the Miami Group, developing countries having been excluded from this last round. One hundred and thirty States adopted the Protocol by consensus, which was then opened for signature at the fifth COP in May 2000 and entered into force in September 2003. The Protocol now has 173 Parties [838], with some major absentees. In addition to the United States, which has still not ratified the Convention and therefore could not ratify the Protocol, Canada and Argentina, which are major GMO producers, have signed it but not ratified it. On the other hand, Brazil and India, other major producers, are parties to the Protocol.

2) A progressive approach

457. The outcome of the negotiations was more favourable to the views of the European Union and developing countries than to those of the Miami Group. The European Commission boasted that it had achieved all its major objectives [839]. The Protocol was given a relatively broad scope of application; an advance informed agreement procedure was established that allows a State to refuse the import of GMOs; the precautionary principle was endorsed and the labelling of GMOs became mandatory.

a) *A relatively broad scope of application*

458. The definition of the scope *ratione materiae* of the Protocol was one of the major issues in the negotiations. Some wanted the Protocol to cover only GMOs intended for introduction in the environment, such

---

837. The ExCOP decided in Cartagena that the Protocol would be called so, knowing that it would not be adopted in Cartagena. This allows the Biosafety Protocol to be distinguished from the Protocol on Substances that Deplete the Ozone Layer, referred to as the Montreal Protocol (1987). See decision on the resumption of the first extraordinary meeting of the Conference of the Parties to the Convention on Biological Diversity, UNEP/CBD/ExCOP/1/3, p. 17.
838. On 13 March 2022.
839. Proposal for a Council Decision on the signature, on behalf of the European Community, of the Cartagena Protocol on Biosafety, COM(2000)182 final, 30 March 2000, p. 2. The European Union has been a Party to the Protocol since 11 September 2003.

as seeds, which are the only ones likely to threaten the environment and biological diversity. Others envisaged a much broader scope, including not only agricultural products, but also GMOs used for food or feed, either directly or after processing, and GMOs used for medicine. An intermediate approach was eventually adopted.

459. The Protocol does not use the usual term "genetically modified organism"; it focuses on "living modified organisms", defined as "any living organism that possesses a novel combination of genetic material obtained through the use of modern biotechnology"[840]. The notion of genetic modification is difficult to pin down and it is the use of biotechnological techniques that makes it possible to define modified organisms. A "living" organism is "any biological entity capable of transferring or replicating genetic material, including sterile organisms, viruses and viroids".

460. This definition from the Protocol was later used in the Codex Alimentarius[841]. By "living", the Protocol means that it covers only biologically active products, such as seeds and unprocessed agricultural products for food or feed use. Derived products, such as oil or flour, which cannot reproduce or pass on genetic material, are therefore excluded from the scope of the Protocol. The same approach was adopted by the aforementioned Community Directive 90/220 on the deliberate release of GMOs in the environment[842].

461. That said, in the end a fairly broad scope was agreed, as the Protocol applies "to the transboundary movement, transit, handling and use of all living modified organisms that may have adverse effects on the conservation and sustainable use of biological diversity, taking also into account risks to human health"[843]. The reference to human health is significant, as the Protocol could have been limited to risks to biological diversity given its ties to the Rio Convention. Moreover, the Protocol does not cover solely transnational aspects of biosafety (which are admittedly difficult to disentangle from national aspects),

---

840. Meaning "the application of: *a. In vitro* nucleic acid techniques, including recombinant deoxyribonucleic acid (DNA) and direct injection of nucleic acid into cells or organelles, or *b.* Fusion of cells beyond the taxonomic family, that overcome natural physiological reproductive or recombination barriers and that are not techniques used in traditional breeding and selection" (Art. 3).

841. See the Principles for the Risk Analysis of Foods Derived from Modern Biotechnology, CAC/GL 44-2003, modified in 2011; Guideline for the Conduct of Food Safety Assessment of Foods Derived from Recombinant-DNA Plants, CAC/GL 45-2003, modified in 2008.

842. See above, paragraph 444.

843. Article 4.

and in particular the border-crossing of LMOs. On the contrary, it also imposes obligations with regard to the purely domestic handling of LMOs, at all stages of the handling process. Lastly, the Protocol also regulates accidental leakage in Articles 16 and 17. With regard to "unintentional transboundary movement", it lays down an obligation of prevention and specifies a number of emergency measures in the event of such movement, based on co-operation and exchange [844].

462. This relatively broad scope was achieved by allowing for a series of exceptions which mean that the obligations defined vary greatly according to the categories of LMOs [845]. For instance, pharmaceutical LMOs are *a priori* excluded from the scope of application, although Parties are free to subject them to a risk assessment before accepting their import. In the case of transit or contained use, the AIA procedure does not apply, but the rest of the Protocol's provisions do. Similarly, the Protocol distinguishes between agricultural LMOs and those intended for direct use as food or feed, for which it establishes a much simplified approval procedure compared to the AIA procedure.

463. There is also disagreement among the Parties as to whether the Protocol covers organisms derived from synthetic biology, the development of which took place after the adoption of the Protocol.

b) *The advance informed agreement procedure*

464. This procedure requires the exporting State to notify the importing State in writing of the export of LMOs, not for each export but only once, "prior to the first intentional transboundary movement of living modified organisms" [846]. The notification must be accompanied by a wide range of information, the minimum content of which is specified in Annex I. The importing country must indeed decide on the basis of

---

844. An "unintentional transboundary movement" was defined as "a transboundary movement of a living modified organism that has inadvertently crossed the national borders of a Party where the living modified organism was released, and the requirements of Article 17 of the Protocol apply to such transboundary movements only if the living modified organism involved is likely to have significant adverse effects on the conservation and sustainable use of biological diversity, taking also into account risks to human health, in the affected or potentially affected States". Decision VIII/16 (2016), *Unintentional Transboundary Movements and Emergency Measures (Art. 17)*.
845. Articles 5 and 6.
846. Article 7. Such a procedure existed under the 1989 Basel Convention on the Control of Transboundary Movements of Hazardous Wastes and their Disposal, and the 1998 Rotterdam Convention on the Prior Informed Consent Procedure for Certain Hazardous Chemicals and Pesticides in International Trade. Another example is the permits required by CITES.

a risk assessment using environmental and public health criteria. The Protocol describes in great detail the risk assessment procedure and methodology. It thus provides a valuable tool for the harmonisation of scientific assessment procedures. However, it opts for a decentralised, national assessment rather than establishing an international environmental and food safety agency capable of providing independent and international expert assessments. States were probably not ready yet to commit to this approach [847]. Another notable feature is that the assessment relies both on the importer and the exporter. The importing country may even require the exporter to conduct a risk analysis and the cost of this assessment to be borne by the exporter [848]. To some extent, the Protocol reverses the way traditional procedures usually work. It should be noted that the Parties may rely on the (optional) *Guidance on Risk Assessment of Living Modified Organisms* defined by the Meeting of the Parties, which is intended to be progressively improved [849].

465. The Party of import must acknowledge receipt of the notification, in writing, to the notifier within ninety days of its receipt. It must then indicate whether the movement can take place after ninety days (without subsequent written consent) or only after the importer has given its written consent. In the latter case, the importer has a relatively long period of 270 days (from the date of receipt of the notification) to notify the exporter of its decision, in writing. The importer may authorise the import (with or without conditions), prohibit it, request additional information or even extend the review period [850]. Except when the importing State's consent is unconditional, reasons must be provided for the decision.

466. The Protocol also enables the suspension of the import if a risk is identified [851]. This is an important provision, as the AIA procedure only applies to the first movement of a LMO:

> "A Party of import may, at any time, in light of new scientific information on potential adverse effects on the conservation and sustainable use of biological diversity, taking also into account the

---

847. See, for instance, European Commission, *White Paper of Food Safety*, COM(1999)719 final, 12 January 2000.
848. Article 15.
849. See Decision BS-VII/12 (2014), *Risk Assessment and Risk Management (Arts. 15 and 16)*.
850. Article 10.
851. Article 12.

risks to human health, review and change a decision regarding an intentional transboundary movement." [852]

The right to import is thus never final.

467. The AIA procedure, which is particularly strict and onerous, applies to agricultural LMOs intended for direct introduction into the environment (e.g. seeds, live fish). It does not apply to pharmaceuticals, LMOs in transit or intended for contained use, or LMOs defined by the Conference of the Parties "as being not likely to have adverse effects on the conservation and sustainable use of biological diversity, taking also into account risks to human health" [853]. More notably, LMOs intended for direct use as food or feed or for processing are subject to a much more flexible procedure set out in Article 11. Thus, fruits, vegetables and cereals intended for consumption are not subject to the AIA procedure. The Miami Group and the United States were successful on this point. Here, the Protocol institutionalises and generalises the exchange of information between the Parties through the Biosafety Clearing-House, established by the Protocol and operating under the aegis of its secretariat [854]. The importer's agreement is still required prior to import, but no notification is required. On this point, the Protocol is particularly vague and difficult to implement [855]. It must be noted that developing countries and countries with economies in transition enjoy a special, in-between regime for as long as they do not have a domestic regulatory framework [856]. As for the Biosafety Clearing-House, its implementation is proving delicate and the way it works could be improved [857]. It depends largely on the funding of the Parties, but the COP has had to

---

852. Article 12.
853. Article 7.
854. The Clearing-House is the focal point of the Convention. In addition to specific information on their legislation, Parties are required to provide the Clearing-House with summaries of risk assessments or ecological studies on LMOs, final decisions on the import or release of LMOs, written reports under the reporting system, etc. The modalities have been clarified by the Decision BS-I/3 (2004), *Information-Sharing and the Biosafety Clearing-House (Art. 20): Modalities of Operation of the Biosafety Clearing-House.*
855. F. Burhenne-Guilmin, "The Biosafety Protocol is Adopted in Montreal" (n. 833), p. 48.
856. They may declare, through the Clearing-House, that their decision prior to the first import of a LMO in this category will be taken following a risk assessment undertaken in accordance with Annex III, and within a foreseeable time period not exceeding 270 days (Art. 11 (6)).
857. See Decision BS-IV/2 (2008), *Operation and Activities of the Biosafety Clearing-House*; Decision VIII/2 (2016), *Operation and Activities of the Biosafety Clearing-House;* Decision 9/2 (2018), *Operation and Activities of the Biosafety Clearing-House (Art. 20).*

remind them of their obligations in this respect on several occasions. This has required a great deal of thought and work on harmonisation, accessibility of data and information, inclusion of data from other sources, as well as targeted assistance to many countries.

468. More generally, the Protocol sets out obligations in terms of access to information, public participation and consultation "in the decision-making process regarding living modified organisms" (Art. 23). Indeed, a more democratic decision-making process – which in the case of GMOs is generally characterised by opacity – would be welcome. However, the Protocol is significantly less precise than what had been envisaged during the negotiations. On this point, it lags behind current trends in international law [858].

469. It should be noted, though, that the Convention on Access to Information, Public Participation in Decision-Making and Access to Justice in Environmental Matters (1998) was amended in 2005 with a view to facilitating the earliest possible and most effective public participation before decisions are made on whether or not to authorise the deliberate release into the environment and placing on the market of GMOs. The amendment clarifies the relationship between the Aarhus Convention and the Protocol as it states the following:

> "The requirements made by Parties in accordance with the provisions of paragraph 1 of this article should be complementary and mutually supportive to the provisions of their national biosafety framework, consistent with the objectives of the Cartagena Protocol on Biosafety." [859]

---

[858]. The Protocol provides that Parties shall "[e]ndeavour to ensure that public awareness and education encompass access to information on living modified organisms identified in accordance with this Protocol that may be imported". It was envisaged that the Parties would be obliged to provide the public with "full" or "appropriate" information.

[859]. Decision II/1 (Almaty, 2005), *Genetically Modified Organisms*. The amendment has not yet entered into force. One ratification was missing by 19 December 2023. The Convention will be open for accession by States Members of the United Nations Economic Commission for Europe and by regional economic integration organisations constituted by sovereign States which are members of the Economic Commission for Europe and which have transferred competence over matters governed by this Convention to such organisations, and also by any other State with the approval of the Meeting of the Parties. In contrast, the Convention's corresponding treaty for the Latin American and Caribbean region, the Regional Agreement on Access to Information, Public Participation and Access to Justice in Environmental Matters in Latin America and the Caribbean (Escazu, 4 March 2018), does not contain specific provisions on GMOs.

470. The AIA procedure carries the risk of deadlock. The explicit agreement of the importer is required; the option of implicit agreement after a "reasonable" period was ruled out. A State that fails to make a decision within the time limit is in breach, but the Protocol does not say how to resolve the issue.

c) *The endorsement of the precautionary principle*

471. The content and scope of the precautionary principle were intensely debated; what some viewed as a customary principle was in fact not that consensual. The Protocol was undoubtedly guided by a precautionary approach, but was the principle to be included as such in its provisions? If so, was it to be in the preamble or in the body of the Protocol? And what scope was it to have? These questions remained contentious almost until the end of the negotiations. The reference – rather neutral – to Principle 15 of the Rio Declaration on Environment and Development was fairly easily accepted by the Miami Group. It thus appears both in the preamble and Article 1 of the Protocol. However, it was much harder for the Miami Group to accept the inclusion of the precautionary principle in Articles 9 and 10, i.e. as a basis for refusing the import of LMOs for food, agriculture or processing. Indeed, here the principle takes on an operational dimension, as wanted by the Europeans [860]. In line with the COP of the Convention on Biological Diversity, the Meeting of the Parties stressed the importance of this approach with regard to products and organisms derived from synthetic biology [861].

472. This inclusion *a priori* strengthened the EU's position in favour of a stronger influence of the precautionary principle in WTO law [862]. The hesitations of legal academics and the timidity of the International Court of Justice and the International Tribunal for the Law of the Sea had until then led the WTO Appellate Body to deny the precautionary principle any autonomy [863]. It was clear from the Appellate Body's earlier decisions that the principle – which could not be conceived as a general principle to be referred to in the event of a dispute –

---

860. The wording of Article 11, para. 8 is similar to that of Article 10, para. 6 applicable to agricultural GMOs.
861. Decision 9/13 (2018), *Risk Assessment and Risk Management (Arts. 15 and 16)*.
862. N. de Sadeleer, "Le principe de précaution : du slogan à la règle de droit", *Droit de l'environnement*, April 2000, No. 77, p. 14.
863. Appellate Body Report, *European Communities – Measures Concerning Meat and Meat Products (Hormones)*, WT/DS26/AB/R, WTDS48/AB/R, 16 January 1998, para. 123.

only applied insofar as it was substantially embedded in the SPS Agreement, but not to the extent that it overrode the provisions of that Agreement [864]. The SPS Agreement's references to the precautionary principle did not amount to incorporation, and could not override the requirement imposed elsewhere for scientific proof of risk. Given this lack of autonomy, the precautionary principle thus risked being treated differently under WTO law, depending on whether measures were assessed under the SPS Agreement, the TBT Agreement or the GATT [865]. While the Appellate Body had recognised in the *Hormones* case that the SPS Agreement left a wide discretion to States, it had also sought to restrict the application of the principle [866]. A State whose restrictions on international GMO trade were to be challenged before the WTO was therefore well-advised to have the dispute decided under the TBT Agreement or the 1994 GATT. The SPS Agreement being the most demanding, with its many references to scientific justification and proof, what is accepted under this agreement could be applied *a fortiori* under less demanding agreements [867]. The GATT seemed to be the most flexible instrument, the *Asbestos* case having opened up interesting prospects with regard to derogations falling within the scope of Article XX [868].

473. The Protocol seemed to be sufficiently precise on this point to reduce the risk of conflict in the WTO, at least between Parties to the Protocol. The position of the WTO's Committee on Trade and Environment, as well as that of the Appellate Body in the *Shrimp-Turtle* case, calling for multilateral solutions to environmental problems, has already been discussed above. Article 3 (2) of the WTO's *Understanding on Rules and Procedures Governing the Settlement of Disputes* requires disputes to be settled on the basis of covered agreements and not the application of international law as a whole, but the Appellate Body has already had the opportunity to state that "the General Agreement

---

864. See para. 125 of the abovementioned report.
865. A. Laudon and C. Noiville, *Le principe de précaution, le droit de l'environnement et l'OMC*, rapport remis au Ministère de l'Environnement, France, 16 November 1998, p. 75.
866. Appellate Body Report, aforementioned, footnotes 92 and 93, para. 123; WT Douma, "The Beef Hormones Dispute and the Use of National Standards under WTO Law", *European Environmental Law Review*, May 1999, p. 137.
867. H. Ruiz-Fabri, "La prise en compte du principe de précaution par l'OMC", *Revue juridique de l'environnement*, 2000, pp. 55-66.
868. Report of the Panel, *European Communities – Measures Affecting Asbestos and Asbestos – Containing Products*, WT/DS135/R, 8 September 2000. The Panel admitted that the French ban measures, challenged by Canada, fall within the scope of Article XX *b)*.

is not to be read in clinical isolation from public international law" [869]. As such, it seemed that a panel could potentially take into account the content of the Cartagena Protocol.

474. It should be added that, under the SPS Agreement, if a State complies with international standards and norms, it enjoys a presumption of compatibility. To ensure coherence, the Protocol could potentially become such a standard, like the *Codex Alimentarius*, if the SPS Committee recognised it as such [870]. This would be especially significant as the Codex does not deal with environmental risks, but only with food-related risks.

d) *The labelling obligation*

475. This was one of the issues that almost caused the collapse of the Protocol negotiations. The US was of the opinion that imposing the labelling of these products would be unnecessary – its argument being that if they are authorised for marketing, they are safe – and too costly. Thus, the Miami Group fought to the bitter end to avoid the separation of LMOs and their labelling, while the EU firmly maintained the opposite position. Based on the necessary freedom of choice for consumers, but also on health and environmental safety requirements, the labelling of GMOs – not only genetically modified bacteria, animals or plants, but also agricultural and food products – was a key priority for European countries. Traceability, which limits the need for controls that are inherently difficult and costly to put in place, relies on the organisation of separate channels. However, it cannot be implemented if labelling is not an international obligation, as shown by cases of accidental contamination. It was therefore in the EU's interest that the Protocol lay down clear obligations on this subject.

476. As a compromise, the Protocol provides that LMOs intended for direct use as food or feed or for processing must be labelled as "may contain" LMOs. The wording of course allows for more information to

---

869. Appellate Body Report, *United States – Standards for Reformulated and Conventional Gasoline*, WT/DS2/AB/R, 29 April 1996, p. 19. In the *Shrimp-Turtle* case, the Appellate Body interpreted the GATT in the light of international environmental law, aforementioned report, para. 125 *et seq*.

870. See Annex 1, paragraph 2 of the Agreement, which also refers to the International Plant Protection Convention. The Codex has also drawn heavily on the Cartagena Protocol and the work done within it. See Principles for the Risk Analysis of Foods Derived from Modern Biotechnology, CAC/GL 44-2003, revised in 2011; Guideline for the Conduct of Food Safety Assessment of Foods Derived from Recombinant-DNA Plants, CAC/GL 45-2003, revised in 2008.

be provided, but the Protocol itself contains no obligation to specify the nature of the products, nor to guarantee their presence or absence [871]. Here as well, the difficulty was postponed: the Protocol gave two years to the Meeting of the Parties after the entry into force of the Protocol to decide at a later stage on more specific and detailed requirements for the identification of LMOs (Art. 18). This was the focus of one of the first decisions of the Meeting of the Parties, which only laid down very general principles but set up a group of technical experts on this subject [872]. Today still, Article 18 remains under negotiation [873]. This is especially difficult as various international standards deal with this subject, and their contents are not harmonised. As it stands, Parties to the Protocol and "other States" are simply invited

> "to take measures to ensure the use of a commercial invoice or other document required or utilized by existing documentation systems, or documentation as required by domestic regulatory and/or administrative frameworks, as documentation that should accompany living modified organisms that are intended for direct use as food or feed, or for processing".

This documentation "should include the information in paragraph 4 below and allow for easy recognition, transmission and effective integration of the information requirements, with consideration of standard formats" [874]. For the time being, the Meeting of the Parties has

---

871. F. Burhenne-Guilmin, "The Biosafety Protocol is Adopted in Montreal" (n. 833), p. 47. It must also be said that they are not likely to be released into the environment.

872. Decision BS-I/6 (2004).

873. CBD, *Report on Analysis of Information on Standards Relevant to the Handling, Transport, Packaging and Identification of Living Modified Organisms*, Note by the Executive Secretary, UNEP/CBD/BS/COP-MOP/6/INF/24, 13 August 2012, p. 3.

874. Parties have to clearly state:

> "*(a)* In cases where the identity of the living modified organisms is known through means such as identity preservation systems, that the shipment contains living modified organisms that are intended for direct use as food or feed, or for processing; *(b)* In cases where the identity of the living modified organisms is not known through means such as identity preservation systems, that the shipment may contain one or more living modified organisms that are intended for direct use as food or feed, or for processing; *(c)* That the living modified organisms are not intended for intentional introduction into the environment; *(d)* The common, scientific and, where available, commercial names of the living modified organisms; *(e)* The transformation event code of the living modified organisms or, where available, as a key to accessing information in the Biosafety Clearing-House, its unique identifier code; *(f)* The Internet address of the Biosafety Clearing-House for further information".

See Decision BS-III/10 (2006), *Handling, Transport, Packaging and Identification of Living Modified Organisms: paragraph 2 (a) of Article 18.*

left it at that, having dropped – at least for now – the idea of a unique identifier [875].

477. The Protocol is a little bit more specific for LMOs intended for contained use, which must be clearly identified; safety requirements for transport, storage and use must also be specified. But it is for LMOs intended to be intentionally introduced into the environment, such as seeds, that the obligations are the most stringent. These must be clearly identified. Their identity must be specified, as well as their relevant features and characteristics, and the safety rules to be observed.

478. The provisions of the Protocol on labelling could conflict with WTO rules. The WTO's Committee on Trade and Environment has recognised the need for harmonisation and further progress on equivalence and mutual recognition to avoid the crystallisation of disputes before the WTO. In this respect, the Protocol on Biosafety may have influenced the more reluctant States. Indeed, even the US recently introduced a labelling requirement, at least for food ingredients containing GMOs [876].

3) The implementation of the Protocol

479. Four issues can be identified with regard to the implementation of the Protocol, which remained a question mark when the Protocol was adopted: taking into account the needs of developing countries, the force of attraction of WTO law, monitoring procedures and co-operation with other international institutions.

a) *Taking into account the needs of developing countries*

480. Like other MEAs and in line with the Convention on Biological Diversity, the Cartagena Protocol adopts the differentiation technique, establishing a special status for developing countries and countries in transition. However, the principle of "common but differentiated responsibilities" is not explicitly mentioned in its provisions, despite the wishes of developing countries [877].

---

875. Decision BS-VII/8 (2014).
876. Department of Agriculture, Agricultural Marketing Service 7 CFR Part 66, [Doc. No. AMS-TM-17-0050] RIN 0581–AD54, *National Bioengineered Food Disclosure Standard*.
877. *Earth Negotiation Bulletin*, Summary Report, 14-23 February 1999, Sixth Session of the Open-ended *Ad Hoc* Working Group on Biosafety (BSWG-6) and First Extraordinary Meeting of the CBD Conference of the Parties (ExCOP).

481. Many developing countries have been overwhelmed by the rapid development of biotechnology and have highlighted their weak or inadequate capacity to manage biosafety. The development of their technical as well as scientific and legal "capacities" is an important condition for the effective implementation of the Protocol. Rather disappointingly, the Protocol simply provides that

> "[a] Party may indicate its needs for financial and technical assistance and capacity-building with respect to living modified organisms intended for direct use as food or feed, or for processing. Parties shall cooperate to meet these needs in accordance with Articles 22 and 28" [878].

Article 22, which focuses on capacity-building, lays down an obligation to co-operate, which may be bilateral or multilateral. The areas mentioned are: scientific and technical training in the proper and safe use of biotechnology, in risk assessment and risk management, as well as the enhancement of technical and institutional capacities in biosafety. But the content of this obligation is probably too general given the issues at stake. In terms of funding, the Global Environmental Facility, which is the financing mechanism of the Rio Convention and is managed jointly by the World Bank, UNEP and UNDP, has by extension become the financing mechanism of the Protocol [879]. But: "The developed country Parties may also provide, and the developing country Parties and the Parties with economies in transition avail themselves of, financial and technological resources . . . through bilateral, regional and multilateral channels". Once more, the wording of the Protocol – "may also" – is not very demanding.

482. Nevertheless, in both respects, the Protocol has had a real impact. The treaty institutions have attached great importance to these issues. The COP has defined and regularly reviewed a relatively precise plan of action in this regard [880]. A large number of countries – over 100 according to the secretariat – have received capacity-building assistance through the Global Environmental Facility's implementing agencies to support their efforts to develop and implement their national legal and administrative frameworks for biosafety. The number of bilateral, sub-regional and regional co-operation agreements for biosafety capacity-building has also increased in recent years. Finally, a roster of experts

---

878. Article 11 (9).
879. Article 28.
880. Decisions BS-V/3 (2010) and BS-VI/3 (2012).

was established. The COP even regretted not the lack of available resources, but the "low number of projects and the total amount of funding requested by Parties" [881].

483. Concerned about the economic and social consequences of the development of biotechnology, developing countries also obtained that the Protocol recognise that States may take socio-economic considerations into account when making decisions under the Protocol (Art. 26). In this regard, the Meeting of the Parties developed *Guidance on the Assessment of Socio-Economic Considerations in the Context of Article 26 of the Cartagena Protocol on Biosafety*, which is optional [882]. It has set up an online forum on the subject and runs an active expert group on the issue.

b) *The Protocol versus WTO law*

484. In negotiating the Cartagena Protocol, the objective of the European Union and of many developing countries was to light a "backfire" against WTO law, as Hélène Ruiz Fabri rightly put it [883].

485. The prospect of a conflict before the WTO was envisaged from the start of the Protocol negotiations and was especially credible as its ratification by some major exporting countries such as Canada and Argentina was far from certain. It was also quite clear that the United States would not participate. As mentioned before, since it has not ratified the Convention on Biological Diversity, it is not in a position to ratify the Protocol even if it wanted to do so. However, the United States has repeatedly threatened to use WTO dispute settlement procedures to ensure free trade in these products [884].

486. In practice, two scenarios can be envisaged. In the first scenario, the conflicting States are all Parties to the Protocol. In this instance, it is generally accepted that trade measures agreed between the Parties to that treaty – even if they are not consistent with WTO rules (in this case the 1994 GATT or the SPS or TBT agreements) –

---

881. Decision BS-VII/5 (2014).
882. Decision 9/14 (2018).
883. H. Ruiz Fabri, "Concurrence ou complémentarité entre les mécanismes de règlement des différends du Protocole de Carthagène et ceux de l'OMC?", *Le commerce international des organismes génétiquement modifiés*, La Documentation française, Monde européen et international, J Bourrinet and S Maljean-Dubois (dir. publ.), 2002, p. 149 (our translation).
884. B. Marre, De la mondialisation subie au développement contrôlé. Les enjeux de la Conférence de Seattle, rapport d'information, Assemblée nationale, France, 30 November-3 December 1999, p. 154.

could be considered as *lex specialis* and should not raise legal issues at the WTO.[885] Furthermore, the WTO's Committee on Trade and Environment has noted: "In practice, in cases where there is a consensus among Parties to an MEA to apply among themselves specifically mandated trade measures, disputes between them over the use of such measures are unlikely to occur in the WTO." [886] In fact, the Committee strongly supports multilateral solutions as the best way for governments to address environmental issues. The Appellate Body itself quoted the Committee:

> "We note that WTO Members in the Report of the CTE, forming part of the Report of the General Council to Ministers on the occasion of the Singapore Ministerial Conference, endorsed and supported: . . . multilateral solutions based on international cooperation and consensus as the best and most effective way for governments to tackle environmental problems of a transboundary or global nature. WTO Agreements and multilateral environmental agreements (MEAs) are representative of efforts of the international community to pursue shared goals, and in the development of a mutually supportive relationship between them, due respect must be afforded to both." [887]

487. In the second scenario, the States in dispute are not all Parties to the Protocol. This was a likely possibility given that some major GMO producers (United States, Canada, Argentina) have not ratified the Protocol and it became a reality with the constitution of a panel against the European Union at the request of the United States, of Canada and Argentina [888].

488. The problem was thus likely to be most acute in relation to restrictions on trade between on the one hand, States that are both a Party to the Protocol and a member of the WTO, and on the other hand, States that are a member of the WTO but not a Party to the Protocol. The purpose of restricting trade with non-Parties is to tighten the regulatory net; such restrictions simultaneously extend the scope of conventions, at least partially, and encourage participation. CITES, the Montreal Protocol and the Basel Convention all include such

---

885. TEC, *Information Document on Trade and Environment,* WTO High level Symposium on Trade and Environment, 15-16 March 1999, p. 11.
886. Aforementioned report WT/CTE/1, 12 November 1996.
887. *United States – Import Prohibition of Certain Shrimp and Shrimp Products,* Appellate Body Report, WT/DS58/AB/R, para. 78, footnote 65.
888. See below.

restrictions. However, the Protocol is less precise and less strict than these three conventions. In stark contrast to the proposals of some States – especially developing countries – that called for a total ban on trade with non-Parties, it simply provides that "[t]ransboundary movements of living modified organisms between Parties and non-Parties shall be consistent with the objective of this Protocol" [889]. It does not therefore require strict compliance, and "consistency" only needs to be assessed in relation to the objectives of the Protocol. The Miami Group succeeded in changing the original wording which initially required consistency with "objectives and principles" of the Protocol.

489. What leeway do the Parties have? Can they still prohibit or restrict trade with non-Parties if they do not consider it sufficiently safe? From the perspective of the Protocol, the answer is yes. Article 2 (4) of the Protocol allows Parties to take more protective measures than those specified. However, this right is restricted in two ways. First, these measures must be compatible with the objectives and – this time – the provisions of the Protocol. On the other hand, and this is again the work of the Miami Group, they must be "consistent with the objective and the provisions of this Protocol and . . . in accordance with that Party's other obligations under international law". The measures must therefore be consistent with WTO law. From this point of view, the relationship of the Biosafety Protocol with WTO law is less problematic than the WTO's relationship with the Basel Convention, CITES or the Montreal Protocol. The Protocol is more in keeping with the position of the WTO's Committee on Trade and Environment, which considers that particular care should be taken in applying restrictions to non-Parties. This is especially true since the Protocol also encourages Parties to conclude bilateral, regional and multilateral agreements and arrangements with non-Parties regarding the transboundary movement of LMOs (Art. 24), which is another way to avoid disputes arising and being submitted to WTO panels [890].

490. From mid-May 2003, the United States, Canada and Argentina requested consultations with the European Communities on measures affecting the approval and marketing of products that contain, are

---

889. Article 24 (1).
890. It should be noted that the adoption of more stringent measures could also give rise to disputes between the Parties, and that the same requirement of consistency with international law, and thus WTO law, is then imposed, as is the requirement of consistency with the objective and provisions of the Protocol. In fact, the right for the Parties to take more stringent measures is considerably restricted and the scenarios in which it could come into play seem very limited.

composed of or are produced from GMOs. In the absence of a mutually satisfactory settlement, the three countries requested on 7 August 2003 the institution of a panel to examine the issue. The Panel issued its report on the *Biotech Products* case in 2006 [891], and it did not give rise to an appeal. The particularly interesting question here was what weight the Cartagena Protocol would have in this scenario. Would WTO law be interpreted in "clinical isolation" from this widely ratified piece of international environmental law?

491. Since the term had been coined by the WTO Appellate Body in 1996 in its first report on the *Gasoline* case, the threat of "clinical isolation" had haunted not only the corridors of the WTO, but also many books and legal journals. The Appellate Body had relied on Article 3 (2) of the *Understanding on Rules and Procedures Governing the Settlement of Disputes*. Pursuant to this provision, a WTO Dispute Settlement Body is supposed to rule only on the "covered agreements": "Recommendations and rulings of the DSB cannot add to or diminish the rights and obligations provided in the covered agreements". However, according to the same provision, a settlement body must also "clarify the existing provisions of those agreements in accordance with customary rules of interpretation of public international law". In the opinion of the Appellate Body, "[t]hat direction reflects a measure of recognition that the General Agreement is not to be read in clinical isolation from public international law" [892].

492. The rejection of "clinical isolation", from the very first Appellate Body report, was thus a sign of openness to external rules. It established that WTO law was not a self-contained regime, assuming such regimes even exist: WTO law is of and exists within international law – it is not clinically isolated from it – and it can be interpreted and construed using customary rules of interpretation of international law.

493. However, Article 3 (2) of the *Understanding* itself is only directly concerned with rules of interpretation of public international law. It only indirectly or by ricochet allows substantive rules to be taken into account. By ricochet, since the rules of interpretation of international law – in particular Articles 31 and 32 of the Vienna Convention on the Law of Treaties, which the Appellate Body very quickly viewed as setting out customary rules – provide for substantive

---

891. WTO, *European Communities – Measures Affecting the Approval and Marketing of Biotech Products*, (DS 291/292/293), Report of the Panel, 29 September 2006.
892. *Ibid.*

public international law to be taken into account. The exercise of the WTO judge's jurisdiction must therefore be "controlled by the normative environment" [893].

494. This was the line of reasoning that the Appellate Body had unfolded little by little, not without some audacity given the many limitations that the *Understanding on Rules and Procedures Governing the Settlement of Disputes* sets on its power to develop the law. Indeed, its case law reflects, in small increments, a very clear evolution in terms of taking into account rules outside the WTO, an evolution compared with the 1947 GATT, which was much more "clinically isolated" than WTO law is today. Thus, it is now established that the covered agreements constitute the primary source of law when examining a dispute, but not the unique source [894]. But how far should the Appellate Body go in taking into account exogenous rules, other international instruments and principles? The *Gasoline* case had not ended the debate, far from it.

495. The interplay between WTO rules and other international instruments and principles was one of the key issues in the *Biotech Products* case. Indeed, the European Communities, to defend themselves, abundantly relied on other international rules and instruments belonging to the sphere of international environmental and health law, in particular the Cartagena Protocol. As for the complainants, they categorically rejected the relevance of the other international rules and instruments invoked to settle the dispute, inviting the Panel to limit itself to "covered agreements", i.e. WTO law and internal rules.

496. In this regard, the principle of systemic integration referred to in Article 31 (3) *(c)* of the 1969 Vienna Convention on the Law of Treaties must prompt the interpreter to take into account "together with the context: ... any relevant rules of international law applicable in the relations between the parties". In this case, the Panel refused to apply this principle. It found that, for a treaty rule to be interpreted in the light of another treaty rule, the latter (the Cartagena Protocol) must be applicable to all parties to the former (WTO law) [895]. This requirement,

---

893. Fragmentation of International Law: Difficulties Arising from the Diversification and Expansion of International Law Report of the Study Group of the International Law Commission, finalized by Martti Koskenniemi, A/CN.4/L.682, 13 April 2006, p. 31.
894. E. Canal-Forgues, *Le règlement des différends à l'OMC*, Bruylant, 2nd ed., 2004, p. 100.
895. In the same vein, J. Pauwelyn, "The Role of Public International Law in the WTO: How Far Can We Go?", *AJIL*, 2001, p. 577; *Conflict of Norms in Public International Law, How WTO Law Relates to other Rules of International Law* (CUP 2003), p. 257. The issue had been raised, only to be set aside, by the Panel, *Chile –*

which was not met and is only rarely met, means that in practice, Article 31 (3) *(c)* essentially makes it possible only to interpret treaty rules in the light of customary rules.

497. According to the Panel,

> "[i]ndeed, it is not apparent why a sovereign State would agree to a mandatory rule of treaty interpretation which could have as a consequence that the interpretation of a treaty to which that State is a party is affected by other rules of international law which that State has decided not to accept".

Acknowledging the contrary would mean great danger for legal certainty – one could undo what it has built on one side by making a different commitment on the other side. Would it be acceptable for the Communities to dismantle WTO law by negotiating and entering into the Cartagena Protocol, which the United States refuses to join? It would not be reasonable, says the Panel. Its report was neither overturned nor confirmed by the Appellate Body [896]. The attempt by the EU and developing countries to light a backfire against WTO law thus proved unavailing [897].

c) *The institution of a non-compliance mechanism*

498. The Protocol is largely non-self-executing and relies mostly on the Parties' national legislation for its implementation. Monitoring implementation and sanctioning non-compliance are thus of particular importance.

499. Conferring on the Meeting of the Parties the traditional, relatively broad remit of COPs, the Protocol provides that it "shall keep under regular review the implementation of this Protocol and shall make, within its mandate, the decisions necessary to promote its effective implementation" (Art. 29 (4)). Article 33 introduces the system of reports, the periodicity and content of which the Meeting of

---

Price Band System and Safeguard Measures relating to Certain Agricultural Products, WT/DS207/R, 3 May 2002, p. 161.

896. See *European Communities and Certain Member States – Measures Affecting Trade in Large Civil Aircraft*, Appellate Body Report, WT/DS316/AB/R, 18 May 2011, p 406. However, the Appellate Body urges caution in such a situation.

897. According to the words of H. Ruiz Fabri, "Concurrence ou complémentarité entre les mécanismes de règlement des différends du Protocole de Carthagène et ceux de l'OMC?" (n. 883), p. 149.

the Parties has specified, in particular by way of guidelines [898]. Article 34 also provided for the adoption of a non-compliance procedure by the Meeting of the Parties at its first meeting, more specifically:

> "cooperative procedures and institutional mechanisms to promote compliance with the provisions of this Protocol and to address cases of non-compliance. These procedures and mechanisms shall include provisions to offer advice or assistance, where appropriate".

Indeed, as early as 2004, the first Meeting of the Parties established the procedure and created a Compliance Committee [899].

500. In comparison to other similar procedures, this procedure is very flexible and mindful of sovereignty. Although "[t]he objective of the compliance procedures and mechanisms shall be to promote compliance with the provisions of the Protocol, to address cases of non-compliance by Parties, and to provide advice or assistance, where appropriate", it is specified that: "The compliance procedures and mechanisms shall be simple, facilitative, non-adversarial and cooperative in nature" [900]. The Committee has two roles. First of all, it must "identify the specific circumstances and possible causes of individual cases of non-compliance referred to it"; cases can be referred to the Committee by "any Party with respect to itself" or "any Party, which is affected or likely to be affected, with respect to another Party". The Committee looked at whether it was appropriate for it to receive and analyse a submission made by an NGO stating that a Party had failed to comply with its obligations under the Protocol. It came to the logical conclusion that it was not within its role to examine such a submission [901].

---

898. See, in particular, Decision BS-III/14 (2006) *Monitoring and Reporting*, which sets out the periodicity, format and guidelines for reporting. See also BS-VI/14 (2012) *Monitoring and Reporting (Art. 33)*; BS-VII/14 (2014), *Monitoring and Reporting (Art. 33)*; Decision 9/5 (2018) *Monitoring and Reporting (Art. 33)*. To facilitate the work of States, the timetable is now synchronised with that of the Convention on Biological Diversity itself.
899. See Decision BS-I/7 (2004) *Establishment of Procedures and Mechanisms on Compliance under the Cartagena Protocol on Biosafety*. See also Decision 9/1 (2018), *Compliance*.
900. Point *I)*.
901. Compliance Committee under the Cartagena Protocol on Biosafety, Montreal Item 6 of the provisional agenda* Report of the Compliance Committee under the Cartagena Protocol on Biosafety on the work of its sixth meeting, UNEP/CBD/BS/CC/6/4, 27 November 2009.

501. When non-compliance is detected, the possible response measures are very mindful of State sovereignty and focus more on guidance and assistance towards a return to compliance. There was talk of tightening this procedure as part of the periodic assessment of the Protocol's effectiveness, scheduled for five years after its entry into force, and then at least every five years thereafter [902]. However, "*recognizing* the need for building further the confidence of Parties in the role of the Compliance Committee", the COP actually further relaxed the consequences of non-compliance [903]. Yet the trade dimension of the Protocol meant that trade sanctions could have been envisaged, and could have been very dissuasive.

502. Second, the Compliance Committee must "review general issues of compliance by Parties with their obligations under the Protocol, taking into account the information provided in the national reports communicated in accordance with Article 33 of the Protocol and also through the Biosafety Clearing-House". The Committee held its seventeenth meeting in 2020. For the most part, it focuses on general issues and contributes to the five-yearly assessment of the Protocol's effectiveness. Its work has informed many decisions of the Meeting of the Parties and it is involved in the reflection on the post-2020 strategic framework. It has looked at whether different Parties were complying with the Convention, but its review appears to be rather formal and procedural. (Have Parties submitted their national reports on time? Have they designated a focal point? Have they taken legal and administrative measures to implement the Protocol?) In terms of follow-up action, the decisions of the Meeting of the Parties are very soft. Indeed, in the event of non-compliance, Parties are not named. Consequences have included statements urging Parties that have not yet put in place all the legal, administrative and other measures required in order to comply with their obligations under the Protocol to do so, with particular attention given to the importance of establishing monitoring systems as a prerequisite for effective reporting, or noting with regret that a Party has not submitted its interim, first, second or third national report. In reality, the Meeting of the Parties is rather powerless in cases of repeated or persistent non-compliance [904].

---

902. Article 35.
903. Decision BS-V/1 (2010), *Report of the Compliance Committee.*
904. Decision VIII/1 (2016), *Compliance.*

d) Co-operation with other organisations

503. The Cartagena Protocol institutions are not the only ones interested in biotechnology at the international level. In a fragmented governance, this sensitive and controversial subject gives rise to competition and games of influence between different international institutions. In these circumstances, it is essential for the treaty institutions to co-operate with other institutions, first so they can inform each other, but above all to promote their approach and try to influence these other institutions. If the Protocol's approach, if the principles and rules defined therein are endorsed by other institutions, if the work of its expert groups is used outside the conventional sphere, this would place the Protocol at the heart of the international governance of biotechnology. Failing this, it could be left on the sidelines and lose much of its effectiveness.

504. Indeed, the decisions of the Meeting of the Parties reveal that it is very open and attentive to what is happening outside the framework of the Protocol. On risk assessment, handling, transport, packaging and identification of LMOs, the Protocol has tried to position itself as a leader among different organisations and institutions. This is clearly part of the mandate of the secretariat and one of the objectives defined as strategic by the Meeting of the Parties in the Strategic Plan of the Cartagena Protocol on Biosafety [905]. Co-operation with other organisations is on the agenda of almost every meeting of the Parties and is usually the subject of a decision. Thus, the Meeting of the Parties early on requested that the secretariat reinforce co-operation on issues of mutual interest with various institutions, such as the Codex Alimentarius Commission, the World Organisation for Animal Health or the International Plant Protection Convention, as well as with the secretariat of the Aarhus Convention on issues related to public awareness and participation [906]. The secretariat has indeed developed useful connections with these institutions, but also with the WTO, the FAO and even the OECD. It has also concluded a partnership agreement with the World Customs Organisation [907]. In 2006, it joined the Green Customs Initiative which brings together the United Nations Environment Programme, the secretariat of the Basel Convention on the Control of Transboundary

---

905. Third assessment and review of the effectiveness of the Cartagena Protocol and mid-term evaluation of the Strategic Plan, UNEP/CBD/BS/COP-MOP/8/1.
906. Decision BS-II/6 (2002).
907. Decisions BS-IV/6 (2008); BS-V/6 (2010); BS-VI/ (2012); BS-VII/6 (2014); VIII/6 (2016).

Movements of Hazardous Wastes and their Disposal, the Convention on International Trade in Endangered Species of Wild Fauna and Flora, the Stockholm Convention on Persistent Organic Pollutants, the Rotterdam Convention on the Prior Informed Consent Procedure for Certain Hazardous Chemicals and Pesticides in International Trade, the Montreal Protocol on Substances that Deplete the Ozone Layer, the United Nations Office on Drugs and Crime, the Organization for the Prohibition of Chemical Weapons, the World Customs Organisation and Interpol. This programme aims to strengthen the capacity of customs and enforcement officials to monitor trade and to detect and prevent illegal trade in environmentally sensitive goods or substances under the relevant international treaties. The Green Customs Initiative complements and strengthens existing training and capacity-building efforts under these agreements [908]. These co-operative efforts have borne fruit. We have already mentioned the amendment to the Aarhus Convention on access to information and public participation [909]. It is also worth mentioning, in the context of the International Plant Protection Convention, the adoption in April 2004, by the Interim Commission on Phytosanitary Measures, of a supplement on risk analysis for LMOs [910]. However, the secretariat has stressed that it lacks resources to carry out this collaborative work [911].

Section 2. The Nagoya-Kuala Lumpur Supplementary Protocol on Liability and Redress to the Cartagena Protocol on Biosafety

505. The result of lengthy negotiations, the Supplementary Protocol on Liability and Redress is very flexible in its content. However, it has not been ratified by many countries.

1) Lengthy negotiations

506. The need to develop rules on liability and redress for damage caused by GMOs quickly became apparent to the Parties to the Convention on Biological Diversity. The issue was highly controversial

---

908. CBD, Cooperation with Other Organizations, Conventions and Initiatives, Note by the Executive Secretary, UNEP/CBD/BS/COP-MOP/8/6 6 September 2016.
909. See *supra*, para. 400.
910. This supplement was incorporated into the International Standard for Phytosanitary Measures NIMP 11 Rév. 1., http://www.fao.org/3/a-j1302f.pdf, accessed on 25 October 2023.
911. CBD, Cooperation with Other Organizations, Conventions and Initiatives, Note by the Executive Secretary, UNEP/CBD/BS/COP-MOP/8/66, September 2016.

during the negotiation of the Cartagena Protocol. As the Parties were unable to agree on this issue, they decided to defer the adoption of rules on this issue. Article 27 of the Cartagena Protocol thus provided that the COP-MOP should at its first meeting initiate a process to define appropriate rules and procedures in the field of liability and redress for damage resulting from transboundary movements of LMOs.

507. Indeed, at its first meeting in Kuala Lumpur in February 2004, the COP-MOP set up an Open-ended *Ad Hoc* Working Group on Liability and Redress under the Cartagena Protocol, to formulate options and propose international rules and procedures in this respect. It took five meetings of the Working Group followed by four meetings of a Group of the Friends of the Co-Chairs, in almost seven years of negotiations, before a new instrument was finalised[912]. The Nagoya-Kuala Lumpur Supplementary Protocol on Liability and Redress to the Cartagena Protocol on Biosafety was adopted on 15 October 2010 at COP 10 in Nagoya. It was named so to distinguish it from the other protocol adopted in Nagoya, which pertains to access and benefit-sharing. In legal terms, it takes the very original form of a protocol to a first protocol to the Convention on Biological Diversity. As a protocol to a protocol, it does not create new institutions, but relies on those existing under the Rio Convention and the Cartagena Protocol[913]. Moreover, it is necessary to be a Party to the latter in order to ratify the new instrument. One might say that it "fits" legally and institutionally into the Cartagena Protocol, which in turns "fits" into the Convention on Biological Diversity.

508. The entry into force of the Supplementary Protocol required forty ratifications; it took place on 5 March 2018. The Protocol currently has fifty-four Parties[914]. Lengthy negotiations, its late entry into force (after more than seven years) and the limited number of Parties nine years later all reflect the limited enthusiasm of States for this Protocol.

2) The content of the Protocol

509. The objective of the Supplementary Protocol on Liability and Redress is "to contribute to the conservation and sustainable use of biological diversity, taking also into account risks to human health, by

---

912. On these negotiations, D. Tladi, "Civil Liability in the Context of the Cartagena Protocol: To Be or Not To Be (Binding)?", *Int. Environ. Agreements* (2010) 10, pp. 15-27.
913. See its Articles 14 and 15.
914. On 19 December 2023.

providing international rules and procedures in the field of liability and redress relating to living modified organisms" [915]. In this respect, it is in keeping with Principle 13 of the Rio Declaration, to which it refers in its preamble, and which provides as follows:

> "States shall develop national law regarding liability and compensation for the victims of pollution and other environmental damage. States shall also cooperate in an expeditious and more determined manner to develop further international law regarding liability and compensation for adverse effects of environmental damage caused by activities within their jurisdiction or control to areas beyond their jurisdiction."

510. The Protocol is intended both to prevent damage to biological diversity and human health and to allow for redress or response measures when such damage occurs. In this respect, it is supposed to contribute, in line with the Cartagena Protocol, to the safe use of GMOs by minimising their impact on biological diversity. In practice however, its scope is relatively narrow. The measures to be taken are quite broad but States Parties have a very wide discretion as to their implementation.

a) *The scope of the Protocol*

511. According to Article 2 (2), the Protocol defines "damage" as follows:

> "An adverse effect on the conservation and sustainable use of biological diversity, taking also into account risks to human health, that: *(i)* Is measurable or otherwise observable taking into account, wherever available, scientifically-established baselines recognized by a competent authority that takes into account any other human induced variation and natural variation; and *(ii)* Is significant as set out in paragraph 3 below."

It should be noted that it does not apply to socio-economic damage. The "significant" nature of an adverse effect is to be determined on the basis of factors, such as:

> "*(a)* The long-term or permanent change, to be understood as change that will not be redressed through natural recovery within

---

[915]. Article 1.

a reasonable period of time; *(b)* The extent of the qualitative or quantitative changes that adversely affect the components of biological diversity; *(c)* The reduction of the ability of components of biological diversity to provide goods and services; *(d)* The extent of any adverse effects on human health in the context of the Protocol." [916]

512. This list of factors for determining whether or not the damage – which must be observable – is significant, is therefore not exhaustive ("such as"). Meanwhile, and this is another very important limitation, the Protocol only applies "to damage resulting from living modified organisms which find their origin in a transboundary movement". In addition, the Protocol specifies that the LMOs referred to are those intended for direct use as food or feed, or for processing; those intended for contained use; and those intended for intentional introduction into the environment [917]. This therefore only pertains to LMOs, and excludes products derived from LMOs or those that have required the use of LMOs at some point in their production (rapeseed oil, soya cake, eggs from hens fed with transgenic maize, etc.).

513. The Protocol covers intentional movements (authorised use) as well as unintentional movements, whether legal or illegal, but it does not cover damage caused in areas beyond the national jurisdiction of Parties [918]. This excludes, for instance, the high seas, even though the use of genetically modified fish is increasing and could have consequences for marine biodiversity. Article 4 further requires that "[a] causal link shall be established between the damage and the living modified organism in question in accordance with domestic law".

b) *Administrative and civil liability*

514. When damage occurs, Parties must require that a number of measures be taken by the "appropriate operator(s)". The operator is defined as follows:

> "Any person in direct or indirect control of the living modified organism which could, as appropriate and as determined by domestic law, include, *inter alia*, the permit holder, person who

---

916. Article 2, paras. 1 and 3.
917. Article 3.
918. Article 3.

placed the living modified organism on the market, developer, producer, notifier, exporter, importer, carrier or supplier." [919]

515. Response measures are broad. They are defined as

"reasonable actions to: *(i)* Prevent, minimize, contain, mitigate, or otherwise avoid damage, as appropriate; *(ii)* Restore biological diversity through actions to be undertaken in the following order of preference: *(a)* Restoration of biological diversity to the condition that existed before the damage occurred, or its nearest equivalent; and where the competent authority determines this is not possible; *(b)* Restoration by, *inter alia*, replacing the loss of biological diversity with other components of biological diversity for the same, or for another type of use either at the same or, as appropriate, at an alternative location" [920].

516. When damage occurs, measures include immediately informing the competent authority, assessing the damage and adopting "appropriate response measures". As for the competent authority, it "shall: *(a)* Identify the operator which has caused the damage; *(b)* Evaluate the damage; and *(c)* Determine which response measures should be taken by the operator" [921]. Furthermore:

"Where relevant information, including available scientific information or information available in the Biosafety Clearing-House, indicates that there is a sufficient likelihood that damage will result if timely response measures are not taken, the operator shall be required to take appropriate response measures so as to avoid such damage." [922]

The authority may act in the place of the operator(s) if they fail to do so and recover the related costs from them [923]. In any case, "[r]esponse measures shall be implemented in accordance with domestic law" and the Parties may provide exemptions, in particular for "act of God or *force majeure*" or "act of war or civil unrest" [924]. Thus, like the European Directive on environmental liability, the Protocol ultimately adopts an

---

919. Article 2.
920. Article 2, para. 2.
921. Article 5, para. 2.
922. Article 5, para. 3.
923. Article 5, paras. 4-5.
924. Article 5, para. 8 and Article 6.

administrative rather than a civil approach to liability [925]. As regards civil liability, the Protocol simply provides an incentive. Parties *may* apply and/or develop their national civil liability rules [926]. The Protocol did not need to authorise this, so this does not add anything. A more prescriptive approach was among the initial options, preferred by a large majority of developing countries, but it was dropped along the way because it was far from unanimous [927].

517. The Protocol thus places responsibility on operators and transfers the issue to national law. At the same time, it is explicitly stated that the Supplementary Protocol "shall not affect the rights and obligations of States under the rules of general international law with respect to the responsibility of States for internationally wrongful acts" [928]. Thus, even if the Protocol does not exclude inter-State responsibility in theory, if properly implemented it could effectively lead to such responsibility being excluded.

3) The impact of the Protocol

518. What is the impact of this instrument, five years after its entry into force? The Protocol is the result of a compromise between States that argued that LMOs do not present specific risks and called for the application of ordinary rules of civil liability (the position of exporting countries in particular), and those that defended a stronger international framework taking into account the specific challenge of establishing the causal link or the "irreversible" nature of the damage [929] (the EU, African countries, Malaysia, Norway, etc.). Multinational GMO companies had a major influence during the negotiations, and this partly explains why the Protocol has a limited scope and is not very demanding. It relies mostly on national law, which States have a wide discretion to define, and on the national competent authorities. It lays down obligations in terms of administrative but not civil liability. Regarding the latter, it only provides an incentive. It does not set up a compulsory insurance

---

925. Directive 2004/35/EC of the European Parliament and of the Council of 21 April 2004 on environmental liability with regard to the prevention and remedying of environmental damage, OJ L 143, 30 April 2004, pp. 56-75.
926. Articles 10 and 12.
927. D. Tladi, "Civil Liability in the Context of the Cartagena Protocol: To Be or Not to Be (Binding)?" (n. 912), pp. 15-27.
928. Article 11.
929. M.-A. Hermitte, S. Maljean-Dubois and E. Truilhé-Marengo, "Actualités de la Convention sur la diversité biologique: science et politique, équité, biosécurité", *Annuaire français de droit international*, 2011, Vol. 57, p. 428.

system or an international guarantee fund, unlike other international conventions [930]. There is no real international liability regime like some were calling for. As for administrative liability, it must be based on a regulatory framework and adequate means, without which the Protocol risks being inoperative [931]. However, many countries lack such framework and means.

519. It should be added that the Protocol has been not been ratified by many countries, least of all the main GMO producers. Thus, neither the United States, nor Canada, nor Argentina have signed it, nor can they do so as they are not parties to the Cartagena Protocol. The fact that the Protocol provides that "[d]omestic law implementing this Supplementary Protocol shall also apply to damage resulting from transboundary movements of living modified organisms from non-Parties" [932] turns out to be of little practical use.

520. These weaknesses are easy to understand. On the whole, States do not seem to be ready to take a strong stand on civil liability for environmental damage. Audacity has been punished in the past: for example, the Lugano Convention on Civil Liability for Damage Resulting from Activities Dangerous to the Environment (1993) never came into force, even though it required only three ratifications. In the end, it received none. But as a result of these weaknesses, the scope of the Protocol is limited.

---

930. See the Brussels Convention relating to Civil Liability in the Field of Maritime Carriage of Nuclear Material or the 1999 Protocol on Liability and Compensation to the Basel Convention on the Control of Transboundary Movements of Hazardous Wastes and their Disposal.

931. M.-A. Hermitte, S. Maljean-Dubois and E. Truilhé-Marengo, "Actualités de la Convention sur la diversité biologique : science et politique, équité, biosécurité" (n. 929), p. 431.

932. Article 3, para. 7.

CHAPTER V

INTERNATIONAL LAW AND ACCESS
AND BENEFIT-SHARING

521. From the colonial period onwards, even though plants and animals were often the object of monopolistic struggles between competing European powers, there was a gradual move towards treating them as raw material openly available to scientists [933]. Moreover, while it was not possible to patent "products of nature", by the end of the nineteenth century, processes exploiting the properties of living organisms (including biochemical reactions of micro-organisms) were patentable. During the second half of the twentieth century, patent law progressively recognised the patentability of such "products", gradually removing all legal obstacles to patenting life [934]. At the same time, biological resources – and the indigenous or local traditional knowledge that may be associated with these resources – were appropriated by companies and research institutions through patent or trademark applications. These appropriations were considered illegitimate because they were not authorised by the populations or States concerned, nor did they give rise to fair compensation. The neologism "biopiracy" was coined. Developments in genetic engineering amplified this phenomenon, making agricultural, pharmaceutical and even cosmetic companies all the more eager to take advantage of these resources. While it is true that patenting a plant is not possible in the light of the patentability criteria, especially requirements for novelty and inventiveness, patenting a gene from such a plant isolated in a laboratory has become possible. Biopiracy has mostly affected biodiversity *hot spots*, located mainly in the countries of the South, and has been perpetrated primarily by companies or research centres from the North. The debate therefore very quickly crystallised as a North/South debate. The very political term biopiracy was used in this context, but also to signal opposition to the commodification/privatisation of life [935].

---

933. F. Thomas, "Ressources génétiques : garantir l'accès à un bien public mondial ou compenser sa marchandisation ?", *Entreprises et histoire*, 2017/3, No. 88, p. 105.
934. *Ibid.*, p. 112.
935. V. Shiva, *Biopiracy: The Plunder of Nature and Knowledge*, South Press, 1997.

522. On these issues, the Convention on Biological Diversity established a general framework consisting of a number of principles, which was completed in 2010 by the adoption of the Nagoya Protocol on Access to Genetic Resources and the Fair and Equitable Sharing of Benefits Arising from their Utilization. This Protocol was designed to ensure a level playing field in accessing biological resources in the South. As pointed out by Marie-Angèle Hermitte, the aim was to put an end to the practice of free and unrestricted prospecting, which was suspected of allowing tremendous profits to be made when prospectors returned. Negotiators from the South all had in mind the legendary Merck-InBio contract pursuant to which Costa Rica had granted the pharmaceutical company access to part of its tropical forest, in return for the payment of an entry free and possible royalties in the event of the marketing of products derived from it [936]. The Rio Convention and its Nagoya Protocol intersect here with issues of environmental protection, human rights, indigenous peoples' rights and international trade law. But in this matter, the institutions created pursuant to the Convention and the Protocol do not operate alone at the international level. Therefore, they must promote their approach well beyond the treaty sphere or risk being ineffective.

Section 1. The need for a Protocol to the Convention on Biological Diversity on access and benefit-sharing

523. On this issue, the 1992 Convention on Biological Diversity appeared at first to be taking a novel approach. Supposed to put an end to "biopiracy" practices, it did raise high hopes in this respect when it was adopted. But its substance is in fact rather ambiguous, and its implementation has been very slow.

1) A novel approach?

524. The Convention on Biological Diversity contains provisions on access to genetic resources and the sharing of benefits arising from their use, which is one of its three objectives [937].

---

936. M.-A. Hermitte, S. Maljean-Dubois and E. Truilhé-Marengo, "Actualités de la Convention sur la diversité biologique: science et politique, équité, biosécurité" (n. 929), p. 412.
937. See its Article 2.

a) *Access to genetic resources*

525. As previously discussed, the Convention on Biological Diversity refused to consider biodiversity as a common heritage of mankind, a status that schematically made some (the countries of the North) fear financial implications, while others (the countries of the South) feared a limitation of their sovereign rights [938]. On the contrary, it reinforced the customary status of natural resources, placed under the sovereignty of the territorial State. Since genetic resources are natural resources, Article 15 (1) of the Convention drew a logical conclusion: "Recognizing the sovereign rights of States over their natural resources, the authority to determine access to genetic resources rests with the national governments and is subject to national legislation". Access "shall be subject to prior informed consent of the Contracting Party providing such resources, unless otherwise determined by that Party" [939]. This statement is clear: companies from the North cannot access the genetic resources of the countries of the South – which are the main suppliers thereof – without the latter's consent. However, supplier countries have limited room for manoeuvre. They cannot systematically refuse access, but must instead endeavour to "create renditions to facilitate access to genetic resources" [940]. Furthermore, once granted, access is to be "on mutually agreed terms" [941].

526. In return for this facilitated access, the Convention on Biological Diversity lays down the obligation to share in a "fair and equitable way the results of research and development and the benefits arising from the commercial and other utilization of genetic resources with the Contracting Party providing such resources", which in conventional language has become "benefit-sharing" [942].

b) *Benefit-sharing*

527. To ensure "benefit-sharing", each Party "shall take legislative, administrative or policy measures, as appropriate"; sharing "shall be upon mutually agreed terms" [943]. Beyond contractual initiatives, Parties have a more general obligation to provide and/or facilitate access to

---
938. M. A. Hermitte, "La Convention sur la diversité biologique" (n. 103), p. 859.
939. Article 15, para. 5.
940. Article 15, para. 2.
941. Article 15, para. 4.
942. Article 15, para. 6.
943. Article 15, para. 7.

and the transfer of the necessary technologies [944]. Access to developing countries "shall be provided and/or facilitated under fair and most favourable terms" [945]. In this respect, the Parties "shall take legislative, administrative or policy measures, as appropriate" [946], including "with the aim that the private sector facilitates access to, joint development and transfer of technology . . . for the benefit of both governmental institutions and the private sector of developing countries" [947]. Article 19 of the CBD, which focuses specifically on the handling of biotechnology, reiterates these obligations and clarifies them a little. Developed countries must "provide for the effective participation in biotechnological research activities" by developing countries and "promote and advance priority access on a fair and equitable basis" to "the results and benefits arising from biotechnologies based upon genetic resources" of these countries. Article 17 (2) completes this section by laying down obligations on the exchange of information, in particular on biotechnology, be it "specialized knowledge" or "indigenous and traditional knowledge".

528. Special attention is given to the latter. Article 8 (j) provides that each Party shall "as far as possible and as appropriate":

> "[s]ubject to its national legislation, respect, preserve and maintain knowledge, innovations and practices of indigenous and local communities embodying traditional lifestyles relevant for the conservation and sustainable use of biological diversity and promote their wider application with the approval and involvement of the holders of such knowledge, innovations and practices and encourage the equitable sharing of the benefits arising from the utilization of such knowledge".

The Convention thereby recognises the role of indigenous communities in the preservation of biological diversity. Indigenous peoples are in fact represented at the COP. Here, the Convention addresses a gap in the international legal order. Indeed, in 1992, while international law increasingly took into account indigenous peoples, it did not address the issue of the legal protection of their knowledge [948]. Significantly, the Convention does not refer to the notion of indigenous "peoples"

---
944. Article 16, para. 1.
945. Article 16, para. 2.
946. Article 16, para. 3.
947. Article 16, para. 4.
948. J.-P. Beurier, "Le droit de la biodiversité", *Revue juridique de l'environnement*, 1996, Nos. 1-2, p. 19.

International Biodiversity Law 297

but to "communities", contrary to the demands of the United Nations Permanent Forum in Indigenous Issues [949]. The COP itself only began to refer to these communities in 2014 [950].

529. It was necessary to combine the technology transfer obligations with financial obligations. Developed countries undertake to provide "new and additional financial resources" to developing countries in order to enable them to meet the additional costs of implementing the Convention [951]. "The extent to which developing country Parties will effectively implement their commitments under this Convention will depend on the effective implementation by developed country Parties of their commitments under this Convention related to financial resources and transfer of technology." [952] Under Article 21, the Global Environmental Facility (GEF) is designated as the financial mechanism.

530. At first, the Convention seems to be part of development law, as developing countries appear to have obtained so many concessions. However, on closer inspection, the Convention features several ambiguities. It was therefore doubtful that the Convention would usher in "a new era concerning access to genetic resources which is subject to the provisions of Article 15 of the Convention and is characterized by a fair and equitable sharing of the benefits arising out of the use of such resources", as the COP itself had claimed [953].

2) The ambiguities of the Convention

531. The endorsement of the patenting of genetic resources as well as its relationship with the FAO reflect the ambiguities of the Convention.

a) *The Convention and patent law*

532. In this respect, the ambiguity of the Convention stems from the compromise on which it is based. While recognising in principle

---

949. *Report of the Tenth Session of the UN Permanent Forum on Indigenous Issues (2011)* UN Doc. E/2011/43-E/C.19/2011/14, paras. 26-27.
950. See Decisions XI/19 and XI/22.
951. Article 20, para. 2.
952. Article 20, para. 3.
953. Statement from the Conference of the Parties to the Convention on Biological Diversity to the Commission on Sustainable Development at its third session, Annex, Decision I/8 Preparation of the Participation of the Convention on Biological Diversity in the third session of the Commission on Sustainable Development, p. 87.

the sovereignty of States over their natural resources, in practice, it opens up access to genetic resources to all States, while providing for "benefit-sharing".

533. Article 15 seeks to protect traditional technologies and knowledge through a system of intellectual property rights. But such rights face many challenges and seem largely illusory [954]. As for "benefit-sharing" between countries of the North and South, the provisions of the Convention are not sufficiently precise or prescriptive. They do not guarantee that developing countries will share in the benefits of exploitation once derived products have been produced; they simply encourage it [955]. Article 15 thus encourages bioprospecting contracts between States (or public bodies) and companies [956]. Pursuant to such contracts, the payment of royalties is in reality largely conditional on the filing of patents [957]. Technology transfers also depend on the adoption by Southern countries of legislation protecting intellectual property. As pointed out by an OECD report, strong intellectual property laws and enforcement procedures are a prerequisite for foreign investment, technology transfer agreements and co-operation under the Convention on Biological Diversity, as in other contexts [958]. Accordingly, in order to achieve "benefit-sharing", countries in the South have to accept both the patenting of their biological resources and the development of protective intellectual property legislation.

534. Thus, although it does constitute progress, the Convention does not put an end to biopiracy [959]. While it fails to guarantee benefit-sharing, it contributes to accelerating the progressive extension of patents to living organisms. Yet beyond the ethical considerations that this raises (what right does a company have to claim a monopoly on the

---

[954]. C. Noiville, *Ressources génétiques et droit* (n. 825), p. 353 *et seq.*
[955]. M. Grandbois, "Le droit de l'environnement et le commerce international: quelques enjeux déterminants", *Les cahiers de droit*, Vol. 40, No. 3, September 1999, p. 560.
[956]. It also overlooks the potential adverse consequences of these agreements, which are unsuitable for many situations with regard to the "conservation" objective. C. Aubertin and F. D. Vivien, *Les enjeux de la biodiversité*, Economica, Paris, 1998, p. 63. On the many weaknesses and inadequacies of these agreements, C. Noiville, *Ressources génétiques et droit* (n. 825), p. 375 *et seq.*
[957]. C. Aubertin and F. D. Vivien, *Les enjeux de la biodiversité* (n. 956), p. 55.
[958]. OCDE, *Propriété intellectuelle, transfert de technologie et ressources génétiques. Pratiques et politiques actuelles*, OCDE, Paris, 1996, p. 23.
[959]. C. Aubertin and F. D. Vivien, *Les enjeux de la biodiversité* (n. 956), p. 91. See the example cited of the Hoodia Agreement, in GRAIN, *Privatisation des moyens de survie: la commercialisation de la biodiversité en Afrique*, Commerce mondial et biodiversité en conflit, No. 5, May 2000.

exploitation of living beings? [960], the patent system has many perverse effects.

535. Compared to *sui generis* systems designed to address the specificities of plant varieties, the patent system increases the protection of the breeder and accordingly restricts the principle of open access. It does not recognise the research exemption: it prevents the free and unrestricted use of patented varieties as genetic resources to create new ones. As the payment of royalties can be a deterrent, the patent system thus authorises a sort of confiscation of knowledge and ultimately constitutes a brake on innovation, or at least on its dissemination and the sharing of knowledge. It is clear that it constitutes a mode of knowledge exploitation, the social return of which is undoubtedly lower than an "open science" system [961]. The patent system also marks the end of the farmer's privilege: farmers lose their right to replant, free of charge, the seeds from the harvest the following year [962].

536. But even the *sui generis* systems of intellectual property have gradually evolved to be closer to the patent system [963]. This is particularly true of the system of plant breeders' rights (PBR) established by the International Convention for the Protection of New Varieties of Plants of 2 December 1961 (UPOV) [964]. In a balanced way, it protected the breeder of plant varieties while recognising the research exemption and the farmer's privilege [965]. Long before the advent of biotechnology, this system was already subject to vigorous criticism, accused of causing, among other things, an erosion of agricultural biodiversity as well as the growing control of a few agrochemical firms over the world's seed stocks [966]. But in 1991, the UPOV Convention was amended to limit the research exemption and the farmer's privilege by recognising stronger

---

960. A. Apotheker, *Du poisson dans les fraises. Notre alimentation manipulée*, La Découverte, Paris, 1999, p. 95.
961. D. Foray, "La privatisation de l'activité de connaissance menace de bloquer l'innovation", *Le Monde, Eco.*, 30 May 2000, p. III.
962. C. Aubertin and F. D. Vivien, *Les enjeux de la biodiversité* (n. 956), p. 33.
963. C. Noiville, *Ressources génétiques et droit* (n. 825), p. 108.
964. Seventy-eight countries are members of the International Union for the Protection of New Varieties of Plants (UPOV) as of 20 December 2023.
965. The competing breeder did not have to seek permission to access the genetic resources of the protected variety, access to the gene pool was free. The farmer had the right to reuse for further sowing part of the seed from a first harvest of the protected variety but within reasonable limits and subject to the safeguarding of the legitimate interests of the breeders. J. Bizet, *Transgéniques : pour des choix responsables*, Sénat, France, Rapport d'information 440 (97-98), p. 60.
966. GRAIN, *Dix bonnes raisons de ne pas adhérer à l'UPOV,* Commerce mondial et biodiversité en conflit, No. 2, May 1998, p. 2; *La protection des obtentions végétales pour nourrir l'Afrique. Rhétorique contre réalité*, octobre 1999.

exclusive rights for breeders. Both the farmer's privilege and the research exemption were eroded. Developing countries were pushed to adhere to the UPOV Convention [967], while the adoption of the WTO Agreement on Trade-Related Aspects of Intellectual Property Rights (TRIPS Agreement) further strengthened its position.

537. Indeed, intellectual property has become one of the new domains regulated by the WTO, compared to the former GATT, in part at least as it only comes within the jurisdiction of the WTO insofar as it relates to trade. This entry into the realm of the WTO reflects the growing importance of intellectual property as well as its internationalisation, both of which make it necessary to ensure global and harmonised protection [968]. The TRIPS Agreement was a first step in this endeavour. However, it only lays down minimum rules, which States are free to tighten. It does not prohibit the patentability of living organisms, which raises the issue of the interplay of this agreement with existing international instruments, first and foremost the Convention on Biological Diversity.

538. According to the TRIPS Agreement, WTO Member States

> "may exclude from patentability inventions, the prevention within their territory of the commercial exploitation of which is necessary to protect *ordre* public or morality, including to protect human, animal or plant life or health or to avoid serious prejudice to the environment, provided that such exclusion is not made merely because the exploitation is prohibited by their law".

But TRIPS requires Member States to establish a protection system for plant varieties, be it a patent system, an "effective" *sui generis* system or "any combination thereof". Article 27 was one of the most debated provisions during the negotiation of this agreement. It was included under pressure from the Europeans and its paragraph 3 *(b)* reproduces the wording of the European Patent Convention. The United States, on the other hand, wanted a broader scope and only accepted this restriction on condition that it would be reviewed in 1999. As a result, it was added that "[t]he provisions of this subparagraph shall be reviewed four years after the date of entry into force of the WTO

---

967. E. Tsioumani, "Beyond Access and Benefit-Sharing: Lessons from the Law and Governance of Agricultural Biodiversity", *Journal of World Intellectual Property*, 2018, Vol. 21, p. 109.
968. B. Boval, "L'Accord sur les droits de propriété intellectuelle qui touchent au commerce", in *La réorganisation mondiale des échanges*, Société française pour le droit international, Pedone, Paris, 1996, p. 132.

Agreement". The TRIPS Council did undertake a review of Article 27.3 *(b)*, although this did not lead to a revision[969]. But advances in genetic engineering are breaking down barriers between kingdoms and between species. As a result, the differences established between plants and animals, and micro-organisms or plant varieties start to no longer make sense and the relative vagueness of TRIPS allows for expansive interpretations of what constitutes a patentable subject matter, even in Europe where patentability ended up being recognised despite strong initial reluctance[970]. Derogations – in particular the research exemption and the farmer's privilege –, which are restricted under UPOV since the 1991 revision, are even more limited under patent law.

539. The TRIPS Agreement has also de facto sidelined the World Intellectual Property Organisation system, because of the direct effect of its provisions – guaranteeing greater effectiveness – and the wide range of control mechanisms provided at national and international level. Although the preamble to TRIPS refers to the necessary "mutually supportive relationship between the WTO and the World Intellectual Property Organization", WIPO has been significantly weakened by the existence of TRIPS and is gradually being relegated to a technical role of assessment and implementation[971]. This shift in the centre of gravity is not neutral for developing countries. WIPO has very little room for manoeuvre to promote alternatives to existing forms of intellectual property rights and tends to concur with TRIPS. This sidelining of an institution that could use well-established expertise to develop specific legal tools or frameworks is unfortunate. For example, WIPO is conducting interesting work on the legal protection of indigenous peoples' knowledge, which is relevant to Article 8 *(j)* of the Convention on Biological Diversity.

540. The question of the relationship between TRIPS and the Rio Convention is no less tricky. Participation in the WTO must not compromise the implementation of undertakings made under the Convention and *vice versa*. The two instruments do not pursue the same objective and it is not surprising that there are certain inconsistencies, or even more general incompatibilities, between their respective content.

---

969. OMC, IP/C/19, 22 October 1999, (99-4590), *Annual Report (1999) of the TRIPS Council*.
970. C. Noiville, *Ressources génétiques et droit* (n. 825), p. 108 *et seq*. E. Tsioumani, "Beyond Access and Benefit-Sharing: Lessons from the Law and Governance of Agricultural Biodiversity" (n. 967), p. 110.
971. B. Boval, "L'Accord sur les droits de propriété intellectuelle qui touchent au commerce" (n. 968), p. 149. See also TRIPS Article 68.

Where the Convention on Biological Diversity appears to be based on notions such as the common good, the need to protect biological diversity and balanced North/South relations, TRIPS focuses on the protection of innovations and the principles of international trade. Thus, while the Rio Convention attempts to organise "benefit-sharing", TRIPS makes no reference to it. While the Convention requires prior State consent for access to biological resources, in order to combat biopiracy, TRIPS, by failing to regulate the issue, could instead encourage biopiracy.

541. But the relationship between the Convention on Biological Diversity and the TRIPS Agreement is not doomed to be seen in terms of opposition. It is difficult to identify a specific substantive contradiction or even an incompatibility between the two instruments. The CBD does not reject intellectual property rights outright. On the contrary, Article 16 of the CBD stresses the need for "adequate and effective protection". TRIPS is in keeping with the Convention in some respects. For example, Article 28 of TRIPS allows for the possibility of licensing contracts, which can be the basis for technology transfers. Article 66 encourages technology transfer to LDCs, which can be done through compulsory licences [972]. However, developed countries are not under any obligation in this respect. Ultimately, like the CBD, TRIPS relies here on contractual solutions.

542. The conflict between TRIPS and the CBD is therefore only on the surface. The reality is more that the two instruments are intertwined [973] even though TRIPS does not refer to the Rio Convention, which was the first to tackle this issue. The CBD COP tried to build bridges and successfully applied for observer status in the WTO's Trade and Environment Committee in 2000 [974]. It has repeatedly stressed the importance of the equitable sharing of benefits arising from the use of traditional knowledge and has forwarded its conclusions to the WTO [975].

543. Nonetheless, as it encourages patentability – and despite its assertions that "patents and other intellectual property rights" must be "supportive of and do not run counter to its objectives" [976] – the Rio

---

972. Article 30. C. Noiville, *Ressources génétiques et droit* (n. 825), p. 359.
973. J.-P. Maréchal, "Quand la biodiversité est assimilée à une marchandise", *Le Monde diplomatique*, July 1999, pp. 6-7.
974. *Access to Genetic Resources*, Note by the Executive Secretary, UNEP/CBD/COP/5/21, 24 February 2000, p. 6 (COP Decision IV/15). The COP requested the secretariat to liaise with the WTO secretariat and to consider participation in the work of the WTO Trade and Environment Committee.
975. Decision V/16, para. 14.
976. Article 16, para. 5.

Convention ultimately proves powerless to reverse an international division of labour that is unfavourable to the South, which is a supplier of raw materials exploited for high returns by the North. The bypassing of sovereign States continues to foster unequal relations with local communities, who surrender their heritage in exchange for derisory payments [977].

544. When defining intellectual property regimes, a growing number of developing countries are moving away from the patent system or the UPOV system [978]. It is particularly interesting to look at what is happening in Africa. The OAU and then the African Union have advocated a *sui generis* system, which recognises both the research exemption and the farmer's privilege. Opposing both the patent system and the UPOV system, the African Union sought to propose a compromise solution between the interests of breeders – the only ones ultimately protected by patents – and those of farmers. It thus drafted a "model law" for "the Protection of the Rights of Local Communities Farmers and Breeders and the Regulation of Access to Biological Resources", designed as a framework to harmonise the legislation of African countries [979]. Attempting to rebalance this new "unequal exchange", it established the principle of prior consent for both the States and the local populations or communities concerned. Thus, access to any biological resource and/or knowledge or technology of local communities in any part of the country in question is to be subject to an application for prior consent and written authorisation. The permit must be issued by the competent national authority after the State as well as the local communities concerned have all given their consent. The authority must determine the amount of royalties payable by the breeder who has developed a variety from one of the national biological resources. Based on the sales of the new variety, royalties are to be paid into a fund in order to finance projects proposed by local communities for the development, conservation and sustainable use of agricultural genetic resources [980]. The system also recognises the farmer's privilege, which is of particular importance when farmers cannot afford to buy seeds every year. It also protects the research exemption, which is particularly necessary here too, since farmers, small seed companies

---

977. GRAIN, *L'ADPIC contre la Convention sur la diversité biologique*, Commerce mondial et biodiversité en conflit, No. 1, April 1998, p. 5.
978. GRAIN, *Au-delà de l'UPOV*, July 1999, p. 1.
979. F. Seuret and R. Ali Brac de la Perrière, "L'Afrique refuse le brevetage du vivant", *Le Monde diplomatique*, July 2000, p. 24.
980. *Ibid.*

and public research are the ones that develop new varieties, and not large corporations as in the North [981].

545. Presented as the implementation of the Convention on Biological Diversity, this system goes against the one adopted in February 1999 by the African Intellectual Property Organization (OAPI), which promotes legislation very similar to the PBR system. Fifteen French-speaking OAPI member countries signed an agreement in 1998 – the Revised Bangui Agreement – updating their common legislation on intellectual property rights to establish a plant variety protection regime that draws heavily on the 1991 version of the UPOV Convention. This agreement is more favourable to the "genetic-industrial complex" and to the seed industry, which is largely dominated by Northern countries, than to African farmers [982].

546. The African Union's initiative allows African countries to be at the forefront on this issue in international fora, particularly at the WTO. Thus, they sent a communication to the WTO secretariat in which they spoke out against the patenting of life forms. In their view, the review process should clarify that plants and animals as well as micro-organisms and all other living organisms and their parts cannot be patented [983]. African countries also called for the TRIPS Agreement to explicitly recognise the possibility for national legislation to include provisions to protect the innovations of indigenous communities and local farming communities in developing countries, as well as the right to save and exchange seeds and to sell their harvest [984]. It must be added that the regional approach has many advantages. It avoids unnecessary competition by establishing common conditions for access and benefit-sharing. It also makes it possible to establish a less restrictive procedure for the movement of genetic resources between Member States. Such initiatives have been developed under the Andean Pact, or the South Asian Association for Regional Cooperation (SAARC) [985].

---

981. *Ibid.*
982. GRAIN, *Privatisation des moyens de survie: la commercialisation de la biodiversité en Afrique* (n. 966).
983. Communication from the Permanent Mission of Kenya on behalf of the African Group (29 July 1999), *cit.* F. Seuret and R. Ali Brac de la Perrière, "L'Afrique refuse le brevetage du vivant" (n. 979), p. 24.
984. *Ibid.*
985. See Decision 391 of the Andean Pact Common Regime on Access to Genetic Resources (July1996) applicable in Bolivia, Colombia, Ecuador, Peru and Venezuela. See also the initiative of the South Asian Association for Regional Cooperation (Bangladesh, Bhutan, India, Maldives, Nepal, Pakistan and Sri Lanka), which agreed in March 1999 not to transfer plant genetic resources to non-member countries, while allowing free exchange among member countries for research purposes. Review of

b) *The relationship between the CBD and the FAO on agricultural biodiversity*

547. Established in 1983, the FAO International Undertaking on Plant Genetic Resources for Food and Agriculture went against the trend towards privatisation and instead described these resources as a heritage of mankind, therefore not appropriable. The FAO saw this as a way to guarantee both freedom of research and free access to resources as well as the farmer's privilege, and to promote North/South technology transfer. Although they share a common purpose, the underlying principle of this Undertaking is therefore the opposite of that of the Convention on Biological Diversity, which specifically refused to view biodiversity as a common heritage of mankind in order to assert the sovereignty of States over their natural resources. This characterisation also seems difficult to reconcile with the patent system, which is based on private appropriation and monopolisation. The disconnect of international law here was especially strong [986]. Non-binding, the Undertaking was rather ineffective. Its institutional positioning was not well defined; many industrialised countries, the US in particular, did not join [987].

548. In 1989, the Undertaking had already been reinterpreted in an attempt to reconcile it with the industrial property system, introducing compensation in return for access to resources. Negotiations were then launched, within the framework of the FAO Commission on Plant Genetic Resources, for a treaty to bring the Undertaking in line with the Convention on Biological Diversity. In 1994, the Conference of the Parties of the Convention on Biological Diversity expressed the wish for co-ordination and collaboration in order to avoid duplication [988]. The relationship between the two systems grew [989]. In the end, the CBD had a strong influence on the agreement adopted on 3 November 2001, the

---

options for access and benefit-sharing mechanisms, Note by the Executive Secretary, UNEP/CBD/ISOC/3, 11 May 1999, para. 18.

986. S. Maljean-Dubois, "Biodiversité, biotechnologies, biosécurité : le droit international désarticulé", *Journal du droit international*, No. 4, 2000, p. 955.

987. C. Aubertin and F.-D. Vivien, *Les enjeux de la biodiversité* (n. 956), p. 35.

988. Decision *I/8. Preparation of the Participation of the Convention on Biological Diversity in the Third Session of the Commission on Sustainable Development*, Annex, Statement from the Conference of the Parties to the Convention on Biological Diversity to the Commission on Sustainable Development at its Third Session, UNEP/CBD/COP/1/17, p. 87.

989. See Resolution 7/93 of FAO Conference. The FAO presents itself as a service available to the Parties to the Rio Convention to assist them in the implementation of this instrument and provide them with assistance and advice. It has also offered to link its information systems with the clearing-house established under the Rio Convention.

International Treaty on Plant Genetic Resources for Food and Agriculture (referred to as the "seed treaty"), which replaced the 1983 Undertaking. This new treaty shares the three objectives of the Convention and recognises the role of indigenous peoples [990]. Thus, according to Article 1:

> "1.1. The objectives of this Treaty are the conservation and sustainable use of plant genetic resources for food and agriculture and the fair and equitable sharing of the benefits arising out of their use, in harmony with the Convention on Biological Diversity, for sustainable agriculture and food security.
> 1.2. These objectives will be attained by closely linking this Treaty to the Food and Agriculture Organization of the United Nations and to the Convention on Biological Diversity."

549. Like the Convention, it is based on the recognition of the sovereign rights of States over plant genetic resources for food and agriculture, but it also recognises the rights of farmers and establishes a multilateral system of access and benefit-sharing with regard to the crops covered by the treaty. Access is to be granted according to a standard material transfer agreement [991]. The latter places sixty-four of our most important crops (thirty-five crop types and twenty-nine forage species), representing 80 per cent of our global crop consumption, in a global reserve of genetic resources, a sort of pool which is made available for research, breeding and training purposes to countries that ratify the Treaty. This solution, which usefully complements and strengthens the provisions of the Rio Convention, constituted a step forward. This system is very elaborate but struggles to generate – and therefore share – real financial benefits [992].

---

990. P. Le Prestre, "The Long Road to a New Order", in *Governing Global Biodiversity. The Evolution and Implementation of the Convention on Biological Diversity*, P. Le Prestre (ed.), Ashgate, 2004, p. 315. The Treaty came into force in 2004 and has 155 Parties as of 20 December 2023.
991. Article 12.4 (SMTA for *Standard Material Transfer Agreement*). The SMTA is a mandatory template for Parties wishing to supply and receive material in the Multilateral System. It cannot be modified or abridged. A revised version is currently being negotiated, in particular to take account of advances in digital sequencing.
992. E. Tsioumani, "Beyond Access and Benefit-Sharing: Lessons from the Law and Governance of Agricultural Biodiversity" (n. 967), p. 113.

3) The need to expand the rules laid down in the Rio Convention and the launch of negotiations for a new Protocol to the Convention

550. In this context, work under the Convention progressed very slowly. An expert group was established to work specifically on access and benefit-sharing [993]. It helped to do the spadework on the issue, focusing mainly on defining the concepts and the types of measures needed for their implementation [994]. This work revealed a need to harmonise national laws that are both incomplete and disparate. The Group of Experts called for the establishment of guidelines on prior informed consent and suggested the adoption of a protocol. The secretariat was tasked with putting together a proposal [995]. The initiative was supported by work showing that, under the Global Environmental Facility, there had been no technology transfer on biotechnology pursuant to Article 16 of the Convention [996]. More generally, according to a UNCTAD study, almost two-thirds of global North-South technology transfers were in fact transfers between subsidiaries and parent companies [997].

551. At its fourth meeting, in 1998, the COP decided to establish an Expert Panel on Access and Benefit-Sharing, which was tasked with clarifying the principles and concepts related to access and benefit-sharing [998]. The Panel met twice. At the COP's fifth meeting, in 2000, an *Ad Hoc* Open-ended Working Group on Access and Benefit-sharing (ABS) was set up as a subsidiary body, with the mandate to develop guidelines and other approaches to assist Parties in implementing the access and benefit-sharing provisions of the Convention [999].

552. Indeed, in 2002, it adopted *The Bonn Guidelines on Access to Genetic Resources and the Fair and Equitable Sharing of Benefits Arising out of their Utilization* with the objective of assisting Parties

---

993. COP Decisions IV/8 and V/16, para. 14.
994. Report of the Panel of Experts on Access and Benefit-Sharing, CBD, UNEP/CBD/COP/5/8, 2 November 1999, p. 4.
995. *Ibid.*, p. 33 *et seq.* Parties are invited to provide the secretariat with information on the role of intellectual property rights in the implementation of access and benefit-sharing arrangements before the end of the year.
996. K. Stokes and J. Mugabe, *Biotechnology, TRIPS and the Convention on Biological Diversity*, UNEP/CBD/ISOC/inf.3, 1999, p. 8.
997. GRAIN, *Droits de propriété intellectuelle et biodiversité: les mythes économiques*, Commerce mondial et biodiversité en conflit, No. 3, October 1999, p. 5.
998. Decision IV/8 (1998).
999. Decision V/26 (2000).

in establishing administrative, legislative or policy measures on access and benefit-sharing, and in negotiating contractual arrangements for access to genetic resources and benefit-sharing.

553. In February 2002, twelve countries from the South – Brazil, China, Columbia, Costa Rica, Ecuador, India, Indonesia, Kenya, Mexico, Peru, South Africa and Venezuela, representing 70 per cent of the world's biodiversity – met in Cancun and formed a consultation and co-ordination group, with the aim of improving the legal framework. This is the group of Like-Minded Megadiverse Countries (LMMC) of which there are now seventeen [1000].

554. In the summer of 2002, the World Summit on Sustainable Development was held in Johannesburg, South Africa. The action plan adopted at the end of the conference acknowledged the need to "negotiate within the framework of the Convention on Biological Diversity, bearing in mind the Bonn Guidelines, an international regime to promote and safeguard the fair and equitable sharing of benefits arising out of the utilization of genetic resources" [1001].

555. The Conference of the Parties to the CBD addressed this demand at its seventh meeting, in 2004, by mandating the *Ad Hoc* Open-ended Working Group on Access and Benefit-Sharing to develop and negotiate an international regime on access to genetic resources and benefit-sharing in order to effectively implement Articles 15 (access to genetic resources) and 8 *(j)* (traditional knowledge) of the Convention.

556. In order to achieve this, the Working Group met eleven times between 2005 and 2010. From its ninth meeting, it worked on a draft protocol proposed by the Columbian and Canadian co-chairs. On 29 October 2010, after six years of negotiations, the Nagoya Protocol on Access to Genetic Resources and the Fair and Equitable Sharing of Benefits Arising from their Utilization to the Convention on Biological Diversity was finally adopted at the tenth meeting of the Conference of the Parties in Nagoya, Japan [1002]. It came into force in October 2014 and now has 140 Parties [1003].

1000. H. Ilbert Hélène and S. Louafi, "Biodiversité et ressources génétiques : la difficulté de la constitution d'un régime international hybride", *Revue Tiers Monde*, 45(177), pp. 107-127.
1001. Plan of Implementation of the World Summit on Sustainable Development, UN, A/CONF.199/20, 2002, para. 44 *(o)*.
1002. Decision X/1 (2010).
1003. On 19 December 2023.

Section 2. The contribution of the Nagoya Protocol on Access to Genetic Resources and the Fair and Equitable Sharing of Benefits Arising from their Utilization

557. The Nagoya Protocol fulfils the third objective of the Convention: the "fair and equitable sharing of the benefits arising out of the utilization of genetic resources, including by appropriate access to genetic resources and by appropriate transfer of relevant technologies"[1004]. The aim of the Protocol is to provide "a strong basis for greater legal certainty and transparency for both providers and users of genetic resources"[1005]. Thus, it seeks to encourage the use of genetic resources and associated traditional knowledge. It meets the objectives of legal certainty as well as equity and justice[1006].

1) The general economy of the Protocol

558. The substance of the Protocol reflects a delicate balance between the concerns of countries of origin and those of user countries, between guaranteeing the "fair and equitable" sharing of the benefits derived from the use of genetic resources which are mainly located in developing countries, and guaranteeing safe access to these resources for companies and research organisations from the North. In this regard, it aims to establish an international framework so that the benefits of the use of genetic resources by various industries can be shared with the countries of origin, based on prior informed consent and the signing of a contract with the State in question. It also encourages the parties to direct benefits from this system towards activities aimed at the conservation and sustainable use of biodiversity.

a) *The principles governing access and benefit-sharing*

559. The Nagoya Protocol reaffirms in its preamble the sovereignty of States over their natural resources, which include genetic resources. It therefore sets the following objective:

1004. Article 1.
1005. Secretariat of the Convention on Biological Diversity, Nagoya Protocol on Access to Genetic Resources and the Fair and Equitable Sharing of Benefits Arising from their Utilization to the Convention on Biological Diversity, text and annex, Montreal, 2011, p. 1.
1006. Preamble.

> "The fair and equitable sharing of the benefits arising from the utilization of genetic resources, including by appropriate access to genetic resources and by appropriate transfer of relevant technologies, taking into account all rights over those resources and to technologies, and by appropriate funding, thereby contributing to the conservation of biological diversity and the sustainable use of its components." [1007]

560. It states that benefits are shared in a fair and equitable manner, including with "indigenous and local communities". However, such sharing is "based on mutually agreed terms". Each Party "shall take legislative, administrative or policy measures, as appropriate" to this effect [1008].

561. With regard to access, the principle is as follows:

> "In the exercise of sovereign rights over natural resources, and subject to domestic access and benefit-sharing legislation or regulatory requirements, access to genetic resources for their utilization shall be subject to the prior informed consent of the Party providing such resources that is the country of origin of such resources or a Party that has acquired the genetic resources in accordance with the Convention, unless otherwise determined by that Party." [1009]

In particular, the Parties must "provide for the issuance at the time of access of a permit or its equivalent as evidence of the decision to grant prior informed consent and of the establishment of mutually agreed terms, and notify the Access and Benefit-sharing Clearing-House accordingly" [1010]. Furthermore,

> "In accordance with domestic law, each Party shall take measures, as appropriate, with the aim of ensuring that traditional knowledge associated with genetic resources that is held by indigenous and local communities is accessed with the prior and informed consent or approval and involvement of these indigenous and local communities, and that mutually agreed terms have been established." [1011]

1007. Article 1.
1008. Article 5.
1009. Article 6.
1010. *Ibid.*, para. 3 *e)*.
1011. Articles 6 and 7. See also Article 12.

562. The Protocol provides, where appropriate, for "transboundary cooperation" [1012]. The Protocol also contemplates the subsequent creation of

> "a global multilateral benefit sharing mechanism to address the fair and equitable sharing of benefits derived from the utilization of genetic resources and traditional knowledge associated with genetic resources that occur in transboundary situations or for which it is not possible to grant or obtain prior informed consent" [1013].

Due to the divergent views of the Parties, such a mechanism is still not in place.

563. The Protocol also provides that the Parties must encourage providers and users of genetic resources and/or traditional knowledge associated with genetic resources to include in the mutually agreed terms provisions "to cover, where appropriate, dispute resolution" and also encourage "the development, update and use of sectoral and cross-sectoral model contractual clauses for mutually agreed terms" [1014]. In 2016, the COP of the Convention on Biological Diversity adopted voluntary guidelines "to ensure the 'prior and informed consent', 'free, prior and informed consent' or 'approval and involvement', depending on national circumstances, of indigenous peoples and local communities". These do not apply to traditional knowledge associated with genetic resources under the Nagoya Protocol, but the COP clarified that they could be used, "where appropriate", to develop specific instruments under the Protocol [1015].

564. According to Article 9 of the Protocol: "The Parties shall encourage users and providers to direct benefits arising from the utilization of genetic resources towards the conservation of biological diversity and the sustainable use of its components".

1012. Article 11.
1013. Article 10.
1014. Articles 18, 19 and 20.
1015. Decision XIII/18 (2016), *Article 8 (j) and related provisions, Mo'otz Kuxtal Voluntary Guidelines, Voluntary Guidelines for the Development of Mechanisms, Legislation or Other Appropriate Initiatives to Ensure the "prior and informed consent", "free, prior and informed consent" or "approval and involvement", Depending on National Circumstances, of Indigenous Peoples and Local Communities for Accessing their Knowledge, Innovations and Practices, for Fair and Equitable Sharing of Benefits Arising from the Use of their Knowledge, Innovations and Practices Relevant for the Conservation and Sustainable Use of Biological Diversity, and for Reporting and Preventing Unlawful Appropriation of Traditional Knowledge.*

565. When prior informed consent has been obtained and mutually agreed terms have been defined, a permit or equivalent document is to be issued. When forwarded to the Convention's Clearing-House, this document becomes "an internationally recognized certificate of compliance".

b) *Adapting to technological change*

566. Technological developments have become an intense topic of discussion in the context of the Convention and its protocols. They are part of the issues for which a coherent international approach will be needed. New technologies, such as synthetic biology, the production and increasing use of digital sequence information (DSI) and its publication in large public and private databases, are significantly reshaping the context surrounding access and benefit-sharing. It is no longer always possible to link digital sequencing information back to the genetic resource from which it was produced. Duplication of a genetic resource becomes possible on the basis of genetic information alone, without the need for physical access to the resource. These technological developments leading to the "dematerialisation" of genetic information thus threaten to render the Convention, the Nagoya Protocol and the FAO Treaty obsolete [1016]. Is accessing such data also subject to prior informed consent, traceability of exchanges and benefit-sharing? Is such traceability even technically possible?

567. Deeply divided on this matter, the CBD COP established an expert group to conduct various assessments in order to clarify the issue [1017]. The decision of the 2018 COP specified that "the term 'digital sequence information' may not be the most appropriate term and that it is used as a placeholder until an alternative term is agreed". The definition of digital sequence information is indeed fundamental in order to determine whether it falls within the scope of the Convention and the Protocol, and whether or to what extent the ABS provisions apply to such DSI and should influence the conditions surrounding access to databases of digitised genetic sequences. This is an intangible

---

[1016]. E. Tsioumani, "Beyond Access and Benefit-Sharing: Lessons from the Law and Governance of Agricultural Biodiversity" (n. 967), p. 117.

[1017]. Decision 14/20 (2018), *Digital Sequence Information on Genetic Resources*. The *Ad Hoc* Technical Expert Group on Digital Sequencing Information is mandated to develop options to clarify the concept of digital sequencing information for genetic resources and to identify key areas in need of capacity-building, for consideration by the Working Group on the Post-2020 Framework.

International Biodiversity Law   313

form of knowledge about living organisms to which the countries of the South are demanding free access [1018]. The COP 15 decision admitted that there "are divergent views on digital sequence information on genetic resources" and decided to establish "a multilateral mechanism for benefit-sharing from the use of digital sequence information on genetic resources, including a global fund". A new *ad hoc* open-ended working group was established "to undertake further development" [1019].

568. As for the development of synthetic biology, the COP is also sharply divided on this issue and has been reflecting on it since its tenth meeting. It also set up a group of technical experts in 2018. While awaiting the results of the discussions and work in progress, it called on the Parties to apply a precautionary approach and, in particular, to consider "introducing organisms containing engineered gene drives into the environment, including for experimental releases and research and development purposes" only under very limited conditions. It did not however prohibit such introduction [1020]. After rough negotiations, the COP 15 decision established a "process for broad and regular horizon scanning, monitoring and assessment of the most recent technological developments in synthetic biology" and a multidisciplinary *ad hoc* technical expert group to support the process [1021]. Thus, despite some progress, it has not yet been possible to resolve the differences and the negotiation process is therefore continuing on these very sensitive issues.

c) *Implementation mechanisms under the Protocol*

569. In terms of implementation, the Protocol relies on a number of institutions. Parties must designate national focal points who liaise with the secretariat, but also provide information to access-seekers. They must also designate one or more national authorities to be responsible for, among other things,

> "granting access or, as applicable, issuing written evidence that access requirements have been met and be responsible for

---

1018. C. Aubertin and F. Pinton, "Compenser plutôt que reconquérir", *Natures Sciences Sociétés* 2018/2 (Vol. 26), p. 128. See also IUCN, *Genetic Frontiers for Conservation, An Assessment of Synthetic Biology and Biodiversity Conservation Synthesis and Key Messages*, IUCN Task Force on Synthetic Biology and Biodiversity Conservation, IUCN, Gland, 2019.
1019. Decision 15/9 (2022), *Digital Sequence Information on Genetic Resources*.
1020. Decision 14/19 (2018), *Synthetic Biology*, para. 11. See the outcome of the group, CBD/SBSTTA/24/4/Rev.1, Annex I.
1021. Decision 15/31 (2022), *Synthetic Biology*.

advising on applicable procedures and requirements for obtaining prior informed consent and entering into mutually agreed terms" [1022].

They must also designate a checkpoint "to monitor and to enhance transparency about the utilization of genetic resource" [1023].

570. Furthermore, an Access and Benefit-sharing Clearing-House was established as part of the clearing-house mechanisms referred to in Article 18 (3) of the Convention. It "shall serve as a means for sharing of information related to access and benefit-sharing. In particular, it shall provide access to information made available by each Party relevant to the implementation of this Protocol" [1024]. The Parties must provide it with information on measures taken under the Protocol, permits or documents issued, and where appropriate the relevant competent authorities of indigenous and local communities, as well as information on standard contractual clauses, methods and tools developed to monitor genetic resources, but also codes of conduct and best practices [1025]. This Clearing-House is still in its early stages. Not all States have submitted the required information. In 2018, the Meeting of the Parties to the Protocol (COP-MOP) adopted the joint operating modalities of the Convention's Clearing-House, the Biosafety Clearing-House and the Access and Benefit-sharing Clearing-House, which can be found in the annex to COP decision 14/25 [1026]. An Informal Advisory Committee was set up to assist the COP in operationalising this mechanism.

571. The Protocol also provides the following:

> "The Parties shall cooperate in the capacity-building, capacity development and strengthening of human resources and institutional capacities to effectively implement this Protocol in developing country Parties, in particular the least developed countries and small island developing States among them, and Parties with economies in transition, including through existing global, regional, subregional and national institutions and organizations." [1027]

1022. Article 13, para. 2.
1023. Article 17.
1024. Article 14, para. 1.
1025. Article 14.
1026. See its Decision NP-3/3 (2018), *The Access and Benefit-sharing Clearing-House and Information Sharing (Art. 14)*.
1027. Article 22.

Furthermore, the Parties "undertake to promote and encourage access to technology by, and transfer of technology to, developing country Parties, in particular the least developed countries and small island developing States among them, and Parties with economies in transition" [1028]. The Protocol designated the financial mechanism of the Convention (the GEF) as its financial mechanism. The same is true for the secretariat and subsidiary bodies of the CBD [1029]. The Conference of the Parties serves as the meeting of the Parties to the Protocol (COP-MOP) [1030]. However, the Protocol provides that the COP-MOP will establish its own reporting and compliance mechanism [1031].

572. The COP-MOP did in fact agree on a format and guidelines for the submission of an interim report, and requested Parties to submit it twelve months before the third meeting of the Parties to the Protocol, i.e. by 1 November 2017 [1032]. Only 39 out of 100 Parties fulfilled this request, despite financial assistance from the Global Environmental Facility being provided to Parties facing difficulties [1033].

573. The COP-MOP also set up at its first meeting a compliance mechanism, based on a committee to promote compliance, the Compliance Committee [1034]. This is a relatively standard procedure. However, it should be noted that the Committee includes two representatives of indigenous and local communities, who are elected by the COP-MOP. There are three possibilities for the Committee to receive submissions: by "[a]ny Party with respect to itself", "[a]ny Party with respect to another Party", which is relatively standard, but also by the COP-MOP, which is more original and constitutes an additional option compared to the Cartagena Protocol. The Committee may also "examine systemic issues of general non-compliance that come to its attention". Compared to other such committees, the Committee has broader means of obtaining information. Indeed:

> "1. The Committee may seek, receive and consider information from relevant sources, including from affected indigenous and

---

1028. Article 23.
1029. Articles 25, 27 and 28. See below.
1030. Article 26.
1031. Articles 29 and 30.
1032. Decision NP-1/3 (2014), *Monitoring and Reporting (Art. 29)*.
1033. Compliance Committee, Second meeting, Montreal, Canada, 24-26 April 2018, First Assessment and Review of the Nagoya Protocol and General Issues of Compliance, Note by the Executive Secretary, CBD/ABS/CC/2/3 5 April 2018, p. 2.
1034. See Decision NP-1/4 (2014), *Cooperative Procedures and Institutional Mechanisms to Promote Compliance with the Nagoya Protocol and to Address Cases of Non-Compliance.*

local communities. The reliability of the information should be ensured.

2. The Committee may seek advice from independent experts, including, in particular where indigenous and local communities are directly affected, from an indigenous and local community expert.

3. The Committee may undertake, upon invitation of the Party concerned, information gathering in the territory of that Party."

574. If there are issues as to the implementation of the Protocol, the Committee can take various measures to accompany the non-compliant Party towards a return to compliance. But it is mainly the COP-MOP that has the means to react by taking positive or negative measures. It can decide to put in place incentives such as facilitating financial or technical assistance, technology transfer, training or capacity-building. It may also "issue a written caution, statement of concern or a declaration of non-compliance to the Party concerned" or "decide on any other measure, as appropriate, in accordance with Article 26, paragraph 4 of the Protocol and the applicable rules of international law, bearing in mind the need for serious measures in cases of grave or repeated non-compliance". As it has not yet received submissions on individual cases of non-compliance, it has primarily worked pursuant to the provision that allows it to consider "systemic issues" [1035].

2) The challenging relationship of the Protocol with other international agreements

575. As with the Cartagena Protocol, the relationship between the Nagoya Protocol and other international agreements is a key aspect of its effectiveness. Few international environmental agreements raise the issue of institutional complexity in such a fundamental way [1036]. It was obvious during the negotiation process and it remains a major issue more than ten years after its adoption, in an ever-changing context.

1035. See the last Committee's report, *Report of the Compliance Committee under the Nagoya Protocol on Access to Genetic Resources and the Fair and Equitable Sharing of Benefits Arising from their Utilization on the Work of its Third Meeting*, CBD/NP/CC/3/5 23 April 2020.

1036. S. Oberthür and J. Pozarowska., "Managing Institutional Complexity and Fragmentation: The Nagoya Protocol and the Global Governance of Genetic Resources", *Global Environmental Politics,* 13:3, August 2013, p. 113.

Developments contrary to the letter or spirit of the Protocol in other fora can considerably weaken and even sideline the Protocol [1037].

576. The Protocol devotes its long Article 4 to its relationship with other international instruments. It states that it "shall be implemented in a mutually supportive manner with other international instruments relevant to this Protocol" and mentions the absence of "hierarchy" with the latter. As a rule, the "provisions of this Protocol shall not affect the rights and obligations of any Party deriving from any existing international agreement", "except where the exercise of those rights and obligations would cause a serious damage or threat to biological diversity". Thus, even though it asserts the absence of a hierarchy, it still suggests that the Protocol's provisions should prevail in this particular case. On the other hand,

> "[w]here a specialized international access and benefit-sharing instrument applies that is consistent with, and does not run counter to the objectives of the Convention and this Protocol, this Protocol does not apply for the Party or Parties to the specialized instrument in respect of the specific genetic resource covered by and for the purpose of the specialized instrument".

The Protocol does not define which instruments fall into the category of "specialized instruments". Discussions are ongoing as to the criteria for defining them [1038].

577. The relationship between the Protocol, the UPOV's International Convention for the Protection of New Varieties of Plants and the FAO's International Treaty on Plant Genetic Resources for Food and Agriculture are particularly worth looking into. In theory, there is no opposition between these three treaties. They establish distinct but related and potentially conflicting legal regimes covering different fields. International and national implementation is therefore crucial to ensure real "mutual support" as called for by Article 4 of the Protocol [1039].

1037. K. Rosendal and S. Andresen, "Realizing Access and Benefit Sharing from Use of Genetic Resources between Diverging International Regimes: The Scope for Leadership", *International Environmental Agreements* (2016) 16, p. 596.
1038. Study into Criteria to Identify a Specialized International Access and Benefit-Sharing Instrument, and a Possible Process for its Recognition, UN Doc. UNEP/CBD/SBI/2/INF/17. The COP-MOP took note of the report. See Decision 3/14 (1996), *Implementation of Article 8 (j)*.
1039. J. Cabrera Medaglia, C. Oguamanam, O. Rukundo and F. Perron-Welch, *Comparative Study of the Nagoya Protocol, the Plant Treaty and the UPOV Convention: The Interface of Access and Benefit Sharing and Plant Variety*, CISDL, 2019, p. 41 et seq.

578. The Protocol does in fact recognise the "fundamental role" of the International Treaty on Plant Genetic Resources for Food and Agriculture and the Commission on Genetic Resources for Food and Agriculture of the FAO [1040]. The Parties also recall the "Multilateral System of Access and Benefit-sharing established under the International Treaty on Plant Genetic Resources for Food and Agriculture developed in harmony with the Convention". This Treaty defines, for agricultural biodiversity, the most sophisticated international regime of access and benefit-sharing [1041]. In the same vein, the United Nations Declaration on the Rights of Peasants and Other People Working in Rural Areas, a new instrument that brings together farmers' rights, human rights and rights over natural resources, recalls the Convention and the Nagoya Protocol as well the FAO Treaty [1042].

579. Indeed, there is extensive co-operation between the Convention, the Nagoya Protocol and the FAO Treaty, going well beyond cross-representation at various meetings. For example, the secretariats of the two treaties have collaborated on the development of indicators and the provision of data as part of the Global Indicator Framework for the 2030 Agenda for Sustainable Development, including Indicator 15.6.1 that will assess progress towards Target 15.6 (to "promote fair and equitable sharing of the benefits arising from the utilization of genetic resources and promote appropriate access to such resources, as internationally agreed") [1043]. At its second meeting, the Meeting of the Parties to the Nagoya Protocol adopted a decision in which, among other things, it invited Parties and other governments to implement the International Treaty on Plant Genetic Resources for Food and Agriculture and the Nagoya Protocol in a mutually supportive manner, as appropriate [1044]. The Conference of the Parties to the CBD adopted a similar decision [1045]. The Multilateral System created by the FAO Treaty is currently being renegotiated. In the revised version, negotiators are struggling with

---

1040. Preamble.
1041. E. Tsioumani, "Beyond Access and Benefit-Sharing: Lessons from the Law and Governance of Agricultural Biodiversity" (n. 967), p. 108.
1042. Resolution UNGA 73/165 (17 December 2018), *United Nations Declaration on the Rights of Peasants and Other People Working in Rural Areas*.
1043. CBD, *Cooperation with Other Conventions, International Organizations and Initiatives*, Note by the Executive Secretary, CBD/NP/MOP/3/9, 9 September 2018.
1044. Decision 2/1 (2016), *Review of Progress Towards Aichi Biodiversity Target 16 on the Nagoya Protocol*.
1045. Decision XIII/3 (2016), *Strategic Actions to Enhance the Implementation of the Strategic Plan for Biodiversity 2011-2020 and the Achievement of the Aichi Biodiversity Targets, Including with respect to Mainstreaming and the Integration of Biodiversity within and across Sectors*, para. 41.

the issue of benefit-sharing with respect to data derived from genetic sequencing. The idea here is to achieve a common agenda between the two conventions. Some countries are trying to limit access to genetic sequencing data, even though it is a potentially very useful tool for the conservation and sustainable use of genetic resources for food and agriculture.

580. The Parties further state in the preamble to the Nagoya Protocol that they are "[m]indful of the International Health Regulations (2005) of the World Health Organization and the importance of ensuring access to human pathogens for public health preparedness and response purposes". Co-operation is ongoing on the potential public health impact of the implementation of the Protocol on pathogen exchange [1046]. They also note the United Nations Declaration on the Rights of Indigenous Peoples. They recognise the ongoing work on access and benefit-sharing in other international fora. In practice, the secretariat is, for example, participating in the UN negotiations on marine biodiversity beyond national jurisdictions, to share its experience and ensure that the framework to be developed on access and benefit-sharing will be compatible with the Protocol. The status of marine genetic resources and the issues of access and benefit-sharing with regard to these resources are indeed part of the package being negotiated, bearing in mind that the UN General Assembly has specified that "this process and its result should not undermine existing relevant legal instruments and frameworks and relevant global, regional and sectoral bodies" [1047].

581. Similarly, one should probably not overstate the existence of real normative conflicts between the Nagoya Protocol and the WTO agreements on trade in goods or intellectual property rights. In itself, the Protocol does not require the implementation of measures that go against WTO law; Parties have much discretion. Thus, if there is to be a conflict, it would not be because of the substance of the Protocol,

---

1046. CBD, *Cooperation with Other Conventions, International Organizations and Initiatives*, Note by the Executive Secretary, CBD/NP/MOP/3/9, 9 September 2018.

1047. Resolution UNGA, 24 December 2017, No. 72/249, *International Legally Binding Instrument under the United Nations Convention on the Law of the Sea on the Conservation and Sustainable Use of Marine Biological Diversity of Areas Beyond National Jurisdiction*. See J. Mossop, "Towards a Practical Approach to Regulating Marine Genetic Resources", *ESIL Reflections* 8:3 (2019); V. De Lucia, "Rethinking the Conservation of Marine Biodiversity Beyond National; Jurisdiction: From 'Not Undermine' to Ecosystem-Based Governance", *ESIL Reflections* 8:4 (2019); G. Voigt-Hanssen, "Current 'Light' and 'Heavy' Options for Benefit-sharing in the Context of the United Nations Convention on the Law of the Sea", in D. Freestone (ed.), *Conserving Biodiversity in Areas Beyond National Jurisdiction*, Leiden Brill Nijhoff, 2019, pp. 243-266.

but rather because of the nature of this instrument which allows Parties to adopt laws that may conflict with WTO rules [1048]. According to Article 24 of the Protocol, Parties are only asked to encourage non-Parties to comply with the Protocol. This provision is quite different from the one that defines the relationship of the Cartagena Protocol with other international agreements; it is much more flexible.

582. The link with regional frameworks is also important. In this respect, mention can be made of the African Convention of Maputo: compared to the laconic Article XI of the Algiers Convention on "Customary Rights" [1049], it includes a more detailed provision on the subject. This provision is entitled "Traditional Rights of Local Communities and Indigenous Knowledge", in keeping with Agenda 21 and the Rio Convention on Biological Diversity [1050]. New references to intellectual property rights, "including farmers' rights" in particular, are included, as well as the need to make access to and use of traditional knowledge subject "to the prior informed consent of the concerned communities and to specific regulations recognizing their rights to, and appropriate economic value of, such knowledge". Here, the Convention highlights the need for harmonised implementation of the relevant provisions, as provided for in the African Union Model Law on Rights of Local Communities, Farmers, Breeders and the Regulation for Access to Biological Resources. As noted before [1051], adopted under the auspices of the OAU in 1998, this model legislation is intended to assist African States in developing and implementing the legal instruments required to meet their obligations under TRIPS and the Convention on Biological Diversity [1052]. However, in reality, few countries have adopted this model [1053].

[1048]. R. Pavoni, "Droit du commerce International et biodiversité après le Protocole de Nagoya", in *Diversité dans la gouvernance internationale : perspectives culturelles, écologiques et juridiques*, V. Négri (ed.), Bruylant, 2016, p. 125.

[1049]. "Les Etats contractants prendront les mesures législatives nécessaires pour mettre les droits coutumiers en harmonie avec les dispositions de la présente Convention."

[1050]. Article XVII.

[1051]. See above, para. 544.

[1052]. IUCN, *An Introduction to the African Convention on the Conservation of Nature and Natural Resources*, Environmental Policy and Law Paper No. 56 Rev., 2nd ed., Gland, 2006, p. 52.

[1053]. S. Yamthieu, "Loi Modèle Africaine", in Dictionnaire juridique de la sécurité alimentaire dans le monde, F. Collard-Dutilleul and J.-P. Bugnicourt (eds.), Larcier, Bruxelles, 2013, pp. 414-416.

3) A limited impact

583. The Protocol is a compromise instrument which essentially reflects the views of the more moderate industrialised countries, such as those of the European Union, but which is far from meeting the needs of the countries of the South [1054]. For the most part, it ultimately relies on national legislation. As pointed out by Marie-Angèle Hermitte, the question of how to share any potential benefits derived from the use of genetic resources has not really been settled, not even in broad terms. Although the Protocol did reaffirm the need for prior consent from the provider country and for "mutually agreed terms", although it distinguished between the regimes applicable to exchanges of tangible things (resources) and intangible things (knowledge), and although suggestions were made to ensure that the agreement would be equitable, almost everything has been left to the discretion of national legislators. According to this author, this is both a liberal and procedural vision of equity based on the law-makers' capacity, in the North as well as in the South, to implement it and on the negotiation and control abilities of the Parties to the agreement [1055]. From this point of view, the Protocol is slow to produce its effects, as shown by the first review of its implementation that took place in 2018 [1056]. States must develop national legislation in this respect and the clearing-house mechanism will need to be progressively strengthened, which cannot be done if States do not provide it with the required information. Thus, as of 22 February 2018, only 51 per cent of the Parties had provided the Clearing-House with information on measures taken, designation of national competent authorities, focal points or international certificates of compliance [1057]. Provisions on technology transfer are also slow to take effect [1058]. Only a small portion of the GEF's funds is dedicated to

---

1054. S. Oberthur and G. K. Rosendal (eds.), *Global Governance of Genetic Resources. Access and Benefit Sharing After the Nagoya Protocol*, Routledge, 2013, p. 233.
1055. *Ibid.*, p. 413.
1056. See Decision NP-3/1 (2018), *Assessment and Review of the Effectiveness of the Protocol (Art. 31)*. The next review will take place in 2024.
1057. Compliance Committee, Second meeting, Montreal, Canada, 24-26 April 2018, *First Assessment and Review of the Nagoya Protocol and General Issues of Compliance*, Note by the Executive Secretary, CBD/ABS/CC/2/3, 5 April 2018, p. 8.
1058. See Decision NP-3/5 (2018), *Measures to Assist in Capacity-Building and Capacity Development (Art. 22)*.

the implementation of the Protocol [1059]. The global multilateral benefit-sharing mechanism is still under consideration [1060].

584. Two major challenges have been underlined by States: ensuring the participation of local and indigenous communities and key stakeholders in access and benefit-sharing mechanisms, but also, at the institutional level, ensuring better co-ordination between the various institutions, ministries and agencies given that this is such a broad issue. Developing countries also regret the lack of financial and human resources.

585. The Protocol also fails to provide specific protection for indigenous peoples; there are no additional guarantees compared to that which would be conferred by national legislation. As many international initiatives exist in this respect, this has consequences for the (lack of) coherence of national policies. Thus, the Nagoya Protocol does not specify its relationship with WIPO or the WTO with regard to the intellectual rights of indigenous peoples over their genetic resources and traditional knowledge. Yet, as noted by Marie-Angèle Hermitte, the existence of such rights, recognised by the international community pursuant to a common legal instrument, in the same way as patents or trademarks, is the only way to overcome the very uncertain nature of the implementation of the benefit-sharing principle as conceived under the Protocol [1061]. Reflection is taking place in a compartmentalised manner within the framework of Article 8 *(j)* of the Convention, for which a working group on the intellectual rights of indigenous peoples has been set up, and within WIPO, which has set up an Intergovernmental Committee on Intellectual Property and Genetic Resources, Traditional Knowledge and Folklore (IGC) under the auspices of which draft articles are being negotiated [1062]. The idea of listing traditional knowledge on biodiversity conservation as an Intangible Cultural Heritage according to UNESCO has also been raised by some with regard to great apes, in

---

1059. Fifty millions of US dollars programmed by GEF-6 out of 1,296 dedicated to biodiversity. See *Financial mechanism and resources (Art. 25)*, Note by the Executive Secretary, CBD/NP/MOP/3/5, 24 September 2018, p. 2.

1060. Decision NP-3/13 (2018), *Global Multilateral Benefit-Sharing Mechanism (Art. 10)*.

1061. M.-A. Hermitte, in M.-A. Hermitte, S. Maljean-Dubois and E. Truilhé-Marengo, "Actualités de la Convention sur la diversité biologique : science et politique, équité, biosécurité" (n. 929), p. 425.

1062. Intergovernmental Committee on Intellectual Property and Genetic Resources, Traditional Knowledge and Folklore, Twenty-Fourth Session, Geneva, 22 to 26 April 2013, *The Protection of Traditional Knowledge: Draft Articles, Document prepared by the Secretariat*, WIPO/GRTKF/IC/24/4, January 2013.

order to prevent the disappearance of this local knowledge, to encourage the reconnection of local populations that live near these threatened species and to help better protect great apes and their habitats [1063].

1063. C. Vincent, "Comment l'Unesco veut sauver les grands singes", *Le Monde*, 18 November 2018.

CHAPTER VI

SUPPORTING STATES IN THE IMPLEMENTATION OF THE INTERNATIONAL LAW ON BIODIVERSITY

"It is a distortion of the human and social reality that is expressed in modern legal systems to focus only on a need for order, for regularity and therefore for the prompt and complete effectiveness of legal rules. Antagonistic interests intersect: the propensity to compromise, leniency, even the principle of least effort, all of which mean that legal rules are inclined to an equally natural ineffectiveness." [1064]

586. Indeed, the effectiveness of legal rules faces much resistance. This is particularly true of international environmental law and, within it, of the international law on biodiversity. When comparing the impressive development of the international law on biodiversity – which began over a century ago – and the rapid deterioration in the state of biodiversity frequently mentioned in environmental reports, including the recent IPBES reports, one must admit that the proliferation of rules has not produced the desired effects. Various tools are in place to support States in the implementation of their international commitments, from technical and financial co-operation tools to international monitoring and compliance procedures.

Section 1. Technical and financial co-operation tools

587. The development of technical and financial co-operation is both a means to strengthen the implementation of international conventions and an incentive to join them.

1) Technical co-operation

588. International conventions encourage technical co-operation, which in practice is implemented on a bilateral and multilateral level. Such co-operation depends on the scope and purpose of conventions,

---

1064. J. Carbonnier, "Effectivité et ineffectivité de la règle de droit", *L'année sociologique*, Vol. 9, 1957-1958, p. 13 (our translation).

but it generally takes the form of "capacity-building" initiatives for developing countries: provision of technology and know-how, assistance in the training of management staff, legal assistance, etc. Co-operation also takes place between countries with similar levels of development and know-how in terms of biodiversity conservation, when it is made necessary by environmental constraints, such as the presence of wetlands or other important habitats for migratory species on each side of borders. The institutions of many conventions conduct valuable field work in this respect.

589. Thus, technical co-operation is an important component of the Rio Convention on Biological Diversity, as set out in Article 18. This provision states that the Parties encourage technical and scientific co-operation, in particular with developing countries. They also promote "cooperation in the training of personnel and exchange of experts". In addition, Article 18 contemplates the establishment of a clearing-house mechanism to promote and facilitate technical and scientific co-operation. This mechanism, known as the CHM, was indeed put in place at the first COP [1065]. Designed to provide information and facilitate the exchange of information between the Parties, it consists of a website serving as a central hub and a network of national clearing-houses [1066]. It operates in an integrated manner for the Convention and its protocols, which contain mirror provisions on technical co-operation, each in relation to their specific subject matter [1067].

590. The secretariat also produces tools to facilitate the implementation of the Convention (such as a toolkit provided by the clearing-house mechanism) and organises various training courses and workshops (regional workshops, workshops focusing on indigenous peoples or local communities, etc.). In its 2010 Decision X/2, which adopted the Strategic Plan for Biodiversity 2011-2020 and the Aichi Targets, the COP declared the following:

> "The extent to which developing country Parties will effectively implement their commitments under this Convention will depend on the effective implementation by developed country Parties

---

1065. Decision I/3 (1994), *Clearing-House Mechanism for Technical and Scientific Cooperation*.
1066. See *Information Services of the Central Clearing-House Mechanism*, UNEP/CBD/CHM/IAC/2010/1/3, 27 September 2010.
1067. See Articles 20 and 22 of the Cartagena Protocol and Article 23 of the Nagoya Protocol.

of their commitments under this Convention related to financial resources and transfer of technology." [1068]

This provision echoes the previously mentioned Article 20 (4) of the Convention. A similar provision can be found in the United Nations Framework Convention on Climate Change [1069].

591. The action plan combines various capacity-building actions. A number of programmes have been implemented, such as the Bio-Bridge Initiative and the Global Taxonomy Initiative. However, the COP has recognised the difficulty of mobilising resources [1070]. It regularly calls on the Parties but also on all potential financial donors – international financial institutions, regional development banks and other multilateral financing institutions – to contribute to capacity-building in relation to the treaty objectives by providing financial, technical and human resources. Developing countries are the main beneficiaries, especially least developed countries, small island developing States and countries with economies in transition, including also countries that are centres of origin and diversity of genetic resources. The COP adopted in 2022 a long-term strategic framework for capacity-building beyond 2020 [1071]. In order to support joint capacity-building activities, synergies and areas of co-operation with the other Rio and biodiversity-related conventions are at the heart of the plan. Technical co-operation is indeed a key aspect of the co-operation between the secretariats of the various conventions [1072].

592. As a matter of fact, all biodiversity conventions place emphasis on technical co-operation. This is true of the Ramsar Convention, which does not contain a very precise provision on technical co-operation, but rather vaguely provides that the Parties must "endeavour to co-ordinate and support present and future policies and regulations concerning

---

1068. Decision X/2 (2010), *The Strategic Plan for Biodiversity 2011-2020 and the Aichi Biodiversity Targets*, UNEP/CBD/COP/DEC/X/2 (2010), p. 117, para. 10.
1069. Article 4, para. 7.
1070. Decision XIII/23 (2016), *Capacity-Building, Technical and Scientific Cooperation, Technology Transfer and the Clearing-House Mechanism.*
1071. Decision 15/8 (2022), *Capacity-Building and Development and Technical and Scientific Cooperation* (Annex I).
1072. See, for example, in relation to the implementation of the Nagoya Protocol and other access and benefit-sharing instruments, CBD, *Cooperation with Other Conventions, International Organizations and Initiatives*, Note by the Executive Secretary, CBD/NP/MOP/3/9, 9 September 2018. See also, in the same vein, UNEP, World Conservation Monitoring Centre, *Mapping Multilateral Environmental Agreements to the Aichi Biodiversity Targets*, Cambridge, 2015.

the conservation of wetlands and their flora and fauna" [1073]. However, the Convention does give rise to significant technical co-operation activities, be it the identification of potential Ramsar Site, the training of reserve wardens, the preparation of management projects for Ramsar Sites, or technical assistance under what is referred to as a monitoring procedure when sites are threatened [1074].

593. Under CITES, the secretariat has responsibilities in terms of technical co-operation. Indeed, it undertakes

> "scientific and technical studies in accordance with programmes authorized by the Conference of the Parties as will contribute to the implementation of the present Convention, including studies concerning standards for appropriate preparation and shipment of living specimens and the means of identifying specimens"

and makes "recommendations for the implementation of the aims and provisions of the present Convention, including the exchange of information of a scientific or technical nature" [1075]. The COP has instructed it to provide targeted technical support for capacity-building and to deliver general and specialised training for CITES Management Authorities and Scientific Authorities, customs and law enforcement authorities, the judiciary, legislators and other stakeholders, including for new Parties, developing Parties, Parties identified through the Convention's compliance mechanism, and small island developing States. The secretariat develops and regularly updates capacity-building materials made available to States online. It must work in conjunction with other relevant international institutions and organisations. It collects capacity-building requests from Parties. The COP seeks to improve activities and has asked the Standing Committee to consider ways to consolidate, streamline and improve the coherence of the capacity-building activities referred to in the resolutions and decisions, and to make recommendations to the Conference of the Parties to this end [1076]. Several activities are undertaken with the aim of promoting the Convention and assisting its implementation. For the most part, they involve technical assistance and training for national authorities

---

1073. Article 5.
1074. See below, Section 2.
1075. Article XII, paras. *(c)* and *(h)*.
1076. CITES, Seventieth meeting of the Standing Committee, Rosa Khutor, Sochi (Russian Federation), 1-5 October 2018, *Strategic Matters Capacity-Building, Capacity-Building Needs of Developing Countries and Countries with Economies in Transition: Report of the Secretariat.*

designated by developing countries. The latter's national focal points are often lacking, for want of resources and/or staff. The secretariat carries out important work to assist member countries in drafting their national legislation and strengthening their "legal capacities". It organises training (for example, the Wildlife Crime and Anti-Money Laundering Training Programme in 2016), develops various tools and manuals (recent examples include the Best Practice Guide for Forensic Timber Identification, Guidelines on Methods and Procedures for Ivory Sampling and Laboratory Analysis or the ICCWC Wildlife and Forest Crime Analytic Tool) and has created a "virtual college" which provides online capacity-building activities and reference materials. In addition, the secretariat encourages bilateral and regional co-operation. Regional meetings of national scientific authorities are also organised.

594. In the Convention concerning the Protection of the World Cultural and Natural Heritage too, technical assistance is an important feature. It can take different forms: assistance in the identification of potential sites for inscription, in the preparation of nominations or requests for technical co-operation, etc. This is known as preparatory assistance. Assistance can also be provided on an emergency basis in the event of sudden and unexpected damage to the site (landslides, floods, etc.). In this case, it enables the production of an emergency plan for the safeguarding of the site, or the undertaking of emergency measures. Furthermore, States Parties may ask for support in the training of staff specialised at all levels in fields covered by the Convention. Assistance may also consist of strictly technical co-operation, regarding works planned pursuant to safeguarding projects [1077].

595. As for the Convention on the Conservation of Migratory Species of Wild Animals, it does not include a provision on technical assistance. The development of co-operation is instead provided for in its daughter agreements. However, the COP adopts initiatives on issues common to all agreements. For example, the Agreement on the Conservation of African-Eurasian Migratory Waterbirds calls on Parties to provide training as well as technical and financial support to other Parties on a multilateral or bilateral basis to help them implement its provisions [1078]. It also provides that they must analyse their training

---

1077. Intergovernmental Committee for the Protection of the World Cultural and Natural Heritage, UNESCO, Intergovernmental Committee for the Protection of the World Cultural and Natural Heritage, UNESCO, *Operational Guidelines for the Implementation of the World Heritage Convention,* WHC.17/01, 12 July 2017, para. 75, para. 170 and p. 65.

1078. Article V (4).

requirements, particularly in relation to surveys, monitoring and the ringing of migratory waterbirds, as well as wetland management, in order to identify priority issues and areas where training is needed and to co-operate in the development and implementation of appropriate training programmes [1079]. Much training is provided within this framework, and a number of useful manuals and documents have also been made available. One example is the Manual for National Focal Points for the CMS instruments, which was developed after the COP of the CMS requested that the secretariat work with the Standing Committee, the Scientific Council and secretariats of the CMS daughter agreements and their scientific advisory bodies to develop tools to strengthen the capacity of CMS Parties [1080]. Another example is the development of an online platform for the National Focal Points of all CMS daughter agreements [1081]. The aim is to provide them with information, examples of best practices, practical tools such as checklists, information on funding programmes and training activities, but also to enable them to communicate and share their experience. This tool was established with the support of the European Commission and UNEP. Lastly, a range of capacity-building measures have been implemented through the 2008 AEWA African Initiative [1082].

2) Financial co-operation

596. In accordance with the principle of "common but differentiated responsibilities" laid down in the Rio Declaration on Environment and Development, and even though it does not formally appear in the CBD [1083], developed countries, by ratifying the Convention on biological diversity, undertake to provide "new and additional financial resources" to developing counties so that they can meet the additional costs of implementing the Convention [1084]. Furthermore:

1079. Article III (2) *(i)*.
1080. See paragraph 4 of CMS COP Resolution 10.6, *Capacity-Building Activities 2012-2014*.
1081. See below.
1082. See AEWA COP Resolution 4.9 (2008), *African Initiative for the Conservation of Migratory Waterbirds and their Habitats in Africa*.
1083. M.-P. Lanfranchi, "Le principe des responsabilités communes, mais différenciées dans les instruments internationaux relatifs à la protection de la biodiversité", *Droit International et développement, Colloque de Lyon*, Société française pour le droit international, 1995, pp. 387-397.
1084. Article 20 (2).

"The extent to which developing country Parties will effectively implement their commitments under this Convention will depend on the effective implementation by developed country Parties of their commitments under this Convention related to financial resources and transfer of technology." [1085]

These provisions must be read in conjunction with Article 28 of the Cartagena Protocol and Article 25 of the Nagoya Protocol. In preparation for the Hyderabad COP in 2012, a group of experts calculated the funding needs under the aegis of the Convention. It estimated the amount needed to be invested in developing countries: calculated for the 2014-2018 period, it ranges from 74 billion US dollars (low scenario) to 191 billion US dollars (high scenario) (i.e. 57 to 147 billion euros). This group found that over a period of four years, this represented a budget three to eight times greater than the amount expected at the time to be spent on biodiversity by public and private financial donors. WWF International arrived at an estimated amount close to the higher end (200 billion US dollars or 153 billion euros).

597. After intense and difficult negotiations, the COP agreed to double biodiversity funding by 2015, and to maintain at that level, at least until 2020, the overall international financial flows for biodiversity protection in developing countries, least developed countries, small island developing States and economies in transition. In reality, as there was no consensus at the time on the amount of biodiversity funding required and estimates were approximate and incomplete, with different CBD Parties completing the CBD financial reporting framework in different ways, this financial commitment was much weaker than it seemed.

598. Progress was made recently in this regard, allowing the negotiation of post-2020 commitments by Parties to be placed on a more solid footing. Thus, a recent OECD report concluded that, based on currently available data, global biodiversity finance is estimated between 78 and 91 billion US dollars per year (2015-2017 average), comprising public domestic expenditure at 67.8 billion US dollars per year, international public expenditure from 3.9 to 9.3 billion US dollars per year, and private expenditure on biodiversity from 6.6 to 13.6 billion US dollars per year. As the report adds, meanwhile, governments spend approximately 500 billion US dollars per year in

---

1085. Article 20 (3).

support that is potentially harmful to biodiversity, roughly five to six times more than total spending for biodiversity. The total volume of finance flows that are harmful to biodiversity, encompassing all public and private expenditure, is even likely to be many times larger [1086]. Another report from the Paulson Institute pointed that the financing gap for biodiversity would average 711 billion US dollars, or between 598 and 824 billion US dollars per year [1087].

599. These reports are more than helpful as

> "[u]p-to-date estimates of biodiversity finance flows are needed to establish a baseline from which governments and other stakeholders can track biodiversity finance trends over time. They are also useful for identifying and assessing any shortfalls in biodiversity finance, and for identifying opportunities for scaling up finance in support of biodiversity objectives" [1088].

In this context, COP 15 defined a new objective, Goal D, acknowledging the "biodiversity finance gap":

> "Adequate means of implementation, including financial resources, capacity-building, technical and scientific cooperation, and access to and transfer of technology to fully implement the Kunming-Montreal Global Biodiversity Framework are secured and equitably accessible to all Parties, especially developing country Parties, in particular the least developed countries and small island developing States, as well as countries with economies in transition, *progressively closing the biodiversity finance gap of FFF700 billion per year, and aligning financial flows with the Kunming-Montreal Global Biodiversity Framework and the 2050 Vision for biodiversity.*"[1089]

This goal is completed by Targets 18 and 19. According to Target 18, CBD Parties have to "identify by 2025, and eliminate, phase out or reform incentives, including subsidies, harmful for biodiversity, in a proportionate, just, fair, effective and equitable way, while substantially and progressively reducing them by at least FFF500 billion per year by

---

1086. OECD, *A Comprehensive Overview of Global Biodiversity Finance*, OECD, Paris, 2021, p. 4.
1087. See also Paulson Institute, *Financing Nature: Closing the Global Biodiversity Financing Gap*, 2021.
1088. OECD, *A Comprehensive Overview of Global Biodiversity Finance*, OECD, Paris, 2021, p. 7.
1089. Decision 15/4 (2022), *Kunming-Montreal Global Biodiversity Framework*, CBD/COP/DEC/15/4, 19 December 2022. Emphasis added.

2030, starting with the most harmful incentives, and scale up positive incentives for the conservation and sustainable use of biodiversity". Under Target 19, Parties shall "substantially and progressively increase the level of financial resources from all sources . . . mobilizing at least 200 billion per year by 2030" [1090]. These numbers are intended to close the biodiversity finance gap. They represent progress compared with the Aichi Targets, even if the Southern countries regret that they concern both public and private sources, and that public development aid is not quantified.

600. Under Article 21 of the Convention, the Global Environmental Facility (GEF) was designated as the multilateral financial mechanism for the Convention and is also the financial mechanism for its two protocols. The COP concluded a Memorandum of Understanding with the Council of the GEF that makes the GEF the mechanism for implementing the policies and criteria established by the COP [1091]. The GEF, which is the main financial tool of environmental conventions, is an original instrument, which operates with flexibility and pragmatism [1092]. But the GEF is criticised by developing countries for its governance and functioning [1093]. The amount of money at its disposal is substantial (5.33 billion US dollars for four years during the 2023-2026 replenishment), however, it is rather modest given the needs identified. Moreover, this amount is to be shared between various environmental conventions [1094]. In this context, the last CBD COP requested the GEF to establish, in 2023, and until 2030 unless the Conference of the Parties decides otherwise, a special trust fund to support the implementation of the Kunming-Montreal Global Biodiversity Framework, "to complement existing support and scale up financing to ensure its timely implementation, taking into account the need for adequacy, predictability, and timely flow of funds" [1095].

601. Originally, with regard to biodiversity, the GEF only funded activities within the framework of the Convention on Biological Diversity and its protocols. However, by making the Aichi Targets their

---

1090. *Ibid.*
1091. Decision III/8 (1996), *Memorandum of Understanding between the Conference of the Parties to the Convention on Biological Diversity and the Council of the Global Environment Facility.*
1092. L. Boisson de Chazournes, "Le Fonds pour l'environnement mondial: recherche et conquête de son identité", *in AFDI*, 1995, pp. 612-632.
1093. M. Daval, "Un nouveau 'cadre mondial pour la biodiversité': enjeux et perspectives", *Revue juridique de l'environnement*, 2/2023, p. 331.
1094. See Work Program for GEF Trust Fund, GEF/C.56/08/Rev.01, 6 June 2019.
1095. Decision 15/7 (2022), *Resource Mobilization*, para. 30.

own, other biodiversity conventions have been able to benefit from GEF funding. Following an appeal by the Secretary-General of CITES, the GEF Council even asked the GEF secretariat to organise meetings between the biodiversity conventions to facilitate the co-ordination of their priorities for inclusion in the Sixth GEF Strategy.

602. In addition to the GEF, a number of funds were set up pursuant to various conventions [1096]. This was the case under the Ramsar Convention, for which the COP established, at its Montreux Conference in 1990, a Wetland Conservation Fund to finance technical assistance activities in developing countries (also known as the "Small Grants Fund") [1097]. States submit their projects to the Bureau, which makes a selection and prioritises them [1098]. The beneficiary Contracting Parties must send reports on the use of the funding obtained as well as reports on the implementation of projects. The Fund finances preparatory work before designation, such as national wetland inventories, emergency interventions in sites that have suffered significant damage or are at risk of damage, as well as technical assistance including the promotion of wise use, specific site conservation or restoration projects, preparation of management plans, etc [1099]. In addition, the existence of the Fund and the development of projects enabled the Bureau to act as a lobby group for wetland conservation with international institutions dealing with development and the funds allocated thereto, in particular the Inter-American Development Bank, the World Bank, the OECD, the European Union, or even more directly with the Global Environment Facility. However, given the modest sums allocated and the fact that the Fund's operation is based on voluntary contributions, the latest COP decided to phase it out and to focus instead on strengthening financial partnerships with the relevant international organisations and other

---

1096. L. Boisson de Chazournes, "International Environmental Law: Technical and Financial Assistance", in *Oxford Yearbook of International Environmental Law*, OUP, Oxford, 2007, p. 947; C. Streck, "Financial Instruments and Cooperation in Implementing International Agreements for the Global Environment", in *Multilevel Governance of Global Environmental Change: An Interdisciplinary Approach*, A. Jordan, R. Wurzel and A. R. Zito (eds.), Cambridge University Press, 2006, p. 493 *et seq*.
1097. Developing countries are eligible, without resorting to a formal list of developed versus developing countries, as is the case under the Convention on Biological Diversity. Minutes of the Fifteenth Meeting of the Standing Committee (SC15), 1994.
1098. The non-selection of projects can be compensated by the allocation of bilateral funding. See, for example, the proposals of France or the United Kingdom, *ibid.*
1099. D. Navid, "The Wetland Fund", Report of the Fifth Meeting of the Conference of the Parties, Kushiro, Japan, 9-16 June 1993, Vol. II, Annex 7, p. 309.

entities and to explore new funding opportunities through their existing financial mechanisms [1100].

603. On the other hand, the World Heritage Fund created under the UNESCO Convention is still in place. Established pursuant to Article 15 of the Convention, it receives compulsory and voluntary contributions. The former represent 1 per cent of the annual contribution of States to the UNESCO budget. The Fund may also receive funding from non-governmental organisations or individuals. It amounts to about 3 million US dollars per year, divided roughly equally between natural and cultural sites. The budget is allocated to a wide range of activities: identification and inventory of sites to be designated, study of the status of conservation, assessment of works or developments to be undertaken, provision of expert services, technical assistance and specialised equipment, training of qualified staff, emergency assistance, etc. [1101].

604. Another example is the Benefit-Sharing Fund set up under the International Treaty on Plant Genetic Resources for Food and Agriculture for the benefit of farmers in developing countries.

605. Even when added together, including with the GEF, these mechanisms are still too modest given the needs at stake. It is therefore particularly important that development aid allocated outside these funds take into account biodiversity-related issued. This is now the case for most multilateral financial donors. For example, since 1989, the World Bank requires an impact assessment of its projects pursuant to an internally developed standard [1102]. The borrower is responsible for carrying out the assessment, with the help of the World Bank's environmental department. The assessment is based on ten environmental and social safeguard policies which are mandatory for loans; the Bank indicates which ones must be specifically addressed in the impact assessment [1103]. It applies to the Bank's projects, but also to those of the GEF, which is significant as it can help ensure that GEF funding

---

[1100]. Resolution XIII.2 (2018), *Financial and Budgetary Matters*.

[1101]. About the use of funds, Intergovernmental Committee for the Protection of the World Cultural and Natural Heritage, UNESCO, Intergovernmental Committee for the Protection of the World Cultural and Natural Heritage, UNESCO, *Operational Guidelines for the Implementation of the World Heritage Convention*, WHC.19/01, 10 July 2019, para. 223 *et seq.*

[1102]. Operational Directive 4.00 of 21 September 1989, revised in October 1991 (OD 4.01 OP 4.01, *Environmental Assessment*). See also OP/BP 4.02, *Environmental Action Plans*.

[1103]. M. Prieur, "Instruments internationaux et évaluation environnementale de la biodiversité : enjeux et obstacles", *Revue juridique de l'environnement* 36 (1), p. 7.

International Biodiversity Law 335

under conventions other than biodiversity conventions (for example, climate conventions) does not have a negative impact on biodiversity. According to Operational Manual Statement 2.36 (para. 9 *(b)*), the World Bank does not finance projects that are likely to cause severe and irreversible damage to the environment, including species extinctions, without mitigatory measures acceptable to the Bank. In particular, according to paragraph 9 *(g)*, the Bank will not finance projects that would significantly alter natural areas designated by the Convention concerning the Protection of the World Cultural and Natural Heritage, or classified as biosphere reserves, national parks, wildlife refuges or other protected areas. Since 1992, the African Development Bank and the Asian Development Bank have also introduced such mechanisms. Complaints mechanisms have been set up by most donors, inspired by the Inspection Panel of the World Bank, to enable affected local people to challenge funding that does not comply with internal policies and procedures to protect people and the environment [1104]. Thus, increasing attention is being paid to the impacts of projects on biodiversity, under the influence of the Convention on Biological Diversity [1105].

Section 2. International implementation monitoring and sanctions for non-compliance

606. International biodiversity law is one of those new branches of international law that "constitute unique and complex conglomerations of domestic and international law, thus reconstructing large parts of traditional law into a new material and spatial dimension", what Robert Kolb calls "amphibious" areas of law [1106]. Here, we witness the blurring and gradual disappearance of the clear-cut boundary between what is international and what is domestic [1107]. International law is for "internal consumption" [1108], which means that most provisions of international biodiversity conventions, given that they are not self-executing, are intended to be transposed into the national law of States Parties.

1104. L. Boisson de Chazournes, "Le Panel d'inspection de la Banque mondiale : à propos de la complexification de l'espace public international", in *Revue générale de droit international public*, No. 1/2001, pp. 145-162.
1105. See the operational policies on natural habitats (PO 4.04) and forests (PO 4.36).
1106. R. Kolb, "Mondialisation et droit international", *Relations internationales*, 05/3, No. 123, p. 78 (our translation).
1107. *Ibid.*, 70.
1108. S. Laghmani, "Droit international et droits internes : vers un renouveau du *jus gentium*?", *Droit international et droits internes. Développements récents*, R. Ben Achour and S. Laghmani (eds.), Pedone, 1999, p. 34 (our translation).

607. In this context, in order to build confidence among the Parties, help struggling Parties and measure collective efforts, monitoring procedures have been put in place. Their purpose is to monitor the States' implementation of their international obligations, but not only. They also make it possible to clarify and give concrete form to these – often initially vague – obligations, for which they encourage collective *learning by doing*. They are known as *non-compliance* procedures.

608. In theory, compliance by subjects of international law is presumed, so that a State does not have to demonstrate *ab initio* that it is acting in accordance with the law [1109]. The creation of multilateral bodies to monitor implementation and compliance and to define appropriate procedures is a relatively new feature of international life. In the past, possible violations were very rarely explicitly contemplated in international instruments, as States were reluctant to place themselves at the receiving end of such potential reactions. The commitments they make are generally aligned with their interests and therefore they have no reason to ignore them. However, with regard to the environment in general and biodiversity especially, States often do not derive a direct and immediate benefit from adhering to a convention, which may even conflict with their interests. Challenges in their implementation are all the greater.

609. Monitoring is recognised as one of the means to ensure a more effective implementation of international obligations. Analysis even shows that comprehensive monitoring is partly able to compensate for the relative softness of international environmental law [1110]. This goal certainly has an influence on the techniques that are used. It has led to the development of non-judicial procedures. Judicial review is little suited to the specificities of these issues and thus has been sidelined even further. In spite of this, biological diversity has been at the heart of several international disputes decided by international courts.

1) The institution of specific and non-judicial compliance procedures

610. Since judicial intervention is exceptional and in several respects inadequate, Parties have established specific non-judicial procedures for monitoring the implementation and compliance with treaty obligations,

---

[1109]. J. Combacau and S. Sur, *Droit international public,* Montchrestien, 13th ed., 2019, p. 169 *et seq.*

[1110]. P. Sand, *The Effectiveness of International Environmental Agreements: A Survey of Existing Legal Instruments*, Cambridge University Press, 1992.

which constitute the bulk of the international environmental corpus. Based in part on techniques that were tested in other fields, some of them are also quite innovative. Such procedures have been developed by several international conventions on biodiversity and we will present their content.

a) *The development of these procedures in the field of biodiversity*

611. The first biodiversity conventions did not include specific and internalised techniques for monitoring compliance, nor did they institutionalise co-operation between Contracting Parties, which is a *sine qua non* for this type of monitoring. These conventions were hardly effective. From the mid-1970s onwards, co-operation was institutionalised and various compliance monitoring techniques were tested, inspired in some respects by the human rights sector. The most widely used technique is undoubtedly the reporting system. Although it is useful, it is not one of the most advanced means of monitoring international law and has important limitations. From the 1990s onwards, mechanisms were systematised and improved in certain treaty spheres, with the development of non-compliance procedures.

612. Such procedures are usually formalised, in one or more resolutions of the convention's plenary political body. A compliance committee is established, whose composition, mandate, decision-making processes and relations with other bodies are specified. In addition to this formalisation, these procedures differ from other implementation techniques or procedures tested in the environmental field because of their comprehensive and coherent nature. Ideally, they must prevent non-compliance through co-operation, monitor compliance and provide assistance in the event of non-compliance as well as a dispute settlement mechanism and enforcement measures. While these different aspects can in theory be distinguished, in practice, they are very closely intertwined: these processes are dynamic and the same facts can over time trigger the full range of measures.

613. The initial model is the non-compliance procedure adopted under the Montreal Protocol on the ozone layer [1111]. While all procedures are largely based on this model, they each have their own specificities.

1111. Decision IV/5, Report of the Fourth Meeting of the Parties to the Montreal Protocol on Substances that Deplete the Ozone Layer, UNEP/OzL. Pro.4/15, Annexes IV and V, 25 November 1992.

- *At the universal level*

614. At the universal level, non-compliance procedures have been established under CITES, the UNESCO World Heritage Convention, the Ramsar Convention, the two protocols of the CBD, the International Treaty on Plant Genetic Resources for Food and Agriculture and most recently the Convention on the Conservation of Migratory Species of Wild Animals.

615. In the case of CITES, the procedure emerged gradually from practice, in small steps. It was then formalised as a comprehensive and coherent non-compliance procedure, which has proven to be effective [1112]. The UNESCO World Heritage Convention set up in its Article 11 a procedure applicable to the World Heritage sites "in danger" [1113]. Under the Ramsar Convention, the non-compliance procedure is called the "Monitoring Procedure". It was established by the Standing Committee in 1988 to provide assistance to Parties with issues in the management of an area included in the Ramsar List of Wetlands of International Importance [1114]. It is applied primarily to sites on the Montreux Record, a record of Ramsar Sites where ecological change may occur, maintained by the Bureau in collaboration with the relevant Contracting Parties [1115]. A procedure was also established under the International Treaty on Plant Genetic Resources for Food and Agriculture at the fourth session of the Governing Body in March 2011 [1116]. Lastly, a "Review Mechanism" procedure was recently agreed by the Standing Committee of the Bonn Convention, which has yet to be operationalised by the next Conference of the Parties [1117]. We

---

[1112]. See details in Resolution Conf. 14.3 (Rev. CoP18), CITES Compliance Procedures, to which is annexed Guide to CITES Compliance Procedures.

[1113]. The details were specified as early as 1977 in the Operational Guidelines for the World Heritage Committee, CC-77/CONF.001, Paris, 30 June 1977, World Heritage Committee (first session) Paris, 27 June-1 July 1977, last revision in 2021 (WHC.21/01, 31 July 2021).

[1114]. The Montreux Conference of the Parties endorsed this procedure in its Recommendation C.4.7 (Montreux, 1990), *Mechanisms for Improved Application of the Ramsar Convention*. See also Resolution XIII.11 (Dubai, 2018), *Ramsar Advisory Mission*.

[1115]. Recommendation C.4.8 (Montreux, 1990), *Change in Ecological Character of Ramsar Sites*.

[1116]. Governing Body, Resolution 2/2011, *Procedures and Operational Mechanisms to Promote Compliance and Address Issues of Non-Compliance*.

[1117]. UNEP/CMS/Resolution 12.9 on the Establishment of a Review Mechanism and a National Legislation Programme.

International Biodiversity Law 339

have previously discussed the institution of compliance mechanisms under the two protocols of the Convention on Biological Diversity, the Cartagena Protocol [1118] and the Nagoya Protocol [1119]. In addition, COP 15 adopted an "enhanced multidimensional approach to planning, monitoring, reporting and review" for the CBD itself, which leads to a more comprehensive control of the implementation of the agreement, without being strictly a compliance mechanism [1120].

- *At the regional level*

616. Although they were not contemplated in initial provisions, non-compliance procedures have been put in place pursuant to the Bern Convention [1121], the Alpine Convention and its protocols [1122], as well as the Barcelona Convention for the Protection of the Mediterranean Sea against Pollution and its protocols [1123]. Another example is the procedure set up by the Meeting of the Parties to the Agreement on the Conservation of African-Eurasian Migratory Waterbirds [1124].

b) *The content of these procedures*

617. Here, we will present the main characteristics of these procedures, the techniques used and the possible reactions to non-compliance.

1118. COP-MOP Decision BS-I/7 (2004), *Establishment of Procedures and Mechanisms on Compliance under the Cartagena Protocol on Biosafety.*
1119. See COP-MOP Decision NP-1/4 (2014), *Cooperative Procedures and Institutional Mechanisms to Promote Compliance with the Nagoya Protocol and to Address Cases of Non-Compliance.*
1120. Decision 15/6, *Mechanisms for Planning, Monitoring, Reporting and Review.*
1121. See Convention on the Conservation of European Wildlife and Natural Habitats, Standing Committee, *Application of the Convention - Summary of Case Files and Complaints – Reminder on the Processing of Complaints and New Online Form, Secretariat Memorandum prepared by the Directorate of Culture and Cultural and Natural Heritage,* T-PVS (2008) 7, 25 August 2008. The procedure was set up in 1982.
1122. The Compliance Committee of the Alpine Convention was established by Decision VII/4 of the Conference of the Parties (2004), without any specific provision in the Convention itself, but as an extension of the reporting provisions (Alpine Convention, Art. 5, para. 4).
1123. The procedure was adopted at the Fifteenth Conference of the Contracting Parties, held in Almeria, Spain, in 2008, and covers the Barcelona Convention and its protocols. See Decision IG 17/2 (2008), *Procedures and Mechanisms on Compliance under the Barcelona Convention and its Protocols.*
1124. Resolution 4.6 (2018), *Establishment of an Implementation Review Process.*

- *The main characteristics of these procedures*

618. Non-compliance procedures are primarily intended to promote the law, although they should also be able to deal with cases of non-compliance. For example, under the Cartagena Protocol, "[the objective of the compliance procedures and mechanisms shall be to *promote* compliance with the provisions of the Protocol, to address cases of non-compliance by Parties, and to provide advice or assistance, where appropriate". "The compliance procedures and mechanisms shall be simple, facilitative, non-adversarial and cooperative in nature." [1125] Under the Nagoya Protocol, "[t]he objective of the compliance procedures and mechanisms is to promote compliance with the provisions of the Protocol and to address cases of non-compliance. These procedures and mechanisms shall include provisions to offer advice or assistance, where appropriate"; "[t]he compliance procedures and mechanisms shall be non-adversarial, cooperative, simple, expeditious, advisory, facilitative, flexible and cost-effective in nature" [1126]. As for CITES, its *Guide to CITES Compliance Procedures* states that its objective is "to inform Parties and others of CITES procedures concerning promoting, facilitating and achieving compliance with obligations under the Convention and, in particular, assisting Parties in meeting their obligations regarding such compliance" [1127].

619. In this context, the procedures have two main characteristics: compliance monitoring is institutionalised and systematic.

620. First of all, the procedures are institutionalised. Performed collectively, monitoring loses its traditional reciprocal dimension: it is entrusted to *ad hoc* bodies created by the various conventions – compliance or implementation committees, Conference of the Parties, standing committees and secretariats – which play a fundamental role here [1128]. Thus, it loses its traditional reciprocal nature and becomes multilateral, which also contributes to better acceptance by States. The involvement of the various bodies varies depending on the treaty systems. Secretariats, expert bodies and NGOs may be entrusted with

---

1125. COP-MOP Decision BS-I/7, *Establishment of Procedures and Mechanisms on Compliance under the Cartagena Protocol on Biosafety*. Emphasis added.
1126. Decision COP-MOP NP-1/4 (2014), *Cooperative Procedures and Institutional Mechanisms to Promote Compliance with the Nagoya Protocol and to Address Cases of Non-Compliance* (emphasis added).
1127. Resolution Conf. 14.3 (Rev. CoP18), *CITES Compliance Procedures*.
1128. R. R. Churchill and G. Ulfstein, "Autonomous Institutional Arrangements in Multilateral Environmental Agreements: A Little-Noticed Phenomenon in International Law", *American Journal of International Law*, Vol. 94, 2000, p. 623 *et seq*.

monitoring functions in the strict sense, and in particular with reviewing and processing information, or they may intervene unofficially. In some cases, NGOs provide important support. However, in general, only the political body controls what happens after the monitoring takes place, i.e. has the power to make recommendations and impose sanctions should a State be found to be in breach. This multiplicity of actors makes it possible to speak of a real "control chain", according to Jean Charpentier: the successive or parallel intervention of several bodies – sometimes independent, sometimes political – ultimately minimising the disadvantages and maximising the advantages of each monitoring method, thereby contributing to better effectiveness [1129].

621. Moreover, the procedures are carried out in a systematic way. Indeed, because compliance monitoring is preventive, it is not exercised in response to the violation of an obligation; it is not reactive. On the contrary, it tends to be continuous. It can thus be called systematic monitoring, which in most cases is exercised before a potential breach occurs. It focuses not only on violations, but also on the threat of such violations.

- *Monitoring and compliance techniques*

622. Institutionalised monitoring generally involves the establishment of an *ad hoc* committee in charge of non-compliance. In rarer cases, it relies on a body that has other functions. This is the case under CITES, where the body responsible for compliance monitoring is the Standing Committee. Such a body can generally be asked to intervene by a Party that encounters difficulties or by a Party against another Party. In the latter case, it may be required that the "requesting" Party has reached out to the "defending Party" [1130]. In some procedures, but

---

1129. J. Charpentier, "Le contrôle par les organisations internationales de l'exécution des obligations des Etats", *Recueil des cours*, Vol. 182 (1983), pp. 193 and 195 (our translation); S .Maljean-Dubois and V. Richard, *Mechanisms for Monitoring and Implementation of International Environmental Protection Agreements*, IDDRI, Paris, November 2004.

1130. This is required, for example, by the procedure defined for the Barcelona Convention and its protocols. See Decision IG 17/2 (2008), *Procedures and Mechanisms on Compliance under the Barcelona Convention and its Protocols*, para. 18, according to which: "The Committee shall consider submissions by: *(a)* a Party in respect of its own actual or potential situation of non-compliance, despite its best endeavours; and *(b)* a Party in respect of another Party's situation of non-compliance, after it has undertaken consultations through the Secretariat with the Party concerned and the matter has not been resolved within three months at the latest, or a longer period as the circumstances of a particular case may require, but not later than six month".

less often, the secretariat also has the power to submit matters to the body in charge of compliance. This is the case for CITES: "If the Party fails to take sufficient remedial action within a reasonable time limit, the compliance matter is brought to the attention of the Standing Committee by the Secretariat, in direct contact with the Party concerned." [1131] In other cases, it is also provided that the COP may refer the matter to the compliance body. For example, under the FAO International Treaty on Plant Genetic Resources for Food and Agriculture, where the Governing Body is the COP, there are three possibilities for the Committee to receive submissions: "The Committee shall receive, through the Secretary, any submissions relating to issues of non-compliance from: *a)* Any Contracting Party with respect to itself; *b)* Any Contracting Party with respect to another Contracting Party; or *c)* The Governing Body." [1132]

623. Monitoring techniques *per se* combine systematic monitoring – where the focus is mainly on preventing violations or identifying them as early as possible – which is present in all procedures, and reactive monitoring – where the focus is on reacting to suspected breaches.

– *Systematic monitoring*

624. The aim of monitoring is to find out as precisely as possible how the conventions are being implemented in practice in the various Member States and to monitor this implementation on a regular basis. State obligations in this respect are often broad, formalised by a *reporting system* which is generally the cornerstone of the monitoring procedure. This monitoring technique is based on the obligation for each State Party to periodically submit a report on its activities that pertain to the convention. The obligation is generally included in the treaty, but COP decisions reinforce it by further specifying the content of such reports (questionnaires, report templates, fact sheets, guidelines etc.).

625. The Convention on Biological Diversity illustrates this well. According to Article 26 of the Convention:

> "Each Contracting Party shall, at intervals to be determined by the Conference of the Parties, present to the Conference of the Parties, reports on measures which it has taken for the

---

1131. Resolution Conf. 14.3 (Rev. CoP18), *CITES Compliance Procedures*, para. 23.
1132. Governing Body, Resolution 2/2011, *Procedures and Operational Mechanisms to Promote Compliance and Address Issues of Non-Compliance.*

implementation of the provisions of this Convention and their effectiveness in meeting the objectives of this Convention."

This provision must be read together with Article 23 (4) of the Convention, which provides that the COP shall review the implementation of the Convention and, to this end, "[e]stablish the form and the intervals for transmitting the information to be submitted in accordance with Article 26 and consider such information as well as reports submitted by any subsidiary body" (a). Article 26 is very laconic, but the COP has gradually clarified the content of the reporting obligation by determining the periodicity of the reports (every four years), but also by gradually establishing guidelines and a format to be followed [1133]. In addition to the general report, a number of thematic reports are required. In 2006, the COP recognised "the need to align the national reporting process with the framework for evaluating implementation of the Convention and progress towards the 2010 target" [1134]. In 2010, it decided to conduct various reviews of the progress made in implementing the Strategic Plan and achieving the Aichi Biodiversity Targets [1135]. The Strategic Plan provides that the subsidiary bodies shall support the COP in this task [1136]. Thus, the COP decided that the fifth national reports should

> "[f]ocus on the implementation of the Strategic Plan for Biodiversity 2011-2020, and progress toward the Aichi Biodiversity Targets, using indicators where possible and feasible, including application, as appropriate, of global headline indicators contained in decision VIII/15 and additional indicators that may be adopted at its eleventh meeting for measuring progress towards the Aichi Biodiversity Targets"

and "[i]nclude, as appropriate, information concerning contributions of the implementation of the Strategic Plan towards the achievement of relevant Millennium Development Goals" [1137]. The latest (sixth) reports were due on 31 December 2018 and were to follow relatively precise

---

1133. See in particular the annex to the Decision II/17 (1995). See also Decision IV/14 (1998); Decision V/19 (2000); Decision VI/25 (2002); Decision VII/25 (2004); Decision X/10 (2010); Decision XIII/27 (2013); Decision XIV/27 (2018).
1134. Decision VIII/14 (2006), *National Reporting and the Next Global Biodiversity Outlook.*
1135. CBD, Decision X/2 (2010), *The Strategic Plan for Biodiversity 2011-2020 and the Aichi Biodiversity Targets*, UNEP/CBD/COP/DEC/X/2 (2010), p. 117.
1136. See the updated multi-year programme of work of the Conference of the Parties until 2020 (Decision XII/3, annex).
1137. CBD, Decision X/10 (2010), *National Reporting: Review of Experience and Proposals for the Fifth National Report.*

guidelines as well as a resource manual developed to provide guidance and assistance to Parties [1138]. According to these guidelines:

> "The sixth national reports should provide a final review of progress in the implementation of the Strategic Plan for Biodiversity 2011-2020 and towards the Aichi Biodiversity Targets, including relevant national targets, based on information concerning the implementation of national biodiversity strategies and action plans and other actions taken to implement the Convention." [1139]

Indeed, the proposed framework theoretically has made it possible to determine to what extent Parties have or have not transposed the Aichi Targets into their national legislation and how they were implementing them [1140]. With the "enhanced multidimensional approach to planning, monitoring, reporting and review", the COP will be able to monitor more closely the implementation of the new post-2020 Global Framework and the Kunming-Montreal Targets, thanks to more precise guidelines, and in particular a comprehensive guidance and draft template for the seventh and eighth national report (2026 and 2029) [1141].

626. The risk inherent to relying on governmental sources of information is that States may reveal only a small amount of information, providing a distorted or even idealised picture of reality. The other difficulty is that States do not fulfil their reporting obligations well. They do not systematically send reports, or do so late, and may provide reports that are somewhat inaccurate and incomplete. It must be said that for many States, particularly developing States, this is a heavy burden for which they have insufficient human and financial resources. Some secretariats have started to look at ways to relieve the burden placed on States and help developing countries to fulfil their obligations under the *reporting system*. The Global Environmental Facility provides support for reporting to the Rio Conventions, including the Convention on Biological Diversity [1142]; such support is

---

1138. See Decision XIII/27 (2013), *National Reporting*.
1139. See Decision XIII/27 (2013), *National Reporting*.
1140. See also the standard reporting format of the International Treaty on Plant Genetic Resources for Food and Agriculture, Fifth Session of the Governing Body, Oman), 24-28 September 2013, Resolution 9/2013, *Procedures and Operational Mechanisms to Promote Compliance and Address Issues of Non-Compliance*.
1141. Decision 15/6 (2022), *Mechanisms for Planning, Monitoring, Reporting and Review*.
1142. CBD, Decision X/20 (2010), *Cooperation with Other Conventions and International Organizations and Initiatives*.

provided under most conventions. There have been some proposals for standardisation and harmonisation of reporting between several treaty spheres, but they have not yet been successful at the international level. For example, a proposed harmonised reporting system between the five global conventions on biodiversity (international trade, biodiversity, wetlands, migratory species, world heritage) is under consideration within the framework of the Liaison Group of Biodiversity-related Conventions, but achieving concrete results is proving difficult [1143]. A first step has however been achieved in the European Union, where the use of the reporting system is also generalised in environmental protection directives [1144].

627. The technique is also more advanced when the treaty institutions' task (usually the secretariats) is not simply to receive reports and forward them to the Parties without dealing with the substance of these reports. This is the case when, after State reports have been collected, the administrative structures process and analyse the information to draw up their own reports referred to as "summary reports" or "Report on National Reports" (according to CITES terminology). These summary reports are more easily exploited than just a series of reports in isolation. They are valuable in that they provide a breakdown of the implementation of each convention, provision by provision. In addition, by processing the information received in the reports, the monitoring bodies are able to uncover issues of non-compliance.

628. But the quality of the summary report depends on the timely provision of the national reports and their own quality. It also varies according to how much leeway the secretariats have and whether, for example, they can rely on additional sources of information, especially non-governmental sources. Indeed, in this respect, NGOs are providing growing support by revealing, thanks to their own monitoring, the existence of implementation challenges or violations in certain States. Involving them tempers the disadvantages linked to the governmental origin of the information contained in the reports. This involvement is more or less developed depending on the treaty systems. Sometimes the intervention of NGOs is unofficial, sometimes it is formalised, with

---

1143. CBD, Decision, X/20 (2010), *Cooperation with Other Conventions and International Organizations and Initiatives*, and XII/29 (2014), *Improving the Efficiency of Structures and Processes under the Convention: Other Matters*, para. 6.

1144. Council Directive of 23 December 1991 standardizing and rationalizing reports on the implementation of certain Directives relating to the environment (91/692/EEC), *JOCE* No. L 377, 31 December 1991, p. 48.

the NGOs being given observer status. It can even go further [1145]. Some NGOs are recognised as "partner" NGOs.

629. Thus, under CITES, the secretariat draws up its own report on the implementation of the Convention, based on the Parties' reports [1146]. This is referred to as the Report on National Reports. It assesses the national legislation of each Party, highlighting its weaknesses with regard to the Convention, and sometimes even suggests improvements. All of the data is digitised, enabling comparative analyses that provide new information and, most importantly, the identification of certain frauds and violations, despite the imperfection of the reports. But this identification can also be made on the basis of other information, from non-governmental or governmental sources. In this respect, "partner NGOs" are very valuable. *TRAFFIC* monitors trade flows and regularly reports its estimations in its publications. IUCN has also established a monitoring group, the *World Trade Monitoring Unit*, which tracks and reports on legal trade, often on behalf of the CITES secretariat itself. More generally, there is an increasing focus on field monitoring with regard to the implementation of the Convention. For example, a compromise adopted in 1997 on the ivory trade was conditional on the establishment of a monitoring system for illegal killing of elephants and elephant population trends *(MIKE Programme)* and an elephant trade information system (ETIS) [1147].

630. Similarly, under the Bern Convention on the Conservation of European Wildlife and Natural Habitats (1979), NGOs frequently submit complaints and now have a "right to petition", which can trigger the opening of "files" on certain States [1148].

631. Systematic monitoring is still rarely supported by independent mechanisms in charge of collecting environmental data. However, in some treaty spheres, the reporting system is complemented by a systematic inspection mechanism, which means that inspections are carried out on a regular basis irrespective of whether non-compliance with international obligations is suspected or has been identified. Thus, the Whaling Convention was revised in 1977 to establish an

---

1145. See above, the recognition of the status of partners to certain NGOs in the framework of CITES or the fact that IUCN acts as the secretariat of the Ramsar Convention.
1146. Article XII *(g)* of the Convention.
1147. Resolution Conf. 10.10 (Rev. CoP18), *Trade in Elephant Specimens*.
1148. See also Bern Convention, Standing Committee, *Application of the Convention – Summary of Case Files and Complaints – Reminder on the Processing of Complaints and New Online Form, Secretariat Memorandum*, T-PVS (2008) 7, 2008, p. 3.

International Monitoring System (IMS), which operates through bilateral exchanges – on a voluntary basis – of observers on vessels or land. These observers then report to the Whaling Commission, in particular on any infringements found [1149].

632. It should be noted that in addition to individual monitoring, most committees are also in charge of examining systemic issues, which impact a large number of parties or the implementation of the convention in general. By way of example, under the Barcelona Convention for the Protection of the Mediterranean Sea against Pollution and its protocols, the Compliance Committee examines

> "at the request of the Meeting of the Contracting Parties, general compliance issues, such as recurrent non-compliance problems, including in relation to reporting, taking into account the reports referred to in Article 26 of the Convention and any other report submitted by the Parties" [1150].

633. If the systematic monitoring of the implementation of conventions reveals suspicions or evidence of non-compliance, monitoring bodies must be able to react. Monitoring becomes *reactive*.

– *Reactive monitoring*

634. When a problem is identified, monitoring bodies must in particular be able to obtain additional information, by conducting investigations or even on-site inspections. These mechanisms go back a long time – see the Rhine Commission – but are still being developed. A growing number of conventions allow monitoring bodies to conduct investigations, understood in a broad way as including all means by which they can play an active role in the processing of information. In other words, they do not simply receive such information passively, but can request additional information from the Parties.

635. Thus, under CITES, the data contained in national reports is digitised, enabling comparative analyses and thereby providing new information. Most importantly, it can help identify certain frauds and violations. This identification can also be based on other information provided by non-governmental or governmental sources. When the

---

[1149]. A. Chayes, *The New Sovereignty. Compliance with International Regulatory Agreements*, Harvard University Press, Cambridge, 1998, p. 186.
[1150]. Decision IG 17/2, *Procedures and Mechanisms on Compliance under the Barcelona Convention and its Protocols* (2008).

CITES secretariat finds that the Convention is being implemented incorrectly, it informs the relevant Party, which must send a reply and provide any information required within a maximum of one month [1151]. An investigation may take place. If "the Party fails to take sufficient remedial action within a reasonable time limit, the compliance matter is brought to the attention of the Standing Committee by the Secretariat, in direct contact with the Party concerned" [1152].

636. As the most comprehensive form of investigation, "reactive" inspection is of course the most effective means as it allows information to be collected at source, limiting State interference. In environmental matters, although this remains exceptional, inspections – the term itself is not always used, but that is what is actually taking place – are organised pursuant to certain conventions. They are carried out by independent experts, accompanied by administrative staff. However, the prior consent of the State concerned is required. In fact, inspections cannot be carried out without its co-operation. From this point of view, the environmental field is less advanced than other sectors of international co-operation, such as disarmament.

637. Since 1984, when the Standing Committee approved the idea, on-the-spot appraisals can be conducted under the Bern Convention on the Conservation of European Wildlife and Natural Habitats. They are performed at the request of the Standing Committee, and with the authorisation of the State concerned, particularly when sensitive files – in the case of serious situations – are opened. They are carried out by an independent expert, appointed by the Secretary General of the Council of Europe with the approval of the Party concerned. This expert is given specific mandate by the Committee. At the request of the Committee or its Chairperson, the expert is accompanied during his or her visit by a member of the secretariat and a representative of the Party in question. Following this appraisal, the expert provides the Committee with an expert report. Several such appraisals have been carried out, and the reports have not always been to the liking of the States involved [1153].

638. A similar mechanism known as an "advisory mission" takes place within the framework of the Convention on Wetlands of International Importance. However, this procedure, which cleverly

---

[1151]. See Resolution 14/3 of the Conference of the Parties to the CITES (2007), as revised by COP 18.

[1152]. *Ibid.*, para. 21.

[1153]. See remarks by Greece on the report following the inspection of the Zakynthos area, in Standing Committee, Bern Convention, Ninth Meeting, 5-8 December 1989, Doc. T-PVS (89) 50, p. 45.

combines technical assistance and monitoring, is probably more cooperative. It is part of the monitoring procedure, which allows the Bureau to contact certain Parties when it receives information from whatever source that there are difficulties in preserving the ecological character of Ramsar Sites. If necessary, the Bureau can then offer its assistance, including by organising an Advisory Mission. Nearly 100 missions have taken place since the procedure was created, usually with regard to sites listed on the Montreux Record [1154]. The possibility is used mostly but not exclusively in developing countries. The monitoring mission, which consists of sending Bureau members accompanied by experts, allows the measures taken by the Parties to be viewed in an international context. These missions have an important national audience. They provide examples of comparable issues and appropriate solutions applied by other Parties. The Party involved receives a report with specific recommendations for remedial action at the site in question. These recommendations may include support for ongoing measures, a call for the stricter enforcement of legislation or a report advising further investigation or remedial action, in particular of a financial nature. Subsequently, the Party in question must provide information on the measures taken in response to the recommendations.

639. The procedure cannot be implemented without the consent of the Party concerned [1155]. Likewise, a site cannot be listed on the Montreux Record without such consent. Thus, NGOs regularly challenge Sates for failing to request the inscription of a site on the Record. Furthermore, the scope of the procedure is necessarily limited due to the lack of financial means, but the mission's conclusions are often used by the Bureau to put together funding projects for the Contracting Parties or multilateral bodies. Lastly, the Ramsar Convention also lacks the financial resources to implement the mission's recommendations or to monitor the sites that have been subject to the procedure. Still, in exchange for technical assistance, the Bureau gains a right of supervision over the implementation of the Convention in the territory of the Party involved, even if this right is heavily restricted and cannot be exercised without the latter's consent [1156].

1154. List of Ramsar Advisory Missions, https://www.ramsar.org/sites/default/files/documents/library/listoframsaradvisorymissions.pdf, as of 19 December 2023.

1155. Resolution 5.4, *The Record of Ramsar Sites Where Changes in Ecological Character Have Occurred, Are Occurring, or Are Likely to Occur (Montreux Record)*.

1156. The Advisory missions were set up by COP Recommendation C.4.7.

640. Where weaknesses are identified, monitoring bodies must be able to adopt measures to restore compliance.

- *The response to identified violations*

641. Unlike traditional dispute settlement mechanisms, non-compliance procedures do not generally result in States being condemned for non-compliance, but more often and first and foremost, they give rise to support measures or assistance with the implementation of the convention, either financial, technical, legal or otherwise. A facilitative approach is preferred to a coercive approach. Only as a last resort, in the event of repeated failure and a refusal to co-operate, would such procedures lead to the adoption of real sanctions. Thus, in a "compliance continuum"[1157], the range of reactions is gradual, from support to incentives to sanctions. These procedures combine reactions, sanctions, incentives and promotion aspects so well that it becomes difficult to distinguish between these different facets.

642. Bearing in mind that the conventions were adopted for the "common good", with no short- or medium-term benefit to States, it is more important to promote the implementation of the obligations they contain than to sanction non-compliance. The use of sanctions might not serve the purpose of the convention and in particular it might discourage States from participating. Thus, the term "violation" is no longer used, but rather a "situation" of non-compliance, or even a "file". Terms like "dispute", "States Parties to a dispute", "defendants", "applicants", or "claimants" are replaced by "Parties concerned" or Parties "interested" in a "situation" or simply by the – most neutral – expression of "Contracting Parties". This vocabulary reflects the desire to move away from traditional litigation procedures, even though it is clearly a mechanism for reacting to unlawful situations[1158]. There are few actual means of sanctioning non-compliance. When they do exist, they have a deterrent value and are actually designed to prevent violations.

1157. J. Brunnée, "Multilateral Environmental Agreements and the Compliance Continuum", in *Multilevel Governance of Global Environmental Science*, G. Winter (ed.), Cambridge University Press, Cambridge, 2006, p. 387.

1158. P.-M. Dupuy, "Où en est le droit international de l'environnement à la fin du siècle?", *Revue générale de droit international public*, 1997, No. 4, Vol. 101, p. 886.

International Biodiversity Law 351

– *Incentives and measures to promote compliance*

643. Measures that can be taken by the Compliance Committee of the Nagoya Protocol are a good example of measures to promote compliance:

> "The Committee, with a view to promoting compliance and addressing cases of non-compliance, may:
>
> *(a)* Offer advice or facilitate assistance to the Party concerned, as appropriate;
>
> *(b)* Request or assist, as appropriate, the Party concerned to develop a compliance action plan to be submitted identifying appropriate steps, an agreed timeframe and indicators to assess satisfactory implementation;
>
> *(c)* Invite the Party concerned to submit progress reports on its efforts to comply with its obligations under the Protocol." [1159]

644. This range of measures can be found in most procedures. Committees are really in the business of supporting States, providing them with advice and assistance, and demanding that States submit an action plan to return to compliance, which they can also help prepare. The party in question must then report regularly on the efforts it has made. It is under a kind of international scrutiny until the Committee is satisfied that it has returned to compliance.

645. Incentive measures are essentially technical, legal or financial assistance and are primarily, if not exclusively, aimed at developing Parties. They can be used in addition to support measures. These measures are relatively limited, due to insufficient resources, either through the Global Environmental Facility or through treaty-based financial mechanisms, which are funded by voluntary contributions. These contributions are inherently variable and unpredictable, and on the whole rather limited.

646. Not all treaties contemplate sanctions. While the Nagoya Protocol provides that the COP can adopt sanctions [1160], in contrast, the FAO International Treaty on Plant Genetic Resources for Food and Agriculture provides for a whole range of support and assistance measures, but no sanctions. Thus:

1159. Decision NP-1/4 (2014), *Cooperative Procedures and Institutional Mechanisms to Promote Compliance with the Nagoya Protocol and to Address Cases of Non-Compliance*.
1160. See below.

"The Committee, with a view to promoting compliance and addressing issues of non-compliance, . . . taking into account such factors as the cause, type, degree, and frequency of non-compliance, may:
(a) Provide advice or facilitate assistance, including legal advice or legal assistance, to the Contracting Party concerned, as appropriate;
(b) Request or assist, as appropriate, the Contracting Party concerned to develop an action plan, which addresses the issue of non-compliance within a timeframe to be agreed upon between the Committee and the Contracting Party concerned, taking into account its existing capacity to address the issue; and
(c) Invite the Contracting Party concerned to submit progress reports to the Committee on the efforts it is making to comply with its obligations under the International Treaty."

As for the Governing body, it may, 'upon the recommendations of the Committee, decide to:

"*(a)* Provide assistance, including, as appropriate, legal, financial and technical assistance, to the Contracting Party concerned;
(b) Take any other actions it deems appropriate, including for capacity-building, in accordance with the International Treaty and for the fulfilment of its objectives." [1161]

– *Sanctions*

647. Generally speaking, in the context of a multilateral treaty, international law accepts that a State respond to another State's violation of a treaty obligation by itself suspending, partially or totally, the application of such a treaty [1162]. In the context of environmental protection conventions, this type of reaction appears to be inadequate since State obligations are non-reciprocal (not *do ut des*) and based on a general and overriding interest: the pursuit of a "common good".

648. Nevertheless, treaty institutions are not entirely without solutions. Some sanctions are theoretically possible and are in fact imple-

---

1161. Governing Body, Resolution 2/2011, *Procedures and Operational Mechanisms to Promote Compliance and Address Issues of Non-Compliance.*
1162. Article 60 of the Vienna Convention of 23 May 1969 on the Law of Treaties: "Termination or suspension of the operation of a treaty as a consequence of its breach".

mented. These collective responses are more appropriate than individual ones when treaties contain non-reciprocal obligations and the goal is compliance with an objective rule.

649. These may be "moral" or "psychological" sanctions: the *name and shame* effect is particularly adapted in the environmental field, where it can be useful and effective. Thus, the publication of a declaration of non-compliance is usually one of the measure taken in response to a situation of non-compliance. The stigmatisation of a State through the publication of reports, resolutions or even debates at Conferences of the Parties is reinforced by the presence of NGOs, which represent public opinion. NGOs thus play the role of a "soundbox", expanding the reach of the debates held at the Conferences of the Parties.

650. By way of example, under the Nagoya Protocol, in addition to the support measures already mentioned above,

> "[t]he Conference of the Parties serving as the meeting of the Parties to the Nagoya Protocol, upon the recommendations of the Committee, may also, with a view to promoting compliance and addressing cases of non-compliance:
>
> *(a)* Take any of the measures set out in paragraphs 2 *(a)-(c)* above *[measures that the Committee may decide, see above]*;
>
> *(b)* Facilitate, as appropriate, access to financial and technical assistance, technology transfer, training and other capacity-building measures;
>
> *(c)* Issue a written caution, statement of concern or a declaration of non-compliance to the Party concerned;
>
> *(d)* Decide on any other measure, as appropriate, in accordance with . . . the applicable rules of international law, bearing in mind the need for serious measures in cases of grave or repeated non-compliance".

651. A scale of reactions is therefore envisaged, ranging from positive reactions (financial assistance, technology transfer, capacity-building) to serious measures, to written warnings or declarations of non-compliance based on *naming and shaming*. Serious measures may include disciplinary sanctions: the suspension of voting rights or even the suspension of all rights and privileges that Parties inherently enjoy by joining the treaty. Lastly, there may be economic sanctions, mainly the withdrawal of the benefits that States derive from participation in the Protocol: withdrawal of financial subsidies, suspension of technical assistance, etc.

652. Depending on the conventions, withdrawal of benefits can also involve the exclusion of a site from an international list, or trade measures. This is still quite rare, as some conventions do not provide such benefits and are therefore not in a position to withdraw them, but also because the conventions that do provide them very seldom choose to do so. Indeed, as it goes against the conventions' purpose, such a reaction can only be a last resort. Thus, under the 1972 UNESCO Convention on World Heritage, the exclusion of a property from the "List" is envisaged if it has lost the characteristics that determined its inscription, or if its intrinsic qualities were already threatened at the time of its nomination and the necessary corrective measures outlined by the State Party have not been taken within the proposed timeframe [1163]. The Committee seeks to avoid this, in particular through technical co-operation, of which IUCN is in charge with regard to natural sites. In any case, the exclusion of a site will not promote its conservation, which is the desired objective. On the other hand, the threat of exclusion may contribute to this goal. The inclusion of a site on an international list is an acknowledgement of its importance and international value. In this respect, it is flattering for a State, which *a priori* has no interest in its downgrading. Even if it wanted to have a free hand over the site, the publicity surrounding the downgrading could discourage it from doing so. In this respect, the downgrading of a site is ultimately akin to a psychological sanction, similar to the simple finding of a violation, even if it has material consequences. At the same time, this sanction goes further. Insofar as the classification of a site facilitates access to international funding, downgrading is likely to mean an actual loss of financial benefits.

653. The same applies to the withdrawal of financial subsidies. It penalises the State, which will therefore seek to avoid it, but contradicts the objectives of the Convention given that these funds are meant for the implementation of the convention. Thus, this type of sanction is not frequently used.

654. Under the Bern Convention, when implementation challenges are identified with regard to a measure, a site or a species, a "file" is opened. The procedure is proving effective, as a State implicated by a complaint often takes corrective measures before being required to defend itself. There have been some 170 files opened and closed once

---

[1163]. Intergovernmental Committee for the Protection of the World Cultural and Natural Heritage, UNESCO, *Operational Guidelines for the Implementation of the World Heritage Convention*, WHC.08/01, 2019, paras. 192-198.

the problem was resolved. However, the Committee is powerless to deal with repeated violations of the Convention. When the tools of diplomacy have failed, it has sometimes decided to close an unresolved file in order to leave the matter to the European Union institutions, which have real means of making States comply with the Convention by bringing an action for failure to fulfil obligations before the European Court of Justice in Luxembourg. This was the case, for example, in the emblematic file opened in 1986 regarding the endangered loggerhead marine turtles *(Caretta Caretta)* whose main nesting place in the Mediterranean is in Greece. In the end, Greece was condemned by the European Court of Justice for not having taken all the necessary measures to protect these animals and avoid disturbing them during the breeding season [1164].

655. It should be added that conventions that include trade-related measures are better off than strictly environmental conventions, such as nature conservation ones, for example. Indeed, they are able to suspend – temporarily – trade in regulated products between the defaulting State and other States Parties. Such sanctions are regularly adopted under CITES. Indeed, it is provided that

> "[i]n certain cases, the Standing Committee decides to recommend the suspension of commercial or all trade in specimens of one or more CITES-listed species, consistent with the Convention. Such a recommendation may be made in cases where a Party's compliance matter is unresolved and persistent and the Party is showing no intention to achieve compliance or a State not a Party is not issuing the documentation referred to in Article X of the Convention. Such a recommendation is always specifically and explicitly based on the Convention and on any applicable Resolution and Decision of the Conference of the Parties" [1165].

For the receiving State, this is indeed a sanction. However, for the States that are supposed to implement the measure, it is only a recommendation; they are free to follow it or not, but they generally comply, "bound" by various political constraints. Over 100 such

---

1164. CJEU, Judgment of the Court (Fourth Chamber), 10 November 2016, Case C504/14, ECLI:EU:C:2016:847; Judgment of the Court (Sixth Chamber), C-103/00, ECLI:EU:C:2002:60, 30 January 2002.
1165. Resolution Conf. 14.3, mentioned above, para. 30.

decisions have been taken [1166]. The possibility is only used as a last resort; its symbolic power is all the stronger for it [1167].

656. In reality, CITES is one of the few environmental agreements that can give rise to real sanctions. This unique specificity stems from its commercial nature.

2) Judicial review

657. The States' compliance with international law can be reviewed by international courts, but also by national courts.

a) *International judicial review*

658. In environmental matters, States have long shown a certain mistrust of international judicial mechanisms, but with the densification of environmental protection obligations, international judicial review tends to increase.

659. The States' traditional reluctance to turn to international courts is even more pronounced here, because the obligations defined are often vague, even at the treaty level, because many elements of the environment have no or little market value, and also because of the specific nature of environmental damage, which may discourage such proceedings [1168].

660. Principle 22 of the Stockholm Declaration called on States to develop further the international law "regarding liability and compensation for the victims of pollution and other environmental damage caused by activities within the jurisdiction or control of such States to areas beyond their jurisdiction". Principle 13 of the 1992 Rio Declaration went in the same direction, as did Article 235 of the Montego Bay Convention at the treaty level. But practice has not contributed much to the development of a liability regime, as almost all inter-State disputes have been settled by the negotiation of compensation agreements

---

[1166]. P. H. Sand, "Endangered Species, International Protection", *Max Planck Encyclopedia of Public International Law [MPEPIL]*, March 2017, para. 18.

[1167]. M.-L. Lambert, *Le commerce des espèces sauvages : entre droit international et gestion locale*, L'Harmattan, Paris, 2000.

[1168]. M.-P. Lanfranchi and S. Maljean-Dubois, "Le contrôle du juge international. Un jeu d'ombres et de lumières", in *L'effectivité du droit européen de l'environnement. Contrôle de la mise en œuvre et sanction du non-respect*, S. Maljean-Dubois (ed.), La Documentation française, Paris, 2000, p. 247 *et seq.*

concluded without reference to rules of international litigation [1169], at least when there wasn't a shift towards private international law [1170]. As previously discussed, the development of such a liability regime was one of the goals during the negotiations of the Nagoya-Kuala Lumpur Supplementary Protocol on Liability and Redress to the Cartagena Protocol on Biosafety. But the result is rather disappointing in this respect [1171]. The Protocol only pertains to transboundary movements of LMOs between the fifty-four States that joined it. The contributions of the International Law Commission have also been limited [1172].

661. Traditional dispute settlement mechanisms are considered too cumbersome, often uncertain and politically damaging to use [1173]. States usually prefer amicable settlement. This reflects a general trend in international society, whereby disputes are resolved through flexible and political procedures rather than judicial ones. Traditional diplomatic mechanisms are more flexible and often more discrete, allowing disputes to be smoothed out while at the same time respecting sensitivities. International liability and peaceful dispute settlement mechanisms appear less suitable for dealing with cases of non-compliance than the specific procedures adopted by conventions. They do not have the same preventive function, as they are necessarily triggered after a violation. They are more suited to the resolution of bilateral conflicts, whereas non-compliance procedures allow for a collective response to the collective nature of the issues at stake and the multilateral nature of obligations. In this respect, Linos-Alexandre Sicilianos draws a distinction between bilateral obligations, which generate "bilateralizable" relations, obligations creating multilateral relations

---

1169. L. Boisson de Chazournes, "La mise en œuvre du droit international dans le domaine de l'environnement: enjeux et défis", *Revue générale de droit international public*, 1/1995, Footnote 106, p. 48.
1170. A. Nollkaemper, "Responsibility of Transnational Corporations in International Environmental Law: Three Perspectives", in *Multilevel Governance of Global Environmental Science*, G Winter (ed.), Cambridge University Press, Cambridge, 2006, p. 186.
1171. See above, para. 505 *et seq.*
1172. See the International Law Commission's Draft Articles on Prevention of Transboundary Harm from Hazardous Activities. Text with commentaries, adopted in 2001, Yearbook of the International Law Commission, 2001, Vol. II, Part Two. See also UNGA Resolution No. 61/36, *Allocation of Loss in the Case of Transboundary Harm Arising Out of Hazardous Activities*.
1173. P.-M. Dupuy, "A propos des mésaventures de la responsabilité internationale des Etats dans ses rapports avec la protection de l'environnement", in M. Prieur and C. Lambrechts (eds.), *Les hommes et l'environnement: quels droits pour le XXIe siècle?*, *Etudes en hommage à Alexandre Kiss*, Paris, Frison Roche, 1998, p. 275.

and obligations creating relations of a universal nature [1174]. Lastly, given their global and gradual treatment of the challenges involved, specific non-compliance procedures also seem more appropriate.

662. International environmental protection conventions do however usually include a standard dispute settlement clause (varying in sophistication) devoted to the peaceful settlement of disputes, which can be relied on to bring legal action against a State for violations of treaty obligations. Dispute settlement clauses whereby Parties recognise the jurisdiction of a court – for example, the International Court of Justice – or an arbitral tribunal are however almost always optional and very few States do agree to them [1175].

663. These instruments do not clearly recognise a right of *actio popularis*, unlike what is possible in matters of human rights, for instance. However, the terms used ("In the event of a dispute between Contracting Parties concerning the interpretation or application of this Convention..."), as well as the fact that these are treaties in respect of which every State Party has a legal interest, may suggest that such a clause could be interpreted very broadly. Collective action by several States may also be a possibility, perhaps more acceptable given the past inter-State cases before the European Convention on Human Rights bodies.

664. To use a very representative example of the practice in international biodiversity conventions, the Convention on Biological Diversity contains a dispute settlement clause that applies *mutatis mutandis* to its protocols. Indeed, Article 27 contains an "optional clause of compulsory jurisdiction", which may lead to the institution of an arbitral tribunal or referral to the International Court of Justice. But if the Parties have not accepted either of these, or if they have accepted different procedures, then the dispute is subject to conciliation proceedings; this does not, however, lead to a binding decision (the

---

1174. L. A. Sicilianos, "The Classification of Obligations and the Multilateral Dimension of the Relations of International Responsibility", *European Journal of International Law*, Vol. 13, No. 5, 2002, pp. 1132-1137.

1175. In the *Mox Plant* case, however, Ireland requested the constitution of an arbitral tribunal to settle its dispute with the United Kingdom under Article 32 of the OSPAR Convention for the Protection of the Marine Environment of the North-East Atlantic, which contains – a very exceptional occurrence – a compulsory arbitration clause at its Article 32 ("Any disputes between Contracting Parties relating to the interpretation or application of the Convention, which cannot be settled otherwise by the Contracting Parties concerned, for instance, by means of inquiry or conciliation within the Commission, shall at the request of any of those Contracting Parties, be submitted to arbitration under the conditions laid down in this Article").

Conciliation Commission "shall render a proposal for resolution of the dispute, which the parties shall consider in good faith" according to Annex II). This explains why the clause has never been relied on and is unlikely to be used in the future. In reality, acceptance of the ICJ's jurisdiction could only be relied on between Austria, Latvia and the Netherlands, and arbitration proceedings could only take place between Austria, Cuba, the Netherlands and Latvia. That being said, the substance of the provisions of the Convention are so weak that they would be unlikely to give rise to international disputes. The few substantive obligations are very much weakened by means of the conditional or expressions such as "as far as possible and as appropriate". Thus, in the Costa Rica/Nicaragua case, the International Court took this into account. Nicaragua claimed that Costa Rica was required to carry out an environmental impact assessment under CBD Article 14. Here, the Court recalled the content of this provision:

> "Each Contracting Party, as far as possible and as appropriate, shall: *(a)* Introduce appropriate procedures requiring environmental impact assessment of its proposed projects that are likely to have significant adverse effects on biological diversity with a view to avoiding or minimizing such effects and, where appropriate, allow for public participation in such procedures." [1176]

Then the Court, without any further explanation, stated the following:

> "The provision at issue *does not create an obligation* to carry out an environmental impact assessment before undertaking an activity that may have significant adverse effects on biological diversity. Therefore, the Court did not establish that Costa Rica breached CBD Article 14 by failing to conduct an environmental impact assessment for its road project." [1177]

It is true that the obligation contained in CBD Article 14 ("shall") is qualified by the expression "as far as possible and as appropriate". But it has been argued that these qualifications, which are quite common in other international biodiversity-related conventions [1178], should not

---

[1176]. *Certain Activities Carried Out by Nicaragua in the Border Area (Costa Rica v. Nicaragua)* and *Construction of a Road in Costa Rica along the San Juan River (Nicaragua v. Costa Rica)* (Judgment) [2015] *ICJ Reports*, para. 164, p. 62.

[1177]. *Ibid.*, para. 164. Emphasis added.

[1178]. The High Court of Australia (1983) has considered qualifications used in the Word Heritage Convention similar to those contained in the CBD. In this instance, the Court held that "[t]hese articles impose a legally binding obligation that is 'real' and

be interpreted as calling into question the existence of an international obligation, but only as a way to allow a margin of discretion for different Parties to choose different ways to implement the obligation [1179]. In addition, it has been argued that the recognition of a customary rule to conduct EIAs implies that a State is under a positive obligation towards potentially affected States to assess harm to biodiversity where that harm extends beyond national borders in relation to impacts on biodiversity, despite the qualified language of the environmental impact assessment obligation under the CBD [1180]. It is also conceivable that in the future the Cartagena or Nagoya Protocols, which contain more specific obligations, could give rise to litigation. But in almost all cases, the involvement of the ICJ or the constitution of an arbitral tribunal can only be decided with the consent of the Parties, once the dispute has arisen. This considerably limits the potential application of this provision.

665. Some conventions are bolder, particularly at the regional level; for instance, the Maputo African Convention on the Conservation of Nature and Natural Resources (Revised Version) relies on the Court of Justice of the African Union for the settlement of disputes. Indeed, when a dispute between two Parties regarding the interpretation or application of the provisions cannot be settled by other means, the Parties are entitled to unilaterally refer the matter to the Court whose decision is final and not subject to appeal [1181]. Another example is Article 18 of the Bern Convention on the Conservation of European Wildlife and Natural Habitats, which provides as follows:

> "Any dispute between Contracting Parties concerning the interpretation or application of this Convention which has not been

---

'substantive' and could not be read as a mere statement of intention: it was expressed in the form of a command requiring each party to endeavour to bring about the matters dealt with – although there is an element of discretion and value judgment on the part of the State to decide what measures are necessary and appropriate, the discretion only concerns the manner of performance – not the issue of whether to perform or not". The argument that these qualifications pertain to how the obligations will be implemented, not whether or not they need to be implemented can also be applied by analogy to the CBD and other international biodiversity-related treaties.

1179. E. Morgera, "Biodiversity as a Human Right and its Implications for the EU's External Action" (2020), Report to the European Parliament, https://www.europarl.europa.eu/RegData/etudes/STUD/2020/603491/EXPOSTU(2020)603491EN.pdf, accessed 12 December 2023.

1180. N. Craik, "Biodiversity-Inclusive Impact Assessments", in E. Morgera and J. Razzaque (eds.), *Encyclopedia of Environmental Law: Biodiversity and Nature Protection Law*, Edward Elgar, 2017, pp. 431-444.

1181. Article XXX.

settled on the basis of the provisions of the preceding paragraph or by negotiation between the parties concerned shall, unless the said parties agree otherwise, be submitted, *at the request of one of them*, to arbitration." [1182]

666. But international litigation on biodiversity issues has so far developed on a basis other than the dispute settlement clauses of the biodiversity conventions, as an incidental issue before the ICJ [1183], the ITLOS, the WTO DSB or before arbitral tribunals. This type of litigation is still rare, but it will probably increase in the future, given the densification of international obligations as well as the growing awareness of threats to biodiversity. One thinks in particular of the potential development of transnational litigation in the human rights field or regarding the protection of investments [1184].

667. In its judgment of 2 February 2018, the International Court of Justice sent a clear signal by recognising for the first time that general international law entitles to compensation for environmental damage in and of itself, as long as it is the consequence of an intentionally wrongful act. It is true that the UN Compensation Commission had been given the competence to award compensation for environmental damage caused by Iraq on the territory of Kuwait in particular [1185]. But never before had it been stated so clearly that the general international law on the international liability of States requires compensation for such damage:

> "It is consistent with the principles of international law governing the consequences of internationally wrongful acts, including the principle of full reparation, to hold that compensation is due for damage caused to the environment, in and of itself, in addition to

---

1182. Emphasis added.
1183. As in the *Whaling* case, where the basis was a request under Article 36, para. 2 of the Statute of the Court, Whaling in the Antarctic *(Australia v. Japan: New Zealand intervening)* (Judgment) [2014] *ICJ Reports*, p. 226.
1184. See, for example, the award *Compañia del Desarollo de Santa Elena SA v. Costa-Rica,* ICSID Case No. ARB/96/1, Award of 17 February 2000. Similarly, see S. Maljean-Dubois and E. Morgera, "International Biodiversity Litigation. The Increasing Emphasis on Biodiversity Law before International Courts and Tribunals", in *Biodiversity Litigation*, G. Futhazar, J. Razzaque and S. Maljean-Dubois (eds.), OUP, 2022.
1185. J.-C. Martin, "La pratique de la Commission d'indemnisation des Nations Unies pour l'Irak en matière de réclamations environnementales", in *Le droit international face aux enjeux environnementaux*, Pedone, Paris, 2010, pp. 257-274. See *Report and Recommendations Made by the Panel of Commissioners concerning the Fifth Instalment of "F4" Claims*, United Nations Security Council, S/AC.26/2005/10, 30 June 2005.

expenses incurred by an injured State as a consequence of such damage." [1186]

In this decision, the ICJ highlights that, in relations between States, damage only gives rise to a right to compensation when there "is a sufficient causal nexus between the wrongful act and the injury suffered" [1187]. But it also recognises that, in the case of environmental damage, this causal link may be problematic. Because it is possibly due to several concurrent causes or because the causal link cannot always be demonstrated with certainty given the state of scientific knowledge, the Court will assess evidential difficulties "in light of the facts of the case at hand and the evidence presented to the Court" [1188]. This clarification, which echoes the case law of the European Court of Human Rights on this issue [1189], demonstrates the desire not to overload the burden of proof in environmental matters and leaves open the possibility, for example, of accepting probabilistic proof of causation, based on statistics, for instance.

668. So far, the relationship between judicial review and non-compliance procedures has not been defined in this respect. However, judicial intervention could be the next step after violations are discovered in non-compliance procedures, especially in cases of repeated non-compliance and refusal to co-operate. Non-compliance procedures are without prejudice to traditional dispute settlement procedures. For example, with respect to the Cartagena and Nagoya Protocols, it is made clear that these procedures shall be "separate from, and without prejudice to, the dispute settlement procedures and mechanisms under Article 27 of the Convention" [1190]. In the same vein, the CITES procedure provides that "[t]he procedures described in this Guide are without prejudice to any rights and obligations and to any

---

1186. *Certain Activities Carried Out by Nicaragua in the Border Area (Costa Rica v. Nicaragua)*, Compensation, Judgment, *ICJ Reports 2018*, p. 15, para. 41, emphasis added. Y. Kerbrat and S. Maljean-Dubois, "La contribution en demie teinte de la CIJ au droit international de l'environnement dans les affaires Costa Rica-Nicaragua", *Journal du droit international*, 2018, pp. 1133-1154; "La reconnaissance du préjudice écologique par la Cour internationale de Justice", *Droit de l'environnement*, March 2018, No. 265, pp. 90-91.
1187. *Ibid.*, para. 72.
1188. *Ibid.*, para. 34.
1189. E. Lambert Abdelgawad, "La Cour européenne des droits de l'homme et le traitement de la connaissance scientifique sur la nocivité des ondes électromagnétiques, produits chimiques et autres activités polluantes", *VertigO – la revue électronique en sciences de l'environnement* [online], Special Issue 27, December 2016.
1190. Article 34 of the Cartagena Protocol. See also, in the same vein, Article 30 of the Nagoya Protocol.

dispute settlement procedure under the Convention"[1191]. Reliance on traditional liability mechanisms has been and remains possible, even though they are less suited than *ad hoc* non-compliance procedures[1192]. They still play a subsidiary role, however, if not in theory, at least in practice, compared to the special procedure defined by the Parties[1193].

b) *Judicial review by national courts*

669. As for national courts, they have so far played only a relatively small role in reviewing the implementation of international environmental law, but this role will undoubtedly grow in the future. Isn't the judge "the most universalisable, but also the most univeralising of the three powers described by Montesquieu"[1194]? In matters of environmental protection, the universalisation of the judicial power is particularly striking. This is due to various factors.

670. Universalisation is due first of all to the influence of international law on domestic law. In essence, environmental law is itself cosmopolitan and crosses borders. It reflects the rise of "porous legality"[1195] and "internormativity" between more or less open and permeable systems that establish various relationships between them – total or partial subordination, co-ordination, indifference. For instance, EU environmental law has had very significant effects on the domestic legislations of Member States. In most Member States, the environmental legal framework is simply equivalent to EU environmental law[1196]. EU policy has largely contributed to the diffusion and strengthening of environmental law, and has allowed its harmonisation among the Member States according to relatively high standards. EU environmental law is also in constant interaction with international environmental law. Large parts of EU environmental law are being developed under international influence. This is the case,

---

1191. Resolution Conf. 14.3 (Rev. CoP18), *CITES Compliance Procedures*.
1192. P.-M. Dupuy, "Où en est le droit international de l'environnement à la fin du siècle?" (n. 1158), p. 897.
1193. M. Koskenniemi, "Breach of Treaty or Non-Compliance? Reflections on the Enforcement of the Montreal Protocol", in *Yearbook of International Environmental Law*, 1992, p. 134.
1194. J. Allard and A. Garapon, *Les juges dans la mondialisation. La nouvelle révolution du droit*, La République des idées, Seuil, Paris, 2005, p. 84 (our translation).
1195. F. Ost and M. van de Kerchove, *De la pyramide au réseau? Pour une théorie dialectique du droit*, Facultés universitaires Saint-Louis, 2002, p. 198 (our translation).
1196. L. Kramer, *EU Environmental Law*, Sweet & Maxwell, 2011.

for example, in areas such as trade in endangered wildlife species, protection of the ozone layer, transportation of hazardous waste, acid rain or climate change. EU environmental law is, in some respects, a "communitisation" of the contents of international environmental law. Conversely, because it often goes further, EU law has had an impact on international environmental law, which it has in turn helped to develop. The issue of access to environmental information is a very good illustration of the dynamic interactions between international and EU law [1197]. Through the definition of global or regional frames of reference, and increasingly precise legal regimes, international law and EU environmental law bring about, to a certain extent, an acculturation or standardisation of the law. Globalisation is shaping internal legal orders, which are undergoing a real transmutation [1198]. The environment thus unquestionably reflects the development of a global or globalised law, through the "spontaneous" convergence of national laws seeking to align themselves with dominant standards and models [1199]. The internationalisation of environmental law allows a certain emancipation of judges, who are as if freed from domestic law in favour of international law, the imprecision of which has the effect of expanding their scope of interpretation [1200].

671. The judicialisation of the international legal order also fuels this cosmopolitanism. International courts too, including regional courts, contribute to uniformity through their case law. Of course, the uniformising force of such case law varies, depending in particular on its quantity and on the authority of the courts reaching these decisions [1201]. But the "reciprocal reception of case law" [1202] is more of a practice than an actual legal principle.

672. The internationalisation of national courts is also the result of more intense exchanges between judges, facilitated by new information

---

1197. M. Pallemaerts, *The Aarhus Convention at Ten: Interactions and Tensions between Conventional International Law and EU Environmental Law*, Europa Law Publishing, 2011.

1198. J. Chevallier, "Mondialisation du droit ou droit de la mondialisation?", in *Le droit saisi par la mondialisation*, C.-A. Morand (ed.) Bruylant, Bruxelles, 2001, p. 38.

1199. F. Ost and M. van de Kerchove, *De la pyramide au réseau? Pour une théorie dialectique du droit* (n. 1195), p. 97.

1200. M. Delmas-Marty, *La refondation des pouvoirs*, tome 3, *Les forces imaginantes du droit,* Seuil, Paris, 2007, p. 45.

1201. G. Canivet, "Les influences croisées entre juridictions nationales et internationales: éloge de la 'bénévolence' des juges", *RSC*, 2005, p. 799.

1202. *Ibid.* (our translation).

technologies and the creation of judicial networks [1203]. This global judicial dialogue is particularly developed in the environmental field. A world forum of environmental law judges was set up under the aegis of the United Nations Environment Programme (UNEP), which took the initiative of bringing together all the presidents of the supreme courts and chief justices from around the world at the international summit on sustainable development held in Johannesburg from 18 to 20 August 2002. Judges from sixty countries and international courts were present. In Europe, a European Union Forum of Judges for the Environment was created in Paris in 2004, on the initiative of a number of judges from different European countries. It aims to contribute to the implementation of national, European and international environmental law by improving judges' knowledge of environmental law, exchanging judicial decisions and by sharing experience in the area of environmental law training. It is not easy to measure the impact of these initiatives, but they can at least be seen as the expression of a need felt by judges. This dialogue continues beyond these initiatives, if only through "judicial" [1204] or "friendly civility between equals" [1205]. UNEP itself has taken the initiative to produce a *Judicial Handbook on Environmental Law*: a sort of "practical guide" published in French and English which aims to help national judges in all types of courts identify the environmental problems they come across and be aware of the range of options available to them in interpreting and applying the law [1206].

673. This movement is abundantly supported by legal academics, but also by civil society [1207]. The latter exercises an increasingly widely recognised right of access to justice or intervenes as *amicus curia*, which is also increasingly accepted [1208]. Climate litigation reflects the interest now shown in national courts when it comes to ensuring the implementation of a State's international commitments. The rapid

---

1203. M. Delmas-Marty, *La refondation des pouvoirs* (n. 1200); p. 42; J. Allard and A. Garapon, *Les juges dans la mondialisation. La nouvelle révolution du droit*, La République des idées, Seuil, Paris, 2005, p. 7.
1204. *Ibid.*, p. 49.
1205. *Ibid.*, p. 59.
1206. G. Canivet, L. Lavrysen and D. Guihal (eds.), *UNEP Judicial Handbook on Environmental Law*, UNEP, 2006, p. 2.
1207. See, for instance, A. Gargule, *Beyond the Institutional Fix? The Potential of Strategic Litigation to Target Natural Resource Corruption*, TNRC Topic Brief series, February 2022.
1208. H. Ascencio, "L'*amicus curiae* devant les juridictions internationales", *RGDIP*, 2004, p. 897.

development of this type of strategic litigation, which is spreading internationally, could lead to the emergence of national trials on other global threats, including biodiversity [1209]. International provisions promoting broad access to justice in environmental matters could support such developments [1210]. This new risk of biodiversity litigation is now a concern not only for governments but also for companies [1211].

1209. G. Futhazar, J. Razzaque and S. Maljean-Dubois (eds.), *Biodiversity Litigation*, OUP, 2022.

1210. See, for example, the Aarhus Convention (1998) on Access to Information, Public Participation in Decision-Making and Access to Justice in Environmental Matters; Article XVI of the Maputo African Convention (2003) on the Conservation of Nature and Natural Resources; the Escazu Regional Agreement (2018) on Access to Information, Public Participation in Decision-Making and Access to Justice in Environmental Matters in Latin America and the Caribbean (2018). See S. Maljean-Dubois and E. Morgera, "International Biodiversity Litigation. The Increasing Emphasis on Biodiversity Law before International Courts and Tribunal" (n. 1184); J. Phelps, "Environmental Liability Litigation Could Remedy Biodiversity Loss", *Conservation Letters*, 2021, 14:e12821. For an illustration, East African Court of Justice, *African Network for Animal Welfare (ANAW) v. the Attorney General of the United Republic of Tanzania*, Reference No. 9 of 2010, 20 June 2014; see also N. Klein and N. Hughes, "National Litigation and International Law: Repercussions for Australia's Protection of Marine Resources", *Melbourne University Law Review*, 33 (1), 2009, pp. 163-204.

1211. N. Brook *et al.*, Clyde & Co, *Biodiversity Liability and Value Chain Risk*, March 2022.

CONCLUSION

674. Biodiversity conservation has been recognised as a common concern of humankind and biodiversity is *de facto* a resource shared by all States on a global scale. However, apart from exceptional cases, it remains *de jure* under the sovereignty of States, which does not facilitate its joint management. Given the explosion in the number of international instruments and institutions interested in biodiversity and the deterioration in the state of biodiversity, one is led to question the effectiveness of the international law on biodiversity and even, beyond that, its usefulness.

675. It seems to us that in this matter, international law has played its promotional function quite effectively, as remarkably highlighted by Norberto Bobbio [1212]. To quote the distinction made by this author, the international law of biodiversity is a tool, not of "social control", but of "social orientation". It points in one or more directions and positively supports and encourages States in the implementation of their international obligations. Thus, international law has made a major contribution to raising awareness of these issues and their importance, among States and their administrations as well as their citizens, and from North to South. It has put biodiversity issues on the "agenda" at all levels, from local to global. It has led to a better understanding of the issues and needs at stake. IPBES has begun to play a major role in this respect. International law has fostered international co-operation at various levels, for the protection of various species of fauna and flora, and of various sites or regions. It has inspired national laws, many of which now take into account biodiversity issues.

676. It is important to note and even admire the plasticity of international law and its ability to take into account complex and politically sensitive issues with vast financial implications. Yet, despite significant progress, international law has been powerless to halt the erosion of biodiversity, which is expected to accelerate considerably in the years to come. Biodiversity issues remain encapsulated in the international law on biodiversity, without sufficiently spreading to other areas and branches of international law. A great deal of progress

---

1212. N. Bobbio, *De la structure à la fonction. Nouveaux essais de théorie du droit*, Dalloz, Paris, 2012.

has been made since the adoption of the 1992 Convention on Biological Diversity, whose institutions are gradually succeeding in injecting some coherence into a hitherto multipolar and fragmented international law and environmental governance. However, this reorganisation is struggling to go beyond the borders of international environmental law to cover the whole of international law. Commitments are not always followed by action. The objectives, principles and tools promoted at the international level are far from being fully implemented at the national level. International biodiversity law focuses more on the symptoms than on the root causes of biodiversity loss. Economic growth and population explosion across the world are undermining the efforts that have been made by eroding the space left to the "wild". Economic incentives more often support the destruction than the conservation of biodiversity. The "commodification" of nature remains the dominant vision [1213]. Economic logic takes precedence over ecological logic.

677. While much has been done, it is not enough. Here, as is often the case, international law can only do so much. It is only a tool, and a tool of necessarily limited scope in the absence of a strong political will to instil real ambition. The apprehension by law and by human institutions – essentially simplifying and fixist – of this living, complex, evolving and still unknown object that is biodiversity is very delicate. Biodiversity resists our attempts to manage it. As we enter the Anthropocene and face the threat of environmental collapse, the challenge remains immense and must be taken more seriously than ever if we wish to achieve the objective of "Living in harmony with nature" set by the Conference of the Parties of the Convention on Biological Diversity, according to which "[b]y 2050, biodiversity is valued, conserved, restored and wisely used, maintaining ecosystem services, sustaining a healthy planet and delivering benefits essential for all people" [1214]. If we do not want to find ourselves fighting a new war with old and inadequate weapons [1215], the objective of "rewilding" our world will need us to combine both intelligence and imagination [1216].

1213. O. de Schutter, "Préface", in *Biodiversité. Quand les politiques européennes menacent le vivant. Connaître la nature pour mieux légiférer,* ed. Yves Michel, Gap, 2017, p. 15.
1214. Decision X/2 (2010), *The Strategic Plan for Biodiversity 2011-2020 and the Aichi Biodiversity Targets,* UNEP/CBD/COP/DEC/X/2 (2010), p. 117.
1215. L. J. Kotze and T. M. P. Marauhn (eds.), *Transboundary Governance of Biodiversity,* Brill, Nijhoff, 2014, p. 22.
1216. V. Maris, *La part sauvage du monde. Penser la nature dans l'anthropocène,* Seuil, Paris, 2018, p. 237.

BIBLIOGRAPHY

Books

Allard, J., and A. Garapon, *Les juges dans la mondialisation. La nouvelle révolution du droit*, La République des idées, Seuil, Paris, 2005.
Andrassy, J., "Les relations internationales de voisinage", *Recueil des cours*, tome 79 (1951), pp. 73-182.
Apotheker, A., *Du poisson dans les fraises. Notre alimentation manipulée*, La Découverte, Paris, 1999.
Aubertin, C., and F. D. Vivien, *Les enjeux de la biodiversité*, Economica, 1998.
Barberis, J., *Los recursos naturales compartidos entre Estados*, Tecnos, Madrid, 1979.
Baya-Laffite, N., M. V. Berros and R. Míguez Núñez (eds.), *Le droit à l'épreuve de la société des sciences et des techniques. Liber amicorum en l'honneur de Marie-Angèle Hermitte*, Academia University Press, 2022.
Beer-Gabel, J., and B. Labat, *La protection internationale de la faune et de la flore sauvages*, Bruylant, Bruxelles, 1999.
Beer-Gabel, J., and V. Lestang, *Les commissions de pêche et leur droit : la conservation et la gestion des ressources marines vivantes*, Bruylant, Bruxelles, 2003.
Beigbeder, Y., *Le rôle international des organisations non gouvernementales*, Bruylant, Bruxelles, 1992.
Bellivier, F., and C. Noiville (eds.), *La bioéquité : batailles autour du partage du vivant*, éd. Autrement, impr. 2009.
Bettati, M., and P.-M. Dupuy (eds.), *Les ONG et le droit international*, Economica, Droit international serie, 198.
Beurier, J.-P., *Droit international de l'environnement*, Pedone, Paris, 2017.
Bhattarai, A. M., *Protection of Himalayan Biodiversity: International Environmental Law and a Regional Legal Framework*, Sage Law, 2010.
Bilderbeek, S. (ed.), *Biodiversity and International Law: The Effectiveness of International Environmental Law*, 1992, IOS Press.
Billet, P. (ed.), *"Des petits oiseaux aux grands principes" : mélanges en l'honneur au professeur Jean Untermaier*, Mare & Martin, 2018.
Blandin, P., *De la protection de la nature au pilotage de la biodiversité*, ed. Quæ, 2009.
Boardman, R., *The International Politics of Bird Conservation: Biodiversity, Regionalism and Global Governance*, Edward Elgar, Cheltenham, 2006.
Bobbio, N., *De la structure à la fonction – Nouveaux essais de théorie du droit*, Dalloz, Paris, 2012.
Bonneuil, C., and J.-P. Fressoz, *L'événement anthropocène, la terre, l'histoire et nous*, Points Seuil, 2016.
Bourrinet, J., and S. Maljean-Dubois (eds.), *Le commerce international des organismes génétiquement modifiés*, La Documentation française, Monde européen et international, 2002.
Bowman, M., P. Davies and C. Redgwell, *Lyster's International Wildlife Law*, Cambridge University Press, 2nd ed., 2010.
Bowman, M., P. G. G. Davies and E. J. Goodwin (eds.), *Research Handbook on Biodiversity and Law*, Research Handbooks in Environmental Law, Cheltenham, UK, Edward Elgar, Cheltenham, 2016.
Bowman, M., and C. Redgwell, *International Law and the Conservation of Biological Diversity*, Kluwer Law International, 1996.
Boyd, D. R., *The Rights of Nature: A Legal Revolution That Could Save the World*, ECW Press, Canada, 2017.

Bradnee Chambers, W., *Interlinkages and the Effectiveness of Multilateral Environmental Agreements*, United Nations University Press, 2008.
Brownlie, I., "Legal Status of Natural Resources in International Law. Some Aspects", in Collected Courses of The Hague Academy of International Law, tome 162 (1979), pp. 245-318.
Buffon, G.-L. Leclerc de, Œuvres, Bibliothèque de la Pléiade, Paris, Gallimard, 2007.
Butler, W. E. (ed.), *Control over Compliance with International Law*, Martinus Nijhoff Publishers, Pays-Bas, 1991.
Canal-Forgues, E., *Le règlement des différends à l'OMC*, Bruylant, 2ᵉ éd., 2004.
Caroll, J. E., *International environmental diplomacy: The management and resolution of transfrontier environmental problems*, Cambridge University Press, Cambridge, MA, USA, 1988.
Carson, R., *Silent spring*, 1962, réédition Mariner Books, 2002.
Charpentier, J., "Le contrôle par les organisations internationales de l'exécution des obligations des États", *Recueil des cours*, tome IV (1983), Vol. 182, pp. 143-245.
Chayes, A., and A. Chayes, *The New Sovereignty. Compliance with International Regulatory Agreements*, Harvard University Press, Cambridge, 1998.
Chege, E. K., and G. Winter (eds.), *Common Pools of Genetic Resources: Equity and Innovation in International Biodiversity Law*, Routledge, 2013.
Chevassus-au-Louis, B., *La biodiversité, c'est maintenant*, ed. de l'Aube, 2013.
Colas-Belcour, F., and J. Guilbaud, *La chasse et le droit*, Litec droit, Paris, 1999, 15e éd..
Combacau, J., and S. Sur, *Droit international public*, Montchrestien, Paris, 13ᵉ éd., 2019.
Compagnon, D., and E. Rodary (eds.), *Les politiques de biodiversité*, Presses de Sciences Po, 2017.
Conquy Beer-Gabel, J., and B. Labat, *La protection internationale de la faune et de la flore sauvages*, ed. Bruylant, Collection de droit international, Bruxelles, 1999.
Couzens, E., *Whales and Elephants in International Conservation Law and Politics: A Comparative Study*, Routledge, 2013.
Curci, J., *The Protection of Biodiversity and Traditional Knowledge in International Law of Intellectual Property*, Cambridge Intellectual Property and Information Law, Cambridge: Cambridge University Press, 2010.
Daillier, P., M. Forteau and A. Pellet, *Droit international public*, LGDJ, Paris, 8ᵉ éd., 2009.
De Klemm, C., and C. Shine, *Biological Diversity Conservation and the Law: Legal Mechanisms for conserving Species and ecosystems*, IUCN Bonn, Germany, 1993.
De La Bigne, Y., C. André, G. Bœuf, N. Chaï, T. Chekchak, P. Lavagne, F. Pichard and P. Pascal Picq, *L'animal est-il l'avenir de l'homme ?*, Larousse, Paris, 2917.
De Sadeleer, N., and C.-H. Born, *Droit international et communautaire de la biodiversité*, Dalloz, 2004.
De Sombre, E. R., *Global Environmental Institutions*, Routledge, London, 2017.
Delmas-Marty, M., *La refondation des pouvoirs*, tome 3, *Les forces imaginantes du droit*, Seuil, Paris, 2007.
–, *Les forces imaginantes du droit*, Vol. II: Le pluralisme ordonné, Seuil, Paris, 2006.
Devictor, V., *Nature en crise. Penser la biodiversité*, Seuil, Anthropocène, 2017.
Dryzek, J. S., and J. Pickering, *The Politics of the Anthropocene*, Oxford University Press, Oxford, 2019.
Dupuy, P.-M., and J. Vinales, *Introduction au droit international de l'environnement*, Bruylant, Bruxelles, 2015.
Dupuy, R.-J. (ed.), *L'Avenir du droit international de l'environnement: colloque, La Haye, 12-14 novembre 1984 = The future of the international law of the environment: workshop, The Hague, 12-14 November 1984*, M. Nijhoff, Dordrecht, Netherlands, Boston, Mass., 1985.
–, *L'humanité dans l'imaginaire des nations*, Juillard, Paris, 1991.

Edelman, B., M. A. Hermitte (eds.), *L'homme, la nature et le droit*, Bourgois, Paris, 1988.
Fitzmaurice, M., "International Protection of the Environment", Collected Courses of The Hague Academy of International Law, 2001, tome 293, pp. 9-488.
Forteau, M., J.-M. Thouvenin (eds.), *Traité de droit international de la mer*, Pedone, Paris, 2017.
Freestone, D. (ed.), *Conserving Biodiversity in Areas Beyond National Jurisdiction*, Leiden Brill Nijhoff, 2019.
Futhazar, G., Maljean-Dubois and J. Razzaque (eds.) *Biodiversity Litigation*, OUP, 2022.
Gillespie, A., *Conservation, Biodiversity and International Law*, Edward Elgar, Cheltenham, 2012.
Glowka, L., F. Burhenne-Guilmin, H. Synge, en collaboration avec J. A. McNeely et L. Gündling, *Guide de la Convention sur la diversité biologique*, UICN, Environmental Policy and Law Paper No. 30, 1996.
Gros, F., and C. Puigelier, *Biologie et droit* : les étapes du vivant, Bruylant, Paris, 2016.
Guruswamy, L. D., and J. A. McNeely (eds.), *Protection of Global Biodiversity: Converging Strategies*, Durham, NC: Duke University Press, 1998.
Haas, P. M., R. O. Kehoane and M. A. Levy, *Institutions for the Earth, Sources of Effective International Environmental Protection*, Cambridge, MIT Press, 1994.
Heams, T., *Infravies – le vivant sans frontière*, Paris, Le Seuil, 2019.
Hrabanski, M., and D. Pesche (eds.), *The Intergovernmental Platform on Biodiversity and Ecosystem Services (IPBES): Meeting the Challenge of Biodiversity Conservation and Governance*, Routledge, 2016.
Jacob, F., *The Logic of Life. A History of Heredity*, Gallimard, Paris, 1970, Princeton University Press, 1993.
Jeffery, M. I., *Biodiversity Conservation, Law and Livelihoods – Bridging the North-South Divide,* IUCN Academy of Environmental Law Research Studies, CUP, 2008.
Juniper, T., *What Has Nature Ever Done for Us? How Money Really Does Grow on Trees*, Synergetic Press, 2018.
Kamau, E. C, G. Winter and P.-T. Stoll (eds.), *Research and Development on Genetic Resources: Public Domain Approaches in Implementing the Nagoya Protocol*, Routledge Research in International Environmental Law, Abingdon, Oxon UK, Routledge, 2015.
Kanie N., and F. Biermann (eds.), *Governing Through Goals: Sustainable Development Goals as Governance Innovation*, Cambridge, MA, MIT Press, 2017.
Kiss, A., *L'écologie et la loi : le statut juridique de l'environnement*, L'Harmattan, Paris, 1989.
Klemm, C. de, and C. Shine, *Biological Diversity Conservation and the Law: Legal Mechanisms for Conserving Species and Ecosystems*, International Union for Conservation of Nature and Natural Resources, IUCN Environmental Policy and Law Paper, No. 29. Gland, 1993.
Kotze, L. J., and T. M. P. Maruahn (eds.), *Transboundary Governance of Biodiversity*, Brill, Nijhoff, 2014.
Krasner, S. (ed.), *International Regimes*. Ithaca, Cornell University Press, 1983.
Lambert, M.-L., *Le commerce des espèces sauvages, entre droit international et gestion locale*, L'Harmattan, Paris, 2000.
Lambrechts, C., "L'œuvre de Cyrille De Klemm dans le domaine du droit de la protection de la nature et de la biodiversité", *International Colloquy in Tribute to the Memory of Cyrille De Klemm, Biological Diversity and Environment Law: Proceedings: Paris (Jean Monnet Faculty, Paris-Sud University), 30-31 March 2000: Actes: Paris (faculté Jean Monnet, Université Paris-Sud) 30-31 Mars 2000*, Conseil de l'Europe, 2001.
Larrère, C., and R. Larrère, *Penser et agir avec la nature. Une enquête philosophique*, La Découverte, 2015.

Lavieille, J.-M. (ed.), *Conventions de protection de l'environnement. Secrétariats, Conférences des Parties, Comités d'experts*, PULIM, Limoges, 2000.
Lawson, C., and A. Kamalesh (eds.), *Biodiversity, Genetic Resources and Intellectual Property: Developments in Access and Benefit Sharing*, Routledge Research in Intellectual Property, Routledge, New York, 2018.
Le Prestre, P., *Governing Global Biodiversity. The Evolution and Implementation of the Convention on Biological Diversity*, Ashgate, 2004.
–, *Protection de l'environnement et relations internationales. Les défis de l'écopolitique mondiale*, Paris, Armand Colin, 2005.
Lochak, D., *Le droit et les paradoxes de l'universalité*, Presses Universitaires de France, Paris, 2010.
Lyster, S., *International Wildlife Law: An Analysis of International Treaties concerned with the Conservation of Wildlife*, CUP, 1985, 1st ed., CUP, 2012.
McConnell, F., *The Biodiversity Convention: A Negotiating History: A Personal Account of Negotiating the United Nations Convention on Biological Diversity, and After*, Kluwer Law International, 1996.
Maes, F. et al. (ed.), *Biodiversity and Climate Change: Linkages at International, National and Local Levels*, Edward Elgar, Cheltenham, the IUCN Academy of Environmental Law, 2013.
Magnin, T., *Penser l'humain au temps de l'homme augmenté*, Albin Michel, Paris, 2017.
Maljean-Dubois, S. (ed.), *Circulations de normes et réseaux d'acteurs dans la gouvernance internationale de l'environnement*, coll. Confluence des droits, DICE, Aix-en-Provence, 2017.
–, "Le droit international de la biodiversité", *Recueil des cours*, Brill/Martinus Nijhoff, 2020, tome 407, pp. 123-538.
Maris, V., *La part sauvage du monde. Penser la nature dans l'anthropocène*, Seuil, Paris, 2018.
–, *Philosophie de la biodiversité. Petite éthique pour une nature en péril*, Buchet Chastel, La Verte, 2ᵉ éd., 2016.
McManis *Biodiversity and the Law: Intellectual Property, Biotechnology and Traditional Knowledge*, Routledge, 2012.
McManis, C., and O. Burton (eds.), *Handbook of Biodiversity and the Law*, Routledge, 2017.
Morgera E. (ed.), *The 2010 Nagoya Protocol on Access and Benefit-sharing in Perspective*, Martinus Nijhoff Publishers, Leiden, 2013.
Morgera E., and K. Kulovesi (eds.), *Research Handbook on International Law and Natural Resources*, Research Handbooks in International Law, Cheltenham, UK, Edward Elgar, Cheltenham, 2016.
Morgera, E., and J. Razzaque (eds.), *Biodiversity and Nature Protection Law*, Edward Elgar, Cheltenham, 2017.
Nègre, C. (ed.), *La convention internationale sur la biodiversité : Enjeux de la mise en œuvre*, La Documentation française, coll. Monde Européen et International, Paris, 2010.
Noiville C., *Ressources génétiques et droit. Essai sur les régimes juridiques des ressources génétiques marines*, Pedone, Paris, 1997.
Oberthur, S., and G. K. Rosendal (eds.), *Global Governance of Genetic Resources. Access and Benefit Sharing After the Nagoya Protocol*, Routledge, 2013.
Oguamanam, C. (ed.), *Genetic Resources, Justice and Reconciliation: Canada and Global Access and Benefit Sharing*. Cambridge, United Kingdom, Cambridge University Press, 2019.
Olivier, J., *L'Union mondiale pour la nature (UICN) : Une organisation singulière au service du droit de l'environnement*, Bruylant, Bruxelles, 2005.
Ost, F., and M. van de Kerchove, *De la pyramide au réseau ? Pour une théorie dialectique du droit*, Facultés universitaires Saint-Louis, 2002.
Pauwelyn, J., *Conflict of Norms in Public International Law, How WTO Law Relates to other Rules of International Law*, CUP, Cambridge, 2003.
Rabitz, F., *The Global Governance of Genetic Resources*, Routledge, 2017.

Ranjeva, R., "Les organisations non gouvernementales et la mise en œuvre du droit international", *Recueil des cours*, 1997, Vol. 270, pp. 9-106.
Reid, C. T., and W. Nsoh, *The Privatization of Biodiversity? New Approaches to Conservation Law*, Edward Elgar, Cheltenham, 2016.
Ricard, P., *La conservation de la biodiversité dans les espaces maritimes internationaux. Un défi pour le droit international*, Pedone, Paris, 2019.
Rifkin, J., *Le siècle Biotech. Le commerce des gènes dans le meilleur des mondes*, La Découverte, Paris, 1998.
Robinson, D. F., *Biodiversity, Access and Benefit-Sharing: Global Case Studies*, Milton Park, Abingdon, Oxon: Routledge, 2015.
Romi, R., *Les espaces humides. Le droit entre protection et exploitation des terres*, L'Harmattan, Paris, 1992.
Roqueplo, P., *Entre savoir et décision, l'expertise scientifique*, INRA eds., 1997.
Sand, P., *The Effectiveness of International Environmental Law. A Survey of Existing Legal Instruments*, Cambridge, Grotius Publications, 1992.
Scholtz, W. (ed.), *Animal Welfare and International Environmental Law. From Conservation to Compassion*, Edward Elgar, Cheltenham, 2019.
Shibata, A., *International Liability Regime for Biodiversity Damage: The Nagoya-Kuala Lumpur Supplementary Protocol*, Routledge Research in International Environmental Law, 2014.
Shiva V., *Biopiracy: The Plunder of Nature and Knowledge*, South Press, 1997.
Slaughter, A.-M., *The Chessboard and the Web: Strategies of Connection in a Networked World*, New Haven, CT: Yale University Press, 2017.
Snape, W. J. (ed.)., *Biodiversity and the Law*, Island Press, 2013.
Soulé, M. E, *Conservation Biology. The Science of Scarcity and Diversity*, Sinauer Associates, 1986.
Susskind, L., and S. H. Ali, *Environmental Diplomacy: Negotiating More Effective Global Agreements*, Oxford University Press, Oxford, 2015.
Swanson, T. M., *The International Regulation of Extinction*, New York University Press, Washington Square, NY, 1994.
Tegner Anker, H., and B. Egelung Olsen (eds.), *Sustainable Management of Natural Resources. Legal Instruments and Approaches*, Intersentia, Cambridge, Antwerp, Portland, 2018.
Thibierge, C., *La force normative. Naissance d'un concept*, Paris, LGDJ, 2009.
Trépant, I., *Biodiversité. Quand les politiques européennes menacent le vivant. Connaître la nature pour mieux légiférer*, ed. Yves Michel, Gap, 2017.
Tsioumani, E., E. Morgera and M. Buck, *Unraveling the Nagoya Protocol: A Commentary on the Nagoya Protocol on Access and Benefit-Sharing to the Convention on Biological Diversity*, M. Nijhoff, Leiden, 2014.
Usha, T. M. (ed.), *Biodiversity: Law, Policy and Governance*, Routledge India, 2017.
Visscher, C. de, *Problèmes de confins en droit international public*, Pedone, Paris, 1969.
Voigt, C. (ed.), *Rule of Law for Nature: New Dimensions and Ideas in Environmental Law*, Cambridge University Press, 2013.
Westra L., K. Bosselmann and R. Westra, *Reconciling Human Existence with Ecological Integrity: Science, Ethics, Economics and Law*, Earthscan, London, 2008.
Wolfrum, R., "Means of Ensuring Compliance with and Enforcement of International Environmental Law", Collected Courses of The Hague Academy of International Law, tome 272, pp. 9-154.
World Commission on Environment and Development, *Our Common Future*, Oxford paperbacks, 1987.
Young, M., *Regime Interaction in International Law: Facing Fragmentation*, Cambridge University Press, 2012.
–, *Trading Fish, Saving Fish: The Interaction between Regimes in International Law*, CUP, 2011.

Articles

Abbott, K. W., R. O. Keohane, A. Moravcsik, A.-M. Slaughter and D. Snidal, "The Concept of Legalization", *International Organisations*, 2000, Vol. 54, pp. 401-419.

Adel, S., "L'émergence de l'idée de parc national en France. De la protection des paysages à l'expérimentation coloniale", Raphaël Larrère (ed.), *Histoire des parcs nationaux. Comment prendre soin de la nature ?*, Versailles, éditions Quæ, 2009, pp. 43-58.

Aguilar, S., "The International Finance for Biodiversity and the Global Environment Facility", *Elgar Encyclopedia of Environmental Law*, 2017, Edward Elgar, Cheltenham, Vol. 3, pp. 477-487.

Alvarado-Quesada, I., and H. P. Weikard, "International Environmental Agreements for Biodiversity Conservation: A Game-Theoretic Analysis", *International Environmental Agreements*, 2017, Vol. 17, pp. 731-754.

Arjjumend, H., K. Koutouki and S. Alam, "Evolution of International Governance of Biodiversity", *Journal of Global Resources*, Vol. 3, July 2016, pp. 1-15.

Ascencio, H., "L'*amicus curiae* devant les juridictions internationales", *RGDIP*, 2001, tome 105, n° 4, pp. 897-930.

Aubertin, C., "L'ascension fulgurante d'un concept flou", *La Recherche*, vol 13, n° 4, pp. 15-21.

Aubertin, C., V. Boisvert and F.-D. Vivien, "La construction sociale de la question de la biodiversité", *Natures, Sciences, Sociétés*, Vol. 6, 1998, pp. 7-19.

Aubertin, C., and G. Filoche, "The Nagoya Protocol on the Use of Genetic Resources: One Embodiment of an Endless Discussion", *Sustentabilidade em Debate*, 2011, 2 (1), pp. 51-63.

Aubertin C., and F. Pinton, "Compenser plutôt que reconquérir", *Natures Sciences Sociétés*, 2018/2, Vol. 26, pp. 127-128.

Bastmeijer, K., M. J. S. Bowman, P. Davies and E. J. Goodwin, "Ecological Restoration in International Biodiversity Law: A Promising Strategy to Address Our Failure to Prevent", *Research Handbook on Biodiversity and Law*, Edward Elgar, Cheltenham, 2016, pp. 387-413.

Bell, D. E., "The 1992 Convention on Biological Biodiversity: The Continuing Significance of US Objections at the Earth Summit", *George Washington Journal of International Law and Economics*, Vol. 26,1993, pp. 479-537.

Bellard, C. *et al.*, "Impacts of Climate Change on the Future of Biodiversity" (2012) 15 *Ecology Letters*, 2012, Vol. 15, pp. 365-377.

Bellevue, C., "GMOs, International Law and Indigenous Peoples", *Pace International Law Review*, Winter 2017, Vol. 30, Issue 1, pp. 1-41.

Bernau, B. M., "Help for Hotspots: NGO Participation in the Preservation of Worldwide Biodiversity", *Indiana Journal of Global Legal Studies*, Vol. 13, Issue 2 (Summer 2006), pp. 617-644.

Beslier, S., "Gouvernance de la haute mer : vers un accord d'application pour 'la conservation et l'exploitation durable de la biodiversité marine' au-delà de la juridiction nationale", *Annuaire du droit de la mer*, Indemer, Vol. 20 (2015), pp. 57-71.

Bétaille, J., "Rights of Nature: Why It Might Not Save the Entire World", *Journal for European Environmental & Planning Law*, Vol. 16, Issue 1, 2019, pp. 35-64.

Betsill, M. *et al.*, "Building Productive Links between the UNFCCC and the Broader Global Climate Governance Landscape", *Global Environmental Politics*, Global Environmental Politics, Vol. 15, Issue 2, May 2015, pp.1-10.

Beurier, J.-P., "Le droit de la biodiversité", *Revue juridique de l'environnement*, 1996, n°s 1-2, pp. 5-28.

Beyerlin, U., and V. Holzer, "Conservation of Natural Resources", *Max Planck Encyclopedia of Public International Law [MPEPIL]*, October 2013.

Biermann, F., "Planetary Boundaries and Earth System Governance: Exploring the Links", *Ecological Economics*, 2012, Vol. 81, pp. 4-9.

Biermann, F., P. Pattberg and H. Van Asselt, "The Fragmentation of Global

Governance Architectures: A Framework for Analysis", *Global Environmental Politics*, Vol. 9, Issue 4, November 2009, pp.14-40.

Bikundo, E., "Aligning Means and Ends to Benefit Indigenous Peoples under the Convention on Biological Diversity and the Nagoya Protocol", in *Biodiversity, Genetic Resources and Intellectual Property: Developments in Access and Benefit Sharing*, K. Adhikari and C. Lawson (eds.), Routledge, 2018, pp. 33-40.

Bled, A., "Business Participation to Global Biodiversity Governance: Challenging Theory with Empirical Data", *Revista de gestão social e Ambiental*, 2009, Vol. 2, n° 3, pp. 75-91.

Böckenförde, M., "Biological Safety", *Max Planck Encyclopedia of Public International Law [MPEPIL]*, April 2011.

Bodansky, D., "International Law and the Protection of Biological Diversity", *Vanderbilt Journal of Transnational Law*, Vol. 28 (4), pp. 623-634.

Boisson de Chazournes, L., "International Environmental Law: Technical and Financial Assistance", in *Oxford Yearbook of International Environmental Law*, OUP, Oxford, 2007, pp. 947-973.

–, "La mise en œuvre du droit international dans le domaine de l'environnement : enjeux et défis", *Revue générale de droit international public*, 1/1995, pp. 37-76.

–, "Le Fonds pour l'environnement mondial : recherche et conquête de son identité", in *Annuaire français de droit international*, 1995, pp. 612-632.

–, "Le Panel d'inspection de la Banque mondiale : à propos de la complexification de l'espace public international", in *Revue générale de droit international public*, n° 1/2001, pp. 145-162.

–, "The Global Environment Facility (GEF) as a Pioneering Institution", *Philippine Law Journal*, Vol.11, 2002.

Boisson de Chazournes L., and M. M. Mbengue, "A propos des convergences entre le Protocole de Cartagena et les accords de l'OMC", *Revue québécoise de droit international*, 2007, Vol. 20-2, pp. 1-39.

Boisvert, V., and F.-D. Vivien, "Gestion et appropriation de la nature entre le nord et le sud. Trente ans de politiques internationales relatives à la biodiversité", *Revue Tiers Monde*, 2010/2, n° 202, pp. 15-32.

–, "Tiers monde et biodiversité : Tristes tropiques ou tropiques d'abondance ? La régulation internationale des ressources génétiques mise en perspective", *Revue Tiers Monde*, 2005/1, n° 181, pp. 185-206.

Bombay, P., "The Role of Environmental NGOs in International Environmental Conferences and Agreements: Some Important Features", *European Environmental Law Review*, July 2001, pp. 228-231.

Bonnin, M., "L'émergence des services environnementaux dans le droit international de l'environnement : une terminologie confuse", *VertigO – la revue électronique en sciences de l'environnement* [En ligne], Vol. 12, n° 3, décembre 2012.

Born, C.-H., "Le diable dans les détails : les défis de la régulation des marchés d'unités de biodiversité : l'exemple du 'Conservation Banking' dans le cadre de l'"endangered Species Act' (Etats-Unis)", *Revue Internationale de Droit Économique*, 2015, Vol. 29, n° 2, pp. 151-181.

Bourg, D., "L'impératif écologique", *Esprit*, décembre 2009, p. 7.

Boval, B., "L'Accord sur les droits de propriété intellectuelle qui touchent au commerce", in *La réorganisation mondiale des échanges*, Colloque de Nice de la SFDI, Pedone, Paris, 1996, pp. 131-152.

Boyd, D., "Les droits comme réponse à l'apocalypse écologique", *OpenGlobalRights*, 25 mars 2019.

Boyd, W, "Ways of Seeing in Environmental Law: How Deforestation Became an Object of Climate Governance", *Ecology Law Quarterly*, 2010, Vol. 37, pp. 843-916.

Boyle, A., "The Environmental Jurisprudence of the International Tribunal for the Law of the Sea", *International Journal of Marine & Coastal Law*, Sep. 2007, Vol. 22, Issue 3, pp. 369-381.

Bragdon, S. H., "National Sovereignty and Global Environmental Responsibility: Can the Tension Be Reconciled for the Conservation of Biological Biodiversity?", *Harvard International Law Journal*, 1992, Vol. 33, n° 2, pp. 381-392.
Breton, J.-M., "Biodiversité, écologie et droit", Etudes caribéennes [En ligne], Vol. 41, Décembre 2018.
Brilman, M., "Environmental Rights and the Legal Personality of the Amazon Region", *EJIL: Talk*, Blog of the European Society of International Law, April 24, 2018 [En ligne].
Broder, S. P., "International Governance of Ocean Fertilization and Other Marine Geoengineering Activities", *Ocean Law and Policy, 20 Years under Unclos*, 2017, pp. 304-343.
Brölmann, C., "Sustainable Development Goal 6 as a Game Changer for International Water Law", *ESIL Reflections* 7:5 (2018).
Brown-Weiss, E., "The Five International Treaties: A Living History", in E. Brown Weiss and H. K. Jacobson (eds.), *Engaging Countries: Strenthening Compliance with International Environmental Accords*, MIT Press, Cambridge and London, pp. 89-172.
Brunnee, J., "COPing with Consent: Law-Making under Multilateral Environmental Agreements", *Leiden Journal of International Law*, Vol. 15, 2002, pp. 1-52.
–, "Multilateral Environmental Agreements and the Compliance Continuum", in *Multilevel Governance of Global Environmental Science*, G. Winter (ed.), Cambridge University Press, Cambridge, 2006, pp. 387-406.
Buck, M., and C. Hamilton, "The Nagoya Protocol on Access to Genetic Resources and the Fair and Equitable Sharing of Benefits Arising from their Utilization to the Convention on Biological Diversity", *Review of European Community and International Environmental Law*, 2011, Vol. 20 (1), pp. 47-61.
Burhenne-Guilmin, F., "The Biosafety Protocol is Adopted in Montreal", *EPL*, 30/1-2 (2000), pp. 46-49.
Burke, A., "Blue Screen Biosphere: The Absent Presence of Biodiversity in International Law", *International Political Sociology* (2019) 13, pp. 333-351.
Butchart, S. H. *et al.*, "Global Biodiversity: Indicators of Recent Declines", *Science*, Vol. 328, 2010, pp. 1164-1168.
Caddel, R., " 'Only connect'? Regime Interaction and Global Biodiversity Conservation", in M. Bowman, P. Davies and E. Goodvin, *Research Handbook on Biodiversity and Law*, Edward Elgar, Cheltenham, 2016, pp. 437-471.
–, "Inter-Treaty Cooperation, Biodiversity Conservation and the Trade in Endangered Species", *Review of European Community and International Environmental Law* 22 (3) 2013, pp. 264-280.
Canivet, G., "Les influences croisées entre juridictions nationales et internationales : éloge de la 'bénévolence' des juges", *Revue de science criminelle et de droit pénal comparé*, 2005, pp. 799-817.
Carbonnier, J., "Effectivité et ineffectivité de la règle de droit", *L'année sociologique*, Vol. 9, 1957-58, pp. 3-17.
Cardoso, F. J., "Le régime juridique de la haute mer et la sauvegarde de la biodiversité dans le cadre des activités de pêche : le contexte international et l'approche de l'Union Européenne", *L'évolution et l'état actuel du droit international de la mer, Mélanges de droit de la mer offerts à Daniel Vignes*, Bruylant, Bruxelles, 2010, pp. 159-184.
Chami, R., T. Cosimano, C. Fullenkamp and S. Oztosun, "Nature's Solution to Climate Change. A Strategy to Protect Whales Can Limit Greenhouse Gases and Global Warming", *Finance and Development*, December 2019, pp. 34-38.
Chandler, M., "The Biodiversity Convention: Selected Issues of Interest to the International Lawyer", *Colorado Journal of International Environmental law and Policy*, 1993, Vol. 4, pp. 141-175.
Chassany, J.-P., and J.-M. Salles, "Potentiels et limites des paiements pour services environnementaux dans les programmes de lutte contre la désertification", Sécheresse 23, 2012, pp. 177-184.

Chemillier-Gendreau, M., "Le droit international et le rapport des sociétés modernes à la nature", *L'Homme et la société*, Année 1989, Vol. 91-92, pp. 31-43.

Chen, J. M., "The Fragile Menagerie: Biodiversity Loss, Climate Change, and the Law", *Indiana Law Journal*, Vol. 93, Issue 2 (Spring 2018), pp. 303-368.

Chevallier, J., "Mondialisation du droit ou droit de la mondialisation?", in *Le droit saisi par la mondialisation*, C.-A. Morand (ed.) Bruxelles, Bruylant, 2001, pp. 37-61.

Churchill, R. R., and G. Ulfstein, "Autonomous Institutional Arrangements in Multilateral Environmental Agreements: A Little-Noticed Phenomenom in International Law", *American Journal of International Law*, Vol. 94, 2000, pp. 623-659.

Collot, P. A., "La protection des savoirs traditionnels, du droit international de la propriété intellectuelle au système de protection *sui generis*", *Droit et cultures*, 2007, Vol. 53, pp. 181-209.

Coombe, R. J., "Intellectual Property, Human Rights & (and) Sovereignty: New Dilemmas in International Law Posed by Recognition of Indigenous Knowledge and the Conservation of Biodiversity", *Indiana Journal of Global Legal Studies*, Vol. 6, Issue 1 (Fall 1998), pp. 59-116.

Costanza, R., R. d'Arge, R. De Groot, S. Farber, M. Grasso, B. Hannon, K. Limburg, S. Naeem, R. V. Oneill, J. Paruelo, R. G. Raskin, P. Sutton and M. Van den Belt, "The Value of the World's Ecosystem Services and Natural Capital", *Nature*, 1997, Vol. 387, pp. 253-260.

Craig, R. K., "Protecting International Marine Biodiversity: International Treaties and National Systems of Marine Protected Areas", *Journal of Land Use & Environmental Law*, Spring 2005, Vol. 20, Issue 2, pp. 333-369.

Daccache, M., "Questioning Biodiversity Governance through its Articulations", *Science Technology & Society*, 2013, Vol. 18, pp. 51-62.

Daval, M., "Un nouveau 'cadre mondial pour la biodiversité' : enjeux et perspectives", *Revue juridique de l'environnement*, 2023/2, Vol. 48, pp. 319-336.

David, V., "La lente consécration de la nature, sujet de droit : le monde est-il enfin Stone?", *Revue juridique de l'environnement*, 2012, 3, pp. 469-485.

–, "La nouvelle vague des droits de la nature. La personnalité juridique reconnue aux fleuves Whanganui, Gange et Yamuna", *Revue juridique de l'environnement*, 2017, n° 3, pp. 409-424.

Davidson, N., and D. Coates, "The Ramsar Convention and Synergies for Operationalizing the Convention on Biological Diversity's Ecosystem Approach for Wetlands Conservation and Wise Use", *Journal of International Wildlife Law and Policy*, Vol. 14, n° 3, 2011, pp. 199-205.

De Klemm C., "Conservation of Species, the Need for a New Approach", in *EPL*, Vol. 9, 1982, pp. 117-128.

De Klemm, C., "Des 'Red Data Books' à la diversité biologique", in *A Law for the Environnement*, Mélanges en l'honneur de W. E. Burhenne, UICN, Gland, 1994, pp. 173-179.

–, "Des qualifications et des règles fondées sur l'appropriation permettent-elles de protéger l'environnement?", in *Le droit et l'environnement*, Actes des Journées de l'environnement du CNRS, 30 novembre-1er décembre 1988, PIREN, CNRS, Paris, 1989, pp. 233-244.

–, "Further Accessions to Convention?", in *EPL*, Vol. 20, 1990, n° 1/2, pp. 25-27.

–, "L'évolution de la protection de la faune et de la flore marines dans les conventions internationales", in *Droit de l'environnement marin, développements récents*, Economica, Paris, 1988, pp. 24-49.

–, "La conservation de la diversité biologique, obligation des Etats et devoir des citoyens", in *RJE*, 4/1989, pp. 397-408.

–, "La Convention de Ramsar et la conservation des zones humides côtières, particulièrement en Méditerranée", in *RJE*, 4/1990, pp. 577-598.

–, "La gestion internationale des populations d'oiseaux migrateurs", in *RJE*, n° 3-4, 1976, pp. 115-121.

–, "La protection des zones d'intérêt écologique", in *Tendances actuelles de la politique et du droit de l'environnement*, M. Bothe (ed.), IUCN, Gland, Suisse, 1981, pp. 169-197.

–, "Le patrimoine naturel de l'humanité", in *L'avenir du droit international de l'environnement*, colloque de l'Académie de droit international de La Haye, 12-14-XI-1985, Martinus Nijhoff Publishers, Boston, Lancaster, 1985, pp. 117-150.

–, "Les apports du droit comparé", in *Le dommage écologique en droit interne, communautaire et comparé*, Colloque de la SFDE, coll. Droit et économie de l'environnement, Economica, 1992, pp. 143-164.

–, "Migratory Species in International Law", in *Natural Resources Journal*, 1989, 29 (4), pp. 935-978.

–, "Migratory Species. A Review of Existing International Instruments", in *EPL*, Vol. 15, 1985, pp. 81-91.

–, "Principes juridiques applicables à la gestion des espèces migratrices", in *Environmental Policy and Law*, Vol. 2, 1976, pp. 16-20.

–, "Species and Habitat Preservation: An International Task", in *EPL*, n° 1, 1975, pp. 10-16.

–, "The Conservation of Migratory Animals Through International Law", in *Natural Resources Journal*, 1972, Vol. 2, n° 2, pp. 271-277.

–, "The Management of Migratory Game Birds and International Law in Proceeding of First Technical Meeting on West Palearctic Migratory Bird Management", Proceedings of First Technical Meetings on Western Palearctic Migratory Bird Management, Paris, 12-13 décembre 1977, pub. IWRB, Paris, 12-13 Dec. 1977, pp. 168-175.

–, "The Problem of Migratory Species in International Law", in *Green Globe Yearbook*, Fridjhoff Nansen Institute, Norway, Oxford University Press, 1994, pp. 67-78.

De Klemm, C., and S. Maljean-Dubois, "L'Accord du 16 juin 1995 relatif à la conservation des oiseaux d'eau migrateurs d'Afrique-Eurasie", *Revue juridique de l'environnement*, n° 1/1998, pp. 5-30.

De Klemm, C., and J. Olivier, "Le rôle des ONG dans le droit de l'environnement : l'exemple de l'UICN", *Les Nations Unies et la protection de l'environnement : la promotion d'un développement durable*, Septièmes rencontres internationales d'Aix-en-Provence, S. Maljean-Dubois and R. Mehdi (eds.), Pedone, 1999, pp. 175-186.

De la Fayette, L. A., "A New Regime for the Conservation and Sustainable Use of Marine Biodiversity and Genetic Resources Beyond the Limits of National Jurisdiction", *International Journal of Marine and Coastal Law*, Vol. 24, Issue 2 (2009), pp. 221-280.

De Lucia, V., "Rethinking the Conservation of Marine Biodiversity Beyond National Jurisdiction: From 'Not Undermine' to Ecosystem-Based Governance", *ESIL Reflections* 8:4 (2019).

De Sadeleer, N., "De la protection à la sauvegarde de la biodiversité", in Ecologie politique, n° 9, printemps 1994, pp. 25-48.

–, "Le principe de précaution : du slogan à la règle de droit", *Droit de l'environnement*, avril 2000, n° 77, pp. 14-15.

De Schutter, O., "Préface", in *Biodiversité. Quand les politiques européennes menacent le vivant. Connaître la nature pour mieux légiférer*, I. Trépant, ed. Yves Michel, Gap, 2017, pp. 13-18.

Deleuil, T., "La CITES et la protection internationale de la biodiversité", *Revue juridique de l'environnement*, 2011, 36 (1), pp. 45-62.

Demogue, R., "Le sujet de droit", *Revue trimestrielle de droit civil*, 1909, pp. 611-655.

Dias Varella, M., "Le rôle des organisations non-gouvernementales dans le développement du droit international de l'environnement", *Journal du droit international*, 1/2005, pp. 41-76.

Diaz, A. "Permanent Sovereignty over Natural Resources", in *EPL,* 24/4, June 1994, pp. 157-173.
Doelle, M., "Linking the Kyoto Protocol and Other Multilateral Environmental Agreements: From Fragmentation to Integration?", *Journal of Environmental Law and Practice*, 2004, Vol. 14, pp. 75-104.
Dolzer, R., "Global Environment Facility (GEF)", *Max Planck Encyclopedia of Public International Law [MPEPIL]*, November 2010.
Douma, W. T., "The Beef Hormones Dispute and the Use of National Standards under WTO Law", *European Energy and Environmental Law Review*, 1999, Issue 5, pp. 137-144.
Doussan, I., "Les services écologiques : un nouveau concept pour le droit de l'environnement?", in *La responsabilité environnementale, prévention, imputation, réparation*, C. Cans (ed.), Paris, Dalloz, 2009 pp. 125-141.
–, "Nature à vendre", in *Etudes foncières*, n° 154, 2011, pp. 10-14.
Doyen, L., P. Roch and M. Tichit, "Concepts et formalismes de la durabilité pour la biodiversité et les services écosystémiques. Perspectives interdisciplinaires", *Valeurs de la biodiversité et services écosystémiques*, Editions Quæ, 2016, pp. 175-190.
Dubos, O., and J.-P. Marguénaud, "La protection internationale et européenne des animaux", *Pouvoirs,* 2009, n° 4, Vol. 131, pp. 113-126.
Duléry, F., "L'Affaire du lac Lanoux", *Revue générale de droit international public*, tome LXII, 1958, pp. 469-514.
Dupont, V., and M. Lucas, "La loi pour la reconquête de la biodiversité : vers un renforcement du régime juridique de la compensation écologique?", *Cahiers droit, sciences et technologies*, Vol. 7, 2017, pp. 143-165.
Dupuy, P.-M., "A propos des mésaventures de la responsabilité internationale des États dans ses rapports avec la protection de l'environnement", in *Les hommes et l'environnement quels droits pour le XXIe siècle ? Mélanges en hommage a Alexandre Kiss*, Paris, Frison-Roche, 1998, pp. 269-282.
–, "La frontière et l'environnement", in *La frontière*, Colloque de la SFDI, Pedone, Paris, 1980, pp. 268-286.
–, "Où en est le droit international de l'environnement à la fin du siècle?", *Revue générale de droit international public* (1997), Vol. 101, n° 4, p.873-903.
Dupuy R.-J., "Le statut de l'Antarctique", in *AFDI,* 1958, pp. 196-229.
Dutreuil, S., "Is the Decisive Issue in Geoengineering Debates Really One of Representation of Nature? Gaia Against (or with?) Prometheus?", *Carbon & Climate Law Review*, Vol. 13, Issue 2, 2019, pp. 94-103.
Dutton, P. H., and D. Squires, "Reconciling Biodiversity with Fishing: A Holistic Strategy for Pacific Sea Turtle Recovery", *Ocean Development and International Law*, Vol. 39, Issue 2 (2008), pp. 200-222.
Duțu, M., "Le protocole sur la conservation et l'utilisation durable de la biodiversité des Carpates : une nouvelle étape dans le développement du droit international de la montagne", *Revue juridique de l'environnement,* n° 3, 2011, pp. 305-316.
Duvic-Paoli, L.-A., "The Intergovernmental Science-Policy Platform for Biodiversity and Ecosystem Services or the Framing of Scientific Knowledge within the Law of Sustainability", *International Community Law Review*, 2017, Vol. 19, No. 2-3, pp. 231-269.
Farber, D. A., "Separated at Birth: Addressing the Twin Crises of Biodiversity and Climate Change", *Ecology Law Quarterly*, Vol. 42, Issue 4, 2015, pp. 841-888.
Farrier, D., and L. Tucker, "Wise Use of Wetlands under the Ramsar Convention: A Challenge for Meaningful Implementation of International Law", *Journal of Environmental Law*, 2000, 12 (1), pp. 21-42.
Fauchille, P., "Protection des animaux en Afrique. Convention de Londres du 19 mai 1900", Chronique des faits internationaux, *RGDIP,* 1900, pp. 520-523.
Filoche, G., "Les connaissances, innovations et pratiques traditionnelles en matière de biodiversité : un kaléidoscope juridique / Traditional Knowledge, Innovations,

and Practices Concerning Biodiversity: A Legal Kaleidoscope", *Droit et société*, 1985, Vol. 72, pp. 433-456.

Francioni, F., "Natural Resources and Human Rights", *Research Handbook on International Law and Natural Resources*, Edward Elgar, Cheltenham, 2016, E. Morgera and K. Kulovesi (eds.), pp. 66-85.

Freestone, D., "Fisheries, Commissions and Organizations", *Max Planck Encyclopedia of Public International Law [MPEPIL]*, December 2010.

Freestone, D., and F. Bulger, "Sargasso Sea Commission: An Innovative Approach to the Conservation of Areas Beyond National Jurisdiction", *Ocean Yearbook*, Vol. 30, 2016, pp. 80-90.

Freestone, D., and K. Killerlain Morrison, "The Signing of the Hamilton Declaration on Collaboration for the Conservation of the Sargasso Sea: A New Paradigm for High Seas Conservation?", *Conserving Biodiversity in Areas Beyond National Jurisdiction*, 2019, pp. 159-176.

Futhazar, G., "The Diffusion of the Strategic Plan for Biodiversity and its Aichi Biodiversity Targets within the Biodiversity Cluster: An Illustration of Current Trends in the Global Governance of Biodiversity and Ecosystems", *Yearbook of international Environmental Law*, Vol. 25, No. 1 (2015), pp. 133-166.

Gambardella, S., "Le processus de Kobé : un vecteur de circulation des normes et des acteurs dans un contexte de gouvernance internationale fragmentée", in Sandrine Maljean-Dubois (ed.), *Circulations de normes et réseaux d'acteurs dans la gouvernance internationale de l'environnement*, coll. Confluence des droits, DICE, Aix-en-Provence, 2017, pp. 147-164.

–, "Le rôle des organisations régionales de gestion des pêches dans la lutte contre la pêche illicite, non déclarée et non règlementée", *AFDI*, Vol. LXIV, 2018, pp. 577-591.

Gervais, A., "La sentence arbitrale du 16 novembre 1957 réglant le litige franco-espagnol relatif à l'utilisation des eaux du Lac Lanoux", *Annuaire français de droit international*, 1957, pp. 178-180.

Gillespie, A., "Biodiversity, Indigenous Peoples and Equity in International Law", *New Zealand Journal of Environmental Law*, 2000, Vol. 4, pp. 1-47.

Glennon, M. J., "Has International Law Failed the Elephant?", *AJIL*, Vol. 84, Issue 1, January 1990, pp. 1-43.

Godard, O., "Stratégies industrielles et conventions d'environnement : de l'univers stabilisé aux univers controversés", *Environnement, Économie,* INSEE méthodes, n° 39-40, pp. 145-174.

Gomar, J. O. V., L. C. Stringer and J. Paavola, "Regime Complexes and National Policy Coherence: Experiences in the Biodiversity Cluster", *Global Governance*, Vol. 20, Issue 1 (January-March 2014), pp. 119-146.

Gosselin, M., "Biodiversity Values in International Laws and Conventions", *Sciences, Eaux & Territoires*, Vol. 2011, Issue 3*bis*, pp. 9-9.

Grandbois, M., "Le droit de l'environnement et le commerce international : quelques enjeux déterminants", *Les cahiers de droit*, Vol. 40, n° 3, September 1999, pp. 545–590.

Granjou, C., and I. Mauz, "Gouverner par les scénarios ? Comment les institutions environnementales anticipent l'avenir de la biodiversité", *Quaderni*, 2011/3 (n° 76), pp. 5-11.

Green Nylen, N., "To Achieve Biodiversity Goals, the New Forest Service Planning Rule Needs Effective Mandates for Best Available Science and Adaptive Management", *Ecology Law Quarterly*, Vol. 38, Issue 2 (2011), pp. 241-292.

Groen, L., "Explaining European Union Effectiveness (Goal Achievement) in the Convention on Biological Diversity: The importance of Diplomatic Engagement", *International Environmental Agreements: Politics, Law and Economics*, February 2019, Vol. 19, Issue 1, pp. 69-87.

Guillaume, G., "Le statut juridique de l'Antarctique", in *Les grandes crises du droit*, ed. du Seuil, Paris, 1994, pp. 127-153.

Gupta, A., and A. Orsini, "Liability, Redress and the Cartagena Protocol", *Elgar*

Encyclopedia of Environmental Law, Edward Elgar, Cheltenham, 2017, Vol. 3, pp. 445-454.

Gutiérrez, C., and L. Víctor, "La conservation et l'exploitation durable de la biodiversité en Méditerranée", in *Droit international de la mer et droit de l'Union Européenne: cohabitation, confrontation, coopération?*, Colloque International, Musée Océanographique de Monaco, 17 et 18 octobre 2013, Pedone, Paris, 2014, pp. 291-320.

Haas, P., "Introduction: Epistemic Communities and International Policy Coordination", *International Organization*, Vol. 46, 1992, pp. 1-35.

Hajjami, N., "CIJ, Certaines activités menées par le Nicaragua dans la région frontalière *(Costa Rica c. Nicaragua)*, arrêt du 2 février 2018, Indemnisation", AFDI, Vol. LXIII, 2017, pp. 163-176.

Hallmann, C. A. *et al.*, "More Than 75 Percent Decline over 27 Years in Total Flying Insect Biomass in Protected Areas", *PLOS One*, 18 October 2017.

Hamman, E., "Bilateral Agreements for the Protection of Migratory Birdlife: The Implementation of the China-Australia Migratory Bird Agreement (CAMBA)", *Asia Pacific Journal of Environmental Law*, Vol. 22, n° 1, 2019, pp. 137-159.

Harrop, S. R., and D. J. Pritchard, "A Hard Instrument Goes Soft: The Implications of the Convention on Biological Diversity's Current Trajectory", *Global Environmental Change*, 2011, Vol. 21, pp. 474-480.

Hassanali, K., "Approaching the Implementing Agreement to UNCLOS on Biodiversity in ABNJ: Exploring Favorable Outcomes for CARICOM", *Marine Policy*, December 2018, Vol. 98, pp. 92-96,

Hecht, J. E., and B. Orlando, "Dialogues: Can the Kyoto Protocol Support Biodiversity Conservation? Legal and Financial Challenges", *The Environmental Law Reporter*, 2000, Vol. XXVIII, No. 9.

Herkenrath, P., "The Implementation of the Convention on Biological Diversity – A Non-Government Perspective Ten Years on", *Review of European, Comparative and International Environmental Law*, 2002, Vol. 11, pp. 29-37.

Hermitte, M.-A., "Artificialisation de la nature et droit(s) du vivant", *La lettre du Collège de France* [En ligne], 44 | 2017-2018.

–, "La convention sur la biodiversité biologique et les droits intellectuels des peuples autochtones: une lacune française", *revue juridique de l'environnement*, 2007, 32(1), pp. 191-213.

–, "La convention sur la diversité biologique", *Annuaire français de droit international*, 1992, Vol. 38, pp. 844-870.

Hermitte, M.-A., I. Doussan, S. Mabile, S. Maljean-Dubois, C. Noiville and F. Bellivier, "La convention sur la diversité biologique a quinze ans", *Annuaire français de droit international*, 2006, Vol. 52, pp. 351-390.

Hermitte, M.-A., S. Maljean-Dubois and E. Truilhé-Marengo, "Actualités de la convention sur la diversité biologique: science et politique, équité, biosécurité", *Annuaire français de droit international*, 2011, Vol. 57, pp. 399-437.

Hey, E., "Wetlands", *Max Planck Encyclopedia of Public International Law [MPEPIL]*, January 2011.

Hufty, M., "La gouvernance internationale de la biodiversité", *Etudes internationales*, Vol. 32, n° 1, 2001, pp. 5-29.

Huneman, P., "Introduction. Diversités théoriques et empiriques de la notion de biodiversité. Enjeux philosophiques, éthiques et scientifiques", *La biodiversité en question*, ed. Matériologiques, 2014, pp. 13-28.

Ilbert, H., and S. Louafi, "Biodiversité et ressources génétiques : la difficulté de la constitution d'un régime international hybride", *Revue Tiers Monde*, 45 (177), 2004, pp. 107-127.

Iles, A., "Rethinking Differential Obligations: Equity under the Biodiversity Convention", *Leiden Journal of International Law*, Vol. 16, Issue 2 (June 2003), pp. 217-252.

Iorns Magallanes, C. J., "Nature as an Ancestor: Two Examples of Legal Personality for Nature in New Zealand", *Vertigo*, Vol. 22, September 2015 [En ligne].

Ituarte-Lima, C., "Transformative Biodiversity Law and 2030 Agenda: Mainstreaming Biodiversity and Justice Through Human Rights", *Risk, Resilience, Inequality and Environmental Law*, 2017, pp. 84-107.

Jacquemont, F., and A. Caparrós, "The Convention on Biological Diversity and the Climate Change Convention 10 Years After Rio: Towards a Synergy of the Two Regimes?", *Review of European Community and International Environmental Law*, Vol. 11 (2), 2002, pp. 169-180.

Jerome, J. S., "How International Legal Agreements Speak About Biodiversity", *Anthropology Today*, Vol. 14, No. 6 (Dec. 1998), pp. 7-9.

Jinnah, S, "Marketing Linkages: Secretariat Governance of the Climate-Biodiversity Interface", *Global Environmental Politics*, 2011, Vol. 11, pp. 23-43.

Johannsdottir, A., I. Cresswell and P. Bridgewater, "The Current Framework for International Governance of Biodiversity: Is It Doing More Harm Than Good?", *Review of European Community and International Environmental Law*, 2010, Vol. 19, pp. 139-149.

Jones, K. R. et al., "One-Third of Global Protected Land is under Intense Human Pressure", *Science*, 18 May 2018, Vol. 360, Issue 6390, pp. 788-791.

Joyner, C. C., and Z. Tyler, "Marine Conservation Versus International Free Trade: Reconciling Dolphins with Tuna and Sea Turtles with Shrimp", *Ocean Development & International Law*, Jan-June 2000, Vol. 31, Issue 1/2, pp. 127-150.

Kaczka, D., "WTO's Shrimp-Sea Turtle Decision", *Review of European Community and International Environmental Law*, Vol. 7 (E 3), pp. 308-311.

Kameri-Mbote, A., and P. Cullet, "Agro-Biodiversity and International Law – A Conceptual Framework", *Journal of Environmental Law*, Vol. 11, Issue 2 (1999), pp. 257-280.

Kamto, M., "Les conventions régionales sur la conservation de la nature et des ressources naturelles en Afrique et leur mise en œuvre", *Revue juridique de l'environnement*, 1991/4, pp. 417-442.

Karlsson-Vinkhuyzen, S. I., M. Groff, P. A. Tamás, A. L. Dahl, M. Harder and G. Hassall, "Entry into Force and Then? The Paris Agreement and State Accountability", *Climate Policy*, Vol. 18, 2017, pp. 593-599.

Karsenty, A., "REDD+ : les bases ambigues du 'paiement aux résultats' obtenu par le Gabon", *WillAgri*, 7 octobre 2019.

Kearns, B., "When Bonobos Meet Guerillas: Preserving Biodiversity on the Battlefield", *Georgetown International Environmental Law Review*, Vol. 24 (2), pp. 123-168.

Keohane, R. O., and D. G. Victor, "Cooperation and Discord in Global Climate Policy", *Nature Climate Change*, 9 May 2016, pp. 570-575.

–, "The Regime Complex for Climate Change", *Perspectives on Politics*, Vol. 9, No. 1, March 2011, pp. 7-23.

Kerbrat, Y., and S. Maljean-Dubois, "La contribution en demie teinte de la CIJ au droit international de l'environnement dans les affaires Costa Rica-Nicaragua", *Journal du droit international*, novembre 2018, pp. 1133-1154.

–, "La Cour internationale de justice face aux enjeux de protection de l'environnement : réflexions critiques sur l'arrêt du 20 avril 2010", *Usines de pâte à papier sur le fleuve Uruguay (Argentine c. Uruguay)*, RGDIP, n° 1, 2011, tome CXV, pp. 39-75.

Kerbrat Y., and S. Maljean-Dubois, "La reconnaissance du préjudice écologique par la Cour internationale de Justice", *Droit de l'environnement*, mars 2018, n° 265, pp. 90-91.

Keune, H. et al., "One Health and Biodiversity", *Transforming Biodiversity Governance*, I. J. Visseren-Hamakers (ed.), CUP, 2022, pp. 93-114.

Kim, J. A., "Regime Interplay: The Case of Biodiversity and Climate Change", *Global Environmental Change*, Vol. 14, Issue 4, December 2004, pp. 315-324.

Kim, R. E., "Is a New Multilateral Environmental Agreement on Ocean Acidification

Necessary?", *Review of European Community and International Environmental Law*, (2012) 21, pp. 243-258.
Kimball, L. A., "Institutional Linkages between the Convention on Biological Diversity and Other International Conventions", *Review of European Community and International Environmental Law*, 1997, Vol. 6, No. 3, pp 239-248.
Kirk, E. A., "The Ecosystem Approach and the Search for an Objective and Content for the Concept of Holistic Ocean Governance", *Ocean Development & International Law*, 2015, Vol. 46:1, pp. 33-49.
Klein, C. B. "New Leadership Needed: The Convention on Biological Diversity", *Emory International Law Review*, 2017, Vol. 31, No. 1, pp. 135-165.
Klein, N., and N. Hughes, "National Litigation and International Law: Repercussions for Australia's Protection of Marine Resources", *Melbourne University Law Review*, 33 (1), 2009, pp. 163-204.
Kleining, B., "Biodiversity Protection under the Habitats Directive: Is Habitat Banking Our New Hope", *Environmental Law Review*, Vol. 19, Issue 2, June 2017, pp. 113-125.
Koester, V., "The Biodiversity Convention Negotiation Process and Some Comments on the Outcome", *Environmental Policy and Law*, 1997, 27, pp. 175-192.
Koetz, T., K. N. Farrell and P. Bridgewater, "Building Better Science-Policy Interfaces for International Environmental Governance: Assessing Potential within the Intergovernmental Platform for Biodiversity and Ecosystem Services", *International Environmental Agreements*, March 2012, Vol. 12, pp. 1-21.
Kohler, F., "Diversité culturelle et diversité biologique : une approche critique fondée sur l'exemple brésilien", *Natures Sciences Sociétés*, 2/2011, Vol. 19, pp. 113-124.
Koivurova, T., and R. Caddell, "Managing Biodiversity Beyond National Jurisdiction in the Changing Arctic", *AJIL Unbound*, 2018, Vol. 112, pp. 134-138.
Kolb, R., "Mondialisation et droit international", *Relations internationales*, 05/3, n° 123, pp. 69-86.
Koskenniemi, M., "Breach of Treaty or Non-Compliance? Reflections on the Enforcement of the Montreal Protocol", in *Yearbook of International Environmental Law, Yearbook of International Environmental Law*, Vol. 3, Issue 1, 1992, pp. 123-162.
Kotzé, J., "The Sustainable Development Goals: An Existential Critique Alongside Three New-Millennial Analytical Paradigms", in D. French and L. J. Kotzé (eds.), *Sustainable Development Goals: Law, Theory and Implementation*, Edward Elgar, 2018, pp. 41-65.
Kundis Craig, R., "Protecting International Marine Biodiversity: International Treaties and National Systems of Marine Protected Areas", *Journal of Land Use & Environmental Law*, 20 (2), pp. 333-369.
Kwiatkowska, B., "Southern Bluefin Tuna (*New Zealand* v. *Japan*; *Australia* v. *Japan*), Order on Provisional Measures (ITLOS Cases Nos. 3 and 4)", *The American Journal of International Law* (2000), 94 (1), pp. 150-155.
Laghmani, S., "Droit international et droits internes : vers un renouveau du *jus gentium* ?", *Droit international et droits internes. Développements récents*, R. Ben Achour and S. Laghmani (eds.), Pedone, Paris, 1999, pp. 23-44.
Lambert Abdelgawad, E., "La Cour européenne des droits de l'homme et le traitement de la connaissance scientifique sur la nocivité des ondes électromagnétiques, produits chimiques et autres activités polluantes", *VertigO – la revue électronique en sciences de l'environnement* [En ligne], Hors-série 27, décembre 2016.
Lanfranchi, M.-P., "Gestion durable des ressources minérales marines et droit international", *Journal du droit international*, 2019, pp. 717-738.
–, "Le principe des responsabilités communes, mais différenciées dans les instruments internationaux relatifs à la protection de la biodiversité", *Droit international et développement*, Colloque de Lyon de la Société française de droit international, Pedone, Paris, 1995, pp. 387-397.
Lanfranchi, M.-P., and S. Maljean-Dubois, "Le contrôle du juge international. Un jeu

d'ombres et de lumières", in *L'effectivité du droit européen de l'environnement. Contrôle de la mise en œuvre et sanction du non-respect*, S. Maljean-Dubois (ed.), La Documentation française, Paris 2000, pp. 247-284.

Le Bœuf, R., "Différend en mer de Chine méridionale *(Philippines c. Chine)*, Sentence arbitrale du 12 juillet 2016", *Annuaire français de droit international*, 2016, pp. 159-182.

Le Bot, O., "Les grandes évolutions du régime juridique de l'animal en Europe : constitutionnalisation et déréification", *Revue québécoise de droit international*, 2011, Vol. 24-1, pp. 249-257.

Le Guyader, H., "La biodiversité : un concept flou ou une réalité scientifique ?", *Le Courrier de l'environnement*, n° 55, 2008, pp. 11-12.

Leary, D., "The Standing of Civil Society to Enforce Commonwealth Environmental Law under Section 475 of the Environment Protection and Biodiversity Conservation Act and its International Implications: The Japanese Whaling Case and the Law of Unintended Consequences", *Macquarie Law Journal*, 01 January 2008 (8), pp. 153-178.

Levantis, E., "Vers une application efficace de la Convention de Berne", *Revue européenne de droit de l'environnement*, 2002, 6-1 pp. 42-47.

Lévêque, C., "Chapitre 8. Biodiversité : mythes et dénis de réalité", in E. Casetta *et al.* (ed.), *La biodiversité en question*, editions Matériologiques "Sciences & philosophie", 2014, pp. 209-228.

Lim, M., "Is Water Different from Biodiversity? Governance Criteria for the Effective Management of Transboundary Resources", *Review of European Comparative & International Environmental Law*, April 2014, Vol. 23, Issue 1, pp. 96-110.

–, "Strengthening the Legal and Institutional Effectiveness of Transboundary Biodiversity Conservation in the 'Heart of Borneo'", *Asia Pacific Journal of Environmental Law*, 2014, Vol. 17, pp. 65-89.

Louafi, S., "Epistemic Community and International Governance of Biological Diversity: A Reinterpretation of the Role of IUCN", in S. Thoyer and B. Martimor-Asso (eds.) *Participation for Sustainability in Trade*, Abingdon, Oxon: Ashgate, 2007, pp. 111-120.

Lovejoy, T., "Changes in Biological Diversity", in *The Global 2000 Report to the President*, Vol. 2, 1980.

Lugo, E., "Ecosystem Services, the Millenium Ecosystem Assessment, and the Conceptual Difference between Benefits Provided by Ecosystems and Benefits Provided by People", *Journal of Land Use*, 23 (2), 2008, pp. 243-262.

MacKenzie, C. P., "Lessons from Forestry for International Environmental Law", *Review of European Community and International Environmental Law*, 2012, Vol. 21, Issue 2, pp. 114-126.

Magda, D., I. Doussan, "Quelle(s) éthique(s) pour les relations hommes-biodiversité ?", *Natures Sciences Sociétés*, 2018/1, Vol. 26, pp. 60-66.

Mahiou, A., "Procédures de décision et droit international", in *Revue Tiers Monde*, tome XXXIII, n° 130, avril-juin 1992, pp. 429-453.

Mair, S. *et al.*, "A Critical Review of the Role of Indicators in Implementing the Sustainable Development Goals", in W. Leal Filho (ed.), *Handbook of Sustainability Science and Research* (Springer, 2017), pp. 41-56.

Maljean-Dubois, S., "Biodiversité, biotechnologies, biosécurité. Le droit international désarticulé", *Journal du droit international*, n° 4/2000, pp. 947-994.

–, "La contribution de l'Union africaine à la protection de la nature en Afrique : de la Convention d'Alger à la Convention de Maputo", in *Liber Amicorum* Raymond Ranjeva, *L'Afrique et le droit international. Variations sur l'organisation internationale*, Pedone, Paris, 2013, pp. 205-218.

–, "Le spectre de l'isolation clinique : quelle articulation entre les règles de l'OMC et les autres règles du droit international ?", in *Revue européenne de droit de l'environnement*, n° 2/2008, pp. 159-176.

Maljean-Dubois, S., and M. Wemaëre, "Climate Change and Biodiversity", in

Encyclopedia of Environmental Law – Biodiversity and Nature Protection Law, Edward Elgar Publishing, J. Razzaque and E. Morgera (eds.), 2016, pp. 295-308.

Maris, V., V. Devictor, I. Doussan and A. Béchet, "Chapitre 1. Les valeurs en question", in Philip Roche *et al.* (ed.), *Valeurs de la biodiversité et services écosystémiques* Editions Quæ "Update Sciences & Technologies", 2016, pp. 21-38.

Martin, J.-C., "La pratique de la Commission d'indemnisation des Nations Unies pour l'Irak en matière de réclamations environnementales", in Colloque de la Société française de droit international d'Aix-en-Provence, *Le droit international face aux enjeux environnementaux*, Pedone, Paris, 2010, pp. 257-274.

Mashaw, J. L., "Accountability and Institutional Design: Some Thoughts on the Grammar of Governance", in M. Dowdle (ed.), *Public Accountability: Designs, Dilemmas and Experiences*, Cambridge University Press, pp. 115-156.

Maurel, R., "Une décision historique : l'indemnisation du dommage environnemental par la Cour internationale de Justice, Note sous l'arrêt de la CIJ du 2 février 2018, Certaines activités menées par le Nicaragua dans la région frontalière *(Costa Rica c. Nicaragua)*", *La Revue du Centre Michel de l'Hospital – éd. électronique*, Centre Michel de l'Hospital, 2018, pp. 51-61.

Mauro, F., and P. D. Hardison, "Traditional Knowledge of Indigenous and Local Communities: International Debate and Policy Initiatives", *Ecological Applications*, 2000, 10 (5), pp. 1263-1269.

Mekouar, M. A., "Un secrétariat dynamique pour la Convention de Maputo, aiguillon de sa vitalité", *Revue Africaine de Droit de l'Environnement-African Journal of Environmental Law*, n° 4/2019, pp. 27-38.

Merson, J., "Bio-Prospecting or Bio-Piracy: Intellectual Property Rights and Biodiversity in a Colonial and Postcolonial Context", *Osiris*, Vol. 15, Nature and Empire: Science and the Colonial Enterprise, 2000, pp. 282-296.

Michallet, I., "Cour Européenne des droits de l'homme et biodiversité", *L'environnement et la Convention européenne des droits de l'homme*, L. Robert (ed.), Bruylant, 2013, pp. 91-102.

Michallet, I., "L'Accord sur la conservation des albatros et des pétrels : la protection de la biodiversité marine face à l'industrie de la pêche", *Revue juridique de l'environnement*, n° 6, 2007, pp. 187-201.

–, "La notion de diversité biologique en droit international", in *La diversité dans la gouvernance internationale. Perspectives culturelles, écologiques et juridiques*, V. Négri (ed.), Bruylant, Bruxelles, 2016, pp. 75-95.

Molenaar, E. J., "Managing Biodiversity in Areas Beyond National Jurisdiction", *International Journal of Marine and Coastal Law*, Vol. 22, Issue, April 2007, pp. 89-124.

Mongruel, R., P. Méral, I. Doussan and H. Levrel, "L'institutionnalisation de l'approche par les services écosystémiques : dimensions scientifiques, politiques et juridiques", in *Valeurs de la biodiversité et services écosystémiques*, P. Roche *et al.* (ed.), Editions Quæ, Paris, 2016, pp. 191-216.

Morgera, E, "Faraway, So Close: A Legal Analysis of the Increasing Interactions between the Convention on Biological Diversity and Climate Change Law", (2011) 2, *Climate Law*, pp. 85-115.

–, "The Need for an International Legal Concept of Fair and Equitable Benefit Sharing", *European Journal of International Law*, Vol. 27, n° 2, 2016, pp. 353-383.

–, "Against All Odds: The Contribution of the Convention on Biological Diversity to International Human Rights Law", in *Unity and Diversity of International Law: Essays in Honour of Professor Pierre-Marie Dupuy*, D. Alland et al. (ed.), 2014, pp. 983-995.

–, "Dawn of a New Day: The Evolving Relationship between the Convention on Biological Diversity and International Human Rights Law", *Wake Forest Law Review*, 2018, Vol. 53, No. 4, 2018, pp. 691-712.

–, "No Need to Reinvent the Wheel for a Human Rights-Based Approach to

Tackling Climate Change: The Contribution of International Biodiversity Law", in *Climate Change and the Law*, Hollo, Kulovesi and Mehling, Springer 2013,
–, "The Ecosystem Approach and the Precautionary Principle", *Elgar Encyclopedia of Environmental Law*, Edward Elgar, Cheltenham, Vol. 3, 2017, pp. 70-80.
–, "The Need for an International Legal Concept of Fair and Equitable Benefit Sharing", *European Journal of International Law*, May 2016, Vol. 27, Issue 2, pp. 353-383.
Morgera, E., "Fair and Equitable Benefit-Sharing at the Cross-Roads of the Human Right to Science and International Biodiversity Law", *Laws*, 2015, 4, pp. 803-831.
Morgera, E., and M. Ntona, "Linking Small-Scale Fisheries to International Obligations on Marine Technology Transfer", *Marine Policy*, July 2018, Vol. 93, pp. 295-306.
Morgera, E., and E. Tsioumani, "Yesterday, Today, and Tomorrow: Looking Afresh at the Convention on Biological Diversity", *Yearbook of International Environmental Law*, 2011, 21, pp. 3-40.
Morin, J.-F. *et al.*, "Boundary Organizations in Regime Complexes: A Social Network Assessment of IPBES", *Journal of International Relations and Development*, Vol. 20, No. 3, pp. 543-577.
–, "A Southern Reaction to the Extension of Patent Law: Biodiversity in the International Regime of Intellectual Property", *Droit et Société*, Vol. 58, 2004, pp. 633-656.
–, "La brevetabilité dans les récents traités de libre-échange américains", *Revue internationale de droit économique*, 2004, Vol. XVIII, 4, pp. 483-501.
–, "Une réplique du Sud à l'extension du droit des brevets : la biodiversité dans le régime international de la propriété intellectuelle", *Droit et société*, 2004/3 (n° 58), pp. 633-653.
Morin, J.-F., and A. Orsini, "Policy Coherency and Regime Complexes: The Case of Genetic Resources", *Review of International Studies*, 40 (2), 2014, pp. 303-324.
Morin, J.-F., and A. Orsini, "Regime Complexity and Policy Coherency: Introducing a Co-adjustments Model", *Global Governance*, 2013, Vol. 19, pp. 41-51.
Mossop, J., "Can We Make the Oceans Greener? The Successes and Failures of UNCLOS as an Environmental Treaty", *Victoria University of Wellington Law Review*, 2018, Vol. 49, Issue 4, pp. 573-593.
Mossop, J., "Towards a Practical Approach to Regulating Marine Genetic Resources", *ESIL Reflections* 8:3 (2019).
Moynihan, R., "Inland Water Biodiversity: International Law on Protection of Transboundary Freshwater Ecosystems and Biodiversity", *Elgar Encyclopedia of Environmental Law*, Edward Elgar, Cheltenham, 2017, pp. 189-202.
Murombo, T., "The Role on International Environmental Diplomacy in the Sustainable Use of Marine Biodiversity in Areas Beyond National Jurisdiction: Ending Deep Sea Trawling", *Comparative and International Law Journal of Southern Africa*, Vol. 40, Issue 2 (2007), pp. 172-192.
Nagle, J. C., "The Effectiveness of Biodiversity Law", *Journal of Land Use & Environmental Law*, Vol. 24, Issue 2, Spring 2009, pp. 203-252.
Naim-Gesbert, E., "Biodiversité et changement climatique : la méthode et le discours. Des mots du droit au droit des mots", *Revue juridique de l'environnement*, 2012, n° 2, pp. 295-303.
Nain Gill, G., N. Chowdhury and N. Srivastava, "Biodiversity and the Indian Judiciary: Tracing the Trajectory", *Brics Law Journal*, Vol. VIII (2021), Issue 2, pp. 10-40.
Natarajan, U., and K. Khoday, "Locating Nature: Making and Unmaking International Law", *Leiden Journal of International Law* (2014), 27, pp. 573-593.
Nele, M.-L., "Biological Diversity, International Protection", *Max Planck Encyclopedia of Public International Law [MPEPIL]*, December 2008.
Nijar, G. S., "Traditional Knowledge Systems, International Law and National Challenges: Marginalization or Emancipation?", *European Journal of International Law*, 2013 24 (4), pp. 1205-1221.

Nijar, G. S., S. Louafi and E. W. Welch, "The Implementation of the Nagoya ABS Protocol for the Research Sector: Experience and Challenges", *International Environmental Agreements*, 2017, 17, pp. 607-621.

Nilsson, M., and Å. Persson, "Reprint of 'Can Earth System Interactions Be Governed? Governance Functions for Linking Climate Change Mitigation with Land Use, Freshwater and Biodiversity Protection", 2012, 81 *Ecological Economics*, pp. 10-20.

Noiville, C., "La mise en œuvre de la Convention de Rio sur la conservation de la diversité biologique et ses relations avec l'accord de l'OMC sur les ADPIC. Analyse juridique de l'outil économique", in *L'outil économique en droit international et européen de l'environnement*, S. Maljean-Dubois (ed.), La Documentation française, Paris, 2002, pp. 281-303.

Nollkaemper, A., "Responsibility of transnational corporations in international environmental law: three perspectives", in *Multilevel Governance of Global Environmental Science*, G. Winter (ed.), Cambridge University Press, Cambridge, 2006, pp. 179-199.

Oberthür, S, "Clustering of Multilateral Environmental Agreements: Potentials and Limitations", *International Environmental Agreements: Politics, Law and Economics*, (2002) 2, pp. 317-340.

–, "Interplay Management: Enhancing Environmental Policy Integration among International Institutions", *International Environmental Agreements: Politics, Law and Economics*, 2009, 9, pp. 371-391.

Oberthür, S., and J. Pozarowska, "Managing Institutional Complexity and Fragmentation: The Nagoya Protocol and the Global Governance of Genetic Resources", *Global Environmental Politics,* August 2013, Vol. 13:3, pp. 100-115.

Odendahl, K., "Nature, International Protection", *Max Planck Encyclopedia of Public International Law [MPEPIL]*, July 2015.

Olivier, J., "Les nouveaux acteurs du droit de l'environnement. Le rôle de l'UICN dans l'élaboration du droit de l'environnement", *Revue européenne de droit de l'environnement*, 2005, Vol. 9, n° 3, pp. 274-296.

Ollitrault, S., "Les ONG protectrices de la biodiversité donneuses d'alerte ou expertes savantes?", *Le droit international et européen du vivant : quel rôle pour les acteurs privés?*, E. Brosset (ed.), La Documentation française, Paris, 2009, pp. 79-86.

Oral, N., "1982 UNCLOS +30: Confronting New Complexities in the Protection of Biodiversity and Marine Living Resources in the High Seas", *American Society of International Law Proceedings*, Vol. 106, Issue 1, 28-31 March 2012, pp. 403-406.

Orsini, A, J.-F. Morin and O. Young, "Regime Complexes: A Buzz, a Boom, or a Boost for Global Governance?", *Global Governance*, 2013, Vol. 19, pp. 27-39.

Ortiz, M.-J., "Aichi Biodiversity Targets on Direct and Indirect Drivers of Biodiversity Loss", *Environmental Law Review*, Vol. 13, Issue 2, 2011, pp. 100-106.

Oubenal, M., J.-C. Vandevelde and M. Hrabanski, "Le 'consensus d'Antalya': les avancées de la Plateforme intergouvernementale scientifique et politique sur la biodiversité et les services écosystémiques (IPBES)", *Natures Sciences Sociétés*, Vol. 22, 2014, pp. 240-246.

Paavola, J., A. Gouldson and T. Kluvánková-Oravská, "Interplay of Actors, Scales, Frameworks and Regimes in the Governance of Biodiversity", *Environmental Policy and Governance*, 2009, Vol. 19, pp. 148-158.

Pancracio, J.-P., "La protection de la biodiversité au-delà des zones sous juridiction nationale", *Annuaire français de droit international*, Vol. 62, 2016, pp. 541-563.

–, "La sentence arbitrale sur la mer de Chine méridionale du 12 juillet 2016", *Annuaire français de relations internationales*, Vol. XVIII, 2017, pp. 639-657.

Pattberg, P., O. Widerberg and M. T. J. Kok, "Towards a Global Biodiversity Action Agenda", *Global Policy*, 2019, pp. 385-390.

Pauwelyn, J., "The Role of Public International Law in the WTO: How Far Can We Go?", *AJIL*, 2001, pp. 535-578.

Pavoni, R., "Droit du commerce international et biodiversité après le Protocole de Nagoya", in *Diversité dans la gouvernance internationale: perspectives culturelles, écologiques et juridiques*, V. Négri (ed.), Bruylant, Bruxelles, 2016, pp. 119-154.

Peña-Neira, S., "International Law and its Application: Biodiversity and International Obligations Derived from Natural Genetic Resources in Costa Rica/El derecho internacional y su aplicación: la biodiversidad y las obligaciones internacionales derivadas de los recursos naturales genéticos en Costa Rica", *Anuario mexicano de derecho internacional*, January 2012, Vol. 12, pp. 673-696.

Penca, J., "Biodiversity Offsetting in Transnational Governance", *Review of European Comparative & International Environmental Law*, April 2015, Vol. 24, Issue 1, pp. 93-102.

Pereira, H. M. et al., "Scenarios for Global Biodiversity in the 21st Century", *Science*, Vol. 330, 2010, pp. 1496-1501.

Persson, L. et al., "Outside the Safe Operating Space of the Planetary Boundary for Novel Entities", 56 (2022) 3 *Environmental Science Technology*, pp. 1510-1521.

Peters, A., "Liberté, Égalité, Animalité: Human-Animal Comparisons in Law", *Transnational Environmental Law*, 2016, pp. 1-29.

Phelps, J., "Environmental Liability Litigation Could Remedy Biodiversity Loss", *Conservation Letters*, 2021, 14:e12821.

Prieur, M., "Instruments internationaux et évaluation environnementale de la biodiversité : enjeux et obstacles", *Revue juridique de l'environnement*, Vol. 36 (1), pp. 7-28.

Prisner-Levyne, Y., "For a New Legal Status for Wild Animal under International Law", *L'Observateur des Nations Unies*, Vol. 45, 2018, pp. 143-175.

Pritchard, D., "International Biodiversity-Related Treaties and Impact Assessment – How Can They Help Each Other?", *Impact Assessment and Project Appraisal*, 2005, Vol. 23:1, pp. 7-16.

Qureshi, W. A., "Marine Biodiversity Conservation: The International Legal Framework and Challenges", *Houston Journal of International Law*, Vol. 40, Issue 3 (Summer 2018), pp. 845-936.

Rashbrooke, G., "The International Tribunal for the Law of the Sea: A Forum for the Development of Principles of International Environmental Law?", *International Journal of Marine & Coastal Law*, December 2004, Vol. 19, Issue 4, pp. 515-535.

Raustiala, K., and D. G. Victor, "The Regime Complex for Plant Genetic Resources", *International Organization*, Vol. 58, Issue 2, April 2004, pp. 277-309.

Rayfuse, R., "Precaution and the Protection of Marine Biodiversity in Areas Beyond National Jurisdiction", *International Journal of Marine and Coastal Law*, Vol. 27, Issue 4, 2012, pp. 773-782.

Redgwell, C., "Biotechnology, Biodiversity and International Law", *Current Legal Problems*, 2005, Vol. 58, pp. 543-569.

Richardson, B. J., "Indigenous Peoples, International Law and Sustainability", *Review of European Community & International Environmental Law*, 2001, Vol. 10, Issue 1, pp. 1-12.

Riffel, C., "Traditional Knowledge", *Max Planck Encyclopedia of Public International Law [MPEPIL]*, April 2014.

Rigal, S. et al., "Farmland Practices Are Driving Bird Population Decline across Europe", 120 (2023) 21 *PNAS*.

Rockström, J., W. Steffen and K. Noone et al., "A Safe Operating Space for Humanity", *Nature*, Vol. 461, 2009, pp. 472–475.

Rodary, E., and C. Castellanet, "Les trois temps de la conservation", in E. Rodary, C. Castellanet and G. Rossi (eds.), *Conservation de la nature et développement : l'intégration impossible ?*, Paris, Karthala/GRET, "Economie et développement", 2004, pp. 5-44.

Rogalla von Bieberstein, K., E. Sattout, M. Christensen, B. Pisupati, N. Burgess,

D. Harrison and Geldmann, "Improving Collaboration in the Implementation of Global Biodiversity Conventions", *Conservation Biology*, Vol. 33, No. 4, pp. 821-831.

Romi, R., "Convention-révolution ou convention inutile ? Premières réflexions sur les conséquences de l'introduction dans le droit interne de la Convention de Berne", in *Les Petites Affiches*, n° 130, 29 octobre 1990, pp. 13-17.

Rosendal, G. K., "Impacts of Overlapping International Regimes: The Case of Biodiversity", *Global Governance*, Vol. 7, No. 1 (Jan.-Mar. 2001), pp. 95-117.

Rosendal, G. K., "Overlapping International Regimes. The Case of the Intergovernmental Forum on Forests (IFF) between Climate Change and Biodiversity", *International Environmental Agreements: Politics, Law and Economics*, 2001, Vol. 1, pp. 447-468.

Rosendal, G. K., and S. Andresen, "Realizing Access and Benefit Sharing from Use of Genetic Resources between Diverging International Regimes: The Scope for Leadership", *International Environmental Agreements*, 2016, Vol. 16, pp. 579-596.

Rossi, G. G., and V. André, "La biodiversité : questions de perspectives", *Annales de géographie*, 2006, Vol. 5, n° 651, pp. 468-484.

Roué, M., "Entre cultures et natures", *Revue internationale des sciences sociales*, 2006/1, n° 187, 2006/1 (n° 187), pp. 11-18.

Ruiz Fabri, H., "La prise en compte du principe de précaution par l'OMC", *Revue juridique de l'environnement*, 2000, pp. 55-66.

Ryngaert, C., "Climate Change Mitigation Techniques and International Law: Assessing the Externalities of Reforestation and Geoengineering", *Ratio Juris.*, September 2017, Vol. 30, Issue 3, pp. 273-289.

Sagemüller, I., "Forest Sinks under the United Nations Framework Convention on Climate Change and the Kyoto Protocol: Opportunity or Risk for Biodiversity?", *Columbia Journal of Environmental Law*, 2006, Vol. 31, pp. 191-204.

Sánchez-Bayo, F., and A. G. Wyckhuys Kris, "Worldwide Decline of the Entomofauna: A Review of its Driver", *Biological Conservation*, Vol. 232, April 2019, pp. 8-27.

Sand, P. H, "Endangered Species, International Protection", *Max Planck Encyclopedia of Public International Law [MPEPIL]*, March 2017.

Sare, S., "OAU's Model Law: lo schéma legislativo dell'Unione Africana per salvaguardare le comunità agricole tradizionali. Analisi e qualche commento / OAU's MODEL LAW: The legislative schéma of the African Union to safeguard the agricultural traditional communities. Analysis and comment", *Africa*, 62 (1), pp. 78-99.

Savaresi, A., "Reducing Emissions from Deforestation in Developing Countries under the United Nations Framework Convention on Climate Change. A New Opportunity for Promoting Forest Conservation?", in F. Maes *et al.* (eds), *Biodiversity and Climate Change: Linkages at International, National and Local Levels*, Edward Elgar, Cheltenham, 2013, pp. 237-267.

Savaresi, A., "The Emergence of Benefit-Sharing under the Climate Regime. A Preliminary Exploration and Research Agenda", Edinburgh School of Law Research Paper Series, 2014/43.

Schofield, C., "International Arctic Change and the Law and Politics of the Arctic Ocean Seabed: Boundaries, Biodiversity, Resources, and Increasing Maritime Activities: Emerging Oceans Governance Challenges for Canada in the Arctic Ocean", *Vermont Law Review*, 2009/10/01, Vol. 34, pp. 35-56.

Scott, K, "Non Compliance Procedures and the Implementation of Commitments under Wildlife Treaties", in *Research Handbook on Biodiversity and Law*, M. Bowman, P. Davies and E. Goodvin (eds.), Edward Elgar, Cheltenham, 2016, pp. 414-436.

–, "International Environmental Governance: Managing Fragmentation Through Institutional Connection", *Melbourne Journal of International Law*, 2011, Vol. 12, pp. 1-40.

Shaffer, G., "The WTO Shrimp-Turtle Case (United States – Import Prohibition of Certain Shrimp and Shrimp Products)", *American Journal of International Law*, 1999, Vol. 93, p. 507, pp. 507-514.

Shaffer, R., "Biodiversity and the Courts: Endangered Species Law in the US, Australia and Canada", *Berkeley Undergraduate Journal*, 2011, Vol. 24 (2), pp. 43-50.

Sharom, A., "A Critical Study of the Laws Relating to the Indigenous Peoples of Malaysia in the Context of Article 8 *(j)* of the Biodiversity Convention", *International Journal on Minority and Group Rights*, Vol. 13, Issue 1 (2006), pp. 53-68.

Sian Koh, N., C. Ituarte-Lima and T. Hahn, "Mind the Compliance Gap: How Insights from International Human Rights Mechanisms Can Help to Implement the Convention on Biological Diversity", *Transnational Environmental Law*, pp. 1-29.

Sicilianos, L. A., "The Classification of Obligations and the Multilateral Dimension of the Relations of International Responsibility", *EJIL*, Vol. 13, No. 5, 2002, pp. 1127-1145.

Soulé, M. E., "What is Conservation Biology? A New Synthetic Discipline Addresses the Dynamics and Problems of Perturbed Species, Communities and Ecosystems", *Biosciences*, Vol. 35, No. 11, December1985, pp. 727-734.

Stephens, T., "The Collateral Damage from China's 'Great Wall of Sand': The Environmental Dimensions of the 'South China Sea Case'", *Australian Yearbook of International Law*, Vol. 34, 2016, pp. 41-52.

Stoett, P., "Framing Bioinvasion: Biodiversity, Climate Change, Security, Trade, and Global Governance", *Global Governance* 103 (2010), Vol. 16, Issue 1, pp. 103-120.

Stokke, O. S., and S. Oberthür, "Introduction: Institutional Interaction in Global Environmental Change", in *Managing Institutional Complexity: Regime Interplay and Global Environmental Change*, S. Oberthür and O. S. Stokke (eds.), MIT Press, Cambridge, 2011, pp. 1-23.

Stone, C. D., "Should Trees Have Standing? Towards Legal Rights for Natural Objects", *Southern California Law Review*, 45 (1972), pp. 450-501.

Streck, C., "Financial Instruments and Cooperation in Implementing International Agreements for the Global Environment", in *Multilevel Governance of Global Environmental Change: An Interdisciplinary Approach*, A. Jordan, R. Wurzel and A. R. Zito, Cambridge University Press, 2006, pp. 493-516.

–, "Synergies between the Kunming-Montreal Global Biodiversity Framework and the Paris Agreement: The Role of Policy Milestones, Monitoring Frameworks and Safeguards", *Climate Policy*, 2023, pp. 1-12.

Sturtz, L., "Southern Bluefin Tuna Case: *Australia and New Zealand v. Japan*", *Ecology Law Quarterly*, 28(2), pp. 455-486.

Swanson, T., "Why is There a Biodiversity Convention? The International Interest in Centralized Development Planning", *International Affairs*, Royal Institute of International Affairs, 1999, Vol. 75 (2), pp. 307-331.

Sykes, K., "The Appeal to Science and the Formation of Global Animal Law", *European Journal of International Law*, Vol. 27, No. 2, pp. 497-518.

Tanaka, Y., "*Costa Rica v. Nicaragua* and *Nicaragua v. Costa Rica*: Some Reflections on the Obligation to Conduct an Environmental Impact Assessment", *Review of European Comparative & International Environmental Law*, April 2017, Vol. 26 Issue 1, pp. 91-99.

Tekayak, D., "Protecting Earth Rights and the Rights of Indigenous Peoples: Towards an International Crime of Ecocide", *Fourth World Journal*, Vol. 14, No. 2, Winter 2016, pp. 5-13.

Thomas, F., "Biodiversité, biotechnologies et savoirs traditionnels. Du patrimoine commun de l'humanité aux ABS", *Revue Tiers Monde*, 2006, Vol. 188, pp. 825-842.

–, "Ressources génétiques : garantir l'accès à un bien public mondial ou com-

penser sa marchandisation ?", *Entreprises et histoire*, 2017/3, n° 88, pp. 103-120.
Tinker, C., "A 'New Breed' of Treaty: The United Nations Convention on Biological Diversity", *Pace Environmental Law Review*, Vol. 13, Issue 1, Fall 1995, September 1995, pp. 191-218.
Tittensor, D. P. et al., "A Mid-Term Analysis of Progress Toward International Biodiversity Targets", *Science*, Vol. 346, 2014, pp. 241-244.
Tladi, D., "Civil Liability in the Context of the Cartagena Protocol: To Be or Not to Be (Binding)?", *International Environmental Agreements*, 2010, Vol. 10, pp. 15-27.
Tladi, D., "The Proposed Implementing Agreement: Options for Coherence and Consistency in the Establishment of Protected Areas Beyond National Jurisdiction", *International Journal of Marine & Coastal Law*, December 2015, Vol. 30, Issue 4, pp. 654-673.
Tremblay-Huet, S., "Should Environmental Law Learn from Animal Law? Compassion as a Guiding Principle for International Environmental Law Instead of Sustainable Development", *Revue québécoise de droit international*, 2018, Vol. 1 (1), pp. 125-144.
Trouwborst, A., "Conserving European Biodiversity in a Changing Climate: The Bern Convention, the European Union Birds and Habitats Directives and the Adaptation of Nature to Climate Change", *Review of European Community & International Environmental Law*, 2011, Vol. 20, pp. 62-77.
–, "International Nature Conservation Law and the Adaptation of Biodiversity to Climate Change: A Mismatch?", *Journal of Environmental Law*, Vol. 21, No. 3, 2009, pp. 419-442.
–, "Managing the Carnivore Comeback: International and EU Species Protection Law and the Return of Lynx, Wolf and Bear to Western Europe", *Journal of Environmental Law*, 22 (3), pp. 347-372.
–, "Transboundary Wildlife Conservation in a Changing Climate: Adaptation of the Bonn Convention on Migratory Species and its Daughter Instruments to Climate Change", *Diversity*, 2012, Vol. 4, pp. 258-300.
–, "Climate Adaptation and Biodiversity Law", *Research Handbook on Climate Adaptation Law*, Edward Elgar, Cheltenham, 2013, pp. 298-324.
–, "Global Large Carnivore Conservation and International Law", *Biodiversity and Conservation*, 2015 July, Vol. 24, n° 7, pp. 1567-1588.
Tsioumani, E., "Beyond Access and Benefit-Sharing: Lessons from the Law and Governance of Agricultural Biodiversity", *Journal of World Intellectual Property*, 2018, Vol. 21, pp. 106-122.
–, "Conservation, Biodiversity and International Law – By Alexander Gillespie", *Review of European Community & International Environmental Law*, 2012, Vol. 21, Issue 3, pp. 297-298.
Tully, S. R., "Corporate-NGO Partnerships and the Regulatory Impact of the Energy and Biodiversity Initiative", *Non-State Actors and International Law*, Vol. 4, Issue 1, 2004, pp. 111-134.
Ulloa, A. M., K. Jax and S. I. Karlsson-Vinkhuyzen, "Enhancing Implementation of the Convention on Biological Diversity: A Novel Peer-Review Mechanism Aims to Promote Accountability and Mutual Learning", *Biological Conservation*, 2018, Vol. 217, pp. 371-376.
Untermaier, J., "Biodiversité et droit de la biodiversité", *Revue juridique de l'environnement*, 33 (1), 2008, pp. 21-32.
Van Asselt, H., "Dealing with the Fragmentation of Global Climate Governance. Legal and Political Approaches in Interplay Management", *Global Governance Working Paper* (2007).
–, "Integrating Biodiversity in the Climate Regime's Forest Rules: Options and Tradeoffs in Greening REDD Design", *Review of European Community and International Environmental Law*, (2011) 20, pp. 139-149.
–, "Managing the Fragmentation of International Environmental Law: Forests at

the Intersection of the Climate and Biodiversity Regimes", *NYU J. Int'l L. & Pol.*, 2011-2012, Vol. 44, pp. 1205-1278.

–, "The Role of Non-State Actors in Reviewing Ambition, Implementation, and Compliance under the Paris Agreement", *Climate Law*, 2016, Vol. 6, pp. 91-108.

Van Asselt, H., F. Sindico and M. A. Mehling, "Global Climate Change and the Fragmentation of International Law", *Law and Policy*, October 2008, Vol. 30, No. 4, pp. 423-449.

Van Asselt, H. D., "Managing the Fragmentation of International Environmental Law: Forests at the Intersection of the Climate and Biodiversity Regimes", Environmental Policy Analysis, Amsterdam Global Change Institute, *New York University Journal of International Law & Politics*, Vol. 44 (4), 2012, pp. 1205-1278.

Vanagt, T., A. Broggiato, L. E. Lallier, M. Jaspars, G. Burton and D. Muyldermans, "*Mare Geneticum*: Towards an Implementing Agreement for Marine Genetic Resources in International Waters", in *Conserving Biodiversity in Areas Beyond National Jurisdiction*, D. Freestone (ed.), Brill, 2019, pp. 267-297.

Velázquez Gomar, J. O., L. C. Stringer and J. Paavola, "Regime Complexes and National Policy Coherence: Experiences in the Biodiversity Cluster", *Global Governance*, Vol. 20, 2014, pp. 119-145.

Verhoosel, G., "Prospecting for Marine and Coastal Biodiversity: International Law in Deep Water", *International Journal of Marine and Coastal Law*, Vol. 13, Issue 1 (February 1998), pp. 91-104.

Villavicencio Calzadilla, P., and L. J. Kotzé, "Living in Harmony with Nature? A Critical Appraisal of the Rights of Mother Earth in Bolivia", *Transnational Environmental Law*, 2018, pp. 1-28.

Vivien, F.-D., "De Rio à Johannesburg les négociations autour de la diversité biologique", *Ecologie & politique*, 2002/3, n° 26, pp. 35-53.

Voigt-Hanssen, G., "Current 'Light' and 'Heavy' Options for Benefit-Sharing in the Context of the United Nations Convention on the Law of the Sea", *The International Journal of Marine and Coastal Law*, 2018, Vol. 33, No. 4, pp. 683-705.

–, "Current 'Light' and 'Heavy' Options for Benefit-Sharing in the Context of the United Nations Convention on the Law of the Sea", *Conserving Biodiversity in Areas Beyond National Jurisdiction*, D. Freestone (ed.), Brill, 2019, pp. 243-266.

Von Moltke, K., "Governments and International Civil Society in Sustainable Development: A Framework", *International Environmental Agreements*, No. 2 (4), 2002, pp. 339-357.

Walid, A., "Les contrats internationaux de bioprospection: moyen de protection de la biodiversité et des savoirs traditionnels ou instrument de biopiraterie?", *Revue québécoise de droit international*, 2009, Vol. 22-1, pp. 53-85.

Wang-Erlandsson, L., "A Planetary Boundary for Green Water" 3 (2022), *Nature Reviews Earth & Environment*, pp. 380-392.

Wani, M., and P. Taraporevala, "CoP-11 on Biodiversity: An Opportunity to Go Beyond Business as Usual", *Economic and Political Weekly*, 2012, 47 (38), pp. 10-13; R.B. Mitchell, "International Environmental Agreements. A Survey of their Features, Formation, and Effects", *Annual Review of Environment and Resources*, 2003, Vol. 28, pp. 429-461.

Warren, L. M., "The Convention on Biological Diversity: Will the Decisions Made at Cop10 in Nagoya Make It Easier to Conserve Biodiversity", *Environmental Law Review*, Vol. 12, Issue 4, 2010, pp. 245-255.

Warren, R. *et al.*, "The Projected Effect on Insects, Vertebrates, and Plants of Limiting Global Warming to 1.5°C Rather Than 2°C", *Science*, 18 May 2018, Vol. 360, Issue 6390, pp. 791-795.

Wiederkehr, M.-O., "La Convention européenne sur la reconnaissance de la personnalité juridique des organisations internationales non gouvernementales du 24 avril 1986", *Annuaire français de droit international*, 1987, Vol. 33, pp. 749-761.

Wiersema, A., "Climate Change, Forests, and International Law: REDD's Descent into Irrelevance", *Vanderbilt Journal of Transnational Law*, 2014, Vol. 47, pp. 1-66.
Xue, D., "WEI Guihong, Sheng Wu Duo Yang Xing De Fa Lu Bao Hu, Biodiversity Conservation in Law", *Chinese Journal of International Law*, Vol. 13, Issue 2, June 2014, pp. 471-476.
Yamin, F., "Biodiversity, Ethics and International Law", *International Affairs*, Vol. 71, Issue 3, 1 July 1995, pp. 529-546.
Yamthieu, S., "Loi Modèle Africaine", in *Dictionnaire juridique de la sécurité alimentaire dans le monde*, F. Collard-Dutilleul and J.-P. Bugnicourt (ed.), Larcier, 2013, pp. 414-416.
Yelpaala, K., "Quo Vadis WTO – The Threat of TRIPS and the Biodiversity Convention to Human Health and Food Security", *Boston University International Law Journal*, Vol. 30, Issue 1 (Spring 2012), pp. 55-134.
Yotova, R., "The Principles of Due Diligence and Prevention in International Environmental Law", *Cambridge Law Journal*, Nov. 2016, Vol. 75, Issue 3, pp. 445-448.
Young, M. A., "Climate Change Law and Regime Interaction", *CCLR*, 2011, Vol. 21, pp. 147-157.
Young, M. A., and A. Friedman, "Biodiversity Beyond National Jurisdictions: Regimes and their Interactions", *AJIL Unbound*, Vol. 112, 2018, pp. 123-128.
Zaccai, E., and W. M. Adams, "How Far Are Biodiversity Loss and Climate Change Similar as Policy Issues?", *Environment, Development and Sustainability*, August 2012, Vol. 14, Issue 4, pp. 557-571.
Zorgbibe, C., "La diplomatie non gouvernementale", in *Les ONG et le droit international*, M. Bettati and P.-M. Dupuy (eds.), Economica, 1986, pp. 35-40.

Doctoral Dissertations

Bohigas, I., *Indigenous Peoples, Protected Areas and Biodiversity Conservation: A Study of Australia's Obligations under International Law*, Thesis, Stockholm University, 2015.
Bonnin, M.-A., *Les aspects juridiques des corridors biologiques* : vers un troisième temps de la conservation de la nature, thèse doctorat, Droit de l'environnement, Nantes, 2003.
Bowman, M., *Our Tangled Web: International Relations Theory, International Environmental Law, and Global Biodiversity Protection in a Post-Modern Epoch of Interdependence*, Thesis, McGill University, 2002.
Futhazar, G., *Les modalités d'influence de l'IPBES sur l'évolution du droit international de l'environnement en Méditerranée*, thèse pour le doctorat en droit public, Aix-Marseille Université, 2018.
Gambardella, S., *La gestion et la conservation des ressources halieutiques en droit international. L'exemple de la Méditerranée*, thèse pour le doctorat en droit, Aix-Marseille Université, 2013.
Jóhannsdóttir, A., *The Significance of the Default: A Study in Environmental Law Methodology with Emphasis on Ecological Sustainability and International Biodiversity Law*, Thesis, Uppsala Universitet, 2009.
Maljean-Dubois, S., *La protection internationale des oiseaux sauvages*, thèse pour le doctorat en droit, Université Paul Cézanne, Aix-en-Provence, 1996.
Mercer, H., *La protection des savoirs traditionnels par droits de propriété intellectuelle comme outil contre la biopiraterie*, thèse, Université du Québec à Montréal, 2010.
Oguamanam, C., *International Law, Plant Biodiversity and the Protection of Indigenous Knowledge: An Examination of Intellectual Property Rights in Relation to Traditional Medicine*, Thesis, University of British Columbia, Vancouver, 2003.
Perruso, C., *Le droit à un environnement sain en droit international*, Thèse pour le doctorat en droit, Université Paris 1 Panthéon Sorbonne, Université de Sao Paulo, 2019.

Reports

Antona, M., and M. Bonnin, *Généalogie scientifique et mise en politique des SE (Services environnementaux et services écosystémiques)*, note de synthèse de revue bibliographique et d'entretiens, WP1, Programme SERENA, document de travail, n° 2010-0.

Billé, R., Broughton, L. Chabason, C. Chiarolla, M. Jardin, G. Kleitz, J.-P. Le Duc and L. Mermet, *Global Governance of Biodiversity New Perspectives on a Shared Challenge*, December 2010, Health and Environment Reports n° 6, IFRI, Paris.

Bonnin B., *Genèse des services environnementaux dans le droit. 1 : L'apparition récente et emmêlée des services environnementaux dans le droit international de l'environnement*, programme SERENA, note de synthèse, n° 2010-05.

Braat, L. C., and P. Ten Brink (eds.), *The Cost of Policy Inaction (COPI): The Case of Not Meeting the 2010 Biodiversity Target*, Report to the European Commission under contract, ENV.G.1./ETU/2007/0044, Alterra report 1718, Wageningen/Brussels, Netherlands-Belgium, 2008.

Brook, N. et al., Clyde & Co, *Biodiversity Liability and Value Chain Risk*, March 2022.

Business and Biodiversity Offsets Program (BBOP), *Standard on Biodiversity Offsets*, BBOP, Washington, DC, 2012.

Canivet, G. L. Lavrysen and D. Guihal (ed.), *Manuel judiciaire de droit de l'environnement*, PNUE, 2006.

Convention sur la diversité biologique, *Mo'otz Kuxtal. Voluntary Guidelines for the Development of Mechanisms, Legislation or Other Appropriate Initiatives to Ensure the "prior and informed consent", "free, prior and informed consent" or "approval and involvement", Depending on National Circumstances, of indigenous Peoples and Local Communities for Accessing their Knowledge, Innovations and Practices, for Fair and Equitable Sharing of Benefits Arising from the Use of their Knowledge, Innovations and Practices Relevant for the Conservation and Sustainable Use of Biological Diversity, and for Reporting and Preventing Unlawful Appropriation of Traditional Knowledge*, Montreal, 2019.

Dahan, A., S. Aykut, H. Guillemot and A. Korczak, *Les arènes climatiques : forums du futur ou foires aux palabres*, Rapport de Recherche, February 2009.

De Klemm, C., *L'application et le suivi de la Convention de Berne et la nécessité d'intégrer la prise en compte des processus de destruction de la diversité biologique*, quatorzième réunion, Symposium sur la "Conférence des Nations Unies sur l'environnement et le développement, la convention sur la diversité biologique et la convention de Berne : les prochaines étapes", T-PVS (94) 14, pp. 55-62.

De Klemm, C., *Les introductions d'organismes naturels non indigènes dans le milieu naturel*, quatorzième réunion, 20-24 mars 1995, T-PVS(95)17.

Doswald, N., M. Barcellos Harris and M. Jones et al., *Biodiversity Offsets: Voluntary and Compliance Regimes. A Review of Existing Schemes, Initiatives and Guidance for Financial Institutions*, UNEP-WCMC, Cambridge, UK. UNEP FI, Geneva, Switzerland, 2012.

European Parliament, Directorate-General for Internal Policies of the Union, S. Hodgson, A. Serdy and I. Payne, *Towards a Possible International Agreement on Marine Biodiversity in Areas Beyond National Jurisdiction*, 2014.

Experts Groups of the World Commission on Environment and Development, *Environmental Protection and Sustainable Development*, Graham and Trotman, Martinus Nijhoff Publishers, London, Boston, 1987.

FAO, *La situation mondiale des pêches et de l'aquaculture*, 2018.

Gargule, A., *Beyond the Institutional Fix? The Potential of Strategic Litigation to Target Natural Resource Corruption*, TNRC Topic Brief series, February 2022.

GRAIN, *Au-delà de l'UPOV*, July 1999.

–, *Dix bonnes raisons de ne pas adhérer à l'UPOV*, Commerce mondial et biodiversité en conflit, n° 2, May 1998.

–, *L'Accord sur les Aspects des Droits de Propriété Intellectuelle qui touchent au*

Commerce contre la Convention sur la diversité biologique, Commerce mondial et biodiversité en conflit, n° 1, April 1998.
–, *La mission impossible de l'OMPI?*, Seedling, n° 3, Vol. 15, September 1998.
–, *La protection des obtentions végétales pour nourrir l'Afrique. Rhétorique contre réalité*, October 1999.
–, *Privatisation des moyens de survie : la commercialisation de la biodiversité en Afrique*, Commerce mondial et biodiversité en conflit, n° 5, mai 2000, non paginé.
Human Rights Council, *Report of the Special Rapporteur on the Issue of Human Rights Obligations relating to the Enjoyment of a Safe, Clean, Healthy and Sustainable Environment*, Note by the Secretariat, A/HRC/34/49, 19 January 2017.
IPBES, *Summary for Policymakers of the Global Assessment Report on Biodiversity and Ecosystem Services of the Intergovernmental Science-Policy Platform on Biodiversity and Ecosystem Services*, S. Díaz et al. (eds.), IPBES secretariat, Bonn, Germany, 2019.
–, *The IPBES Regional Assessment Report on Biodiversity and Ecosystem Services for Africa*, E. Archer, L. Dziba, K. J. Mulongoy, M. A. Maoela and M. Walters, (eds.), Secretariat of the Intergovernmental Science-Policy Platform on Biodiversity and Ecosystem Services, Bonn, Germany, 2018.
IUCN, *An Introduction to the African Convention on the Conservation of Nature and Natural Resources – Introduction à la Convention africaine sur la conservation de la nature et des ressources naturelles*, Environmental Policy and Law Paper No. 56 Rev., 2e éd., Gland, 2006.
–, *Genetic Frontiers for Conservation, An Assessment of Synthetic Biology and Biodiversity Conservation Synthesis and Key Messages*, IUCN Task Force on Synthetic Biology and Biodiversity Conservation, IUCN, Gland, 2019.
Laudon A., and C. Noiville, *Le principe de précaution, le droit de l'environnement et l'OMC*, rapport remis au Ministère de l'Environnement, France, 16 novembre 1998.
Lavallée, S., *Guide des négociations. Convention sur la diversité biologique. 14e session de la Conférence des Parties (CdP14, CdP/RdP9 et CdP/RdP3) du 17 au 29 novembre 2018, Charm El-cheikh, Égypte*, Institut de la Francophonie pour le développement durable, Montréal, 2018.
Manuel Ramsar, *Gestion intégrée des zones humides*, 2010, 4e ed.
Marre, B., *De la mondialisation subie au développement contrôlé. Les enjeux de la Conférence de Seattle*, Rapport d'information, Assemblée nationale, France, 30 novembre-3 December 1999.
NEP-WCMC, *Developing Ecosystem Service Indicators: Experiences and Lessons Learned from Sub-Global Assessments and Other Initiatives*. Secretariat of the Convention on Biological Diversity, Montréal, Canada. Technical Series No. 58, 2011.
OCDE, *Financer la biodiversité, agir pour l'économie et les entreprises*, résumé et synthèse, rapport préparé pour la réunion des ministres de l'Environnement du G7, les 5 et 6 mai 2019, 2019.
–, *Propriété intellectuelle, transfert de technologie et ressources génétiques. Pratiques et politiques actuelles*, OCDE, Paris, 1996.
ONU, Evaluation des écosystèmes pour le Millénaire, Les écosystèmes et le bien-être humain : synthèse sur la diversité biologique, 2005.
Ourbak, T., *Analyse rétrospective de la COP 21 et de l'Accord de Paris : un exemple de diplomatie multilatérale exportable*, rapport d'expertise, MAEDI, France, 2017.
Pattberg, P., K. Kristensen and O. Widerberg, *Beyond the CBD: Exploring the Institutional Landscape of Governing for Biodiversity*, Institute for Environmental Studies/IVM, 2017, Report R-17/06, November 2017.
Rankovic, A., S. Maljean-Dubois, M. Wemaëre and Y. Laurans, *Un Agenda de l'action pour la biodiversité : attentes et enjeux à court et moyen termes*, Policy brief, Iddri, April 2018.
Sagne, L., *Les accords internationaux dans le domaine de la protection des habitats*,

Rapport de stage d'études au ministère de l'Environnement, France, August 1992, M. Bigan (ed.).

Secrétariat de la Convention sur la diversité biologique, *Principes et directives d'Addis Abeba pour l'utilisation durable de la diversité biologique (Lignes directrices de la CDB)*, secrétariat de la Convention sur la diversité biologique, Montreal, 2004.

Secretariat of the Convention on Biological Diversity, *Connecting Biodiversity and Climate Change Mitigation and Adaptation: Report of the Second Ad Hoc Technical Expert Group on Biodiversity and Climate Change*, 2009.

Secretariat of the Convention on Biological Diversity, *Global Biodiversity Outlook 3. A Report by the Secretariat of the Convention on Biological Diversity*, Montreal, 2010.

Secretariat of the Convention on Biological Diversity, *Global Biodiversity Outlook 4. A Report by the Secretariat of the Convention*, Montreal, 2014.

Secretariat of the Convention on Biological Diversity, *Handbook of the Convention on Biological Diversity*, Earthscan Publications, London, 2005.

Secretariat of the Convention on Biological Diversity, *Interlinkages between Biological Diversity and Climate Change. Advice on the Integration of Biodiversity Considerations into the Implementation of the United Nations Framework Convention on Climate Change and its Kyoto Protocol*, 2003.

Security Council, *Report and Recommendations Made by the Panel of Commissioners concerning the Fifth Instalment of "F4" Claims*, United Nations Security Council, S/AC.26/2005/10, 30 June 2005.

Seddon, N., S. Sengupta, M. García-Espinosa, I. Hauler, D. Herr and A. Raza Rizvi, *Nature-based Solutions in Nationally Determined Contributions*, IUCN, University of Oxford, Gland, 2019.

Selnes, T. A., and D. A. Kamphorst, *International Governance of Biodiversity, Searching for Renewal*, WOt-technical report 22, Wageningenur.

Special Rapporteur on Human, Rights and the Environment, *Human Rights Depend on a Healthy Biosphere: Good Practices*, Annex to A/75/161, 21 September 2020.

Stokes, K., and J. Mugabe, *Biotechnology, TRIPS and the Convention on Biological Diversity*, UNEP/CBD/ISOC/inf.3, 15 June 1999.

Ten Brink, P. (ed.), *The Economics of Ecosystems and Biodiversity: Mainstreaming the Economics of Nature: A Synthesis of the Approach, Conclusions and Recommendations of TEEBB*, 2010.

The Ecuador Principles, IV, Version 4, November 2019. AA Financial Industry Benchmark for Determining, Assessing and Managing Environmental and Social Risk in Projects, 2019.

The Shift Project, *Biodiversité et changement climatique : The Shift Project défend une vision coordonnée, Note d'analyse et proposition à destination des pouvoirs publics*, Paris, March 2019.

UICN, *An Introduction to the African Convention on the Conservation of Nature and Natural Resources*, IUCN Environmental Policy and Law Paper No. 56 Rev., 2nd ed., 2006.

–, *Stratégie mondiale de la conservation. La conservation des ressources vivantes au service du développement durable*, 1980.

UN Secretary-General, *Human Rights Obligations relating to the Enjoyment of a Safe, Clean, Healthy and Sustainable Environment*, Note by the Secretary-General, A/75/161, 15 July 2020.

UNEP-WCMC, IUCN and NGS (2018). *Protected Planet Report 2018*, UNEP-WCMC, IUCN and NGS: Cambridge UK; Gland, Switzerland; and Washington, DC, USA.

UNEP, *Advancing the Biodiversity Agenda. A UN System-Wide Contribution. A Report by the Environment Management Group*, UNEP, WCMC, 2010.

–, *Gap Analysis for the Purpose of Facilitating the Discussions on How to Improve and Strengthen the Science-Policy Interface on Biodiversity and Ecosystem Services*, UNEP/IPBES/2/INF/1, 19 August 2009.

–, WCMC, Ministry of Environment of Finland, *Promoting Synergies within the Cluster of Biodiversity-Related Multilateral Environmental Agreements*, WCMC, Cambridge, April 2012.
–, World Conservation Monitoring Centre, *Mapping Multilateral Environmental Agreements to the Aichi Biodiversity Targets*, Cambridge, 2015.
Unesco, *Diversité culturelle et biodiversité pour un développement durable: table ronde de haut niveau organisée conjointement par l'Unesco et le PNUE le 3 septembre 2002 à Johannesburg à l'occasion du Sommet mondial pour le développement durable*, Paris, Unesco, 2003.
UNODC, *World Wildlife Crime Report,* United Nations Office on Drugs and Crime, Vienna, 2016.
World Bank, *Illegal Logging, Fishing and Wildlife Trade. The Costs and How to Combat It*, World Bank, 2019.

Newspaper Articles

Bouvier, P., "Aux Etats-Unis, le lac Erié a désormais le droit légal 'd'exister et de prospérer naturellement'", *Le Monde*, 22 February 2019.
Fontaine, B. *et al.*, "Espèces en voie d'extinction, le compte n'y est pas", *The Conversation*, 14 January 2018.
Foray, D., "La privatisation de l'activité de connaissance menace de bloquer l'innovation", *Le Monde, Eco.,* 30 May 2000, p. III.
Gabbatiss, J., "Earth Will Take Millions of Years to Recover from Climate Change Mass Extinction, Study Suggests. 'Speed Limit' on Rate of Evolution Means Diversity Would Be Slow Return to Previous Levels", *The Independent*, 9 April 2019.
Geffroy, L., "Où sont passés les oiseaux des champs?", *Le Journal du CNRS*, 6 May 2019.
Le temps, "L'annonce de bébés aux gènes modifiés crée la polémique en Chine", *Le temps*, 26 November 2018.
Lynn, W., "Réensauvager la moitié de la Terre: la dimension éthique d'un projet spectaculaire", *The Conversation*, 20 September 2015.
Maréchal, J.-P., "Quand la biodiversité est assimilée à une marchandise", *Le Monde diplomatique*, July 1999, pp. 6-7.
Musacchio, S., "Ces animaux stars menacés d'extinction", *Le Journal du CNRS*, 13 April 2018.
Seuret, F., and A. Ali Brac de la Perrière, "L'Afrique refuse le brevetage du vivant", *Le Monde diplomatique*, July 2000, p. 24.
Vincent, C., "Comment l'Unesco veut sauver les grands singes", *Le Monde*, 18 November 2018.

PUBLICATIONS DE L'ACADÉMIE
DE DROIT INTERNATIONAL
DE LA HAYE

PUBLICATIONS OF THE
HAGUE ACADEMY OF INTERNATIONAL
LAW

RECUEIL DES COURS Depuis 1923, les plus grands noms du droit international ont professé à l'Académie de droit international de La Haye. Tous les tomes du *Recueil* qui ont été publiés depuis cette date sont disponibles, chaque tome étant, depuis les tout premiers, régulièrement réimprimé sous sa forme originale.

Depuis 2008, certains cours font l'objet d'une édition en livres de poche.

En outre, toute la collection existe en version électronique. Tous les ouvrages parus à ce jour ont été mis en ligne et peuvent être consultés moyennant un des abonnements proposés, qui offrent un éventail de tarifs et de possibilités.

INDEX A ce jour, il a paru sept index généraux. Ils couvrent les tomes suivants :

1 à 101	(1923-1960)	379 pages	ISBN 978-90-218-9948-0
102 à 125	(1961-1968)	204 pages	ISBN 978-90-286-0643-2
126 à 151	(1969-1976)	280 pages	ISBN 978-90-286-0630-2
152 à 178	(1976-1982)	416 pages	ISBN 978-0-7923-2955-8
179 à 200	(1983-1986)	260 pages	ISBN 978-90-411-0110-5
201 à 250	(1987-1994)	448 pages	ISBN 978-90-04-13700-4
251 à 300	(1995-2002)	580 pages	ISBN 978-90-04-15387-7

A partir du tome 210 il a été décidé de publier un index complet qui couvrira chaque fois dix tomes du *Recueil des cours*. Le dernier index paru couvre les tomes suivants :

311 à 320	(2004-2006)	392 pages	Tome 320A	ISBN 978-90-04-19695-7

COLLOQUES L'Académie organise également des colloques dont les débats sont publiés. Les derniers volumes parus de ces colloques portent les titres suivants : *Le règlement pacifique des différends internationaux en Europe : perspectives d'avenir* (1990) ; *Le développement du rôle du Conseil de sécurité* (1992) ; *La Convention sur l'interdiction et l'élimination des armes chimiques : une percée dans l'entreprise multilatérale du désarmement* (1994) ; *Actualité de la Conférence de La Haye de 1907, Deuxième Conférence de la Paix* (2007).

CENTRE D'ÉTUDE ET DE RECHERCHE Les travaux scientifiques du Centre d'étude et de recherche de droit international et de relations internationales de l'Académie de droit international de La Haye, dont les sujets sont choisis par le Curatorium de l'Académie, faisaient l'objet, depuis la session de 1985, d'une publication dans laquelle les directeurs d'études dressaient le bilan des recherches du Centre qu'ils avaient dirigé. Cette série a été arrêtée et la dernière brochure parue porte le titre suivant : *Les règles et les institutions du droit international humanitaire à l'épreuve des conflits armés récents*. Néanmoins, lorsque les travaux du Centre se révèlent particulièrement intéressants et originaux, les rapports des directeurs et les articles rédigés par les chercheurs font l'objet d'un ouvrage collectif.

Les demandes de renseignements ou de catalogues et les commandes doivent être adressées à

MARTINUS NIJHOFF PUBLISHERS

B.P. 9000, 2300 PA Leyde   Pays-Bas   http://www.brill.nl

COLLECTED COURSES Since 1923 the top names in international law have taught at The Hague Academy of International Law. All the volumes of the *Collected Courses* which have been published since 1923 are available, as, since the very first volume, they are reprinted regularly in their original format.

Since 2008, certain courses have been the subject of a pocketbook edition.

In addition, the total collection now exists in electronic form. All works already published have been put "on line" and can be consulted under one of the proposed subscription methods, which offer a range of tariffs and possibilities.

INDEXES Up till now seven General Indexes have been published. They cover the following volumes:

1 to 101	(1923-1960)	379 pages	ISBN 978-90-218-9948-0
102 to 125	(1961-1968)	204 pages	ISBN 978-90-286-0643-2
126 to 151	(1969-1976)	280 pages	ISBN 978-90-286-0630-2
152 to 178	(1976-1982)	416 pages	ISBN 978-0-7923-2955-8
179 to 200	(1983-1986)	260 pages	ISBN 978-90-411-0110-5
201 to 250	(1987-1994)	448 pages	ISBN 978-90-04-13700-4
251 to 300	(1995-2002)	580 pages	ISBN 978-90-04-15387-7

From Volume 210 onwards it has been decided to publish a full index covering, each time, ten volumes of the *Collected Courses*. The latest Index published covers the following volumes:
311 to 320 (2004-2006) 392 pages Volume 320A ISBN 978-90-04-19695-7

WORKSHOPS The Academy publishes the discussions from the Workshops which it organises. The latest titles of the Workshops already published are as follows: *The Peaceful Settlement of International Disputes in Europe: Future Prospects* (1990); *The Development of the Role of the Security Council* (1992); *The Convention on the Prohibition and Elimination of Chemical Weapons: A Breakthrough in Multilateral Disarmament* (1994); *Topicality of the 1907 Hague Conference, the Second Peace Conference* (2007).

CENTRE FOR STUDIES AND RESEARCH The scientific works of the Centre for Studies and Research in International Law and International Relations of The Hague Academy of International Law, the subjects of which are chosen by the Curatorium of the Academy, have been published, since the Centre's 1985 session, in a publication in which the Directors of Studies reported on the state of research of the Centre under their direction. This series has been discontinued and the title of the latest booklet published is as follows: *Rules and Institutions of International Humanitarian Law Put to the Test of Recent Armed Conflicts*. Nevertheless, when the work of the Centre has been of particular interest and originality, the reports of the Directors of Studies together with the articles by the researchers form the subject of a collection published by the Academy.

Requests for information, catalogues and orders for publications must be addressed to

MARTINUS NIJHOFF PUBLISHERS

P.O. Box 9000, 2300 PA Leiden   The Netherlands   **http://www.brill.nl**

TABLE PAR TOME DES COURS PUBLIÉS CES DERNIÈRES ANNÉES
INDEX BY VOLUME OF THE COURSES PUBLISHED THESE LAST YEARS

Tome/Volume 326 (2007)

Collins, L. : Revolution and Restitution : Foreign States in National Courts (Opening Lecture, Private International Law Session, 2007), 9-72.
Gotanda, J. Y. : Damages in Private International Law, 73-408.
(ISBN 978-90-04-16616-5)

Tome/Volume 327 (2007)

Mayer, P. : Le phénomène de la coordination des ordres juridiques étatiques en droit privé. Cours général de droit international privé (2003), 9-378.
(ISBN 978-90-04-16617-2)

Tome/Volume 328 (2007)

Garcimartín Alférez, F. J., Cross-border Listed Companies, 9-174.
Vrellis, S., Conflit ou coordination de valeurs en droit international privé. A la recherche de la justice, 175-486. (ISBN 978-90-04-16618-9)

Tome/Volume 329 (2007)

Pellet, A. : L'adaptation du droit international aux besoins changeants de la société internationale (conférence inaugurale, session de droit international public, 2007), 9-48.
Gaillard, E. : Aspects philosophiques du droit de l'arbitrage international, 49-216.
Schrijver, N. : The Evolution of Sustainable Development in International Law : Inception, Meaning and Status, 217-412.
(ISBN 978-90-04-16619-6)

Tome/Volume 330 (2007)

Pamboukis, Ch. P. : Droit international privé holistique : droit uniforme et droit international privé, 9-474.
(ISBN 978-90-04-16620-2)

Tome/Volume 331 (2007)

Pinto, M. : L'emploi de la force dans la jurisprudence des tribunaux internationaux, 9-160
Brown Weiss, E. : The Evolution of International Water Law, 161-404.
(ISBN 978-90-04-17288-3)

Tome/Volume 332 (2007)

Carlier, J.-Y. : Droit d'asile et des réfugiés. De la protection aux droits, 9-354.
Fatouros, A. A. : An International Legal Framework for Energy, 355-446.
(ISBN 978-90-04-17198-5)

Tome/Volume 333 (2008)

Müllerson, R. : Democracy Promotion : Institutions, International Law and Politics, 9-174.

Pisillo Mazzeschi, R. : Responsabilité de l'Etat pour violation des obligations positives relatives aux droits de l'homme, 174-506.

(ISBN 978-90-04-17284-5)

Tome/Volume 334 (2008)

Verhoeven, J. : Considérations sur ce qui est commun. Cours général de droit international public (2002), 9-434. (ISBN 978-90-04-17289-0)

Tome/Volume 334 (2008)

Verhoeven, J. : Considérations sur ce qui est commun. Cours général de droit international public (2002), 9-434.

(ISBN 978-90-04-17289-0)

Tome/Volume 335 (2008)

Beaumont, P. R. : The Jurisprudence of the European Court of Human Rights and the European Court of Justice on the Hague Convention on International Child Abduction, 9-104.

Moura Vicente, D. : La propriété intellectuelle en droit international privé, 105-504.

(ISBN 978-90-04-17290-6)

Tome/Volume 336 (2008)

Decaux, E. : Les formes contemporaines de l'esclavage, 9-198.
McLachlan, C. : *Lis Pendens* in International Litigation, 199-554.

(ISBN 978-90-04-17291-3)

Tome/Volume 337 (2008)

Mahiou, A. : Le droit international ou la dialectique de la rigueur et de la flexibilité. Cours général de droit international public, 9-516.

(ISBN 978-90-04-17292-0)

Tome/Volume 338 (2008)

Thürer, D. : International Humanitariam Law : Theory, Practice, Context, 9-370.

(ISBN 978-90-04-17293-7)

Tome/Volume 339 (2008)

Sicilianos, L.-A. : Entre multilatéralisme et unilatéralisme : l'autorisation par le Conseil de sécurité de recourir à la force, 9-436. (ISBN 978-90-04-17294-4)

Tome/Volume 340 (2009)

Beaumont, P. R. : Reflections on the Relevance of Public International Law to Private International Law Treaty Making (Opening Lecture, Private International Law Session, 2009), 9-62.

Carbone, S. M. : Conflits de lois en droit maritime, 63-270.

Boele-Woelki, K. : Unifying and Harmonizing Substantive Law and the Role of Conflict of Laws, 271-462. (ISBN 978-90-04-17295-1)

Tome/Volume 341 (2009)

Bucher, A.: La dimension sociale du droit international privé. Cours général, 9-526.
(ISBN 978-90-04-18509-8)

Tome/Volume 342 (2009)

Musin, V.: The Influence of the International Sale of Goods Convention on Domestic Law Including Conflict of Laws (with Specific Reference to Russian Law), 9-76.
Onuma, Y.: A Transcivilizational Perspective on International Law. Questioning Prevalent Cognitive Frameworks in the Emerging Multi-Polar and Multi-Civilizational World of the Twenty-First Century, 77-418.
(ISBN 978-90-04-18510-4)

Tome/Volume 343 (2009)

Abou-el-Wafa, A.: Les différends internationaux concernant les frontières terrestres dans la jurisprudence de la Cour internationale de Justice, 9-570.
(ISBN 978-90-04-18513-5)

Tome/Volume 344 (2009)

Villiger, M. E.: The 1969 Vienna Convention on the Law of Treaties – 40 Years After, 4-192.
Alvarez, J. E.: The Public International Law Regime Governing International Investment, 193-452. (ISBN 978-90-04-18512-8)

Tome/Volume 345 (2009)

Meziou, K.: Migrations et relations familiales, 9-386.
Lauterpacht, Sir Elihu: Principles of Procedure in International Litigation, 387-530.
(ISBN 978-90-04-18514-2)

Tome/Volume 346 (2009)

Kawano, M.: The Role of Judicial Procedures in the Process of the Pacific Settlement of International Disputes, 9-474.
(ISBN 978-90-04-18515-9)

Tome/Volume 347 (2010)

Salmon, J.: Quelle place pour l'Etat dans le droit international d'aujourd'hui? 9-78.
Boisson de Chazournes, L.: Les relations entre organisations régionales et organisations universelles, 79-406.
(ISBN 978-90-04-18516-6)

Tome/Volume 348 (2010)

Bogdan, M.: Private International Law as Component of the Law of the Forum. General Course, 9-252.
Baratta, R.: La reconnaissance internationale des situations juridiques personnelles et familiales, 253-500.
(ISBN 978-90-04-18517-3)

Tome/Volume 349 (2010)

Malenovský, J.: L'indépendance des juges internationaux, 9-276.
Wang, G.: Radiating Impact of WTO on Its Members' Legal System: The Chinese Perspective, 277-536. (ISBN 978-90-04-18518-0)

Tome/Volume 350 (2010)

Van Gerven, W.: Plaidoirie pour une nouvelle branche du droit: le «droit des conflits d'ordres juridiques» dans le prolongement du «droit des conflits de règles» (conférence inaugurale), 9-70.
Bonomi, A.: Successions internationales: conflits de lois et de juridictions, 71-418.
Oxman, B. H.: Idealism and the Study of International Law (Inaugural Lecture), 419-440. (ISBN 978-90-04-18519-7)

Tome/Volume 351 (2010)

Reisman, W. M.: The Quest for World Order and Human Dignity in the Twenty-first Century: Constitutive Process and Individual Commitment. General Course on Public International Law, 9-382.
(ISBN 978-90-04-22725-5)

Tome/Volume 352 (2010)

Daví, A.: Le renvoi en droit international privé contemporain, 9-522.
(ISBN 978-90-04-22726-2)

Tome/Volume 353 (2011)

Meeusen, J.: Le droit international privé et le principe de non-discrimination, 9-184.
Gowlland-Debbas, V.: The Security Council and Issues of Responsibility under International Law, 185-444. (ISBN 978-90-04-22727-9)

Tome/Volume 354 (2011)

Lamm, C. B.: Internationalization of the Practice of Law and Important Emerging Issues for Investor-State Arbitration (Opening Lecture), 9-64.
Briggs, A.: The Principle of Comity in Private International Law, 65-182.
Davey, W. J.: Non-discrimination in the World Trade Organization: The Rules and Exceptions, 183-440. (ISBN 978-90-04-22728-6)

Tome/Volume 355 (2011)

Chemillier-Gendreau, M.: A quelles conditions l'universalité du droit international est-elle possible? (conférence inaugurale), 9-40.
Xue Hanqin: Chinese Contemporary Perspectives on International Law – History, Culture and International Law, 41-234.
Arrighi, J. M.: L'Organisation des Etats américains et le droit international, 235-438. (ISBN 978-90-04-22729-3)

Tome/Volume 356 (2011)

Talpis, J.: Succession Substitutes, 9-238.
Lagrange, E.: L'efficacité des normes internationales concernant la situation des personnes privées dans les ordres juridiques internes, 239-552.
(ISBN 978-90-04-22730-9)

Tome/Volume 357 (2011)

Dugard, J.: The Secession of States and Their Recognition in the Wake of Kosovo, 9-222.
Gannagé, L.: Les méthodes du droit international privé à l'épreuve des conflits de cultures, 223-490. (ISBN 978-90-04-22731-6)

Tome/Volume 358 (2011)

Brand, R. A.: Transaction Planning Using Rules on Jurisdiction and the Recognition and Enforcement of Judgments, 9-262.

Hafner, G.: The Emancipation of the Individual from the State under International Law, 263-454. (ISBN 978-90-04-22732-3)

Tome/Volume 359 (2012)

Opertti Badán, D.: Conflit de lois et droit uniforme dans le droit international privé contemporain: dilemme ou convergence? (conférence inaugurale), 9-86.

Chen Weizuo: La nouvelle codification du droit international privé chinois, 87-234.

Kohler, Ch.: L'autonomie de la volonté en droit international privé: un principe universel entre libéralisme et étatisme, 285-478. (ISBN 978-90-04-25541-8)

Tome/Volume 360 (2012)

Basedow, J.: The Law of Open Societies — Private Ordering and Public Regulation of International Relations. General Course on Private International Law, 9-516. (ISBN 978-90-04-25550-0)

Tome/Volume 361 (2012)

Pinto, M. C. W.: The Common Heritage of Mankind: Then and Now, 9-130.

Kreindler, R.: Competence-Competence in the Face of Illegality in Contracts and Arbitration Agreements, 131-482.

(ISBN 978-90-04-25552-4)

Tome/Volume 362 (2012)

Arsanjani, M. H.: The United Nations and International Law-Making (Opening Lecture), 9-40.

Alland, D.: L'interprétation du droit international public, 41-394.

(ISBN 978-90-04-25554-8)

Tome/Volume 363 (2012)

Sur, S.: La créativité du droit international. Cours général de droit international public, 9-332.

Turp, D.: La contribution du droit international au maintien de la diversité culturelle, 333-454. (ISBN 978-90-04-25556-2)

Tome/Volume 364 (2012)

Gaja, G.: The Protection of General Interests in the International Community. General Course on Public International Law (2011), 9-186.

Glenn, H. P.: La conciliation des lois. Cours général de droit international privé (2011), 187-470.

(ISBN 978-90-04-25557-9)

Tome/Volume 365 (2013)

Crawford, J.: Chance, Order, Change: The Course of International Law. General Course on Public International Law, 9-390.

(ISBN 978-90-04-25560-9)

Tome/Volume 366 (2013)

Hayton, D.: "Trusts" in Private International Law, 9-98.
Hobér, K.: *Res Judicata* and *Lis Pendens* in International Arbitration, 99-406.
(ISBN 978-90-04-26395-6)

Tome/Volume 367 (2013)

Kolb, R.: L'article 103 de la Charte des Nations Unies, 9-252.
Nascimbene, B.: Le droit de la nationalité et le droit des organisations d'intégration régionales. Vers de nouveaux statuts de résidents?, 253-454.
(ISBN 978-90-04-26793-0)

Tome/Volume 368 (2013)

Caflisch, L: Frontières nationales, limites et délimitations. – Quelle importance aujourd'hui? (conférence inaugurale), 9-46.
Benvenisti, E.: The International Law of Global Governance, 47-280.
Park, K. G.: La protection des personnes en cas de catastrophes, 281-456.
(ISBN 978-90-04-26795-4)

Tome/Volume 369 (2013)

Kronke, H.: Transnational Commercial Law and Conflict of Laws: Institutional Co-operation and Substantive Complementarity (Opening Lecture), 9-42.
Ortiz Ahlf, L.: The Human Rights of Undocumented Migrants, 43-160.
Kono, T.: Efficiency in Private International Law, 161-360.
Yusuf, A. A.: Pan-Africanism and International Law, 361-512.
(ISBN 978-90-04-26797-8)

Tome/Volume 370 (2013)

Dominicé, Ch.: La société internationale à la recherche de son équilibre. Cours général de droit international public, 9-392. (ISBN 978-90-04-26799-2)

Tome/Volume 371 (2014)

Lagarde, P.: La méthode de la reconnaissance est-elle l'avenir du droit international privé?, 9-42.
Charlesworth, H.: Democracy and International Law, 43-152.
de Vareilles-Sommières, P.: L'exception d'ordre public et la régularité substantielle internationale de la loi étrangère, 153-272.
Yanagihara, M.: Significance of the History of the Law of Nations in Europe and East Asia, 273-435. (ISBN 978-90-04-28936-9)

Tome/Volume 372 (2014)

Bucher, A.: La compétence universelle civile, 9-128.
Cordero-Moss, G.: Limitations on Party Autonomy in International Commercial Arbitration, 129-326.
Sinjela, M.: Intellectual Property: Cross-Border Recognition of Rights and National Development, 327-394.
Dolzer, R.: International Co-operation in Energy Affairs, 395-504.
(ISBN 978-90-04-28937-6)

Tome/Volume 373 (2014)

Cachard, O. : Le transport international aérien de passagers, 9-216.
Audit, M. : Bioéthique et droit international privé, 217-447.

(ISBN 978-90-04-28938-3)

Tome/Volume 374 (2014)

Struycken, A. V. M. : Arbitration and State Contract, 9-52.
Corten, O., La rébellion et le droit international : le principe de neutralité en tension, 53-312.
Parra, A. : The Convention and Centre for Settlement of Investment Disputes, 313-410.

(ISBN 978-90-04-29764-7)

Tome/Volume 375 (2014)

Jayme, E. : Narrative Norms in Private International Law – The Example of Art Law, 9-52.
De Boer, Th. M. : Choice of Law in Arbitration Proceedings, 53-88.
Frigo, M. : Circulation des biens culturels, détermination de la loi applicable et méthodes de règlement des litiges, 89-474. (ISBN 978-90-04-29766-1)

Tome/Volume 376 (2014)

Cançado Trindade, A. A. : The Contribution of Latin American Legal Doctrine to the Progressive Development of International Law, 9-92.
Gray, C. : The Limits of Force, 93-198.
Najurieta, M. S. : L'adoption internationale des mineurs et les droits de l'enfant, 199-494.

(ISBN 978-90-04-29768-5)

Tome/Volume 377 (2015)

Kassir, W. J. : Le renvoi en droit international privé – technique de dialogue entre les cultures juridiques, 9-120.
Noodt Taquela, M. B. : Applying the Most Favourable Treaty or Domestic Rules to Facilitate Private International Law Co-operation, 121-318.
Tuzmukhamedov, B. : Legal Dimensions of Arms Control Agreements, An Introductory Overview, 319-468.

(ISBN 978-90-04-29770-8)

Tome/Volume 378 (2015)

Iwasawa, Y. : Domestic Application of International Law, 9-262.
Carrascosa Gonzalez, J. : The Internet – Privacy and Rights relating to Personality, 263-486. (ISBN 978-90-04-32125-0)

Tome/Volume 379 (2015)

Lowe, V. : The Limits of the Law.
Boele-Woelki, K. : Party Autonomy in Litigation and Arbitration in View of The Hague Principles on Choice of Law in International Commercial Contracts.
Fresnedo de Aguirre, C. : Public Policy : Common Principles in the American States.
Ben Achour, R. : Changements anticonstitutionnels de gouvernement et droit international. (ISBN 978-90-04-32127-4)

Tome/Volume 380 (2015)

Van Loon, J. H. A.: The Global Horizon of Private International Law.
Pougoué, P.-G.: L'arbitrage dans l'espace OHADA.
Kruger, T.: The Quest for Legal Certainty in International Civil Cases.
(ISBN 978-90-04-32131-1)

Tome/Volume 381 (2015)

Jayme, E.: Les langues et le droit international privé, 11-39.
Bermann, G.: Arbitrage and Private International Law. General Course on Private International Law (2015), 41-484.
(ISBN 978-90-04-33828-9)

Tome/Volume 382 (2015)

Cooper, D., and C. Kuner: Data Protection Law and International Dispute Resolution, 9-174.
Jia, B. B.: International Case Law in the Development of International Law, 175-397.
(ISBN 978-90-04-33830-2)

Tome/Volume 383 (2016)

Bennouna, M.: Le droit international entre la lettre et l'esprit, 9-231.
Iovane, M.: L'influence de la multiplication des juridictions internationales sur l'application du droit international, 233-446. (ISBN 978-90-04-34648-2)

Tome/Volume 384 (2016)

Symeonides, S. C.: Private International Law Idealism, Pragmatism, Eclecticism, 9-385. (ISBN 978-90-04-35131-8)

Tome/Volume 385 (2016)

Berman, Sir F.: Why Do we Need a Law of Treaties?, 9-31.
Marrella, F.: Protection internationale des droits de l'homme et activités des sociétés transnationales, 33-435. (ISBN 978-90-04-35132-5)

Tome/Volume 386 (2016)

Murphy, S. D.: International Law relating to Islands, 9-266.
Cataldi, G.: La mise en œuvre des décisions des tribunaux internationaux dans l'ordre interne, 267-428.
(ISBN 978-90-04-35133-2)

Tome/Volume 387 (2016)

Lequette, Y.: Les mutations du droit international privé: vers un changement de paradigme?, 9-644. (ISBN 978-90-04-36118-8)

Tome/Volume 388 (2016)

Bonell, M. J.: The Law Governing International Commercial Contracts: Hard Law versus Soft Law, 9-48.
Hess, B.: The Private-Public Divide in International Dispute Resolution, 49-266.
(ISBN 978-90-04-36120-1)

Tome/Volume 389 (2017)

Muir Watt, H. : Discours sur les méthodes du droit international privé (des formes juridiques de l'inter-altérité). Cours général de droit international privé, 9-410.

(ISBN 978-90-04-36122-5)

Tome/Volume 390 (2017)

Rau, A. S. : The Allocation of Power between Arbitral Tribunals and State Courts, 9-396. (ISBN 978-90-04-36475-2)

Tome/Volume 391 (2017)

Cançado Trindade, A. A. : Les tribunaux internationaux et leur mission commune de réalisation de la justice : développements, état actuel et perspectives, Conférence spéciale (2017), 9-101.
Mariño Menéndez, F. M. : The Prohibition of Torture in Public International Law, 103-185.
Swinarski, C. : Effets pour l'individu des régimes de protection de droit international, 187-369.
Cot, J.-P. : L'éthique du procès international (leçon inaugurale), 371-384.

(ISBN 978-90-04-37781-3)

Tome/Volume 392 (2017)

Novak, F. : The System of Reparations in the Jurisprudence of the Inter-American Court of Human Rights, 9-203.
Nolte, G. : Treaties and their Practice – Symptoms of their Rise or Decline, 205-397. (ISBN 978-90-04-39273-1)

Tome/Volume 393 (2017)

Tiburcio, C. : The Current Practice of International Co-Operation in Civil Matters, 9-310.
Ruiz De Santiago, J. : Aspects juridiques des mouvements forcés de personnes, 311-468. (ISBN 978-90-04-39274-8)

Tome/Volume 394 (2017)

Kostin, A. A. : International Commercial Arbitration, with Special Focus on Russia, 9-86.
Cuniberti, G. : Le fondement de l'effet des jugements étrangers, 87-283.

(ISBN 978-90-04-39275-5)

Tome/Volume 395 (2018)

Salerno, F. : The Identity and Continuity of Personal Status in Contemporary Private International Law, 9-198.
Chinkin, C. M. : United Nations Accountability for Violations of International Human Rights Law, 199-320. (ISBN 978-90-04-40710-7)

Tome/Volume 396 (2018)

Jacquet, J.-M. : Droit international privé et arbitrage commercial international, 9-36.
Brown Weiss, E. : Establishing Norms in a Kaleidoscopic World. General Course on Public International Law, 37-415. (ISBN 978-90-04-41002-2)

Tome/Volume 397 (2018)

D'Avout, L. : L'entreprise et les conflits internationaux de lois, 9-612.
(ISBN 978-90-04-41221-7)

Tome/Volume 398 (2018)

Treves, T. : The Expansion of International Law, General Course on Public International Law (2015), 9-398.
(ISBN 978-90-04-41224-8)

Tome/Volume 399 (2018)

Kanehara, A. : Reassessment of the Acts of the State in the Law of State Responsibility, 9-266.
Buxbaum, H. L. : Public Regulation and Private Enforcement in a Global Economy: Strategies for Managing Conflict, 267-442.
(ISBN 978-90-04-41670-3)

Tome/Volume 400 (2018)

Chedly, L. : L'efficacité de l'arbitrage commercial international, 9-624.
(ISBN 978-90-04-42388-6)

Tome/Volume 401 (2019)

Wood, P. : Extraterritorial Enforcement of Regulatory Laws, 9-126.
Nishitani, Yuko : Identité culturelle en droit international privé de la famille, 127-450.
(ISBN 978-90-04-42389-3)

Tome/Volume 402 (2019)

Kinsch, P. : Le rôle du politique en droit international privé. Cours général de droit international privé, 9-384.
Dasser, F. : "Soft Law" in International Commercial Arbitration, 385-596.
(ISBN 978-90-04-42392-3)

Tome/Volume 403 (2019)

Daudet, Y. : 1919-2019, le flux du multilatéralisme, 9-48.
Kessedjian, C. : Le tiers impartial et indépendant en droit international, juge, arbitre, médiateur, conciliateur, 49-643.
(ISBN 978-90-04-42468-5)

Tome/Volume 404 (2019)

Rajamani, L. : Innovation and Experimentation in the International Climate Change Regime, 9-234.
Sorel, J.-M. : Quelle normativité pour le droit des relations monétaires et financières internationales?, 235-403.
(ISBN 978-90-04-43142-3)

Tome/Volume 405 (2019)

Paulsson, J. : Issues arising from Findings of Denial of Justice, 9-74.
Brunée, J. : Procedure and Substance in International Environmental Law, 75-240.
(ISBN 978-90-04-43300-7)

Tome/Volume 406 (2019)

Bundy, R.: The Practice of International Law, Inaugural Lecture, 9-26.
Gama, L.: Les principes d'UNIDROIT et la loi régissant les contrats de commerce, 27-343.
(ISBN 978-90-04-43611-4)

Tome/Volume 407 (2020)

Wouters, J.: Le statut juridique des standards publics et privés dans les relations économiques internationales, 9-122.
Maljean-Dubois, S.: Le droit international de la biodiversité, 123-538.
(ISBN 978-90-04-43643-5)

Tome/Volume 408 (2020)

Cançado Trindade, A. A.: Reflections on the Realization of Justice in the Era of Contemporary International Tribunals, 9-88.
González, C.: Party Autonomy in International Family Law, 89-361.
(ISBN 978-90-04-44504-8)

Tome/Volume 409 (2020)

Shany, Y: The Extraterritorial Application of International Human Rights Law, 9-152.
Besson, S.: La *due diligence* en droit international, 153-398.
(ISBN 978-90-04-44505-5)

Tome/Volume 410 (2020)

Koh, H. H.: American Schools of International Law, 9-93.
Peters, A.: Animals in International Law, 95-544.
(ISBN 978-90-04-44897-1)

Tome/Volume 411 (2020)

Cahin, G: Reconstrution et construction de l'Etat en droit international, 9-573.
(ISBN 978-90-04-44898-8)

Tome/Volume 412 (2020)

Momtaz, D: La hiérarchisation de l'ordre juridique international, cours général de droit international public, 9-252.
Grammaticaki-Alexiou, A.: Best Interests of the Child in Private International Law, 253-434.
(ISBN 978-90-04-44899-5)

Tome/Volume 413 (2021)

Ferrari, F.: Forum Shopping Despite Unification of Law, 9-290.
(ISBN 978-90-04-46100-0)

Tome/Volume 414 (2021)

Pellet, A.: Le droit international à la lumière de la pratique: l'introuvable théorie de la réalité. Cours général de droit international public, 9-547.
(ISBN 978-90-04-46547-3)

Tome/Volume 415 (2021)

Trooboff, P. D.: Globalization, Personal Jurisdiction and the Internet. Responding to the Challenge of adapting settled Principles and Precedents. General Course of Private International Law, 9-321.   (ISBN 978-90-04-46730-9)

Tome/Volume 416 (2021)

Wolfrum, R: Solidarity and Community Interests: Driving Forces for the Interpretation and Development of International Law. General Course on Public International Law, 9-479.   (ISBN 978-90-04-46827-6)

Tome/Volume 417 (2021)

d'Argent, P.: Les obligations internationales, 9-210.
Schabas, W. A.: Relationships Between International Criminal Law and Other Branches of International Law, 211-392.   (ISBN 978-90-04-47239-6)

Tome/Volume 418 (2021)

Bollée, S.: Les pouvoirs inhérents des arbitres internationaux, 9-224.
Tladi, D.: The Extraterritorial Use of Force against Non-State Actors, 225-360.
(ISBN 978-90-04-50380-9)

Tome/Volume 419 (2021)

Kolb, R.: Le droit international comme corps de «droit privé» et de «droit public». Cours général de droit international public, 9-668.
(ISBN 978-90-04-50381-6)

Tome/Volume 420 (2021)

Perrakis, S.: La protection internationale au profit des personnes vulnérables en droit international des droits de l'homme, 9-497.   (ISBN 978-90-04-50382-3)

Tome/Volume 421 (2021)

Estrella Faria, J. A.: La protection des biens culturels d'intérêt religieux en droit international public et en droit international privé, 9-333.
(ISBN 978-90-04-50829-3)

Tome/Volume 422 (2021)

Karayanni, M.: The Private International Law of Class Actions: A Functional approach, 9-248.
Mahmoudi, S.: Self-Defence and "Unwilling or Unable" States, 249-399.
(ISBN 978-90-04-50830-9)

Tome/Volume 423 (2022)

Kinnear, M.: The Growth, Challenges and Future Prospects for Investment Dispute Settlement, 9-36.
Weller, M.: "Mutual Trust": A Suitable Foundation for Private International Law in Regional Integration Communities and Beyond?, 37-378.
(ISBN 978-90-04-51411-9)

Tome/Volume 424 (2022)

Asada, M.: International Law of Nuclear Non-proliferation and Disarmament, 9-726. (ISBN 978-90-04-51769-1)

Tome/Volume 425 (2022)

Metou, B. M.: Le contrôle international des dérogations aux droits de l'homme, 9-294.
Silva Romero, E.: Legal Fictions in the Language of International Arbitration, 295-423. (ISBN 978-90-04-51770-7)

Tome/Volume 426 (2022)

Kuijper, P. J.: Delegation and International Organizations, 9-240.
McCaffrey, S. C.: The Evolution of the Law of International Watercourses, 241-384.

(ISBN 978-90-04-51771-4)

Tome/Volume 427 (2022)

Kaufmann-Kohler, G.: Indépendance et impartialité du juge et de l'arbitre dans le règlement des différends entre investisseurs et Etats (leçon inaugurale), 9-50.
Boyle, A.: International Lawmaking in an Environmental Context, 51-108.
Weller, M.-P.: La méthode tripartite du droit international privé: désignation, reconnaissance, considération, 109-210.
Mourre, A.: La légitimité de l'arbitrage, 211-288. (ISBN 978-90-04-52770-6)

Tome/Volume 428 (2023)

Laghmani, S.: Islam et droit international, 9-128.
Oyarzábal, M. J. A.: The Influence of Public International Law upon Private International Law in History and Theory and in the Formation and Application of the Law, 129-525.

(ISBN 978-90-04-54440-6)

Tome/Volume 429 (2023)

Moreno Rodríguez, J. A.: Private (And Public) International Law In Investment Arbitration, 9-702.

(ISBN 978-90-04-54462-8)

Tome/Volume 430 (2023)

Casella, P. B.: Droit international, histoire et culture, 9-610.

(ISBN 978-90-04-54463-5)

Tome/Volume 431 (2023)

Yeo, T. M.: Common Law, Equity and Statute. The Effect of Juridical Sources on Choice-of-Law Methodology, 9-88.
Frigessi Di Rattalma, M.: New Trends in Private International Law of Insurance Contracts, 89-200.
Roosevelt III, K.: The Third Restatement of Conflict of Laws, 201-284.
Sands, P.: Colonialism: A Short History of International Law in Five Acts, 285-410.

(ISBN 978-90-04-54464-2)

Tome/Volume 432 (2023)

Ruiz Fabri, H.: La justice procédurale en droit international, 9-44.
Shaw, M.: A House of Many Rooms: The Rise, Fall and Rise Again of Territorial Sovereignty?, 45-78.
Kovács, P.: L'individu et sa position devant la Cour pénale internationale, 79-421.
(ISBN 978-90-04-54465-9)

Tome/Volume 433 (2023)

Eyffinger, A.: The Hague Academy at 100: Its Rationale, Role and Record, 9-97.
Thorn, K.: The Protection of Small and Medium-Sized Enterprises in Private International Law, 99-205.
Moollan, S.: Parallel Proceedings in International Arbitration. Theoretical Analysis and the Search for Practical Solutions, 207-303. (ISBN 978-90-04-54469-7)

Tome/Volume 434 (2023)

Stephan, Paul B.: Applying Municipal Law in International Disputes, 9-214
Casado Raigón, R.: La contribution des juridictions internationales au développement du droit de la mer, 215-511.
(ISBN 978-90-04-69182-7)

Tome/Volume 435 (2023)

Salam, N.: Rethinking the United Nations: 75 and Beyond, 9-32.
Hascher, D.: Le rôle du droit international dans le contrôle des sentences arbitrales, 33-72.
Blokker, N.: Legal Facets of the Practice of International Organizations, 73-324.
(ISBN 978-90-04-69432-3)

Tome/Volume 436 (2024)

Corten, O.: Le champ juridique interntational, Cours général de droit international, 9-389. (ISBN 978-90-04-69912-0)

Tome/Volume 437 (2024)

Lim, Chin Leng: The Aims and Methods of Postcolonial International Law, 9-193.
Tanzi, Attila M.: The Principle *Jura Novit Curia* in International Judicial and Arbitral Proceedings, A Window on International Adjudication, 195-382.
(ISBN 978-90-04-69913-7)

Tome/Volume 438 (2024)

Lehmann, M.: Crypto-économie et droit international, 9-384.
(ISBN 978-90-04-70670-5)

Tome/Volume 439 (2024)

Hey, E.: Making Sense of Soft Law, 9-114.
Galindo, G. R. B.: The Inviolabilities of the Diplomatic Mission, 115-288.
Gomez-Robledo, J. M.: Le droit international du désarmement: entre idéalisme et réalisme, 289-3974.
(ISBN 978-90-04-70671-2)